Acknowledgments

The editor gratefully wishes to thank the Consultants of the *NIV Thematic Study Bible*: Alister McGrath, Donald J. Wiseman, J. I. Packer, Stephen Travis, Gordon McConville, and all those who compiled and edited the Thematic Section of the *NIV Thematic Study Bible*, on which this work is based.

THIS IS OUR GOD

Doctrinal themes from the Bible

Edited by Martin H. Manser

Hodder & Stoughton
LONDON SYDNEY AUCKLAND

Selection copyright © Martin H. Manser 1997

Scripture quotations taken from the HOLY BIBLE, NEW INTERNATIONAL VERSION. Copyright © 1973, 1978, 1984 by International Bible Society. First published in Great Britain 1979. Inclusive language version 1995, 1996. Used by permission of Hodder & Stoughton, a member of the Hodder Headline Group.

All rights reserved. No part of this publication may be reproduced, stored in a retrieval system, or transmitted, in any form or by any means without the prior written permission of the publisher, nor be otherwise circulated in any form of binding or cover other than that in which it is published and without a similar condition being imposed on the subsequent purchaser.

10 9 8 7 6 5 4 3 2 1

A CIP catalogue record for this title is available from the British Library

ISBN 0 340 65649 2

Typeset by Hewer Text Composition Services, Edinburgh
Printed and bound in Great Britain by
Caledonian International Book Manufacturing Ltd, Glasgow

Hodder & Stoughton Ltd
A Division of Hodder Headline PLC
338 Euston Road
London NW1 3BH

Contents

Introduction	vii
How to study a theme	ix
Abbreviations	xi
Bible themes	1
Index of themes	267

Introduction

The study of Scripture lies at the heart of the Christian faith. It is therefore important that readers of Scripture are given every means of help so that they will derive as much benefit and enjoyment as possible out of reading the Bible. *This is our God* is a selection of some 300 themes from the acclaimed *NIV Thematic Study Bible* published by Hodder and Stoughton.

Thematic study of the Bible is important because it draws together from different parts of the Bible what Scripture says on a particular subject. *This is our God* is a selection of doctrinal themes relating to *God*: who God is and what he is like. The *Trinity* is the characteristically Christian doctrine about God: *Jesus Christ* and *the Holy Spirit* are equal to God the Father in eternity, nature and status. God created the *human race*; to deal with the problem of *sin* we see the plan of *salvation* unfolded with the person and work of Jesus Christ and the ministry of the Holy Spirit.

The ultimate aim of thematic study is not simply to group together truths intellectually but to respond to God in *repentance, faith, prayer* and *worship* to come to know God personally.

A thematic study is different from a lexical study in that the former is based on related ideas, the latter on individual words. The difference between them can be appreciated by considering the theme of "the gospel". A word-based approach would be limited to identifying biblical passages in which the word "gospel" appears. A thematic approach, however, goes far beyond this and explores all the various elements of the theme. It identifies its basic concepts, its presuppositions and its consequences, in order that the theme in all its fulness can be unfolded to the reader. For example the material that deals with the gospel covers the *basic essentials* of the gospel (that Jesus Christ is both Lord and Saviour), the *promises of the gospel*,

Introduction

including forgiveness of sins, new life in Jesus Christ and adoption into God's family, the *requirements* of and *responses* to the gospel.

In this selection the actual text of key verses is quoted from the inclusive-language (gender-neutral) NIV Bible text. Many other verse references are also included to provide a wealth of biblical material.

A thorough system of cross-references allows the interrelationship of biblical themes to be understood and explored. For example, from "the gospel" the reader is referred to the following: access to God; forgiveness; grace; Holy Spirit, gift of; Jesus Christ as Saviour; Jesus Christ, responses to; Jesus Christ, the Lord; Jesus, the Christ; salvation.

Martin H. Manser
Aylesbury 1997

How to study a theme

Themes in this edition are arranged alphabetically by title. Each theme consists of a precise summary of the nature and importance of the theme, followed by a detailed analysis of its main parts. The text of Scripture for the main references appears in full, and many other scriptural references document each of the theme's aspects. At the end of the themes cross-references are provided to related themes included in this book.

Theme name →

Holy Spirit, indwelling
The Holy Spirit dwells within Jesus Christ and his disciples. Recognisable results in believers' lives include Christlikeness and the fruit of the Spirit.

Introduction gives a concise definition of the theme to show its contents and importance

Major headings set out clearly the key aspects of the theme

The indwelling of the Holy Spirit in the OT
Ge 41:38 So Pharaoh asked them [his officials], "Can we find anyone like this man [Joseph], one in whom is the spirit of God?"
Ex 35:31 "... and he [the LORD] has filled him [Bezalel] with the Spirit of God, with skill, ability and knowledge in all kinds of crafts—" See also **Nu** 27:18; **1Sa** 10:6–7; **Isa** 59:21; **Hag** 2:5

Main verse reference printed in bold type (e.g., Ge 41:38)

Scripture text given for main references

Comment or explanation is in reduced type. If it relates to a single verse reference it follows it; if it relates to a group of refernces it proceeds them

The Holy Spirit indwells believers
2Ti 1:14 ... the Holy Spirit who lives in us.
Believers are described as the temple of the Holy Spirit:
1Co 3:16; 6:19
Eph 2:22; **1Jn** 2:27; 3:24

If there are further secondary references after such a group, they start on a new line

Results of the Holy Spirit's indwelling in believers
Preaching and public testimony is aided Mt 10:20 pp Mk 13:11 pp Lk 12:12; **Ac** 4:8–12; 5:29–32
The fruit of the Spirit is displayed
Gal 5:22–23 ... the fruit of the Spirit is love, joy, peace, patience, kindness, goodness, faithfulness, gentleness and self-control ...
See also **Ro** 5:5; 14:17; 15:13,30

Parallel passages are preceded by "pp" and are not in bold type

Subheadings

Secondary verses support the main verse, preceded by See also. The Bible book name only is printed in bold type (e.g., Ro 5:5)

Cross-references to other themes are in italics. These enable you to look up related material

Those without the Holy Spirit's indwelling are not Christlike
Gal 5:17; **Jude** 18–19 See also *Christlikeness; Holy Spirit in life of Jesus Christ; Holy Spirit, filling with;*

Abbreviations

A.D.	since the birth of Jesus Christ
B.C.	before the birth of Jesus Christ
c.	about
fn	footnote
NT	New Testament
OT	Old Testament
pp	parallel passage

The Old Testament

Genesis	Ge	2 Chronicles	2Ch	Daniel	Da
Exodus	Ex	Ezra	Ezr	Hosea	Hos
Leviticus	Lev	Nehemiah	Ne	Joel	Joel
Numbers	Nu	Esther	Est	Amos	Am
Deuteronomy	Dt	Job	Job	Obadiah	Ob
Joshua	Jos	Psalms	Ps	Jonah	Jnh
Judges	Jdg	Proverbs	Pr	Micah	Mic
Ruth	Ru	Ecclesiastes	Ecc	Nahum	Na
1 Samuel	1Sa	Song of Songs	SS	Habakkuk	Hab
2 Samuel	2Sa	Isaiah	Isa	Zephaniah	Zep
1 Kings	1Ki	Jeremiah	Jer	Haggai	Hag
2 Kings	2Ki	Lamentations	La	Zechariah	Zec
1 Chronicles	1Ch	Ezekiel	Eze	Malachi	Mal

The New Testament

Matthew	Mt	Ephesians	Eph	Hebrews	Heb
Mark	Mk	Philippians	Php	James	Jas
Luke	Lk	Colossians	Col	1 Peter	1Pe
John	Jn	1 Thessalonians	1Th	2 Peter	2Pe
Acts	Ac	2 Thessalonians	2Th	1 John	1Jn
Romans	Ro	1 Timothy	1Ti	2 John	2Jn
1 Corinthians	1Co	2 Timothy	2Ti	3 John	3Jn
2 Corinthians	2Co	Titus	Tit	Jude	Jude
Galatians	Gal	Philemon	Phm	Revelation	Rev

BIBLE THEMES

Abba

The Aramaic word "Abba" is thought to be a very intimate term for "Father" suggesting that those who use it to refer to God enjoy a close relationship with him. Jesus Christ uses the term as a consequence of his natural sonship of God; believers may use it as a consequence of their adopted sonship of God through faith.

"Abba" used in addressing God
By Jesus Christ Mk 14:36
By believers Ro 8:15; **Gal** 4:6 *See also fellowship with God; God, fatherhood; God, titles and names of; Holy Spirit and prayer; Jesus Christ, Son of God; Jesus Christ, sonship of; knowing God; Trinity.*

abiding in Christ

The NT stresses the need for believers to remain in Christ. The reality of this close personal relationship with Jesus Christ is expressed in obedience to his word and is essential to effective discipleship.

Jesus Christ tells his disciples to abide in him
Jn 15:4–9 "Remain in me, and I will remain in you . . ." *See also* **Mt** 24:10–13; **Lk** 9:62; **Jn** 6:67

NT writers exhort believers to abide in Christ
Col 2:6 . . . as you received Christ Jesus as Lord, continue to live in him, *See also* **Gal** 4:9; 5:5–6; **Col** 3:1–3; **Heb** 12:1–3

Abiding in Christ depends upon holding on to his teaching
1Jn 2:24 See that what you have heard from the beginning remains in you. If it does, you also will remain in the Son and in the Father. *See also* **Jn** 8:31; **2Th** 2:15; **2Ti** 3:14; **2Jn** 9; **3Jn** 3–4

It depends on obedience to him
Jn 15:10 "If you [disciples] obey my [Jesus'] commands, you will remain in my love, just as I have obeyed my Father's commands and remain in his love." *See also* **Mt** 7:24–25; **Jn** 14:23; **Jas** 1:25; **1Jn** 3:24

It requires living like Jesus Christ
1Jn 2:6 Whoever claims to live in him must walk as Jesus did.

Aids to abiding in Christ
Eating his flesh and drinking his blood
Jn 6:56 "Those who eat my [Jesus'] flesh and drink my blood remain in me, and I in them."
The Spirit's anointing
1Jn 2:27 . . . the anointing you [believers] received from him [the Holy One] remains in you, and you do not need anyone to teach you . . . *See also* **Jn** 14:17,23; **Ro** 8:9; **1Jn** 3:24

Jesus Christ abides in believers
Jn 15:4 "Remain in me [Jesus], and I will remain in you [disciples] . . ." *See also* **Jn** 17:23; **Col** 1:27; **1Jn** 3:24; **Rev** 3:20
By his Spirit Jn 14:17; **Ro** 8:9–10; **1Co** 3:16; **1Jn** 2:27
By faith Eph 3:17–19; **Gal** 2:20

Results of abiding in Christ
Fruitfulness
Jn 15:4–5 "I [Jesus] am the vine; you are the branches. If you remain in me and I in you, you will bear much fruit . . ." *See also* **Gal** 5:22–23

access to God

Answered prayer Jn 15:7,16
Freedom from persistent sin
1Jn 3:6–9 No-one who lives in him [Jesus] keeps on sinning . . .
Relationship with God the Father Jn 14:23; 2Jn 9
Confidence in the face of the last day 1Jn 2:28

Warnings to those who fail to abide in Christ
Mt 24:12–13; Jn 15:2,6; 1Co 15:2; Heb 6:4–6
See also Holy Spirit, fruit of; Holy Spirit, indwelling; prayer.

access to God
The privilege of entering into the presence of God through the work of Jesus Christ.

Only the pure have access to God
Ps 24:3–4 Who may ascend the hill of the LORD? Who may stand in his holy place? Those who have clean hands and pure hearts, who do not lift up their souls to an idol or swear by what is false.
1Jn 3:21–22 Dear friends, if our hearts do not condemn us, we have confidence before God and receive from him anything we ask, because we obey his commands and do what pleases him.
See also Ps 41:12; 66:18–19; 73:28; Mt 5:8; 1Pe 3:12; Ps 34:15–16

The wicked do not have access to God
Ps 101:7 No-one who practises deceit will dwell in my house; no-one who speaks falsely will stand in my presence.
Isa 59:2 But your iniquities have separated you from your God; your sins have hidden his face from you, so that he will not hear. *See also* Ge 4:14,16; Lev 22:3; Dt 31:18; Ps 5:5; Isa 1:15; 64:7; Jer 7:15; 15:1; 23:39; 52:3; Eze 39:23; Hos 5:6; Mic 3:4

Access to God through the priests and sacrificial system
Access to God by this means in the OT
Ex 29:44–45 "So I will consecrate the Tent of Meeting and the altar and will consecrate Aaron and his sons to serve me as priests. Then I will dwell among the Israelites and be their God."
See also Ex 29:29–30,36,38–39
This OT access to God fulfilled in Jesus Christ
Heb 4:14–16 Therefore, since we have a great high priest who has gone through the heavens, Jesus the Son of God . . . Let us then approach the throne of grace with confidence, so that we may receive mercy and find grace to help us in our time of need.
Heb 7:23–25 Now there have been many of those priests, since death prevented them from continuing in office; but because Jesus lives for ever, he has a permanent priesthood. Therefore he is able to save completely those who come to God through him, because he always lives to intercede for them. *See also* Heb 2:17; 7:18–19; 10:10–12; 12:18–24
Access to God by the priesthood of all believers
1Pe 2:5 . . . you [God's elect] also, like living stones, are being built into a spiritual house to be a holy priesthood, offering spiritual sacrifices acceptable to God through Jesus Christ.
See also 1Pe 2:9; Rev 1:6

Access to God through the Tent of Meeting and the tabernacle
Access to God by this means in the OT
Ex 33:7–11 . . . Anyone enquiring of the LORD would go to the tent of meeting outside the camp . . . *See also* Ex 40:1–2,34–35; Nu 1:51; 3:10,38; 18:7,22; 2Ch 1:3
This OT access to God fulfilled in Jesus Christ
Heb 9:23–24 . . . For Christ did not enter a sanctuary made with human hands that was only a copy of the true one; he entered heaven itself, now to appear for us in God's presence.
See also Ac 7:44; Heb 8:1–2,5–6; 9:11

Access to God through the Most Holy Place
Access to God by this means in the OT
Heb 9:7–8 But only the high priest entered the inner room, and that only once a year, and never without blood, which he offered for himself and

for the sins the people had committed in ignorance. The Holy Spirit was showing by this that the way into the Most Holy Place had not yet been disclosed as long as the first tabernacle was still standing. See also **Lev** 16:2,12–17, 32–33; **1Ki** 6:16; 8:6 pp 2Ch 5:7; **1Ki** 8:10–11 pp 2Ch 5:13–14; **2Ch** 3:8

Access to God by this means fulfilled in Jesus Christ

Heb 9:12 . . . he [Christ] entered the Most Holy Place once for all by his own blood, having obtained eternal redemption. See also **Heb** 9:3–5

Heb 10:19–22 Therefore, brothers and sisters, since we have confidence to enter the Most Holy Place by the blood of Jesus, by a new and living way opened for us through the curtain, that is, his body, and since we have a great priest over the house of God, let us draw near to God with a sincere heart in full assurance of faith, having our hearts sprinkled to cleanse us from a guilty conscience and having our bodies washed with pure water. See also **Mt** 27:51 pp Mk 15:38; **Heb** 6:19–20

Believers have access to God by grace

Ps 21:6 Surely you have granted him eternal blessings and made him glad with the joy of your presence. See also **Ps** 51:10–11; 145:18; **Hos** 6:1–2; **Ac** 17:27; **2Co** 4:14; **Jas** 4:8; **Jude** 24

Believers have access to God through Jesus Christ

Ro 5:1–2 Therefore, since we have been justified through faith, we have peace with God through our Lord Jesus Christ, through whom we have gained access by faith into this grace in which we now stand. And we rejoice in the hope of the glory of God.

Eph 2:18 For through him [Christ Jesus] we both [Jew and Gentile] have access to the Father by one Spirit.

Eph 3:12 In him [Christ Jesus our Lord] and through faith in him we may approach God with freedom and confidence. See also **Jn** 10:9; 14:6 See also God, holiness of; grace; Jesus Christ, high priest; prayer; repentance; sin.

Christlikeness

The process by which believers are conformed to the likeness of Jesus Christ, especially in relation to obedience to and trust in God. Through the Holy Spirit, God refashions believers in the image of his Son, who is set before them as a model of the form of the redeemed life.

Believers are to become Christlike

1Co 11:1 Follow my [Paul's] example, as I follow the example of Christ.

Php 2:5 Your attitude should be the same as that of Christ Jesus: See also **Jn** 13:15; **Ro** 8:29; **Eph** 4:11–13; **Php** 3:8–11,20–21; **1Jn** 2:6

The Holy Spirit makes believers Christlike

2Co 3:18 And we, who with unveiled faces all reflect the Lord's glory, are being transformed into his likeness with ever-increasing glory, which comes from the Lord, who is the Spirit. See also **Ro** 8:5–9; **Gal** 5:22–23; **1Th** 1:6

Christlikeness is the aim of discipleship

Mt 10:25 "It is enough for students to be like their teachers, and the servants like their masters . . ." See also **Lk** 6:40; **1Jn** 2:6

Christlikeness is based on total commitment to Jesus Christ

Lk 9:57–62 As they were walking along the road, someone said to him [Jesus], "I will follow you wherever you go." Jesus replied, "Foxes have holes and birds of the air have nests, but the Son of Man has nowhere to lay his head." He said to another man, "Follow me." But he replied, "Lord, first let me go and bury my father." Jesus said to him, "Let the dead bury their own dead, but you go and proclaim the kingdom of God." Still another said, "I will follow you, Lord; but first let me go back and say good-bye to my family." Jesus replied, "No-one who takes hold of the plough and looks back is fit for service in the kingdom of God." See also **Mt** 9:9 pp Mk 2:14 pp Lk 5:27; **Mt** 19:21 pp Lk 18:22; **Jn** 1:43; 10:27; 12:26; 15:10; **2Jn** 9

Christlikeness

The demonstration of Christlikeness

In costly sacrifice
Mk 8:34–35 Then he [Jesus] called the crowd to him along with his disciples and said: "Those who would come after me must deny themselves and take up their cross and follow me. For those who want to save their lives will lose them, but those who lose their lives for me and for the gospel will save them." pp Mt 16:24 pp Lk 9:23–24

1Pe 2:21–23 To this you were called, because Christ suffered for you, leaving you an example, that you should follow in his steps. "He committed no sin, and no deceit was found in his mouth." When they hurled their insults at him, he did not retaliate; when he suffered, he made no threats. Instead, he entrusted himself to him who judges justly. *See also* Mt 10:38; Lk 14:26–27; Jn 12:26; 21:19; Php 3:10; 1Pe 4:1

In humility and service
Mt 20:26–28 [Jesus said] ". . . whoever wants to become great among you must be your servant, and whoever wants to be first must be your slave—just as the Son of Man did not come to be served, but to serve, and to give his life as a ransom for many." pp Mk 10:43–45 *See also* Mt 11:29; Mk 9:35; Lk 22:24–26; Jn 13:14–15; Php 2:4–5

In love for other believers
Jn 15:12 [Jesus said] "My command is this: Love each other as I have loved you."

1Jn 3:16 This is how we know what love is: Jesus Christ laid down his life for us. And we ought to lay down our lives for one another. *See also* Jn 13:34; 15:17; Eph 5:2,25

In a readiness to forgive others
Col 3:13 Bear with each other and forgive whatever grievances you may have against one another. Forgive as the Lord forgave you. *See also* Mt 6:12 pp Lk 11:4

In sharing Jesus Christ's mission to the world
Mt 4:19 "Come, follow me," Jesus said, "and I will make you fishers of men and women." pp Mk 1:17 *See also* Jn 20:21

By following godly examples that imitate Jesus Christ
1Co 11:1 Follow my [Paul's] example, as I follow the example of Christ. *See also* Eph 5:1; 1Th 1:5–6; 2:14; Heb 6:12; 13:7–8; 3Jn 11

Christlikeness is part of God's re-creation
Ge 1:26–27 Then God said, "Let us make human beings in our image, in our likeness, and let them rule over the fish of the sea and the birds of the air, over the livestock, over all the earth, and over all the creatures that move along the ground." So God created human beings in his own image, in the image of God he created them; male and female he created them.

2Co 4:4 The god of this age [the devil] has blinded the minds of unbelievers, so that they cannot see the light of the gospel of the glory of Christ, who is the image of God.

Eph 4:24 and to put on the new self, created to be like God in true righteousness and holiness.

Col 3:10 and have put on the new self, which is being renewed in knowledge in the image of its Creator.

The process of becoming Christlike

It is the purpose for which believers are saved
Ro 8:28–29 And we know that in all things God works for the good of those who love him, who have been called according to his purpose. For those God foreknew he also predestined to be conformed to the likeness of his Son, that he might be the firstborn among many brothers and sisters. *See also* Eph 2:10; 2Pe 1:4

It continues in the experience of believers
2Co 3:18 And we, who with unveiled faces all reflect the Lord's glory, are being transformed into his likeness with ever-increasing glory, which comes from the Lord, who is the Spirit.

It will be complete when believers finally share Jesus Christ's glory
1Jn 3:2–3 Dear friends, now we are children of God, and what we will be has not yet been made known. But we know that when he appears, we shall be like him, for we shall see him as he is. All who have this hope in them purify themselves, just as he is pure. *See also* Ps 17:15; Jn 17:24; 1Co 15:49–53; Gal 4:19;

Php 3:20–21; **Col** 3:4; **1Jn** 4:17   *See also faith; holiness; Holy Spirit, fruit of; Holy Spirit, indwelling; Jesus Christ, example of.*

church
The community of faithful believers, of whom Jesus Christ is the head, called out from the world to serve God down the ages. Scripture emphasises that the church is the body of Christ whose members are intended to be filled with the Holy Spirit. Scriptural understanding of the church is corporate, rather than solitary or individual.

church, life of
The church lives its life in union with Christ and in the power of the Holy Spirit. It is called to mutual love, holy living, and to worship.

The church lives its life in union with Christ
The church lives in Christ and Christ lives in the church
1Co 1:30 It is because of him [God] that you are in Christ Jesus . . .   *See also* **Mt** 18:20; **Jn** 15:5; 17:21; **1Co** 8:6; **Gal** 2:20; **Col** 1:27; 2:6; **1Jn** 4:13
Believers are united with Christ in baptism
Gal 3:27 for all of you who were baptised into Christ have clothed yourselves with Christ. *See also* **Ac** 2:38; 19:5; **Ro** 6:3–4; **Col** 2:12

The church lives its life in the power of the Holy Spirit
The church lives in the Spirit, and the Spirit lives in the church
Ro 8:9–11 You, however, are controlled not by the sinful nature but by the Spirit, if the Spirit of God lives in you. And if anyone does not have the Spirit of Christ, that person does not belong to Christ . . .   *See also* **1Co** 3:16; **Gal** 5:16,25; **Eph** 2:22; **2Ti** 1:14; **1Jn** 2:27
The Spirit is given to the church
Ac 1:4–5 . . . "Do not leave Jerusalem, but wait for the gift my [Jesus'] Father promised, which you have heard me speak about. For John baptised with water, but in a few days you will be baptised with the Holy Spirit."   *See also* **Jn** 20:22; **Ac** 2:4; 15:8; **Ro** 7:6; 15:16; **1Co** 6:11; **Gal** 3:3; **1Pe** 1:1–2
The Spirit seals the church
Eph 1:13 . . . Having believed, you were marked in him [Christ] with a seal, the promised Holy Spirit,   *See also* **2Co** 1:22; 5:5; **Eph** 4:30
The Spirit guides the church
Rev 2:7 Those who have ears, let them hear what the Spirit says to the churches . . . *See also* **Ac** 8:29; 10:19; 11:12; 13:2; 20:23; 21:4
The Spirit teaches the church
1Co 2:13 . . . we speak, not in words taught us by human wisdom but in words taught by the Spirit . . .   *See also* **Jn** 16:13; **Eph** 1:17
The Spirit sanctifies the church
Ro 15:16 . . . so that the Gentiles might become an offering acceptable to God, sanctified by the Holy Spirit.   *See also* **1Co** 6:11; **2Th** 2:13; **1Pe** 1:2
The Spirit endows the church with gifts
1Co 12:7 Now to each one the manifestation of the Spirit is given for the common good. *See also* **Ro** 12:6–8; **1Co** 12:8–11,28; **Eph** 4:11

The church as a fellowship
As a fellowship of mutual love
1Th 5:11 Therefore encourage one another and build each other up, just as in fact you are doing.   *See also* **Ro** 15:2; **1Co** 14:12; **Gal** 6:10; **1Th** 4:18; **Heb** 10:25
As a fellowship of ordinary people
1Co 1:26–27 . . . But God chose the foolish things of the world to shame the wise; God chose the weak things of the world to shame the strong.   *See also* **Lk** 6:20; **Jas** 2:5

The distinctiveness of the church
The church as a chosen people
1Pe 2:9 But you are a chosen people, a royal priesthood, a holy nation, a people belonging to God . . .   *See also* **Eph** 1:4; **Col** 3:12
The church as a holy people
Heb 12:14 Make every effort . . . to be holy; without holiness no-one will see the Lord. *See also* **Ro** 11:16; 15:16; **1Co** 1:2; **Eph** 2:21; 5:3; **1Th** 3:13; **Heb** 2:11; **1Pe** 1:15–16; **2Pe** 3:11

The church as a people set apart
2Co 7:1 Since we have these promises, dear friends, let us purify ourselves from everything that contaminates body and spirit, perfecting holiness out of reverence for God. *See also* 1Co 5:9–12; 2Co 6:14–18; Eph 5:7; 2Th 3:14; 2Ti 3:1–5; Tit 3:10–11

The church as a heavenly people
Jn 17:14–16 ". . . They [the disciples] are not of the world, even as I [Jesus] am not of it." *See also* Lk 10:20; 1Co 15:48; Gal 4:26; Eph 2:6; Php 3:20; Col 3:1–4; Heb 11:16; 12:22–23

The church and worship
Praise in the life of the church
Heb 13:15 Through Jesus, therefore, let us continually offer to God a sacrifice of praise—the fruit of lips that confess his name. *See also* Ac 2:47; 1Co 14:26; Eph 5:18–20; Php 3:3; Col 3:16

Prayer in the life of the church
Corporate prayer in the church: **Ac 1:14; 2:42; 4:24–31; 12:5,12; 20:36; 21:5**
Prayer for church leaders: **Ro 15:30; Eph 6:19–20; Col 4:2–4; 1Th 5:25; 2Th 3:1; Heb 13:18**
Eph 6:18; 1Ti 2:1–2

Baptism in the life of the church
Ac 2:38; 1Co 1:13; Gal 3:26–27; Eph 4:4–5; Col 2:11–12; 1Pe 3:21

The Lord's Supper in the life of the church
1Co 10:16–17 Is not the cup of thanksgiving for which we give thanks a participation in the blood of Christ? And is not the bread that we break a participation in the body of Christ? Because there is one loaf, we, who are many, are one body, for we all partake of the one loaf. *See also* Ac 2:42,46; 20:7; 1Co 10:21; 11:17–34

The suffering of the church
Suffering persecution from a hostile world
Jn 16:33 "I [Jesus] have told you these things, so that in me you may have peace. In this world you will have trouble. But take heart! I have overcome the world." *See also* Mt 5:10–12; 1Co 4:12; 2Co 4:9; 1Th 3:4; 2Ti 3:12

Sharing in the sufferings of Christ
Php 3:10 I [Paul] want to know Christ and the power of his resurrection and the fellowship of sharing in his sufferings, becoming like him in his death, *See also* Jn 15:20; Ro 8:17; 2Co 4:10–11; 1Pe 4:13

Suffering as the road to glory
Jas 1:12 Blessed are those who persevere under trial, because when they have stood the test, they will receive the crown of life that God has promised to those who love him. *See also* Ro 5:3; 8:18; 2Co 4:17; 2Ti 2:11–12; 1Pe 5:10
See also holiness; Holy Spirit in the church; life, spiritual; prayer in the church; worship.

---

church, nature of
The church is the people called by God, who are united by their faith in Christ and by their common life in him. Various descriptions and metaphors emphasise the continuity between the people of God in the OT and NT.

NT images of the church
The body of Christ
Ro 12:4–5 Just as each of us has one body with many members, and these members do not all have the same function, so in Christ we who are many form one body, and each member belongs to all the others. *See also* 1Co 12:12,27; Eph 3:6; 5:23; Col 1:18,24; 2:19; 3:15

God's building or temple
1Co 3:16–17 Don't you know that you yourselves are God's temple and that God's Spirit lives in you? . . . *See also* 1Co 3:10; 2Co 6:16; Eph 2:21–22; Heb 3:6; 10:21; 1Pe 2:5

A plant or vine
Jn 15:1–8 ". . . I [Jesus] am the vine; you [the disciples] are the branches . . ."
See also Ro 11:17–24; 1Co 3:6–8

Jesus Christ's flock
Jn 10:14–16 "I [Jesus] am the good shepherd; I know my sheep and my sheep know me . . . there shall be one flock and one shepherd." *See also* Mt 25:33; Lk 12:32; Ac 20:28–29; 1Pe 5:2–4

The bride of Christ
Rev 21:2 I [John] saw the Holy City, the new

Jerusalem, coming down out of heaven from God, prepared as a bride beautifully dressed for her husband.   *See also* **Eph** 5:25–27,31–32; **Rev** 19:7; 22:17

God's household or family
Eph 2:19 . . . you [Gentile believers] are no longer foreigners and aliens, but fellow-citizens with God's people and members of God's household,   *See also* **Jn** 8:35–36; **Gal** 6:10; **Eph** 3:15; **1Ti** 3:15; **Heb** 2:11; **1Pe** 2:17; 4:17

NT descriptions of the church
Emphasising continuity with the OT church
Abraham's offspring: **Ro** 4:16; **Gal** 3:7,29
The people of God: **Ro** 9:25; **2Co** 6:16; **Heb** 13:12; **1Pe** 2:9–10
The new Jerusalem: **Gal** 4:26; **Heb** 12:22; **Rev** 3:12; 21:2,9–10
Gal 6:16

Emphasising God's call and authority in the church
Sons of God: **Mt** 5:9; **Jn** 1:12; **Ro** 8:15–16; **2Co** 6:18; **Gal** 3:26; 4:5–6; **1Jn** 3:10
The elect: **Mt** 24:22; **Ro** 11:7; **2Ti** 2:10; **1Pe** 1:1
Heirs of God and God's inheritance: **Ro** 8:17; **Gal** 3:29; 4:7; **Tit** 3:7; **Heb** 1:14; 6:17; **1Pe** 1:4
A priesthood: **1Pe** 2:5,9; **Rev** 1:6; 5:10; 20:6

Descriptions applied to the church by outsiders
Followers of the Way: **Ac** 9:2; 19:9,23; 22:4; 24:14
Ac 11:26; **Ac** 24:5

Descriptions used by Christians
The believers: **Ac** 1:15; 2:44; 5:12; **Gal** 6:10; **1Ti** 4:12; **1Pe** 2:17
The disciples: **Ac** 6:1–2; 9:19; 11:26; 14:22; 20:1
Saints: **Ro** 1:7; 15:25; **1Co** 6:1; 14:33; **Eph** 1:1; **Php** 4:21; **Col** 1:12; **Jude** 3
Other NT descriptions of the church **1Ti** 3:15; **Heb** 12:23

The foundation of the church
Jesus Christ as the church's foundation-stone
1Co 3:11 For no-one can lay any foundation other than the one already laid, which is Jesus Christ.   *See also* **Mt** 7:24–25; 21:42 pp **Mk** 12:10 pp **Lk** 20:17; **Ac** 4:11; **Eph** 2:20; **1Pe** 2:6; **Isa** 28:16; **1Pe** 2:7; **Ps** 118:22

Apostles and prophets as founders of the church
Eph 2:19–20 . . . God's household, built on the foundation of the apostles and prophets, with Christ Jesus himself as the chief cornerstone.
See also **Mt** 16:18–19; **Rev** 21:14

The church as God's people
A people chosen by God
1Pe 2:9 But you are a chosen people, a royal priesthood, a holy nation, a people belonging to God, that you may declare the praises of him who called you out of darkness into his wonderful light.   *See also* **Jn** 15:16; **Ro** 8:33; **Eph** 1:4; **Col** 3:12; **2Th** 2:13; **Jas** 2:5; **1Pe** 1:2

A people called by God
Ro 1:6 And you also [Christians in Rome] are among those who are called to belong to Jesus Christ.   *See also* **Ac** 2:39; **1Co** 1:2,9; **Gal** 1:6; **2Th** 2:14; **2Ti** 1:9; **Jude** 1

A people loved by God
1Pe 2:10 Once you were not a people, but now you are the people of God; once you had not received mercy, but now you have received mercy.   *See also* **Eph** 2:1–5; **Tit** 3:4–7

God's covenant people
Heb 8:8–10 ". . . This is the covenant I will make with the house of Israel after that time, declares the Lord. I will put my laws in their minds and write them on their hearts. I will be their God, and they will be my people."
See also **Ro** 11:27; **Isa** 59:20–21; **Heb** 10:16; **Jer** 31:31–33   *See also* Holy Spirit, indwelling; Jesus Christ, head of the church.

church, purpose
The church is called to praise and glorify God, to establish Jesus Christ's kingdom, and to proclaim the gospel throughout the world.

God's purposes for the church
To praise God
1Pe 2:9 But you are a chosen people, a royal priesthood, a holy nation, a people belonging to God, that you may declare the praises of him who called you out of darkness into his wonderful light.
See also **Eph** 1:5–6,11–12,14; **Heb** 13:15; **1Pe** 2:5

church, purpose

To share God's glory
Ro 8:29–30 For those God foreknew he also predestined to be conformed to the likeness of his Son, that he might be the firstborn among many brothers and sisters. And those he predestined, he also called; those he called, he also justified; those he justified, he also glorified. *See also* **Mt** 13:43; **Jn** 17:24; **Ro** 9:23; **1Co** 2:7; **Php** 3:21; **Col** 3:4; **2Th** 2:14; **Rev** 2:26–27; 3:4–5,21

God will build his church
Mt 16:18–19 "And I [Jesus] tell you that you are Peter, and on this rock I will build my church, and the gates of Hades will not overcome it. I will give you the keys of the kingdom of heaven; whatever you bind on earth will be bound in heaven, and whatever you loose on earth will be loosed in heaven." *See also* **Mt** 27:40 pp **Mk** 15:29; **Jn** 2:19–22; **1Co** 3:9; **Eph** 2:21–22; 4:11–13; **Heb** 3:3–6; **1Pe** 2:5

To challenge Satan's dominion
Eph 3:10–11 His [God's] intent was that now, through the church, the manifold wisdom of God should be made known to the rulers and authorities in the heavenly realms . . .
See also **Mt** 16:18; **Eph** 6:12; **1Jn** 2:14

To go into the world in mission
2Co 5:18 All this is from God, who reconciled us to himself through Christ and gave us the ministry of reconciliation: *See also* **Mt** 5:13–16; 28:19–20; **Mk** 16:15; **Lk** 24:48; **Jn** 20:21; **Ac** 1:8; **Php** 2:15–16; **Col** 1:27

The church's mission
To preach the gospel to the world
Mk 13:10 And the gospel must first be preached to all nations. pp **Mt** 24:14 *See also* **Mt** 28:19; **Lk** 24:47; **Jn** 10:16; **Ac** 13:47

To do good to all
Gal 6:10 Therefore, as we have opportunity, let us do good to all people, especially to those who belong to the family of believers. *See also* **Mt** 25:37–40; **Lk** 6:35; **Ac** 9:36; **Eph** 2:10; **1Ti** 6:18; **Jas** 1:27; **1Pe** 2:12

Images of the church's mission
Mt 5:13–16 "You are the salt of the earth . . . You are the light of the world . . ."
Jn 15:5–8 "I [Jesus] am the vine; you are the branches. If you remain in me and I in you, you will bear much fruit . . ."
A fruitful plant in a fruitless world: **Mt** 7:18–19; **Ro** 7:4; **Eph** 5:9–10; **Php** 1:11; **Col** 1:6,10; **Jas** 3:17
Salt in an insipid world: **Mk** 9:50; **Lk** 14:34–35
Light in a dark world: **Ro** 13:12–14; **Eph** 5:8; **Php** 2:15; **1Th** 5:5–6

The growth of the church
Numerical growth among the first Christians
Ac 11:21 The Lord's hand was with them, and a great number of people believed and turned to the Lord. *See also* **Ac** 2:41,47; 4:4; 5:14; 6:1,7; 9:31,42; 11:24; 12:24; 13:49; 16:5; 17:4; 18:8; 19:20

The church is to grow to maturity
Eph 4:12–13 . . . so that the body of Christ may be built up until we all reach unity in the faith and in the knowledge of the Son of God and become mature, attaining to the whole measure of the fulness of Christ. *See also* **Php** 1:6; 3:13–15; **2Th** 1:3

Aspects of growth
Growth in character: **2Co** 9:10; **1Th** 3:12
Growth into Christ: **Eph** 4:15; **Col** 1:10; **2Pe** 3:18
Heb 6:1

Prayers for the growth of the church
Eph 3:14–19 . . . And I [Paul] pray that you, being rooted and established in love, may have power, together with all the saints, to grasp how wide and long and high and deep is the love of Christ, and to know this love that surpasses knowledge—that you may be filled to the measure of all the fulness of God. *See also* **Eph** 1:17–19; **Php** 1:9–11; **Col** 1:9–12; **1Th** 3:11–13; **2Th** 1:11–12

Visions of the church's final destiny
Rev 7:9–10 After this I looked and there before me was a great multitude that no-one could count, from every nation, tribe, people and language, standing before the throne and in front of the Lamb . . . *See also* **Mt** 24:31; **Jn** 10:16; **Eph** 1:10; **1Th** 4:16–17; **Heb** 12:22–23; **Rev** 21:2 *See also God, glory of; God, purpose of; kingdom of God.*

church, unity

The church is one in essence, because it is founded on one gospel, united to one Lord and indwelt by one Spirit. Its unity is under constant threat because of the tendency to division that is inherent in fallen humanity, and needs to be continually maintained and actively expressed in fellowship.

The unity of the church
The church is one
Ro 12:5 . . . in Christ we who are many form one body, and each member belongs to all the others. *See also* **1Co** 12:12,20; **Eph** 4:25

The church transcends all barriers
Col 3:11 Here there is no Greek or Jew, circumcised or uncircumcised, barbarian, Scythian, slave or free, but Christ is all, and is in all. *See also* **Jn** 10:16; **Ac** 10:28–29,47; 15:8–9; **Gal** 3:28; **Eph** 2:14–16; 3:6

The church's unity reflects the unity within the Trinity
Eph 4:4–6 There is one body and one Spirit—just as you were called to one hope when you were called—one Lord, one faith, one baptism; one God and Father of all, who is over all and through all and in all. *See also* **Jn** 17:11; **Ro** 3:29–30; 10:12–13; **Gal** 3:27–28

The church's unity is the work of the Trinity
Eph 2:16–18 . . . in this one body to reconcile both of them to God through the cross, by which he [Christ] put to death their hostility . . . For through him we both have access to the Father by one Spirit. *See also* **Jn** 11:52; **Ac** 10:45–47; **1Co** 12:13; **Eph** 2:22; 4:3

The purpose of the church's unity
To lead others to faith
Jn 17:23 ". . . May they [all believers] be brought to complete unity to let the world know that you sent me [Jesus] and have loved them even as you have loved me." *See also* **Jn** 17:21

To lead believers to maturity
Eph 4:13 . . . until we all reach unity in the faith and in the knowledge of the Son of God and become mature, attaining to the whole measure of the fulness of Christ.

The nature of the church's unity
Php 2:1–2 . . . then make my [Paul's] joy complete by being like-minded, having the same love, being one in spirit and purpose. *See also* **2Co** 13:11; **Php** 1:27; **Col** 2:2

Appeals for unity in the church
Eph 4:3 Make every effort to keep the unity of the Spirit through the bond of peace. *See also* **Ro** 12:10; 15:5,7; **1Co** 12:25; **Col** 3:14; **1Pe** 3:8

The church's unity is expressed in fellowship
Fellowship with God
1Co 1:9 God, who has called you into fellowship with his Son Jesus Christ our Lord, is faithful. *See also* **2Co** 13:14; **Php** 2:1; **2Pe** 1:4; **1Jn** 1:3, 6–7

Fellowship expressed by meeting together
Ac 2:46 Every day they continued to meet together in the temple courts. They broke bread in their homes and ate together with glad and sincere hearts, *See also* **Ac** 2:1,42; 5:12; 6:2; **1Co** 14:26; **Heb** 10:25

Fellowship expressed through sharing resources
Ac 2:44–45 All the believers were together and had everything in common. Selling their possessions and goods, they gave to anyone who had need. *See also* **Ac** 4:32,34–37; 11:27–30; **Ro** 15:26; **1Co** 16:1–2; **2Co** 8:2–5,13–14; 9:13; **Php** 4:14–18

Fellowship through suffering
Rev 1:9 I, John, your brother and companion in the suffering and kingdom and patient endurance that are ours in Jesus . . . *See also* **Ro** 8:17; **2Co** 1:7; **Php** 3:10; 4:14; **Heb** 10:33–34; 13:3

Fellowship through shared spiritual blessings
1Co 9:23 I [Paul] do all this for the sake of the gospel, that I may share in its blessings. *See also* **Ro** 11:17; **Php** 1:7; **2Th** 2:14; **1Pe** 5:1; **Jude** 3

Specific actions which express fellowship and unity in the church
Sharing in the Lord's Supper
1Co 10:16–17 Is not the cup of thanksgiving for which we give thanks a participation in the blood of Christ? And is not the bread that we break a participation in the body of Christ? . . .   *See also* **Ac** 2:46; 20:7; **1Co** 11:33
Baptism as an expression of unity
Eph 4:4–6 There is one body and one Spirit—just as you were called to one hope when you were called—one Lord, one faith, one baptism; one God and Father of all, who is over all and through all and in all.   *See also* **1Co** 12:13
Extending hospitality Ac 28:7; **Ro** 12:13; 16:23; **1Ti** 5:10; **Tit** 1:8; **1Pe** 4:9; **3Jn** 8
Greeting one another Ac 18:27; **Ro** 16:3–16; **1Co** 16:19–20; **Col** 4:10; **Phm** 17
Welcoming former opponents Ac 9:26–27; **2Co** 2:5–8; **Gal** 2:9

Divisions in the church
Causes of division in the NT church
Personal ambition: **Mk** 9:34; 10:35–41 pp **Mt** 20:20–24
Ethnic tension: **Ac** 6:1
Differences of opinion: **Ac** 15:37–40; **Php** 4:2
Troublesome heretical leaders: **Ro** 16:17; **Jude** 19
Partisan spirit: **1Co** 1:11–12; 3:3–4
1Co 6:1–6
Greed: **1Co** 11:18,20–21; **Jas** 4:1–3
Warnings against divisions in the church
1Co 1:10 I [Paul] appeal to you, brothers and sisters, in the name of our Lord Jesus Christ, that all of you agree with one another so that there may be no divisions among you and that you may be perfectly united in mind and thought. *See also* **Ro** 12:16; 16:17; **2Co** 12:20; **Eph** 4:31; **Jas** 4:11
Acceptable differences in the church
In secondary matters of conscience, Christians are to respect rather than judge each other. These things need not impair the essential unity that is in Christ: **Ro** 14:1–3,5–6; **1Co** 8:9–13
In varieties of spiritual gifts: **1Co** 12:4–6,14–25; **Gal** 2:7

Necessary divisions in the church
Between the true gospel and heretical alternatives: **2Co** 11:2–6,13–15; **Gal** 1:6–9; **Col** 2:8,16–19; **1Ti** 4:1–6; **1Jn** 2:18–19; **2Jn** 9–11; **Jude** 18–20
Between those truly committed to Jesus Christ, and those apparently part of the church but living sinful lives: **1Co** 5:9–10; **2Th** 3:6; **1Ti** 6:3–5; **2Ti** 3:2–9; **2Pe** 1:20–21; 2:1–3; **Rev** 2:20,24; 3:1,4
Over essential gospel principles: **Ac** 15:2,5–6,19; **Gal** 2:11   *See also God, unity of.*

creation and God
The natural world is sustained by God and speaks of God.

God sustains the creation
He upholds the natural order
Heb 1:3 The Son is the radiance of God's glory and the exact representation of his being, sustaining all things by his powerful word. After he had provided purification for sins, he sat down at the right hand of the Majesty in heaven.
See also **Job** 38:33–37; **Ps** 104:1–35; 135:6–7; 145:16–17; **Mt** 10:29–30; **Col** 1:17
He sustains humanity
Ac 17:28 " 'For in him we live and move and have our being.' As some of your own poets have said, 'We are his offspring.' "   *See also* **Job** 33:4; **Ps** 36:6; **Da** 4:34–35; **1Co** 8:6
Creation is upheld for the good of humanity
Ge 8:22 "As long as the earth endures, seedtime and harvest, cold and heat, summer and winter, day and night will never cease."
See also **Ge** 9:12–16; **Mt** 6:11
God's sustaining power reserves the world for judgment
2Pe 3:7 By the same word the present heavens and earth are reserved for fire, being kept for the day of judgment and destruction of the ungodly.   *See also* **2Pe** 3:9–12

God has given humanity responsibility to preserve creation
Ge 1:28 God blessed them and said to them [male and female], "Be fruitful and increase in number; fill the earth and subdue it. Rule over the

fish of the sea and the birds of the air and over every living creature that moves on the ground."   See also **Ge** 2:15; 9:1–3; **Ps** 8:6–8; 115:16; **Heb** 2:8; **Jas** 3:7

Creation is spoilt by sin
Ge 3:17–19 To Adam he [the LORD God] said, "Because you listened to your wife and ate from the tree about which I commanded you, 'You must not eat of it,' "Cursed is the ground because of you; through painful toil you will eat of it all the days of your life. It will produce thorns and thistles for you, and you will eat the plants of the field. By the sweat of your brow you will eat your food until you return to the ground, since from it you were taken; for dust you are and to dust you will return."   See also **Ro** 8:20–22; **Heb** 6:8

Creation speaks of God's nature and character
His revelation of himself
Job 12:7–10 "But ask the animals, and they will teach you, or the birds of the air, and they will tell you; or speak to the earth, and it will teach you, or let the fish of the sea inform you. Which of all these does not know that the hand of the LORD has done this? In his hand is the life of every creature and the breath of all people."
His eternal power and divine nature
Ro 1:20 For since the creation of the world God's invisible qualities—his eternal power and divine nature—have been clearly seen, being understood from what has been made, so that they are without excuse.   See also **Jer** 32:17
His authority Job 38:4–39:30; **Jer** 33:2
His glory and majesty
Ps 19:1–2 The heavens declare the glory of God; the skies proclaim the work of his hands. Day after day they pour forth speech; night after night they display knowledge.   See also **Ps** 8:1–9
His love and faithfulness
Ps 36:5 Your love, O LORD, reaches to the heavens, your faithfulness to the skies.   See also **Mt** 6:30

His power
Isa 40:25–28 "To whom will you compare me? Or who is my equal?" says the Holy One. Lift your eyes and look to the heavens: Who created all these? He who brings out the starry host one by one, and calls them each by name. Because of his great power and mighty strength, not one of them is missing. Why do you say, O Jacob, and complain, O Israel, "My way is hidden from the LORD; my cause is disregarded by my God"? Do you not know? Have you not heard? The LORD is the everlasting God, the Creator of the ends of the earth. He will not grow tired or weary, and his understanding no-one can fathom.
His wisdom
Ps 136:5 who by his understanding made the heavens . . .   See also **Pr** 8:27–29
His unchangeableness and eternity
Ps 102:25–27 In the beginning you laid the foundations of the earth, and the heavens are the work of your hands. They will perish, but you remain; they will all wear out like a garment. Like clothing you will change them and they will be discarded. But you remain the same, and your years will never end.   See also **Ps** 90:1–2; **Heb** 1:11
His spiritual work in believers' lives Mt 13:3–43   See also God, faithfulness; God, glory of; God, the Creator; God, the provider; God, wisdom of; Holy Spirit in creation; Holy Spirit in the world; Jesus Christ as creator; providence; revelation, creation; sin.

---

faith
A constant outlook of trust towards God, whereby human beings abandon all reliance on their own efforts and put their full confidence in him, his word and his promises.

---

faith and blessings
Confidence in the ability and willingness of God to act in supernatural power to advance his kingdom, and a commitment, expressed in prayer and action, to being the means by which he does so.

God's power is released through faith
Mt 17:20 He [Jesus] replied, "Because you

have so little faith. I tell you the truth, if you have faith as small as a mustard seed, you can say to this mountain, 'Move from here to there' and it will move. Nothing will be impossible for you." *See also* **Mk** 9:23; **Lk** 17:6

Praying in faith
Mt 21:21–22 Jesus replied, "I tell you the truth, if you have faith and do not doubt, not only can you do what was done to the fig-tree, but also you can say to this mountain, 'Go, throw yourself into the sea,' and it will be done. If you believe, you will receive whatever you ask for in prayer." pp Mk 11:22–24 *See also* **Jas** 1:5–7; 5:14–15

Praying in Jesus Christ's name
Jn 14:12–14 I [Jesus] tell you the truth, all who have faith in me will do what I have been doing, and they will do even greater things than these, because I am going to the Father. And I will do whatever you ask in my name, so that the Son may bring glory to the Father. You may ask me for anything in my name, and I will do it.

In the OT, faith in God's power
Heb 11:32–34 . . . who through faith conquered kingdoms, administered justice, and gained what was promised; who shut the mouths of lions, quenched the fury of the flames, and escaped the edge of the sword; whose weakness was turned to strength; and who became powerful in battle and routed foreign armies. *See also* **Heb** 11:11–12; **Jos** 14:6–14; **1Sa** 14:6; 17:32–47; **2Ch** 20:20; 32:7–8; **Da** 6:23

In the NT, healing in response to faith
Mt 9:22 Jesus turned and saw her [the woman with a severe haemorrhage]. "Take heart, daughter," he said, "your faith has healed you." And the woman was healed from that moment. pp Mk 5:34 pp Lk 8:48 *See also* **Mt** 9:29–30; **Mk** 10:52 pp **lk** 18:42; **Lk** 17:19; **Ac** 3:16; 14:8–10

Powerful ministries marked by faith
Ac 11:24 He [Barnabas] was a good man, full of the Holy Spirit and faith, and a great number of people were brought to the Lord. *See also* **Ac** 6:5–10; **1Co** 12:9

Faith and spiritual warfare
Eph 6:16 In addition to all this, take up the shield of faith, with which you can extinguish all the flaming arrows of the evil one.
See also **1Th** 5:8; **1Jn** 5:4–5

The importance of love accompanying faith
1Co 13:2 ". . . if I have a faith that can move mountains, but have not love, I am nothing.
See also God, power of; Holy Spirit, power; Jesus Christ, miracles; miracles; prayer and faith.

faith and salvation
Both in the OT and in the NT faith is the only basis of salvation. Faith is the means by which God's grace in Christ, and with him the blessings of salvation, is received. Paul's doctrine of justification by faith emphasises the centrality of faith in the Christian life.

Salvation by faith in the OT
Hab 2:4 ". . . the righteous will live by their faith . . ."

The faith of Abraham and other individuals
Ge 15:6 Abram believed the LORD, and he credited it to him as righteousness. *See also* **Ro** 4:9–16; **Heb** 11:4–5, 7

Salvation by faith in the NT
Ro 1:16–17 . . . in the gospel a righteousness from God is revealed, a righteousness that is by faith from first to last, just as it is written: "The righteous will live by faith." *See also* **1Co** 1:21; **Php** 3:8–9

Salvation through faith alone
Eph 2:8–9 For it is by grace you have been saved, through faith—and this not from yourselves, it is the gift of God—not by works, so that no-one can boast. *See also* **Ro** 3:27–28; 4:1–8; **Ps** 32:1–2; **Ro** 9:30–32; **Gal** 3:10–14; **Dt** 27:26

Salvation is by faith in Jesus Christ
Jn 3:14–16 "Just as Moses lifted up the snake

in the desert, so the Son of Man must be lifted up, that everyone who believes in him may have eternal life. For God so loved the world that he gave his one and only Son, that whoever believes in him shall not perish but have eternal life."
Ro 10:9-10 . . . if you confess with your mouth, "Jesus is Lord," and believe in your heart that God raised him from the dead, you will be saved . . .
See also Jn 8:24; Ac 8:37 fn; 13:38-39; Ro 3:21-26; 4:24; 2Co 4:13-14; Gal 3:22

Salvation is for all who believe
Ro 10:4 Christ is the end of the law so that there may be righteousness for everyone who believes. *See also Ac 15:7-9; Ro 3:29-30*

Salvation is for those who persevere in their faith
Col 1:21-23 . . . if you continue in your faith, established and firm, not moved from the hope held out in the gospel . . . *See also Heb 3:14; 6:11-12*

Saving faith shows itself in action
Jas 2:14 What good is it, my brothers and sisters, if people claim to have faith but have no deeds? Can such faith save them?

Blessings of salvation received through faith

Justification and peace with God Ro 5:1-2; Gal 2:15-16; 5:5
Forgiveness Lk 7:48-50; Ac 10:43
Adoption into God's family Jn 1:12; Gal 3:26

The gift of the Holy Spirit Jn 7:38-39; Gal 3:2; Eph 1:13
Jesus Christ in the heart Eph 3:17
Protection through God's power 1Pe 1:5
Access to God Eph 3:12; Heb 10:22
Sanctification Ac 26:17-18
New life Gal 2:20
Eternal life Jn 3:16,36; 5:24; 6:40,47
Victory over death Jn 11:25-27 *See also forgiveness; Holy Spirit, gift of; Jesus Christ, death of; salvation.*

---

faith, nature of
Confidence in and commitment to God and Jesus Christ. These attitudes remain sure even though the objects of faith are unseen. True faith is seen in obedient action, love and continuing good works.

The object of faith
God as the object of faith
Heb 11:6 And without faith it is impossible to please God, because anyone who comes to him must believe that he exists and that he rewards those who earnestly seek him. *See also Ps 25:1-2; 26:1; Pr 29:25; 1Pe 1:21*

Jesus Christ as the object of faith
Jn 14:1 "Do not let your [the disciples'] hearts be troubled. Trust in God; trust also in me [Jesus]." *See also Jn 3:16,18,36; 6:68-69*

False objects of faith
Human resources: Ps 20:7; Hos 10:13
Ps 118:9; Pr 28:26; Isa 42:17

Faith is personal trust in God
2Sa 22:31 "As for God, his way is perfect; the word of the LORD is flawless. He is a shield for all who take refuge in him." *See also Ps 18:2-6; 27:13-14; 1Pe 2:23*

True faith cannot be second-hand
2Ti 1:5 I [Paul] have been reminded of your [Timothy's] sincere faith, which first lived in your grandmother Lois and in your mother Eunice and, I am persuaded, now lives in you also.
See also Jn 4:42

Faith and assurance
Assurance accompanies faith
Heb 11:1 Now faith is being sure of what we hope for and certain of what we do not see.
See also Ro 4:19-21; 1Ti 3:13; Heb 10:22

Faith may be mixed with doubt Mt 14:31; Mk 9:24; Jn 20:24-28

Faith and sight
2Co 5:7 We live by faith, not by sight.
Faith as trust in what is unseen
Jn 20:29 Then Jesus told him [Thomas], "Because you have seen me, you have believed; blessed are those who have not seen and yet have believed." *See also 2Co 4:18; Heb 11:1-3,7,27*

Faith looks towards an unseen future
Heb 11:13–14 All these people [Abel, Enoch, Noah, Abraham] were still living by faith when they died. They did not receive the things promised; they only saw them and welcomed them from a distance. And they admitted that they were aliens and strangers on earth. People who say such things show that they are looking for a country of their own. *See also* **Heb 11:8–10, 20–22, 24–26**

Faith and obedience
True faith is demonstrated in obedience
Ro 1:5 Through him and for his name's sake, we received grace and apostleship to call people from among all the Gentiles to the obedience that comes from faith.
Heb 4:2 For we also have had the gospel preached to us, just as they did; but the message they heard was of no value to them, because those who heard did not combine it with faith. *See also* **Ro 16:26; 2Co 9:13; 1Pe 1:2**

Examples of obedient faith
Noah builds the ark: **Ge 6:22; Heb 11:7**
Abraham leaves Haran: **Ge 12:4; Heb 11:8**
Abraham offers Isaac: **Ge 22:1–10; Heb 11:17**
Ex 14:15–16
Caleb and Joshua: **Nu 13:30; 14:8–9**
Jos 3:5–13
Joshua at Jericho **Jos 6:2–5; Heb 11:30**
Jn 21:4–6; Ac 26:19

Faith and works
True faith is demonstrated in good deeds
Jas 2:14–26 . . . faith by itself, if it is not accompanied by action, is dead. But someone will say, "You have faith; I have deeds." Show me your faith without deeds, and I will show you my faith by what I do . . . *See also* **Php 2:17; 1Th 1:3; Tit 1:1; 2Pe 1:5**

True faith issues in love
Gal 5:6 For in Christ Jesus neither circumcision nor uncircumcision has any value. The only thing that counts is faith expressing itself through love. *See also* **Eph 1:15; 6:23; 1Th 3:6; 5:8; 1Ti 1:5,14; 4:12**

True faith is constantly productive
Lk 8:15 "But the seed on good soil stands for those with a noble and good heart, who hear the word, retain it, and by persevering produce a crop." pp **Mt 13:23** pp **Mk 4:20** *See also* **Jn 15:1–5** *See also Jesus Christ, responses to; life of faith.*

---

faith, necessity
A fundamental duty for all people and the necessary response to God's self-revelation. The only channel through which God's blessings may be received, and the only means by which life may be made meaningful, in relationship with God.

The call to faith
In the OT
Ps 37:3–5 Trust in the LORD and do good; dwell in the land and enjoy safe pasture. Delight yourself in the LORD and he will give you the desires of your heart. Commit your way to the LORD; trust in him and he will do this: *See also* **Pr 3:5–6; Isa 26:4; 50:10**

In the NT
Jn 6:28–29 . . . Jesus answered, "The work of God is this: to believe in the one he has sent." *See also* **Mk 1:15; Ac 16:30–31; 19:4; 20:21; Ro 1:5; 1Jn 3:23**

God's self-revelation leaves no excuse for unbelief
Jn 14:8–11 . . . Jesus answered: "Don't you know me, Philip, even after I have been among you such a long time? Anyone who has seen me has seen the Father. How can you say, 'Show us the Father'? . . ."
Ro 10:17–18 Consequently, faith comes from hearing the message, and the message is heard through the word of Christ. But I ask: Did they not hear? Of course they did: "Their voice has gone out into all the earth, their words to the ends of the world." *See also* **Ps 19:4; Jn 1:10–12; Ro 1:18–21; 3:1–4; Ps 51:4; Ro 16:25–27**

The need for faith in God
The LORD is the only true God
Hab 2:18–20 "Of what value is an idol, since someone has carved it? Or an image that teaches lies? For those who make them trust in their own creations; they make idols that cannot speak . . . But the LORD is in his holy temple; let all the earth be silent before him." *See also* Ps 115:2–11

God alone can be trusted absolutely
Ps 9:10 Those who know your name will trust in you, for you, LORD, have never forsaken those who seek you. *See also* Ps 91:1–4; Isa 12:2; Na 1:7

Faith in God is the basis for peace
Isa 26:3 You will keep in perfect peace those whose minds are steadfast, because they trust in you. *See also* Ps 42:11; Jn 14:1; Ro 15:13; 2Pe 1:1–2

Faith is necessary to receive God's blessing
Heb 11:6 And without faith it is impossible to please God, because anyone who comes to him must believe that he exists and that he rewards those who earnestly seek him. *See also* Ps 40:4; Jer 17:7–8; Jn 5:24

Faith is necessary to avoid God's judgment
Jn 3:36 "Those who believe in the Son have eternal life, but those who reject the Son will not see life, for God's wrath remains on them." *See also* Jn 3:18; 2Th 2:12; 1Pe 2:6–8; Isa 28:16; Ps 118:22; Isa 8:14

Actions not springing from faith are sinful
Ro 14:23 . . . and everything that does not come from faith is sin. *See also* Ro 14:5–8,14

Unbelief challenged
Heb 3:12–18; Ps 95:7–8; Isa 7:9; Jer 17:5–6; Mk 16:14 *See also* God as Saviour; God, grace and mercy; God, unique; Jesus Christ as Saviour; repentance; revelation; salvation, necessity of.

---

faith, origins of
Faith is a gift from God himself and is not to be seen as the result of human striving or achievement. Faith is inspired by the word and works of God.

Faith is a gift from God
Jn 6:63–65 "The Spirit gives life; the flesh counts for nothing. The words I have spoken to you are spirit and they are life. Yet there are some of you who do not believe." For Jesus had known from the beginning which of them did not believe and who would betray him. He went on to say, "This is why I told you that no-one can come to me unless the Father has enabled them."

Eph 2:8–9 For it is by grace you have been saved, through faith—and this not from yourselves, it is the gift of God—not by works, so that no-one can boast. *See also* Mt 16:15–17; Mk 9:24; Lk 17:5; Ac 3:16; 14:27; 18:27; Ro 12:3; 1Co 4:7; 12:9; Php 1:29; Jas 2:5

Faith comes through God's word
Faith following a direct word from God
Heb 11:29–30; Ex 14:15; Jos 6:2–5; Ac 27:23–25
Faith through the Scriptures
Jn 2:22; 20:30–31; 2Ti 3:15

Faith comes through hearing God's word preached
Ro 10:14–17 How, then, can they call on the one they have not believed in? And how can they believe in the one of whom they have not heard? And how can they hear without someone preaching to them? And how can they preach unless they are sent? As it is written, "How beautiful are the feet of those who bring good news!" . . . Consequently, faith comes from hearing the message, and the message is heard through the word of Christ. *See also* Isa 52:7; 53:1; Jn 1:7; 4:41–42; 17:20; Ac 11:19–21; 1Co 2:4–5

Faith comes through a personal encounter with Jesus Christ
Jn 9:35–38; 20:26–28

Faith comes through witnessing miracles
Jn 14:11 "Believe me [Jesus] when I say that I am in the Father and the Father is in me; or at least believe on the evidence of the miracles themselves." *See also* Jn 2:11; 4:53

The raising of Lazarus: **Jn** 11:45; 12:11
Ac 9:42

Faith based on knowledge of God
Knowledge of God's faithfulness leads to faith
Ps 46:1–3; **La** 3:19–24; **Na** 1:7; **Ac** 2:25–26
Knowledge of God's achievements leads to faith Dt 3:21–22; **1Sa** 17:34–37; **Jer** 14:22
See also God, power of; grace and salvation; Jesus Christ, miracles; miracles, nature of; Scripture.

---

fellowship with God

The relationship with God, disrupted by sin yet established through Jesus Christ, which provides the only proper basis for true human fellowship. God's desire for fellowship with humanity is made known through his calling of a people to be his own and to reflect his holiness and love.

God's fellowship with his people is shown by his presence
God's presence with Israel
Lev 26:12 "'I will walk among you [Israel] and be your God, and you will be my people.'" *See also* **Ex** 33:14; **Isa** 63:9; **Hag** 1:13
God's presence in the tabernacle
Ex 25:8 "Then have them [the Israelites] make a sanctuary for me, and I [the LORD] will dwell among them." *See also* **Ex** 29:45–46; 40:34–36; **Lev** 26:11; **Dt** 12:11
God's presence in the temple
1Ki 6:12–13 ". . . I [the LORD] will live among the Israelites and will not abandon my people Israel." *See also* **1Ki** 8:29 pp 2Ch 6:20; **2Ch** 7:1–2; **Isa** 6:1
God's presence in the new Jerusalem
Zec 2:10–13 "Shout and be glad, O Daughter of Zion. For I am coming, and I will live among you," declares the LORD . . . *See also* **Eze** 37:26–28; 43:4–7; 48:35; **Rev** 21:3

The church's fellowship with God
Fellowship with the Father, Son and Holy Spirit
Jn 14:23 Jesus replied, "Those who love me will obey my teaching. My Father will love them, and we will come to them and make our home with them." *See also* **Jn** 14:7,16–17
Fellowship is made possible through Jesus Christ
Eph 2:18–19 For through him [Christ Jesus] we both have access to the Father by one Spirit . . . *See also* **Ro** 5:10; **2Co** 5:18–19; **Col** 1:20–22; **Heb** 10:19–22
Fellowship with Jesus Christ
1Co 1:9 God, who has called you into fellowship with his Son Jesus Christ our Lord, is faithful. *See also* **Mt** 28:20; **Jn** 15:4–5; **Ro** 6:4–5; **1Co** 10:15–16; **Php** 3:10
Fellowship with God is inseparable from fellowship with one another
1Jn 1:3 We [the apostles] proclaim to you what we have seen and heard, so that you also may have fellowship with us. And our fellowship is with the Father and with his Son, Jesus Christ.
See also **Mt** 18:20; **Mk** 9:37; **Jn** 17:21; **2Co** 13:11

The demands of fellowship with God
Holiness
Lev 20:26 "'You [Israel] are to be holy to me because I, the LORD, am holy, and I have set you apart from the nations to be my own.'"
2Co 6:14–18 . . . What agreement is there between the temple of God and idols? For we are the temple of the living God. As God has said: "I will live with them and walk among them, and I will be their God, and they will be my people." "Therefore come out from them and be separate, says the Lord. Touch no unclean thing, and I will receive you." . . . *See also* **Ex** 34:12–14; **Ezr** 6:21; **1Co** 5:11; **Eph** 5:8–11; **Jas** 4:4
Obedience to God's will
1Jn 3:24 Those who obey his [God's] commands live in him, and he in them. And this is how we know that he lives in us: We know it by the Spirit he gave us. *See also* **Isa** 57:15; **Mt** 12:49–50 pp Mk 3:34–35 pp Lk 8:21; **Jn** 14:21

Sin separates people from fellowship with God
Isa 59:2 But your iniquities have separated you

from your God; your sins have hidden his face from you, so that he will not hear.

1Jn 1:5-6 . . . If we claim to have fellowship with him [God] yet walk in the darkness, we lie and do not live by the truth. *See also* **Ge** 3:8; **Eze** 39:23

Examples of fellowship with God
Ge 5:22; 6:9; **2Ch** 20:7
Moses: **Ex** 33:11; **Nu** 12:3
Jos 1:9; **Mal** 2:6 *See also abiding in Christ; forgiveness; heaven, community of redeemed; holiness; prayer, response to God; sin; Trinity.*

forgiveness
The freeing of a person from guilt and its consequences, including punishment; usually as an act of favour, compassion or love, with the aim of restoring a broken personal relationship. Forgiveness can involve both the remission of punishment and the cancellation of debts.

forgiveness, divine
God forgives the sins of believers on the basis of the once for all sacrifice offered by Jesus Christ on the cross. Believers' sins are no longer held against them, on account of the atoning death of Jesus Christ.

God's nature and forgiveness
Ex 34:5-7 Then the LORD came down in the cloud and stood there with him and proclaimed his name, the LORD. And he passed in front of Moses, proclaiming, "The LORD, the LORD, the compassionate and gracious God, slow to anger, abounding in love and faithfulness, maintaining love to thousands, and forgiving wickedness, rebellion and sin . . ." *See also* **Nu** 14:17-20; **Ne** 9:16-17; **Ps** 103:1-18; **Isa** 43:25; **Mic** 7:18-20; **1Jn** 1:8-9

God's promise of forgiveness
Jer 31:31-34 "The time is coming," declares the LORD, "when I will make a new covenant with the house of Israel and with the house of Judah. It will not be like the covenant I made with their ancestors when I took them by the hand to lead them out of Egypt, because they broke my covenant, though I was a husband to them," declares the LORD. "This is the covenant that I will make with the house of Israel after that time," declares the LORD. "I will put my law in their minds and write it on their hearts. I will be their God, and they will be my people. No longer will they teach their neighbours, or say to one another, 'Know the LORD,' because they will all know me, from the least of them to the greatest," declares the LORD. "For I will forgive their wickedness and will remember their sins no more." *See also* **2Ch** 7:14; **Isa** 55:6-7; **Heb** 8:8-12

People's need of forgiveness
1Jn 1:8-10 If we claim to be without sin, we deceive ourselves and the truth is not in us. If we confess our sins, he is faithful and just and will forgive us our sins and purify us from all unrighteousness. If we claim we have not sinned, we make him out to be a liar and his word has no place in our lives. *See also* **Ps** 51:1-5; **Isa** 6:1-5; **Ro** 3:9,23

The means of forgiveness
Under the old covenant
Heb 9:22 In fact, the law requires that nearly everything be cleansed with blood, and without the shedding of blood there is no forgiveness. *See also* **Lev** 4:27-31; 5:17-18
Under the new covenant
Mt 26:27-28 Then he [Jesus] took the cup, gave thanks and offered it to them, saying, "Drink from it, all of you. This is my blood of the covenant, which is poured out for many for the forgiveness of sins." *See also* **Jn** 1:29; **Eph** 1:7-8; **Col** 2:13-15

The assurance of forgiveness
1Jn 1:8-9 If we claim to be without sin, we deceive ourselves and the truth is not in us. If we confess our sins, he is faithful and just and will forgive us our sins and purify us from all unrighteousness. *See also* **Ps** 51:7; 103:8-12; 130:3-4; **Pr** 28:13; **Isa** 1:18; **Ac** 2:38;

forgiveness, Jesus Christ's ministry 20

Jas 5:13–16; 1Jn 2:1–2   *See also grace; Holy Spirit, conviction; repentance; sin, remedy for.*

forgiveness, Jesus Christ's ministry

A central feature of Jesus Christ's ministry was his declaration that believers' sins were forgiven through their faith in him.

Jesus Christ's ministry of forgiveness was foretold

Mt 1:20–21 ... "Joseph son of David, do not be afraid to take Mary home as your wife, because what is conceived in her is from the Holy Spirit. She will give birth to a son, and you are to give him the name Jesus, because he will save his people from their sins."

Jn 1:29 The next day John saw Jesus coming towards him and said, "Look, the Lamb of God, who takes away the sin of the world!"

Jesus Christ's exercise of forgiveness

Lk 23:33–34 When they came to the place called the Skull, there they crucified him, along with the criminals—one on his right, the other on his left. Jesus said, "Father, forgive them, for they do not know what they are doing." ...
See also Jn 8:3–11

Jesus Christ has authority on account of his divinity to forgive sins

Mt 9:1–8 Jesus stepped into a boat, crossed over and came to his own town. Some people brought to him a paralytic, lying on a mat. When Jesus saw their faith, he said to the paralytic, "Take heart, son; your sins are forgiven." At this, some of the teachers of the law said to themselves, "This fellow is blaspheming!" Knowing their thoughts, Jesus said, "Why do you entertain evil thoughts in your hearts? Which is easier: to say, 'Your sins are forgiven,' or to say, 'Get up and walk'? But so that you may know that the Son of Man has authority on earth to forgive sins. ..." Then he said to the paralytic, "Get up, take your mat and go home." And the man got up and went home. When the crowd saw this, they were filled with awe; and they praised God, who had given such authority to human beings. pp Mk 2:1–12 pp Lk 5:17–26

People's offence at Jesus Christ's exercise of forgiveness

Mk 2:5–7 When Jesus saw their faith, he said to the paralytic, "Son, your sins are forgiven." Now some teachers of the law were sitting there, thinking to themselves, "Why does this fellow talk like that? He's blaspheming! Who can forgive sins but God alone?" pp Mt 9:2–3 pp Lk 5:20–21

Parables of forgiveness

Mt 18:23–35; **Lk** 7:36–50; 15:11–32

The church's ministry of forgiveness in Jesus Christ's name

Jn 20:21–23 Again Jesus said, "Peace be with you! As the Father has sent me, I am sending you." And with that he breathed on them and said, "Receive the Holy Spirit. If you forgive the sins of anyone, their sins are forgiven; if you do not forgive them, they are not forgiven."
See also Ac 2:38; 13:38; 26:15–18   *See also gospel, promises; Jesus Christ, authority; Jesus Christ, death of; Jesus Christ, miracles; Jesus Christ, opposition to; Jesus Christ, parables.*

freedom through Jesus Christ

Jesus Christ, the promised deliverer, sets his people free from the present effects of sin and from the power of sin and will finally deliver them completely from its presence.

The OT points ahead to a new and greater freedom and to a new deliverer

The OT predicts Jesus Christ as the deliverer
Isa 61:1 ... He [the Sovereign LORD] has sent me to bind up the broken-hearted, to proclaim freedom for the captives and release from darkness for the prisoners.   *See also* Isa 42:6–7
The redemption of the exodus foreshadows the redemption achieved by Jesus Christ
Col 1:13–14 For he [the Father] has rescued

us from the dominion of darkness and brought us into the kingdom of the Son he loves, in whom we have redemption, the forgiveness of sins. *See also* **1Co** 10:1–4

Jesus Christ fulfils the OT predictions of him as deliverer
Lk 4:18–19 ". . . He [the Lord] has sent me to proclaim freedom for the prisoners and recovery of sight for the blind, to release the oppressed . . ." *See also* **Ro** 11:26; **Isa** 59:20

The freedom that comes through Jesus Christ
Jn 8:32–36 ". . . So if the Son sets you free, you will be free indeed." *See also* **Mt** 1:21

Jesus Christ sets his people free from the penalty of sin
1Th 1:10 . . . Jesus, who rescues us from the coming wrath. *See also* **Jn** 3:36; **Ro** 8:1–2; **Heb** 9:15; **Rev** 1:5

Jesus Christ sets his people free from the spiritual death that accompanies sin
Ro 6:1–7 . . . because anyone who has died has been freed from sin. *See also* **Eph** 2:1–5; **Heb** 9:14

Jesus Christ sets his people free from the fear of death
Heb 2:14–15 Since the children have flesh and blood, he too shared in their humanity so that by his death he might destroy him who holds the power of death—that is, the devil—and free those who all their lives were held in slavery by their fear of death.

Jesus Christ will finally set his people free from death itself
1Co 15:22–23 For as in Adam all die, so in Christ all will be made alive. But in this order: Christ, the firstfruits; then, when he comes, those who belong to him. *See also* **Ro** 5:12–17; 7:24

Jesus Christ sets his people free from the power of sin
Ro 6:11–14 In the same way, count yourselves dead to sin but alive to God in Christ Jesus. Therefore do not let sin reign in your mortal body so that you obey its evil desires. Do not offer the parts of your body to sin, as instruments of wickedness, but rather offer yourselves to God, as those who have been brought from death to life; and offer the parts of your body to him as instruments of righteousness. For sin shall not be your master, because you are not under law, but under grace. *See also* **Ro** 6:22–23

Jesus Christ sets his people free from the pollution of sin
2Pe 1:2–4 . . . Through these [God's glory and goodness] he has given us his very great and precious promises, so that through them you may participate in the divine nature and escape the corruption in the world caused by evil desires. *See also* **Gal** 1:3–4

Jesus Christ sets his people free from the power of Satan
Col 1:13–14 . . . he [the Father] has rescued us from the dominion of darkness and brought us into the kingdom of the Son he loves, in whom we have redemption, the forgiveness of sins. *See also* **Mk** 3:27; **Ac** 26:17–18

Jesus Christ will set his people free from the presence of sin
Php 3:21 who [the Lord Jesus Christ], by the power that enables him to bring everything under his control, will transform our lowly bodies so that they will be like his glorious body. *See also* **Eph** 5:27; **Col** 1:22; **1Th** 3:13; 5:23; **Rev** 21:4

Freedom as the result of being rescued from trials by Jesus Christ
2Ti 3:11 persecutions, sufferings—what kinds of things happened to me in Antioch, Iconium and Lystra, the persecutions I endured. Yet the Lord rescued me from all of them. *See also* **Ac** 26:17; **2Ti** 4:18; **2Pe** 2:9 *See also Jesus Christ as redeemer; Jesus Christ, second coming; Messiah, coming of; sin, deliverance from.*

glory
The distinctive feature of the presence of God, often compared to power, weight or brightness. Scripture affirms that God's glory is made known through his work of creation, his acts of intervention in history and supremely in the life and resurrection of Jesus Christ.

glory, divine and human

Through the death and resurrection of Jesus Christ, believers will finally be glorified. All human glory derives from God.

Human glory in the creation
Human glory as God's intention
Heb 2:6–7 . . . "What is a human being that you [God] are mindful of him, the son of man that you care for him? You made him a little lower than the angels; you crowned him with glory and honour"   *See also* **Ps** 8:4–5

People are created in God's image
Ge 5:1 . . . When God created human beings, he made them in the likeness of God.
See also **Ge** 1:26–27; 9:6; **1Co** 11:7; **Jas** 3:9

Human beings have precedence over the rest of creation
Mt 6:26 "Look at the birds of the air; they do not sow or reap or store away in barns, and yet your heavenly Father feeds them. Are you [humans] not much more valuable than they?" pp Lk 12:24   *See also* **Mt** 10:29–31 pp Lk 12:6–7; **Mt** 12:12

Human responsibility for creation
Ge 2:19–20 Now the LORD God had formed out of the ground all the beasts of the field and all the birds of the air. He brought them to the man to see what he would name them . . . So the man gave names to all the livestock, the birds of the air and all the beasts of the field. But for Adam no suitable helper was found.
See also **Ge** 1:28; **Ps** 8:6–8; **Heb** 2:8; **Jas** 3:7

Human glory diminished after the fall
Ro 3:23 for all have sinned and fall short of the glory of God,   *See also* **Ge** 5:3; **Ecc** 7:29; **Ro** 5:12

The imperfect nature of human glory
1Pe 1:24–25 . . . "All human beings are like grass, and all their glory is like the flowers of the field; the grass withers and the flowers fall . . ."   *See also* **Isa** 40:6–8; **Ps** 49:10–11,16–17; 103:15; **2Co** 3:7–8,10,13

Human glory is given and taken by God
Ps 82:6–7 "I [God] said, 'You are "gods"; you are all sons of the Most High.' But you will die like mere mortals; you will fall like every other ruler."   *See also* **Ex** 9:16; **1Ki** 3:13 pp 2Ch 1:12; **Jer** 27:6–7; **Da** 2:37–39; 4:29–31,36; **Jn** 19:11; **Ro** 13:1

The temporary nature of the glory of the wicked
Php 3:19 Their [Christ's enemies'] destiny is destruction, their god is their stomach, and their glory is in their shame . . .   *See also* **Isa** 5:15; **Lk** 16:25; **Rev** 18:14–17

The temptation associated with human glory
Mt 4:8–9 . . . the devil took him [Jesus] to a very high mountain and showed him all the kingdoms of the world and their splendour. "All this I will give you," he said, "if you will bow down and worship me." pp Lk 4:5–7   *See also* **2Ti** 4:10; **1Jn** 2:15

The uniqueness of God's glory
Job 40:9–10 "Do you [Job] have an arm like God's, and can your voice thunder like his? Then adorn yourself with glory and splendour, and clothe yourself in honour and majesty."
See also **Ex** 15:11; **1Ch** 16:24–28 pp Ps 96:3–7; **Isa** 42:8; 48:11

God's glory revealed to human beings
Ex 24:17 To the Israelites the glory of the LORD looked like a consuming fire on top of the mountain.   *See also* **Ex** 16:10; **Ps** 26:8; **Eze** 1:25–28; **Lk** 2:9; **Ac** 7:55

Glory is not to be sought from other human beings but from God
Mt 6:2 "So when you give to the needy, do not announce it with trumpets, as the hypocrites do in the synagogues and on the streets, to be honoured by others. I tell you the truth, they have received their reward in full."   *See also* **Jer** 9:23–24; **Hos** 4:7; **Jn** 5:41–44; **Php** 3:3; **1Th** 2:4–6; **Jas** 4:16

It is a human duty to glorify God
Ps 34:3 Glorify the LORD with me: let us exalt his name together. *See also* **Ps** 63:3; 86:12; **Da** 4:37; **Ro** 15:6; **Gal** 1:3–5

Glory is restored to redeemed humanity by the death of Jesus Christ
Ro 8:30 . . . those he [God] predestined, he also called; those he called, he also justified; those he justified, he also glorified.
See also **Ro** 9:23; **1Co** 15:47–49; **Col** 3:10

Spiritual glory is divinely given
Jn 17:22 "I [Jesus] have given them [the disciples] the glory that you [God] gave me . . ." *See also* **Ps** 84:11; **2Co** 3:18

Glorification when Jesus Christ returns
Col 3:4 When Christ, who is your life, appears, then you also will appear with him in glory.
See also **Ro** 8:18; **Php** 3:21; **1Th** 2:20; **1Jn** 3:2
See also God, glory of; God, unique; heaven; Jesus Christ, glory of; Jesus Christ, transfiguration; sin.

---

glory, revelation of
God's majestic brilliance shown to the world through Israel and the church, and supremely in and through Jesus Christ.

God's glory revealed in nature
Ps 19:1 The heavens declare the glory of God; the skies proclaim the work of his hands.
See also **Ge** 1:31; **Ps** 29:3–9; 104:1–4; **Ro** 1:20

God's glory revealed through Israel
In the exodus
Ex 15:11 "Who among the gods is like you, O LORD? Who is like you—majestic in holiness, awesome in glory, working wonders?"
See also **Ex** 16:7,10; 24:9–11

At his sanctuary
Ex 40:34–35 Then the cloud covered the Tent of Meeting, and the glory of the LORD filled the tabernacle . . . *See also* **Ex** 29:43; **Lev** 9:6,23; **Nu** 20:6; **1Ki** 8:10–11 pp **2Ch** 5:13–14; **2Ch** 7:1–3; **Isa** 6:1; **Eze** 44:4; **Hag** 2:7

In the nation as a whole
Isa 44:23 . . . Burst into song, you mountains, you forests and all your trees, for the LORD has redeemed Jacob, he displays his glory in Israel.
See also **Ps** 85:9; **Isa** 43:6–7; 46:13; 49:3; 55:5; **Zec** 2:4–5

To individuals in Israel
Moses: **Ex** 24:15–17; 33:18–23
Ezekiel: **Eze** 1:28; 3:23; 8:4; 9:3; 10:4,18–19; 11:22–23; 43:2–5

God's glory revealed through the church
2Co 3:18 And we, who with unveiled faces all reflect the Lord's glory, are being transformed into his likeness with ever-increasing glory, which comes from the Lord, who is the Spirit. *See also* **Eph** 1:12; 3:21; **1Pe** 4:14

God's glory revealed to the whole earth
To all peoples
Ps 57:5 Be exalted, O God, above the heavens; let your glory be over all the earth. pp **Ps** 108:5
Hab 3:3 God came from Teman, the Holy One from Mount Paran . . . His glory covered the heavens and his praise filled the earth.
See also **Ps** 57:11; 72:19; 97:6; **Isa** 6:3; 40:5

God's glory revealed in his judgments
Rev 19:1–2 After this I heard what sounded like the roar of a great multitude in heaven shouting: "Hallelujah! Salvation and glory and power belong to our God, for true and just are his judgments . . ." *See also* **Nu** 14:10,21–23; 16:19–20; **Isa** 2:10,19,21; **Eze** 39:21; **Rev** 15:8

God's glory revealed in the future
Isa 60:19–20 "The sun will no more be your light by day, nor will the brightness of the moon shine on you, for the LORD will be your everlasting light, and your God will be your glory . . ."
See also **Isa** 4:5; 24:23; 35:2; 58:8; 60:1–2

God's glory revealed through Jesus Christ
Jesus Christ reveals God's glory
Heb 1:3 The Son is the radiance of God's glory

God

and the exact representation of his being ...
See also **Lk** 2:9; **Jn** 11:40; 14:8–9; **Ac** 7:55
Jesus Christ reveals his own glory
Jn 1:14 The Word became flesh and made his dwelling among us. We have seen his glory, the glory of the One and Only, who came from the Father, full of grace and truth.   See also **Lk** 9:32; **Jn** 2:11; 12:41; 17:24; **Heb** 2:9; **2Pe** 1:16–17
Glory revealed in Jesus Christ's death
Jn 12:23 Jesus replied, "The hour has come for the Son of Man to be glorified."   See also **Jn** 12:27–33; 13:31–32
Glory revealed at Jesus Christ's second coming
Mt 16:27 pp **Mk** 8:38 pp **Lk** 9:26; **Mt** 24:30 pp **Mk** 13:26 pp **Lk** 21:27; **Mt** 25:31; **2Th** 1:10

God's glory revealed in the new Jerusalem
Rev 21:10–11 ... he [one of the seven angels] ... showed me the Holy City, Jerusalem, coming down out of heaven from God. It shone with the glory of God ...   See also **Rev** 21:23   See also *God, glory of; God, power of; God, revelation; Holy Spirit, power; Jesus Christ, glory of; Jesus Christ, second coming; Jesus Christ, Son of God.*

God
The Creator and Redeemer of the world, who reveals himself in Scripture and in Jesus Christ, and who is loved, worshipped and adored by believers. Scripture stresses the personal nature of God, and also his total reliability and trustworthiness. God is the Father of Jesus Christ and of all believers.

God as judge
As a part of his sovereignty and authority, God is executor of his righteousness within the created order. Jesus Christ shares in this ongoing work.

God has authority to judge
God's status as judge
Ps 75:7 ... it is God who judges: He brings one down, he exalts another.   See also **Ps** 50:6; 76:8–9; **Ecc** 11:9; **Isa** 33:22; 66:16; **2Ti** 4:8; **Heb** 12:23; **Jas** 4:12

He decides disputes
Jdg 11:27 "... Let the LORD, the Judge, decide the dispute this day between the Israelites and the Ammonites."   See also **Ge** 16:5; 31:53; **1Sa** 24:15; **Isa** 2:4 pp **Mic** 4:3; **Jas** 5:9
He presides in the heavenly court
Isa 3:13 The LORD takes his place in court; he rises to judge the people.   See also **Ps** 50:4; 82:1; **Da** 7:9–10; **Joel** 3:12; **Rev** 20:11–15

God is judge over the whole of creation
He judges the earth
Ge 18:25 "... Will not the Judge of all the earth do right?"   See also **Ps** 9:8; 58:11; 82:8; 94:2; 96:13; 98:9
He judges every individual
Eze 33:20 "... I [the LORD] will judge each of you according to your own ways."   See also **Ecc** 3:17; **Heb** 9:27; **1Pe** 4:5; **Jude** 15; **Rev** 20:12
He judges the nations
Joel 3:12 "... I [the LORD] will sit to judge all the nations on every side."   See also **Ps** 9:19–20; 110:6; **Ob** 15; **Zep** 3:8
He judges rulers of nations **Isa** 40:23; **Jer** 25:17–27; **Rev** 6:15–17
He judges his own people
Heb 10:30 ... "The Lord will judge his people."   See also **Dt** 32:36; **Ps** 78:62; **Jer** 1:16; **1Pe** 4:17
He judges angels **2Pe** 2:4; **Jude** 6
He judges Satan **Ge** 3:14–15; **Mt** 25:41; **1Ti** 3:6; **Rev** 20:10

God's judgment is inescapable
No-one can hide from God
Ob 4 "Though you soar like the eagle and make your nest among the stars, from there I will bring you down," declares the LORD.   See also **Ge** 3:8–9; **Job** 11:20; **Jer** 11:11; **Am** 9:1–4
God searches human hearts
Jer 17:10 "I the LORD search the heart and examine the mind, to reward everyone according to their conduct, according to what their deeds deserve."   See also **1Ch** 28:9; **Ps** 7:9; **Pr** 5:21; **Jer** 11:20

God reveals secrets
Ro 2:16 . . . God will judge everyone's secrets through Jesus Christ . . . *See also* **Ecc** 12:14; **Jer** 16:17; **1Co** 4:5; **Heb** 4:13

Examples of God acting as judge
His judgment of the earth in sending the flood Ge 6:7,13,17; 7:21–23
His judgment of individuals Ge 4:9–12; **Ac** 5:3–10; 13:8–11
His judgment of families Jos 7:24–25; **1Sa** 3:12–13
His judgment of cities Ge 19:24–25; **Jos** 6:24
His judgment of nations Dt 7:1–5
His judgment of the rulers of nations 2Ch 26:16–21; **Da** 4:31–33; 5:22–30; **Ac** 12:22–23
His judgment of his own people Jdg 2:11–15; **2Ch** 36:15–20; **Isa** 33:22

God's character is revealed through his righteous judgments
His sovereignty Ps 9:7; 96:10; 99:4; **Eze** 6:14
His power Ex 6:6; 14:31; **Eze** 20:33–36; **Rev** 18:8
His holiness Lev 10:1–3; **1Sa** 6:19–20; **Eze** 28:22; **Rev** 16:5
His anger Na 1:2–3; **Ro** 2:5
His truth Ps 96:13; **Ro** 2:2; **Rev** 16:7
His impartiality 2Ch 19:7; **Ro** 2:9–11; **Col** 3:25; **1Pe** 1:17
His compassion La 3:31–33; **Hos** 11:8–9; **Jnh** 3:10; 4:2
His patience Nu 14:18; **Ne** 9:30; **2Pe** 3:9
His mercy Ne 9:31; **Job** 9:15; **Ps** 78:38; **Mic** 7:18

Jesus Christ continues God's work as judge
Jn 5:22 ". . . the Father judges no-one, but has entrusted all judgment to the Son," *See also* **Jn** 5:27; **Ac** 10:42

God will act as judge on the last day
Rev 20:12 And I saw the dead, great and small, standing before the throne, and books were opened. Another book was opened, which is the book of life. The dead were judged according to what they had done as recorded in the books. *See also* **Isa** 2:17; **Zep** 1:14–18; **Jn** 12:48; **Ac** 17:31; **Ro** 2:16; 14:10; **1Co** 4:5; **2Ti** 4:1; **1Pe** 4:5; **2Pe** 2:9; 3:7 *See also God, anger of; God, grace and mercy; God, holiness of; God, justice of; God, patience of; God, righteousness; Jesus Christ as judge.*

God as redeemer

God alone has the ability to save his people from slavery and captivity. God's redemptive will and power is demonstrated in his deliverance of Israel from bondage in Egypt, and supremely through the death and resurrection of Jesus Christ.

God as the sole redeemer of Israel
Isa 47:4 Our Redeemer—the LORD Almighty is his name—is the Holy One of Israel. *See also* **Dt** 13:5; **Ps** 19:14
He redeems because of his love Dt 7:8; **Ps** 44:26
He is able to redeem because of his power Dt 9:26; **2Sa** 7:23 pp **1Ch** 17:21; **Ne** 1:10

God acts as Israel's redeemer
Ps 78:35; 111:9; **Isa** 43:1; 48:17; 54:5; 63:16
He promises to redeem Israel from Egypt
Ex 3:8–10 "So I [God] have come down to rescue them [the Israelites] from the hand of the Egyptians and to bring them up out of that land into a good and spacious land, a land flowing with milk and honey . . . I am sending you to Pharaoh to bring my people the Israelites out of Egypt." *See also* **Ex** 3:21; 14:4
He redeems Israel in the exodus from Egypt
Dt 5:15 "Remember that you were slaves in Egypt and that the LORD your God brought you out of there with a mighty hand and an outstretched arm . . ." *See also* **Dt** 15:15; 21:8; 24:18; **Ne** 9:9–11; **Ps** 77:14–20; 105:23–38; **Hos** 13:4; **Mic** 6:4; **Ac** 7:30–36
He redeems Israel from Babylonian exile
Isa 41:14 "Do not be afraid, O worm Jacob, O little Israel, for I myself will help you," declares the LORD, your Redeemer, the Holy One of Israel. *See also* **Isa** 43:4; 44:6,24; 49:26; 54:5; 60:16; 62:12; **Jer** 50:33–35; 51:12; **Mic** 4:10; **Zec** 10:8

God redeems his people from difficult personal circumstances
Ps 34:22 The LORD redeems his servants . . . *See also* **Isa** 29:22; **Job** 19:25; **Ps** 31:4–5; **La** 3:58
He brings deliverance from enemies Ps 69:18; 106:10; 107:2; **Jer** 15:21; 31:11

God redeems his people from the bondage and guilt of sin
Ps 130:7–8 . . . with him [the Lord] is full redemption. He himself will redeem Israel from all their sins. *See also* **Ps** 34:22; **Isa** 59:20
Those who remain sinful do not find redemption
Hos 7:13 "Woe to them, because they have strayed from me! Destruction to them, because they have rebelled against me! I long to redeem them but they speak lies against me." *See also* **Ps** 26:11; **Isa** 1:27–28

God redeems his people from death
Ps 49:15 But God will redeem my life from the grave . . . *See also* **Job** 19:25–27; **Ps** 103:4

Jesus Christ is central to God's redemptive purposes
Col 1:13–14 For he [God] has rescued us from the dominion of darkness and brought us into the kingdom of the Son he loves, in whom we have redemption, the forgiveness of sins. *See also* **Lk** 1:68; **Ro** 3:23–24; **1Co** 1:30; 7:23; **Gal** 3:13–14; 4:4–5; **Eph** 1:7; **Heb** 9:11–12; **1Pe** 1:18–21
God will finally redeem all creation at Jesus Christ's second coming
Ro 8:19–23 The creation waits in eager expectation for the children of God to be revealed. For the creation was subjected to frustration, not by its own choice, but by the will of the one who subjected it, in hope that the creation itself will be liberated from its bondage to decay and brought into the glorious freedom of the children of God. We know that the whole creation has been groaning as in the pains of childbirth right up to the present time. Not only so, but we ourselves, who have the firstfruits of the Spirit, groan inwardly as we wait eagerly for our adoption, the redemption of our bodies. *See also* **Lk** 21:28; **Eph** 1:13–14; 4:30; **Tit** 2:13–14

God's redemptive work brings him praise and worship
Eph 1:3–7 Praise be to the God and Father of our Lord Jesus Christ, who has blessed us in the heavenly realms with every spiritual blessing in Christ . . . In him we have redemption through his blood, the forgiveness of sins, in accordance with the riches of God's grace *See also* **Ex** 15:1–21; **Ps** 71:23; 111:9; 119:134; 136:1–26; **Isa** 35:4–10; 44:22–23; 48:20; 51:11; 52:9 *See also God as Saviour; God, love of; God, power of; Jesus Christ as redeemer; repentance; salvation; worship, reasons.*

God as Saviour
God is the only Saviour and deliverer of his people. His work of salvation is inaugurated in the OT, and reaches its climax in the work of Jesus Christ.

God is the only Saviour
Isa 45:21–22 ". . . there is no God apart from me, a righteous God and a Saviour; there is none but me. Turn to me and be saved, all you ends of the earth; for I am God, and there is no other." *See also* **Jdg** 10:13–14; **Isa** 43:11; **Jer** 2:28; 3:23; 11:12

God's deliverance can be worked through a human agent
Jdg 2:16 Then the LORD raised up judges, who saved them out of the hands of these raiders. *See also* **Ge** 45:5–7; **Ex** 3:10; **Jos** 10:6–10; **Jdg** 2:18; 6:14–16; **2Ki** 13:5; **Isa** 45:1,13

Examples of God's saving deeds
God delivers his people from Egypt: **Ex** 6:6–7; 14:13–14,21–23,27–28; **Ps** 77:19–20; **Hos** 13:4
God delivers David from various dangers: **1Sa** 17:37; **2Sa** 22:1–3 pp Ps 18:2; **2Sa** 22:18 pp Ps 18:17; **Ps** 3:8
Da 6:16–22
God delivers the apostles from prison: **Ac** 5:18–19; 12:6–11; 16:25–26

God's acts of deliverance reveal his nature and character
Isa 52:10 The LORD will lay bare his holy arm in the sight of all the nations, and all the ends of the earth will see the salvation of our God.
See also **Ps 98:2; Isa 49:6; Lk 3:4–6; Isa 40:3–5; Ro 1:16**

His strength is seen
Ps 18:2 The LORD is my rock, my fortress and my deliverer; my God is my rock, in whom I take refuge. He is my shield and the horn of my salvation, my stronghold. *See also* **Ex 15:2 pp Ps 118:14; 1Sa 2:1; 2Sa 22:2–3,47 pp Ps 18:46; Ps 28:8**

His glory is seen
Ex 14:4 ". . . I will gain glory for myself through Pharaoh and all his army, and the Egyptians will know that I am the LORD."
See also **Ex 14:17–18; Nu 14:22; Ps 85:9; Isa 66:19; Eze 39:21**

God's deliverance is anticipated
Ps 31:2 Turn your [the LORD'S] ear to me, come quickly to my rescue; be my rock of refuge, a strong fortress to save me. *See also* **Ge 49:18; Ps 35:4; 69:13–15; Isa 33:22; 35:4**

God's deliverance is promised
Ex 6:6 "Therefore, say to the Israelites: 'I am the LORD, and I will bring you out from under the yoke of the Egyptians. I will free you from being slaves to them, and I will redeem you with an outstretched arm and with mighty acts of judgment.'" *See also* **Ps 50:15; 91:14; Isa 38:6; 46:4; Eze 34:12**

Implications of God's deliverance for believers
God is able to deliver believers from trials and testing
2Ti 4:18 The Lord will rescue me from every evil attack and will bring me safely to his heavenly kingdom . . . *See also* **Da 12:1; Mt 6:13; 1Co 10:13; 2Pe 2:9; Rev 3:10**

God is able to deliver believers from sin and death
Ro 7:24–25 What a wretched man I [Paul] am! Who will rescue me from this body of death? Thanks be to God—through Jesus Christ our Lord! . . . *See also* **2Sa 12:13; Ps 33:19; Eze 37:23; 1Co 15:56–57; 2Co 1:9–10**

Testimony to God as Saviour and deliverer
Ge 50:20 "You intended to harm me, but God intended it for good to accomplish what is now being done, the saving of many lives."
See also **Ps 13:5; 18:46–48; Isa 61:10; Da 6:27; Hab 3:18; Lk 1:47; 1Ti 4:10** *See also God as redeemer; Jesus Christ as Saviour; salvation; sin, deliverance from.*

God as shepherd
The image of God as a shepherd points to his continual direction, guidance and care for his people.

Shepherd as a title for God
Ps 80:1 . . . O Shepherd of Israel, you who lead Joseph like a flock . . . *See also* **Ge 49:24; Ecc 12:11**

God's people are his flock
Israel is God's flock
Ps 95:7 . . . he is our God and we are the people of his pasture, the flock under his care . . . *See also* **Ps 79:13; 100:3; Jer 50:7; Eze 34:31**

The church is God's flock
1Pe 5:2 Be shepherds of God's flock . . .
See also **Lk 12:32; Ac 20:28–29**

The tasks undertaken by God the shepherd
The shepherd leads and guides
Ps 23:2–3 . . . he leads me beside quiet waters, he restores my soul. He guides me in paths of righteousness for his name's sake.
See also **Isa 40:11**

The shepherd provides
Ps 23:1 The LORD is my shepherd, I shall not be in want. *See also* **Ge 48:15; Ps 23:5–6; Hos 4:16; Mic 7:14**

The shepherd protects
Ps 28:9 . . . be their [God's people's] shepherd and carry them for ever. *See also* **Ge** 49:23-24

The shepherd saves those who are lost or scattered
Jer 31:10 ". . . 'He who scattered Israel will gather them and will watch over his flock like a shepherd.'" *See also* **Ps** 119:176; **Isa** 53:6; **Eze** 34:11-16; **Mt** 18:12-14 pp **Lk** 15:3-7

The shepherd judges
Eze 34:17-22 "'As for you, my flock, this is what the Sovereign LORD says: I will judge between one sheep and another, and between rams and goats . . .'" *See also* **Jer** 23:1; **Zec** 10:2-3; 11:16; **Mt** 25:32-46

God gives shepherds to be leaders over his people

He gives David's line
Eze 34:23 "'I will place over them one shepherd, my servant David, and he will tend them; he will tend them and be their shepherd.'" *See also* **2Sa** 5:2 pp **1Ch** 11:2; **Ps** 78:70-72; **Eze** 34:23-24; 37:24; **Mic** 5:4; **Mt** 2:6

He gives individual leaders Isa 44:28; 63:11

He gives faithful leaders
Jer 3:15 "Then I will give you shepherds after my own heart, who will lead you with knowledge and understanding." *See also* **Jer** 23:4; **1Pe** 5:2-4 *See also God, compassion; God, the provider; Holy Spirit, guidance; Jesus Christ as shepherd.*

God as Spirit

God has no material body and he is not subject to human limitations. While his spiritual nature is clearly inferred in Scripture, it is seldom directly stated; the emphasis is on his dynamic, living personhood.

God as spirit

Jn 4:24 "God is spirit, and his worshippers must worship in spirit and in truth." *See also* **Isa** 28:5-6; 31:3

God is not subject to physical limitations 1Sa 16:7; **1Ki** 18:27; **Job** 10:4-8; **Ps** 121:3-4

God as the Spirit
Ps 139:7 Where can I go from your Spirit? Where can I flee from your presence? *See also* **Ps** 51:11; 143:10; **Isa** 34:16; **2Co** 3:17-18

God cannot be represented physically
Images of God are prohibited Ex 20:4; 34:17; **Lev** 26:1; **Ac** 17:29

God transcends spacial limitations
Ac 17:24 "The God who made the world and everything in it is the Lord of heaven and earth and does not live in temples built by hands." *See also* **1Ki** 8:27 pp **2Ch** 6:18; **2Ch** 2:6; **Ac** 7:48-50

God is invisible
1Ti 6:15-16 . . . God, the blessed and only Ruler, the King of kings and Lord of lords, who alone is immortal and who lives in unapproachable light, whom no-one has seen or can see . . .
See also **Ex** 33:20; **Dt** 4:15-19; **Jn** 1:18; **Col** 1:15; **1Ti** 1:17 *See also God, human descriptions of; God, present everywhere; God, transcendent; God, unity of; Holy Spirit; life, spiritual.*

God of the fathers

God's particular association with Abraham, Isaac and Jacob, the fathers of the nations of Israel, highlights his faithfulness in fulfilling the promises made to them. He is the God who establishes a covenant with his people for their everlasting blessing.

God's relationship with the fathers

The God of Abraham, Isaac and Jacob
Ac 7:32 "'I [the LORD] am the God of your fathers, the God of Abraham, Isaac and Jacob.' . . ." *See also* **Ex** 3:6,15; 4:5

The God of Jacob
Ps 20:1 May the LORD answer you when you are in distress; may the name of the God of Jacob protect you. *See also* **Ge** 32:27-28; **Ps** 14:7; 46:7,11; 75:9; 76:6; 114:7

Such a relationship served as an encouragement to others
Abraham's servant was encouraged to trust God in his mission by the example of Abraham's faith: **Ge** 24:12,27,42,48

God's people were frequently encouraged by the relationship they saw between God and other individuals (e.g., Jos 1:5; 2Ki 2:14); **Ge** 26:24; 31:42,53 **Ge** 46:1–3

God's covenant with the fathers
God's promises that they will be the fathers of a great nation
Ge 28:13–15 . . . "I am the LORD, the God of your father Abraham and the God of Isaac. I will give you [Jacob] and your descendants the land on which you are lying . . ."
See also **Ge** 26:2–4; **Ex** 3:16–17
God remembers and fulfils his promises
Ex 2:24 God heard their [the Israelites] groaning and he remembered his covenant with Abraham, with Isaac and with Jacob. *See also* **Ex** 6:3–5; 32:13; **Lev** 26:42; **Dt** 1:8; **Ac** 7:17
God makes a covenant with his people to be their God
Dt 29:12–13 You [the Israelites] are standing here in order to enter into a covenant with the LORD your God, a covenant the LORD is making with you this day and sealing with an oath, to confirm you this day as his people, that he may be your God as he promised you and as he swore to your fathers, Abraham, Isaac and Jacob. *See also* **Ge** 17:7; **Ex** 6:7–8; **Ps** 105:8–11

Characteristics of the God of the fathers
He blesses his people
Dt 1:11 "May the LORD, the God of your ancestors, increase you a thousand times and bless you as he has promised!" *See also* **Dt** 30:20
He is powerful **1Ki** 18:36–39
He is gracious and compassionate **2Ki** 13:23
He keeps his people faithful **1Ch** 29:18
He gives wisdom **Da** 2:23
He is the God of the living
Mt 22:32 "'I am the God of Abraham, the God of Isaac, and the God of Jacob'? He is not the God of the dead but of the living."
pp **Mk** 12:26–27 pp **Lk** 20:37–38

People sometimes fail to respond to the God of their fathers
Jos 18:3 . . . Joshua said to the Israelites: "How long will you wait before you begin to take possession of the land that the LORD, the God of your ancestors, has given you?"
See also **Nu** 32:11; **Dt** 6:10–12; 9:27; **2Ch** 30:7
See also God, faithfulness.

God, activity of
God is not passive or remote from his creation but dynamically involved in all that he has made. In the past, this activity was seen in the history of Israel and in the ministry of Jesus Christ. In the present, God's activity can be seen in the life of believers and of the church.

God is active by nature
He actively works out his purposes
Jn 5:17 Jesus said to them [the Jews], "My Father is always at his work to this very day, and I, too, am working." *See also* **Nu** 23:19; **Ps** 115:3; **Pr** 16:4; **Isa** 43:13
His names reflect his activity and involvement in his people's lives **Ge** 22:14; **Ex** 15:26; 17:15; **Ps** 95:6
His word is active
Isa 55:10–11 ". . . my [the LORD'S] word that goes out from my mouth: It will not return to me empty, but will accomplish what I desire and achieve the purpose for which I sent it."
See also **Ge** 1:3; **Eze** 37:4,7

God is active in the creation
In making the universe
Ne 9:6 "You alone are the LORD. You made the heavens, even the highest heavens, and all their starry host, the earth and all that is on it, the seas and all that is in them. You give life to everything, and the multitudes of heaven worship you." *See also* **Ge** 1:1,31; 2:2; 5:1–2; **Ps** 102:25; **Am** 4:13; **Ac** 17:24; **Rev** 4:11
In sustaining the created order
Ps 103:19 The LORD has established his throne in heaven, and his kingdom rules over all. *See also* **Ps** 104:10–17; 107:33–35; **Mt** 6:28–30; **Ac** 14:17; **Eph** 1:11; **Col** 1:16–17
In bringing about changes in the weather **Job** 37:10; 38:22–30,34–35; **Ps** 107:25; 147:8; **Mt** 5:45; **Ac** 14:17

In the stars and other heavenly bodies Job
38:31–33; Ps 104:19; 147:4; Isa 40:26; Jas 1:17
In the animal creation Job 39:1–30; 40:15–24;
41:1–11; Ps 104:20–27; 147:9; Mt 10:29 pp Lk 12:6

God is active in Israel's history
In the calling and creation of Israel as a people
Ex 6:6–8 "'... I [the LORD] will take you
[Israel] as my own people, and I will be your
God. Then you will know that I am the LORD your
God, who brought you out from under the yoke
of the Egyptians...'" *See also* Ge 12:1–3;
Ex 19:3–6; Dt 4:32–34; Isa 51:2; Eze 16:6–7;
Hos 11:1–4; Mal 2:10
In saving and delivering his people
Ps 106:2 Who can proclaim the mighty acts of
the LORD or fully declare his praise? *See also*
Ex 33:16–17; 2Sa 7:7–11; 1Ki 18:36–38; Ps
28:8–9; 107:2–3
In judgment Nu 25:3–4; 1Sa 2:25; 12:16–18;
2Sa 21:1
In bringing victory in battle Ex 14:27–28;
17:8–16; Nu 21:1–3; Jos 6:2; 10:30; Jdg 7:9,22;
1Sa 17:47; 2Ch 20:22–23
**In raising up and sending leaders to the
people** 2Sa 7:8–9; 2Ch 24:19; Est 4:14; Jer
7:25; Zec 7:7

God is active in the nations of the world
His rule over the nations
Ps 22:28 ... dominion belongs to the LORD
and he rules over the nations. *See also* Ge
11:8; Dt 32:8; Jdg 2:20–23; Job 12:23; Ps
46:8–10; 66:7; Isa 41:2; Ac 17:26
Examples of nations through which God acts
Assyria: 2Ki 17:18–23; Isa 28:11
Babylon: 2Ki 24:10–14; 2Ch 36:15–18
2Ch 36:22–23 pp Ezr 1:1–4

God is active in human life
He determines the course of human lives
Ac 17:28 "'For in him [God] we live and
move and have our being.'..." *See also* 1Ch
29:12; Ps 8:3–6; 75:6–7; 139:16; Lk 1:52;
Jn 1:4

Examples of God's intervention in human lives
Nu 22:21–23; 1Sa 1:19–20; 2Ki 5:14–15; Jnh
1:17
Paul: Ac 9:3–6; 13:1–3; 16:6,10

God is active in Jesus Christ's ministry
Ac 10:38 "how God anointed Jesus of Nazareth
with the Holy Spirit and power, and how he went
around doing good and healing all who were
under the power of the devil, because God was
with him." *See also* Lk 5:17; 11:20; Jn 3:2;
5:17–19; 9:3–4; 14:10; 2Co 5:19

God is active through the Holy Spirit
Ge 1:2; 2Ki 2:16; Eze 8:3; 11:1; 43:5

God is active in the church
1Co 12:6 There are different kinds of working,
but the same God works all of them in
everyone. *See also* 1Co 14:24–25; Gal 2:8;
3:5; Eph 3:10,20–21; Php 1:6; 2:13 *See also*
church; God as judge; God as Saviour; God, living; God,
present everywhere; God, purpose of; God, sovereignty;
God, the Creator; Holy Spirit in the church; Jesus Christ,
mission.

God, all-knowing
The omniscience of God is that attribute by which
he knows all things past, present and future.
What is hidden from human sight is still known
by God. Scripture stresses the wisdom of God in
all his actions, and often grounds this in his
all-embracing knowledge.

God's unique self-knowledge within the Trinity
Mt 11:27 "All things have been committed to
me by my Father. No-one knows the Son except
the Father, and no-one knows the Father except
the Son and those to whom the Son chooses to
reveal him." *See also* Jn 10:15; 1Co 2:10–11

The nature of God's knowledge
God's knowledge originates within himself
Isa 40:13–14 Who has understood the mind
of the LORD, or instructed him as his counsellor?
Whom did the LORD consult to enlighten him, and

who taught him the right way? Who was it that taught him knowledge or showed him the path of understanding? *See also* **Job** 21:22; **Ro** 11:33–34; **1Co** 2:16

God's knowledge is complete
Mt 10:30 And even the very hairs of your head are all numbered. pp **Lk** 12:7 *See also* **Ps** 147:4; **Isa** 40:26

God knows things that are hidden from human understanding
Dt 29:29 The secret things belong to the LORD our God, but the things revealed belong to us and to our children for ever . . . *See also* **Job** 37:15–16; **Da** 2:22; **Mt** 24:36 pp **Mk** 13:32; **Ac** 1:7; **2Co** 12:2–4

God's comprehensive knowledge of people

God's knowledge of people's actions
Job 34:21 "His [God's] eyes are on the ways of mortals; he sees their every step." *See also* **Job** 24:23; 31:4; **Ps** 33:13–15; 139:2–3; **Jer** 23:24

God's knowledge of people's needs
Mt 6:8 ". . . your Father knows what you need before you ask him." *See also* **Mt** 6:31–32 pp **Lk** 12:29–30

God's knowledge of people's hearts and minds
1Ch 28:9 ". . . the LORD searches every heart and understands every motive behind the thoughts . . ." *See also* **Ps** 44:20–21; 139:1–2; **Jer** 17:10; **Eze** 11:5; **Heb** 4:12–13

God's knowledge of individuals Ge 20:1–7; **1Sa** 16:1–12; **Ac** 5:1–10

God's knowledge of people's sin
Jer 16:17 "My [the LORD'S] eyes are on all their ways; they are not hidden from me, nor is their sin concealed from my eyes." *See also* **Job** 10:14; **Ps** 69:5; **Jer** 2:22; **Hos** 7:2; **Am** 5:12

God's foreknowledge
Isa 46:10 "I [God] make known the end from the beginning, from ancient times, what is still to come . . ." *See also* **Isa** 42:9; 44:7; **Da** 2:28

God's foreknowledge of Jesus Christ's passion
Ac 2:23 This man [Jesus] was handed over to you by God's set purpose and foreknowledge . . . *See also* **Ac** 3:18; 4:27–28

God's foreknowledge of those who would become disciples
Ro 8:29 For those God foreknew he also predestined to be conformed to the likeness of his Son, that he might be the firstborn among many brothers and sisters. *See also* **Jer** 1:5; **Ro** 11:2; **1Pe** 1:2

God's foreknowledge of people's free actions
Ps 139:4 Before a word is on my tongue you know it completely, O LORD. *See also* **Ex** 3:19; **Dt** 31:21; **1Sa** 23:10–13

Implications of God's knowledge

God's knowledge ensures that all will be judged fairly
Heb 4:13 Nothing in all creation is hidden from God's sight. Everything is uncovered and laid bare before the eyes of him to whom we must give account. *See also* **1Sa** 2:3; **Job** 34:22–23; **Ecc** 12:14; **Ro** 2:16; **1Co** 4:5

God's knowledge ensures that he knows those who are his
2Ti 2:19 . . . "The Lord knows those who are his," . . . *See also* **Nu** 16:5; **Ex** 33:12; **Job** 23:10

Jn 10:14 "I am the good shepherd; I know my sheep and my sheep know me—" *See also* **1Co** 8:3; **Gal** 4:9; **1Jn** 3:19–20; **Rev** 3:8

See also God as judge; God, present everywhere; God, purpose of; God, sovereignty; God, wisdom of; Jesus Christ, knowledge of.

God, anger of

The punitive and vindicatory reaction, legitimate and controlled, yet awesomely emphatic, of God the righteous judge to unrighteousness in his human creatures. Up to the present, the expression of God's anger and wrath has had the purpose of drawing sinners to repentance and conversion, but this will not be the case at the final judgment.

The nature of God's anger
It is fearsome
Na 1:6 Who can withstand his indignation? Who can endure his fierce anger? His wrath is poured out like fire; the rocks are shattered before

God, anger of

him. See also Jos 7:26; Eze 38:18

It is reluctant and short-lived
Ex 34:6 ... "The LORD, the LORD, the compassionate and gracious God, slow to anger, abounding in love and faithfulness,"
See also Isa 54:7–8; Ne 9:16–18

It is consistent with his righteous and merciful character
Ps 7:11 God is a righteous judge, a God who expresses his wrath every day.
See also Hab 3:2

It fulfils God's purposes
Jer 23:20 "The anger of the LORD will not turn back until he fully accomplishes the purposes of his heart..." See also Jer 30:24

The causes of God's anger

Idolatry and unbelief
Nu 25:3 So Israel joined in worshipping the Baal of Peor. And the LORD's anger burned against them. See also Ex 32:8–10; Dt 8:19; Jdg 2:10–14; 1Ki 14:9; 16:32–33; 22:53; 2Ki 23:19; 2Ch 28:25; 34:25; Jer 8:19; 32:29; 44:3; Jn 3:36; Ro 1:18–23; 2:8

Disobedience and disloyalty
Jos 7:1 But the Israelites acted unfaithfully in regard to the devoted things; Achan son of Carmi, the son of Zimri, the son of Zerah, of the tribe of Judah, took some of them. So the LORD's anger burned against Israel. See also Dt 9:7; 2Ki 22:13; 1Ch 13:10; Ps 106:29; Jer 32:32; Zec 7:13; Eph 5:6

Ungodly living
God's judgment against the ungodly is a sign of his anger against actions that contradict his righteous character and purposes: **2Ti 3:1–9; Jude 14–16**

Pride, arrogance and hypocrisy
Mt 23:27–28 "Woe to you, teachers of the law and Pharisees, you hypocrites! You are like whitewashed tombs, which look beautiful on the outside but on the inside are full of the bones of the dead and everything unclean. In the same way, on the outside you appear to people as righteous but on the inside you are full of hypocrisy and wickedness." See also 2Ch 32:25; Pr 3:34; 8:13; Isa 13:11; Hos 12:14; Mal 4:1

Complaints against, and opposition to, God's purposes
Nu 11:1 Now the people complained about their hardships in the hearing of the LORD, and when he heard them his anger was aroused. Then fire from the LORD burned among them and consumed some of the outskirts of the camp.
See also Nu 14:27; 21:5

Injustice
Zec 7:9–12 "This is what the LORD Almighty says: 'Administer true justice; show mercy and compassion to one another. Do not oppress the widow or the fatherless, the alien or the poor. In your hearts do not think evil of each other.' "But they refused to pay attention; stubbornly they turned their backs and stopped up their ears. They made their hearts as hard as flint and would not listen to the law or to the words that the LORD Almighty had sent by his Spirit through the earlier prophets. So the LORD Almighty was very angry." See also 2Ch 19:7; Jer 22:13; Eze 9:9; Mal 3:5; Mt 23:23

The rejection of God's servants
Heb 10:29–31 How much more severely do you think those deserve to be punished who have trampled the Son of God under foot, who have treated as an unholy thing the blood of the covenant that sanctified them, and who have insulted the Spirit of grace? For we know him who said, "It is mine to avenge; I will repay," and again, "The Lord will judge his people." It is a dreadful thing to fall into the hands of the living God. See also Dt 32:35–36; Ps 135:14; Ne 9:26; Zec 7:12; Mt 21:33–41; Ac 7:35–37

God reveals his anger

In present times
Ro 1:18 The wrath of God is being revealed from heaven against all the godlessness and wickedness of those who suppress the truth by their wickedness. See also Jer 10:10

On a future "day of wrath" which is anticipated
Ro 2:5 ... you are storing up wrath against yourself for the day of God's wrath, when his righteous judgment will be revealed.
See also Isa 13:9,13; Eze 7:19; Zep 1:15,18; 2:2

The consequences of God's anger
God allows those who reject righteousness to remain in their sin
Ro 1:18–32 . . . For although they knew God, they neither glorified him as God nor gave thanks to him, but their thinking became futile and their foolish hearts were darkened . . . Furthermore, since they did not think it worth while to retain the knowledge of God, he gave them over to a depraved mind, to do what ought not to be done . . . Although they know God's righteous decree that those who do such things deserve death, they not only continue to do these very things but also approve of those who practise them. *See also* **1Ki** 14:16; **2Ch** 12:5; **Ne** 9:28; **Isa** 54:7–8; **Jer** 7:27–29; 12:7–8

Punishment will be experienced by rebellious people
Dt 8:19 If you ever forget the LORD your God and follow other gods and worship and bow down to them, I testify against you today that you will surely be destroyed. *See also* **Isa** 59:18; **Jer** 21:14; **Mt** 18:34–35; 25:28–30
Punishment of death: **Ex** 12:12; **Nu** 32:13; **Jos** 7:25–26; **Isa** 13:9–13; **Da** 5:30; **Ac** 5:5,10
Punishment of exile: **1Ki** 14:15; **Jer** 15:13–14; 25:7–11
Destruction of the whole nation of Israel: **La** 2:1–9; **Eze** 38:19–21

God will be feared as his holiness and greatness are revealed
Isa 59:18–19 According to what they have done, so will he repay wrath to his enemies and retribution to his foes; he will repay the islands their due. From the west, people will fear the name of the LORD, and from the rising of the sun, they will revere his glory. For he will come like a pent-up flood that the breath of the LORD drives along. *See also* **Eze** 38:22–23

Ultimately God will purify and restore his people for service
Mal 3:2–4 But who can endure the day of his coming? Who can stand when he appears? For he will be like a refiner's fire or a launderer's soap. He will sit as a refiner and purifier of silver; he will purify the Levites and refine them like gold and silver. Then the LORD will have people who will bring offerings in righteousness, and the offerings of Judah and Jerusalem will be acceptable to the LORD, as in days gone by, as in former years. *See also* **Jer** 15:19–21
See also God as judge; God, grace and mercy; God, justice of; God, righteousness; Jesus Christ, anger of.

God, compassion
An aspect of God's nature which is reflected in his sympathetic understanding of human weakness and his restoration of those in trouble.

God is compassionate by nature
2Co 1:3 Praise be to the God and Father of our Lord Jesus Christ, the Father of compassion and the God of all comfort, *See also* **Ex** 33:19; 34:6; **Ps** 86:15; 103:8; 116:5; 119:156; **Hos** 1:7; **Joel** 2:13

God shows compassion as a parent
Ps 103:13–14 As a father has compassion on his children, so the LORD has compassion on those who fear him; for he knows how we are formed, he remembers that we are dust. *See also* **Isa** 49:15–16; 63:15–16; **Jer** 31:20

God shows compassion to all
Ps 145:8–9 . . . The LORD is good to all; he has compassion on all he has made.

God shows compassion to those in deep trouble
Isa 49:13 . . . For the LORD comforts his people and will have compassion on his afflicted ones. *See also* **Ex** 22:27; **2Ki** 13:22–23; **Ps** 40:1–2,11–12; 69:16–17; **Isa** 30:18; **La** 3:22,32; **Zec** 10:6; **Jas** 5:11

God shows compassion towards sinners
Ne 9:17 "They [the Israelites] refused to listen and failed to remember the miracles you performed among them. They became stiff-necked and in their rebellion appointed a leader in order to return to their slavery. But you are a forgiving God, gracious and compassionate, slow to anger and abounding in love. Therefore you did not desert them," *See also* **Dt** 13:17; **Ne** 9:28; **Ps** 51:1–2; 103:3–4; **Isa** 54:7–8; 60:10; **Da** 9:9; **Mic** 7:19

God, faithfulness

The return from exile shows God's compassion to sinners
Eze 39:25 "Therefore this is what the Sovereign LORD says: I will now bring Jacob back from captivity and will have compassion on all the people of Israel, and I will be zealous for my holy name." *See also* **Dt 30:2–3; Jer 12:15; 30:18; 33:26**

God's deeds show his compassion
Ps 111:3–4 . . . He has caused his wonders to be remembered; the LORD is gracious and compassionate. *See also* **Ps 102:14; Isa 14:1; 63:7**

God's compassion is essential to believers' well-being
Ps 119:77 Let your compassion come to me that I may live . . . *See also* **Ps 77:8–9; Isa 63:15**

God's compassion is reflected in acts of human compassion
Col 3:12 Therefore, as God's chosen people, holy and dearly loved, clothe yourselves with compassion, kindness, humility, gentleness and patience. *See also* **2Ch 30:9; Jer 42:12; Zec 7:9; Lk 6:36; Eph 4:32**

Jesus Christ reflects God's compassion
Heb 4:15 For we do not have a high priest who is unable to sympathise with our weaknesses, but we have one who has been tempted in every way, just as we are—yet was without sin. *See also* **Lk 1:72; 15:20** *See also* forgiveness; God, grace and mercy; God, love of; Jesus Christ, compassion; Jesus Christ, grace and mercy.

God, faithfulness
God's perfect loyalty and consistency in being true to his name, his character and his word.

God's faithfulness is an integral part of his nature
Nu 23:19 "God is not human, that he should lie, nor a human being, that he should change his mind. Does he speak and then not act? Does he promise and not fulfil?"

La 3:22–23 Because of the LORD's great love we are not consumed, for his compassions never fail. They are new every morning; great is your faithfulness. *See also* **Ex 34:6; Dt 7:8–9; 32:4; Ro 4:21; 2Ti 2:13**

God is faithful to his name and character
2Ti 2:13 if we are faithless, he will remain faithful, for he cannot disown himself. *See also* **Ne 9:8; Ps 106:8; 1Th 5:24; Heb 6:13–18**
Jos 23:14 ". . . not one of all the good promises the LORD your God gave you has failed. Every promise has been fulfilled; not one has failed."

God's faithfulness is known through fulfilled promises
Jos 21:45; 1Ki 8:56; 1Ch 16:15; Ps 145:13; 2Pe 3:9

Examples of God's faithfulness in fulfilled promises
Abraham's fatherhood Ge 12:2–3; 15:4; 21:1–2; Ro 9:9; Gal 4:28; Heb 6:13–15; 11:11
The building of the temple 2Sa 7:12–13 pp 1Ch 17:11–12; 1Ki 8:17–21 pp 2Ch 6:7–11
The exile in Babylon
Jer 25:8–11 . . . "Because you have not listened to my words . . . This whole country will become a desolate wasteland, and these nations will serve the king of Babylon for seventy years." *See also* **2Ki 25:8–12 pp 2Ch 36:17–21 pp Jer 52:12–16; Ezr 1:1–3; Jer 52:27; 29:10; Da 9:2–3,15–19**

God's faithfulness is revealed to the faithful
2Sa 22:26 "To the faithful you show yourself faithful, to the blameless you show yourself blameless, *See also* **Gal 3:14; Heb 10:23**

God's faithfulness is constant
Ro 3:3–4 What if some did not have faith? Will their lack of faith nullify God's faithfulness? Not at all! Let God be true, and every person a liar . . . *See also* **Eze 12:25; Hab 2:3; 2Ti 2:13**

Jesus Christ is the ultimate evidence of God's faithfulness
Ac 13:32–33 "We tell you the good news: What God promised our ancestors he has fulfilled for us, their children, by raising up Jesus. As it is written in the second Psalm: 'You are my Son; today I have become your Father.'" *See also* **Jn 14:9–11; Ro 15:8–9; 2Co 1:20–22; Rev 1:5; Heb 3:2–6; Rev 19:11** *See also God, the Rock; God, truth of; Jesus Christ, faithfulness.*

God, fatherhood

Primarily signifying God's paternal relationship to Jesus Christ, the term also refers to God's fatherly relationship to his creation, especially to believers as the "children of God".

Aspects of the fatherhood of God

He is the Creator and provider
1Co 8:6 . . . there is but one God, the Father, from whom all things came and for whom we live . . . *See also* **Dt 32:6; Isa 64:8; Dt 32:18; Ac 17:24–28**

He shows love and compassion
Hos 11:1 "When Israel was a child, I loved him, and out of Egypt I called my son." *See also* **Ps 103:13; Jer 3:19; 2Co 1:3**

He exercises his providence and care
Ps 68:5 A father to the fatherless, a defender of widows, is God in his holy dwelling. *See also* **Mt 6:26,31–33 pp Lk 12:29–31; Mt 7:11 pp Lk 11:13**

He disciplines and corrects
Dt 8:5 . . . as a man disciplines his son, so the LORD your God disciplines you. *See also* **Pr 3:11–12; Heb 12:5–6**

God as the Father of Jesus Christ
Mt 3:17 And a voice from heaven said, "This is my Son, whom I love; with him I am well pleased." pp **Mk 1:11** pp **Lk 3:22** *See also* **Mt 11:27; Lk 2:49; Jn 5:17–18; 17:11; 20:17; Ro 15:6; Eph 1:3; 1Jn 1:3**

God is the father of Israel
He cares for his covenant people
Jer 31:9 ". . . I [the LORD] am Israel's father, and Ephraim is my firstborn son." *See also* **Ex 4:22; Dt 14:1; 32:6,18; Isa 63:16; Mal 2:10**

He is the father of the kings of Israel
2Sa 7:13–14 "'. . . I will be his father, and he shall be my son . . .'" pp **1Ch 17:12–13** *See also* **Ps 2:7; 89:26–27**

God is the father of Christian believers

He has an intimate relationship with believers
Mt 6:9 "This, then, is how you should pray: "'Our Father in heaven, hallowed be your name,'" pp **Lk 11:2** *See also* **Jn 20:17; 2Co 6:18; Gal 3:26; 1Jn 2:13**

He adopts believers into his family
Jn 1:12–13 Yet to all who received him, to those who believed in his name, he gave the right to become children of God—children born not of natural descent, nor of human decision or a husband's will, but born of God. *See also* **Ro 8:14–17; Gal 4:5–7; 1Jn 3:1**

The fatherhood of God has implications for the church

Character: children are to reproduce the Father's likeness
Mt 5:48 "Be perfect, therefore, as your heavenly Father is perfect."

Unity: one Father means one family
Eph 4:3–6 Make every effort to keep the unity of the Spirit through the bond of peace. There is one body and one Spirit—just as you were called to one hope when you were called—one Lord, one faith, one baptism; one God and Father of all, who is over all and through all and in all. *See also* **Mal 2:10; Mt 23:9; Eph 3:14–15**

Status: believers are related to Jesus Christ
Mt 12:50 "For whoever does the will of my Father in heaven is my brother and sister and mother." pp **Mk 3:35** pp **Lk 8:21** *See also* **Ro 8:29; Heb 2:11**

Inheritance: believers are heirs of the Father's kingdom
Ro 8:17 Now if we are children, then we are heirs—heirs of God and co-heirs with Christ . . . *See also* **Lk 12:32; Gal 3:29; Col 1:12; Tit 3:7**

Submission: believers are to revere the Father
1Pe 1:17 Since you call on a Father who judges each person's work impartially, live your lives as strangers here in reverent fear. *See also* **Mt 6:9** pp **Lk 11:2**; **Eph 3:14** *See also* Abba; God of the fathers; God, compassion; God, love of; Jesus Christ, Son of God; kingdom of God; Trinity.

God, feminine descriptions of
Some expressions attribute feminine qualities to God, especially relating to motherhood.

Descriptions of God relating to childbirth
God gives birth to his people
Isa 44:2 "This is what the LORD says—he who made you, who formed you in the womb . . ." *See also* **Nu 11:12**; **Dt 32:18**; **Isa 44:24**
God gives birth to individuals
Ps 139:13 For you [O LORD] created my inmost being; you knit me together in my mother's womb. *See also* **Ge 29:31**; **30:22**; **Ecc 11:5**; **Isa 49:5**; **Jer 1:5**
God as a midwife
Ps 22:9 Yet you [my God] brought me out of the womb . . . *See also* **Job 10:18**; **Ps 71:6**; **Isa 66:9**

Descriptions of God relating to motherhood
God nurses his people
Isa 49:15 "Can a mother forget the baby at her breast and have no compassion on the child she has borne? Though she may forget, I will not forget you!"
God comforts his people
Isa 66:13 "As a mother comforts her child, so will I comfort you . . ." *See also* **Isa 40:11**
God as a mother bird protecting her young
Dt 32:10–11 . . . he [the LORD] guarded him [his people] as the apple of his eye, like an eagle that stirs up its nest and hovers over its young, that spreads its wings to catch them and carries them on its pinions.
Mt 23:37 ". . . how often I [Jesus] have longed to gather your children together, as a hen gathers her chicks under her wings . . ." pp **Lk 13:34** *See also* **Ru 2:12**; **Ps 17:8**; **91:4**
See also God, compassion; God, human descriptions of.

God, glory of
The revelation of God's power and characteristics, sometimes accompanied by visible phenomena.

Glory as an attribute of God
Ps 24:7–8 Lift up your heads, O you gates; be lifted up, you ancient doors, that the King of glory may come in. Who is this King of glory? The LORD strong and mighty, the LORD mighty in battle. *See also* **Ps 29:3**; **Jn 11:40**; **Ac 7:2**; **Rev 19:1**

Visible phenomena accompanying God's glory
The appearance of God's glory
Hab 3:4 His [God's] splendour was like the sunrise; rays flashed from his hand, where his power was hidden. *See also* **Dt 5:24**; **2Sa 22:8–16** pp **Ps 18:7–15**; **Ps 104:1**; **Eze 1:26–28**
God's glory as a cloud
Ex 24:15–16 When Moses went up on the mountain, the cloud covered it, and the glory of the LORD settled on Mount Sinai . . . *See also* **Ex 33:9–10**; **Isa 4:5**; **Mt 17:5** pp **Mk 9:7** pp **Lk 9:34**; **Lk 21:27** pp **Mt 24:30** pp **Mk 13:26**
God's glory in the tabernacle and the temple
2Ch 5:13–14 . . . Then the temple of the LORD was filled with a cloud, and the priests could not perform their service because of the cloud, for the glory of the LORD filled the temple of God. pp **1Ki 8:10–11** *See also* **Ex 40:34–35**; **2Ch 7:1–3**; **Eze 8:4**; **9:3**; **10:19**; **43:1–5**; **Rev 15:8**

God's glory revealed
In Jesus Christ
Heb 1:3 The Son is the radiance of God's glory and the exact representation of his being, sustaining all things by his powerful word . . . *See also* **Isa 49:3**; **Jn 1:14**; **13:31–32**; **17:5**; **2Co 4:6**; **2Pe 1:17**
In his people
Col 1:27 . . . God has chosen to make known among the Gentiles the glorious riches of this

mystery, which is Christ in you, the hope of glory.   *See also* **Isa** 60:19–21; 62:3; **2Co** 3:18; **Eph** 3:21

In the whole world
Isa 6:3 . . . "Holy, holy, holy is the LORD Almighty; the whole earth is full of his glory."   *See also* **Nu** 14:21; **Ps** 57:5,11 pp Ps 108:5; **Hab** 2:14; 3:3

In heaven
Rev 21:23 The city does not need the sun or the moon to shine on it, for the glory of God gives it light, and the Lamb is its lamp.   *See also* **Ro** 8:17; **Heb** 2:9; **1Pe** 5:10

In his name
Ne 9:5 . . . "Blessed be your glorious name, and may it be exalted above all blessing and praise."   *See also* **Dt** 28:58; **1Ch** 29:13; **Ps** 8:1; 79:9

In his works
Ps 111:3 Glorious and majestic are his deeds, and his righteousness endures for ever.   *See also* **Ps** 19:1; **Isa** 12:5; 35:2; **Jn** 11:40–44; 17:4

In his kingdom
Ps 145:11-12 They [the saints] will tell of the glory of your kingdom . . .   *See also* **1Ch** 29:11; **Mt** 6:13 fn; **1Th** 2:12

God's glory cannot be fully seen
1Ti 6:15-16 . . . God, the blessed and only Ruler, the King of kings and Lord of lords, who alone is immortal and who lives in unapproachable light, whom no-one has seen or can see . . .
To see God face to face means certain death: **Ex** 33:18–20; **Jdg** 6:22–23; 13:20–22; **Isa** 6:5; **Jn** 1:18

God's glory experienced
Ac 7:55 . . . Stephen, full of the Holy Spirit, looked up to heaven and saw the glory of God, and Jesus standing at the right hand of God.   *See also* **Ex** 3:2; **Isa** 6:1–4; **Lk** 2:9

The effects of God's glory
God's glory is acknowledged
Ps 72:19 Praise be to his glorious name for ever; may the whole earth be filled with his glory . . .   *See also* **Ps** 29:2; **Ro** 11:36; **Rev** 4:11; 5:13; 19:1

God's glory brings guilt and fear
Ro 3:23 for all have sinned and fall short of the glory of God,   *See also* **Isa** 2:10,19,21; **Rev** 11:13; 15:8   *See also* glory; God, greatness of; God, majesty of; God, revelation; Jesus Christ, glory of; Jesus Christ, Son of God.

God, goodness of
All God's perfect qualities are made freely available to all for the benefit of the whole world.

God alone is good
Mk 10:18 "Why do you call me good?" Jesus answered. "No-one is good—except God alone."   pp Mt 19:17 pp Lk 18:19

God demonstrates his goodness
In his actions
Ps 119:68 You are good, and what you do is good . . .   *See also* **2Ch** 30:18; **Ne** 9:20; **Ps** 73:1; 143:10; **Ac** 10:38; **Ro** 2:4

In his work of creation
1Ti 4:4 For everything God created is good, and nothing is to be rejected if it is received with thanksgiving,   *See also* **Ge** 1:4,31; **Ps** 145:9

In his love
Ps 86:5 You are forgiving and good, O Lord, abounding in love to all who call to you.   *See also* **1Ch** 16:34 pp Ps 106:1; **Ps** 25:7–8; 69:16; 100:5

In his gifts
Jas 1:17 Every good and perfect gift is from above, coming down from the Father of the heavenly lights, who does not change like shifting shadows.   *See also* **Nu** 13:27; **Dt** 8:7; 26:11; **Heb** 9:11

In his promises
Jos 23:14-15 ". . . You know with all your heart and soul that not one of all the good promises the LORD your God gave you has failed. Every promise has been fulfilled; not one has failed . . .   *See also* **2Sa** 7:28 pp 1Ch 17:26; **1Ki** 8:56; **Jer** 29:10

In his commands
Ps 119:39 Take away the disgrace I dread, for your laws are good.   *See also* **Ps** 19:7; **Ro** 7:12,16; 12:2

God's goodness is to be experienced
God is good to those who trust him
Ps 34:8 Taste and see that the LORD is good; blessed are those who take refuge in him.
Na 1:7 The LORD is good, a refuge in times of trouble. He cares for those who trust in him . . . *See also* **Ex** 33:19; **2Ch** 7:10; **Job** 42:11; **Ps** 31:19–20; 84:11; 86:17; **La** 3:25; **Am** 5:14–15; **1Pe** 2:3

God's people can rely on his goodness
Jer 32:40 "I will make an everlasting covenant with them: I will never stop doing good to them, and I will inspire them to fear me, so that they will never turn away from me." *See also* **Ps** 23:6; 27:13; **Mt** 7:11 pp **Lk** 11:13; **Php** 1:6

God works positively for good in unfavourable circumstances
Ge 50:20 "You intended to harm me [Joseph], but God intended it for good to accomplish what is now being done, the saving of many lives." *See also* **Ac** 2:23–24; **Ro** 8:28; **2Co** 4:17; **Heb** 12:10

God's goodness is to be praised
Ps 135:3 Praise the LORD, for the LORD is good; sing praise to his name, for that is pleasant. *See also* **Dt** 8:10; **2Ch** 5:13; 7:3; **Ps** 86:5; 136:1; 145:7 *See also God, compassion; God, grace and mercy; God, love of; God, the provider; prayer as praise and thanksgiving.*

God, grace and mercy
The qualities of God's character by which he shows himself compassionate, accepting, and generous to sinful human beings, shielding them from his wrath, forgiving them, and bestowing on them his righteousness so that they can live and grow in faith and obedience. Grace and mercy are particularly expressed through God's covenant with his chosen people and through Jesus Christ's atoning death on the cross.

God's grace and mercy are made known in Jesus Christ
Jn 1:16–17 From the fulness of his grace we have all received one blessing after another. For the law was given through Moses; grace and truth came through Jesus Christ.

The abundance of God's grace and mercy
Eph 2:4–8 But because of his great love for us, God, who is rich in mercy, made us alive with Christ even when we were dead in transgressions—it is by grace you have been saved. And God raised us up with Christ and seated us with him in the heavenly realms in Christ Jesus, in order that in the coming ages he might show the incomparable riches of his grace, expressed in his kindness to us in Christ Jesus. For it is by grace you have been saved, through faith—and this not from yourselves, it is the gift of God— *See also* **2Sa** 24:14 pp **1Ch** 21:13; **Ps** 69:13; 84:11; 102:13; **Ro** 2:4; 5:17; 9:23; **1Ti** 1:14

God's grace and mercy are always unearned and unmerited
Dt 7:7–8 The LORD did not set his affection on you and choose you because you were more numerous than other peoples, for you were the fewest of all peoples. But it was because the LORD loved you . . . *See also* **Dt** 9:5–6; **Eze** 36:22; **Da** 9:18; **Ro** 9:16; **Eph** 1:6; 2:8–9; 3:8; **Tit** 3:5

God's grace and mercy are a source of blessing
Ge 21:1–2 Now the LORD was gracious to Sarah as he had said, and the LORD did for Sarah what he had promised. Sarah became pregnant and bore a son to Abraham in his old age, at the very time God had promised him. *See also* **Ge** 33:11; **1Sa** 2:21

God's grace and mercy are expressed in the covenant relationship
Jer 31:3 The LORD appeared to us in the past, saying: "I have loved you with an everlasting love; I have drawn you with loving-kindness." *See also* **Ex** 34:6; **Dt** 7:9,12; **Ne** 9:17; **Ps** 6:4; **Isa** 55:3; **La** 3:22,32

Salvation comes by grace
Tit 2:11 For the grace of God that brings salvation has appeared to all people. *See also* **Mk** 10:25–27; **Ro** 5:15; **Eph** 1:5–6; 2:8; **2Ti** 1:9–10

This is ultimately shown in the cross of Jesus Christ
Ro 3:24–25 . . . [all] are justified freely by his grace through the redemption that came by Christ Jesus. God presented him as a sacrifice of atonement, through faith in his blood . . .
See also **Ro** 5:8; **Eph** 1:7; **Heb** 2:9; **2Pe** 1:10–11

God's grace and mercy are offered to sinners
Punishment is withheld
Ezr 9:13 ". . . you have punished us less than our sins have deserved and have given us a remnant like this." *See also* **2Ki** 13:22–23; **Eze** 20:15–17; **Hos** 11:8; **Joel** 2:13

Sin is forgiven
Mic 7:18 Who is a God like you, who pardons sin and forgives the transgression of the remnant of his inheritance? You do not stay angry for ever but delight to show mercy.
1Jn 1:9 If we confess our sins, he is faithful and just and will forgive us our sins and purify us from all unrighteousness. *See also* **Ps** 32:5; **Pr** 28:13; **Isa** 55:7; **Jer** 3:12; 33:8; **Da** 9:9

Sinners' prayers are heard
Ps 51:1 Have mercy on me, O God, according to your unfailing love; according to your great compassion blot out my transgressions.
Lk 18:13–14 ". . . but [the tax collector] beat his breast and said, 'God, have mercy on me, a sinner.' "I tell you that this man, rather than the other, went home justified before God. For all those who exalt themselves will be humbled, and those who humble themselves will be exalted." *See also* **Ps** 6:2–3; 123:3; **Hab** 3:2

The favour of God
Examples of those who found favour with God
Ge 4:4; 6:8; **Ex** 33:12; **Jdg** 6:17–18; **1Sa** 2:26 **Ezr** 7:27–28; **Lk** 1:30; 2:52; **Ac** 7:46

Examples of those who seek the favour of God
Ex 32:11; **2Ki** 13:4; **2Ch** 33:12
Nehemiah: **Ne** 5:19; 13:31
Da 9:17

Promises relating to the favour of God
Lev 26:9; **Ps** 5:12; 30:5

The OT predicts a future age of God's favour
Isa 49:8 This is what the LORD says: "In the time of my favour I will answer you, and in the day of salvation I will help you; I will keep you and will make you to be a covenant for the people, to restore the land and to reassign its desolate inheritances," *See also* **Isa** 60:10; 61:2; **Eze** 36:9

Implications for believers of the grace and mercy of God
God's grace and mercy are to influence the character and conduct of believers
Ro 6:1–2 What shall we say, then? Shall we go on sinning, so that grace may increase? By no means! We died to sin; how can we live in it any longer? *See also* **Ac** 11:23; **Ro** 6:14; 12:1; **Tit** 2:11–12

Believers must humbly rely on God's grace and mercy
Gal 2:21 "I do not set aside the grace of God, for if righteousness could be gained through the law, Christ died for nothing!" *See also* **Pr** 3:34; **Jas** 4:6; **Jnh** 2:8; **Ro** 2:4; **2Co** 6:1–2

God's grace strengthens believers for service
Eph 3:7–8 I [Paul] became a servant of this gospel by the gift of God's grace given me through the working of his power. Although I am less than the least of all God's people, this grace was given me: to preach to the Gentiles the unsearchable riches of Christ, *See also* **1Co** 3:10; **2Co** 12:7–9; **Gal** 1:15–16; **Eph** 4:7,11

Illustrations of God's grace and mercy
God shows grace to Noah, saving him from the flood and afterwards establishing a covenant with him: **Ge** 6:8,22; 9:9–11

Jnh 1:1–3, 17; 2:1–3; 3:1–10; **Lk** 15:11–32
See also forgiveness; God, compassion; God, love of; gospel; grace; Jesus Christ, grace and mercy; prayer; salvation; sin, remedy for.

God, greatness of
God's nature, deeds and attributes are incomparable, for which he deserves all praise.

God is great
Jer 10:6 No-one is like you, O LORD; you are great, and your name is mighty in power. *See also* **1Ch** 16:25 pp **Ps** 96:4; **1Ch** 29:11; **Ne** 1:5; **Isa** 12:6

God's name is great
Eze 36:23 "'I will show the holiness of my great name, which has been profaned among the nations . . .'" *See also* **Jos** 7:9; **1Sa** 12:22; **1Ki** 8:42 pp **2Ch** 6:32

God is a great king
Ps 47:2 How awesome is the LORD Most High, the great King over all the earth! *See also* **Ps** 47:7; 48:2; **Mal** 1:14; **Mt** 5:35; **1Ti** 6:15

God's deeds are great
He does great things
Ps 136:4 to him who alone does great wonders . . . *See also* **Jdg** 2:7; **Isa** 55:9; **Jer** 32:19; **Lk** 1:49; **Eph** 3:20
His acts are powerful
Dt 9:29 "But they are your people, your inheritance that you brought out by your great power and your outstretched arm." *See also* **Ex** 15:7; **Dt** 9:26
His great victories in the promised land: **1Sa** 19:5; **2Sa** 23:10
His powerful act of creation: **Isa** 40:26; **Jer** 32:17 **Na** 1:3; **Eph** 1:19–20

God's attributes are great
His great love
Ps 108:4 For great is your love, higher than the heavens; your faithfulness reaches to the skies. *See also* **Nu** 14:19; **2Ch** 1:8; **La** 3:22; **Eph** 2:4; **1Jn** 3:1
His great mercy
1Ch 21:13 David said to Gad, "I am in deep distress. Let me fall into the hands of the LORD, for his mercy is very great; but do not let me fall into human hands." *See also* **Ne** 9:31; **Ro** 5:17; **1Pe** 1:3
His great anger
2Ki 22:13 ". . . Great is the LORD's anger that burns against us because those who have gone before us have not obeyed the words of this book; they have not acted in accordance with all that is written there concerning us." *See also* **Ps** 90:11; 102:10; **Jer** 21:5; 32:37

God's gifts are great
He bestows great gifts
Da 5:18 "O king, the Most High God gave your father Nebuchadnezzar sovereignty and greatness and glory and splendour." *See also* **Ge** 12:2; **1Sa** 26:25; **1Ch** 29:25
He gives great joy
Ne 12:43 And on that day they offered great sacrifices, rejoicing because God had given them great joy. The women and children also rejoiced. The sound of rejoicing in Jerusalem could be heard far away. *See also* **Ezr** 6:22; **Ps** 4:7; 126:3

The effects of God's greatness
God's power is known in the nations
Ps 126:2 Our mouths were filled with laughter, our tongues with songs of joy. Then it was said among the nations, "The LORD has done great things for them." *See also* **2Ch** 9:6; 20:6; **Ps** 99:2; **Da** 4:3
People are astonished
Lk 9:43 And they [the crowd] were all amazed at the greatness of God . . . *See also* **Hab** 1:5; **Lk** 5:26
God must be praised for his greatness
Ps 48:1 Great is the LORD, and most worthy of praise . . . *See also* **Dt** 32:3; **Ps** 89:1; 96:4; 145:3

God's greatness makes him unique
There is no-one like him
Ps 150:2 Praise him for his acts of power; praise him for his surpassing greatness. *See also* **2Sa** 7:22; **Ps** 71:19; 86:10; 145:3
He is greater than other gods
Ex 18:11 "Now I [Jethro] know that the LORD is greater than all other gods, for he did this to

those who had treated Israel arrogantly." *See also* **Dt** 4:7; 10:17; **2Ch** 2:5; **Ps** 135:5; **1Co** 8:4–6
God is greater than human power and pride
Job 33:12 "... God is greater than any mortal." *See also* **2Ch** 32:7–8; **Isa** 40:6–7; **1Jn** 3:20   *See also* God as Saviour; God, all-knowing; God, anger of; God, love of; God, majesty of; God, power of; God, sovereignty; God, unique; Jesus Christ, pre-eminence; miracles, nature of; worship, reasons.

God, holiness of
The moral excellence of God that unifies his attributes and is expressed through his actions, setting him apart from all others. Believers are called to be holy as God is holy.

God's nature is holy
He is perfect
Dt 32:4 He is the Rock, his works are perfect, and all his ways are just. A faithful God who does no wrong, upright and just is he.
Isa 6:3 And they were calling to one another: "Holy, holy, holy is the LORD Almighty; the whole earth is full of his glory."
Rev 4:8 ... "Holy, holy, holy is the Lord God Almighty, who was, and is, and is to come." *See also* **2Sa** 22:31; **Job** 6:10; **Ps** 18:30; 22:3; 71:22; 78:41; **Isa** 41:14; 43:15; **Hab** 1:13; **Jn** 17:11; **Rev** 6:10
He is uniquely holy
1Sa 2:2 "There is no-one holy like the LORD; there is no-one besides you ...   *See also* **Ex** 15:11; **Ps** 77:13; **Isa** 40:25; **Rev** 15:4

God's name is holy
Eze 36:21–23 "'... I will show the holiness of my great name ...'"   *See also* **Lev** 22:32; **1Ch** 16:35; 29:16; **Ps** 33:21; 97:12; **Isa** 57:15; **Eze** 39:25; **Lk** 1:49

God's dwelling-place is holy
Isa 57:15 ... "I live in a high and holy place ..."   *See also* **2Ch** 8:11; 30:27; **Ps** 2:6; 3:4; 5:7; 11:4; 15:1; 20:6; 47:8; 48:1; 65:4; **Isa** 63:15; **Joel** 3:17; **Ob** 16–17; **Jnh** 2:4; **Mic** 1:2; **Hab** 2:20; **Zec** 2:13; **Ac** 21:28; **Eph** 2:21–22; **Heb** 10:19–22; **Rev** 22:19

God's holiness is revealed in his righteous activity
Isa 5:16 ... the holy God will show himself holy by his righteousness.   *See also* **Jdg** 5:11; **1Sa** 12:7; **Ps** 77:13; 145:17; **Da** 9:14,16; **Zep** 3:5

God's holiness affects worship
It is celebrated in worship
Ps 99:5 Exalt the LORD our God and worship at his footstool; he is holy.   *See also* **1Ch** 16:29; **Ps** 29:2; 99:5; 103:1; 105:3; 145:21; **Isa** 6:3
Coming before a holy God requires preparation
Ex 3:5 "Do not come any closer," God said. "Take off your sandals, for the place where you are standing is holy ground."   *See also* **Ex** 29:37; **Ps** 24:3–4; **1Co** 11:28; **Heb** 10:1–2,22
Special requirements and tasks are given to worship leaders Lev 21:7–8, 10–15
Aaron and his family: **Ex** 28:1–43; **Lev** 21:16–23
2Ch 29:5

God's holiness is to be seen in his people
God's people are to be holy because he is holy
Lev 19:2 "Speak to the entire assembly of Israel and say to them: 'Be holy because I, the LORD your God, am holy.'"
2Ti 1:9 [God] who has saved us and called us to a holy life—not because of anything we have done but because of his own purpose and grace ...   *See also* **Ex** 19:6; 22:31; **Lev** 11:44; **Mt** 5:48; **Ro** 12:1; **1Co** 1:2; **2Co** 11:2; **Eph** 1:4; 5:3; **Php** 4:8; **Col** 1:22; 3:12; **1Th** 3:13; 4:3–7; **Tit** 1:8; **Heb** 2:11; 3:1; 12:10; **1Pe** 1:15–16
Becoming holy involves striving after God
2Pe 3:14 ... make every effort to be found spotless, blameless and at peace with him.   *See also* **2Co** 7:1; 13:11; **Eph** 4:22–24; **1Ti** 5:22; **Heb** 12:14; **Jas** 1:20–21; **2Pe** 3:11–12
The holiness of believers originates from God
Ex 31:13 "Say to the Israelites, 'You must observe my Sabbaths. This will be a sign between me and you for the generations to come, so that you may know that I am the LORD, who makes you holy.'"   *See also* **Lev** 22:9; **Dt** 28:9; **Ps** 4:3; **1Jn** 3:1–3

Jesus Christ purifies Christian believers

1Jn 1:7 But if we walk in the light, as he is in the light, we have fellowship with one another, and the blood of Jesus, his Son, purifies us from all sin. *See also* **Heb** 7:26–28; 9:26–28; 10:10,14; **1Jn** 3:4–6

God's holiness makes sin objectionable to him

Hab 1:13 Your eyes are too pure to look on evil; you cannot tolerate wrong . . . *See also* **Jos** 24:19–20; **Jer** 50:29

God's holiness necessitates dependence upon him for forgiveness

Ps 51:1–17 . . . Against you, you only, have I sinned and done what is evil in your sight, so that you are proved right when you speak and justified when you judge . . . Cleanse me with hyssop, and I shall be clean; wash me, and I shall be whiter than snow . . . Do not cast me from your presence or take your Holy Spirit from me . . . *See also* **Da** 9:4–19; **1Jn** 1:9
See also Christlikeness; fellowship with God; forgiveness; God, perfection; God, righteousness; God, zeal of; holiness; Jesus Christ, holiness; worship.

God, human descriptions of

Figures of speech which describe God in human terms, sometimes referred to as anthropomorphisms. Since God is Spirit, these expressions help the human mind to understand God, and enable God to reveal himself to human beings.

Bodily form ascribed to God

Ex 33:23 "Then I [the LORD] will remove my hand and you will see my back; but my face must not be seen." *See also* **Ge** 18:2–14; **Jos** 5:13–15; **Eze** 1:26–28

His face

Nu 6:25–26 "'"the LORD make his face shine upon you and be gracious to you; the LORD turn his face towards you and give you peace."'"
See also **Ps** 27:8; 51:9; **Mt** 18:10; **Rev** 22:4

His heart

2Ch 7:16 "I [the LORD] have chosen and consecrated this temple so that my Name may be there for ever. My eyes and my heart will always be there." *See also* **Ge** 6:6; 8:21; **1Sa** 13:14; **Ac** 13:22

His hands

Isa 14:27 For the LORD Almighty has purposed, and who can thwart him? His hand is stretched out, and who can turn it back? *See also* **1Ch** 28:19; 29:14,16; **Ps** 45:4; **Ac** 2:33–34; **1Pe** 3:22; 5:6

His eyes

2Ch 16:9 "For the eyes of the LORD range throughout the earth to strengthen those whose hearts are fully committed to him . . ." *See also* **Dt** 11:12; **Pr** 15:3; **Am** 9:8; **Zec** 4:10; **1Pe** 3:12; **Ps** 34:15

His feet

Eze 43:7 He [God] said: "Son of man, this is the place of my throne and the place for the soles of my feet. This is where I will live among the Israelites for ever . . ." *See also* **Dt** 33:3; **2Sa** 22:10 pp **Ps** 18:9; **Ps** 45:5; **Isa** 60:13

His arm

Isa 59:1 Surely the arm of the LORD is not too short to save . . .

Jer 32:21 "You brought your people Israel out of Egypt with signs and wonders, by a mighty hand and an outstretched arm and with great terror." *See also* **Ex** 6:6; **Dt** 5:15; **Job** 40:9; **Isa** 51:9; 52:10; 63:5; **Lk** 1:51; **Jn** 12:38; **Isa** 53:1

His mind

Ro 11:34 "Who has known the mind of the Lord? Or who has been his counsellor?" *See also* **Isa** 40:13; **1Sa** 15:29; **Jer** 7:31; **Heb** 7:21; **Ps** 110:4

Human actions ascribed to God

He walks

Ge 3:8 Then the man and his wife heard the sound of the LORD God as he was walking in the garden in the cool of the day . . . *See also* **Lev** 26:12; **2Co** 6:16

He speaks

Dt 4:12 Then the LORD spoke to you out of the fire. You heard the sound of words but saw no form; there was only a voice. *See also* **Job** 40:6; **Ps** 29:3–9; 33:6,9; **Eze** 1:24; **Mt** 3:17 pp **Mk** 1:11 pp **Lk** 3:22; **Ac** 7:6

He rests
Ge 2:2 . . . so on the seventh day he [God] rested from all his work. *See also* **Ex** 20:11; **Heb** 4:4

He rides
Ps 68:4 Sing to God, sing praise to his name, extol him who rides on the clouds—his name is the LORD . . . *See also* **Dt** 33:26; **2Sa** 22:11 pp Ps 18:10; **Ps** 68:33; **Hab** 3:8

He laughs
Ps 59:8 But you, O LORD, laugh at them; you scoff at all those nations. *See also* **Ps** 2:4; 37:13

Other actions Isa 5:26; Rev 3:20

Human senses ascribed to God
He hears
Ps 4:3 . . . the LORD will hear when I call to him. *See also* **Ge** 16:11; **2Ch** 7:14; **Ps** 94:9; **Lk** 1:13; **Jn** 11:42; **Heb** 5:7

He sees
Ge 16:13 She [Hagar] gave this name to the LORD who spoke to her: "You are the God who sees me," for she said, "I have now seen the One who sees me." *See also* **Ge** 1:4; **2Ch** 12:7; **Ne** 9:9; **Pr** 24:18; **Eze** 8:12–13; **Jnh** 3:10

He smells
Ge 8:21 The LORD smelled the pleasing aroma and said in his heart: "Never again will I curse the ground because of human beings, even though every inclination of the human heart is evil from childhood. And never again will I destroy all living creatures, as I have done." *See also* **Lev** 1:9

God experiences emotion
He shows delight
Zep 3:17 ". . . He [the LORD] will take great delight in you, he will quiet you with his love, he will rejoice over you with singing." *See also* **Dt** 30:9; **Ps** 149:4; **Isa** 5:7; 62:4

He is compassionate
Jas 5:11 . . . The Lord is full of compassion and mercy. *See also* **Ps** 145:9; **Isa** 54:10; **Hos** 2:19; 11:8; **2Co** 1:3

He is angry
Ps 95:10–11 For forty years I was angry with that generation; I said, "They are a people whose hearts go astray, and they have not known my ways." So I declared on oath in my anger, "They shall never enter my rest." *See also* **2Ki** 17:11; **Ps** 78:58; 106:29; **Isa** 5:25; 54:8

He experiences pain
Ge 6:6 The LORD was grieved that he had made human beings on the earth, and his heart was filled with pain. *See also* **1Sa** 15:11,35; **2Sa** 24:16 pp 1Ch 21:15; **Eze** 6:9

Human occupations ascribed to God
Isa 29:16 You turn things upside down, as if the potter were thought to be like the clay! Shall what is formed say to the one who formed it, "You did not make me"? Can the pot say to the potter, "You know nothing"? *See also* **Ex** 15:3; **Ps** 23:1; **Heb** 11:10

Human relationships ascribed to God
God as a loving husband
Isa 54:5–8 "For your Maker is your husband—the LORD Almighty is his name . . ." *See also* **Jer** 3:14; 31:32; **Hos** 2:16

God as a loving father
Ps 103:13 As a father has compassion on his children, so the LORD has compassion on those who fear him; *See also* **Isa** 1:2–3; **Jer** 31:9; **Hos** 11:1–4; **Mt** 11:27; **Jn** 16:27

God is not to be brought down to human levels
Hos 11:9 ". . . For I am God, and not a human being—the Holy One among you . . ." *See also* **Nu** 23:19; **Job** 9:32; **Ps** 50:21; **Isa** 55:8–9 *See also* God as shepherd; God, anger of; God, compassion; God, fatherhood; God, feminine descriptions of; God, suffering of; word of God.

God, joy of
God rejoices in the well-being and faithfulness of his covenant people, and in the repentance and conversion of sinners. He brings joy to his people, who rejoice in his presence and faithfulness.

God is the source of joy
Ps 37:4 Delight yourself in the LORD and he will give you the desires of your heart. *See also*

1Sa 2:1; Ne 1:11; 12:43; Isa 61:10; Jn 15:11; Php 4:4

God rejoices in the restoration of his people
Jer 32:41 "I will rejoice in doing them good and will assuredly plant them in this land with all my heart and soul." *See also* Isa 62:4–5; 65:19; Jer 31:20; Zep 3:17

Joy can be found in the heavenly presence of God
1Ch 16:27 Splendour and majesty are before him; strength and joy in his dwelling-place.
At creation: Job 38:4–7; Pr 8:30–31
Lk 15:7

Causes of God's joy
His own works Jer 9:24
His chosen servant Mt 12:18; Isa 42:1; Heb 1:9; Ps 45:7
Jesus Christ Mt 3:17 pp Mk 1:11 pp Lk 3:22; Mt 17:5
The restored temple Hag 1:8
His people and their worship
Ps 149:4–9 For the LORD takes delight in his people; he crowns the humble with salvation. Let the saints rejoice in this honour and sing for joy on their beds . . . *See also* Ps 69:30–31
Repentance Dt 30:9
Obedience, honesty and integrity
1Sa 15:22 . . . "Does the LORD delight in burnt offerings and sacrifices as much as in obeying the voice of the LORD? . . ."
Pr 12:22 The LORD detests lying lips, but he delights in those who are truthful. *See also* 1Ch 29:17; Ps 147:10–11; Pr 11:1,20

God's face shining on his people
Nu 6:25 " ' "the LORD make his face shine upon you and be gracious to you;" ' "
See also Ps 67:1; 80:19; 119:135
By contrast God's face is against evil, showing his displeasure: Ps 34:16; 1Pe 3:12 *See also God as redeemer; God as Saviour; God, righteousness; Holy Spirit, joy of; Jesus Christ, joy of.*

God, justice of
The moral righteousness of God is revealed in his laws and expressed in his judicial acts. God's commands and judgments meet perfect standards of justice, and his apportioning of punishments and rewards is also perfectly just. God's justice is impartial. Special praise is his for vindicating the penitent and the needy who have no human champions. Ultimately, all God's ways will be seen as just and equitable.

God's justice displays his righteousness
It conforms to his moral law
Job 34:12 "It is unthinkable that God would do wrong, that the Almighty would pervert justice." *See also* Dt 32:4; Ps 9:16; 11:7; Zep 3:5; Ro 2:2; 2Ti 2:13; Rev 15:3
It is seen in his perfect will
Ps 99:4 The King is mighty, he loves justice— you have established equity . . . *See also* Ps 40:8; Isa 53:10; Mt 6:10; 26:39 pp Mk 14:36 pp Lk 22:42; Heb 10:9–10

God acts with justice
Ps 33:5–15 The LORD loves righteousness and justice; the earth is full of his unfailing love . . . From heaven the LORD looks down and sees all humanity; from his dwelling-place he watches all who live on earth—he who forms the hearts of all, who considers everything they do.
See also Ne 9:33
God's justice is exercised fairly and equitably
Ps 9:7–8 The LORD reigns for ever; he has established his throne for judgment. He will judge the world in righteousness; he will govern the peoples with justice. *See also* Ps 96:13; 98:9; 99:4
He judges people according to their deeds
Rev 20:12–13 . . . The dead were judged according to what they had done as recorded in the books. The sea gave up the dead that were in it, and death and Hades gave up the dead that were in them, and everyone was judged according to what they had done. *See also* Ex 34:6–7; Ps 62:12; Jer 17:10; Eze 18:20; Mt 16:27; Rev 22:12

He punishes wickedness
Eze 18:20 "The soul who sins is the one who will die. The child will not share the guilt of the parent, nor will the parent share the guilt of the child . . ." *See also* Ex 34:7; Dt 32:35; Isa 59:18; 66:24; Mt 25:41–46; Col 3:25; 2Th 1:8–9

He rewards righteousness
Ps 58:11 Then people will say, "Surely the righteous still are rewarded; surely there is a God who judges the earth." *See also* Isa 62:11; Mt 5:12 pp Lk 6:23; Mt 25:34–40,46; Ro 2:7; 8:1–2; 2Ti 4:8

God establishes justice
He upholds the cause of the oppressed
Ps 103:6 The LORD works righteousness and justice for all the oppressed. *See also* Dt 10:18; Ps 140:12; 146:7–9; Isa 61:8; Lk 1:52–53

He vindicates those who have been wronged
1Sa 25:39 When David heard that Nabal was dead, he said, "Praise be to the LORD, who has upheld my cause against Nabal for treating me with contempt. He has kept his servant from doing wrong and has brought Nabal's wrongdoing down on his own head." . . . *See also* 1Sa 24:15; Ps 135:14; Ro 12:19; Dt 32:35; 1Pe 2:23

He is completely impartial
Job 34:18–19 "Is he [God, the mighty one] not the One who says to kings, 'You are worthless,' and to nobles, 'You are wicked,' who shows no partiality to princes and does not favour the rich over the poor, for they are all the work of his hands?" *See also* Dt 10:17; 2Ch 19:7; Ac 10:34–35; Eph 6:9

God's ways in exercising justice
God's justice is not always immediately apparent
Jer 12:1 You are always righteous, O LORD, when I bring a case before you. Yet I would speak with you about your justice: Why does the way of the wicked prosper? Why do all the faithless live at ease? *See also* Job 21:7; Ps 73:3–14; Ecc 7:15; Hab 1:2–4; Mal 2:17; 3:14–15; Mt 20:10–12

God warns before punishing
2Ch 36:15 The LORD, the God of their ancestors, sent word to them through his messengers again and again, because he had pity on his people and on his dwelling-place. *See also* 2Ki 17:23; Ne 9:29–30; Jer 7:13; Jnh 3:4; Heb 12:25

God gives opportunity for people to change their ways
Jer 18:8–10 "and if that nation I [the LORD] warned repents of its evil, then I will relent and not inflict on it the disaster I had planned . . ." *See also* Jer 7:5–7; Eze 18:25–32; Mt 21:28–32; 1Jn 1:9

God's justice is truly equitable
Gal 6:7–8 Do not be deceived: God cannot be mocked. People reap what they sow. Those who sow to please their sinful nature, from that nature will reap destruction; those who sow to please the Spirit, from the Spirit will reap eternal life. *See also* Ge 18:25; Nu 32:23; Ps 73:17; Lk 16:25; 18:7–8; Col 3:24–25

God's justice is satisfied by the work of Jesus Christ
Ro 3:25–26 God presented him [Jesus Christ] as a sacrifice of atonement, through faith in his blood. He did this to demonstrate his justice, because in his forbearance he had left the sins committed beforehand unpunished—he did it to demonstrate his justice at the present time, so as to be just and the one who justifies those who have faith in Jesus. *See also* Isa 53:10–11; Heb 9:22; 1Jn 1:9; 2:1–2

God's justice will be established in the reign of Jesus Christ
Mt 25:31–33 "When the Son of Man comes in his glory, and all the angels with him, he will sit on his throne in heavenly glory. All the nations will be gathered before him, and he will separate the people one from another as a shepherd separates the sheep from the goats. He will put the sheep on his right and the goats on his left." *See also* Isa 9:6–7; Ac 17:31; Rev 19:11–16

Heaven and earth will rejoice when God's justice is established
Ps 96:10–13 pp 1Ch

God, living

16:30–33; **Ps** 98:4–9; **Rev** 15:3–4; 16:5–7; 19:1–2

God requires people to reflect his justice

Pr 21:3 To do what is right and just is more acceptable to the LORD than sacrifice. *See also* **Lev** 19:15; **Dt** 16:20; 24:17; **1Ki** 10:9 pp **2Ch** 9:8; **Ps** 82:3–4; **Isa** 56:1; **Mic** 6:8; **Zec** 7:9–10; **Col** 4:1; **1Ti** 5:21 *See also God as judge; God, patience of; Jesus Christ as judge; Jesus Christ, righteousness; law.*

God, living

God is alive and active. In contrast to idols, he is uncreated and the source of all continuing life.

God is alive

Jer 10:10 But the LORD is the true God; he is the living God, the eternal King . . . *See also* **Ge** 1:1; **Dt** 5:26; **Jos** 3:10; **Jer** 23:36; **Mt** 26:63; **1Ti** 3:15; **Heb** 3:12; 12:22

God lives for ever

Isa 57:15 For this is what the high and lofty One says—he who lives for ever, whose name is holy . . . *See also* **Da** 4:34; 12:7; **Rev** 4:9–10; 10:6; 15:7

God is self-existent

Jn 5:26 "For as the Father has life in himself, so he has granted the Son to have life in himself." *See also* **Ex** 3:14; **Jn** 8:58; **Ac** 17:25

The living God is Father, Son and Holy Spirit

Jn 6:57 "Just as the living Father sent me [Jesus] and I live because of the Father, so the one who feeds on me will live because of me." **2Co 3:3** You [Corinthian Christians] show that you are a letter from Christ, the result of our ministry, written not with ink but with the Spirit of the living God . . . *See also* **Mt** 16:16; **1Co** 8:6; **Heb** 7:24

The living God is to be worshipped

Da 6:26 "I [King Darius] issue a decree that in every part of my kingdom people must fear and reverence the God of Daniel. For he is the living God and he endures for ever; his kingdom will not be destroyed, his dominion will never end." *See also* **Da** 6:20; **Ro** 9:26; **Hos** 1:10; **2Co** 6:16; **1Ti** 4:10; **Heb** 9:14

Turning away from the living God is sin

Heb 3:12 See to it, brothers and sisters, that none of you has a sinful, unbelieving heart that turns away from the living God. *See also* **1Sa** 17:26,36; **2Ki** 19:4 pp **Isa** 37:4; **2Ki** 19:16 pp **Isa** 37:17; **Heb** 10:31

The living God contrasts with dead idols

Ac 14:15 ". . . We [Barnabas and Paul] are bringing you good news, telling you to turn from these worthless things to the living God, who made heaven and earth and sea and everything in them." *See also* **1Ki** 18:26–29; **Ps** 115:2–7; **Isa** 46:1–4; **Jer** 10:3–6; **1Th** 1:9

God is the source of life

Dt 30:20 . . . For the LORD is your life . . . *See also* **Jn** 1:4

God gives life to created beings

Ge 2:7 the LORD God formed a man from the dust of the ground and breathed into his nostrils the breath of life, and the man became a living being. *See also* **Job** 27:3; **Ps** 104:30; **Isa** 40:28; **Ac** 17:25,28

God sustains the life of all people

Ps 54:4 Surely God is my help; the Lord is the one who sustains me. *See also* **1Ch** 29:14; **Ps** 3:5; 18:35; 146:9; 147:6; **Isa** 46:4; **Heb** 1:3

God gives spiritual life

Jn 10:28 "I [Jesus] give them eternal life, and they shall never perish; no-one can snatch them out of my hand." *See also* **Jn** 5:21; 11:25; 14:6; **1Pe** 1:23

God is the source of new life

Ps 42:2 My soul thirsts for God, for the living God. When can I go and meet with God? *See also* **Ps** 63:1; 84:2; **Jn** 3:1–8 *See also God, the Creator; God, the eternal; Holy Spirit, life-giver; life, spiritual.*

God, love of

The deepest possible expression of God's character. Though God loves all people, he is especially committed to sacrificial, loyal relationships with his people.

God's nature is love
1Jn 4:8 . . . God is love.   *See also* **1Jn** 4:16
His love is perfectly expressed within the Trinity
Mk 1:10–11 . . . a voice came from heaven: "You [Jesus] are my Son, whom I love; with you I am well pleased." pp **Mt** 3:16–17 pp **Lk** 3:21–22
See also **Jn** 5:20; 10:17; 14:23; **Eph** 1:6; **Col** 1:13

Characteristics of God's love
It is eternal
Jer 31:3 . . . "I [the LORD] have loved you with an everlasting love; I have drawn you with loving-kindness."   *See also* **Ps** 103:17; 136:1–26; **Isa** 49:15–16; 54:8,10
It is a covenant love
Dt 7:9 Know therefore that the LORD your God is God; he is the faithful God, keeping his covenant of love to a thousand generations of those who love him and keep his commands.
See also **Ex** 20:6 pp **Dt** 5:10; **Dt** 7:12; **1Ki** 8:23 pp **2Ch** 6:14; **Ps** 106:45; **Da** 9:4
It is lavish
Ex 34:6–7 . . . he passed in front of Moses, proclaiming, "The LORD, the LORD, the compassionate and gracious God, slow to anger, abounding in love and faithfulness, maintaining love to thousands, and forgiving wickedness, rebellion and sin . . ."   *See also* **Ne** 9:17; **Ps** 103:8; **Joel** 2:13; **Jnh** 4:2; **1Jn** 3:1
It is holy and just
Ps 33:5 The LORD loves righteousness and justice; the earth is full of his unfailing love.
See also **Ps** 37:28; 99:4; **Isa** 61:8

Images of God's love
God as a father: **Dt** 1:31; **Hos** 11:1–4; **Lk** 15:11–32; **Heb** 12:6; **Pr** 3:12
God as a husband: **Jer** 31:32; **Hos** 2:14–20; **Rev** 21:2

God's loving actions
The gift of God's Son is a unique act of love
1Jn 4:9–10 This is how God showed his love among us: He sent his one and only Son into the world that we might live through him. This is love: not that we loved God, but that he loved us and sent his Son as an atoning sacrifice for our sins.   *See also* **Jn** 3:16; 15:13; **Ro** 5:7–8
God sets his love on the unlovely
Dt 7:7–8 The LORD did not set his affection on you [Israel] and choose you because you were more numerous than other peoples, for you were the fewest of all peoples. But it was because the LORD loved you . . .   *See also* **Eze** 16:1–14; **Ro** 5:8; **Eph** 2:4–5
God always acts in love towards believers
Ro 8:38–39 For I am convinced that neither death nor life, neither angels nor demons, neither the present nor the future, nor any powers, neither height nor depth, nor anything else in all creation, will be able to separate us from the love of God that is in Christ Jesus our Lord.
See also **2Co** 13:14; **2Jn** 3

God's love for his people
Israel
Isa 43:4 "Since you [Israel] are precious and honoured in my sight, and because I love you, I will give nations in exchange for you, and peoples in exchange for your life."   *See also* **Dt** 10:15; **2Ch** 9:8; **Mt** 15:24; **Ro** 9:15–16; **Ex** 33:19; **Ro** 11:28
The church
Rev 1:5 . . . To him who loves us and has freed us from our sins by his blood,   *See also* **Jn** 16:27; 17:23

God's love for the world
Dt 10:18 He defends the cause of the fatherless and the widow, and loves the alien, giving them food and clothing.
Jn 3:16–17 "For God so loved the world that he gave his one and only Son, that whoever believes in him shall not perish but have eternal life. For God did not send his Son into the world to condemn the world, but to save the world through him."   *See also* **Ps** 145:9,17; **Mt** 5:45; **Ac** 14:17; 17:25

God's love for individuals
2Sa 12:24-25 ... She [Bathsheba] gave birth to a son, and they named him Solomon. The LORD loved him; and because the LORD loved him, he sent word through Nathan the prophet to name him Jedidiah. *See also* **Dt** 33:12
David: 2Sa 7:15 pp **1Ch** 17:13; **Isa** 55:3 **Ezr** 7:28; **Ne** 13:26

God's love transforms human love
Human love must respond to God's love
1Jn 4:19 We love because he first loved us. *See also* **Dt** 6:5; 30:6; **Eph** 5:1; **Col** 3:12-14
Human love must be modelled on God's love
Mt 5:44-45 "But I tell you: Love your enemies, and pray for those who persecute you, that you may be children of your Father in heaven ..." *See also* **Hos** 3:1; **1Jn** 2:15; 4:7-8,11-12 *See also God, compassion; God, fatherhood; God, grace and mercy; Holy Spirit and love; Jesus Christ, love of.*

God, majesty of
The greatness and splendour of God, revealed in his creation and mighty works of deliverance. On account of his majesty, God is worthy of praise and adoration from all people.

God is majestic
Heb 8:1 ... We do have such a high priest, who sat down at the right hand of the throne of the Majesty in heaven, *See also* **1Sa** 15:29; **Ps** 24:10; **Heb** 1:3-4

Majesty belongs to God
1Ch 29:11 "Yours, O LORD, is the greatness and the power and the glory and the majesty and the splendour, for everything in heaven and earth is yours. Yours, O LORD, is the kingdom; you are exalted as head over all." *See also* **Ps** 145:12; **Jude** 25

God's majesty is awesome
Job 37:22 "... God comes in awesome majesty." *See also* **Isa** 2:10,19,21

God's character is majestic
Ps 93:1 The LORD reigns, he is robed in majesty; the LORD is robed in majesty and is armed with strength ... *See also* **Ex** 15:11; **Ps** 104:1; 145:5; **Isa** 24:14; 26:10

God's activity is majestic
Ex 15:6-7 "Your right hand, O LORD, was majestic in power. Your right hand, O LORD, shattered the enemy. In the greatness of your majesty you threw down those who opposed you. You unleashed your burning anger; it consumed them like stubble." *See also* **Dt** 9:26; 11:2-3; **2Ch** 20:6; **Ps** 111:3; **Lk** 9:43

God's name is majestic
Ps 8:1 O LORD, our Lord, how majestic is your name in all the earth! You have set your glory above the heavens. *See also* **Ps** 8:9

God's voice is majestic
Ps 29:4 The voice of the LORD is powerful; the voice of the LORD is majestic. *See also* **Job** 37:4; **Isa** 30:30

God's presence is majestic
1Ch 16:27 Splendour and majesty are before him; strength and joy in his dwelling-place. *See also* **Ps** 96:6; **2Th** 1:9; **2Pe** 1:17

The risen Christ shares in God's majesty
2Pe 1:16-17 We did not follow cleverly invented stories when we told you about the power and coming of our Lord Jesus Christ, but we were eye-witnesses of his majesty. For he received honour and glory from God the Father when the voice came to him from the Majestic Glory, saying, "This is my Son, whom I love; with him I am well pleased." *See also* **Heb** 1:3-4; 8:1

God's delegated majesty
To the Messiah
Mic 5:4 He will stand and shepherd his flock in the strength of the LORD, in the majesty of the name of the LORD his God ... *See also* **Zec** 9:9
To kings
Ps 21:5 Through the victories you gave, his

glory is great; you have bestowed on him splendour and majesty. *See also* **Ps** 45:3–4; 110:2–3

God's majesty provides help for his people
Ps 68:34–35 Proclaim the power of God, whose majesty is over Israel, whose power is in the skies. You are awesome, O God, in your sanctuary; the God of Israel gives power and strength to his people. Praise be to God! *See also* **Ex** 15:6; **Dt** 33:26–27

Experiences of God's majesty
Isa 6:1–4; **Eze** 1:4–28; **Hab** 3:3–6; **Rev** 4:1–11

Human responses to the majesty of God
An awareness of sin
Isa 6:5 "Woe to me!" I cried. "I am ruined! For I am a man of unclean lips, and I live among a people of unclean lips, and my eyes have seen the King, the LORD Almighty."
An awareness of insignificance Isa 40:15
Worship and adoration of God 1Ch 16:29; **Ps** 92:1–8; 93:1; 95:3–6; **Lk** 1:46   *See also* glory, revelation of; God, glory of; God, greatness of; God, holiness of; God, power of; God, present everywhere; God, sovereignty; God, titles and names of; God, transcendent; Jesus Christ, majesty of; worship.

God, patience of
God shows forbearance in his character, decisions and actions. Above all, he waits patiently for people to turn to him for salvation.

God's patient character
God is slow to anger
Nu 14:18 "'The LORD is slow to anger, abounding in love and forgiving sin and rebellion . . .'"   *See also* **Ex** 34:6; **Ne** 9:16–17; **Ps** 86:15; 103:8; 145:8; **Joel** 2:13; **Jnh** 4:2; **Na** 1:3
God imparts patience
Ro 15:5 May the God who gives endurance and encouragement give you a spirit of unity among yourselves as you follow Christ Jesus,   *See also* **Jer** 15:15; **2Th** 3:5; **1Pe** 3:20

God's patience with sinful people
God's patience lasts a long time
Ac 13:18 "he [God] endured their conduct for about forty years in the desert,   *See also* **Dt** 8:2; **Ne** 9:30; **Ps** 78:38
God is patient in delaying punishment
Isa 42:14 "For a long time I have kept silent, I have been quiet and held myself back . . ."
See also **Ne** 9:30–31; **Ps** 50:20–21; 78:38; **Isa** 48:9; **Hab** 2:3
Sinful people try God's patience
Mal 2:17 You have wearied the LORD with your words . . .   *See also* **Ge** 18:16–33; **Nu** 14:27; **Ps** 78:41,56; **Isa** 1:14; 7:13; 43:24

Examples of God's patience
Ge 8:22; 18:32; **Isa** 3:10
With his people: **Eze** 20:17; **Mic** 7:19
Jnh 3:1

The purpose of God's patience
Repentance
Ro 2:4 Or do you show contempt for the riches of his kindness, tolerance and patience, not realising that God's kindness leads you towards repentance?   *See also* **2Pe** 3:9
Salvation
2Pe 3:15 . . . our Lord's patience means salvation . . .   *See also* **Ro** 9:22–24   *See also* God, compassion; God, grace and mercy; God, love of; Jesus Christ, patience of; repentance; salvation; sin.

God, perfection
God is complete, faultless and totally sufficient in every aspect of his being and ways. That perfection is made known in Jesus Christ, and is the ultimate goal of the Christian life.

God's moral perfection
Ps 25:8 Good and upright is the LORD . . .
See also **Ex** 33:19; **Ps** 18:25–26; 92:15; **Isa** 26:7; **Mk** 10:18 pp **Lk** 18:19
Humanity should emulate God's moral perfection
Mt 5:48 "Be perfect, therefore, as your heavenly Father is perfect."   *See also* **Lev** 19:2; 11:44–45; **1Pe** 1:16; **2Co** 7:1; 13:11

God, power of

God's work is perfect
Dt 32:4 . . . his works are perfect, and all his ways are just. A faithful God who does no wrong, upright and just is he. *See also* **2Sa** 22:31 pp **Ps** 18:30; **Ps** 19:1; 40:5; 96:3; 139:14; 145:4–6; **Jer** 32:19–20

God's will is perfect
Ro 12:2 . . . his [God's] good, pleasing and perfect will. *See also* **Ps** 19:7–11

God's words are perfect
Ps 12:6 And the words of the LORD are flawless, like silver refined in a furnace of clay, purified seven times. *See also* **Ps** 18:30; **Pr** 30:5

Humanity cannot always grasp the perfection of God's ways
Job 42:3 "You [the Lord God] asked, 'Who is this that obscures my counsel without knowledge?' Surely I [Job] spoke of things I did not understand, things too wonderful for me to know." *See also* **Ecc** 3:11; **Eze** 18:25,29; 33:17–20

Examples of the perfection of God's attributes
Perfect knowledge Job 37:16; **Ps** 139:1–6; 147:5
Perfect faithfulness Isa 25:1
Perfect love 1Jn 3:1; 4:8–12,16–19

God's perfection is seen in Jesus Christ
Heb 7:26 Such a high priest meets our need—one who is holy, blameless, pure, set apart from sinners, exalted above the heavens. *See also* **Col** 1:19; 2:9; **Heb** 2:10; 5:8–9; 7:28
See also God, all-knowing; God, goodness of; God, holiness of; God, love of; God, power of; God, purpose of; God, unchangeable; God, unique; God, will of; Jesus Christ, perfection.

God, power of
God is all-powerful (that is omnipotent), and is able to do whatever he wills. His power is limited only by his character.

God is all-powerful
Mk 10:27 Jesus looked at them [the disciples] and said, "Humanly this is impossible, but not with God; all things are possible with God." pp **Mt** 19:26 *See also* **Ge** 18:14; **Ps** 93:1; **Mk** 14:36; **Lk** 1:37; **2Co** 4:7

God cannot be thwarted
Job 42:2 "I [Job] know that you [the LORD] can do all things; no plan of yours can be thwarted." *See also* **Job** 9:12; **Isa** 14:27

God's names denote his power
The uniqueness of God's power
Jer 10:6 No-one is like you, O LORD; you are great, and your name is mighty in power.
He is the Almighty
"the Almighty" is Hebrew "El Shaddai": **Ge** 28:3; 35:11; 43:14; **Ex** 6:3; **Job** 11:7; 31:2
He is the LORD Almighty and God Almighty
"Almighty" in these verses is usually Hebrew "Sabaoth": **Ps** 24:10; 89:8; **Jer** 10:16; **2Co** 6:18; **Rev** 11:17; 19:6
He is the Mighty One Ge 49:24; **Jos** 22:22; **Ps** 50:1; **Isa** 1:24; 10:21; 60:16; **Mk** 14:62; **Lk** 1:49

God's power is seen above all in his acts of redemption
God is powerful to save
Zep 3:17 The LORD your God is with you, he is mighty to save . . .
God shows his power in the exodus
Dt 9:29 ". . . they [Israel] are your [the Sovereign LORD's] people, your inheritance that you brought out by your great power and your outstretched arm." *See also* **Ex** 13:9; 14:31; **Dt** 7:8; 9:26; **Ne** 1:10; **Jer** 32:21
God shows his power through the work of Jesus Christ
Ac 2:24 But God raised him [Jesus] from the dead, freeing him from the agony of death, because it was impossible for death to keep its hold on him. *See also* **Ro** 1:4; **Eph** 1:19–21; **Col** 2:13–15; **Rev** 12:10
God shows his power through the proclamation of the good news about Jesus Christ
Ro 1:16 I [Paul] am not ashamed of the

gospel, because it is the power of God for the salvation of everyone who believes: first for the Jew, then for the Gentile. See also **1Co** 1:18,24–25; **2Co** 10:4; **Col** 2:12

God's power is shown in Jesus Christ's life
God's power in Jesus Christ's earthly ministry
Lk 5:17 . . . And the power of the Lord was present for him to heal the sick. See also **Lk** 6:19; 8:46; **Ac** 10:38; **2Pe** 1:16
God's power in Jesus Christ's heavenly ministry
Heb 7:16 one [our Lord] who has become a priest not on the basis of a regulation as to his ancestry but on the basis of the power of an indestructible life. See also **Ac** 4:10; **2Co** 13:4
God's power seen in Jesus Christ's second coming
Mk 13:26 "At that time people will see the Son of Man coming in clouds with great power and glory." pp Mt 24:30 pp Lk 21:27 See also **2Th** 1:9–10

The Holy Spirit demonstrates God's power
Mic 3:8 But as for me [Micah], I am filled with power, with the Spirit of the LORD, and with justice and might . . . See also **Ac** 1:8; 10:38; **Ro** 15:19; **1Co** 2:4–5; **1Th** 1:5

God's power in the world
God rules the created order
Ro 1:20 For since the creation of the world God's invisible qualities—his eternal power and divine nature—have been clearly seen, being understood from what has been made, so that they are without excuse. See also **Ps** 19:1; 65:6; 68:34; **Isa** 40:26; **Mt** 8:26 pp Mk 4:39; **Mt** 21:19; **Heb** 1:3
God's works are powerful
Dt 3:24 "O Sovereign LORD, you have begun to show to your servant your greatness and your strong hand. For what god is there in heaven or on earth who can do the deeds and mighty works you do?" See also **Ps** 71:18; 77:12; 145:4; **Jer** 32:17–19; **Lk** 1:51

The ark symbolises God's powerful presence
Ps 132:8 "arise, O LORD, and come to your resting place, you and the ark of your might." pp 2Ch 6:41 See also **1Sa** 5:1–12; **2Sa** 6:6–8, 11–12; **Ps** 78:61
God keeps his promises
Ro 4:21 [Abraham] being fully persuaded that God had power to do what he had promised. See also **2Co** 9:8
God gives life to the dead
1Co 6:14 By his power God raised the Lord from the dead, and he will raise us also. See also **Mt** 22:29 pp Mk 12:24; **Php** 3:21

God's power in the lives of believers
God gives his own power to his people
1Ch 29:11–12 "Yours, O LORD, is the greatness and the power . . . In your hands are strength and power to exalt and give strength to all." See also **1Sa** 2:10; **Da** 2:27–28; **2Co** 13:3–4; **Php** 4:13; **2Ti** 1:7; **1Pe** 4:11
God's power achieves his purposes in his people's lives
2Th 1:11 With this in mind, we constantly pray for you, that our God may count you worthy of his calling, and that by his power he may fulfil every good purpose of yours and every act prompted by your faith. See also **Mic** 5:4; **Ac** 4:28; **1Co** 5:4; **Eph** 1:20–21
God's power completes his work of salvation in believers' lives
1Pe 1:5 [believers] who through faith are shielded by God's power until the coming of the salvation that is ready to be revealed in the last time. See also **2Ti** 1:12; **Heb** 7:25; **Jude** 24
God's power gives believers inner strength
Eph 3:16–17 I [Paul] pray that out of his glorious riches he may strengthen you with power through his Spirit in your inner being, so that Christ may dwell in your hearts through faith . . . See also **Eph** 1:18–19; 6:10; **Php** 3:10; **Col** 1:11
God's power is made plain through human weakness
2Co 12:9–10 But he [the Lord] said to me [Paul], "My grace is sufficient for you, for my power is made perfect in weakness." Therefore I

God, present everywhere

will boast all the more gladly about my weaknesses, so that Christ's power may rest on me. That is why, for Christ's sake, I delight in weaknesses, in insults, in hardships, in persecutions, in difficulties. For when I am weak, then I am strong. *See also* **Isa** 53:1–3; **2Co** 4:7; 13:4

God's power gives help to believers in suffering
2Ti 4:16–17 . . . But the Lord stood at my [Paul's] side and gave me strength . . . *See also* **2Ch** 25:8; **Ps** 46:1; **Da** 3:17; **2Co** 6:7; **2Ti** 1:8

God's power is limited only by his character
God cannot deny himself
2Ti 2:13 . . . if we [believers] are faithless, he [God] will remain faithful, for he cannot disown himself. *See also* **Jas** 1:17
God cannot tolerate evil
Hab 1:13 Your eyes [O Lord] are too pure to look on evil; you cannot tolerate wrong . . .
God cannot be tempted
Jas 1:13 When tempted, no-one should say, "God is tempting me." For God cannot be tempted by evil, nor does he tempt anyone;
God cannot lie
Nu 23:19 "God is not human, that he should lie, nor a human being, that he should change his mind. Does he speak and then not act? Does he promise and not fulfil?" *See also* **1Sa** 15:29; **Heb** 6:18

God's power is to be praised
Ps 68:35 You are awesome, O God, in your sanctuary; the God of Israel gives power and strength to his people. Praise be to God! *See also* **Ps** 21:13; 118:14; **1Ti** 6:16; **Jude** 25; **Rev** 5:12 *See also God as Saviour; God, purpose of; God, the Creator; God, the Lord; God, titles and names of; Holy Spirit, power; Jesus Christ, power of; Jesus Christ, resurrection; miracles.*

God, present everywhere
God is omnipresent in that he transcends all limitations of space and is present in the fulness of his being in every place but in varying ways.

God transcends all spatial limitations
1Ki 8:27 "But will God really dwell on earth? The heavens, even the highest heaven, cannot contain you. How much less this temple I [Solomon] have built!" pp 2Ch 6:18
See also **2Ch** 2:6; **Ps** 113:4–6

God is present throughout heaven and earth
Ps 139:7–12 Where can I go from your Spirit? Where can I flee from your presence? If I go up to the heavens, you are there; if I make my bed in the depths, you are there. If I rise on the wings of the dawn, if I settle on the far side of the sea, even there your hand will guide me, your right hand will hold me fast. If I say, "Surely the darkness will hide me and the light become night around me," even the darkness will not be dark to you; the night will shine like the day, for darkness is as light to you.
Jer 23:23–24 "Am I only a God nearby," declares the Lord, "and not a God far away? Who can hide in secret places so that I cannot see him?" declares the Lord. "Do not I fill heaven and earth?" declares the Lord. *See also* **Nu** 14:21; **Dt** 4:39; **Isa** 6:3; 66:1; **Am** 9:2–3

God sees and knows everything
Pr 15:3 The eyes of the Lord are everywhere, keeping watch on the wicked and the good.
See also **2Ch** 16:9; **Zec** 4:10

God is near to all human beings
Ac 17:27–28 ". . . he is not far from each one of us. 'For in him we live and move and have our being.' As some of your own poets have said, 'We are his offspring.'"

God is present with special groups of people
God is especially close to the poor and needy
Ps 34:18 The Lord is close to the broken-hearted and saves those who are crushed in spirit. *See also* **Isa** 57:15
God is especially close to those who call on him
Ps 145:18 The Lord is near to all who call on

him, to all who call on him in truth. *See also* **Ps** 16:8; **Isa** 50:8

God's presence with his people
God is always present with his people
Ex 33:15–16 Then Moses said to him, "If your Presence does not go with us, do not send us up from here. How will anyone know that you are pleased with me and with your people unless you go with us? What else will distinguish me and your people from all the other people on the face of the earth?" *See also* **Ps** 14:5; **Isa** 43:2; **Zep** 3:17; **1Co** 14:25
God's promise to be present
Jos 1:9 ". . . Be strong and courageous. Do not be terrified; do not be discouraged, for the LORD your God will be with you wherever you go." *See also* **Ge** 28:15; 31:3; **Ex** 29:45; **Lev** 26:12; **Dt** 20:1; 31:8; **Mt** 28:20
God is present in believers through the Holy Spirit
1Co 3:16 Don't you [Christians in Corinth] know that you yourselves are God's temple and that God's Spirit lives in you? *See also* **Jn** 14:18; **Eph** 2:22; **1Jn** 3:24

God will be acknowledged everywhere
Ps 113:3 From the rising of the sun to the place where it sets, the name of the LORD is to be praised. *See also* **Ps** 72:19; 96:7–9,11–13; **Mal** 1:11; **Rev** 5:13 *See also God, activity of; God, all-knowing; God, transcendent; Holy Spirit, indwelling; Holy Spirit, presence of; knowing God.*

God, purpose of
God has a plan for his creation which he will certainly accomplish. It is carried out through the control of circumstances and his choice and use of people, and above all in the life, death, resurrection and second coming of Jesus Christ.

God's purpose will be accomplished
Isa 46:10–11 ". . . My [the LORD's] purpose will stand, and I will do all that I please . . . What I have said, that will I bring about; what I have planned, that will I do." *See also* **Ps** 135:6; **Pr** 16:4; **Ecc** 3:14; **Isa** 14:24,26–27; 25:1; 55:11; **Eph** 1:11

God's purpose prevails
It stands for ever
Ps 33:11 But the plans of the LORD stand firm for ever, the purposes of his heart through all generations. *See also* **Job** 42:2; **Jer** 23:20
It cannot be thwarted by human beings
Pr 19:21 Many are the plans in a human heart, but it is the LORD's purpose that prevails. *See also* **Job** 9:12; 23:13; **Isa** 8:10; **Da** 4:35
It cannot be thwarted by evil powers
Rev 17:17 "For God has put it into their [the beast and the ten horns'] hearts to accomplish his purpose by agreeing to give the beast their power to rule, until God's words are fulfilled." *See also* **1Sa** 16:14; **Job** 1:12; 2:6; **2Co** 12:7
It prevails in people's lives and circumstances
Pr 16:9 In your heart you may plan your course, but the LORD determines your steps. *See also* **Pr** 20:24; 21:1
It is fulfilled through his choice of individuals
Eph 1:11 In him [Christ] we were also chosen, having been predestined according to the plan of him who works out everything in conformity with the purpose of his will, *See also* **Ge** 18:19; **Ro** 11:5; **1Co** 1:1; **Eph** 1:4–5; **2Th** 2:13
Examples of the actions of evil people serving God's purpose
Ac 2:23 "This man [Jesus of Nazareth] was handed over to you by God's set purpose and foreknowledge; and you, with the help of wicked people, put him to death by nailing him to the cross." *See also* **Ge** 50:20; **Isa** 10:5–7

God's purpose is founded on divine wisdom
Eph 3:10–11 His intent was that now, through the church, the manifold wisdom of God should be made known to the rulers and authorities in the heavenly realms, according to his eternal purpose which he accomplished in Christ Jesus our Lord. *See also* **Ps** 104:24; **Ro** 11:33

God's purpose is determined from eternity
2Ti 1:9 . . . [God] has saved us and called us

God, purpose of

to a holy life—not because of anything we have done but because of his own purpose and grace. This grace was given us in Christ Jesus before the beginning of time,   See also **2Ki** 19:25; **Isa** 25:1; 46:10; **Mt** 25:34; **Eph** 1:4; **Tit** 1:2; **1Pe** 1:20

God's purpose is for his own glory
Ex 9:16 "'... I [God] have raised you [Pharaoh] up for this very purpose, that I might show you my power and that my name might be proclaimed in all the earth.'"   See also **Ro** 9:17; **Eze** 36:22–23; **Eph** 1:5–6,11–12

God's purpose for his people
God reveals his purpose to his people
Am 3:7 Surely the Sovereign LORD does nothing without revealing his plan to his servants the prophets.   See also **Ge** 18:17; **2Sa** 7:20–21; **1Co** 2:9–10; **Eph** 1:9

Its fulness is beyond human understanding
Ro 11:33 Oh, the depth of the riches of the wisdom and knowledge of God! How unsearchable his judgments, and his paths beyond tracing out!   See also **Dt** 29:29; **1Co** 2:9–10; **Eph** 1:9; 3:4–5

It is good and loving
Ro 8:28 ... we know that in all things God works for the good of those who love him, who have been called according to his purpose. See also **Jer** 29:11; **Ro** 12:2; **Eph** 1:4–5; **2Ti** 1:9

God's purpose is revealed through Jesus Christ
In the church
Eph 3:10–11 His intent was that now, through the church, the manifold wisdom of God should be made known to the rulers and authorities in the heavenly realms, according to his eternal purpose which he accomplished in Christ Jesus our Lord.

It centres on the cross
Isa 53:10 Yet it was the LORD'S will to crush him and cause him to suffer, and though the LORD makes his life a guilt offering, he will see his offspring and prolong his days, and the will of the LORD will prosper in his hand.   See also **Ac** 4:27–28; **1Pe** 1:19–20; **1Jn** 4:10

It is God's purpose to redeem the world through the cross
Mt 26:18, 45 pp **Mk** 14:41; **Jn** 7:6–8; 12:23; 13:1; 17:1

It is God's purpose to exalt and establish Jesus Christ as Lord
Eph 1:9–10 And he [God] made known to us the mystery of his will according to his good pleasure, which he purposed in Christ, to be put into effect when the times will have reached their fulfilment— to bring all things in heaven and on earth together under one head, even Christ.   See also **Ac** 2:36; **Php** 2:8–11; **Col** 1:18; **Heb** 1:2–4

Jesus Christ submits to God's purpose
Jn 6:38 "For I [Jesus] have come down from heaven not to do my will but to do the will of him who sent me."   See also **Mt** 26:39–42 pp **Mk** 14:35–36 pp **Lk** 22:42; **Jn** 4:34; 5:30; **Heb** 5:7–8; 10:7

God's ultimate purpose is to save
The salvation of people through Jesus Christ
Jn 6:40 "For my [Jesus'] Father's will is that all those who look to the Son and believe in him shall have eternal life ..."   See also **Jn** 3:16–17; **Gal** 1:3–4; **1Ti** 2:3–4; **1Pe** 1:2; **2Pe** 3:9

Specific aspects of God's purpose in salvation
Ro 8:29; **2Co** 5:5; **Eph** 1:4; 2:15; 3:10–11

God wills that people submit to his purposes
Jas 4:15 ... you ought to say, "If it is the Lord's will, we will live and do this or that." See also **Ps** 40:8; 143:10; **Mt** 6:10

God's people should pray for the fulfilment of his purposes
Mt 6:9–10 "This, then, is how you should pray: "'Our Father in heaven, hallowed be your name, your kingdom come, your will be done on earth as it is in heaven.'"   pp **Lk** 11:2

People can reject God's purposes in their lives
Lk 7:30; 19:41–42; **Ac** 13:46

Examples of God's purposes being worked out
Ge 45:5–9

Through Cyrus: **Isa** 41:2,25; 45:1,13; 46:11; 48:14
In the life of Paul: **Ac** 18:21; 21:14; **Ro** 1:10; 15:32; **1Co** 4:19   See also God, all-knowing; God, glory of; God, power of; God, sovereignty; God, will of; God, wisdom of; Jesus Christ, mission; Jesus Christ, obedience; law, purpose of; revelation.

God, repentance of
A change in God's plan or intention, often in response to human repentance, but without implying any fault or moral imperfection on God's part.

God's repentance may show his pain and sorrow
Ge 6:6–7 The LORD was grieved that he had made human beings on the earth, and his heart was filled with pain . . .   See also **1Sa** 15:11,35

God's repentance may show his compassion
Jnh 4:2 He [Jonah] prayed to the LORD, "O LORD . . . I knew that you are a gracious and compassionate God, slow to anger and abounding in love, a God who relents from sending calamity."   See also **Dt** 32:36; **2Sa** 24:15–16 pp **1Ch** 21:14–15; **Ps** 106:45; **Isa** 38:1–5; **Hos** 11:8; **Am** 7:1–6

God may repent in response to human repentance
Jer 18:8 "and if that nation I warned repents of its evil, then I will relent and not inflict on it the disaster I had planned."   See also **Ex** 32:14; **2Ch** 12:1–8; **Jer** 26:13,19; **Joel** 2:13; **Jnh** 3:6–10

God never repents of his oath or changes his character
Nu 23:19; **Ps** 110:4; **Heb** 6:17–18   See also forgiveness, divine; God, compassion; God, suffering of; God, unchangeable; repentance; repentance, nature of.

God, revelation
God graciously makes himself known to humanity since people cannot discover him on their own. He achieves this in many ways, but supremely through his Son Jesus Christ.

The necessity of revelation
God is hidden from human view because of sin
Isa 59:2 But your iniquities have separated you from your God; your sins have hidden his face from you, so that he will not hear.   See also **Dt** 31:18; **Isa** 1:15; 45:15; 64:7; **Eze** 39:23; **Mic** 3:4

People are ignorant of God
Ac 17:23 "For as I [Paul] walked around and looked carefully at your objects of worship, I even found an altar with this inscription: TO AN UNKNOWN GOD. Now what you worship as something unknown I am going to proclaim to you [men of Athens]."   See also **Ex** 5:2; **Jdg** 2:10; **Jer** 4:22; **Jn** 4:22; 15:21; **Gal** 4:8; **Eph** 4:18; **1Th** 4:5

People cannot know God unaided
Mt 11:25–27 ". . . All things have been committed to me [Jesus] by my Father. No-one knows the Son except the Father, and no-one knows the Father except the Son and those to whom the Son chooses to reveal him." pp **Lk** 10:21–22   See also **Job** 34:29; **1Co** 1:21

The means by which God reveals himself
In the Scriptures
Ps 119:105 Your word is a lamp to my feet and a light for my path.   See also **Ps** 19:7–10; 119:130; 147:19; **Pr** 6:23; **2Ti** 3:16; **2Pe** 1:19–21

By the Holy Spirit
Eph 1:17 I [Paul] keep asking that the God of our Lord Jesus Christ, the glorious Father, may give you the Spirit of wisdom and revelation, so that you may know him better.   See also **Ne** 9:20; **Lk** 2:26; 12:12; **Jn** 14:26; **1Co** 2:10,12; **1Jn** 2:27

Supremely in Jesus Christ
Heb 1:1–2 . . . but in these last days he has spoken to us by his Son, whom he appointed heir of all things, and through whom he made the universe.   See also **Jn** 1:18; 8:26; 12:49; 14:10; 17:6

In the creation
Ps 19:1 The heavens declare the glory of God; the skies proclaim the work of his hands.   See also **Ps** 97:6; **Ac** 14:17; 17:26–27

God, revelation

Through the prophets
Am 3:7 Surely the Sovereign LORD does nothing without revealing his plan to his servants the prophets.   *See also* **Nu** 12:6; **2Sa** 7:17 pp **1Ch** 17:15; **2Sa** 7:27 pp **1Ch** 17:25; **Isa** 22:14; **1Pe** 1:12

In visions and dreams
Da 1:17 . . . And Daniel could understand visions and dreams of all kinds.   *See also* **Ge** 15:1; **Isa** 1:1; **Eze** 11:24; **Da** 8:1; **Na** 1:1; **Mt** 1:20; 2:12,22; **Ac** 9:10; 16:9; 22:17–18

Face to face
Nu 12:8 "With him [Moses] I [the LORD] speak face to face, clearly and not in riddles; he sees the form of the LORD. Why then were you not afraid to speak against my servant Moses?"   *See also* **Ge** 32:30; **Ex** 24:9–10; **Jdg** 13:22; **Job** 42:5; **Isa** 6:5

In the exodus
Ex 7:5 "And the Egyptians will know that I am the LORD when I stretch out my hand against Egypt and bring the Israelites out of it."   *See also* **Ex** 14:4; **1Sa** 2:27; **Eze** 20:5,9

In special signs Jdg 6:36–40; **1Ki** 13:3–5; **2Ki** 20:9–11 pp **Isa** 38:7–8

The nature of God's self-revelation in Jesus Christ

God reveals Jesus Christ's true identity
Mt 16:17 Jesus replied, "Blessed are you, Simon son of Jonah, for this was not revealed to you by flesh and blood, but by my Father in heaven."   *See also* **Mt** 3:17 pp **Mk** 1:11 pp **Lk** 3:22; **Mt** 17:5 pp **Mk** 9:7 pp **Lk** 9:35; **Jn** 1:31; **Gal** 1:15–16; **2Pe** 1:17–18

Jesus Christ is the visible image of God
Col 1:15 He [Christ] is the image of the invisible God, the firstborn over all creation.   *See also* **2Co** 4:4; **Php** 2:6; **Heb** 1:3

Jesus Christ's glory is still to be fully revealed **Lk** 17:30; **1Co** 1:7; **2Th** 1:7; **1Pe** 1:7,13; 4:13

Things that God reveals

Hidden mysteries
Da 2:22 "He [God] reveals deep and hidden things; he knows what lies in darkness, and light dwells with him."   *See also* **Ge** 41:16; **Job** 12:22; **Da** 2:28–30,47

Future events
Ge 41:25 Then Joseph said to Pharaoh, "The dreams of Pharaoh are one and the same. God has revealed to Pharaoh what he is about to do."   *See also* **1Sa** 9:15–16; **2Ki** 8:10; **Jer** 11:18; 38:21; **Mt** 2:13; **Ac** 18:9–10; 27:22–24

His righteousness
Ro 1:17 For in the gospel a righteousness from God is revealed, a righteousness that is by faith from first to last, just as it is written: "The righteous will live by faith."   *See also* **Isa** 56:1; **Ro** 3:21; **Rev** 15:4

His wrath
Ro 1:18 The wrath of God is being revealed from heaven against all the godlessness and wickedness of those who suppress the truth by their wickedness,   *See also* **Nu** 11:1; **2Sa** 6:7 pp **1Ch** 13:10; **Ps** 7:11; **Ro** 2:5

His salvation
Ps 98:2 The LORD has made his salvation known and revealed his righteousness to the nations.   *See also* **Isa** 52:10; **Lk** 2:30–32; 3:6; **Tit** 2:11

His glory
Isa 40:5 "And the glory of the LORD will be revealed, and all people will see it together . . ."

The pillar of cloud and fire in the wilderness: **Ex** 16:10; 33:9; **Nu** 12:5; **Dt** 1:33; **Ne** 9:12; **Ps** 78:14; 105:39

Ex 33:18–23

The cloud of glory in the tabernacle and the temple: **Ex** 40:34; **Lev** 16:2; **Dt** 31:15; **Eze** 9:3; 10:4

Dt 5:24; **Ps** 97:6; 102:16; **Isa** 35:2; 44:23; 60:2; **Ac** 7:55

The mystery of the gospel
Eph 3:2–3 Surely you have heard about the administration of God's grace that was given to me for you, that is, the mystery made known to me by revelation . . .   *See also* **Mt** 13:11 pp **Mk** 4:11 pp **Lk** 8:10; **Ro** 16:25–26; **Gal** 3:23; **Eph** 3:5–6; **Col** 1:26–27; **2Ti** 1:10

The revelation of God's will
Physical means by which God reveals his will By the Urim and Thummim: **Ex** 28:30; **Nu** 27:21

By casting lots: **Jos** 18:6–10; **Jnh** 1:7; **Ac** 1:26

God's self-revelation makes his will plain
Ro 1:20 For since the creation of the world God's invisible qualities—his eternal power and divine nature—have been clearly seen, being understood from what has been made, so that they are without excuse. *See also* **Zec** 7:11–12; **Jn** 9:41; 16:8; **Ro** 7:7

God's self-revelation is according to his own sovereign purpose
Isa 65:1 "I revealed myself to those who did not ask for me; I was found by those who did not seek me. To a nation that did not call on my name, I said, 'Here am I, here am I.'" *See also* **Da** 2:30; **Ro** 10:20; **Gal** 1:11–12 *See also* God, glory of; God, will of; incarnation; Jesus Christ, Son of God; knowing God, nature of; revelation; Scripture; signs, purposes; word of God.

God, righteousness

An aspect of God's nature which expresses his unique moral perfection and his readiness to save sinners. It is made known especially through the gospel of Jesus Christ.

God's nature is righteous
Ps 119:137 Righteous are you, O LORD, and your laws are right. *See also* **Dt** 32:4; **Ps** 48:10; 97:2; 119:142; 145:17; **Isa** 45:21; **Jer** 12:1; **Jn** 17:25

God's righteousness shows his sovereignty
Ps 71:19 Your righteousness reaches to the skies, O God, you who have done great things. Who, O God, is like you? *See also* **Job** 37:23; **Ps** 36:6; 97:6; **Isa** 5:16

God's righteousness is eternal
Ps 111:3 Glorious and majestic are his [the LORD's] deeds, and his righteousness endures for ever. *See also* **Ps** 112:3,9; 119:142,160; **Isa** 51:8

God's actions are righteous
Da 9:14 ". . . the LORD our God is righteous in everything he does . . ." *See also* **Jdg** 5:11; **1Sa** 12:7; **Jer** 9:24; **Rev** 15:3

God's rule is righteous
Ps 9:8 He [the LORD] will judge the world in righteousness; he will govern the peoples with justice. *See also* **2Sa** 23:3–4; **Ps** 96:13; 99:4; **Jer** 9:23–24

God's righteous acts are saving acts
Ps 65:5 You answer us with awesome deeds of righteousness, O God our Saviour, the hope of all the ends of the earth and of the farthest seas, *See also* **Ps** 40:10; 116:4–6; 129:4; **Isa** 41:10; 46:13; **Da** 9:16; **Mic** 6:5

God's righteousness vindicates his people
Ps 35:24 Vindicate me in your righteousness, O LORD my God; do not let them gloat over me. *See also* **Ps** 4:2–3; 7:9; 9:4; 103:6; **Isa** 50:8; **Mic** 7:9; **Ro** 8:33

God's righteousness shows his faithfulness
Ne 9:8 ". . . You [the LORD God] have kept your promise because you are righteous." *See also* **Ps** 4:1; **Zep** 3:5; **Zec** 8:8

God's righteousness shows his justice
Jer 11:20 But, O LORD Almighty, you who judge righteously and test the heart and mind . . . *See also* **Ge** 18:25; **Job** 8:3; **Ps** 11:7; 50:6; 51:4; **Pr** 21:12; **Ecc** 3:17; **2Ti** 4:8

God's righteousness is seen in his judgments
Ps 7:11 God is a righteous judge, a God who expresses his wrath every day. *See also* **2Ch** 12:5–6; **Ezr** 9:15; **Isa** 10:22; 28:17; **La** 1:18; **Mal** 3:5; **Ro** 2:2,5

God's laws show his righteousness
Ps 19:8–9 . . . The ordinances of the LORD are sure and altogether righteous. *See also* **Dt** 4:8; **Ps** 33:4; 119:7,144; **Ro** 1:32; 7:12; 8:4

God's righteousness contrasts with human unrighteousness
Ro 3:5 But if our unrighteousness brings out God's righteousness more clearly, what shall we say? . . . *See also* **Ex** 9:27; **Ne** 9:33; **Job** 4:17; 9:2; **Da** 9:7; **Ro** 10:3

God's righteousness is revealed primarily in Jesus Christ
Ro 3:21–22 . . . This righteousness from God comes through faith in Jesus Christ to all who

God, sovereignty

believe... *See also* **Isa** 11:2–5; **Jer** 23:6; **Zec** 9:9; **Ac** 3:14; **Ro** 10:4; **1Co** 1:30; **2Pe** 1:1; **1Jn** 2:1

God's righteousness is revealed in the gospel
Ro 1:17 For in the gospel a righteousness from God is revealed, a righteousness that is by faith from first to last, just as it is written: "The righteous will live by faith." *See also* **Php** 3:9

God gives his righteousness to believers
Ro 4:22–24... The words "it was credited to him [Abraham]" were written not for him alone, but also for us, to whom God will credit righteousness—for us who believe in him who raised Jesus our Lord from the dead. *See also* **Ge** 15:6; **Job** 33:26; **Hos** 10:12; **Ro** 3:22; 4:3–8; 5:17; 10:4; **2Co** 5:21

The Holy Spirit reveals God's righteousness
Gal 5:5 But by faith we eagerly await through the Spirit the righteousness for which we hope. *See also* **Jn** 16:8,10; **Ro** 14:17

God's righteousness is to be sought after
Mt 6:33 "But seek first his kingdom and his righteousness, and all these things will be given to you as well." *See also* **Isa** 51:1; **Zep** 2:3

God's righteousness is a pattern for human living
1Jn 3:7 Dear children, do not let anyone lead you astray. He who does what is right is righteous, just as he [God] is righteous. *See also* **Ge** 18:19; **Hos** 14:9; **Eph** 4:24; **1Jn** 2:29; 3:12

God's righteousness is worthy of praise
Isa 24:15–16... From the ends of the earth we hear singing: "Glory to the Righteous One."... *See also* **Ps** 7:17; 22:31; 35:28; 51:14; 71:15,24; 145:7   *See also God as Saviour; God, holiness of; God, justice of; Jesus Christ, righteousness; law; sin and God's character.*

God, sovereignty
The fact that God is free and able to do all that he wills; that he reigns over all creation and that his will is the final cause of all things. This is often expressed in the language of kingship.

God is free to do all he wills
Ps 135:6 The LORD does whatever pleases him, in the heavens and on the earth, in the seas and all their depths. *See also* **Ps** 115:3; **Isa** 46:10; **Da** 4:35; **Ro** 9:19–21

God is able to do whatever he wills
Lk 1:37 "For nothing is impossible with God." *See also* **Job** 42:2; **Mt** 19:26; **Eph** 3:20

God cannot be successfully opposed
Job 42:2 "I know that you can do all things; no plan of yours can be thwarted." *See also* **1Sa** 2:10; **2Ch** 20:6; **Job** 9:12; **Ecc** 7:13; **Isa** 43:13; 45:9–10; **Ac** 5:39

God rules and reigns
He is King
Ps 29:10 The LORD sits enthroned over the flood; the LORD is enthroned as King for ever. *See also* **1Ch** 16:31; **Ps** 47:2; **Isa** 6:5; 43:15; **Jer** 10:7,10; **Zec** 14:9; **1Ti** 1:17; 6:15; **Rev** 15:3; 19:6

He is Lord of heaven and earth
Dt 4:39... the LORD is God in heaven above and on the earth below... *See also* **Ge** 24:3; **Dt** 10:14; **Jos** 2:11; **1Ch** 29:11; **Ne** 9:6; **Ps** 121:2; 134:3; **Lk** 10:21; **Ac** 17:24

His throne is a symbol of his sovereignty **Ex** 17:16; **Ps** 45:6; 93:2; 123:1–2; **Isa** 6:1; 66:1; **Jer** 49:38; **La** 5:19; **Eze** 1:26; **Da** 7:9; **Mt** 5:34; 19:28; **Ac** 7:49; **Heb** 1:8; 8:1; 12:2; **Rev** 4:2; 20:11

God's sovereignty extends over all things
He is sovereign over creation
Rev 4:11 "You are worthy, our Lord and God, to receive glory and honour and power, for you created all things, and by your will they were created and have their being." *See also* **Ps** 93:1; **Isa** 40:22; 41:18–19

He is sovereign over human life
1Ch 29:12 "Wealth and honour come from you; you are the ruler of all things. In your hands are strength and power to exalt and give strength

to all."   See also **2Ch** 25:8; **Lk** 1:51–53; **Ac** 18:21; **Jas** 4:15

He is sovereign over the minutest details of life Mt 10:29–30 pp **Lk** 12:6–7

He is sovereign in electing his people
Eph 1:11 In him [Christ] we were also chosen, having been predestined according to the plan of him who works out everything in conformity with the purpose of his will,   See also **Ro** 8:29; 9:11,18

He is sovereign in the life and salvation of his people
1Co 1:30 It is because of him [God] that you are in Christ Jesus . . .   See also **Jer** 18:6; **1Co** 12:11; **Php** 2:13; **Jas** 1:18

He is sovereign over the sufferings of believers Php 1:29; **1Pe** 3:17

He is sovereign over world history
Pr 21:1 The king's heart is in the hand of the LORD; he directs it like a watercourse wherever he pleases.   See also **Ex** 9:16; **Ps** 22:28; **Jer** 18:7–10; **Da** 4:35

God is sovereign over all other gods and over demonic forces

God is supreme over all gods
Ps 95:3 For the LORD is the great God, the great King above all gods.   See also **Ex** 18:11; **Dt** 10:17; **1Ch** 16:26; **Ps** 96:5; **Da** 2:47; **Col** 1:16

Satan is defeated through God's sovereign purposes at work in Jesus Christ
Col 2:15 . . . having disarmed the powers and authorities, he [Christ] made a public spectacle of them, triumphing over them by the cross.
See also **Jn** 12:31; **Ro** 16:20; **2Th** 2:8; **Heb** 2:14; **2Pe** 2:4; **1Jn** 3:8; **Jude** 6; **Rev** 12:7–10   See also God as judge; God, power of; God, purpose of; God, will of; Holy Spirit, sovereignty; human race and God; Jesus Christ, victory; kingdom of God, coming.

God, suffering of
God suffers on account of the failures and pain of his people, and especially through his Son, Jesus Christ. Scripture often likens God to a parent who suffers pain and grief on account of children.

God feels real suffering

He suffers pain because people sin
Ge 6:6 The LORD was grieved that he had made human beings on the earth, and his heart was filled with pain.   See also **1Sa** 15:10–11,35

He is angered because people sin
Ps 78:58 They [Israel] angered him [God] with their high places; they aroused his jealousy with their idols.   See also **Dt** 32:15–16; **Jdg** 2:12–13; **1Ki** 21:22; **Eze** 8:17; **Hos** 12:14

God identifies with suffering

He suffers with his chosen people
Isa 63:9 In all their [Israel's] distress he [the LORD] too was distressed, and the angel of his presence saved them. In his love and mercy he redeemed them; he lifted them up and carried them all the days of old.   See also **Ex** 3:7; **Jdg** 10:16; **2Ch** 36:15

He suffers with all humanity
Isa 16:11 My [the LORD's] heart laments for Moab like a harp, my inmost being for Kir Hareseth. pp **Jer** 48:31   See also **2Sa** 24:15–17 pp **1Ch** 21:14–17; **Isa** 16:9; **Jer** 48:32–36; **Hos** 11:8–9

He suffers as a parent
Jer 31:20 "Is not Ephraim my dear son, the child in whom I delight? Though I often speak against him, I still remember him. Therefore my heart yearns for him; I have great compassion for him," declares the LORD.   See also **Isa** 42:14; 49:15; **Hos** 11:1–4

God's plan of salvation causes him suffering

He suffered in giving his Son
Ro 8:32 He [God] who did not spare his own Son, but gave him up for us all—how will he not also, along with him, graciously give us all things?   See also **Isa** 7:13–14; **Jn** 3:16; **Ro** 3:25–26; 8:3; **Gal** 4:4; **Heb** 1:2; **1Jn** 4:14

He suffers because he endures the rejection his Son suffers
Lk 10:16 "Whoever listens to you listens to me [Jesus]; whoever rejects you rejects me; but whoever rejects me rejects him who sent me."
See also **1Pe** 2:4

God, the Creator

God's creation reflects his suffering
Ro 8:22 We know that the whole creation has been groaning as in the pains of childbirth right up to the present time. *See also* **Ro** 8:19–21

God's people share his suffering
Ro 8:17 Now if we are children, then we are heirs—heirs of God and co-heirs with Christ, if indeed we share in his sufferings in order that we may also share in his glory. *See also* **Mt** 16:24 pp Mk 8:34 pp Lk 9:23; **Mt** 20:22–23 pp Mk 10:38–39; **Php** 1:29; **1Pe** 2:21 *See also God, anger of; God, compassion; God, fatherhood; God, holiness of; God, righteousness; Jesus Christ, sonship of; Jesus Christ, suffering.*

God, the Creator

God's power is revealed in the initial creation and the continuing sustenance of the universe. Humanity represents the climax of the Creator's purposes.

God is the Creator
Ne 9:6 ". . . You made the heavens, even the highest heavens, and all their starry host, the earth and all that is on it, the seas and all that is in them. You give life to everything . . ." *See also* **Ge** 1:1; **Isa** 45:7; 66:2; **Eph** 3:9; **Rev** 4:11

God's creative activity demonstrates his uniqueness
Ps 96:5 For all the gods of the nations are idols, but the LORD made the heavens. *See also* **Isa** 37:16; **Jer** 10:11

God's creative activity implies that he is good
1Ti 4:4 For everything God created is good . . . *See also* **Ge** 1:4,31

God creates all things
He creates the physical world
Isa 45:18 . . . he who created the heavens, he is God; he who fashioned and made the earth, he founded it . . . *See also* **Ge** 1:1–25
He creates the spiritual world
Ps 148:2–5 Praise him, all his angels, praise him, all his heavenly hosts . . . Let them praise the name of the LORD, for he commanded and they were created. *See also* **Ro** 8:38–39; **Col** 1:16

The human race is the apex of God's creation
Ps 8:3–8 When I consider your heavens, the work of your fingers, the moon and the stars, which you have set in place, what are mere mortals that you are mindful of them, human beings that you care for them? You made them a little lower than the heavenly beings and crowned them with glory and honour. You made them rulers over the works of your hands; you put everything under their feet: all flocks and herds, and the beasts of the field, the birds of the air, and the fish of the sea, all that swim the paths of the seas. *See also* **Ge** 1:26–28; 5:1; 9:6; **Ps** 100:3; 139:13; **Isa** 42:5; **Ac** 17:26–28

The Creator's agents
He creates through Jesus Christ
1Co 8:6 . . . and there is but one Lord, Jesus Christ, through whom all things came and through whom we live. *See also* **Jn** 1:3; **Col** 1:16; **Heb** 1:2
He creates by the Spirit
Job 33:4 "The Spirit of God has made me; the breath of the Almighty gives me life." *See also* **Ge** 1:2; **Ps** 104:30
He creates by his word
Ps 33:6 By the word of the LORD were the heavens made, their starry host by the breath of his mouth. *See also* **Job** 38:8–11; **Ps** 33:9
He creates by wisdom
Pr 3:19 By wisdom the LORD laid the earth's foundations . . . *See also* **Pr** 8:30; **Jer** 10:12–13

He creates from nothing
Heb 11:3 By faith we understand that the universe was formed at God's command, so that what is seen was not made out of what was visible. *See also* **Job** 26:7; **Ro** 4:17

The Creator sustains the created order
Isa 44:24 ". . . I am the LORD, who has made all things, who alone stretched out the heavens, who spread out the earth by myself . . ." *See also* **Dt** 30:20; **Job** 9:8–9; **Ps** 104:2–4; **Isa** 42:5

Examples of God sustaining creation
Mt 5:45 ". . . He causes his sun to rise on the evil and the good, and sends rain on the righteous and the unrighteous."   *See also* **Job** 5:10; 38:31–33; **Mt** 6:28–30

The Creator watches over his creation
Ps 33:14 From his dwelling-place he watches all who live on earth—   *See also* **Ps** 121:2–8

The creation is a vehicle for God's self-revelation
Ro 1:20 For since the creation of the world God's invisible qualities—his eternal power and divine nature—have been clearly seen, being understood from what has been made, so that they are without excuse.   *See also* **Ps** 19:1; **Isa** 40:26; **Am** 4:13

God renews his creation through redemption
Jn 3:17 For God did not send his Son into the world to condemn the world, but to save the world through him.
2Co 5:17 Therefore, if anyone is in Christ, there is a new creation: the old has gone, the new has come!   *See also* **Jn** 1:12–13; **Ro** 4:17; 6:4; 8:19–23; **Gal** 6:15

God renews his new creation of believing people
2Co 4:16 Therefore we do not lose heart. Though outwardly we are wasting away, yet inwardly we are being renewed day by day.   *See also* **Col** 3:10

God will reveal a new universe
Rev 21:1 Then I saw a new heaven and a new earth, for the first heaven and the first earth had passed away, and there was no longer any sea.   *See also* **Rev** 21:5; **Isa** 65:17   *See also creation and God; God, the provider; Holy Spirit in creation; Jesus Christ as creator; revelation, creation.*

God, the eternal
God transcends all limitations of time and endures for ever.

God endures for ever
Ne 9:5 And the Levites . . . said: "Stand up and praise the LORD your God, who is from everlasting to everlasting. Blessed be your glorious name, and may it be exalted above all blessing and praise."   *See also* **Dt** 32:40; 33:27; **Job** 36:26; **Ps** 48:14; 102:12; **Isa** 40:28; **Hab** 1:12

God transcends all concepts of time
Rev 1:8 "I am the Alpha and the Omega," says the Lord God, "who is, and who was, and who is to come, the Almighty."   *See also* **Ps** 90:4; **Isa** 41:4; **1Co** 2:7; **Heb** 13:8; **2Pe** 3:8; **Rev** 11:17; 22:13

He existed before time
Ps 90:2 Before the mountains were born or you brought forth the earth and the world, from everlasting to everlasting you are God.   *See also* **Pr** 8:23; **Jn** 17:5,24; **Eph** 1:4; **1Pe** 1:20

He will exist after time
Heb 1:11–12 "They [the earth and the heavens] will perish, but you [O Lord] remain; they will all wear out like a garment. You will roll them up like a robe; like a garment they will be changed. But you remain the same, and your years will never end."   *See also* **Ps** 102:26–27

The eternity of God's qualities
His love
1Ch 16:34 Give thanks to the LORD, for he is good; his love endures for ever. pp Ps 106:1   *See also* **2Ch** 5:13; **Ps** 103:17; **Jer** 31:3; **Hos** 2:19
His faithfulness
Ps 100:5 For the LORD is good and his love endures for ever; his faithfulness continues through all generations.   *See also* **Ps** 117:2; 146:6
His power
Ps 66:7 He [God] rules for ever by his power . . .   *See also* **Ro** 1:20; **1Pe** 5:11
His righteousness
Ps 111:3 Glorious and majestic are his [the LORD's] deeds, and his righteousness endures for ever.   *See also* **Ps** 112:3; 119:142; **Da** 9:24

God's word is eternal
Ps 119:89 Your word, O LORD, is eternal; it stands firm in the heavens.   *See also* **Mk** 13:31; **1Pe** 1:24–25; **Isa** 40:8

God's covenant is eternal
Ge 17:7 "I will establish my covenant as an everlasting covenant between me and you [Abraham] and your descendants after you for the generations to come, to be your God and the God of your descendants after you." *See also* **Nu** 18:19; **Ps** 105:10; **Isa** 24:5; 54:10; 55:3; **Jer** 32:40

God's kingdom is eternal
Ps 145:13 Your [the LORD's] kingdom is an everlasting kingdom, and your dominion endures through all generations . . . *See also* **Ex** 15:18; **Ps** 9:7; 45:6; **La** 5:19; **Da** 4:3; 7:14,27; **2Pe** 1:11

God's gifts are eternal
Ro 11:29 . . . God's gifts and his call are irrevocable.

He gives eternal life
Jn 10:28 "I [Jesus] give them eternal life, and they shall never perish; no-one can snatch them out of my hand." *See also* **Jn** 5:24; 6:47; **Ro** 2:7; 6:23

He gives eternal salvation
Isa 45:17 But Israel will be saved by the LORD with an everlasting salvation; you will never be put to shame or disgraced, to ages everlasting. *See also* **Heb** 5:9; 9:12

He gives eternal joy
Isa 35:10 . . . the ransomed of the LORD will return. They will enter Zion with singing; everlasting joy will crown their heads. Gladness and joy will overtake them, and sorrow and sighing will flee away. *See also* **Ps** 16:11; **Isa** 51:11; 61:7

He gives eternal possessions
Ge 48:4 "' . . . I will make you [Jacob] a community of peoples, and I will give this land as an everlasting possession to your descendants after you.'" *See also* **Ge** 17:8 *See also God, faithfulness; God, living; God, love of; God, power of; God, righteousness; God, the LORD; God, transcendent; kingdom of God; word of God.*

God, the LORD
The translation of the Hebrew name "Yahweh" which is the personal name of God whose meaning was revealed to Moses. It emphasises that God is the one who is eternal, unique, unchangeable and always actively present with his people. It expresses God's role as Israel's Redeemer and covenant Lord.

The name of God, the LORD
The LORD is the personal name of God
Isa 42:8 "I am the LORD; that is my name! . . ."

The name's meaning
Ex 3:14–15 God said to Moses, "I AM WHO I AM. This is what you are to say to the Israelites: 'I AM has sent me to you.'" God also said to Moses, "Say to the Israelites, 'The LORD, the God of your fathers—the God of Abraham, the God of Isaac and the God of Jacob—has sent me to you.' This is my name for ever, the name by which I am to be remembered from generation to generation."

The name is revealed to Moses
Ex 6:2–3 God also said to Moses, "I am the LORD. I appeared to Abraham, to Isaac and to Jacob as God Almighty, but by my name the LORD I did not make myself known to them."

The name is glorious and awesome
Dt 28:58–59 . . . this glorious and awesome name—the LORD your God . . . *See also* **Jos** 7:9; **1Sa** 12:22

The name is not to be misused
Ex 20:7 "You shall not misuse the name of the LORD your God, for the LORD will not hold anyone guiltless who misuses his name." pp **Dt** 5:11 *See also* **Lev** 19:12; 24:11,15–16

God's character is revealed by his name the LORD
He is unique **Ex** 8:10; **Dt** 4:35,39; **1Ki** 8:60; **Isa** 45:5,18; **Joel** 2:27

He is eternal **Ge** 21:33; **Ps** 9:7; 29:10; 102:12; 135:13; **Isa** 26:4

He is holy **Lev** 11:44; **1Sa** 2:2; **Ps** 30:4; **Isa** 43:15

He is powerful **Ex** 15:6; **Jos** 22:22; **Ps** 93:4; **Jer** 10:6

He is majestic **Ps** 83:18; 93:1; 97:9; **Isa** 2:10,19,21; **Mic** 5:4

He is compassionate and gracious **Ex** 34:6–7;

Ps 103:8; 145:8–9
He is faithful and true Ps 145:13
He is unchangeable Ps 33:11; 110:4; **Mal** 3:6
He is actively present with his people Dt 31:6; **Jos** 1:9; **1Ki** 8:57; **Hag** 1:13

God reveals the relevance of his name the LORD by his actions
In creation
Jer 33:2 "This is what the LORD says, he who made the earth, the LORD who formed it and established it—the LORD is his name:" *See also* **Isa** 42:5; 43:15; 45:18
In the deliverance of his people from Egypt
Ex 6:6 "Therefore, say to the Israelites: 'I am the LORD, and I will bring you out from under the yoke of the Egyptians. I will free you from being slaves to them, and I will redeem you with an outstretched arm and with mighty acts of judgment.'" *See also* **Ex** 12:51; 14:30; 16:6; 20:2; **Lev** 26:13; **Ps** 81:10
In establishing a covenant with his people
Ex 6:7 "I will take you as my own people, and I will be your God. Then you will know that I am the LORD your God, who brought you out from under the yoke of the Egyptians." *See also* **Ex** 29:46; **2Sa** 7:24 pp 1Ch 17:22; **Jer** 14:9
In the judgment of his enemies
Ex 12:12 "... I will bring judgment on all the gods of Egypt. I am the LORD." *See also* **Ex** 7:5; 8:22–23; **1Sa** 17:45–47; **2Ch** 14:11–13
In the restoration of his people
Eze 36:36 "... I the LORD have rebuilt what was destroyed and have replanted what was desolate. I the LORD have spoken, and I will do it.'" *See also* **Ps** 102:15–22; **Isa** 60:15–22; **Eze** 37:6,13–14

God, the LORD denotes God's lordship
He is the Sovereign LORD
Eze 2:4 "... This is what the Sovereign LORD says.'" *See also* **Ge** 15:2,8; **Dt** 3:24; **Jos** 7:7; **Jdg** 6:22; **2Sa** 7:18–29; **Ps** 73:28; **Isa** 61:1; **Jer** 1:6; **Am** 1:8
He is the LORD Almighty
1Sa 1:3 ... [Elkanah] went up from his town to worship and sacrifice to the LORD Almighty at Shiloh ... *See also* **1Ch** 11:9; **Ps** 24:10; 46:7,11; **Isa** 2:12; **Jer** 39:16; **Hag** 2:6–9; **Zec** 1:3–4,6; **Mal** 1:14
He is the Lord, the LORD Almighty
Isa 1:24 ... the Lord, the LORD Almighty, the Mighty One of Israel ... *See also* **Ps** 69:6; **Isa** 3:15; 19:4; **Jer** 2:19; 46:10; 49:5; **Am** 9:5

As the LORD, God interacts with his people
He enforces the moral code
Lev 18:1–5 "... You [God's people] must obey my laws and be careful to follow my decrees. I am the LORD your God ..." *See also* **Lev** 11:44–45; 19:2
He makes his people holy
Lev 22:32 "... I am the LORD, who makes you holy" *See also* **Ex** 31:13; **Lev** 20:8; 21:8; **Eze** 20:12; 37:28
He is the object of his people's worship
Ex 4:22–23 "Then say to Pharaoh, 'This is what the LORD says: Israel is my firstborn son, and I told you, "Let my son go, so that he may worship me." ...'" *See also* **Ex** 12:31; 23:25; **1Ch** 16:29 pp Ps 96:9; **Ps** 29:2; 99:5; 100:2; **Jnh** 1:9

Jesus Christ takes God's name to himself
Jn 8:58–59 "I tell you the truth," Jesus answered, "before Abraham was born, I am!" At this, they picked up stones to stone him ... *See also God, faithfulness; God, sovereignty; God, the Creator; God, the Lord; God, titles and names of; God, unique; Jesus Christ, divinity.*

God, the Lord
God is the almighty ruler to whom everything and everyone is subject. His lordship is seen in his power and his victory over his enemies and also in his deliverance of his people and his loving care for them. He is the recipient of their obedience and their prayers. ("Lord" is the translation of the Hebrew word "Adonai" meaning "Ruler" or "Master" and is distinct from "LORD" which is the translation of the divine name "Yahweh".)

God is the almighty ruler
He is Lord of lords
1Ti 6:15 . . . God, the blessed and only Ruler, the King of kings and Lord of lords,
See also **Dt** 10:17; **Ps** 136:3; **Da** 2:47

He is Lord of all the earth
Ps 97:5 The mountains melt like wax before the LORD, before the Lord of all the earth. *See also* **Jos** 3:11,13; **Mic** 4:13; **Zec** 4:14; **Ac** 17:24

Characteristics of God as Lord
He is great and powerful
Ps 147:5 Great is our Lord and mighty in power . . . *See also* **Ne** 4:14; **Ps** 86:8; 114:7–8; 135:5; **Isa** 28:2; **Da** 9:4; **Ac** 4:24

He is majestic and exalted
Isa 6:1 . . . I [Isaiah] saw the Lord seated on a throne, high and exalted, and the train of his robe filled the temple. *See also* **Ps** 8:1,9; 2Th 1:9

He is righteous
Da 9:16 "O Lord, in keeping with all your righteous acts, turn away your anger and your wrath from Jerusalem, your city, your holy hill . . ." *See also* **Ps** 97:5–6; **Da** 9:7

He is loving and caring
Ps 86:15 But you, O Lord, are a compassionate and gracious God, slow to anger, abounding in love and faithfulness. *See also* **Ps** 62:12; 86:5

He is merciful and forgiving
Da 9:9 "The Lord our God is merciful and forgiving . . ." *See also* **Ps** 86:3–5; 130:2–4

God, the Lord, is triumphant over his enemies
Ps 78:65–66 . . . He [the Lord] beat back his enemies; he put them to everlasting shame. *See also* **Ps** 2:4–5; 37:13; 110:5–6

God, the Lord, delivers his people and cares for them
Ps 68:19 Praise be to the Lord, to God our Saviour, who daily bears our burdens. *Selah* *See also* **Ps** 38:15,22; 40:17; 54:4; 59:11; 77:2; 90:1,17

God is addressed as Lord
As a mark of respect or obedience
Jos 5:14 . . . Joshua fell face down to the ground in reverence, and asked him, "What message does my Lord have for his servant?" *See also* **Ex** 4:10,13; 5:22; **Jdg** 6:15; **Lk** 2:29

In prayer
Ne 1:11 "O Lord, let your ear be attentive to the prayer of this your servant and to the prayer of your servants who delight in revering your name . . ." *See also* **Ge** 18:27,30–32; **Ex** 34:9; **Jos** 7:8; **Jdg** 13:8; **Ps** 30:8; **Da** 9:4,15,19

Jesus Christ is God, the Lord
Jn 20:28 Thomas said to him [Jesus], "My Lord and my God!" *See also* **Mt** 22:41–45 pp **Mk** 12:35–37 pp **Lk** 20:41–44; **Ac** 2:34–36; **Heb** 1:13; **Ps** 110:1 *See also God as Saviour; God, greatness of; God, majesty of; God, power of; God, sovereignty; God, the LORD; God, titles and names of; Jesus Christ, the Lord; Lord's Day.*

God, the provider
God supplies the needs of all creation, but gives special care to his own people.

God is called "The LORD who provides"
Ge 22:13–14 . . . So Abraham called that place The LORD Will Provide. And to this day it is said, "On the mountain of the LORD it will be provided." *See also* **Ge** 22:8

God provides for the needs of all creation
He provides for the earth
Ps 65:9–13 You care for the land and water it; you enrich it abundantly. The streams of God are filled with water to provide the people with corn, for so you have ordained it . . . *See also* **Dt** 11:12,14–15; **Ps** 68:9; 104:10–18; 135:7; 147:8; **Eze** 34:26–29

He provides for the animals
Ps 145:16 You open your hand and satisfy the desires of every living thing. *See also* **Job** 38:41; **Ps** 104:27–28; 147:9; **Mt** 6:26 pp **Lk** 12:24

He provides for all people
Ac 14:17 ". . . He [God] has shown kindness

by giving you rain from heaven and crops in their seasons; he provides you with plenty of food and fills your hearts with joy." See also 1Ch 29:12; Ps 68:5; 107:9; Mt 5:45; Ac 17:28

He provides for the poor and needy
Ps 140:12 I know that the LORD secures justice for the poor and upholds the cause of the needy. See also 1Sa 2:8; Ps 35:10; 145:13–14; 146:7–9; Isa 25:4

Special instances of God's practical provision
Food and water in the wilderness: Ex 16:13–18; 17:3–6; Nu 11:4–9,31–32
God's provision for Elijah: 1Ki 17:6,16; 19:5–8
2Ki 4:42–44; Mt 14:15–21 pp Mk 6:35–44 pp Lk 9:12–17 pp Jn 6:5–13; Mt 15:32–38 pp Mk 8:1–9

God's special provision for his own people
He provides for their practical needs
Php 4:19 And my God will meet all your needs according to his glorious riches in Christ Jesus. See also Dt 2:7; Ps 68:10; 111:5; Mt 6:25–33 pp Lk 12:22–31

He provides for their protection
Ps 5:12 For surely, O LORD, you bless the righteous; you surround them with your favour as with a shield. See also Ge 28:15; Dt 33:27; 1Sa 2:9; Ps 91:9–13; 121:3–8; Isa 46:4; Php 4:7; 1Pe 1:5; Jude 24; Rev 3:10

He provides for their every need
2Pe 1:3 His divine power has given us everything we need for life and godliness through our knowledge of him who called us by his own glory and goodness. See also 1Co 3:21–23; Col 2:10

Examples of God's provision for his people
2Sa 7:10 pp 1Ch 17:9; Isa 61:3; Jer 33:6–9; 1Co 10:13

Implications of God's providential care
Freedom from worry
Mt 6:31–33 "So do not worry, saying, 'What shall we eat?' or 'What shall we drink?' or 'What shall we wear?' For the pagans run after all these things, and your heavenly Father knows that you need them. But seek first his kingdom and his righteousness, and all these things will be given to you as well." pp Lk 12:29–31

Generosity
Lk 6:38 "Give, and it will be given to you. A good measure, pressed down, shaken together and running over, will be poured into your lap. For with the measure you use, it will be measured to you."
See also 1Ch 29:14; 2Co 9:6–11; Php 4:18

Faithfulness
Ro 2:4 Or do you show contempt for the riches of his kindness, tolerance and patience, not realising that God's kindness leads you towards repentance? See also Isa 5:1–7; Hos 10:1–2; 11:1–4 See also God as Saviour; God, compassion; God, fatherhood; God, sovereignty; God, titles and names of; miracles, nature of; providence.

God, the Rock
An OT title for God and a Messianic title signifying that God's people can rely on him for absolute protection and salvation.

Rock as a title for Israel's God
Ps 78:35 They remembered that God was their Rock, that God Most High was their Redeemer. See also Ge 49:24; Dt 32:15,18,30; 2Sa 23:3; Ps 42:9; Isa 30:29; Hab 1:12

God the Rock is unique
2Sa 22:32 "For who is God besides the LORD? And who is the Rock except our God?" pp Ps 18:31 See also 1Sa 2:2; Isa 44:8

The Rock is superior to other gods
Dt 32:31 For their rock is not like our Rock . . . See also Dt 32:37

The Rock is worthy to be praised
Ps 144:1 Praise be to the LORD my Rock, who trains my hands for war, my fingers for battle. See also Dt 32:4; Ps 92:15

God the Rock and his people
God the Rock is a refuge for his people
Ps 62:7 . . . he is my mighty rock, my

refuge. *See also* **Ps** 28:1; 31:1–3; 61:2; 71:3; **Isa** 26:4

God the Rock is his people's fortress
Ps 94:22 . . . the LORD has become my fortress, and my God the rock in whom I take refuge. *See also* **Ps** 28:8; 46:7,11; 48:3; 59:9,16–17; 91:2; 144:2; **Jer** 16:19

God the Rock is his people's security
2Sa 22:3 my God is my rock . . . He is my stronghold, my refuge and my saviour . . . pp Ps 18:2 *See also* **Ps** 9:9; 27:1; 37:39; 43:2; 52:7; **Joel** 3:16

God the Rock saves and delivers his people
Ps 95:1 . . . let us shout aloud to the Rock of our salvation. *See also* **2Sa** 22:47 pp Ps 18:46; **Ps** 19:14; 62:2; 89:26; **Isa** 17:10

Rock as a Messianic title
The Messiah is the rock/stone on which God's living temple stands
Isa 8:14 ". . . he [the LORD Almighty] will be a stone that causes people to stumble and a rock that makes them fall . . ."
Isa 28:16 . . . "See, I lay a stone in Zion, a tested stone, a precious cornerstone for a sure foundation; the one who trusts will never be dismayed." *See also* **Ps** 118:22; **Mt** 21:42 pp Mk 12:10 pp Lk 20:17; **Ac** 4:11; **1Pe** 2:6–7

The Messiah's kingdom is eternal and immovable like a rock
Da 2:34–35 ". . . the rock that struck the statue became a huge mountain and filled the whole earth." *See also* **Da** 2:44–45

Consequences of rejecting the rock/stone Mt 21:44 pp Lk 20:18; **Ro** 9:32–33; **1Pe** 2:4–8
See also God, titles and names of; Jesus Christ, titles and names of; salvation.

God, titles and names of

These reflect the great and varied aspects of God's being and character. They are particularly used by the psalmists to speak of God as a source of strength, security, blessing and hope.

Titles which denote God's greatness
God Almighty
Ge 17:1 When Abram was ninety-nine years old, the LORD appeared to him and said, "I am God Almighty . . ." *See also* **Ge** 28:3; 48:3; **Ex** 6:3; **Ru** 1:20–21; **Job** 5:17
"Almighty" is the favourite divine title in the book of Job: **Job** 6:4; 37:23
Ps 91:1; **Rev** 16:14; 19:15

God Most High
Ge 14:18–20 . . . "Blessed be Abram by God Most High, Creator of heaven and earth. And blessed be God Most High, who delivered your enemies into your hand." . . . *See also* **Ge** 14:22; **Dt** 32:8; **2Sa** 22:14 pp Ps 18:13; **Ps** 9:2; 21:7; 46:4; 47:2; 78:35; 97:9; **Isa** 14:14; **Da** 3:26
Jesus Christ as the Son of the Most High: **Mk** 5:7 pp Lk 8:28; **Lk** 1:32,35
Lk 6:35; **Ac** 16:17

The Eternal God
Ge 21:33 Abraham planted a tamarisk tree in Beersheba, and there he called upon the name of the LORD, the Eternal God. *See also* **Dt** 33:27; **Ro** 16:26

The Ancient of Days Da 7:9,13,22

The Mighty One
Lk 1:49 ". . . the Mighty One has done great things for me [Mary] . . ." *See also* **Jos** 22:22; **Ps** 50:1; 132:2,5; **Isa** 1:24; 49:26; 60:16; **Mk** 14:62

The living God
Ps 84:2 My soul yearns, even faints, for the courts of the LORD; my heart and my flesh cry out for the living God.
Da 6:26–27 ". . . people must fear and reverence the God of Daniel. For he is the living God and he endures for ever . . ." *See also* **Dt** 5:26; **Jos** 3:10; **1Sa** 17:26,36; **2Ki** 19:16 pp Isa 37:17; **Ps** 42:2; **Jer** 10:10; **Mt** 16:16; **Ac** 14:15; **Heb** 10:31

The Holy One of Israel
Isa 12:6 ". . . great is the Holy One of Israel among you." *See also* **2Ki** 19:22 pp Isa 37:23; **Ps** 71:22; 78:41; 89:18; **Isa** 30:12,15; 41:14; 45:11; 55:5; 60:9

The LORD
Ge 4:26 . . . At that time people began to call on the name of the LORD.
Ex 6:2 God also said to Moses, "I am the LORD." *See also* **Ex** 3:15

God, titles and names of

Titles which refer to God as LORD
Ex 34:5–7; Dt 10:17; 28:10; 1Ki 2:3; Ps 146:10; Jer 14:9; Da 9:14

The Lord God Rev 1:8; 22:5

The LORD God Almighty
Ps 89:8 O LORD God Almighty, who is like you? You are mighty, O LORD, and your faithfulness surrounds you. *See also* Ps 80:4; Jer 5:14; 15:16; Hos 12:5; Am 4:13

The LORD Most High
Ps 7:17 I will give thanks to the LORD because of his righteousness and will sing praise to the name of the LORD Most High. *See also* Ps 47:2; 97:9

The Sovereign LORD
2Sa 7:28 "O Sovereign LORD, you are God! Your words are trustworthy . . ." *See also* Dt 9:26; Jos 7:7; Isa 25:8; Jer 32:17; Am 7:2

Titles referring to God as the source of light
2Sa 22:29; Ps 27:1; 84:11; Isa 10:17; Mic 7:8; Jas 1:17

Titles referring to God as the source of strength
Ps 59:9 O my [the psalmist's] Strength, I watch for you; you, O God, are my fortress, *See also* Ex 15:2; Ps 18:1; 22:19; 28:7; 46:1; 59:17; 81:1; Isa 12:2

Titles referring to God as the source of security
A shield
Ge 15:1 . . . the word of the LORD came to Abram in a vision: "Do not be afraid, Abram. I am your shield, your very great reward." *See also* Dt 33:29; 2Sa 22:3 pp Ps 18:2; 2Sa 22:31 pp Ps 18:30; Ps 28:7; 84:11; 115:9; Pr 2:7; 30:5
A refuge
Ps 46:1 God is our refuge and strength, an ever-present help in trouble. *See also* Ps 9:9; 61:3; 91:2,9; 119:114; 142:5; Jer 16:19; Joel 3:16; Na 1:7
A hiding-place Ps 32:7
A fortress 2Sa 22:2 pp Ps 18:2; Ps 31:3; 62:2,6; 91:2; 144:2; Isa 17:10; Jer 16:19

A stronghold 2Sa 22:3 pp Ps 18:2; Ps 9:9; 27:1; 37:39; 43:2; 144:2; Joel 3:16
A defender Dt 10:18; Ps 68:5; Pr 23:11
A Rock Ge 49:24; Dt 32:4; Ps 19:14; Isa 26:4

Titles referring to God as the source of provision
Ge 22:14 So Abraham called that place The LORD Will Provide. And to this day it is said, "On the mountain of the LORD it will be provided."
La 3:24 I [the lamenter] say to myself, "The LORD is my portion; therefore I will wait for him." *See also* Ge 22:8; Ps 73:26; 119:57; 142:5; Jer 10:16; 51:19

Titles referring to God as the source of hope
Jer 14:8 O Hope of Israel, its Saviour in times of distress . . . *See also* Jer 17:13; 50:7

Titles referring to God as the source of peace
Ro 15:33 The God of peace be with you all. Amen. *See also* Jdg 6:24; Ro 16:20; 2Co 13:11; Php 4:9; 1Th 5:23; 2Th 3:16; Heb 13:20

Titles referring to God as the source of comfort
Jer 8:18; 2Co 1:3

Titles referring to God as the source of grace
Ex 34:6; Ne 9:31; Ps 86:15; Jnh 4:2; 1Pe 5:10

Titles referring to God as the source of love
Ps 59:10,17; 144:2; 2Co 13:11; 1Jn 4:7–16

God as shepherd
Ps 23:1 The LORD is my shepherd, I shall not be in want. *See also* Ge 48:15; 49:24; Ps 80:1

The true God
2Ch 15:3; Jer 10:10; Jn 17:3; 1Jn 5:20 *See also* God as Saviour; God of the fathers; God, grace and mercy; God, living; God, power of; God, the eternal; God, the Lord; God, the provider; Holy Spirit, titles and names of; Jesus Christ, titles and names of.

God, transcendent

God is far above, beyond and outside the created order.

God is outside and above all creation
Ps 113:4 The LORD is exalted over all the nations, his glory above the heavens.
Isa 40:22 He sits enthroned above the circle of the earth, and its people are like grasshoppers . . .
Solomon confesses that God transcends containment by the temple: **1Ki** 8:27; **2Ch** 2:6
Job 37:23; **Ps** 8:1; 57:5, 11; 97:9; 108:5; 148:13, **Isa** 33:5; **Ac** 7:49, 17:24; **Eph** 1:20–21; 4:6; **Heb** 7:26

God is able also to draw near to his creatures
Isa 57:15 For this is what the high and lofty One says—he who lives for ever, whose name is holy: "I live in a high and holy place, but also with those who are contrite and lowly in spirit . . .

The invisibility of God
God is invisible to people and hidden from their sight
Ex 33:20 . . . "you cannot see my [the LORD's] face, for no-one may see me and live."
Isa 45:15 . . . you are a God who hides himself . . . *See also* **Ex** 3:6
Job is unable to find God in his suffering: **Job** 9:11; 23:8–9
Ps 10:1; 13:1; 89:46; **Jn** 1:18; 5:37; **Col** 1:15; **1Ti** 1:17; 6:16; **1Jn** 4:12
OT saints who saw God
Ex 33:11 The LORD would speak to Moses face to face, as one speaks to a friend . . .
See also **Ge** 32:30; **Ex** 24:10; **Jdg** 13:22; **Isa** 6:5
God is made visible in Jesus Christ Jn 1:18; 14:9; **2Co** 4:4,6; **Col** 1:15
Redeemed people will be able to look at God's face Mt 5:8; **1Co** 13:12; **1Jn** 3:2; **Rev** 22:4

God's ways are beyond human understanding
Isa 55:8–9 "For my thoughts are not your thoughts, neither are your ways my ways," declares the LORD. "As the heavens are higher than the earth, so are my ways higher than your ways and my thoughts than your thoughts."
See also **Dt** 29:29; **Job** 5:9; 11:7; 36:22–23; **Ps** 139:1–6; **Pr** 25:2; **Ecc** 3:11; **Isa** 40:28; **Ro** 11:33–34; **1Co** 2:11,16   *See also God, holiness of; God, human descriptions of; God, present everywhere; God, sovereignty; God, the Creator; God, the eternal; Jesus Christ, sonship of; revelation.*

God, truth of

God's unique integrity is displayed in his perfection of character and attributes. It is further emphasised by the consistent truth of his words and works, supremely shown in Jesus Christ.

God is the one and only true God
He alone is God
Jer 10:10 . . . the LORD is the true God; he is the living God, the eternal King . . . *See also* **Dt** 4:39; **2Ch** 15:3; **Isa** 43:10–11; 45:5–6,14,21; **Zec** 14:9; **Jn** 1:18; 17:3; **Rev** 6:10
The contrast with other "gods"
Ro 1:25 They [the godless] exchanged the truth of God for a lie, and worshipped and served created things rather than the Creator . . .
See also **Ex** 15:11; **Dt** 4:35; 32:39; **Ps** 86:8; **Isa** 43:3; **1Th** 1:9
The contrast with earthly rulers
Jer 10:6–8 No-one is like you, O LORD; you are great, and your name is mighty in power. Who should not revere you, O King of the nations? This is your due. Among all the wise men of the nations and in all their kingdoms, there is no-one like you. They are all senseless and foolish; they are taught by worthless wooden idols.

God is characterised by truth
Ps 31:5 . . . redeem me, O LORD, the God of truth.   *See also* **Ps** 40:10; 43:3; **Isa** 65:16; **Jn** 3:33; 7:28; 8:26; **1Jn** 5:20; **Rev** 15:3

God's truth is demonstrated in the revelation of himself in Jesus Christ
Jesus Christ is "the truth"
Jn 14:6 Jesus answered, "I am the way and

the truth and the life. No-one comes to the Father except through me." *See also* **1Jn** 5:20
Jesus Christ and the Spirit bring truth Jn 1:14; 14:16–17; **Ro** 15:8

God's words are truthful
His words are consistently true and reliable
Nu 23:19 "God is not human, that he should lie, nor a human being, that he should change his mind. Does he speak and then not act? Does he promise and not fulfil?" *See also* **1Sa** 15:29; **Ps** 12:6; 33:4; 119:151,160; **Ro** 3:4; **Tit** 1:2; **Heb** 6:18; **Jas** 1:17

His words of promise are totally true and trustworthy
Ps 132:11 The LORD swore an oath to David, a sure oath that he will not revoke . . .
See also **2Ti** 2:13; **Heb** 7:21; **Ps** 110:4

God's people live in the light of his truth
Ps 86:11 Teach me your way, O LORD, and I will walk in your truth . . . *See also* **Ps** 26:3; 119:141–142; **Da** 9:13; **Jn** 17:17 *See also God, faithfulness; God, holiness of; God, perfection; God, truthfulness; God, unique; Holy Spirit, teacher.*

God, truthfulness
To call the LORD "the true God" means that he alone has in his being the fulness of deity and is worthy to be worshipped as God. He and his word are a trustworthy foundation for life because he speaks the truth and is utterly reliable and consistent in his character, his revelation of himself, his promises and his pronouncements.

Titles reflecting God's truthfulness
The true God 2Ch 15:3; **Jer** 10:10; **1Th** 1:9
The God of truth Ps 31:5; **Isa** 65:16
Jesus Christ is "the truth"
Jn 14:6 Jesus answered, "I am the way and the truth and the life. No-one comes to the Father except through me." *See also* **Jn** 1:14,17; 6:32; **Jn** 5:20; **Rev** 3:7,14
The Spirit of truth Jn 14:17; 15:26; 16:13; **1Jn** 4:6; 5:6

God is true to his character and his word
He speaks the truth
Isa 45:19 ". . . I, the LORD, speak the truth; I declare what is right." *See also* **2Sa** 7:28; **Ps** 33:4; 119:160; **Jn** 17:17; **Rev** 21:5; 22:6
He does not lie
Nu 23:19 "God is not human, that he should lie, nor a human being, that he should change his mind. Does he speak and then not act? Does he promise and not fulfil?" *See also* **Ro** 3:4; **2Ti** 2:13; **Tit** 1:2; **Heb** 6:18
He is true to himself and his promises Dt 32:4; **Ps** 25:10; 33:4; 145:13; 146:6; **La** 3:23; **2Ti** 2:13

The truthfulness of God undergirds the law
Ps 119:142 . . . your [the LORD's] law is true. *See also* **Ps** 19:7; 119:151,160; **Mal** 2:6–7

The truthfulness of God undergirds the covenant
Ps 25:10 All the ways of the LORD are loving and faithful for those who keep the demands of his covenant. *See also* **Ps** 145:13; **Hos** 2:19–20; **2Ti** 2:13

The truthfulness of God undergirds the prophetic word
Eze 12:25 "'But I the LORD will speak what I will, and it shall be fulfilled without delay . . .'" *See also* **Isa** 55:11; **Jer** 1:12; 28:9; **Eze** 33:33; **Da** 2:45

The truthfulness of God undergirds his promises
Jos 23:14–15 . . . every good promise of the LORD your God has come true . . . *See also* **Nu** 23:19; **1Ki** 8:20; **Ps** 105:42; **Ro** 4:20–21

The truthfulness of God undergirds his judgment
Ps 96:13 . . . He [the LORD] will judge the world in righteousness and the peoples in his truth. *See also* **Ps** 98:9; **Isa** 11:3–5; **Ro** 2:2

The truthfulness of God undergirds the teaching of Jesus Christ
Jn 1:17 . . . grace and truth came through Jesus Christ.   *See also* **Mt** 5:18; 22:16 pp **Mk** 12:14 pp **Lk** 20:21; **Mk** 3:28; **Lk** 4:24; **Jn** 1:51; 8:31–32; 18:37   *See also God, faithfulness; God, justice of; God, purpose of; God, truth of; Holy Spirit in the world; Jesus Christ, preaching and teaching; word of God.*

God, unchangeable
God's nature, plans and actions do not change even though he is active and his relationships do not remain static. His moral consistency guarantees his commitment to unchanging principles.

God's being is unchangeable
Ps 102:27 But you [God] remain the same . . .   *See also* **Heb** 1:12; **Mal** 3:6; **Heb** 13:8; **Jas** 1:17

God's characteristics do not change
God's love is constant
Ps 89:2 I will declare that your love stands firm for ever . . .   *See also* **Ps** 136:1–26; **2Ti** 2:13

God's purposes and plans do not change
Heb 6:17 . . . God wanted to make the unchanging nature of his purpose very clear to the heirs of what was promised . . .   *See also* **Nu** 23:19; **1Sa** 15:29; **Pr** 19:21; **Jer** 44:29; **Heb** 7:21; **Ps** 110:4

God does not revoke his promises
Ps 132:11 The LORD swore an oath to David, a sure oath that he will not revoke . . .
See also **Ps** 145:13; **Heb** 4:1

God's word does not change
Isa 40:8 ". . . the word of our God stands for ever."   *See also* **Ps** 119:89; **Mt** 5:18; **1Pe** 1:23–25

God's failure to inflict promised judgment is a sign of his unchanging grace
Hos 11:8 ". . . My heart is changed within me; all my compassion is aroused."   *See also* **Ex** 32:10–14; **Jnh** 3:10; 4:2   *See also God, faithfulness; God, goodness of; God, grace and mercy; God, love of; God, purpose of; God, repentance of; God, the eternal; God, unity of.*

God, unique
No-one and nothing is comparable to the triune God in his nature or comparable to him in his character and activity.

There is no God except the LORD
Isa 45:5–6 "I am the LORD, and there is no other; apart from me there is no God . . . from the rising of the sun to the place of its setting people may know there is none besides me. I am the LORD, and there is no other."   *See also* **Dt** 4:35; 6:4; 32:3; **1Ki** 8:60; **Ps** 83:18; 86:10; **Isa** 43:10–11; 44:6–8; 45:18; **1Co** 8:4–6; **Eph** 4:6; **1Ti** 2:5

There is no-one like God
Ps 89:6–8 For who in the skies above can compare with the LORD? Who is like the LORD among the heavenly beings? . . . O LORD God Almighty, who is like you? . . .   *See also* **Ex** 8:10; **Isa** 40:18
In his creative power
Isa 40:25–26 "To whom will you compare me? Or who is my equal?" says the Holy One. Lift your eyes and look to the heavens: Who created all these? He who brings out the starry host one by one, and calls them each by name. Because of his great power and mighty strength, not one of them is missing.   *See also* **Jn** 1:3; **Ne** 9:6; **Ac** 14:15; **Col** 1:16; **Rev** 4:11
In his mighty acts
Ps 86:10 For you are great and do marvellous deeds; you alone are God.   *See also* **Ps** 135:5–6
In his character and glory
Ex 15:11 "Who among the gods is like you, O LORD? Who is like you—majestic in holiness, awesome in glory, working wonders?"
See also **2Sa** 7:22; **1Ch** 29:11
In his ability to save
Dt 33:26 "There is no-one like the God of Jeshurun, who rides on the heavens to help you

and on the clouds in his majesty." *See also* **Isa** 45:20–22; **Jer** 10:5–6
In his covenant love
1Ki 8:23 . . . "O LORD, God of Israel, there is no God like you in heaven above or on earth below—you who keep your covenant of love with your servants who continue wholeheartedly in your way." *See also* **2Sa** 7:22–23 pp **1Ch** 17:20–21
Zec 14:9 The LORD will be king over the whole earth. On that day there will be one LORD, and his name the only name.
In his sovereignty **Dt** 4:39; **1Ti** 1:17

Implications of God's uniqueness
God alone is to be worshipped
Ex 20:2–3 "I am the LORD your God, who brought you out of Egypt, out of the land of slavery. You shall have no other gods before me." pp **Dt** 5:6–7 *See also* **Ex** 23:13,24; **Lev** 19:4; **Dt** 6:13–14; **2Ki** 17:35
Idolatry is empty and worthless
Jnh 2:8 "Those who cling to worthless idols forfeit the grace that could be theirs."
See also **Dt** 4:28; **Isa** 44:18–20; 45:20; **Hab** 2:18   *See also God as Saviour; God, glory of; God, greatness of; God, majesty of; God, sovereignty; God, the Creator; God, the Rock; God, transcendent.*

God, unity of
God acts as a unity in all his deeds. The three persons of the Trinity are united in one Godhead. They are interrelated with one another, share the same attributes and co-operate in the same work. God's characteristics are consistent, expressing his integral divine nature.

God is one
Dt 6:4 Hear, O Israel: The LORD our God, the LORD is one. *See also* **Mk** 12:29,32; **1Co** 8:4; **Gal** 3:20; **Eph** 4:5–6; **1Ti** 2:5; **Jas** 2:19

The three persons of the Trinity are united in one Godhead
All three are interrelated
Ro 8:9–11 You, however, are controlled not by the sinful nature but by the Spirit, if the Spirit of God lives in you. And if anyone does not have the Spirit of Christ, that person does not belong to Christ. But if Christ is in you, your body is dead because of sin, yet your spirit is alive because of righteousness . . . *See also* **Jn** 14:23; **2Co** 13:14; **Eph** 2:18; **1Pe** 1:2
The Son is one with the Father
Jn 10:30 "I and the Father are one."
See also **Mt** 10:40; **Mk** 9:37 pp **Lk** 9:48; **Lk** 10:16; **Jn** 8:16; 14:9
The Spirit is one with God
2Sa 23:2–3 "The Spirit of the LORD spoke through me [David]; his word was on my tongue. The God of Israel spoke, the Rock of Israel said to me . . ." *See also* **Ps** 51:11; **1Co** 3:16

The three persons are one in character
All three are eternal **Ro** 16:26; **Isa** 9:6; **Heb** 9:14
All three are all-knowing **Isa** 40:13–14; **Jn** 2:24–25; 21:17 **1Co** 2:10–11
All three are holy **Jn** 17:11
The Son: **Mk** 1:24; **Ac** 3:14
The Spirit: **Jn** 14:26; **Ro** 1:4
All three are called Lord and God
The Father: **Mt** 11:25; **Ac** 3:22; **1Co** 8:6
The Son: **Jn** 1:1; 20:28; **Ac** 10:36; **2Pe** 1:1
The Spirit: **Ac** 5:3–4; **2Co** 3:17–18
All three are glorious
The Father: **Ac** 7:2; **Eph** 1:17
The Son: **Jn** 1:14; 12:41
The Spirit: **2Co** 3:8,18; **1Pe** 4:14

The three persons share in the same work
In creation
Ge 1:1–3 In the beginning God created the heavens and the earth. Now the earth was formless and empty, darkness was over the surface of the deep, and the Spirit of God was hovering over the waters. And God said, "Let there be light," and there was light.
See also **Ps** 33:6; 104:30; **Jn** 1:3–4; **Col** 1:16
In Jesus Christ's ministry
Jn 3:34 "For the one whom God has sent speaks the words of God, for God gives the Spirit without limit." *See also* **Ac** 10:38

God, will of

In salvation
1Pe 1:2 who have been chosen according to the foreknowledge of God the Father, through the sanctifying work of the Spirit, for obedience to Jesus Christ and sprinkling by his blood . . . *See also* **2Co** 1:21–22; **Tit** 3:4–6

In indwelling the church
Eph 2:22 And in him [Christ] you too are being built together to become a dwelling in which God lives by his Spirit.
The Spirit indwells believers: **1Co** 3:16; 6:19
The Son indwells believers: **Gal** 2:20; **Eph** 3:17

In directing the church's mission
Ac 16:6–10 Paul and his companions travelled throughout the region of Phrygia and Galatia, having been kept by the Holy Spirit from preaching the word in the province of Asia. When they came to the border of Mysia, they tried to enter Bithynia, but the Spirit of Jesus would not allow them to . . . After Paul had seen the vision, we got ready at once to leave for Macedonia, concluding that God had called us to preach the gospel to them.
The Father directs mission: **Ac** 14:27; **Gal** 1:1
The Son directs mission: **Mt** 28:18–20; **Ac** 1:7–8
The Spirit directs mission: **Ac** 13:2,4

God's characteristics are consistent
His love and justice are in unity
Ex 34:6–7 And he passed in front of Moses, proclaiming, "The LORD, the LORD, the compassionate and gracious God, slow to anger, abounding in love and faithfulness, maintaining love to thousands, and forgiving wickedness, rebellion and sin. Yet he does not leave the guilty unpunished; he punishes the children and their children for the sin of the parents to the third and fourth generation." *See also* **2Sa** 7:14–15; **Ps** 103:6–8; **Ro** 3:25–26

His wrath and mercy are in unity
Joel 2:11–13 The LORD thunders at the head of his army; his forces are beyond number, and mighty are those who obey his command. The day of the LORD is great; it is dreadful. Who can endure it? . . . Rend your heart and not your garments. Return to the LORD your God, for he is gracious and compassionate, slow to anger and abounding in love, and he relents from sending calamity.
See also **Jn** 3:16–18; **Ro** 2:4, 7–8 *See also God, perfection; God, unchangeable; God, unique; Holy Spirit, divinity; Jesus Christ, Son of God; Trinity.*

God, will of
The intent and purpose of God, as revealed in Scripture. God's will for his creation and his people is set out in the Law and the Prophets, which find their fulfilment in Jesus Christ. A central aspect of the will of God is that his people be faithful and obedient.

The revelation of God's will
in his word
2Ti 3:16 All Scripture is God-breathed and is useful for teaching, rebuking, correcting and training in righteousness, *See also* **2Sa** 7:21 pp **1Ch** 17:19; **Ps** 103:20–21; **Col** 1:25–26; **1Jn** 2:4–5
Through the law Ex 18:15–16; 24:12; **Dt** 30:16; **Ps** 119:43; **Ro** 7:12; **1Ti** 1:8
Through the prophets 1Ki 22:6–7 pp **2Ch** 18:5–6; **2Ki** 3:11; **Jer** 42:3–4; **Eze** 12:25; **Am** 3:7
In the apostolic gospel Ac 20:27; **Gal** 1:11–12

The fulfilment of God's will
God's will is fulfilled in Jesus Christ
Eph 1:9–10 And he [God] made known to us the mystery of his will according to his good pleasure, which he purposed in Christ . . .
See also **Eph** 3:4–11; **Col** 1:27

Jesus Christ obeyed his Father's will
Jn 6:38 "For I [Jesus] have come down from heaven not to do my will but to do the will of him who sent me." *See also* **Mt** 26:39 pp **Mk** 14:36 pp **Lk** 22:42; **Jn** 4:34; 5:30; **Heb** 10:7; **Ps** 40:8

Jesus Christ's death fulfilled God's will
Gal 1:3–4 . . . the Lord Jesus Christ, who gave himself for our sins to rescue us from the present evil age, according to the will of our God and Father, *See also* **Isa** 53:10; **Ac** 2:23

God's will for the world
God desires justice and righteousness
Am 5:24 ". . . let justice roll on like a river, righteousness like a never-failing stream!"

See also **Ps** 33:5; **Isa** 5:7; **Jer** 9:24; **Mic** 6:8

God desires honesty and truth
Pr 12:22 The LORD detests lying lips, but he delights in those who are truthful. See also **Ex** 20:16 pp **Dt** 5:20; **Lev** 19:35–36; **Pr** 11:1; **Zec** 8:16–17

God desires harmony and peace
1Ti 2:2–3 for kings and all those in authority, that we may live peaceful and quiet lives in all godliness and holiness. This is good, and pleases God our Saviour, See also **Isa** 2:3–4 pp **Mic** 4:2–3; **Isa** 11:6–9

God desires the world to be saved
1Ti 2:4 [God our Saviour] who wants all people to be saved and to come to a knowledge of the truth. See also **Eze** 18:23; 33:11; **Mt** 18:14; **Jn** 3:16–17; **2Pe** 3:9

God's will for his redeemed people
God desires loving obedience
Mt 22:35–38 . . . "Teacher, which is the greatest commandment in the Law?" Jesus replied: "'Love the Lord your God with all your heart and with all your soul and with all your mind.' . . ." pp **Mk** 12:28–29 pp **Lk** 10:27 See also **Dt** 6:5
Scripture regularly makes obedience to God a higher priority than performing religious acts: **Ps** 51:16–17; **Isa** 1:11; **Jer** 7:22–23; **1Jn** 2:5

God desires worship
1Pe 2:9 But you are a chosen people, a royal priesthood, a holy nation, a people belonging to God, that you may declare the praises of him who called you out of darkness into his wonderful light.
See also **Ps** 100:4; **Isa** 45:23; **1Th** 5:18; **Rev** 1:6

God desires holiness
1Th 4:3 It is God's will that you should be sanctified . . . See also **Lev** 19:1–2; **1Co** 1:2; **Col** 1:22; **1Th** 4:7; **Heb** 10:10; **1Pe** 1:15–16

God desires love for one another
Jn 13:34–35 "A new command I [Jesus] give you: Love one another. As I have loved you, so you must love one another . . ." See also **Lev** 19:18; **Mt** 22:39 pp **Mk** 12:31 pp **Lk** 10:27; **Jn** 15:12–13; **Gal** 5:14; **1Jn** 3:11

God desires high moral standards
1Pe 2:15 For it is God's will that by doing good you should silence the ignorant talk of foolish people. See also **Mt** 5:16,48; **1Pe** 3:4

God's will may involve suffering
1Pe 3:17 It is better, if it is God's will, to suffer for doing good than for doing evil. See also **Ac** 14:22; 21:13–14; **Heb** 12:5–7; **1Pe** 4:19

Proper responses to God's will
Discovering God's will
Eph 5:17 Therefore do not be foolish, but understand what the Lord's will is. See also **Ro** 2:18; **Col** 1:9

Obeying God's will
Mt 7:21 "Not everyone who says to me [Jesus], 'Lord, Lord,' will enter the kingdom of heaven, but only those who do the will of my Father who is in heaven." See also **Ezr** 10:11; **Mt** 12:50 pp **Mk** 3:35; **Eph** 6:6; **Heb** 13:21; **Jas** 4:15

Praying for God's will
Mt 6:10 "'. . . your kingdom come, your will be done on earth as it is in heaven.'" See also **Ps** 143:10; **Mt** 26:42; **Jn** 14:13–14; **1Jn** 5:14

Making radical changes to do God's will
Ro 12:2 Do not conform any longer to the pattern of this world, but be transformed by the renewing of your mind. Then you will be able to test and approve what God's will is—his good, pleasing and perfect will. See also **Ro** 8:5; **Gal** 5:16–17; **Jas** 1:20; **1Pe** 1:14; 4:2; **1Jn** 2:15–17

Rejecting God's will
Lk 7:30 But the Pharisees and experts in the law rejected God's purpose for themselves . . .
See also **Ps** 107:11; **Isa** 30:1; **Eze** 3:7; **Mt** 23:37 pp **Lk** 13:34; **Jn** 8:44

Examples of people who obeyed God's will
Dt 33:21
David: **1Sa** 13:14; **Ac** 13:22,36
Isa 44:28–45:1
Paul: **Ac** 18:21; 21:14; **Ro** 1:10; 15:32; **1Co** 4:19

Ways of discovering God's will
Ex 18:20; 28:30; **Ps** 86:11; 119:105; **Da** 2:22–23; **Jn** 14:26; **Ac** 1:26

God's will and the human will
God's will overrules human wills
Pr 19:21 Many are the plans in a human heart, but it is the LORD's purpose that prevails. *See also* **Ps 33:10–11; Pr 16:9**
God's will overrides the desires of the wicked
Ge 50:20; Isa 10:5–11; Hab 1:5–11; Ac 2:23
God's will can harmonise with human wills
1Ch 13:2; Ps 37:4; 145:19; Ac 15:28

God's will is sovereign
Over all things
Eph 1:11 . . . according to the plan of him who works out everything in conformity with the purpose of his will,
Over creation
Mt 10:29; Ro 8:20; Rev 4:11
Over evil
Ge 45:8; 1Sa 2:25; Pr 16:4; Isa 65:12; Ro 9:18
Over the gospel
Mic 7:18; Mt 11:25–26 pp Lk 10:21; Jn 5:21; Ac 13:48; Ro 9:18; 1Co 1:21
In the church
1Co 1:1; 12:11,28; Php 2:13; 2Ti 1:1; Heb 2:4 *See also God, purpose of; God, sovereignty; Holy Spirit, guidance; Jesus Christ, cross of; law; prayer and God's will; revelation; Scripture.*

God, wisdom of
Scripture declares that God alone is wise and discerning, and that human wisdom is often unable or unwilling to understand his ways. God's wisdom is expressed in both creation and redemption.

God's wisdom described
Isa 28:29 All this also comes from the LORD Almighty, wonderful in counsel and magnificent in wisdom. *See also* **1Sa 2:3; Ro 16:27**
God's wisdom is beyond measure
Ps 147:5 Great is our Lord and mighty in power; his understanding has no limit. *See also* **Isa 44:7; Jer 10:7; Ro 11:33**
God's wisdom is profound
Isa 40:28 . . . The LORD is the everlasting God, the Creator of the ends of the earth. He will not grow tired or weary, and his understanding no-one can fathom. *See also* **Job 9:4; 28:12–24; Ps 92:5; Ecc 8:17**
God's wisdom is superior to human wisdom
Isa 55:9 "As the heavens are higher than the earth, so are my ways higher than your ways and my thoughts than your thoughts." *See also* **Job 21:22**

God's wisdom exhibited
God's wisdom in creation
Jer 10:12 . . . God made the earth by his power; he founded the world by his wisdom and stretched out the heavens by his understanding. *See also* **Job 28:25–27; 37:14–16; Ps 104:24; 136:5; Pr 3:19–20; Isa 40:12–14**
God's wisdom as an agent in creation
Pr 8:22–31 "The LORD brought me forth as the first of his works, before his deeds of old; I was appointed from eternity, from the beginning, before the world began . . ."
God's wisdom in historical events
Isa 31:2 Yet he [the LORD] too is wise and can bring disaster; he does not take back his words. He will rise up against the house of the wicked, against those who help evildoers. *See also* **Job 12:13–25; Da 2:20–22**
God's wisdom in knowing the human mind
1Ch 28:9 ". . . for the LORD searches every heart and understands every motive behind the thoughts . . ." *See also* **Ps 139:2,4,6**

Jesus Christ the wisdom of God
1Co 1:30 . . . Christ Jesus, who has become for us wisdom from God . . . *See also* **Isa 9:6; 11:2; 1Co 1:24; Col 2:2–3**

God's wisdom in the gospel
1Co 1:25 For the foolishness of God is wiser than human wisdom . . . *See also* **1Co 1:18–21; Eph 3:10**

God gives his wisdom to human beings
Eph 1:17 I keep asking that the God of our Lord Jesus Christ, the glorious Father, may give you the Spirit of wisdom and revelation, so that you may know him better. *See also* **2Ch 1:11–12; Ezr 7:25; Pr 2:6; Ecc 12:11; Da 2:23; 1Co 2:6–16; Jas 1:5**

Examples of God's wisdom
1Sa 16:7; 1Ki 3:28; Isa 28:24–29; Lk 11:49

See also God, all-knowing; God, the Creator; Holy Spirit, wisdom; Jesus Christ, wisdom.

God, zeal of
The intense and protective commitment of God to his people and to his purposes which seeks a passionate and obedient response. The zeal of God is often linked with the idea of the "jealousy of God", in which God refuses to contemplate his people giving their allegiance or affection to another.

God in his zeal demands exclusive loyalty from his people
Ex 20:5 ". . . I, the LORD your God, am a jealous God . . ."   *See also* **Ex** 34:14; **Dt** 4:24; 5:9; **Jos** 24:19; **Na** 1:2

God's zeal for the honour of his name
Isa 42:8 "I am the LORD; that is my name! I will not give my glory to another or my praise to idols."   *See also* **Ex** 20:7; **Dt** 32:51; **Isa** 48:9–11; **Eze** 20:9,14,22; 36:20–23; 39:7,25

God's zeal on behalf of his people
Zec 1:14 ". . . 'I [the LORD Almighty] am very jealous for Jerusalem and Zion,' "   *See also* **2Ki** 19:31 pp Isa 37:32; **Joel** 2:18; **Zec** 8:2

God's zeal to establish the Messiah's reign
Isa 9:7 . . . He [the royal son] will reign on David's throne and over his kingdom, establishing and upholding it with justice and righteousness from that time on and for ever. The zeal of the LORD Almighty will accomplish this.

God's zeal is aroused by his people's idolatry
Dt 32:16 They made him [the LORD] jealous with their foreign gods and angered him with their detestable idols.   *See also* **Dt** 29:20; 32:21; **1Ki** 14:22; **Ps** 78:58; **Eze** 8:3,5; 16:38; 23:25; **1Co** 10:21–22

God's zeal in judgment
He judges the nations Eze 36:5–6; 38:18–19; **Zep** 1:18; 3:8

He restrains his zeal in judgment
Eze 16:42 " ' . . . my jealous anger will turn away from you; I will be calm and no longer angry.' "   *See also* **Nu** 25:11

God's people appeal for his zeal to be shown
Isa 63:15 . . . Where are your [the LORD's] zeal and your might? Your tenderness and compassion are withheld from us.   *See also* **Ps** 74:10–11; **Isa** 26:11

God's people reflect his zeal
Nu 25:11–13 "Phinehas son of Eleazar, the son of Aaron, the priest, has turned my anger away from the Israelites; for he was as zealous as I [the LORD] am for my honour among them, so that in my zeal I did not put an end to them . . . he was zealous for the honour of his God and made atonement for the Israelites."
See also **1Ki** 19:10,14; **Pr** 23:17; **Ro** 12:11
See also God, anger of; God, glory of; God, holiness of; God, justice of; Messiah, coming of.

gospel
The good news of God's redemption of sinful humanity through the life, death and resurrection of his Son Jesus Christ.

gospel, basics of
The chief characteristic and fundamental doctrine of the gospel is that Jesus Christ is both Lord and Saviour.

Jesus Christ as Lord
The universal lordship of Jesus Christ
Mt 28:18 Then Jesus came to them and said, "All authority in heaven and on earth has been given to me."   *See also* **Da** 7:13–14; **Lk** 10:22; **Jn** 3:35; 17:2; **Ac** 10:36; **Ro** 14:9; **1Co** 15:27; **Eph** 1:20–22; **Php** 2:9–10; **Col** 1:15–20
Personal implications of the lordship of Jesus Christ
Lk 12:8–9 "I tell you, those who acknowledge me before others, the Son of Man will also acknowledge before the angels of God. But those who disown me before others will be disowned before the angels of God."

Ro 10:9 . . . if you confess with your mouth, "Jesus is Lord," and believe in your heart that God raised him from the dead, you will be saved. *See also* **Mt** 7:21-27 pp Lk 6:46-49; **Jn** 13:13-14

The lordship of Jesus Christ can only be acknowledged through divine inspiration and revelation

1Co 12:3 . . . I tell you that no-one who is speaking by the Spirit of God says, "Jesus be cursed," and no-one can say, "Jesus is Lord," except by the Holy Spirit. *See also* **Jn** 16:13-15; **1Jn** 4:2-3

Jesus Christ as Saviour
Lk 2:11 "Today in the town of David a Saviour has been born to you; he is Christ the Lord." *See also* **Jn** 1:29; 4:42; **Ac** 5:31; **1Ti** 2:5-6; **Tit** 2:11-14; **1Jn** 4:14

Jesus Christ is the promised Messiah

Mt 1:20-23 ". . . and you are to give him the name Jesus, because he will save his people from their sins." All this took place to fulfil what the Lord had said through the prophet: "The virgin will be with child and will give birth to a son, and they will call him Immanuel"—which means, "God with us." *See also* **Isa** 7:14; **Ps** 130:8; **Isa** 53:11; **Ac** 13:23

Jesus Christ did everything that was required to save his people

Jn 19:30 When he had received the drink, Jesus said, "It is finished." With that, he bowed his head and gave up his spirit. *See also* **Mt** 3:15; **Jn** 4:34; 17:4; **1Co** 15:20-22

Salvation comes only through Jesus Christ

Jn 14:6 . . . "I [Jesus] am the way and the truth and the life. No-one comes to the Father except through me." *See also* **Ac** 4:12; 10:43; 16:30-31; **1Ti** 2:5

Jesus Christ will return to judge the world and bring his people to glory

Mt 16:27 "For the Son of Man is going to come in his Father's glory with his angels, and then he will reward everyone according to what they have done." *See also* **Jn** 14:3; **Ac** 1:11; 17:31; **1Th** 4:16-17; **2Ti** 4:1; **Rev** 1:7; 22:7,12,20 *See also* grace; Jesus Christ, second coming; Jesus Christ, the Lord; Jesus, the Christ; law and gospel; salvation; Jesus Christ as Saviour.

gospel, promises

To all who believe and submit to its demands, the promises of the gospel include forgiveness of sins, new life in Jesus Christ and adoption into the family of God.

Forgiveness of sins
The sin of God's people is imputed to God's Son

Jn 1:29 . . . John saw Jesus coming towards him and said, "Look, the Lamb of God, who takes away the sin of the world!" *See also* **Isa** 53:4-6; **Lk** 24:46-47; **Ac** 5:30-32; 13:38; **Tit** 2:13-14; **Heb** 9:28; **1Pe** 2:24

The righteousness of God's Son is imputed to God's people

Ro 1:16-17 . . . For in the gospel a righteousness from God is revealed, a righteousness that is by faith from first to last, just as it is written: "The righteous will live by faith." *See also* **Ro** 3:21-26; 9:30; **Php** 3:7-9

Peace with God
Ro 5:1-2 Therefore, since we [believers] have been justified through faith, we have peace with God through our Lord Jesus Christ, through whom we have gained access by faith into this grace in which we now stand. And we rejoice in the hope of the glory of God. *See also* **Jn** 14:27; **Ro** 8:1-4,31-35

New birth
1Pe 1:23-25 For you have been born again, not of perishable seed, but of imperishable, through the living and enduring word of God . . . *See also* **Jn** 1:12-13; 3:5-8; **Jas** 1:18

Eternal life
Jn 3:14-16 "Just as Moses lifted up the snake in the desert, so the Son of Man must be lifted up, that everyone who believes in him may have eternal life. For God so loved the world that he gave his one and only Son, that whoever believes in him shall not perish but have eternal life."

See also Jn 1:4; 6:68–69; 10:10; 20:31; 1Jn 1:1–2; 5:12

The gift of the Holy Spirit
Ac 2:38 Peter replied, "Repent and be baptised, every one of you, in the name of Jesus Christ for the forgiveness of your sins. And you will receive the gift of the Holy Spirit." *See also* **Joel** 2:28–32; **Jn** 7:37–39; **Ac** 8:14–17; 19:1–7

Adoption into God's family
Ro 8:12–17 . . . For you did not receive a spirit that makes you a slave again to fear, but you received the Spirit of adoption. And by him we cry, "*Abba*, Father." The Spirit himself testifies with our spirit that we are God's children . . . *See also* **Jn** 1:12–13; **Gal** 3:26; 4:4–6; **Eph** 1:5
See also access to God; forgiveness; Holy Spirit, gift of.

gospel, requirements
The gospel demands an obedient response to all that God has done for humanity in Jesus Christ. This includes faith in God, trust in the work of Jesus Christ, the repenting of sin, being baptised, and becoming like Christ through discipleship.

The requirement of faith
Belief in God
Heb 11:6 And without faith it is impossible to please God, because anyone who comes to him must believe that he exists and that he rewards those who earnestly seek him. *See also* **Jn** 10:38; 11:25–27; 14:8–11
Trust in Jesus Christ
Jn 3:14–16 "Just as Moses lifted up the snake in the desert, so the Son of Man must be lifted up, that everyone who believes in him may have eternal life. For God so loved the world that he gave his one and only Son, that whoever believes in him shall not perish but have eternal life." *See also* **Jn** 1:12–13; 3:36; 7:37–39; 20:31; **Ac** 13:38–39; 16:31; **Ro** 3:22

The requirement of repentance
A conscious change of mind and heart
Ac 3:17–20 ". . . Repent, then, and turn to God, so that your sins may be wiped out . . ." *See also* **Ps** 51:17; **Jer** 3:12–13; 6:16; **Lk** 18:13–14; **Ac** 17:30
Turning away from sin
Ac 8:22 "Repent of this wickedness and pray to the Lord. Perhaps he will forgive you [Simon the sorcerer] for having such a thought in your heart." *See also* **2Ch** 7:14; **Ps** 34:14; **Isa** 59:20; **Jer** 25:4–6
Turning towards God
Ac 20:21 "I [Paul] have declared to both Jews and Greeks that they must turn to God in repentance and have faith in our Lord Jesus." *See also* **Dt** 4:29–31; 30:8–10; **Isa** 44:21–22; 55:6–7; **Hos** 14:1–2; **Jas** 4:8–10

The requirement of baptism
Ac 2:38 Peter replied, "Repent and be baptised, every one of you, in the name of Jesus Christ for the forgiveness of your sins . . ." *See also* **Mt** 28:18–20; **Ac** 8:12,36–38; 10:47–48; 19:1–5; 22:16

The requirement of public confession of Jesus Christ
Ro 10:9–10 . . . if you confess with your mouth, "Jesus is Lord," and believe in your heart that God raised him from the dead, you will be saved. For it is with your heart that you believe and are justified, and it is with your mouth that you confess and are saved. *See also* **Mt** 10:32 pp **Lk** 12:8–9

The requirement of discipleship
Willingness to learn from Jesus Christ
Mt 11:28–30 ". . . Take my yoke upon you and learn from me, for I am gentle and humble in heart, and you will find rest for your souls. For my yoke is easy and my burden is light." *See also* **Jn** 13:14–15; **Php** 2:5; **1Pe** 2:21
Willingness to obey Jesus Christ
Jn 14:15 "If you love me [Jesus], you will obey what I command." *See also* **Jn** 14:21,23; 15:10; **1Jn** 2:3–6; 3:21–24; 5:3; **2Jn** 6
Willingness to suffer for the sake of Jesus Christ
Mt 16:24 Then Jesus said to his disciples, "Those who would come after me must deny

gospel, responses

themselves and take up their cross and follow me." pp Mk 8:34 pp Lk 9:23   *See also* **Ac** 14:21–22; **Php** 1:29; **2Ti** 3:10–12; **Jas** 1:2; **1Pe** 3:14; 4:12–19   *See also faith; repentance.*

gospel, responses
The gospel cannot be subscribed to half-heartedly or in part; it must be either accepted or rejected.

The gospel calls for a positive response
Ro 10:5–13 . . . if you confess with your mouth, "Jesus is Lord," and believe in your heart that God raised him from the dead, you will be saved. For it is with your heart that you believe and are justified, and it is with your mouth that you confess and are saved. As the Scripture says, "Anyone who trusts in him will never be put to shame." . . .   *See also* **Ac** 13:38–39; 16:29–32; **Ro** 3:21–26; **Jn** 6:41–52; **1Jn** 5:1,5,10–12

The command to accept the gospel
Mt 11:28 "Come to me [Jesus], all you who are weary and burdened, and I will give you rest."

Ac 17:30 "In the past God overlooked such ignorance, but now he commands all people everywhere to repent."   *See also* **Mt** 6:19–24 pp Lk 11:34–36; **Mt** 7:7–12 pp Lk 11:9–13; **Mt** 7:24–27 pp Lk 6:47–49; **Jn** 4:13–14; 6:35–40; 8:31–32,36; 10:9–10; 11:25–26; 12:44–46

Examples of people who accepted the gospel
Mk 1:16–18 As Jesus walked beside the Sea of Galilee, he saw Simon and his brother Andrew casting a net into the lake, for they were fishermen. "Come, follow me," Jesus said, "and I will make you fishers of men and women." At once they left their nets and followed him. pp Mt 4:18–22   *See also* **Mk** 1:19–20; **Mt** 9:9 pp Mk 2:14 pp Lk 5:27–28; **Ac** 2:41; 11:19–21; 13:46–48; 16:13–15

Rejection of the gospel
Through lack of perception
Jn 12:37–41 Even after Jesus had done all these miraculous signs in their presence, they still would not believe in him . . .   *See also* **Mt** 13:13–15 pp Mk 4:10–12 pp Lk 8:9–10; **Isa** 6:9; **Ro** 11:8; **Eph** 4:17–19

Through worldly distractions
Mt 13:22 "Those who received the seed that fell among the thorns are the people who hear the word, but the worries of this life and the deceitfulness of wealth choke it, making it unfruitful." pp Mk 4:18–19 pp Lk 8:14   *See also* **Mt** 6:24 pp Lk 16:13; **2Ti** 4:10; **Jas** 4:4; **1Jn** 2:15

Through indifference
Mt 12:30 "Whoever is not with me [Jesus] is against me, and whoever does not gather with me scatters." pp Lk 11:23

Through hostility to God
Ro 8:6–8 . . . the sinful mind is hostile to God. It does not submit to God's law, nor can it do so. Those controlled by the sinful nature cannot please God.   *See also* **Jn** 7:13–20; 10:24–33; **Ac** 4:15–18; 5:17–28; 7:51–53; 19:8–9; 21:27–32; **1Th** 2:14–16

Warnings against rejecting the gospel
Heb 2:1–4 . . . how shall we escape if we ignore such a great salvation? . . .   *See also* **Mk** 8:36–38; **Lk** 12:5,16–21; 13:22–30; **Jn** 12:47–50; **Heb** 6:4–6; 10:29–31; 12:25; **2Pe** 2:17–22

Examples of people who rejected the gospel
Mt 19:16–22 . . . Jesus answered, "If you want to be perfect, go, sell your possessions and give to the poor, and you will have treasure in heaven. Then come, follow me." When the young man heard this, he went away sad, because he had great wealth. pp Mk 10:17–22 pp Lk 18:18–23   *See also* **Ac** 5:29–33; 7:51–58; 17:32; 13:44–47; 19:23–28; 24:24–25; 26:24–28

The gospel evokes opposition
Jn 17:14 "I have given them your word and the world has hated them, for they are not of the world any more than I am of the world."
Ac 17:13 When the Jews in Thessalonica learned that Paul was preaching the word of God at Berea, they went there too, agitating the

crowds and stirring them up.   *See also* **Ac** 13:8; **17:5–9**; **1Th** 2:14–16

The gospel evokes persecution
Ac 8:1–3 And Saul was there, giving approval to his [Stephen's] death. On that day a great persecution broke out against the church at Jerusalem, and all except the apostles were scattered throughout Judea and Samaria. Godly men buried Stephen and mourned deeply for him. But Saul began to destroy the church. Going from house to house, he dragged off both men and women and put them in prison.
1Th 3:7 Therefore, brothers and sisters, in all our distress and persecution we were encouraged about you because of your faith.   *See also* **Ac** 13:49–50; **2Th** 1:4   *See also Jesus Christ, responses to.*

grace
The unmerited favour of God, made known through Jesus Christ, and expressed supremely in the redemption and full forgiveness of sinners through faith in Jesus Christ.

grace and Christian life
The Christian life, from its beginning to its end, is totally dependent upon the grace of God.

God's grace compensates for human weaknesses
2Co 12:8–9 Three times I [Paul] pleaded with the Lord to take it away from me. But he said to me, "My grace is sufficient for you, for my power is made perfect in weakness." Therefore I will boast all the more gladly about my weaknesses, so that Christ's power may rest on me.
1Pe 5:10 And the God of all grace, who called you to his eternal glory in Christ, after you have suffered a little while, will himself restore you and make you strong, firm and steadfast.   *See also* **1Co** 2:1–5; **2Co** 9:8; **Heb** 2:14; 4:15; 5:2; **Jas** 4:6; **2Pe** 3:17–18

Believers are to pray for grace
Heb 4:16 Let us then approach the throne of grace with confidence, so that we may receive mercy and find grace to help us in our time of need.   *See also* **Ps** 25:16; **Hos** 14:1–2; **Col** 1:9; 4:12

Christian experience may be summed up in terms of grace
1Co 15:10 . . . by the grace of God I [Paul] am what I am, and his grace to me was not without effect. No, I worked harder than all of them [the other apostles]—yet not I, but the grace of God that was with me.   *See also* **Ac** 18:27; **Ro** 5:2; **Gal** 1:15; **Php** 1:7

Believers should go on to experience more of God's grace
Ac 20:32 "Now I [Paul] commit you [the Ephesian elders] to God and to the word of his grace, which can build you up and give you an inheritance among all those who are sanctified."   *See also* **Ac** 13:43; **Col** 1:3–6; **Heb** 13:9; **1Pe** 5:12; **2Pe** 3:18

Believers are enabled to serve Jesus Christ by his grace
1Pe 4:10 Each of you should use whatever gift you have received to serve others, faithfully administering God's grace in its various forms. *See also* **Ac** 15:39–40; **Ro** 5:17; 12:6; 15:15; **1Co** 3:10; **2Co** 12:9; **Gal** 2:9; **Eph** 3:7–9

God's grace is seen in Christian character, especially in generosity
2Co 8:6–7 . . . we [Paul and Timothy] urged Titus, since he had earlier made a beginning, to bring also to completion this act of grace on your part. But just as you excel in everything—in faith, in speech, in knowledge, in complete earnestness and in your love for us—see that you also excel in this grace of giving.   *See also* **Ac** 4:33; 11:22–23; **2Co** 9:13–14; **Col** 4:6

An ongoing experience of God's grace requires the believer's co-operation
2Co 6:1 As God's co-workers we [Paul and Timothy] urge you not to receive God's grace in vain.   *See also* **Php** 2:12–13; **Heb** 12:15; **1Pe** 5:5; **Jas** 4:6

grace and Holy Spirit

The Holy Spirit is both an expression of God's grace and the means by which it is experienced.

The Holy Spirit is himself a gracious gift of God

Ac 2:38 Peter replied [to the crowd at Pentecost], "Repent and be baptised, every one of you, in the name of Jesus Christ for the forgiveness of your sins. And you will receive the gift of the Holy Spirit."

Ac 6:5–8 . . . Stephen, a man full of faith and of the Holy Spirit . . . a man full of God's grace and power . . .

Tit 3:4–7 . . . when the kindness and love of God our Saviour appeared, he saved us, not because of righteous things we had done, but because of his mercy. He saved us through the washing of rebirth and renewal by the Holy Spirit, whom he poured out on us generously through Jesus Christ our Saviour, so that, having been justified by his grace, we might become heirs having the hope of eternal life.

1Jn 3:24 Those who obey his [God's] commands live in him, and he in them. And this is how we know that he lives in us: We know it by the Spirit he gave us.   *See also* **Jn** 6:63; 20:21–22; **Ac** 5:32; 11:15–17; 15:6–8; **1Co** 2:12; **Gal** 3:14

Through the Holy Spirit God brings believers out of slavery and into his family

Ro 8:15–16 For you did not receive a spirit that makes you a slave again to fear, but you received the Spirit of adoption. And by him we cry, "*Abba*, Father." The Spirit himself testifies with our spirit that we are God's children.
See also **Gal** 4:6–7; **Eph** 2:17–18

Through the Holy Spirit God equips believers to serve him

1Co 12:4–7 There are different kinds of gifts, but the same Spirit. There are different kinds of service, but the same Lord. There are different kinds of working, but the same God works all of them in everyone. Now to each one the manifestation of the Spirit is given for the common good.   *See also* **Jn** 7:37–39; **Ac** 1:8; 2:4; 4:31; **Ro** 5:5; **Gal** 3:5; **Heb** 2:4

The Holy Spirit in God's gracious work of redemption

Ro 8:1–2 . . . there is now no condemnation for those who are in Christ Jesus, because through Christ Jesus the law of the Spirit of life set me [Paul] free from the law of sin and death.
See also **1Co** 2:4–5,13; **1Th** 1:4–5; **1Pe** 1:12

The Holy Spirit in God's gracious work of sanctifying and sustaining his people

2Co 3:17–18 Now the Lord is the Spirit, and where the Spirit of the Lord is, there is freedom. And we, who with unveiled faces all reflect the Lord's glory, are being transformed into his likeness with ever-increasing glory, which comes from the Lord, who is the Spirit.

2Th 2:13 . . . we ought always to thank God for you, brothers and sisters loved by the Lord, because from the beginning God chose you to be saved through the sanctifying work of the Spirit and through belief in the truth.   *See also* **Ac** 9:31; **Ro** 8:26–27; 14:17–18; 15:13; **Gal** 5:4–5,22–23; 6:8; **Eph** 2:22; 3:16–20; **Php** 1:18–19; **2Ti** 1:14; **Heb** 10:29; **Jas** 4:4–6   *See also abiding in Christ; Holy Spirit and regeneration; Holy Spirit and sanctification; Holy Spirit, filling with; Holy Spirit, fruit of.*

grace and Jesus Christ

Grace is demonstrated pre-eminently in Jesus Christ and the work he came to do.

God's promise of grace has been fulfilled in Jesus Christ

Jn 1:14 The Word became flesh and made his dwelling among us. We have seen his glory, the glory of the One and Only, who came from the Father, full of grace and truth.

Jn 1:16–17 From the fulness of his grace we have all received one blessing after another. For the law was given through Moses; grace and truth came through Jesus Christ.

2Ti 1:8–10 . . . God, who has saved us and called us to a holy life—not because of anything we have done but because of his own purpose and grace. This grace was given us in Christ Jesus before the beginning of time, but it has now been revealed through the appearing of our Saviour,

Christ Jesus . . . See also **Jn** 3:16–17; **Ac** 13:38; **Ro** 1:1–5; 5:8,16–17; **Eph** 1:3–8; **Tit** 2:11–14; 3:4–5; **1Pe** 1:3–5

Grace was expressed in Jesus Christ's life and ministry

Mt 9:36 When he [Jesus] saw the crowds, he had compassion on them, because they were harassed and helpless, like sheep without a shepherd. pp **Mk** 6:34

2Co 8:9 For you [Corinthian Christians] know the grace of our Lord Jesus Christ, that though he was rich, yet for your sakes he became poor, so that you through his poverty might become rich. See also **Mt** 9:10–13 pp **Mk** 2:15–17 pp **Lk** 5:27–32; **Mt** 11:4–5; 19:13–15 pp **Mk** 10:13–16 pp **Lk** 18:15–17; **Lk** 2:40; 4:22; 19:9–10; 23:34; **Jn** 10:11; **Ac** 10:37–38; **Heb** 2:9; **1Jn** 3:16

Grace is demonstrated in Jesus Christ's atoning death on the cross

Jn 1:16–17 From the fulness of his [Christ's] grace we have all received one blessing after another. For the law was given through Moses; grace and truth came through Jesus Christ.

Eph 2:4–5 . . . because of his great love for us, God, who is rich in mercy, made us alive with Christ even when we were dead in transgressions—it is by grace you have been saved.

1Pe 2:10 Once you [Gentile believers] were not a people, but now you are the people of God; once you had not received mercy, but now you have received mercy. See also **Jn** 3:16; **Ro** 3:22–24; 5:1–2; 8:32; **1Co** 1:4–6; **2Co** 5:18–19; **Gal** 2:21; **Eph** 4:7; **2Th** 2:16–17; **1Ti** 1:13–14; **1Pe** 1:3–5; **1Jn** 4:10 See also forgiveness; Jesus Christ's ministry; God, purpose of; Jesus Christ, compassion; Jesus Christ, cross of; Jesus Christ, grace and mercy; Jesus Christ, love of.

---

grace and salvation

Deliverance through Jesus Christ is the result of accepting God's undeserved favour.

Salvation is all God's doing

Ro 5:6–8 . . . at just the right time, when we were still powerless, Christ died for the ungodly. Very rarely will anyone die for a righteous person, though for a good person someone might possibly dare to die. But God demonstrates his own love for us in this: While we were still sinners, Christ died for us.

Ro 9:14–16 What then shall we say? Is God unjust? Not at all! For he says to Moses, "I will have mercy on whom I have mercy, and I will have compassion on whom I have compassion." It does not, therefore, depend on human desire or effort, but on God's mercy.

Eph 1:7 In him [Jesus Christ] we have redemption through his blood, the forgiveness of sins, in accordance with the riches of God's grace

1Ti 1:15–16 Here is a trustworthy saying that deserves full acceptance: Christ Jesus came into the world to save sinners—of whom I [Paul] am the worst. But for that very reason I was shown mercy so that in me, the worst of sinners, Christ Jesus might display his unlimited patience as an example for those who would believe on him and receive eternal life. See also **Ex** 33:19; **Ac** 4:12; 20:24; **Ro** 5:15–17; **2Co** 6:2; **Col** 1:13–14; **2Th** 2:16; **Tit** 2:11; **Heb** 7:23–25; **Rev** 7:10

There is nothing human beings can do to save themselves

Tit 3:4–7 . . . when the kindness and love of God our Saviour appeared, he saved us, not because of righteous things we had done, but because of his mercy. He saved us through the washing of rebirth and renewal by the Holy Spirit, whom he poured out on us generously through Jesus Christ our Saviour, so that, having been justified by his grace, we might become heirs having the hope of eternal life. See also **Lk** 18:9–14; **Ro** 11:5–6

Salvation is not by keeping God's law

Gal 5:4 You who are trying to be justified by law have been alienated from Christ; you have fallen away from grace. See also **Ro** 5:20–21; 6:14; 8:1–4; **Gal** 2:21; 3:17–18; **1Ti** 1:9

Salvation must be accepted as a free gift by faith

Eph 2:4–9 . . . because of his great love for

us, God, who is rich in mercy, made us alive with Christ even when we were dead in transgressions—it is by grace you have been saved. And God raised us up with Christ and seated us with him in the heavenly realms in Christ Jesus, in order that in the coming ages he might show the incomparable riches of his grace, expressed in his kindness to us in Christ Jesus. For it is by grace you have been saved, through faith—and this not from yourselves, it is the gift of God—not by works, so that no-one can boast.   See also **Ac** 15:7–11; 16:30–31; **Ro** 3:21–24; 4:14–16; 5:1–2; **Heb** 4:16   See also access to God; faith; Jesus Christ, death of; law; life, spiritual; salvation.

heaven

God's habitation where he is worshipped and served by angels. Solely on account of the sacrifice of Jesus Christ on the cross, believers will inherit a place in heaven and there for ever enjoy perfect fellowship with God in his worship and service.

heaven, community of redeemed

The community of the redeemed in heaven will represent all peoples and languages. They will owe this solely to the sacrifice of Jesus Christ. They will share in the divine life in perfect fellowship with God, free for ever from suffering and death.

Heaven as a divine gift
Ro 6:23 . . . the gift of God is eternal life in Christ Jesus our Lord.   See also **Lk** 12:32; 22:28–30; **Jn** 17:2

Divine preparations made for believers in heaven
Jn 14:2 "In my Father's house are many rooms . . . I [Jesus] am going there to prepare a place for you."   See also **2Co** 5:1; **Heb** 11:16

The redeemed in heaven come from all peoples
Rev 7:9–10 After this I [John] looked and there before me was a great multitude that no-one could count, from every nation, tribe, people and language, standing before the throne and in front of the Lamb . . .   See also **Isa** 59:19; **Mal** 1:11; **Mt** 8:11 pp Lk 13:29; **Rev** 5:9

The redeemed owe their place in heaven solely to Jesus Christ
Rev 7:14 . . . "These are they who have come out of the great tribulation; they have washed their robes and made them white in the blood of the Lamb."   See also **1Pe** 1:18–19; **Rev** 22:14

The redeemed are identified with Jesus Christ
Jesus Christ acknowledges the redeemed as his own
Lk 12:8 "I [Jesus] tell you, those who acknowledge me before others, the Son of Man will also acknowledge before the angels of God."   See also **Mt** 7:21–23
Believers possess the family likeness to Jesus Christ
1Co 15:49 . . . just as we have borne the likeness of the earthly, so shall we bear the likeness of the heavenly.   See also **2Co** 3:18; **Php** 3:21; **1Jn** 3:2
Believers share divine life
2Pe 1:4 Through these he has given us his very great and precious promises, so that through them you may participate in the divine nature . . .   See also **Rev** 2:7; 3:21

Believers on earth at the second coming will be taken up to heaven
Rev 11:12 Then they heard a loud voice from heaven saying to them, "Come up here." And they went up to heaven in a cloud, while their enemies looked on.   See also **Jn** 11:26; **1Th** 4:16–17

Conditions in heaven for the redeemed
Perpetual and perfect fellowship with the Lord
Rev 21:3 And I heard a loud voice from the throne saying, "Now the dwelling of God is with human beings, and he will live with them. They will be his people, and God himself will be with

them and be their God." *See also* **Ps** 17:15; **Mt** 5:8; **Jn** 14:3; **1Th** 4:17; **Rev** 22:4

Joy in the immediate presence of God
Ps 16:11 You have made known to me the path of life; you will fill me with joy in your presence, with eternal pleasures at your right hand. *See also* **Isa** 51:11; **Mt** 25:21; **Lk** 15:7,10; **Jn** 15:11; **1Th** 2:19–20; **Heb** 12:2,22; **Jude** 24

Restfulness
2Th 1:5–7 . . . God is just: He will pay back trouble to those who trouble you and give relief to you who are troubled, and to us as well. This will happen when the Lord Jesus is revealed from heaven . . . *See also* **Heb** 4:3,9; **Rev** 14:13

There will no longer be any need for the marriage relationship
Mt 22:30 "At the resurrection people will neither marry nor be given in marriage; they will be like the angels in heaven." pp **Mk** 12:25 pp **Lk** 20:35–36

Heaven is filled with the light of God's glory
Rev 21:23 The city does not need the sun or the moon to shine on it, for the glory of God gives it light, and the Lamb is its lamp.
See also **Da** 12:3; **Mt** 13:43; **2Co** 4:17; **1Pe** 2:9

Believers will share Jesus Christ's glory
Col 3:4 When Christ, who is your life, appears, then you also will appear with him in glory.
See also **Jn** 17:24; **1Th** 2:12; **1Pe** 5:4,10

Divine glory will banish the memory of earthly troubles
Ro 8:18 I [Paul] consider that our present sufferings are not worth comparing with the glory that will be revealed in us. *See also* **2Co** 4:17; **1Pe** 5:1

There will be no more death or suffering in heaven
Rev 21:4 "He [God] will wipe every tear from their eyes. There will be no more death or mourning or crying or pain, for the old order of things has passed away." *See also* **Isa** 25:8; 35:10; 51:11; **Lk** 20:35–36; **Rev** 7:17

Believers are citizens of the heavenly Jerusalem
Php 3:20 But our citizenship is in heaven. And we eagerly await a Saviour from there, the Lord Jesus Christ, *See also* **Ps** 87:5; **Isa** 35:9–10; 51:11; **Gal** 4:26; **Heb** 11:16; **Rev** 21:2

Their names are enrolled as citizens of heaven
Lk 10:20 "However, do not rejoice that the spirits submit to you, but rejoice that your names are written in heaven." *See also* **Php** 4:3; **Heb** 12:23; **Rev** 3:5; 13:8; 14:1; 17:8; 20:12; 21:27
See also God, glory of; Jesus Christ, glory of; Jesus Christ, second coming.

heaven, inheritance

Heaven is the secure inheritance, of priceless value, awaiting the redeemed. There, faithful service will be rewarded and the redeemed will be given resurrection bodies for service in the heavenly realm.

Believers inherit the kingdom of heaven
Their inheritance is secure
Mt 25:34 "Then the King will say to those on his right, 'Come, you who are blessed by my Father; take your inheritance, the kingdom prepared for you since the creation of the world.'" *See also* **Lk** 12:32; 22:28–29; **Jas** 2:5

The value of their inheritance is beyond human calculation
1Co 2:9–10 However, as it is written: "No eye has seen, no ear has heard, no mind has conceived what God has prepared for those who love him"—but God has revealed it to us by his Spirit . . . *See also* **Ac** 20:32; **Eph** 1:18; 2:6–7

As those adopted into God's family they are heirs of God and Christ
Ro 8:17 Now if we are children, then we are heirs—heirs of God and co-heirs with Christ, if indeed we share in his sufferings in order that we may also share in his glory. *See also* **Gal** 4:7; **Tit** 3:7; **Heb** 6:17

The nature of the heavenly inheritance
It is inviolable
1Pe 1:3–5 . . . an inheritance that can never perish, spoil or fade—kept in heaven for you . . . *See also* **Rev** 21:25,27

It is a response to faith and love
Jas 2:5 . . . Has not God chosen those who

heaven, nature of

are poor in the eyes of the world to be rich in faith and to inherit the kingdom he promised those who love him? See also **Col** 1:12; 3:24; **Heb** 11:7

It is for overcomers
Rev 21:7 "Those who overcome will inherit all this, and I will be their God and they will be my children." See also **1Jn** 4:4; 5:3–5; **Rev** 2:7,11,17,26–28; 3:5,12,21

The heavenly treasure is to be sought
Mt 6:19–21 "Do not store up for yourselves treasures on earth . . . But store up for yourselves treasures in heaven . . . For where your treasure is, there your heart will be also." See also **Mt** 13:44; 19:21; **Lk** 12:33; **2Co** 4:18; **Php** 3:8; **1Ti** 6:18–19; **Rev** 3:18

Heavenly rewards
Service will be rewarded in heaven
1Co 3:11–14 . . . If the building survives, the builder will receive a reward. See also **Mt** 5:12 pp **Lk** 6:23; **Rev** 22:12

The prospect of heavenly rewards should be a spur to present service
Php 3:14 I [Paul] press on towards the goal to win the prize for which God has called me heavenwards in Christ Jesus. See also **Heb** 11:26

Rewards will vary
Mt 16:27 "For the Son of Man is going to come in his Father's glory with his angels, and then he will reward everyone according to what they have done." See also **Da** 12:3; **Mt** 25:20–23 pp **Lk** 19:15–19; **1Co** 3:8; **2Co** 9:6; **Rev** 22:12

Endurance for Jesus Christ's sake will be specially rewarded
Mt 5:10–12 ". . . Rejoice and be glad, because great is your reward in heaven, for in the same way they persecuted the prophets who were before you." pp **Lk** 6:22–23

Rewards for service include crowns signifying position and authority
1Pe 5:4 And when the Chief Shepherd appears, you [faithful elders] will receive the crown of glory that will never fade away. See also **1Th** 2:19; **2Ti** 4:8

The redeemed will share Jesus Christ's position in glory
Eph 2:6 And God raised us up with Christ and seated us with him in the heavenly realms in Christ Jesus, See also **Jn** 14:3; 17:24; **1Jn** 3:2; **Rev** 22:4

The resurrection body as a heavenly inheritance
Php 3:20–21 But our citizenship is in heaven. And we eagerly await a Saviour from there, the Lord Jesus Christ, who . . . will transform our lowly bodies so that they will be like his glorious body. See also **1Co** 15:42–44; **2Co** 5:1–4
See also *kingdom of God.*

heaven, nature of
Scripture refers to heaven as God's habitation but also uses the term as an alternative for God himself.

Heaven as God's habitation
It is the place where he dwells
Dt 26:15 "Look down from heaven, your holy dwelling-place . . ." See also **Ge** 28:17; **2Ch** 6:21; **Ecc** 5:2; **Rev** 13:6

It is insufficient as God's dwelling-place
1Ki 8:27 "But will God really dwell on earth? The heavens, even the highest heaven, cannot contain you . . ." pp **2Ch** 6:18 See also **Ps** 113:5–6

Heaven as the place of God's throne
Ps 11:4 The LORD is in his holy temple; the LORD is on his heavenly throne . . . See also **Ex** 24:9–11; **1Ki** 22:19; **Isa** 6:1; 63:15; **Da** 7:9; **Mt** 5:34; 23:22; **Ac** 7:49; **Isa** 66:1; **Heb** 8:1; **Rev** 4:1–6; 20:11

Heaven as God's vantage point
Ps 33:13 From heaven the LORD looks down and sees all humanity; See also **Ps** 53:2; 102:19–20; **Ecc** 5:2

Heaven as an alternative term for God
Lk 15:18 "'I will set out and go back to my father and say to him: Father, I [the younger

heaven, nature of

son] have sinned against heaven and against you.'" *See also* Mt 8:11; 13:11; 16:19; 18:18; 21:25 pp Mk 11:30 pp Lk 20:4; Jn 3:29; 17:1

Heaven and the sovereignty of God
Heaven is the place of God's rule
Da 4:26 "The command to leave the stump of the tree with its roots means that your kingdom will be restored to you [Nebuchadnezzar] when you acknowledge that Heaven rules." *See also* Ps 45:6; 103:19; Ac 17:24
God's voice from heaven speaks with divine authority
Dt 4:36 From heaven he [the LORD] made you hear his voice to discipline you . . . *See also* Da 4:31; Jn 12:28; 1Th 4:16; 2Pe 1:17–18

Heaven glimpsed by human eyes
At the baptism of Jesus Christ
Mk 1:10 As Jesus was coming up out of the water, he saw heaven being torn open and the Spirit descending on him like a dove. pp Mt 3:16 pp Lk 3:21–22 *See also* Jn 1:32
In visions
Ac 7:56 "Look," he [Stephen] said, "I see heaven open and the Son of Man standing at the right hand of God." *See also* 2Co 12:2–4; Rev 4:1

Prayer addressed to God in heaven
1Ki 8:30 "Hear the supplication of your servant and of your people Israel when they pray towards this place. Hear from heaven, your dwelling-place, and when you hear, forgive." *See also* Dt 26:15; 2Ch 30:27; Ne 1:4; Ps 20:6; Rev 5:8

The association of oaths with heaven
Mt 23:22 "And anyone who swears by heaven swears by God's throne and by the one who sits on it." *See also* Ge 24:3; Da 12:7; Mt 5:34; Jas 5:12

The place of Jesus Christ in heaven
His pre-existence in heaven
Jn 6:38 "For I [Jesus] have come down from heaven not to do my will but to do the will of him who sent me." *See also* Jn 3:13

His ascension into heaven after his resurrection
Lk 24:51 While he [Jesus] was blessing them, he left them and was taken up into heaven. pp Mk 16:19 *See also* Eph 1:20
His place is now with God the Father
Heb 9:24 . . . he [Christ] entered heaven itself, now to appear for us in God's presence. *See also* Col 3:1
His second coming will be from heaven
1Th 4:16 For the Lord himself will come down from heaven, with a loud command, with the voice of the archangel and with the trumpet call of God . . . *See also* Mt 25:31; Ac 1:11; 1Th 1:10

The new heaven
The new heaven completely replaces the old
Rev 21:1 Then I saw a new heaven and a new earth, for the first heaven and the first earth had passed away, and there was no longer any sea. *See also* Isa 65:17; 66:22; 2Pe 3:13
The new Jerusalem is divinely created in heaven
Rev 21:2 I saw the Holy City, the new Jerusalem, coming down out of heaven from God, prepared as a bride beautifully dressed for her husband. *See also* Isa 2:2–5; Heb 11:16; 13:14; Rev 3:12; 21:10
Fulness of life in heaven is wholly sustained by God
Rev 21:22–23 I did not see a temple in the city, because the Lord God Almighty and the Lamb are its temple. The city does not need the sun or the moon to shine on it, for the glory of God gives it light, and the Lamb is its lamp.
Rev 22:1–2 Then the angel showed me the river of the water of life, as clear as crystal, flowing from the throne of God and of the Lamb down the middle of the great street of the city. On each side of the river stood the tree of life, bearing twelve crops of fruit, yielding its fruit every month. And the leaves of the tree are for the healing of the nations. *See also* Isa 55:1; Eze 47:8–9,12; Jn 7:38–39; Rev 2:7 *See also God, sovereignty; God, titles and names of; Jesus Christ, ascension; last things; prayer.*

heaven, worship and service

All in heaven engage continuously in the worship of God, while they perfectly carry out his will.

All heaven worships God
The multitude in heaven and the twenty-four elders
Rev 19:6–7 Then I heard what sounded like a great multitude, like the roar of rushing waters and like loud peals of thunder, shouting: "Hallelujah! For our Lord God Almighty reigns. Let us rejoice and be glad and give him glory! . . ."   See also **Ne** 9:6; **Rev** 4:6–11; 7:11–12; 11:16; 22:8–9
The redeemed
1Pe 2:9 But you are a chosen people, a royal priesthood, a holy nation, a people belonging to God, that you may declare the praises of him who called you out of darkness into his wonderful light.   See also **Isa** 51:11; **Rev** 19:5–7
The angels Lk 2:13–14; Rev 5:11–12; 7:11
God is worshipped in song
Rev 15:2–3 . . . They [victorious believers] held harps given them by God and sang the song of Moses the servant of God and the song of the Lamb: "Great and marvellous are your deeds, Lord God Almighty. Just and true are your ways, King of the ages."   See also **Rev** 14:3
Jesus Christ is worshipped in heaven
Php 2:10–11 that at the name of Jesus every knee should bow, in heaven and on earth and under the earth, and every tongue confess that Jesus Christ is Lord, to the glory of God the Father.   See also **Da** 7:14; **Heb** 1:6; **Rev** 5:8–14

All heaven serves God
God's will is perfectly done in heaven
Mt 6:10 "'. . . your will be done on earth as it is in heaven.'"   See also **Mt** 12:50
The redeemed will serve God
Rev 22:3 . . . The throne of God and of the Lamb will be in the city, and his servants will serve him.   See also **Rev** 5:10; 7:13–15
The redeemed will reign with Jesus Christ and share his authority Mt 19:28; 25:34; 1Co 6:3; 2Ti 2:12; Heb 12:28; Rev 2:26–27; 3:21; 20:6

The divine service of angels
They have divine authority Rev 8:2; 18:1; 20:1
They serve Jesus Christ Mt 25:31; 26:53; Lk 4:10; 22:43; 2Th 1:7–8; Heb 1:6; 1Pe 3:22
They serve believers 1Ki 19:5–8; Mt 24:31; Heb 1:14
They serve by encouraging Ge 21:17; Lk 22:43; Ac 27:23–24
They serve by guarding Ex 14:19; 2Ki 6:15–17; Ps 91:11; Mt 18:10; Rev 7:2–3
They serve by instructing Ge 22:11,15; Zec 6:5; Mt 1:20; 2:13; 28:5–7; Lk 1:13,19; Ac 8:26; 10:3–5
They serve by delivering believers in trouble Da 6:22; Ac 5:19; 12:7
Their service is continuous Ge 28:12; Jn 1:51
See also *God, will of; Jesus Christ, authority; worship, places.*

holiness

The quality of God that sets him utterly apart from his world, especially in terms of his purity and sanctity. The holiness of God is also manifested in the persons and work of Jesus Christ and the Holy Spirit. Believers are called upon to become like God in his holiness.

holiness in behaviour

Behaviour that reflects the holy character of God himself is to be expressed in both social and personal dimensions of life.

Holiness in practice is a reflection of God's own character
1Pe 1:15–16 . . . just as he who called you is holy, so be holy in all you do; for it is written: "Be holy, because I am holy."   See also **Lev** 11:44–45; 19:2; 20:7; **Eph** 4:24; **1Jn** 3:3

Holiness demands a different way of life
Shunning practices that defile
Lev 18:1–3 The LORD said to Moses, "Speak to the Israelites and say to them: 'I am the LORD your God. You must not do as they do in Egypt, where you used to live, and you must not do as

they do in the land of Canaan, where I am bringing you. Do not follow their practices.' "
Eph 5:11–12 Have nothing to do with the fruitless deeds of darkness, but rather expose them . . .
1Ti 5:22 Do not be hasty in the laying on of hands, and do not share in the sins of others. Keep yourself pure.   *See also* **Lev** 18:21–24, 29–30; 20:1–3,6–7,23–26; 21:7; **2Co** 6:17–7:1; **Gal** 5:19–21,24; **Eph** 5:3–7; **Col** 3:5–10

Obedience to God's law
Lev 20:7–8 " 'Consecrate yourselves and be holy, because I am the LORD your God. Keep my decrees and follow them. I am the LORD, who makes you holy.' "   *See also* **Lev** 18:4–5; 19:37; **Dt** 6:25; 28:9; **Ps** 119:9; **Ro** 7:12; **1Pe** 1:22

Holiness is expressed in social behaviour
Care for the disadvantaged
Lev 19:9–10 " 'When you reap the harvest of your land, do not reap to the very edges of your field or gather the gleanings of your harvest. Do not go over your vineyard a second time or pick up the grapes that have fallen. Leave them for the poor and the alien. I am the LORD your God.' "   *See also* **Lev** 19:14,33–34; **1Ti** 5:3–4,8; **Jas** 1:27

A concern for truth and justice
Lev 19:15–16 " 'Do not pervert justice; do not show partiality to the poor or favouritism to the great, but judge your neighbour fairly. Do not go about spreading slander among your people. Do not do anything that endangers your neighbour's life. I am the LORD.' "   *See also* **Lev** 19:11–13, 35–37

Loving one's neighbour
Lev 19:18 " 'Do not seek revenge or bear a grudge against one of your people, but love your neighbour as yourself. I am the LORD.' "
See also **Lev** 19:16–17

Holiness is expressed in family and sexual relations
1Th 4:3–7 It is God's will that you should be sanctified: that you should avoid sexual immorality; that each of you should learn to control your own body in a way that is holy and honourable, not in passionate lust like the heathen, who do not know God; and that in this matter no-one should wrong or take advantage of a brother or sister. The Lord will punish those who commit all such sins, as we have already told you and warned you. For God did not call us to be impure, but to live a holy life.   *See also* **Lev** 18:5–20,22–23; 19:3; 20:9; **Eph** 5:3; **1Co** 6:13–15,18–19

Holiness is seen in personal character
Col 3:12 . . . as God's chosen people, holy and dearly loved, clothe yourselves with compassion, kindness, humility, gentleness and patience.
See also **Eph** 4:23–24,32–5:2; **2Ti** 2:22
See also God, holiness of; Jesus Christ, holiness.

---

holiness, believers' growth in
Believers are enabled to grow in holiness on account of the sacrificial death of Jesus Christ, foreshadowed by the OT sacrificial system, and through the sanctifying work of the Holy Spirit.

Holiness begins with God's initiative
God chooses who and what is to be holy
2Ch 7:16 "I [the LORD] have chosen and consecrated this temple so that my Name may be there for ever. My eyes and my heart will always be there." pp 1Ki 9:3   *See also* **Ex** 20:11; **Nu** 16:7; **2Ch** 29:11; **Zec** 2:12

God chooses and calls his people to holiness
Dt 7:6 For you [Israel] are a people holy to the LORD your God. The LORD your God has chosen you out of all the peoples on the face of the earth to be his people, his treasured possession.
Eph 1:4 For he [God] chose us [Christians] in him [Christ] before the creation of the world to be holy and blameless in his sight . . .
See also **Dt** 14:2; **Ro** 1:7; **Col** 3:12; **1Pe** 1:2,15

Holiness is conferred by the holy God
Holiness is conferred by the presence of God
Ex 29:42–43 "For the generations to come this burnt offering is to be made regularly at the entrance to the Tent of Meeting before the LORD. There I [the LORD] will meet you and speak to

holiness, believers' growth in

you; there also I will meet with the Israelites, and the place will be consecrated by my glory." *See also* Ex 3:4–5; 19:23; **2Ch** 7:1–2

Holiness is conferred through covenant relationship with God
Ex 19:5–6 "'Now if you obey me [the LORD] fully and keep my covenant, then out of all nations you will be my treasured possession. Although the whole earth is mine, you will be for me a kingdom of priests and a holy nation.' . . ." *See also* **Dt** 28:9; **Eze** 37:26–28; **1Pe** 2:9

Holiness is conferred by the sovereign action of God
1Th 5:23 May God himself, the God of peace, sanctify you through and through. May your whole spirit, soul and body be kept blameless at the coming of our Lord Jesus Christ. *See also* **Lev** 20:8; **Isa** 4:3–4; **Eze** 36:25; **Zep** 1:7; **Ac** 15:9; **Heb** 2:11

Holiness through the OT rituals
Cleansing from what is unclean
Nu 8:6–7 "Take the Levites from among the other Israelites and make them ceremonially clean. To purify them, do this: Sprinkle the water of cleansing on them; then make them shave their whole bodies and wash their clothes, and so purify themselves." *See also* **Ex** 19:14; **Nu** 19:9; **Ne** 12:30

Purification and atonement through sacrifice
Nu 8:12–14 "After the Levites lay their hands on the heads of the bulls, use the one for a sin offering to the LORD and the other for a burnt offering, to make atonement for the Levites. Make the Levites stand in front of Aaron and his sons and then present them as a wave offering to the LORD. In this way you are to set the Levites apart from the other Israelites, and the Levites will be mine." *See also* **Ex** 29:35–37; **Lev** 8:14–15; 16:5–10,15–22,29–30

Consecration by anointing
Lev 8:10–12 Then Moses took the anointing oil and anointed the tabernacle and everything in it, and so consecrated them. He sprinkled some of the oil on the altar seven times, anointing the altar and all its utensils and the basin with its stand, to consecrate them. He poured some of the anointing oil on Aaron's head and anointed him to consecrate him. *See also* **Ex** 29:21; 40:9

Holiness through Jesus Christ
Through the sacrifice of Jesus Christ
Heb 10:10 . . . we have been made holy through the sacrifice of the body of Jesus Christ once for all. *See also* **Eph** 5:25–27; **Col** 1:22; **Heb** 1:3; 9:13–14,23–28; 10:14,19–22; 13:12; **1Jn** 1:7; 2:2; 4:10

Through relationship with Jesus Christ
1Co 1:2 To the church of God in Corinth, to those sanctified in Christ Jesus and called to be holy, together with all those everywhere who call on the name of our Lord Jesus Christ—their Lord and ours: *See also* **1Co** 1:30

Holiness through the sanctifying work of the Holy Spirit
2Th 2:13 But we ought always to thank God for you, brothers and sisters loved by the Lord, because from the beginning God chose you to be saved through the sanctifying work of the Spirit and through belief in the truth. *See also* **Jn** 3:5–8; **Ro** 15:16; **1Co** 6:11; **1Th** 4:7–8; **Tit** 3:5; **1Pe** 1:2

The human response to holiness
Repentance
1Jn 1:9 If we confess our sins, he is faithful and just and will forgive us our sins and purify us from all unrighteousness. *See also* **Ezr** 9:1–7; 10:1–4; **Ps** 51:1–10; **Ac** 2:38; **Ro** 6:11–13; **Jas** 4:8

Faith
Gal 5:5 But by faith we eagerly await through the Spirit the righteousness for which we hope. *See also* **Ro** 1:17–18; **2Th** 2:13

Obedience
1Pe 1:22 Now that you have purified yourselves by obeying the truth so that you have sincere mutual affection, love one another deeply, from the heart. *See also* **Ps** 119:9; **Jn** 17:17; **Ro** 6:16–19 *See also access to God; faith; Holy Spirit and sanctification; Holy Spirit, indwelling; Jesus Christ, holiness; repentance.*

holiness, purpose

God in his holiness desires a holy people amongst whom he can dwell, and who can effectively worship, witness to and serve him as they prepare for a future with God and to be like God.

The goal of holiness is to be like God
Lev 19:2 "Speak to the entire assembly of Israel and say to them: 'Be holy because I, the LORD your God, am holy.'"
Mt 5:48 [Jesus said to his disciples] "Be perfect, therefore, as your heavenly Father is perfect." *See also* **Ro** 8:29; **Heb** 12:10; **1Pe** 1:15–16; **1Jn** 3:2–3

God dwells with holy people
God dwelt with the people of Israel
Dt 23:14 . . . the LORD your God moves about in your camp to protect you and to deliver your enemies to you. Your camp must be holy, so that he will not see among you anything indecent and turn away from you. *See also* **Ex** 29:42–46; **Nu** 5:1–3; **1Ki** 9:3; **Eze** 37:26–28; **Zec** 2:10–12
God dwells with Christians
Eph 2:19–22 . . . you are no longer foreigners and aliens, but fellow-citizens with God's people and members of God's household, built on the foundation of the apostles and prophets, with Christ Jesus himself as the chief cornerstone. In him the whole building is joined together and rises to become a holy temple in the Lord. And in him you too are being built together to become a dwelling in which God lives by his Spirit.
See also **1Co** 3:16–17

Holiness is required for acceptable worship
Heb 10:19–22 Therefore, brothers and sisters, since we have confidence to enter the Most Holy Place by the blood of Jesus, by a new and living way opened for us through the curtain, that is, his body, and since we have a great priest over the house of God, let us draw near to God with a sincere heart in full assurance of faith, having our hearts sprinkled to cleanse us from a guilty conscience and having our bodies washed with pure water. *See also* **Lev** 22:17–22; **2Ch** 29:15–31; **Isa** 56:6–7; **Mt** 15:7–9 pp **Mk** 7:6; **Isa** 29:13; **Ro** 12:1

Holiness is needed for effective witness
1Pe 2:9–12 . . . you are a chosen people, a royal priesthood, a holy nation, a people belonging to God, that you may declare the praises of him who called you out of darkness into his wonderful light. Once you were not a people, but now you are the people of God; once you had not received mercy, but now you have received mercy. Dear friends, I urge you, as aliens and strangers in the world, to abstain from sinful desires, which war against your soul. Live such good lives among the pagans that, though they accuse you of doing wrong, they may see your good deeds and glorify God on the day he visits us. *See also* **Eze** 20:41; 36:20; 39:7; **1Pe** 3:1–2

Holiness is needed for godly service
Heb 9:13–14 The blood of goats and bulls and the ashes of a heifer sprinkled on those who are ceremonially unclean sanctify them so that they are outwardly clean. How much more, then, will the blood of Christ, who through the eternal Spirit offered himself unblemished to God, cleanse our consciences from acts that lead to death, so that we may serve the living God! *See also* **Ex** 28:41; **Lev** 21:6–8; **2Ch** 35:3; **Zep** 3:9; **Lk** 1:74–75; **2Ti** 2:20–21; **Tit** 2:14

Holiness leads to a future hope
Holy people will see God
Heb 12:14 Make every effort to live in peace with everyone and to be holy; without holiness no-one will see the Lord. *See also* **Mt** 5:8; **1Th** 3:13; **2Th** 1:10
Holy people will receive eternal life
Ro 6:22 . . . now that you have been set free from sin and have become slaves to God, the benefit you reap leads to holiness, and the result is eternal life. *See also* **2Pe** 3:11
Holy people will inherit the kingdom
Col 1:12 giving thanks to the Father, who has qualified you to share in the inheritance of the saints in the kingdom of light. *See also* **Da**

Holy Spirit

7:18,22,27; **Eph** 1:18; **Rev** 20:6
Holy people will judge the world 1Co 6:2
Believers' ultimate destiny is to share God's holiness for ever
Eph 5:25–27 . . . Christ loved the church and gave himself up for her to make her holy, cleansing her by the washing with water through the word, and to present her to himself as a radiant church, without stain or wrinkle or any other blemish, but holy and blameless.
Rev 21:2–3 I [John] saw the Holy City, the new Jerusalem, coming down out of heaven from God, prepared as a bride beautifully dressed for her husband. And I heard a loud voice from the throne saying, "Now the dwelling of God is with human beings, and he will live with them. They will be his people, and God himself will be with them and be their God." *See also Christlikeness; fellowship with God; heaven; worship.*

Holy Spirit

The co-equal and co-eternal Spirit of the Father and the Son, who inspired Scripture and brings new life to the people of God. The Spirit of God is often portrayed in Scripture in terms of "breath", "life" or "wind", indicating his role in sustaining and bringing life to God's creation.

Holy Spirit and assurance

The Holy Spirit assures believers of their standing in Christ and their eternal salvation.

The Holy Spirit makes an individual a member of Christ
Ro 8:9 You, however, are controlled not by the sinful nature but by the Spirit, if the Spirit of God lives in you. And if anyone does not have the Spirit of Christ, that person does not belong to Christ. *See also* 1Co 2:12; 6:11,17; 1Th 4:8

The Holy Spirit assures believers that they have been born anew
Ro 2:29 . . . a person is a Jew who is one inwardly; and circumcision is circumcision of the heart, by the Spirit, not by the written code. Such a person's praise is not from others, but from God. *See also* Jn 3:5–6; Ro 7:6; 2Co 3:6; Gal 4:29; Tit 3:5–7

The Holy Spirit assures believers that they are God's children
Ro 8:14–16 . . . those who are led by the Spirit of God are children of God. For you did not receive a spirit that makes you a slave again to fear, but you received the Spirit of adoption. And by him we cry, "*Abba*, Father." The Spirit himself testifies with our spirit that we are God's children. *See also* Gal 4:6

The Holy Spirit assures believers that God loves them
Ro 5:5 . . . God has poured out his love into our hearts by the Holy Spirit, whom he has given us.

The Holy Spirit assures believers that Jesus Christ lives in them and they in him
1Jn 4:13 We know that we live in him and he in us, because he has given us of his Spirit. *See also* 1Co 12:13; 1Jn 3:24

The Holy Spirit assures believers that God's power is within them
Gal 3:5 Does God give you his Spirit and work miracles among you because you observe the law, or because you believe what you heard? *See also* 1Co 2:4–5

The fruit of the Spirit is evidence of the believer's standing in Christ
Mt 7:15–20 ". . . A good tree cannot bear bad fruit, and a bad tree cannot bear good fruit. Every tree that does not bear good fruit is cut down and thrown into the fire. Thus, by their fruit you will recognise them." *See also* Ac 13:52; Ro 8:6; 14:17; 2Co 6:6; Gal 5:16–25; 1Th 1:6

The Holy Spirit assures believers of the significance of Jesus Christ
1Co 2:10–12 . . . The Spirit searches all things, even the deep things of God . . . We have not received the spirit of the world but the

Spirit who is from God, that we may understand what God has freely given us. See also **2Co 3:14–17; Eph 3:5**

The Holy Spirit is the first instalment of the believer's inheritance in the kingdom of God
2Co 1:21–22 . . . He [God] anointed us, set his seal of ownership on us, and put his Spirit in our hearts as a deposit, guaranteeing what is to come. See also **Eph 1:13–14; 4:30**

The Holy Spirit assures believers of their final victory in Christ
2Co 5:5 . . . God . . . has given us the Spirit as a deposit, guaranteeing what is to come. See also **Ro 8:11,15–17,23; Eph 1:14** See also *God, love of; Holy Spirit and regeneration; Holy Spirit, anointing; Holy Spirit, Counsellor; Holy Spirit, fruit of; Holy Spirit, indwelling; Holy Spirit, power; Holy Spirit, sealing of; Jesus Christ, victory.*

Holy Spirit and love
Heartfelt concern and steadfast practical care is part of the evidence of the Holy Spirit's presence in the lives of believers.

The Holy Spirit's work and fruit includes the characteristic of love
Gal 5:22 . . . the fruit of the Spirit is love . . . See also **Ac 9:31; Ro 15:30; Col 1:8; 1Th 4:8–10**

The Holy Spirit fills believers with the love of God
Ro 5:5 . . . God has poured out his love into our hearts by the Holy Spirit, whom he has given us. See also **Eze 11:19; Eph 3:16–19**

The Holy Spirit enables believers to live with one another in love
Eph 4:2–3 . . . bearing with one another in love. Make every effort to keep the unity of the Spirit through the bond of peace. See also **2Co 6:6; Gal 5:14–16,25–26; Php 2:1–2**

The gift of the Holy Spirit results in practical love
Ac 4:31–35 . . . And they were all filled with the Holy Spirit and spoke the word of God boldly. All the believers were one in heart and mind. No-one claimed that any of their possessions was their own, but they shared everything they had . . .

Love is essential in the exercise of the gifts of the Holy Spirit
1Co 13:1–13 If I speak in human or angelic tongues, but have not love, I am only a resounding gong or a clanging cymbal. If I have the gift of prophecy and can fathom all mysteries and all knowledge, and if I have a faith that can move mountains, but have not love, I am nothing . . . See also **1Co 14:1,12,26** See also *church, life of; forgiveness; God, love of; Holy Spirit, fruit of; Jesus Christ, love of.*

Holy Spirit and mission
The Holy Spirit directs and empowers believers in their missionary tasks, bearing witness to Jesus Christ and preparing the hearts of men and women to respond to him in faith.

The Holy Spirit equips God's people
He inspired the prophets Ne 9:30; Job 32:8; Isa 48:16; Mic 3:8; Heb 1:1
He empowered Jesus Christ as Messiah Isa 11:2; 42:1; Mt 3:16 pp Mk 1:10 pp Lk 3:21–22 pp Jn 1:32–34; Ac 10:38
He empowered the first Christians Ac 1:8; 2:16–17; 8:17; 10:44; 11:15; 19:6
He empowers God's people today Jn 14:16; Ro 8:26–27; 1Co 12:3–7

The Holy Spirit accomplishes the mission of God
He convicts of sin
Jn 16:8 "When he [the Counsellor] comes, he will convict the world of guilt in regard to sin and righteousness and judgment:" See also **Ac 2:37; 1Co 14:24–25**
He directs mission
Ac 13:2 While they [Christians at Antioch] were worshipping the Lord and fasting, the Holy Spirit

said, "Set apart for me Barnabas and Saul for the work to which I have called them." *See also* **Ac** 8:29; 10:19–20; 13:4; 16:6–10

He inspires witnesses and speakers
Ac 6:9–10 . . . but they [the opposition] could not stand up against his [Stephen's] wisdom or the Spirit by whom he spoke. *See also* **Mt** 10:19–20 pp Mk 13:11 pp Lk 21:14–15; **Ac** 2:14; 4:31; 11:15; 13:9–10; **1Th** 1:5; **1Pe** 1:12

He gives signs and wonders
Ro 15:18–19 I [Paul] will not venture to speak of anything except what Christ has accomplished through me in leading the Gentiles to obey God by what I have said and done—by the power of signs and miracles, through the power of the Spirit. So from Jerusalem all the way around to Illyricum, I have fully proclaimed the gospel of Christ. *See also* **Jn** 1:50; **Ac** 5:13; **2Co** 12:12; **Gal** 3:5; **Heb** 2:4

The Holy Spirit's missionary activity is ongoing
He cares for God's people involved in mission
Jn 16:13,7; Ac 15:28; 1Pe 5:7

He sanctifies God's people Ro 8:10,14; 15:16; 2Th 2:13

He encourages God's people Ro 8:16,27; 2Th 2:17; 1Jn 3:24; 4:13 *See also Holy Spirit and preaching; Holy Spirit, conviction; Holy Spirit, guidance; Holy Spirit, inspiration; Holy Spirit, power; Holy Spirit, witness of; signs, purposes.*

Holy Spirit and peace
The Holy Spirit brings a sense of well-being, contentment and wholeness to believers whatever their outward circumstances. Peace is therefore an indication of the Holy Spirit's presence.

Peace is part of the nature of the Holy Spirit
The Spirit is likened to a dove, the symbol of peace
Mt 3:16 . . . he [Jesus] saw the Spirit of God descending like a dove . . . pp Mk 1:10 pp Lk 3:22 pp Jn 1:32

As part of the Godhead the Spirit is the God of peace Php 4:9; 1Th 5:23; Heb 13:20

Peace is a resource that the Holy Spirit gives to believers
Ro 14:17 For the kingdom of God is . . . righteousness, peace and joy in the Holy Spirit, *See also* **Jn** 14:15–19; **Ro** 15:13

The fruit of the Spirit includes peace
Gal 5:22–25 . . . the fruit of the Spirit is love, joy, peace, patience, kindness, goodness, faithfulness . . . *See also* **Ro** 8:6

The Holy Spirit brings peace to God's people concerning their circumstances
He changes situations to bring peace
Isa 32:14–18 The fortress will be abandoned, the noisy city deserted; citadel and watchtower will become a wasteland for ever, the delight of donkeys, a pasture for flocks, till the Spirit is poured upon us from on high, and the desert becomes a fertile field . . . The fruit of righteousness will be peace; the effect of righteousness will be quietness and confidence for ever . . . *See also* **Isa** 63:14; **Ac** 9:31

He brings peace of mind to those facing difficult situations
Php 1:19 for I know that through your prayers and the help given by the Spirit of Jesus Christ, what has happened to me will turn out for my deliverance. *See also* **Hag** 2:5; **Jn** 16:5–21; 20:21–22

The Holy Spirit brings peaceful relationships
Between believers
Eph 4:3 Make every effort to keep the unity of the Spirit through the bond of peace.

Between believers and God the Father
Ro 8:1–2 . . . there is now no condemnation for those who are in Christ Jesus, because through Christ Jesus the law of the Spirit of life set me [Paul] free from the law of sin and death. *See also* **Ro** 8:11,14–17 *See also God, present everywhere; gospel, promises; Holy Spirit in life of Jesus Christ; Holy Spirit, Counsellor; Holy Spirit, descriptions; Holy Spirit, fruit of; Holy Spirit, presence of.*

Holy Spirit and praise
The Holy Spirit inspires believers to extol, worship and thank God. His aim is to glorify the Father and the Son.

The promise that the Holy Spirit will bring praise
Isa 61:1–3 The Spirit of the Sovereign LORD is on me, because the LORD has anointed me . . . to bestow on them . . . a garment of praise instead of a spirit of despair . . .

The Holy Spirit inspires praise
True praise must be inspired by the Spirit
Jn 4:23–24 ". . . true worshippers will worship the Father in spirit and truth, for they are the kind of worshippers the Father seeks. God is spirit, and his worshippers must worship in spirit and in truth." *See also* **Php** 3:3
The Spirit prompts praise
2Sa 23:1–2 . . . "The Spirit of the LORD spoke through me [David]; his word was on my tongue."
At Jesus Christ's coming: **Lk** 1:67–68; 2:27–28
Lk 10:21

Evidence of the Holy Spirit's work inspires praise
The Spirit's convicting work inspires praise
1Co 14:24–25
The Spirit's converting work inspires praise
Ac 11:15–18 "As I [Peter] began to speak, the Holy Spirit came on them as he had come on us at the beginning. Then I remembered what the Lord had said: 'John baptised with water, but you will be baptised with the Holy Spirit.' So if God gave them the same gift as he gave us, who believed in the Lord Jesus Christ, who was I to think that I could oppose God?" When they heard this, they had no further objections and praised God, saying, "So then, God has granted even the Gentiles repentance unto life." *See also* **2Th** 2:13

The Holy Spirit activates the church's praise
Eph 5:18–20 . . . be filled with the Spirit. Speak to one another with psalms, hymns and spiritual songs. Sing and make music in your heart to the Lord, always giving thanks to God the Father for everything, in the name of our Lord Jesus Christ. *See also* **Ac** 10:44–46; **Col** 3:16–17 *See also church, life of; Holy Spirit and prayer; Holy Spirit in the church; Holy Spirit, inspiration; prayer; worship.*

Holy Spirit and prayer
The Holy Spirit intercedes for God's people and also prompts their petitions, supplications and thanksgivings.

The Holy Spirit enables God's children to address him as "Abba"
Ro 8:15 . . . you received the Spirit of adoption. And by him we cry, "*Abba,* Father." *See also* **Gal** 4:6

The role of the Holy Spirit in prayer
He prompts supplication
Zec 12:10 "And I will pour out on the house of David and the inhabitants of Jerusalem a spirit of grace and supplication . . ."
He inspires prayers of praise
Lk 10:21 . . . Jesus, full of joy through the Holy Spirit, said, "I praise you . . ."
See also **Eph** 5:18–20
He inspires praying in tongues
Ac 2:4 All of them were filled with the Holy Spirit and began to speak in other tongues as the Spirit enabled them. *See also* **Ac** 10:44–46; 19:6; **1Co** 14:14–19
He intercedes for believers
Ro 8:26–27 In the same way, the Spirit helps us in our weakness. We do not know what we ought to pray for, but the Spirit himself intercedes for us with groans that words cannot express. And he who searches our hearts knows the mind of the Spirit, because the Spirit intercedes for the saints in accordance with God's will.

The evidence of the Holy Spirit's work prompts praise and thanks
1Th 1:2–5 We always thank God for all of you, mentioning you in our prayers. We

Holy Spirit and preaching 94

continually remember before our God and Father your work produced by faith, your labour prompted by love, and your endurance inspired by hope in our Lord Jesus Christ . . .   *See also* **Ac** 11:15–18

Believers are exhorted to pray in the Spirit
Eph 6:18–20 . . . pray in the Spirit on all occasions with all kinds of prayers and requests. With this in mind, be alert and always keep on praying for all the saints . . .   *See also* **Jude** 20

The love of the Holy Spirit is a motive for prayer
Ro 15:30–32 I [Paul] urge you, brothers and sisters, by our Lord Jesus Christ and by the love of the Spirit, to join me in my struggle by praying to God for me . . .   *See also* **Lk** 11:13; **Ac** 8:14–17   *See also God, fatherhood; Holy Spirit and praise; Holy Spirit, inspiration; Jesus Christ, prayers of; prayer.*

Holy Spirit and preaching
True Christian preaching is grounded in the word of God and applied by the Holy Spirit to its audience.

The Holy Spirit is identified with the proclaimed word of God
Eph 6:17 Take the helmet of salvation and the sword of the Spirit, which is the word of God.   *See also* **Jn** 6:63

The Holy Spirit sends God's messengers
Ac 13:4–5 The two of them [Paul and Barnabas], sent on their way by the Holy Spirit, went down to Seleucia and sailed from there to Cyprus. When they arrived at Salamis, they proclaimed the word of God in the Jewish synagogues . . .

The Holy Spirit equips, inspires and instructs God's messengers
He inspires the OT prophets
Mic 3:8 But as for me, I [Micah] am filled with power, with the Spirit of the Lord, and with justice and might, to declare to Jacob his transgression, to Israel his sin.   *See also* **Isa** 61:1–2; **Eze** 2:2–5; **2Pe** 1:21

He inspires Jesus Christ's teaching ministry
Lk 4:18–21 "The Spirit of the Lord is on me, because he has anointed me to preach good news to the poor. He has sent me to proclaim freedom for the prisoners and recovery of sight for the blind, to release the oppressed, to proclaim the year of the Lord's favour." Then he [Jesus] rolled up the scroll, gave it back to the attendant and sat down. The eyes of everyone in the synagogue were fastened on him, and he began by saying to them, "Today this scripture is fulfilled in your hearing."   *See also* **Isa** 61:1–2; **Mt** 12:18; **Isa** 42:1; **Jn** 3:34

The apostles preach in the Spirit's power
1Co 2:4–5 My [Paul's] message and my preaching were not with wise and persuasive words, but with a demonstration of the Spirit's power, so that your faith might not rest on human wisdom, but on God's power.   *See also* **Lk** 24:45–49; **Ac** 4:8–12; 6:10; 13:4–5; **1Th** 1:5; **1Pe**1:12

The Holy Spirit teaches and applies the preached word of God to its hearers
Jn 14:26 "But the Counsellor, the Holy Spirit, whom the Father will send in my name, will teach you all things and will remind you of everything I have said to you."   *See also* **Jn** 16:15; **1Co** 2:13   *See also Holy Spirit in life of Jesus Christ; Holy Spirit, anointing; Holy Spirit, inspiration; Holy Spirit, teacher; Holy Spirit, witness of; Jesus Christ, preaching and teaching; Scripture, inspiration and authority; word of God.*

Holy Spirit and regeneration
God's Spirit works to bring the gift of new birth and renewal to those who have been called to faith.

The Holy Spirit's work is promised
Eze 36:26–27 "'I [the Lord] will give you a new heart and put a new spirit in you; I will remove from you your heart of stone and give you a heart of flesh. And I will put my Spirit in you and move you to follow my decrees and be careful to keep my laws.'"   *See also* **Eze** 37:14

Jesus Christ proclaims the Holy Spirit's work
Jn 3:5-8 . . . "I tell you the truth, no-one can enter the kingdom of God without being born of water and the Spirit. Flesh gives birth to flesh, but the Spirit gives birth to spirit. You should not be surprised at my saying, 'You must be born again.' The wind blows wherever it pleases. You hear its sound, but you cannot tell where it comes from or where it is going. So it is with everyone born of the Spirit."

The Holy Spirit's work brings salvation
Tit 3:5-6 . . . He [God] saved us through the washing of rebirth and renewal by the Holy Spirit, whom he poured out on us generously through Jesus Christ our Saviour,   *See also* **Eph** 5:25-27

Regeneration is a creative work of God's Spirit alone
It cannot be achieved by human means
Jn 6:63 "The Spirit gives life; the flesh counts for nothing . . ."   *See also* **Jn** 1:13; 3:6
It cannot be achieved through the works of the law
2Co 3:6 . . . for the letter kills, but the Spirit gives life.   *See also* **Ro** 2:29; 7:6; 8:2; **Gal** 3:2   *See also gospel, promises; Holy Spirit in the world; Holy Spirit, conviction; Holy Spirit, life-giver.*

Holy Spirit and sanctification
The work of the Holy Spirit in enabling believers to lead holy lives, dedicated to the service of God and conformed to his likeness.

The Spirit of holiness is promised
Mt 3:11 "I [John the Baptist] baptise you with water for repentance. But after me will come one who is more powerful than I, whose sandals I am not fit to carry. He will baptise you with the Holy Spirit and with fire."   pp Lk 3:16

Sanctification is a special work of the Holy Spirit
Ro 15:16 . . . so that the Gentiles might become an offering acceptable to God, sanctified by the Holy Spirit.   *See also* **1Co** 6:11; **Gal** 5:5; **1Pe** 1:2

The Holy Spirit requires believers to be sanctified
2Th 2:13 . . . from the beginning God chose you to be saved through the sanctifying work of the Spirit and through belief in the truth.   *See also* **1Co** 6:18-19

The Holy Spirit enables believers to be sanctified
Ro 8:4 in order that the righteous requirements of the law might be fully met in us, who do not live according to the sinful nature but according to the Spirit.   *See also* **Ro** 8:13; **Eph** 5:18

The Holy Spirit produces sanctification
Gal 5:22-23 But the fruit of the Spirit is love, joy, peace, patience, kindness, goodness, faithfulness, gentleness and self-control . . .   *See also* **Ro** 14:17; **2Ti** 1:7

The process of sanctification
The Holy Spirit makes believers more like Jesus Christ
2Co 3:18 And we, who with unveiled faces all reflect the Lord's glory, are being transformed into his likeness with ever-increasing glory, which comes from the Lord, who is the Spirit.
The Holy Spirit helps mortify sinful human nature
Ro 8:13 For if you live according to the sinful nature, you will die; but if by the Spirit you put to death the misdeeds of the body, you will live,   *See also* **Gal** 5:17
The Holy Spirit is opposed to natural desires
Gal 5:16-17 So I say, live by the Spirit, and you will not gratify the desires of the sinful nature . . .   *See also* **Ro** 8:5-9; **Jude** 19

Examples of people sanctified by the Holy Spirit
Joshua: **Nu** 27:18 fn; **Dt** 34:9 fn
Lk 2:25
The deacons in Jerusalem: **Ac** 6:3,5
Ac 11:24; **2Co** 6:6   *See also Christlikeness; God, holiness of; grace and Holy Spirit; holiness, believers' growth in; Holy Spirit, baptism with; Holy Spirit, fruit of; Jesus Christ, holiness; life, spiritual.*

Holy Spirit and Scripture
The Holy Spirit inspired the original writing of all the Scriptures, and illumines their meaning to believers.

The Holy Spirit inspired the writing of Scripture

The Spirit inspired the writers of the OT
2Sa 23:1-2 These are the last words of David: "The oracle of David son of Jesse, the oracle of the man exalted by the Most High, the man anointed by the God of Jacob, Israel's singer of songs: The Spirit of the LORD spoke through me; his word was on my tongue." *See also* **Ne** 9:30; **Eze** 2:2; 11:24-25; **Mic** 3:8; **Zec** 7:12

The NT recognises OT writings as inspired by the Holy Spirit
2Ti 3:16 All Scripture is God-breathed and is useful for teaching, rebuking, correcting and training in righteousness,
2Pe 1:20-21 . . . For prophecy never had its origin in the human will, but prophets, though human, spoke from God as they were carried along by the Holy Spirit. *See also* **Mt** 22:43 pp **Mk** 12:36; **Ac** 1:16; 4:25; 28:25-27; **Heb** 3:7-11; 10:15-17; **1Pe** 1:11

The Spirit inspired the writers of the NT
Eph 3:4-5 In reading this, then, you will be able to understand my [Paul's] insight into the mystery of Christ, which was not made known to people in other generations as it has now been revealed by the Spirit to God's holy apostles and prophets. *See also* **1Co** 7:40; **Rev** 2:7,11,17,29; 3:6,13,22

The Holy Spirit illumines the meaning of Scripture
1Co 2:12-16 We have not received the spirit of the world but the Spirit who is from God, that we may understand what God has freely given us . . . *See also* **Jn** 14:26; 16:13-15; **2Co** 3:14-17; **Heb** 9:8; **1Jn** 2:20,27

The relationship between the word and the Holy Spirit
The association of God's Spirit and breath with his word(s) **Ps** 33:6; **Isa** 59:21; **Jn** 3:34; 6:63; **Eph** 6:17

The Spirit is essential for obeying God's law
Ro 2:29 . . . a person is a Jew who is one inwardly; and circumcision is circumcision of the heart, by the Spirit, not by the written code . . . *See also* **Ro** 7:6; **2Co** 3:6; **Gal** 3:2,5; 5:18

The Spirit enables believers to fulfil the law
Ro 8:4 . . . that the righteous requirements of the law might be fully met in us, who do not live according to the sinful nature but according to the Spirit. *See also* **Gal** 5:4-5 *See also* Holy Spirit and preaching; Holy Spirit and sanctification; Holy Spirit in Old Testament; Holy Spirit, inspiration; Holy Spirit, teacher; law; life, spiritual; revelation; Scripture; word of God.

Holy Spirit in creation
The Holy Spirit was active with the Father and the Word in creation. He is the active power of God present within creation.

The Holy Spirit is involved in creative activity
Ge 1:2 Now the earth was formless and empty, darkness was over the surface of the deep, and the Spirit of God was hovering over the waters. *See also* **Job** 26:13; **Ps** 33:6

The Holy Spirit is the breath of life throughout creation
Ge 2:7 the LORD God formed a man from the dust of the ground and breathed into his nostrils the breath of life, and the man became a living being. *See also* **Job** 12:10; 32:8; 33:4; 34:14-15; **Ps** 104:30

The Holy Spirit is present everywhere in creation
Ps 139:7-8 Where can I go from your Spirit? Where can I flee from your presence? If I go up to the heavens, you are there; if I make my bed in the depths, you are there.

The Holy Spirit controls nature and history
Isa 34:16 Look in the scroll of the LORD and read: None of these will be missing, not one will

lack her mate. For it is his mouth that has given the order, and his Spirit will gather them together.   *See also* Isa 40:7

The Holy Spirit enables creative achievement

Ex 31:1–5 Then the LORD said to Moses, "See I have chosen Bezalel son of Uri, the son of Hur, of the tribe of Judah, and I have filled him with the Spirit of God, with skill, ability and knowledge in all kinds of crafts . . ."   *See also* Ex 35:30–35   *See also God, present everywhere; God, the Creator; Holy Spirit in Old Testament; Holy Spirit, descriptions; Holy Spirit, life-giver; Holy Spirit, presence of; Holy Spirit, sovereignty; Jesus Christ as creator.*

Holy Spirit in life of Jesus Christ

From the moment of his conception Jesus Christ was empowered by the Holy Spirit. Christ's possession of the Holy Spirit was demonstrated publicly at several points in his ministry. After his resurrection the Holy Spirit demonstrated him to be the Son of God.

OT prophecies of the Holy Spirit in Jesus Christ's life

Isa 11:2 The Spirit of the LORD will rest on him—[the Branch] the Spirit of wisdom and of understanding, the Spirit of counsel and of power, the Spirit of knowledge and of the fear of the LORD—   *See also* Ps 45:2; Isa 42:1; 61:1; Zec 12:10

Jesus Christ was conceived by the Holy Spirit

Lk 1:35 The angel answered, "The Holy Spirit will come upon you [Mary], and the power of the Most High will overshadow you. So the holy one to be born will be called the Son of God."   *See also* Mt 1:18,20

The Holy Spirit at Jesus Christ's baptism

Mt 3:16 As soon as Jesus was baptised, he went up out of the water. At that moment heaven was opened, and he saw the Spirit of God descending like a dove and lighting on him.   pp Mk 1:10 pp Lk 3:22 pp Jn 1:32

Jesus Christ lived by the Holy Spirit

Lk 10:21 At that time Jesus, full of joy through the Holy Spirit . . .   *See also* Mt 4:1 pp Mk 1:12 pp Lk 4:1; Lk 1:80; 1Pe 3:18

Jesus Christ's ministry was empowered by the Holy Spirit

Heb 9:14

In preaching

Lk 4:18 "The Spirit of the Lord is on me, because he has anointed me to preach good news to the poor. He has sent me to proclaim freedom for the prisoners and recovery of sight for the blind, to release the oppressed,"   *See also* Isa 61:1; Mt 12:18; Lk 4:14–15,21; Jn 3:34; Ac 1:2

In working miracles

Ac 10:38 how God anointed Jesus of Nazareth with the Holy Spirit and power, and how he went around doing good and healing all who were under the power of the devil, because God was with him.   *See also* Mt 12:15–18,28 pp Lk 11:20; Lk 5:17

Jesus Christ was vindicated by the Holy Spirit

Ro 1:4 . . . who through the Spirit of holiness was declared with power to be the Son of God, by his resurrection from the dead: Jesus Christ our Lord.   *See also* 1Ti 3:16; 1Pe 3:18

Jesus Christ promises the Holy Spirit to his disciples

Lk 11:13 "If you then, though you are evil, know how to give good gifts to your children, how much more will your Father in heaven give the Holy Spirit to those who ask him!"   *See also* Mt 10:20 pp Mk 13:11; Lk 12:12; Jn 7:39; 14:16–17,26; 15:26; 16:13–15

Jesus Christ gives the Holy Spirit to his disciples

Jn 20:22 And with that he [Jesus] breathed on them [the disciples] and said, "Receive the Holy Spirit."   *See also* Ac 2:33   *See also Abba; Holy*

Spirit, anointing; Holy Spirit, baptism with; Holy Spirit, gift of; Holy Spirit, indwelling; Holy Spirit, promise of; Jesus Christ, baptism of; Jesus Christ, birth of; Jesus Christ, miracles; Jesus Christ, power of; Jesus Christ, preaching and teaching; Jesus Christ, resurrection.

Holy Spirit in Old Testament

The OT portrays the Holy Spirit as being active in creation, in equipping individuals for skilled tasks and in inspiring prophecy and revelation.

The Holy Spirit as the presence of God
He is active in creation
Ge 1:2 . . . the Spirit of God was hovering over the waters. *See also* **Job** 33:4; **Ps** 104:30
He is present everywhere
Ps 139:7 Where can I go from your Spirit? Where can I flee from your presence?
His sovereignty
Isa 34:16 Look in the scroll of the LORD and read: None of these will be missing, not one will lack her mate. For it is his mouth that has given the order, and his Spirit will gather them together. *See also* **Eze** 36:27; 37:14
All life is dependent on the Spirit
Job 34:14–15 "If it were his [God's] intention and he withdrew his spirit and breath, all people would perish together and they would return to the dust." *See also* **Ge** 6:3
He is present with God's people
Isa 63:11–14 . . . they were given rest by the Spirit of the LORD. This is how you guided your people to make for yourself a glorious name. *See also* **Ne** 9:20; **Hag** 2:5

The Holy Spirit equips individuals
For leadership
Jdg 3:10 The Spirit of the LORD came upon him [Othniel], so that he became Israel's judge and went to war . . . *See also* **Nu** 11:17, 25–29; **Nu** 27:18fn; **Dt** 34:9fn; **Jdg** 6:34; 11:29; 13:25; **1Sa** 10:6; 11:6; 16:13
In bringing revelation
Ge 41:38–39 So Pharaoh asked them, "Can we find anyone like this man, one in whom is the spirit of God?" Then Pharaoh said to Joseph, "Since God has made all this known to you, there is no-one so discerning and wise as you." *See also* **Da** 4:8–9,18; 5:11,14
By empowering the prophet Eze 2:2; 3:12,14,24; 8:3; 11:24; 43:5
By giving special strength Jdg 14:6,19; 15:14
By guidance Ps 143:10
In planning 1Ch 28:12
In craftsmanship Ex 31:3–5; 35:31–35
In building Zec 4:6

The Holy Spirit inspires
Prophecy
2Ch 24:20 Then the Spirit of God came upon Zechariah son of Jehoiada the priest. He stood before the people and said, "This is what God says: 'Why do you disobey the LORD's commands? . . . *See also* **Nu** 24:2; **1Sa** 10:6,10; 19:20,23; **2Ch** 15:1; 20:14; **Isa** 48:16; **Eze** 11:5; **Mic** 3:8; **2Pe** 1:21
Teaching Ne 9:20,30
Praise 2Sa 23:1–2
A declaration of allegiance 1Ch 12:18

Examples of the awareness of the Holy Spirit's activity
1Ki 18:12; **2Ki** 2:16

Examples of grieving the Holy Spirit
Isa 63:10 Yet they [God's people] rebelled and grieved his Holy Spirit . . . *See also* **Ge** 6:3; **1Sa** 16:14; **Ps** 51:11; 106:33–48; **Isa** 30:1; **Mic** 2:7; **Zec** 7:12

Promises of the Holy Spirit for the future
The Spirit and the Messiah
Isa 11:2 The Spirit of the LORD will rest on him——the Spirit of wisdom and of understanding, the Spirit of counsel and of power, the Spirit of knowledge and of the fear of the LORD——
See also **Isa** 42:1; 61:1
The outpouring of the Spirit
Joel 2:28–29 ". . . I will pour out my Spirit on all people. Your sons and daughters will prophesy, your old men will dream dreams, your young men will see visions. Even on my servants, both men and women, I will pour out my Spirit

in those days." *See also* **Isa** 32:15; 44:3; 59:21; **Eze** 36:27; 37:14; 39:29 *See also* Holy Spirit and praise; Holy Spirit in creation; Holy Spirit, divinity; Holy Spirit, life-giver; Holy Spirit, presence of; Holy Spirit, promise of; Holy Spirit, resisting; Holy Spirit, sovereignty; Holy Spirit, teacher; Jesus Christ, prophecies concerning; revelation, Old Testament.

Holy Spirit in the church
The church depends upon the activity of the Holy Spirit, without which its effective and faithful service is impossible.

The Holy Spirit forms the church
1Co 12:13 For we were all baptised by one Spirit into one body—whether Jews or Greeks, slave or free—and we were all given the one Spirit to drink. *See also* **Ac** 2:1–4,16–18; **Joel** 2:28–29; **Ac** 10:44–48; **Eph** 2:21–22

The Holy Spirit indwells the church
1Co 3:16 Don't you know that you yourselves are God's temple and that God's Spirit lives in you? *See also* **Eze** 10:4; **Jn** 16:14; **1Co** 6:19; **2Co** 6:16; **1Pe** 4:14

The Holy Spirit enables the church to function as the body of Christ
1Co 12:7 Now to each one the manifestation of the Spirit is given for the common good. *See also* **Ex** 31:1–5; **Nu** 11:24–27; **1Sa** 10:5–11; **Ro** 12:5; **1Co** 12:8–11

The Holy Spirit enables Christian unity
Eph 4:3–4; **Php** 2:1

The church worships, serves and speaks by the Holy Spirit
The church worships by the Spirit
Ac 2:11 ". . . Cretans and Arabs—we hear them declaring the wonders of God in our own tongues!" *See also* **Jn** 4:24; **Ac** 10:45–46; **Ro** 8:15; **1Co** 14:26–33; **Php** 3:3
The church serves by the Spirit
Ro 12:6–8 We have different gifts according to the grace given us . . . *See also* **1Co** 12:7–11; **Eph** 4:7–13

The church speaks by the Spirit
Ac 6:10 but they [the opposition] could not stand up against his [Stephen's] wisdom or the Spirit by whom he spoke. *See also* **Ac** 4:8; **1Co** 14:24–25

The Holy Spirit communicates Jesus Christ's message to the church
Rev 2:7 "Those who have ears, let them hear what the Spirit says to the churches . . ." *See also* **Jn** 14:26; 16:13; **Rev** 2:11,17,29; 3:6,13,22

The Holy Spirit and the church's mission
The church fulfils its mission by the Spirit
Ac 1:8 "But you will receive power when the Holy Spirit comes on you; and you will be my witnesses in Jerusalem, and in all Judea and Samaria, and to the ends of the earth." *See also* **Jn** 15:26–27; 20:21–23; **Ac** 4:31; **Gal** 3:3
The Spirit directs the church's missionary enterprise **Ac** 13:2–3; 15:28; 16:6 *See also* church; Holy Spirit and mission; Holy Spirit and preaching; Holy Spirit, anointing; Holy Spirit, baptism with; Holy Spirit, guidance; Holy Spirit, presence of; Holy Spirit, teacher; Scripture; worship.

Holy Spirit in the world
The Holy Spirit, active in the created world, works to show the futility and sinfulness of life without God, and brings a conviction of the presence of God, his righteousness and coming judgment.

The Holy Spirit is active in the created world
In creation itself
Job 33:4 "The Spirit of God has made me; the breath of the Almighty gives me life."
Ps 33:6 By the word of the LORD were the heavens made, their starry host by the breath of his mouth. *See also* **Ge** 1:2; **Job** 26:13; **Ps** 104:30
In ordering the natural world
Isa 34:11–17 . . . his Spirit will gather them together

Holy Spirit, anointing

The Holy Spirit is present everywhere in the world
Ps 139:7 Where can I go from your Spirit? Where can I flee from your presence?

The unbelieving world will not recognise the Holy Spirit
Jn 14:17 "the Spirit of truth. The world cannot accept him, because it neither sees him nor knows him. But you know him, for he lives with you and will be in you."   See also **1Co** 2:14

The Holy Spirit testifies to the truth
Jn 15:26 "When the Counsellor comes, whom I [Jesus] will send to you from the Father, the Spirit of truth who goes out from the Father, he will testify about me."   See also **Ro** 8:16; **1Co** 2:11–14

The Holy Spirit convicts the world
Jn 16:7–11 ". . . When he [the Counsellor] comes, he will convict the world of guilt in regard to sin and righteousness and judgment . . ."   See also **1Co** 14:24–25

The Holy Spirit empowers the church to serve the world in mission
Ac 1:8 "But you will receive power when the Holy Spirit comes on you; and you will be my witnesses in Jerusalem, and in all Judea and Samaria, and to the ends of the earth."
See also **Jn** 15:26–27   See also *God as Spirit; God, present everywhere; Holy Spirit and mission; Holy Spirit in creation; Holy Spirit, conviction.*

Holy Spirit, anointing

"Anoint" means to set someone apart, to authorise and equip him or her for a task of spiritual importance. Jesus Christ is set apart by the work of the Holy Spirit for his ministry of preaching, healing and deliverance. The Holy Spirit sets Christians apart for their ministry in Christ's name.

Jesus Christ anointed by the Holy Spirit
The Messiah's anointing is predicted
Isa 61:1–3 The Spirit of the Sovereign LORD is on me, because the LORD has anointed me to preach good news to the poor . . .
The Spirit anoints Jesus Christ at the start of his ministry
Mt 3:16 . . . he [Jesus] saw the Spirit of God descending like a dove and lighting on him. pp **Mk** 1:10 pp **Lk** 3:22 pp **Jn** 1:32
Ac 10:38 "how God anointed Jesus of Nazareth with the Holy Spirit and power, and how he went around doing good and healing all who were under the power of the devil, because God was with him."
Jesus Christ declares his anointing
Lk 4:18–21 "The Spirit of the Lord is on me, because he has anointed me to preach good news to the poor . . ." and he [Jesus] began by saying to them, "Today this scripture is fulfilled in your hearing."   See also **Isa** 61:1–2
The first Christians declare Jesus Christ's anointing
Ac 4:26–27 "'The kings of the earth take their stand and the rulers gather together against the Lord and against his Anointed One.' Indeed Herod and Pontius Pilate met together with the Gentiles and the people of Israel in this city to conspire against your holy servant Jesus, whom you anointed."
Evidence pointing to the Spirit's anointing in Jesus Christ's ministry Mt 4:23–25; 7:28–29; 12:28; **Lk** 4:14–15; 5:17; 6:19; 7:14–15

Believers anointed by the Holy Spirit
The Spirit anoints God's chosen people 2Sa 23:1–2
Anointing enables Christians to stand firm 2Co 1:21–22
Anointing guards Christians against falsehood
1Jn 2:20,27   See also *Holy Spirit in life of Jesus Christ; Holy Spirit in Old Testament; Holy Spirit, baptism with; Holy Spirit, filling with; Holy Spirit, gift of; Holy Spirit, power; Jesus, the Christ.*

Holy Spirit, baptism with

A divine act, promised by John the Baptist and by Jesus Christ, whereby the Holy Spirit initiates Christians into realised union and communion with the glorified Jesus Christ, thus equipping and enabling them for sanctity and service.

Baptism with the Holy Spirit promised
John the Baptist anticipates baptism with the Spirit
Jn 1:33 ". . . 'The man on whom you see the Spirit come down and remain is the one who will baptise with the Holy Spirit.'" pp Mt 3:11 pp Mk 1:8 pp Lk 3:16

Jesus Christ promises baptism with the Spirit
Ac 1:4–5 ". . . wait for the gift my Father promised, which you have heard me speak about. For John baptised with water, but in a few days you will be baptised with the Holy Spirit." *See also* **Lk** 24:49; **Ac** 1:8

The gift of the Holy Spirit followed Jesus Christ's glorification
Ac 2:33 "Exalted to the right hand of God, he [Jesus] has received from the Father the promised Holy Spirit and has poured out what you now see and hear." *See also* **Jn** 7:39

Instances of baptism with the Holy Spirit
Ac 2:2–4
On subsequent occasions: **Ac** 8:15–17; 10:44–47; 19:6
A work of God recognised by Jewish Christians as experienced by Gentiles: **Ac** 10:46–47; 11:15–17; 15:8

The gift of the Holy Spirit is for all believers at the outset of their Christian lives
Ac 2:38–39 . . . "Repent and be baptised, every one of you, in the name of Jesus Christ for the forgiveness of your sins. And you will receive the gift of the Holy Spirit. The promise is for you and your children and for all who are far off—for all whom the Lord our God will call." *See also* **Ac** 2:16–18; **Joel** 2:28–29; **Gal** 3:2–5

This gift of the Holy Spirit links believers together in the one body of Christ
1Co 12:13 For we were all baptised by one Spirit into one body—whether Jews or Greeks, slave or free—and we were all given the one Spirit to drink. *See also Holy Spirit in life of Jesus Christ; Holy Spirit, anointing; Holy Spirit, filling with; Holy Spirit, gift of; Holy Spirit, promise of.*

Holy Spirit, blasphemy against
The denial of the action of the Holy Spirit in the ministry of Jesus Christ, or the attribution of his works to demonic influence.

Jesus Christ warns against blasphemy
Mk 3:29 . . . whoever blasphemes against the Holy Spirit will never be forgiven but is guilty of an eternal sin." pp Mt 12:31–32 pp Lk 12:10 *See also* **1Jn** 5:16

Blasphemy as erroneously attributing the work of the Holy Spirit to demonic influence
Jesus Christ is accused of being possessed by demons
Mk 3:22 And the teachers of the law who came down from Jerusalem said, "He is possessed by Beelzebub! By the prince of demons he is driving out demons." pp Mt 12:24 pp Lk 11:15 *See also* **Mt** 10:25; **Jn** 7:20; 8:48,52; 10:20

Jesus Christ is accused of casting out demons by demonic power
Mt 9:34 But the Pharisees said, "It is by the prince of demons that he drives out demons." *See also* **Mt** 12:24 pp Mk 3:22 pp Lk 11:15

Jesus Christ refutes these charges Mt 12:25–29 pp Mk 3:23–27 pp Lk 11:17–22

Blasphemy as acting in ways which deny the Holy Spirit's work
Ac 5:3 . . . "Ananias, how is it that Satan has so filled your heart that you have lied to the Holy Spirit and have kept for yourself some of the money you received for the land?" *See also* **Isa** 63:10; **1Th** 5:19; **Heb** 10:26–31 *See also forgiveness; Holy Spirit, resisting; Holy Spirit, witness of; Jesus Christ, victory; sin.*

Holy Spirit, conviction
The Holy Spirit convinces human beings of sin and of the reality of forgiveness through Jesus Christ.

The Holy Spirit convicts the world of sin and its consequences
Jn 16:8–11 "When he [the Counsellor] comes, he will convict the world of guilt in regard to sin and righteousness and judgment: in regard to sin, because people do not believe in me; in regard to righteousness, because I am going to the Father, where you can see me no longer; and in regard to judgment, because the prince of this world now stands condemned."

Ways in which the Holy Spirit brings conviction
Through preaching
Ac 2:37 When the people heard this, they were cut to the heart and said to Peter and the other apostles, "Brothers, what shall we do?" *See also* **Ac** 16:14; **1Th** 1:5
Through the exercise of spiritual gifts
1Co 14:24–25 But if an unbeliever or someone who does not understand comes in while everybody is prophesying, such people will be convinced by all that they are sinners and will be judged by all . . .

The reality of the Holy Spirit's conviction in the lives of believers
He brings illumination
Eph 1:17–18 I [Paul] keep asking that the God of our Lord Jesus Christ, the glorious Father, may give you the Spirit of wisdom and revelation, so that you may know him better. I pray also that the eyes of your heart may be enlightened in order that you may know the hope to which he has called you, the riches of his glorious inheritance in the saints, *See also* **1Co** 2:8–10, 14–16
He gives assurance about their new relationship with God
Ro 8:15–16 . . . The Spirit himself testifies with our spirit that we are God's children. *See also* **Gal** 4:6

He convicts of the need for constant change
Ro 8:5–9 . . . Those controlled by the sinful nature cannot please God. You, however, are controlled not by the sinful nature but by the Spirit, if the Spirit of God lives in you. And if anyone does not have the Spirit of Christ, that person does not belong to Christ. *See also* **Gal** 5:16–23 *See also Holy Spirit and assurance; Holy Spirit and preaching; Holy Spirit and sanctification; Holy Spirit in the world; Holy Spirit, witness of; repentance.*

Holy Spirit, Counsellor
The Holy Spirit is the one who comforts, advises and strengthens. Christians, drawing them closer to Jesus Christ.

The Holy Spirit is Counsellor in addition to Jesus Christ
Jesus Christ is a Counsellor
1Jn 2:1 . . . we [believers] have one who speaks to the Father in our defence—Jesus Christ . . .
The Spirit is another Counsellor
Jn 14:16–17 "And I [Jesus] will ask the Father, and he will give you another Counsellor to be with you for ever—the Spirit of truth . . .
The Counsellor is the gift of the exalted Christ
Jn 16:7 ". . . Unless I [Jesus] go away, the Counsellor will not come to you; but if I go, I will send him to you." *See also* **Jn** 7:38–39; **Ac** 2:33

The Counsellor comforts and reassures believers
Jn 14:16–18; **Ac** 11:12; **Ro** 8:16

The Counsellor strengthens and equips the church
Eph 3:16 I [Paul] pray that out of his glorious riches he may strengthen you with power through his Spirit in your inner being, *See also* **Ac** 4:31; 9:31; **Ro** 8:26

The Counsellor teaches and instructs believers
The Spirit reminds the disciples of Jesus Christ's teaching
Jn 14:26 "But the Counsellor, the Holy Spirit . . . will teach you all things and will

remind you of everything I [Jesus] have said to you." *See also* Jn 16:14; 1Jn 5:6–8

The Spirit teaches the church further truth
Jn 16:13 "But when he, the Spirit of truth, comes, he will guide you into all truth. He will not speak on his own; he will speak only what he hears, and he will tell you what is yet to come." *See also* 1Co 2:9–10; 1Jn 2:27

The Counsellor helps the church in its mission

The Spirit testifies to Jesus Christ and helps the church to do likewise
Jn 15:26–27 "When the Counsellor comes, whom I [Jesus] will send to you from the Father, the Spirit of truth who goes out from the Father, he will testify about me. And you also must testify, for you have been with me from the beginning." *See also* Ac 1:8

The Spirit convicts the unbelieving world Jn 16:8–11; 1Co 14:24–25

Examples of the Spirit's help in witness and mission Ac 4:8; 1Co 2:3–4; 1Th 1:5

The Counsellor draws believers closer to Jesus Christ
Eph 3:16–17 I pray that out of his glorious riches he may strengthen you with power through his Spirit in your inner being, so that Christ may dwell in your hearts through faith . . . *See also* Jn 14:23; Ro 8:9–11 *See also Holy Spirit and assurance; Holy Spirit and mission; Holy Spirit and preaching; Holy Spirit, conviction; Holy Spirit, gift of; Holy Spirit, indwelling; Holy Spirit, presence of; Holy Spirit, teacher; Holy Spirit, witness of.*

Holy Spirit, descriptions

Though himself invisible, the Holy Spirit may appear in symbolic form and his activities may be described metaphorically.

The dove
Mt 3:16 . . . he [Jesus] saw the Spirit of God descending like a dove and lighting on him. pp Mk 1:10 pp Lk 3:22 *See also* Jn 1:32

The wind or breath
Ac 2:2 Suddenly a sound like the blowing of a violent wind came from heaven and filled the whole house where they were sitting.
See also Eze 37:9–14; Jn 3:8; 20:22

The fire
Ac 2:3–4 They saw what seemed to be tongues of fire that separated and came to rest on each of them. All of them were filled with the Holy Spirit and began to speak in other tongues as the Spirit enabled them. *See also* Isa 4:4; Mt 3:11–12 pp Lk 3:16–17; 1Th 5:19

The oil of anointing
Isa 61:1; Ac 10:38

Water
Jn 7:37–39 ". . . Whoever believes in me, as the Scripture has said, will have streams of living water flowing from within." By this he meant the Spirit . . . the Spirit had not been given, since Jesus had not yet been glorified. *See also* Isa 44:3; Jn 4:14; 1Co 12:13

A seal
Eph 1:13 . . . Having believed, you were marked in him with a seal, the promised Holy Spirit, *See also* Eph 4:30

A deposit
2Co 1:21–22; Eph 1:14

A guide or shepherd
Isa 63:14 like cattle that go down to the plain, they were given rest by the Spirit of the LORD. This is how you guided your people to make for yourself a glorious name. *See also* Isa 34:16

A voice
Heb 3:7–11 So, as the Holy Spirit says: "Today, if you hear his voice, do not harden your hearts . . ." *See also* Eze 2:2; Mt 10:19–20 pp Mk 13:11; Jn 16:13

God's gift
Ac 2:38 . . . "Repent and be baptised, every one of you . . . And you will receive the gift of the Holy Spirit." *See also* Ac 1:4; 8:20; 10:45; 11:17

Holy Spirit, divinity

The power of God
Lk 1:35 ... "The Holy Spirit will come upon you [Mary], and the power of the Most High will overshadow you ..."   *See also* **Lk** 5:17; 6:19; 24:49   *See also God, power of; Holy Spirit in life of Jesus Christ; Holy Spirit, anointing; Holy Spirit, sealing of; Holy Spirit, titles and names of.*

Holy Spirit, divinity
The Holy Spirit's attributes and activities are always those of God. The titles used of the Holy Spirit identify him as part of the triune nature of the divine being.

The Holy Spirit possesses the attributes of God

He is present everywhere
Ps 139:7–8 Where can I go from your Spirit? Where can I flee from your presence? If I go up to the heavens, you are there; if I make my bed in the depths, you are there.   *See also* **Jn** 14:17

He knows all things
Isa 40:13 Who has understood the mind of the LORD, or instructed him as his counsellor?   *See also* **Jn** 16:13; **1Co** 2:10–11

He has infinite power
Zec 4:6 "... 'Not by might nor by power, but by my Spirit,' says the LORD Almighty."   *See also* **Lk** 1:35

He is eternal
Heb 9:14 How much more, then, will the blood of Christ, who through the eternal Spirit offered himself unblemished to God ...   *See also* **Jn** 14:16

He is unique
Eph 4:4–6 There is one body and one Spirit ... one Lord, one faith, one baptism; one God and Father of all ...   *See also* **1Co** 12:4

He is holy
Ro 1:4 ... the Spirit of holiness ...
See also **Ro** 5:5; **1Co** 6:19; **2Co** 6:6

The Holy Spirit is the seal of ownership marking those who belong to God: **Eph** 1:13; 4:30

1Th 1:5; **2Ti** 1:14; **Tit** 3:5; **Heb** 2:4; 9:8; **1Pe** 1:12; **2Pe** 1:21; **Jude** 20

The Holy Spirit performs divine works

He creates
Ps 104:30 ... you send your Spirit, they are created ...   *See also* **Ge** 1:2; **Job** 26:13; 33:4; **Ps** 33:6

He gives life
Eze 37:14 "'I will put my Spirit in you and you will live ...'"   *See also* **Ge** 2:7; **Ro** 8:2

The Holy Spirit is identified with the person and activity of the Godhead
Ro 8:11

"Holy Spirit" and "God" are used interchangeably
Ac 5:3–4 "... you [Ananias] have lied to the Holy Spirit and have kept for yourself some of the money you received for the land? ... You have not lied to us men but to God."   *See also* **1Co** 3:16

The Spirit is called "Lord"
2Co 3:17–18 Now the Lord is the Spirit, and where the Spirit of the Lord is, there is freedom ... which comes from the Lord, who is the Spirit.

It is possible to blaspheme the Spirit Mt 12:32; **Mk** 3:29; **Lk** 12:10

The Spirit is sent by the Father and the Son
Jn 15:26 "When the Counsellor comes, whom I [Jesus] will send to you from the Father, the Spirit of truth who goes out from the Father, he will testify about me."   *See also* **Jn** 16:14–15

The Spirit is identified with the Father and the Son Mt 28:19–20; **2Co** 13:14; **Eph** 2:18
In believers' lives: **Gal** 4:6; **1Pe** 1:1–2

The Holy Spirit is given divine titles
The Spirit of God
2Ch 15:1 The Spirit of God came upon Azariah son of Oded.   *See also* **Ex** 31:3; **1Sa** 10:10; **Nu** 24:2; **1Sa** 19:20; **2Ch** 24:20; **Eze** 11:24; **Mt** 3:16; **1Co** 2:11,14; **2Co** 3:3; **Php** 3:3; **1Pe** 4:14

The Spirit of the LORD
Jdg 3:10 The Spirit of the LORD came upon him [Othniel] ...

Isa 61:1 The Spirit of the Sovereign LORD is on me, because the LORD has anointed me to preach good news to the poor ...   *See also* **Jdg** 6:34;

1Sa 16:13–14; 2Sa 23:2; 1Ki 22:24; 2Ki 2:16; 2Ch 18:23; Isa 11:2; 63:14; Eze 11:5; 37:1
The Spirit of the Lord Lk 4:18; 2Co 3:17
The Spirit of Christ
Ro 8:9 . . . And if anyone does not have the Spirit of Christ, that person does not belong to Christ. *See also* **Gal** 4:6; **1Pe** 1:11; **Php** 1:19
The Spirit of Jesus Ac 16:7 *See also God, living; God, unity of; Holy Spirit in creation; Holy Spirit, blasphemy against; Holy Spirit, life-giver; Holy Spirit, power; Holy Spirit, sovereignty; Holy Spirit, titles and names of; Jesus Christ, divinity; Trinity.*

Holy Spirit, filling with

To be filled with the Holy Spirit is to be energised and controlled by the third person of the Godhead in such a way that under the acknowledged lordship of Jesus Christ the full presence and power of God are experienced. Spirit-filling leads to renewal, obedience, boldness in testimony and an arresting quality in believers' lives.

People filled with the Holy Spirit before the ministry of Jesus Christ
In the OT Ex 31:3; Dt 34:9fn
In the events surrounding the birth of John the Baptist Lk 1:15, 41, 67

Jesus Christ is full of the Holy Spirit
Lk 4:1 Jesus, full of the Holy Spirit . . .
See also Lk 10:21; Jn 3:34; Ac 10:38

NT terminology
Ac 1:5 ". . . in a few days you will be baptised with the Holy Spirit."
Ac 2:4 All of them were filled with the Holy Spirit . . .
Ac 10:47 ". . . They [Gentile believers] have received the Holy Spirit just as we have."
"Be filled with the Spirit": an apostolic command
Eph 5:18 . . . be filled with the Spirit.
"Filled with the Spirit": a conscious experience of God's power
Ac 2:4 All of them [the first Christians] were filled with the Holy Spirit . . . *See also* **Ac** 4:31; 9:17

"Full of the Spirit": a consistent quality of Christian character
Ac 6:3–5 ". . . choose seven men from among you who are known to be full of the Spirit and wisdom . . . They chose Stephen, a man full of faith and of the Holy Spirit . . . *See also* **Ac** 11:24; 13:52
"Filled with the Spirit": the inspiration to speak words of witness, challenge or rebuke
Ac 4:8; 7:55; 13:9

Characteristics of the Spirit-filled life
The Spirit of Christ should rule believers' lives
Ro 8:4–6 . . . those who live in accordance with the Spirit have their minds set on what the Spirit desires . . . *See also* **Gal** 5:16,25
The Spirit produces fruit of Christlike character
Ro 15:13; 2Co 6:6; Gal 5:22–23
The Spirit brings liberty
Ro 7:6 But now, by dying to what once bound us, we have been released from the law so that we serve in the new way of the Spirit, and not in the old way of the written code. *See also* 2Co 3:17; Gal 5:1
Being filled with the Spirit often leads to words of praise
Ac 2:4 All of them were filled with the Holy Spirit and began to speak in other tongues as the Spirit enabled them. *See also* **Ac** 4:31; 10:44–46; 19:6; **Eph** 5:18–20

Characteristics linked with the fulness of the Spirit
Skill: **Ex** 31:3; 35:31
Wisdom: **Dt** 34:9 fn; **Ac** 6:3
Joy: **Lk** 10:21; **Ac** 13:52
Faith: **Ac** 6:5; 11:24 *See also Holy Spirit and praise; Holy Spirit, baptism with; Holy Spirit, fruit of; Holy Spirit, gift of; Holy Spirit, indwelling; Holy Spirit, power; Holy Spirit, witness of; life, spiritual.*

Holy Spirit, fruit of

The living presence of the Holy Spirit in believers leads to Christlike virtues within them, just as a living tree will bear good fruit.

God expects his people to bear spiritual fruit
Isa 5:4 "... When I looked for good grapes, why did it yield only bad?" *See also* **Mt 7:12–20**

The fruit of the Spirit leads to believers becoming Christlike
The gift of the Spirit begins this lifelong process
2Co 3:18 And we, who with unveiled faces all reflect the Lord's glory, are being transformed into his likeness with ever-increasing glory, which comes from the Lord, who is the Spirit.

Christlike qualities are contrasted with sinful ones
Gal 5:16–17 ... live by the Spirit, and you will not gratify the desires of the sinful nature. For the sinful nature desires what is contrary to the Spirit, and the Spirit what is contrary to the sinful nature ... *See also* **Ro 8:5–14; 1Co 12:7; Gal 6:8; Eph 5:8–16; Col 3:1–17**

The fruit of Spirit-filled living
Gal 5:22–23 But the fruit of the Spirit is love, joy, peace, patience, kindness, goodness, faithfulness, gentleness and self-control. Against such things there is no law. *See also* **Eph 5:9**

Examples of the fruit of the Spirit
Love Ro 5:5; **1Co** 13:1–13
Joy Php 1:18–19; **1Th** 1:6
Peace Ro 8:6; 14:17
Patience Heb 6:12; **Jas** 5:7–11
Kindness 2Co 6:6; **Col** 3:12; **2Pe** 1:7
Goodness Ro 15:14; **2Pe** 1:5
Faithfulness 1Co 10:13; **3Jn** 3
Gentleness Mt 11:29–30; **1Th** 2:7
Self-control 2Ti 3:3; **2Pe** 1:6

Other evidence of the Holy Spirit's activity
Ro 14:17
Hope: **Ro** 15:13; **Gal** 5:5
Eph 1:17; 5:18

The evidence of the fruit of the Spirit is a result of divine activity, not of human effort
1Co 3:9,16; Gal 2:20 *See also Christlikeness; God, faithfulness; Holy Spirit and love; Holy Spirit and peace; Holy Spirit and sanctification; Holy Spirit, indwelling; Holy Spirit, joy of; Jesus Christ, example of; kingdom of God, qualities.*

Holy Spirit, gift of
In the OT the gift of the Holy Spirit was restricted to individuals for particular tasks, but at Pentecost and on subsequent occasions, the Holy Spirit is given to all believers.

The gift of the Holy Spirit in the OT
The Spirit is given to individuals for specific tasks
Ex 31:2–5; 1Sa 10:6

The gift of the Spirit can be withdrawn
1Sa 16:14 Now the Spirit of the LORD had departed from Saul, and an evil spirit from the LORD tormented him.
Ps 51:11 Do not cast me from your presence or take your Holy Spirit from me. *See also* **Jdg 16:20; 1Ki 22:24**

The gift of the Holy Spirit is foretold
He is promised by John the Baptist **Mt 3:11** pp **Mk** 1:8 pp **Lk** 3:16 pp **Jn** 1:33
He is promised by Jesus Christ **Lk** 24:49; **Jn** 7:37–39; 14:16,26; 15:26; 16:7; **Ac** 1:4–5,8; 11:16

The gift of the Holy Spirit before Pentecost
Individuals filled with the Spirit
Lk 1:15 "... he [John the Baptist] will be great in the sight of the Lord. He is never to take wine or other fermented drink, and he will be filled with the Holy Spirit even from birth." *See also* **Lk** 1:41,67; 2:25–27

Jesus Christ receives the gift of the Spirit
Mt 3:16 As soon as Jesus was baptised, he went up out of the water. At that moment heaven was opened, and he saw the Spirit of God descending like a dove and lighting on him. pp **Mk** 1:10 pp **Lk** 3:22 pp **Jn** 1:32

Jesus Christ bids his disciples receive the Holy Spirit Jn 20:22

The gift of the Holy Spirit at Pentecost and after
At Pentecost
Ac 2:2-4 ... All of them were filled with the Holy Spirit and began to speak in other tongues as the Spirit enabled them.   *See also* **Ac** 2:33
The Spirit was given on later occasions
Ac 10:44 While Peter was still speaking these words, the Holy Spirit came on all who heard the message.   *See also* **Ac** 8:15–17; 9:17; 19:6; **Gal** 3:5; **Heb** 2:4
The gift of the Spirit is for all believers
Ac 2:38-39 "... you will receive the gift of the Holy Spirit. The promise is for you and your children and for all who are far off—for all whom the Lord our God will call."   *See also* **Ac** 2:17; 5:32; 10:45; 11:17; 15:8; **Ro** 8:9; **Gal** 3:14; **1Th** 4:8; **Heb** 2:4
God's willingness to give the Spirit
Lk 11:13 "If you then, though you are evil, know how to give good gifts to your children, how much more will your Father in heaven give the Holy Spirit to those who ask him!"
See also **Jn** 3:34

God's purposes require the gift of the Holy Spirit
To give assurance of acceptance by God
Ac 15:8 "God, who knows the heart, showed that he accepted them by giving the Holy Spirit to them, just as he did to us."   *See also* **Ac** 10:47; 11:17; **1Jn** 3:24; 4:13
To convict the world of sin Jn 16:7–8; **Ac** 2:37
To provide spiritual gifts Ac 2:4; 10:45–46; 19:6; **1Co** 12:4–11
To work miracles, signs and wonders Ro 15:18–19; **Gal** 3:5; **Heb** 2:4
To give boldness in preaching and witnessing
Ac 1:8 "But you will receive power when the Holy Spirit comes on you; and you will be my witnesses ..."   *See also* **Ac** 4:31; 5:32
To cultivate the fruit of the Spirit
Ro 14:17 For the kingdom of God is not a matter of eating and drinking, but of righteousness, peace and joy in the Holy Spirit,
See also **Ro** 5:5; 15:13; **Gal** 5:16
To sanctify the believer 2Th 2:13; **1Pe** 1:2
See also Holy Spirit and assurance; Holy Spirit and mission; Holy Spirit in Old Testament; Holy Spirit, anointing; Holy Spirit, baptism with; Holy Spirit, conviction; Holy Spirit, filling with; Holy Spirit, indwelling; Holy Spirit, presence of; life, spiritual.

Holy Spirit, guidance
The Holy Spirit gives guidance to groups and individuals facing challenges, decisions and difficulties. Such guidance, however given, effectively specifies the will of God in situations of choice within the biblically established guidelines of righteousness.

Knowing divine guidance is associated with the presence of the Holy Spirit
Isa 63:11-14 ... Where is he who set his Holy Spirit among them ... they were given rest by the Spirit of the LORD. This is how you guided your people to make for yourself a glorious name.   *See also* **1Ki** 18:12; **Ps** 139:7–10

The Holy Spirit guides Jesus Christ in his ministry
Lk 4:1 Jesus, full of the Holy Spirit, returned from the Jordan and was led by the Spirit in the desert, pp Mt 4:1 pp Mk 1:12   *See also* **Ac** 10:37–38

The Holy Spirit guides the church in its corporate decisions
Ac 13:2 ... the Holy Spirit said, "Set apart for me Barnabas and Saul for the work to which I have called them."   *See also* **Ac** 15:28

The Holy Spirit's guidance of believers
The Holy Spirit guides individual believers
Ro 8:14 ... because those who are led by the Spirit of God are children of God.   *See also* **Gal** 5:18
He guides through the word of God, spiritually understood and kept before the mind Isa 59:21
He guides in prayer Ro 8:26–27
He guides through spiritual gifts 1Co 12:7–11

He guides in Christian living Ro 8:14; Gal 5:25
He guides in witness and evangelism
Mk 13:11 "Whenever you are arrested and brought to trial, do not worry beforehand about what to say. Just say whatever is given you at the time, for it is not you speaking, but the Holy Spirit." pp Mt 10:19–20 pp Lk 12:11–12
Ac 8:29 The Spirit told Philip, "Go to that chariot and stay near it." *See also* 1Co 2:13
He guides in ministry Ac 16:6–7; 20:22
He guides into a knowledge of truth Jn 16:13 *See also God, will of; Holy Spirit in life of Jesus Christ; Holy Spirit, teacher.*

Holy Spirit, indwelling

The Holy Spirit dwells within Jesus Christ and his disciples. Recognisable results in believers' lives include Christlikeness and the fruit of the Spirit.

The indwelling of the Holy Spirit in the OT
Ge 41:38 So Pharaoh asked them [his officials], "Can we find anyone like this man [Joseph], one in whom is the spirit of God?"
Ex 35:31 ". . . and he [the LORD] has filled him [Bezalel] with the Spirit of God, with skill, ability and knowledge in all kinds of crafts—" *See also* Nu 27:18; 1Sa 10:6–7; Isa 59:21; Hag 2:5

The Holy Spirit indwells Jesus Christ
Isa 11:2; Mt 12:18; Isa 42:1; Lk 4:18; Isa 61:1; Ac 10:38

The indwelling of the Holy Spirit is promised to believers
Jn 14:17 ". . . he [the Spirit] lives with you and will be in you." *See also* Eze 36:27; 37:14

The Holy Spirit indwells believers
2Ti 1:14 . . . the Holy Spirit who lives in us.
Believers are described as the temple of the Holy Spirit: 1Co 3:16; 6:19
Eph 2:22; 1Jn 2:27; 3:24

Results of the Holy Spirit's indwelling in believers
The Holy Spirit guarantees life
Ro 8:11 . . . he [God] who raised Christ from the dead will also give life to your mortal bodies through his Spirit, who lives in you. *See also* Eze 37:14; Jn 7:38–39

The Holy Spirit assures believers that they belong to God
Ro 8:14–16 . . . but you received the Spirit of adoption. And by him we cry, "*Abba*, Father." The Spirit himself testifies with our spirit that we are God's children. *See also* 2Co 1:21–22; Gal 4:6; Eph 1:13–14; 1Jn 4:13
Wisdom and insight are received Ge 41:38; Dt 34:9 fn; Da 4:8–9,18; 5:11,14
Strength is received Eph 3:16
Preaching and public testimony is aided Mt 10:20 pp Mk 13:11 pp Lk 12:12; Ac 4:8–12; 5:29–32
The moral law is obeyed Eze 36:27; Ro 8:4–5,13; Gal 5:16
The fruit of the Spirit is displayed
Gal 5:22–23 . . . the fruit of the Spirit is love, joy, peace, patience, kindness, goodness, faithfulness, gentleness and self-control . . .
See also Ro 5:5; 14:17; 15:13,30

Those without the Holy Spirit's indwelling are not Christlike
Gal 5:17; Jude 18–19 *See also Christlikeness; Holy Spirit in life of Jesus Christ; Holy Spirit, filling with; Holy Spirit, fruit of; Holy Spirit, gift of; Holy Spirit, life-giver; Holy Spirit, presence of; Holy Spirit, sealing of; life, spiritual.*

Holy Spirit, inspiration

The Holy Spirit inspires prophecy and gives knowledge of God, insight and wisdom. Scripture declares itself to have been inspired by God.

The Holy Spirit inspired the writers of Scripture
2Ti 3:16 All Scripture is God-breathed . . .
See also Mt 22:43 pp Mk 12:36; Ac 1:16; 4:25; 28:25; Heb 3:7; 9:8; 10:15

The Holy Spirit inspires believers to honour Jesus Christ
1Co 12:3 . . . no-one who is speaking by the Spirit of God says, "Jesus be cursed," and no-one

can say, "Jesus is Lord," except by the Holy Spirit.   See also 1Jn 4:2

Purposes of the Holy Spirit's inspiration
Eph 1:17 I keep asking that the God of our Lord Jesus Christ, the glorious Father, may give you the Spirit of wisdom and revelation, so that you may know him better.   See also 2Ti 3:16–17

The Holy Spirit inspired prophecy
Nu 24:2–3 When Balaam looked out and saw Israel encamped tribe by tribe, the Spirit of God came upon him and he uttered his oracle: "The oracle of Balaam son of Beor, the oracle of one whose eye sees clearly,"
2Pe 1:21 For prophecy never had its origin in the human will, but prophets, though human, spoke from God as they were carried along by the Holy Spirit.   See also **Nu** 11:25–29; **1Sa** 10:6,10; 19:20,23; **2Sa** 23:2; **1Ch** 12:18; **2Ch** 15:1; 20:14; 24:20; **Ac** 11:28; 19:6; **1Pe** 1:11–12

People aware of the Holy Spirit's inspiration
2Sa 23:2 "The Spirit of the LORD spoke through me [David]; his word was on my tongue."
See also **Isa** 48:16; **Mic** 3:8; **Ac** 15:28
Paul: **1Co** 2:13; 7:40

The Holy Spirit gives revelation
God's purposes revealed
1Co 2:10–13 but God has revealed it to us by his Spirit. The Spirit searches all things, even the deep things of God . . .   See also **Eph** 1:17; 3:3–6; **1Jn** 2:27
The Messiah revealed to Simeon Lk 2:25–27
Visions given
Ac 7:55 But Stephen, full of the Holy Spirit, looked up to heaven and saw the glory of God, and Jesus standing at the right hand of God.
See also **Joel** 2:28; **Ac** 2:17; **Rev** 1:10; 4:2
Visions interpreted Ac 10:19–20
Dreams interpreted Ge 41:38–39; **Da** 4:8–9,18; 5:11,14
David's plans for the temple 1Ch 28:12

Wisdom and knowledge are given
1Co 12:8 To one there is given through the Spirit the message of wisdom, to another the message of knowledge by means of the same Spirit,   See also **Isa** 11:2; **Ac** 6:10; **Eph** 1:17
God's fatherhood revealed to believers Ro 8:15–16; **Gal** 4:6

Speech is inspired by the Holy Spirit
Testifying to God
Mt 10:20 "for it will not be you speaking, but the Spirit of your Father speaking through you."
pp **Mk** 13:11   See also **Lk** 12:12; **Ac** 4:8,31; 13:9
Instruction
Ne 9:20 "You [God] gave your good Spirit to instruct them [the Israelites] . . ."   See also **Ne** 9:30; **Ac** 1:2; **1Ti** 4:1
Speaking in tongues Ac 2:4; 10:44–46; 19:6
Prayer Ro 8:26–27; **Eph** 6:18   See also God, revelation; Holy Spirit and prayer; Holy Spirit and preaching; Holy Spirit in Old Testament; Holy Spirit, teacher; Scripture, inspiration and authority.

Holy Spirit, joy of
The Holy Spirit brings joy to believers, giving them an inner contentment and happiness which is not dependent upon external circumstances.

The Holy Spirit enables the Messiah to bring joy
Isa 61:1–3 The Spirit of the Sovereign LORD is on me, because the LORD has anointed me . . . to comfort all who mourn, and provide for those who grieve in Zion—to bestow on them a crown of beauty instead of ashes, the oil of gladness instead of mourning, and a garment of praise instead of a spirit of despair . . .   See also **Isa** 9:2–3

The Holy Spirit gives joy
To those anticipating Jesus Christ's birth
Lk 1:41–45 When Elizabeth heard Mary's greeting, the baby leaped in her womb, and Elizabeth was filled with the Holy Spirit. In a loud voice she exclaimed . . . "As soon as the sound of your greeting reached my ears, the baby in my womb leaped for joy. Blessed is she who has

believed that what the Lord has said to her will be accomplished!" *See also* **Lk** 1:67–68
To Jesus Christ
Lk 10:21 At that time Jesus, full of joy through the Holy Spirit, said, "I praise you, Father, Lord of heaven and earth . . ." *See also* **Heb** 1:9
To disciples even in the face of opposition
Ac 13:52 . . . the disciples were filled with joy and with the Holy Spirit. *See also* **Ac** 16:25; **1Th** 1:6; **1Pe** 4:13–14

The Holy Spirit's fruit includes joy
Gal 5:22 . . . the fruit of the Spirit is love, joy . . . *See also* **Ro** 14:17; 15:13

Evidence of the Holy Spirit's work prompts believers to rejoice
Ac 11:15–18 ". . . the Holy Spirit came on them as he had come on us at the beginning . . ." When they heard this, they had no further objections and praised God, saying, "So then, God has granted even the Gentiles repentance unto life." *See also* **Ac** 11:23–24
See also God, joy of; Holy Spirit and praise; Holy Spirit in life of Jesus Christ; Holy Spirit, fruit of; Jesus Christ, joy of.

Holy Spirit, life-giver
Through the Holy Spirit, God gives birth to and supports both natural and spiritual life. For this reason, Scripture likens the Holy Spirit to life-giving water.

The creating Spirit (or breath) of God gives and sustains life
Ge 1:2 . . . and the Spirit of God was hovering over the waters. *See also* **Ge** 2:7; **Job** 26:13; 27:3; 32:8 fn; 33:4; 34:14 fn; **Ps** 33:6; 104:30

The Holy Spirit gives new life
Eze 37:1–14 "' . . . I will put my Spirit in you and you will live . . . '" *See also* **Eze** 36:26–28

The Holy Spirit is the life-giver in the conception of Jesus Christ
Mt 1:18 This is how the birth of Jesus Christ came about: His mother Mary was pledged to be married to Joseph, but before they came together, she was found to be with child through the Holy Spirit. *See also* **Mt** 1:20; **Lk** 1:35

The Holy Spirit gives resurrection life to Jesus Christ
1Pe 3:18 . . . He [Christ] was put to death in the body but made alive by the Spirit, *See also* **Ro** 1:4

The Holy Spirit brings new spiritual life
Jn 3:5 ". . . no-one can enter the kingdom of God without being born of water and the Spirit." *See also* **Jn** 3:6,8; 6:63

The Spirit sets believers free from bondage to works that lead to death
Ro 8:2 because through Christ Jesus the law of the Spirit of life set me [Paul] free from the law of sin and death. *See also* **Ro** 8:6,13; **Gal** 6:8

The Holy Spirit is described as life-giving water
Jn 7:37–39 . . . "Let anyone who is thirsty come to me [Jesus] and drink. Whoever believes in me, as the Scripture has said, will have streams of living water flowing from within." By this he meant the Spirit . . . *See also* **Isa** 32:15; 44:3–4; **Eze** 36:25–27; 39:29; 47:1–12; **Zec** 14:8; **Jn** 4:10,14; **Rev** 22:1–2,17 *See also gospel, promises; Holy Spirit and regeneration; Holy Spirit and sanctification; Holy Spirit in creation; Holy Spirit, descriptions; incarnation; life, spiritual.*

Holy Spirit, personality
The Holy Spirit is not an impersonal power but a real person with his own personality.

The Holy Spirit is involved in personal relationships
He is in relationship with the Father and the Son
Mt 28:19 "Therefore go and make disciples of all nations, baptising them in the name of the Father and of the Son and of the Holy Spirit," *See also* **Jn** 16:14–15; **2Co** 13:14; **1Pe** 1:2; **Jude** 20–21

He is in relationship with Christians
Ac 15:28 It seemed good to the Holy Spirit and to us [the apostles and elders in Jerusalem] not to burden you [the Gentile believers] . . .

The Spirit can be treated in personal ways
Ac 5:3 ". . . you have lied to the Holy Spirit . . ." *See also* **Ac** 5:9; **Heb** 10:29

Personal characteristics of the Holy Spirit

The Spirit is wise
Isa 11:2 The Spirit of the LORD will rest on him—the Spirit of wisdom and of understanding, the Spirit of counsel and of power, the Spirit of knowledge and of the fear of the LORD—
Eph 1:17 I keep asking that the God of our Lord Jesus Christ, the glorious Father, may give you the Spirit of wisdom and revelation, so that you may know him better. *See also* **Jn** 14:26; **Ro** 8:27

The Spirit can experience emotion and pain
Eph 4:30 And do not grieve the Holy Spirit of God, with whom you were sealed for the day of redemption. *See also* **Isa** 63:10; **Heb** 10:29

Grammatical indications of the Holy Spirit's personhood
Jn 14:16 "And I [Jesus] will ask the Father, and he will give you another Counsellor to be with you for ever—" *See also* **Jn** 14:26; 15:26; 16:7

Examples of the Holy Spirit's actions
He teaches: **Lk** 12:12; **1Co** 2:13
Ro 8:16, 26; 20:23
He speaks: **2Sa** 23:2; **Ac** 8:29; 10:19; 11:12; 13:2; **Rev** 2:7
Jn 16:13; **1Co** 2:11; **Gal** 4:6

The Holy Spirit's own personality is seen by the gifts he gives and the attitudes he promotes
Gal 5:22–23 . . . the fruit of the Spirit is love, joy, peace, patience, kindness, goodness, faithfulness, gentleness and self-control . . . *See also* **Lk** 10:21; **Ac** 9:31; **Ro** 5:5; 8:6; 14:17; 15:13; **2Co** 13:14; **1Jn** 1:6; 5:6 *See also* Holy Spirit and love; Holy Spirit and peace; Holy Spirit, divinity; Holy Spirit, fruit of; Holy Spirit, guidance; Holy Spirit, joy of; Holy Spirit, resisting; Holy Spirit, teacher; Holy Spirit, titles and names of; Trinity.

Holy Spirit, power

The Holy Spirit equips and empowers believers so that the reign and reality of God is revealed through them in the world.

The power of the Holy Spirit is witnessed to in the OT
Isa 11:2–3 The Spirit of the LORD will rest on him—the Spirit of wisdom and of understanding, the Spirit of counsel and of power, the Spirit of knowledge and of the fear of the LORD—and he will delight in the fear of the LORD. He will not judge by what he sees with his eyes, or decide by what he hears with his ears; *See also* **Isa** 42:1

The Spirit will show his power on the earth
Isa 32:15 till the Spirit is poured upon us from on high, and the desert becomes a fertile field, and the fertile field seems like a forest.

The Spirit's power will enable people to serve God
Eze 36:26–27 "'I will give you a new heart and put a new spirit in you; I will remove from you your heart of stone and give you a heart of flesh. And I will put my Spirit in you and move you to follow my decrees and be careful to keep my laws.'" *See also* **Jer** 31:33

The Spirit's power will prompt prophecy and visions
Joel 2:28–29 "And afterwards, I will pour out my Spirit on all people. Your sons and daughters will prophesy, your old men will dream dreams, your young men will see visions. Even on my servants, both men and women, I will pour out my Spirit in those days." *See also* **Ac** 2:17–18

The Holy Spirit's power is described by OT imagery
Oil: **1Sa** 10:1; 16:13
Isa 63:11–12
The hand of God: **Eze** 3:14; 37:1

The Holy Spirit's power is demonstrated in the OT

In creation Ge 1:2; Job 33:4; Ps 104:30

In acts of judgment and war
Jdg 14:19 ... the Spirit of the LORD came upon him [Samson] in power. He went down to Ashkelon, struck down thirty of their men ... *See also* Jdg 3:10; 6:34; 11:29; 14:6; 15:14; 1Sa 11:6; 16:13

In the lives of his servants
Mic 3:8 ... I am filled with power, with the Spirit of the LORD, and with justice and might, to declare to Jacob his transgression, to Israel his sin. *See also* Nu 11:17; 1Sa 10:6,10

The Holy Spirit's power is seen in the life of Jesus Christ

In his conception
Lk 1:35 The angel answered, "The Holy Spirit will come upon you [Mary], and the power of the Most High will overshadow you. So the holy one to be born will be called the Son of God.

In his teaching and ministry Mt 7:28–29; 12:28; Mk 1:22,27; Lk 4:14; 5:17; Ac 10:38

In his resurrection
Ro 1:4 ... through the Spirit of holiness was declared with power to be the Son of God, by his resurrection from the dead: Jesus Christ our Lord. *See also* Ro 8:11; 1Ti 3:16; 1Pe 3:18

The Holy Spirit's power is seen in the church's mission

In the church's witness and preaching
Ac 1:8 "But you will receive power when the Holy Spirit comes on you; and you will be my witnesses..." *See also* Lk 24:49; Ac 6:10; 16:7; 1Co 2:4; 1Th 1:5

In the apostolic ministry of signs and wonders
Ro 15:18–19 I [Paul] will not venture to speak of anything except what Christ has accomplished through me in leading the Gentiles to obey God by what I have said and done—by the power of signs and miracles, through the power of the Spirit ... *See also* Heb 2:4

In miraculous works in the church
Gal 3:5 Does God give you his Spirit and work miracles among you because you observe the law, or because you believe what you heard? *See also* 1Co 12:28

The Holy Spirit's power builds Christian character

Ro 15:13 May the God of hope fill you with all joy and peace as you trust in him, so that you may overflow with hope by the power of the Holy Spirit. *See also* 2Ti 1:7

The Holy Spirit's power strengthens the church

Eph 3:16 I [Paul] pray that out of his glorious riches he may strengthen you with power through his Spirit in your inner being, *See also* Ro 1:11; 1Co 1:7–8 *See also God, power of; Holy Spirit and preaching; Holy Spirit and sanctification; Holy Spirit in creation; Holy Spirit in life of Jesus Christ; Holy Spirit, baptism with; Holy Spirit, filling with; Jesus Christ, power of; miracles.*

Holy Spirit, presence of

Present throughout the world, the Holy Spirit convicts the world of sin and brings peace and comfort to believers through his refreshing and restoring presence.

The Holy Spirit is present and active in creation

Ge 1:2 ... the Spirit of God was hovering over the waters. *See also* Job 33:4; Ps 104:30

The Holy Spirit is present everywhere

Ps 139:7 Where can I go from your Spirit? ... *See also* Ac 20:23

He is equated with God's presence
Ps 51:11 Do not cast me from your presence or take your Holy Spirit from me.

He is present with God's people
Hag 2:5 "' ... my Spirit remains among you ... '" *See also* Isa 59:21; 63:10–14; Eze 36:27; 37:14; 1Co 3:16; Eph 2:22

He is present in Jesus Christ's ministry Lk 4:14,18; 5:17; 6:19; 10:21; Ac 10:38

He is present with Jesus Christ's disciples
Jn 14:16–17 "And I will ask the Father, and he will give you another Counsellor to be with

you for ever—the Spirit of truth . . . you know him, for he lives with you and will be in you."   See also Jn 14:26; 15:26—27

The consequences of the Holy Spirit's presence in the church
He convicts of sin Jn 16:7–11; 1Th 1:5
He gives direction Ac 13:2; 15:28
He transforms experience
Php 1:19 for I [Paul] know that through your prayers and the help given by the Spirit of Jesus Christ, what has happened to me will turn out for my deliverance.
He encourages
Ac 9:31 Then the church throughout Judea, Galilee and Samaria enjoyed a time of peace. It was strengthened; and encouraged by the Holy Spirit . . .
He empowers Christians for witness Ac 1:8; 6:10
He sanctifies
2Co 3:18 And we, who with unveiled faces all reflect the Lord's glory, are being transformed into his likeness with ever-increasing glory, which comes from the Lord, who is the Spirit.   See also Ro 15:16; 2Th 2:13; 1Pe 1:2

The Holy Spirit's presence has observable effects
2Co 3:3 You show that you are a letter from Christ, the result of our ministry, written not with ink but with the Spirit of the living God, not on tablets of stone but on tablets of human hearts.   See also Jn 3:21; Ac 11:23
He brings blessing and fellowship
2Co 13:14 May the grace of the Lord Jesus Christ, and the love of God, and the fellowship of the Holy Spirit be with you all.   See also Php 2:1; 1Pe 4:14
He brings freedom and peace
2Co 3:17 . . . where the Spirit of the Lord is, there is freedom.   See also Ro 8:2,5–9
He brings life
Ro 8:10–11 But if Christ is in you, your body is dead because of sin, yet your spirit is alive because of righteousness. And if the Spirit of him who raised Jesus from the dead is living in you, he who raised Christ from the dead will also give life to your mortal bodies through his Spirit, who lives in you.   See also God, present everywhere; Holy Spirit and peace; Holy Spirit and sanctification; Holy Spirit in creation; Holy Spirit in life of Jesus Christ; Holy Spirit in the world; Holy Spirit, Counsellor; Holy Spirit, guidance; Holy Spirit, indwelling; Holy Spirit, life-giver.

Holy Spirit, promise of
The OT foretold and Jesus Christ reaffirmed that the Holy Spirit would be poured out on God's people, transforming, empowering and gifting them.

OT promises of the Holy Spirit fulfilled in the OT
The promised Spirit enables prophecy
1Sa 10:6 "The Spirit of the LORD will come upon you in power, and you will prophesy with them; and you will be changed into a different person."   See also 1Sa 10:10
The Spirit fulfils the promised presence of the LORD
Ex 33:14 The LORD replied, "My Presence will go with you, and I will give you rest."   See also Isa 63:11,14; Hag 2:5

OT promises of the Holy Spirit fulfilled in the NT
The Spirit implements the promised new covenant
Jer 31:33–34 "This is the covenant that I will make with the house of Israel after that time," declares the LORD. "I will put my law in their minds and write it on their hearts. I will be their God, and they will be my people . . ."
See also Ro 8:2,9–10; 2Co 3:3,6; Heb 8:10–11
The promised Spirit will renew Israel
Eze 36:26–27 "I will give you a new heart and put a new spirit in you; I will remove from you your heart of stone and give you a heart of flesh. And I will put my Spirit in you and move you to follow my decrees and be careful to keep my laws."   See also Eze 11:19; 37:14
The promised Spirit is the guarantee for Israel's future
Isa 44:3 ". . . I will pour out my Spirit on

your offspring, and my blessing on your descendants." *See also* **Isa** 32:15; 59:21; **Eze** 39:29

The promised Spirit will empower the life and work of the Messiah
Isa 61:1–2 The Spirit of the Sovereign LORD is on me, because the LORD has anointed me to preach good news to the poor . . . *See also* **Isa** 11:2; **Lk** 4:18–19

The Spirit is promised for all people
Joel 2:28–29 "And afterwards, I will pour out my Spirit on all people. Your sons and daughters will prophesy, your old men will dream dreams, your young men will see visions. Even on my servants, both men and women, I will pour out my Spirit in those days." *See also* **Ac** 2:17–18

Promises of the Holy Spirit in the NT
The promise that Jesus Christ would baptise with the Spirit
Mt 3:11 "I [John] baptise you with water for repentance. But after me will come one who is more powerful than I, whose sandals I am not fit to carry. He will baptise you with the Holy Spirit and with fire." pp Mk 1:8 pp Lk 3:16 *See also* **Jn** 1:33; **Ac** 1:5; 11:16

The Spirit is promised by Jesus Christ
Lk 24:49 "I am going to send you what my Father has promised; but stay in the city until you have been clothed with power from on high." *See also* **Jn** 15:26; 16:7–15; **Ac** 1:5–8

The Spirit is promised for the time after Jesus Christ's resurrection and ascension
Jn 7:39 By this he [Jesus] meant the Spirit, whom those who believed in him were later to receive. Up to that time the Spirit had not been given, since Jesus had not yet been glorified. *See also* **Ac** 2:4,33

The promised Spirit fulfils God's word to Abraham
Gal 3:14 He redeemed us in order that the blessing given to Abraham might come to the Gentiles through Christ Jesus, so that by faith we might receive the promise of the Spirit.

The promised Spirit guarantees to believers their future inheritance
Eph 1:13–14 And you also were included in Christ when you heard the word of truth, the gospel of your salvation. Having believed, you were marked in him with a seal, the promised Holy Spirit, who is a deposit guaranteeing our inheritance until the redemption of those who are God's possession—to the praise of his glory. *See also Holy Spirit and regeneration; Holy Spirit and sanctification; Holy Spirit in life of Jesus Christ; Holy Spirit in Old Testament; Holy Spirit, baptism with; Holy Spirit, filling with; Holy Spirit, gift of; Holy Spirit, inspiration; Holy Spirit, life-giver; Holy Spirit, presence of.*

Holy Spirit, resisting
The work of the Holy Spirit can be resisted through disobedience and unbelief.

Scriptural images of resisting the Holy Spirit
Grieving the Spirit
Isa 63:10 Yet they rebelled and grieved his Holy Spirit. So he turned and became their enemy and he himself fought against them.
Eph 4:30 And do not grieve the Holy Spirit of God, with whom you were sealed for the day of redemption.

Resisting the Spirit
Ac 7:51 "You stiff-necked people, with uncircumcised hearts and ears! You are just like your ancestors: You always resist the Holy Spirit!" *See also* **Ge** 6:3; **Ac** 6:9–10

Blaspheming against the Spirit
Mk 3:29 ". . . whoever blasphemes against the Holy Spirit will never be forgiven but is guilty of an eternal sin." pp Mt 12:31 pp Lk 12:10 *See also* **Heb** 10:29

Quenching the Spirit
1Th 5:19 Do not put out the Spirit's fire;

Lying to the Spirit
Ac 5:3 Then Peter said, "Ananias, how is it that Satan has so filled your heart that you have lied to the Holy Spirit and have kept for yourself some of the money you received for the land?"

Testing the Spirit
Ac 5:9 Peter said to her [Sapphira], "How could you agree to test the Spirit of the Lord? Look! The feet of those who buried your husband are at the door, and they will carry you out also."

Ways in which the Holy Spirit is resisted
Through sin
Gal 5:17 For the sinful nature desires what is contrary to the Spirit, and the Spirit what is contrary to the sinful nature. They are in conflict with each other, so that you do not do what you want. *See also* **Eph** 4:30–31
Through rebellion
Ps 106:33 for they rebelled against the Spirit of God, and rash words came from Moses' lips. *See also* **Isa** 63:10
Through hardness of heart
Zec 7:12 "They made their hearts as hard as flint and would not listen to the law or to the words that the LORD Almighty had sent by his Spirit through the earlier prophets. So the LORD Almighty was very angry." *See also* **Ac** 7:51
Through spiritual blindness
1Co 2:14 The person without the Spirit does not accept the things that come from the Spirit of God but considers them foolishness, and cannot understand them, because they are spiritually discerned. *See also Holy Spirit, blasphemy against; Holy Spirit, personality.*

Holy Spirit, sealing of
Based on the practice of sealing letters, documents and property, the Holy Spirit is described as being a seal on the lives of God's people, affirming their Christian character, marking them out as belonging to God and guarding them from the world and the devil.

The Holy Spirit's seal on the life of Jesus Christ
Jn 6:27 ". . . On him [Jesus] God the Father has placed his seal of approval." *See also* **Isa** 42:1; 61:1

The seal of the Holy Spirit in the life of believers
The seal marks God's ownership
2Co 1:21–22 Now it is God who makes both us and you stand firm in Christ. He anointed us, set his seal of ownership on us, and put his Spirit in our hearts . . . *See also* **Rev** 7:3–4; 9:4; 14:1; 22:4

The seal acts as a guarantee of redemption
Eph 1:13–14 . . . Having believed, you were marked in him with a seal, the promised Holy Spirit, who is a deposit guaranteeing our inheritance until the redemption of those who are God's possession . . . *See also* **2Co** 5:5; **Eph** 4:30; **1Pe** 1:5 *See also Holy Spirit in life of Jesus Christ; Holy Spirit, anointing; Holy Spirit, baptism with; Holy Spirit, descriptions; Holy Spirit, gift of; Holy Spirit, titles and names of; Jesus Christ, baptism of; Trinity, relationships in.*

Holy Spirit, sovereignty
The Holy Spirit has supreme power and acts in accordance with divine purposes, exercising authority and control in the world and over God's people.

The Holy Spirit is Lord
2Co 3:17–18 Now the Lord is the Spirit, and where the Spirit of the Lord is, there is freedom. And we, who with unveiled faces all reflect the Lord's glory, are being transformed into his likeness with ever-increasing glory, which comes from the Lord, who is the Spirit. *See also* **Jdg** 3:10

The Holy Spirit is sovereign in bringing spiritual life
Jn 3:1–8 ". . . The wind blows wherever it pleases. You hear its sound, but you cannot tell where it comes from or where it is going. So it is with everyone born of the Spirit." *See also* **Eze** 37:14; **Jn** 6:63; **Ro** 8:2; **Tit** 3:5; **1Pe** 1:2

The Holy Spirit's will is sovereign
He determines the distribution of spiritual gifts
1Co 12:11 All these [spiritual gifts] are the work of one and the same Spirit, and he gives them to each one, just as he determines. *See also* **1Sa** 10:6,10; 19:20,23; **Heb** 2:4
He controls the appointment of leaders
Ac 13:2 While they were worshipping the Lord and fasting, the Holy Spirit said, "Set apart for me Barnabas and Saul for the work to which I have called them." *See also* **Ac** 20:28

The Holy Spirit demonstrates his sovereignty over creation

He participates in the work of creation
Job 33:4 "The Spirit of God has made me; the breath of the Almighty gives me life." *See also* **Ge** 1:2; **Ps** 104:30

He performs miraculous deeds
Ac 8:39 . . . the Spirit of the Lord suddenly took Philip away, and the eunuch did not see him again . . . *See also* **1Ki** 18:12; **2Ki** 2:16; **Mt** 12:28–38 pp Mk 3:22–30 pp Lk 11:14–23

The Holy Spirit exercises his rule in the lives of individuals

Jesus Christ is led by the Spirit
Mt 4:1 Then Jesus was led by the Spirit into the desert to be tempted by the devil. pp Mk 1:12 pp Lk 4:1

God's people are led by the Spirit
Gal 5:18 But if you are led by the Spirit, you are not under law. *See also* **1Ch** 28:12; **Ps** 143:10; **Mt** 10:20; **Lk** 2:27; **Jn** 16:13; **Ac** 8:29; 20:22

God's people are restrained by the Spirit
Ac 16:6–7 Paul and his companions travelled throughout the region of Phrygia and Galatia, having been kept by the Holy Spirit from preaching the word in the province of Asia. When they came to the border of Mysia, they tried to enter Bithynia, but the Spirit of Jesus would not allow them to.

God's people are given victory by the Spirit
Jdg 3:10 The Spirit of the LORD came upon him [Othniel], so that he became Israel's judge and went to war. The LORD gave Cushan-Rishathaim king of Aram into the hands of Othniel, who overpowered him. *See also* **Jdg** 14:6,19; 15:14

The Holy Spirit's sovereignty is confirmed by the greatness of his attributes

Ps 139:7; **1Co** 2:4; 10–11 *See also God, all-knowing; God, present everywhere; God, sovereignty; Holy Spirit and regeneration; Holy Spirit in creation; Holy Spirit, divinity; Holy Spirit, filling with; Holy Spirit, guidance; Holy Spirit, life-giver; Holy Spirit, power.*

Holy Spirit, teacher

Having instructed God's people in the OT and Jesus Christ's disciples in the NT, the Spirit of truth continues to reveal the truth of God to believers.

The Holy Spirit as teacher in the OT

The Spirit teaches on practical matters
1Ch 28:12–13 He [David] gave him [Solomon] the plans of all that the Spirit had put in his mind . . . *See also* **Ex** 31:2–6 pp Ex 35:30–35; **1Ch** 28:19

The Spirit teaches the ways of God
Ps 143:10 Teach me to do your will, for you are my God; may your good Spirit lead me on level ground. *See also* **Ne** 9:20,30; **Isa** 48:16–17

The Spirit teaches about the salvation which is to come in Jesus Christ
1Pe 1:10–11 Concerning this salvation, the prophets, who spoke of the grace that was to come to you, searched intently and with the greatest care, trying to find out the time and circumstances to which the Spirit of Christ in them was pointing when he predicted the sufferings of Christ and the glories that would follow. *See also* **Heb** 9:8; 10:15–17

The Holy Spirit empowers Jesus Christ's teaching

Lk 4:14–15 Jesus returned to Galilee in the power of the Spirit . . . He taught in their synagogues, and everyone praised him. *See also* **Jn** 3:34; **Ac** 1:2

The Holy Spirit teaches Jesus Christ's disciples

The Spirit will teach the disciples what to say when persecuted
Mt 10:19–20 "But when they arrest you, do not worry about what to say or how to say it. At that time you will be given what to say, for it will not be you speaking, but the Spirit of your Father speaking through you." pp Mk 13:11 pp Lk 12:11–12 *See also* **Ac** 4:8; 6:10

Jesus Christ promises the Spirit's teaching ministry
Jn 14:26 "But the Counsellor, the Holy Spirit, whom the Father will send in my name, will teach you all things..." *See also* **Jn** 14:16; 16:13–15

The Spirit continues to teach believers
1Jn 2:20 But you have an anointing from the Holy One, and all of you know the truth. *See also* **1Jn** 2:27

The Spirit teaches the churches Rev 2:7,11,17,29; 3:6,13,22

The Spirit teaches within believers' hearts, in contrast to the written code Eze 36:27; **Ro** 2:29; **2Co** 3:7–8

The Holy Spirit's teaching centres on Jesus Christ
Jn 16:14–15 "He [the Spirit] will bring glory to me [Jesus] by taking from what is mine and making it known to you. All that belongs to the Father is mine. That is why I said the Spirit will take from what is mine and make it known to you."

The Holy Spirit inspires Scripture for teaching
2Ti 3:16 All Scripture is God-breathed and is useful for teaching, rebuking, correcting and training in righteousness, *See also Holy Spirit and Scripture; Holy Spirit in the church; Holy Spirit, anointing; Holy Spirit, inspiration; Holy Spirit, wisdom; Holy Spirit, witness of; Jesus Christ, preaching and teaching; revelation; Scripture.*

Holy Spirit, titles and names of

The names and terms for the Holy Spirit relate to his power, activity and presence in the world, often indicating the nature of his actions or the gifts which he conveys to believers.

Titles relating the Holy Spirit to God
The Spirit of God
Ge 1:2 ... the Spirit of God was hovering over the waters. *See also* **Ge** 41:38; **1Sa** 10:10; 19:20,23; **Ro** 8:9; **1Co** 6:11; **2Co** 3:3; **Eph** 4:30; **Php** 3:3

The Spirit of the LORD
The Spirit empowered the judges to deliver the people: **Jdg** 3:10; 6:34; 11:29; 13:25; 14:6,19; 15:14
1Sa 10:6; 16:13; **2Sa** 23:2
The Messiah will be empowered by the Spirit: **Isa** 11:2; 61:1
2Co 3:17

Forms of reference to the Spirit of God
My Spirit Ge 6:3; **Isa** 30:1; 59:21; **Joel** 2:28–29; **Hag** 2:5; **Zec** 4:6; 6:8; **Mt** 12:18
His Spirit Isa 34:16; 63:10–11; **Zec** 7:12; **Ro** 8:11; **Eph** 2:22
Your Spirit Ne 9:20,30; **Ps** 51:11; 139:7; 143:10
The Spirit of your Father Mt 10:20
The promised Holy Spirit Ac 2:33; **Eph** 1:13
The Spirit of him who raised Jesus from the dead Ro 8:11
The spirit of the gods
Seen from a pagan viewpoint: **Da** 4:8–9,18; 5:11,14

Titles relating the Holy Spirit to God the Son
Gal 4:6 ... he sent the Spirit of his Son into our hearts, the Spirit who calls out, *"Abba,* Father." *See also* **Ac** 16:7; **Ro** 8:9; **Php** 1:19; **1Pe** 1:11

Titles revealing the Holy Spirit's essential nature
The Spirit of truth
Jn 16:13 "But when he, the Spirit of truth, comes, he will guide you into all truth..." *See also* **Jn** 14:17; 15:26; **1Jn** 4:6
The Spirit of holiness Ro 1:4
The Spirit of life Ro 8:2
The Spirit of glory 1Pe 4:14
The eternal Spirit Heb 9:14

Titles showing the nature of the Holy Spirit's activity
The Counsellor Jn 14:26; 15:26
The Spirit of wisdom and understanding
Isa 11:2 The Spirit of the LORD will rest on him—the Spirit of wisdom and of understanding, the Spirit of counsel and of power, the Spirit of knowledge and of the fear of the LORD—
See also **Dt** 34:9 fn; **Eph** 1:17

Holy Spirit, wisdom

The Spirit of grace and supplication Zec 12:10 fn
The Spirit of adoption Ro 8:15
The Spirit of judgment and fire Isa 4:4 fn
See also God, the Lord; Holy Spirit and sanctification; Holy Spirit in life of Jesus Christ; Holy Spirit, Counsellor; Holy Spirit, descriptions; Holy Spirit, divinity; Holy Spirit, inspiration; Holy Spirit, life-giver; Trinity.

Holy Spirit, wisdom

The quality of being discerning and perceptive which is a characteristic of the Holy Spirit. The Holy Spirit is the source of human wisdom.

Those who knew and can know the wisdom of the Holy Spirit
Joshua
Dt 34:9 Now Joshua son of Nun was filled with the spirit of wisdom because Moses had laid his hands on him. So the Israelites listened to him and did what the Lord had commanded Moses.
The Messiah
Isa 11:2 The Spirit of the Lord will rest on him [the Messiah] —the Spirit of wisdom and of understanding, the Spirit of counsel and of power, the Spirit of knowledge and of the fear of the Lord—
Jesus Christ
Lk 2:40 And the child [Jesus] grew and became strong; he was filled with wisdom, and the grace of God was upon him. *See also* **Col 2:9**
Christians
Eph 1:17 I [Paul] keep asking that the God of our Lord Jesus Christ, the glorious Father, may give you the Spirit of wisdom and revelation, so that you may know him better.

The Holy Spirit is the source of wisdom
Job 32:6–9 "I [Elihu] thought, 'Age should speak; advanced years should teach wisdom.' But it is the spirit in mortals, the breath of the Almighty, that gives them understanding . . ."
Ac 6:9–10 Opposition arose, however, from members of the Synagogue of the Freedmen . . . who began to argue with Stephen, but they could not stand up against his wisdom or the Spirit by whom he spoke.

1Co 2:12–14 We have not received the spirit of the world but the Spirit who is from God, that we may understand what God has freely given us. This is what we speak, not in words taught us by human wisdom but in words taught by the Spirit, expressing spiritual truths in spiritual words . . .
These references to the wisdom of Solomon make it clear that it was a gift from God: **1Ki 3:8–9,12; 4:29–34; 10:1,23–24**

Pr 2:6; **Da** 5:10–16; **Ac** 6:3; 15:28; **1Co** 2:11; 12:8; **Col** 1:9

The Holy Spirit as teacher
Jn 14:26 "But the Counsellor, the Holy Spirit, whom the Father will send in my name, will teach you all things and will remind you of everything I have said to you." *See also* **Ne** 9:20; **Mt** 10:19–20 pp **Mk** 13:11 pp **Lk** 12:12; **1Jn** 2:27 *See also God, wisdom of; Holy Spirit, teacher; Jesus Christ, wisdom.*

Holy Spirit, witness of

The Holy Spirit bears witness to the person and work of Jesus Christ, and enables believers to bear effective witness to him.

The Holy Spirit bears witness to Jesus Christ
The Spirit's testimony
1Jn 4:2–3 This is how you can recognise the Spirit of God: Every spirit that acknowledges that Jesus Christ has come in the flesh is from God, but every spirit that does not acknowledge Jesus is not from God . . . *See also* **Ac** 5:32; **1Co** 12:3
At Jesus Christ's baptism
Jn 1:32–34 Then John gave this testimony: "I saw the Spirit come down from heaven as a dove and remain on him. I would not have known him, except that the one who sent me to baptise with water told me, 'The man on whom you see the Spirit come down and remain is the one who will baptise with the Holy Spirit.' I have seen and I testify that this is the Son of God."
See also **Mt** 3:16 pp **Mk** 1:10 pp **Lk** 3:22
After Jesus Christ's ascension
Jn 15:26 "When the Counsellor comes, whom I

will send to you from the Father, the Spirit of truth who goes out from the Father, he will testify about me."   See also **Jn** 14:26; 16:13–14; **1Jn** 5:6

The Holy Spirit's witness enables believers to be effective

He brings assurance to believers

1Jn 3:24 Those who obey his commands live in him, and he in them. And this is how we know that he lives in us: We know it by the Spirit he gave us.   See also **1Jn** 4:13; 5:7–10

He gives assurance of the finality of Jesus Christ's saving work

Heb 10:14–17 because by one sacrifice he [Jesus] has made perfect for ever those who are being made holy. The Holy Spirit also testifies to us about this. First he says: "This is the covenant I will make with them after that time, says the Lord. I will put my laws in their hearts, and I will write them on their minds." Then he adds: "Their sins and lawless acts I will remember no more."

He gives believers confidence in their status as children of God

Ro 8:15–16 . . . you received the Spirit of adoption. And by him we cry, "Abba, Father." The Spirit himself testifies with our spirit that we are God's children.   See also **Gal** 4:6   See also Holy Spirit and assurance; Holy Spirit and mission; Holy Spirit and preaching; Holy Spirit, power.

human race

Human beings are the high point of God's creation. They alone are created in his image. As a result of sin they are alienated from God and from one another, and are unable by themselves to alter this situation. The salvation of humanity rests totally upon the atoning sacrifice of Jesus Christ, received by grace through faith.

human race and God

Though vastly superior to the human race, God nevertheless loves, sustains and governs it, sending his Son as a human being to redeem humanity.

God is incomparably superior to the human race

Isa 40:15–22 Surely the nations are like a drop in a bucket; they are regarded as dust on the scales; he weighs the islands as though they were fine dust . . . Before him all the nations are as nothing; they are regarded by him as worthless and less than nothing . . . He sits enthroned above the circle of the earth, and its people are like grasshoppers. He stretches out the heavens like a canopy, and spreads them out like a tent to live in.   See also **Job** 25:1–6; 38:1–7; **Ps** 8:3–4; **Isa** 31:1–3; **Ac** 17:24–25; **1Co** 1:20–25

The human race is dependent upon God

Job 34:14–15 "If it were his intention and he withdrew his spirit and breath, all people would perish together and they would return to the dust."   See also **Job** 12:10; **Ps** 36:5–6; **Ac** 17:24–28

The human race is valued and loved by God

The human race is the object of God's care and compassion

Ps 103:13 As a father has compassion on his children, so the LORD has compassion on those who fear him;   See also **Ps** 10:17–18; **La** 3:31–33; **Mt** 6:25–33 pp Lk 12:22–31

God wants to bless the human race **Ge** 12:1–3; **Ro** 10:12

God wants to save the human race

Jn 3:16–17 "For God so loved the world that he gave his one and only Son, that whoever believes in him shall not perish but have eternal life. For God did not send his Son into the world to condemn the world, but to save the world through him."   See also **1Ti** 2:1–4; **2Pe** 3:8–9

God highly values the human race and human life

Ge 9:6 "Whoever sheds human blood, by human beings shall their blood be shed; for in the image of God has God made all people."   See also **Ex** 20:13; **Mt** 16:26 pp Mk 8:36–37 pp Lk 9:25; **1Pe** 1:18–19

God is sovereign and watches over the human race
Ps 33:10–15 The LORD foils the plans of the nations; he thwarts the purposes of the peoples. But the plans of the LORD stand firm for ever, the purposes of his heart through all generations. Blessed is the nation whose God is the LORD, the people he chose for his inheritance. From heaven the LORD looks down and sees all humanity; from his dwelling-place he watches all who live on earth—he who forms the hearts of all, who considers everything they do.   *See also* **Ps 9:7–8; Pr 5:21; Da 5:18–21**

God will judge and punish the wickedness of the human race
Isa 2:12–17 The LORD Almighty has a day in store for all the proud and lofty, for all that is exalted (and they will be humbled) . . . The arrogance of all people will be brought low and human pride humbled . . .   *See also* **Mt 13:40–43; Ac 17:29–31; Ro 2:5–11**

God is to be feared and worshipped by the entire human race
Ps 33:8 Let all the earth fear the LORD; let all the people of the world revere him.
Ro 1:20–25 For since the creation of the world God's invisible qualities—his eternal power and divine nature—have been clearly seen . . . They exchanged the truth of God for a lie, and worshipped and served created things rather than the Creator . . .   *See also* **1Ch 16:28–31; Ps 96:7–10**   *See also God as Saviour; God, grace and mercy; God, love of; God, the provider; Jesus Christ; humanity; salvation.*

human race and redemption
Through Jesus Christ's death on the cross and his redemption, human beings are offered a salvation that will give them spiritual life and freedom, reconcile them to God, and unite them to one another as part of a new humanity.

Salvation is offered to the human race through Jesus Christ
Jn 3:14–17 "Just as Moses lifted up the snake in the desert, so the Son of Man must be lifted up, that everyone who believes in him may have eternal life. For God so loved the world that he gave his one and only Son, that whoever believes in him shall not perish but have eternal life. For God did not send his Son into the world to condemn the world, but to save the world through him."   *See also* **Mt 28:18–20; Lk 24:45–47; Ac 2:38–39; 10:34–35,44–48; 1Ti 2:1–7; Tit 2:11–14; Rev 14:6–7**

The Saviour was himself a human being
Gal 4:4 But when the time had fully come, God sent his Son, born of a woman, born under law,
1Ti 2:5–6 For there is one God and one mediator between God and human beings, Christ Jesus, himself human, who gave himself as a ransom for all—the testimony given in its proper time.   *See also* **Mt 1:1; Ro 1:3–4; 8:3; Php 2:8; Heb 2:17**

The human race is reconciled to God through Jesus Christ's death on the cross
2Co 5:18–21 All this is from God, who reconciled us to himself through Christ and gave us the ministry of reconciliation: that God was reconciling the world to himself in Christ, not counting people's sins against them. And he has committed to us the message of reconciliation. We are therefore Christ's ambassadors, as though God were making his appeal through us. We implore you on Christ's behalf: Be reconciled to God. God made him who had no sin to be sin for us, so that in him we might become the righteousness of God.   *See also* **Ro 5:1–2; Eph 2:14–18; Col 1:19–22; Heb 2:17; 10:19–22**

The human race is united in Jesus Christ
Gal 3:26–28 You are all children of God through faith in Christ Jesus, for all of you who were baptised into Christ have clothed yourselves with Christ. There is neither Jew nor Greek, slave nor free, male nor female, for you are all one in Christ Jesus.   *See also* **Jn 10:14–16; 1Co 12:12–13; Eph 2:13–22; Col 3:9–11; Rev 5:9–14**

The human race is renewed in Jesus Christ
Eph 2:15 . . . His purpose was to create in himself one new humanity out of the two, thus making peace, *See also* **1Co** 15:47–49; **2Co** 5:17

In Jesus Christ the human race is given spiritual life and freedom
Eph 2:4–5 But because of his great love for us, God, who is rich in mercy, made us alive with Christ even when we were dead in transgressions . . . *See also* **Ro** 5:17–18; 8:1–2,9–11; **2Co** 3:13–17 *See also church; Jesus Christ, death of; Jesus Christ, humanity; Jesus Christ, Son of Man; salvation.*

---

human race and sin
As a result of the fall, human beings have become separated from God through sin, and are divided amongst themselves. All are in a condition of spiritual blindness, slavery and death, and are incapable of saving themselves from this situation.

All the human race is sinful
Ro 3:9–12 . . . Jews and Gentiles alike are all under sin. As it is written: "There is no-one righteous, not even one; there is no-one who understands, no-one who seeks God. All have turned away, they have together become worthless; there is no-one who does good, not even one." *See also* **Ps** 14:1–3; 53:1–3; **Ge** 6:5–13; **Job** 15:14–16; **Ecc** 7:20; **Ro** 1:18–32; **Rev** 18:1–5

The human race is estranged from God
Isa 59:1–2 Surely the arm of the LORD is not too short to save, nor his ear too dull to hear. But your iniquities have separated you from your God; your sins have hidden his face from you, so that he will not hear. *See also* **Ge** 3:8–10, 22–24; **Ps** 5:4–5; **Eph** 2:12; 4:17–18; **Col** 1:21

The human race is spiritually callous, blind, enslaved and dead
Eph 2:1–3 As for you, you were dead in your transgressions and sins, in which you used to live when you followed the ways of this world and of the ruler of the kingdom of the air, the spirit who is now at work in those who are disobedient. All of us also lived among them at one time, gratifying the cravings of our sinful nature and following its desires and thoughts. Like the rest, we were by nature objects of wrath.
Eph 4:17–19 So I tell you this, and insist on it in the Lord, that you must no longer live as the Gentiles do, in the futility of their thinking. They are darkened in their understanding and separated from the life of God because of the ignorance that is in them due to the hardening of their hearts. Having lost all sensitivity, they have given themselves over to sensuality so as to indulge in every kind of impurity, with a continual lust for more. *See also* **Ro** 1:21; 5:12–14; 6:16–20; **2Co** 4:4; **1Jn** 5:19

The human race is divided
The human race is divided individual against individual Ge 4:3–9; **Ro** 1:28–29
The human race is divided man against woman Ge 3:8–12,16; **Pr** 21:9
The human race is divided nation against nation Ge 11:1–9; **Mt** 24:6–7
The human race is divided Jew against Gentile Ac 10:27–28; **Eph** 2:11–12
The human race is divided rich against poor Am 8:4–6; **Jas** 2:1–7

The human race has been weakened by sin
The human race has become subject to death
Ge 2:16–17 And the LORD God commanded the man, "You are free to eat from any tree in the garden; but you must not eat from the tree of the knowledge of good and evil, for when you eat of it you will surely die."
Ro 6:23 For the wages of sin is death, but the gift of God is eternal life in Christ Jesus our Lord. *See also* **Ro** 5:12; **1Co** 15:21; **Jas** 1:15
Human beings have become weak and frail
Isa 40:6–7 A voice says, "Cry out." And I said, "What shall I cry?" "All people are like grass, and all their glory is like the flowers of the field. The grass withers and the flowers fall,

human race, destiny

because the breath of the LORD blows on them. Surely the people are grass."   *See also* **Job 14:1–12; Ps 90:3–6; 103:13–16; Ecc 12:1–7; 1Pe 1:24–25**

---

human race, destiny

All human beings must face judgment, when God will reward them according to their attitude towards him.

The human race will face final judgment

Mt 16:27 "For the Son of Man is going to come in his Father's glory with his angels, and then he will reward everyone according to what they have done."

1Co 4:5 Therefore judge nothing before the appointed time; wait till the Lord comes. He will bring to light what is hidden in darkness and will expose the motives of people's hearts. At that time each will receive praise from God.   *See also* **Da 12:1–2; Mal 3:16–18; Mt 13:40–43; Jn 5:24–29; Ro 2:5–11**

Unbelievers will be separated from God

2Th 1:8–10 He will punish those who do not know God and do not obey the gospel of our Lord Jesus. They will be punished with everlasting destruction and shut out from the presence of the Lord and from the majesty of his power on the day he comes to be glorified in his holy people . . .   *See also* **Mt 25:31–46; Mk 9:42–48; Lk 13:22–28; 2Pe 3:7; Rev 20:11–15**

Those who have faith will live in God's presence

Rev 21:1–3 Then I saw a new heaven and a new earth, for the first heaven and the first earth had passed away, and there was no longer any sea. I saw the Holy City, the new Jerusalem, coming down out of heaven from God, prepared as a bride beautifully dressed for her husband. And I heard a loud voice from the throne saying, "Now the dwelling of God is with human beings, and he will live with them. They will be his people, and God himself will be with them and be their God."

Jn 14:1–3 ". . . Trust in God; trust also in me. In my Father's house are many rooms; if it were not so, I would have told you. I am going there to prepare a place for you. And if I go and prepare a place for you, I will come back and take you to be with me that you also may be where I am."   *See also* **Zec 2:10–13; Rev 7:13–17; 22:3–4**

United in the praise of God

Rev 7:9–10 After this I looked and there before me was a great multitude that no-one could count, from every nation, tribe, people and language, standing before the throne and in front of the Lamb. They were wearing white robes and were holding palm branches in their hands. And they cried out in a loud voice: "Salvation belongs to our God, who sits on the throne, and to the Lamb."   *See also* **Isa 2:2–4 pp Mic 4:1–3; Mt 8:11 pp Lk 13:29; Rev 5:9–10; 21:22–27**

Delivered from suffering, pain and death

Rev 21:3–4 And I heard a loud voice from the throne saying, "Now the dwelling of God is with human beings, and he will live with them. They will be his people, and God himself will be with them and be their God. He will wipe every tear from their eyes. There will be no more death or mourning or crying or pain, for the old order of things has passed away."   *See also* **Isa 25:6–8; 65:17–25; Rev 7:16–17; 22:1–3**

Sharing in the glory of Jesus Christ

Col 3:4 When Christ, who is your life, appears, then you also will appear with him in glory.

1Pe 5:4 And when the Chief Shepherd appears, you will receive the crown of glory that will never fade away.   *See also* **2Ti 4:8**   *See also God as judge; heaven; Jesus Christ as Lamb; Jesus Christ as shepherd; last things.*

Immanuel

An OT name given to Jesus Christ, meaning "God with us".

Actual uses of the name Immanuel

Isa 7:14 "Therefore the Lord himself will give you [King Ahaz] a sign: The virgin will be with child and will give birth to a son, and will call him Immanuel."

Isa 8:7-10 ". . . therefore the Lord is about to bring against them the mighty floodwaters of the River—the king of Assyria with all his pomp . . . Its outspread wings will cover the breadth of your [Judah's] land, O Immanuel!" . . .
Mt 1:22-23 All this took place to fulfil what the Lord had said through the prophet: "The virgin will be with child and will give birth to a son, and they will call him Immanuel"—which means, "God with us."

The significance of Immanuel
God is with his people
Ge 28:15 "I [the LORD] am with you [Jacob] and will watch over you wherever you go, and I will bring you back to this land. I will not leave you until I have done what I have promised you." *See also* **Ex** 33:14; **Nu** 14:9; **Dt** 4:7; **2Ch** 13:12; **Ps** 46:7,11; **Hag** 2:4; **Ro** 8:31; **Heb** 13:5
God dwells with his people
Rev 21:3 And I [John] heard a loud voice from the throne saying, "Now the dwelling of God is with human beings, and he will live with them. They will be his people, and God himself will be with them and be their God." *See also* **Lev** 26:11-12; **Eze** 37:27; **2Co** 6:16
Jesus Christ is always with believers
Mt 28:20 ". . . And surely I [Jesus] am with you always, to the very end of the age." *See also* **Jn** 14:18,23; 15:4-5,7; **Ac** 18:10; **Gal** 2:20
The Holy Spirit is always with believers
Jn 14:17 ". . . But you know him, for he [the Spirit of truth] lives with you and will be in you." *See also* **Ro** 8:9-11; **1Co** 3:16; **2Co** 1:22; **Eph** 2:22; **2Ti** 1:14; **1Jn** 4:13 *See also God, faithfulness; incarnation; Jesus Christ, birth of; Jesus Christ, divinity; Jesus Christ, faithfulness; Jesus Christ, humanity; Jesus Christ, Son of God; Jesus Christ, titles and names of; Jesus, the Christ.*

God the Son assumed human nature
Jn 1:14 The Word became flesh and made his dwelling among us. We have seen his glory, the glory of the One and Only, who came from the Father, full of grace and truth. *See also* **Jn** 1:9; 8:56; **1Ti** 3:16; **1Jn** 1:1-2; 4:2; **2Jn** 7

Jesus Christ's incarnation involved a supernatural conception
Lk 1:35 . . . "The Holy Spirit will come upon you [Mary], and the power of the Most High will overshadow you. So the holy one to be born will be called the Son of God." *See also* **Isa** 9:6; **Mt** 1:18; **Jn** 14:9; **Ro** 1:4; **Col** 1:15, 19; **Heb** 1:2-3

Jesus Christ's incarnation involved a virgin birth
Mt 1:22-23 "The virgin will be with child and will give birth to a son . . ." *See also* **Isa** 7:14; **Lk** 1:34; **Ro** 1:3; **Gal** 4:4; **Php** 2:8; **Heb** 2:14

The cost of the incarnation
Php 2:6-7 [Jesus] Who, being in very nature God, did not consider equality with God something to be grasped, but made himself nothing, taking the very nature of a servant, being made in human likeness. *See also* **2Co** 8:9; **Heb** 2:10

The necessity of the incarnation
Ro 8:3 For what the law was powerless to do in that it was weakened by the sinful nature, God did by sending his own Son in the likeness of sinful humanity to be a sin offering . . . *See also* **Ro** 5:17-19; **2Co** 5:19; **Col** 1:22; **1Ti** 2:5; **Heb** 2:17-18; 4:15 *See also Jesus Christ, birth of; Jesus Christ, humanity; Jesus Christ, humility; Jesus Christ, Son of God; word of God.*

---

incarnation
The assuming by God of human nature in the person of Jesus Christ. The incarnation is the fixed and permanent physical dwelling of God in his world, as opposed to the temporary manifestation of the divine presence and power in a theophany.

Jesus Christ
The co-equal and co-eternal Son of the Father, who became incarnate in Jesus Christ for the redemption of the world. Scripture stresses both the divinity and the humanity of the incarnate Son of God, and the necessity and total sufficiency of

his atoning death for human redemption. Through his resurrection and ascension, he intercedes for believers at the right hand of God.

Jesus Christ as creator
Scripture identifies the pre-existent Jesus Christ as involved in the work of creation, and relates this to his work in redemption, by which a new creation is brought out of the ruins of the old.

Jesus Christ's creation of the present world
Jesus Christ created all things
Jn 1:3 Through him [the Word] all things were made; without him nothing was made that has been made.   *See also* **Jn** 1:10; **Ac** 3:15; **1Co** 8:6; **Col** 1:15–16; **Heb** 1:2

Jesus Christ sustains the created universe
Heb 1:3 The Son is the radiance of God's glory . . . sustaining all things by his powerful word . . .   *See also* **1Co** 8:6; **Col** 1:17; **Rev** 3:14

Jesus Christ will bring the entire work of creation to perfection
Eph 1:9–10 And he [God] made known to us the mystery of his will according to his good pleasure, which he purposed in Christ, to be put into effect when the times will have reached their fulfilment—to bring all things in heaven and on earth together under one head, even Christ.   *See also* **Ro** 8:19–22; **Col** 1:20

Jesus Christ makes a new creation possible
Jesus Christ recreates people through a new birth
2Co 5:17 Therefore, if anyone is in Christ, there is a new creation: the old has gone, the new has come!   *See also* **Jn** 1:12–13; 3:5–6; **Gal** 6:15; **Jas** 1:18

Jesus Christ's work of new creation should be evident in believers' lives
Eph 4:24 . . . put on the new self, created to be like God in true righteousness and holiness.   *See also* **Eph** 3:15; **Col** 3:10

Through Jesus Christ a new heaven and earth will be created
2Pe 3:13 But in keeping with his promise we are looking forward to a new heaven and a new earth, the home of righteousness.   *See also* **Rev** 21:1,4–5   *See also God, the Creator; Holy Spirit and regeneration; Holy Spirit in creation; Jesus Christ, divinity; Jesus Christ, pre-eminence.*

Jesus Christ as judge
Jesus Christ executed judgment against the forces of evil through his death on the cross. Individuals will be judged according to their response to his saving grace.

Jesus Christ is appointed judge by God the Father
Jn 5:22 ". . . the Father judges no-one, but has entrusted all judgment to the Son,"   *See also* **Jn** 5:27; **Ac** 10:42; 17:31

Jesus Christ is a just judge
Jn 5:30 ". . . I judge only as I hear, and my [Jesus Christ's] judgment is just, for I seek not to please myself but him who sent me."   *See also* **Isa** 11:3–4; **Mic** 4:3; **Jn** 8:15–16; **Ac** 17:31; **Rev** 19:11

Jesus Christ's death brought judgment on Satan and evil world powers
Jn 12:31–33 "Now is the time for judgment on this world; now the prince of this world will be driven out . . ."   *See also* **Jn** 16:11

Jesus Christ will act as judge at the end of time
2Ti 4:1 . . . Jesus, who will judge the living and the dead . . .   *See also* **Mt** 25:31–32; **Ro** 2:16; **2Th** 1:7–10; **2Ti** 4:8; **Rev** 19:11–16; 22:12

People will be judged according to their response to Jesus Christ
Jn 3:18 "Those who believe in him are not condemned, but those who do not believe stand condemned already because they have not believed in the name of God's one and only Son."   *See also* **Mt** 10:32–33 pp **Lk** 12:8–9; **Mk** 8:38 pp **Lk** 9:26; **Jn** 9:39; 12:48

Jesus Christ's teaching on judgment
Jesus Christ will separate the righteous from the unrighteous
Mt 25:31-32 "When the Son of Man comes in his glory, and all the angels with him, he will sit on his throne in heavenly glory. All the nations will be gathered before him, and he will separate the people one from another as a shepherd separates the sheep from the goats." *See also* **Mt** 3:12; 13:24-30,36-42, 47-50; 25:33-46

Those who reject Jesus Christ will be punished
Da 2:34-35; **Mt** 21:33-44 pp **Mk** 12:1-11 pp **Lk** 20:9-18

Christians will stand before Jesus Christ as judge and be rewarded for what they have done
Mt 16:27 ". . . the Son of Man is going to come in his Father's glory with his angels, and then he will reward everyone according to what they have done." *See also* **Mt** 25:14-30; **Lk** 19:12-27; **2Co** 5:10

The day of Jesus Christ's return as judge is unknown
Mk 13:32-36 "No-one knows about that day or hour, not even the angels in heaven, nor the Son, but only the Father. Be on guard! Be alert! You do not know when that time will come . . ." *See also* **Mt** 24:36-44 pp **Lk** 17:26-37; **Mt** 25:1-13   *See also God as judge; Jesus Christ as Saviour; Jesus Christ, justice of; Jesus Christ, preaching and teaching; Jesus Christ, second coming; Jesus Christ, victory.*

Jesus Christ as king

Jesus Christ is declared king at his birth: he descends from the royal line of David. People rejected his kingly claims at his crucifixion but God exalted him to his rightful place of power and majesty. At the end of time Jesus Christ will rule the nations for ever.

Jesus Christ descends from the royal line of David
He was the Son of David
Mt 1:1 A record of the genealogy of Jesus Christ the son of David, the son of Abraham: *See also* **Mt** 9:27; 12:23; 15:22; **Lk** 1:32-33; 2:4; 3:31

He was born in Bethlehem, the town of David
Jn 7:42 "Does not the Scripture say that the Christ will come from David's family and from Bethlehem, the town where David lived?"   *See also* **Mt** 2:3-6; **Mic** 5:2; **Lk** 2:15-16

Jesus Christ is regarded as king
Jn 1:49 Then Nathanael declared, "Rabbi, you are the Son of God; you are the King of Israel."   *See also* **Mt** 2:1-2; **Jn** 6:15; **Ac** 17:7

Jesus Christ refused worldly kingdoms
Jn 18:36 Jesus said, "My kingdom is not of this world. If it were, my servants would fight to prevent my arrest by the Jews. But now my kingdom is from another place."   *See also* **Mt** 4:8-10 pp **Lk** 4:5-8; **Jn** 6:15

Jesus Christ entered Jerusalem as a king
Mt 21:1-9 . . . "Say to the Daughter of Zion, 'See, your king comes to you, gentle and riding on a donkey, on a colt, the foal of a donkey.'" . . . pp **Jn** 12:12-15   *See also* **Zec** 9:9

Jesus Christ's kingship is an issue at his trial
Pilate questions Jesus Christ
Lk 23:2-3 And they began to accuse him [Jesus], saying, "We have found this man subverting our nation. He opposes payment of taxes to Caesar and claims to be Christ, a king." So Pilate asked Jesus, "Are you the king of the Jews?" "Yes, it is as you say," Jesus replied. pp **Mt** 27:11 pp **Mk** 15:2 pp **Jn** 18:33

Jesus Christ claims to be a spiritual king
Jn 18:36-37 . . . "You are a king, then!" said Pilate. Jesus answered, "You are right in saying I am a king. In fact, for this reason I was born, and for this I came into the world, to testify to the truth. Everyone on the side of truth listens to me."   *See also* **Mt** 27:11 pp **Mk** 15:2 pp **Lk** 23:3

Pilate appeals to the crowd to accept Jesus Christ as their king
Mk 15:9 "Do you want me to release to you

the king of the Jews?" asked Pilate.
The crowd reject Jesus Christ as king
Mk 15:12-13 "What shall I do, then, with the one you call the king of the Jews?" Pilate asked them [the crowd]. "Crucify him!" they shouted.   *See also* **Jn** 19:12-15

Jesus Christ is mocked as king
Mt 27:27-30 ... They [the soldiers] stripped him [Jesus] and put a scarlet robe on him, and then twisted together a crown of thorns and set it on his head. They put a staff in his right hand and knelt in front of him and mocked him. "Hail, king of the Jews!" they said ... pp Mk 15:16-20 pp Jn 19:2-3

Jesus Christ is declared king at his crucifixion
Jn 19:19-22 Pilate had a notice prepared and fastened to the cross. It read: JESUS OF NAZARETH, THE KING OF THE JEWS ... pp Mt 27:37 pp Mk 15:26 pp Lk 23:38

God has exalted Jesus Christ to his rightful place as king
Heb 1:3 ... After he [Jesus] had provided purification for sins, he sat down at the right hand of the Majesty in heaven.   *See also* **Heb** 8:1; 12:2; **Rev** 5:6; 7:17; 22:1-3

As king, Jesus Christ welcomes believers into his kingdom
Lk 23:42-43 Then he [the dying criminal] said, "Jesus, remember me when you come into your kingdom." Jesus answered him, "I tell you the truth, today you will be with me in paradise."   *See also* **2Ti** 4:18; **Rev** 3:20-21

Jesus Christ is king of all kings
He will rule over the nations
Rev 1:5 ... Jesus Christ, who is the faithful witness, the firstborn from the dead, and the ruler of the kings of the earth ...   *See also* **Ps** 2:7-9; **Da** 7:13-14; **Mt** 19:28; 25:31-32; **Ro** 15:12; **1Co** 15:25; **Php** 2:9-10; **Rev** 12:5; 17:14; 19:11-16

He is king for ever
Rev 11:15 ... "The kingdom of the world has become the kingdom of our Lord and of his Christ, and he will reign for ever and ever."   *See also* **Isa** 9:7; **Lk** 1:33; **Heb** 1:8; **Ps** 45:6   *See also* Jesus Christ, cross of; Jesus Christ, exaltation; Jesus Christ, kingdom of; Jesus Christ, prophecies concerning; Jesus Christ, second coming; Jesus Christ, Son of David; Jesus Christ, trial; Jesus Christ, triumphal entry; Jesus Christ, victory; kingdom of God; Messiah, coming of.

Jesus Christ as Lamb

Jesus Christ is referred to as the "Lamb of God". This symbol points to Christ being a perfect sacrifice for sin. It also conveys his meekness and his willingness to submit to suffering and death.

The imagery of the lamb
An image of innocence and attraction
Isa 11:6 The wolf will live with the lamb, the leopard will lie down with the goat, the calf and the lion and the yearling together; and a little child will lead them.   *See also* **Lev** 23:12; **2Sa** 12:3

An image of submissiveness and vulnerability
Jer 11:19 I had been like a gentle lamb led to the slaughter; I did not realise that they had plotted against me, saying, "Let us destroy the tree and its fruit; let us cut him off from the land of the living, that his name be remembered no more."   *See also* **Isa** 40:11; **Lk** 10:3; **Jn** 21:15

An image of quiet suffering
Isa 53:7 He [the servant] was oppressed and afflicted, yet he did not open his mouth; he was led like a lamb to the slaughter, and as a sheep before her shearers is silent, so he did not open his mouth.

An image of sacrifice
Ex 29:38 "This is what you are to offer on the altar regularly each day: two lambs a year old."   *See also* **Ex** 12:27; **Lev** 3:7; 4:32; 14:13; **Eze** 46:13; **Mk** 14:12 pp **Lk** 22:7

Jesus Christ is likened to a lamb
Jn 1:36 When he [John the Baptist] saw Jesus passing by, he said, "Look, the Lamb of God!"   *See also* **Jn** 1:29; **1Co** 5:7; **1Pe** 1:19; **Rev** 5:6

The symbolism of the lamb applies to Jesus Christ

Jesus Christ is innocent and draws people to himself
Lk 23:41 "We are punished justly, for we are getting what our deeds deserve. But this man [Jesus] has done nothing wrong." *See also* **Jn** 12:32; **Heb** 4:15; 7:26; **1Pe** 2:22; **Isa** 53:9

Jesus Christ was submissive and vulnerable
Mt 26:38–39 Then he [Jesus] said to them [Peter and the two sons of Zebedee], "My soul is overwhelmed with sorrow to the point of death. Stay here and keep watch with me." Going a little farther, he fell with his face to the ground and prayed, "My Father, if it is possible, may this cup be taken from me. Yet not as I will, but as you will." pp **Mk** 14:35–36 pp **Lk** 22:41–42 *See also* **Jn** 3:27; **1Co** 1:27; **Php** 2:7–8; **Heb** 4:15

Jesus Christ suffered quietly
Mt 27:28–31 . . . After they [the soldiers] had mocked him, they took off the robe and put his own clothes on him. Then they led him away to crucify him. pp **Mk** 15:17–20 *See also* **Mt** 26:62–63 pp **Mk** 14:60–61; **Mt** 27:12–14 pp **Mk** 15:3–5; **Lk** 23:8–11; **Jn** 19:2–3; **Ac** 8:32–35; **Isa** 53:7–8; **1Pe** 2:23

Jesus Christ is seen as a sacrifice
1Pe 1:18–19 For you know that it was not with perishable things such as silver or gold that you were redeemed from the empty way of life handed down to you from your ancestors, but with the precious blood of Christ, a lamb without blemish or defect. *See also* **Ge** 22:8; **Ex** 13:13; **Isa** 53:4–6,10–11; **Jn** 1:29; **1Co** 5:7; **Rev** 12:11; 13:8

Jesus Christ as the glorious Lamb in the book of Revelation

The Lamb is worthy
Rev 5:8–12 . . . the four living creatures and the twenty-four elders fell down before the Lamb . . . they sang a new song: "You are worthy to take the scroll and to open its seals, because you were slain, and with your blood you purchased for God members of every tribe and language and people and nation . . ."
See also **Rev** 7:9–10; 15:3

The Lamb is upon the throne
Rev 17:14 "They will make war against the Lamb, but the Lamb will overcome them because he is Lord of lords and King of kings . . ."
See also **Rev** 5:6; 7:17; 22:1–3

The Lamb will execute judgment
Rev 6:16 They called to the mountains and the rocks, "Fall on us and hide us from the face of him who sits on the throne and from the wrath of the Lamb!" *See also* **Rev** 6:1–3; 14:10

The Lamb is the bridegroom of the church
Rev 19:7–9 "Let us rejoice and be glad and give him glory! For the wedding of the Lamb has come, and his bride has made herself ready . . ." *See also* **Rev** 21:9 *See also* Jesus Christ, anger of; Jesus Christ, glory of; Jesus Christ, perfection; Jesus Christ, sinlessness; Jesus Christ, suffering; sin, remedy for; worship.

Jesus Christ as prophet

Jesus Christ was acclaimed as a prophet by those who witnessed his miracles and heard his teaching. They recognised him as a bearer of the word of God, who spoke with authority concerning the nature and purposes of God.

Examples of those who recognised Jesus Christ as a prophet

People anticipating the coming prophet
Jn 6:14 After the people saw the miraculous sign that Jesus did, they began to say, "Surely this is the Prophet who is to come into the world." *See also* **Jn** 1:21; 7:40,52

A Samaritan woman Jn 4:17–19

Witnesses of Jesus Christ's miracles Mt 14:1–5 pp **Mk** 6:14–15; **Mt** 16:13–14 pp **Mk** 8:27–28 pp **Lk** 9:18–19

The crowd as Jesus Christ approached Jerusalem Mt 21:10–11,46

Two of Jesus Christ's disciples after his death Lk 24:19

The apostles Peter and Stephen Ac 3:20–23; 7:37; **Dt** 18:15–18

Indications of Jesus Christ being a prophet

He announced coming blessing from God
Jn 7:37–40 ". . . Whoever believes in me, as

the Scripture has said, will have streams of living water flowing from within." By this he meant the Spirit, whom those who believed in him were later to receive . . .   See also **Mt** 5:3-12 pp **Lk** 6:20-23; **Mt** 13:16-17 pp **Lk** 10:23-24; **Jn** 20:19-21,29

He announced coming judgment and woe
Ac 3:23 " 'Anyone who does not listen to that prophet [Jesus] will be completely cut off from among the people.' "   See also **Mt** 11:20-24 pp **Lk** 10:13-15; **Mt** 23:13-39; **Lk** 6:24-26

He possessed supernatural knowledge and insight
Jn 2:24-25 But Jesus would not entrust himself to them, for he knew all people. He did not need human testimony about them, for he knew what was in people.   See also **Mt** 9:4 pp **Mk** 2:8 pp **Lk** 5:22; **Lk** 7:39-43; 9:47; **Jn** 4:16-19

He performed mighty works and miracles Lk 7:12-17; **Jn** 9:17

Jesus Christ's own understanding of himself as a prophet
As a rejected prophet
Lk 13:31-35 ". . . In any case, I [Jesus] must keep going today and tomorrow and the next day—for surely no prophet can die outside Jerusalem! . . ."   See also **Mt** 13:57 pp **Mk** 6:4; **Lk** 4:24-27; **Jn** 5:46

As a prophet anointed by God's Spirit
Jn 3:34 "For the one whom God has sent speaks the words of God, for God gives the Spirit without limit."   See also **Lk** 4:16-21; **Isa** 61:1-2

As a prophet who speaks with authority Mk 1:22; 3:28; **Jn** 7:16; 14:10

The place of Jesus Christ in relation to other prophets
Jesus Christ is greater than other prophets
Mt 12:41 "The people of Nineveh will stand up at the judgment with this generation and condemn it; for they repented at the preaching of Jonah, and now one greater than Jonah is here." pp **Lk** 11:32   See also **Jn** 1:15

Jesus Christ is the Messiah and Son of God
Mt 16:13-17 . . . Simon Peter answered, "You are the Christ, the Son of the living God." . . .   See also **Heb** 1:1-2

The exalted Christ is the source and essence of all prophecy Rev 19:10   See also Holy Spirit in life of Jesus Christ; Jesus Christ, miracles; Jesus Christ, preaching and teaching; Jesus Christ, prophecies concerning; Jesus Christ, Son of God; Jesus Christ, Son of Man; Jesus, the Christ.

Jesus Christ as redeemer
Jesus Christ redeems believers from all forms of sinful bondage and oppression through his death and resurrection. The price of that redemption, his own death, represents a ransom paid to secure the freedom of those held in bondage to sin.

The incarnate God as redeemer
God as redeemer
Isa 63:16 . . . you, O LORD, are our Father, our Redeemer from of old is your name.   See also **Job** 19:25; **Isa** 49:26; 59:20; **Lk** 1:68-75

Jesus Christ as redeemer
1Co 1:30 . . . Christ Jesus, who has become for us wisdom from God—that is, our righteousness, holiness and redemption.

Forms of bondage from which Jesus Christ redeems believers
Jesus Christ redeems from slavery to sin
Rev 1:5 . . . To him who loves us and has freed us from our sins by his blood,   See also **Ps** 130:8; **Ro** 3:23-24; 6:18,22; **Tit** 2:14; 3:3-5; **1Pe** 3:18

Jesus Christ redeems from the curse of the law
Gal 3:13 Christ redeemed us from the curse of the law by becoming a curse for us, for it is written: "Cursed is everyone who is hung on a tree."   See also **Gal** 4:4-5

Jesus Christ redeems from empty religion
1Pe 1:18 For you know that it was not with perishable things such as silver or gold that you were redeemed from the empty way of life handed down to you from your ancestors, See also **Gal** 4:3; **Col** 2:20; **Heb** 9:14 fn

Jesus Christ redeems from the power of Satan
Col 1:13 For he [the Father] has rescued us

from the dominion of darkness and brought us into the kingdom of the Son he loves,
See also **Ac** 26:18; **Gal** 1:4

Jesus Christ redeems from the coming judgment
1Th 1:10 . . . Jesus, who rescues us from the coming wrath. *See also* **Ro** 5:9; 8:1–2; **1Th** 5:9

Jesus Christ redeems from death
Heb 2:14–15 . . . so that by his [Jesus Christ's] death he might destroy him who holds the power of death—that is, the devil—and free those who all their lives were held in slavery by their fear of death. *See also* **Hos** 13:14; **1Co** 15:54–57

The means by which Jesus Christ has redeemed believers

Redemption comes through the incarnation of Jesus Christ
Gal 4:4–5 But when the time had fully come, God sent his Son, born of a woman, born under law, to redeem those under law . . . *See also* **Ro** 8:3; **Heb** 2:14

Jesus Christ redeems by his sacrificial death
Heb 9:12 He [Jesus] did not enter by means of the blood of goats and calves; but he entered the Most Holy Place once for all by his own blood, having obtained eternal redemption. *See also* **2Co** 5:21; **Eph** 1:7; **1Pe** 1:18–19; **Rev** 1:5

Jesus Christ redeems by paying a ransom
Mt 20:28 "just as the Son of Man did not come to be served, but to serve, and to give his life as a ransom for many." pp **Mk** 10:45
See also **Ac** 20:28; **Heb** 9:15; **Rev** 5:9

The purposes for which Jesus Christ redeems believers

Jesus Christ redeems believers so that their sins may be forgiven
Eph 1:7 In him [Jesus] we have redemption through his blood, the forgiveness of sins, in accordance with the riches of God's grace
See also **Ac** 26:18; **Col** 1:14; **Heb** 9:15; **1Jn** 1:7

Jesus Christ redeems believers to make them pure
Tit 2:14 who [Jesus Christ] gave himself for us to redeem us from all wickedness and to purify for himself a people that are his very own, eager to do what is good. *See also* **1Co** 6:19–20; 7:23

Jesus Christ redeems believers so that they may receive God's promised blessings
Gal 3:14 He [Christ] redeemed us in order that the blessing given to Abraham might come to the Gentiles through Christ Jesus . . . *See also* **Gal** 4:5; 5:1; **Heb** 9:15

Jesus Christ redeems believers so that they may receive final redemption
Ro 8:23 Not only so, but we ourselves, who have the firstfruits of the Spirit, groan inwardly as we wait eagerly for our adoption, the redemption of our bodies. *See also* **Lk** 21:28; **Eph** 1:14; 4:30 *See also* forgiveness; God as redeemer; Jesus Christ, death of; Jesus Christ, victory; sin, remedy for.

Jesus Christ as Saviour

God's work of salvation is accomplished supremely through the cross and resurrection of Jesus Christ. Through faith, the believer is able to share in all the saving benefits won by Jesus Christ through his obedience to God.

Jesus Christ is the Saviour

Jesus Christ is called Saviour
Tit 1:4 . . . Grace and peace from God the Father and Christ Jesus our Saviour.
See also **Lk** 2:11; **Tit** 3:6; **2Pe** 1:1; 3:2,18

Jesus Christ is the promised Saviour
Ac 13:23 "From this man's [David's] descendants God has brought to Israel the Saviour Jesus, as he promised." *See also* **Lk** 1:69–75; 2:28–30

Jesus Christ's purpose is to save
Lk 19:10 "For the Son of Man came to seek and to save what was lost." *See also* **Mt** 1:21; **1Ti** 1:15

Jesus Christ's qualities as Saviour

Jesus Christ is the unique Saviour
Ac 4:12 "Salvation is found in no-one else, for there is no other name under heaven given to people by which we must be saved." *See also* **Jn** 6:68–69; 10:9; 14:6; **Ac** 10:42–43

Jesus Christ is the complete Saviour
Heb 7:25 Therefore he [Jesus] is able to save

completely those who come to God through him, because he always lives to intercede for them. *See also* Jn 19:30; Php 3:21; Col 1:19–20; Heb 5:9; 9:26–28; 1Jn 1:9; Jude 24

Jesus Christ is the Saviour of the world
Jn 4:42 They said to the [Samaritan] woman, "We no longer believe just because of what you said; now we have heard for ourselves, and we know that this man really is the Saviour of the world." *See also* Lk 2:30–32; 1Ti 2:5–6; 4:10; 1Jn 4:14

Jesus Christ saves through his grace
Ac 15:11 ". . . We believe it is through the grace of our Lord Jesus that we are saved, just as they are." *See also* Ro 3:24; Eph 5:23–27; Tit 3:4–5

Jesus Christ saves by his mighty acts
Jesus Christ saves by his death
1Pe 1:18–19 For you know that it was not with perishable things such as silver or gold that you were redeemed from the empty way of life handed down to you from your ancestors, but with the precious blood of Christ, a lamb without blemish or defect. *See also* Mt 20:28 pp Mk 10:45; Lk 24:45–47; Jn 1:29,36; 10:15,17–18; 1Co 1:18; Rev 7:10

Jesus Christ saves by his resurrection life
1Pe 3:21 and this water symbolises baptism that now saves you also—not the removal of dirt from the body but the pledge of a good conscience towards God. It saves you by the resurrection of Jesus Christ, *See also* Ro 5:10; 2Ti 1:10

Jesus Christ saves by his coming again
Php 3:20 But our citizenship is in heaven. And we eagerly await a Saviour from there, the Lord Jesus Christ, *See also* Tit 2:13; Heb 9:28; 1Pe 1:5

Jesus Christ saves by defeating Satan
1Jn 3:8 . . . The reason the Son of God appeared was to destroy the devil's work. *See also* Jn 13:31; 16:11; Heb 2:14; Rev 2:10–11

Jesus Christ saves from all forms of evil
Jesus Christ saves from physical danger Mt 8:25–26 pp Mk 4:38–39 pp Lk 8:24–25; Ac 26:17; 2Co 1:10; 2Ti 4:18

Jesus Christ saves from the power of sin
1Jn 1:7 . . . the blood of Jesus, his Son, purifies us from all sin. *See also* Ac 5:31; Ro 3:25–26; 5:18–19; 6:6–7; Gal 1:4; Rev 1:5–6

Jesus Christ saves from the condemnation of law
Gal 3:13 Christ redeemed us from the curse of the law by becoming a curse for us, for it is written: "Cursed is everyone who is hung on a tree." *See also* Ac 13:38–39; Ro 8:1–4; Gal 4:4–5; Eph 2:15

Jesus Christ saves from God's wrath
1Th 1:10 . . . Jesus, who rescues us from the coming wrath. *See also* Ro 5:9; 1Th 5:9; Rev 11:17–18

Jesus Christ saves from the power of death
2Ti 1:10 . . . it has now been revealed through the appearing of our Saviour, Christ Jesus, who has destroyed death and has brought life and immortality to light through the gospel. *See also* 1Co 15:55–57; Heb 2:15; Rev 20:6; 21:4

Jesus Christ saves from Satan's power
Ac 26:18 "'to open their eyes and turn them from darkness to light, and from the power of Satan to God, so that they may receive forgiveness of sins and a place among those who are sanctified by faith in me.'" *See also* Lk 10:18–19; 13:16; Col 1:13; 1Jn 3:8

Jesus Christ saves to bring people to God
Jesus Christ saves for eternal life
Jn 6:40 "For my Father's will is that all those who look to the Son and believe in him shall have eternal life, and I will raise them up at the last day." *See also* Jn 3:14–16,36; 5:24–25; Ro 6:23

Jesus Christ saves so that people may live for God
1Jn 4:9 This is how God showed his love among us: He sent his one and only Son into the world that we might live through him. *See also* Ro 6:8–11; 7:21–25; Gal 2:20; 2Ti 1:9; Heb 9:14–15; 1Pe 2:24; 1Jn 3:5–6; 5:18

Jesus Christ's salvation is received through faith
Ac 16:30–31 . . . "Believe in the Lord Jesus,

and you will be saved—you and your household." *See also* **Ac** 2:21; **Ro** 10:13; **Joel** 2:32; **Ro** 1:16; 10:9; **2Th** 2:13; **2Ti** 3:15 *See also* forgiveness; God as Saviour; Jesus Christ as Lamb; Jesus Christ as redeemer; Jesus Christ, grace and mercy; Jesus Christ, resurrection; Messiah, coming of; salvation; sin.

Jesus Christ as servant
Jesus Christ laid aside his majesty in order to serve humanity. His death is the supreme example of his servanthood: the fulfilling of the will of God his Father.

The prophets speak of the Messiah as a servant
Mt 12:17–21 This was to fulfil what was spoken through the prophet Isaiah: "Here is my servant whom I have chosen . . ." *See also* **Isa** 42:1–4; 49:1–7; 50:4–9; 52:13–53:12; **Eze** 34:23–24; 37:24–25; **Zec** 3:8

Jesus Christ describes himself as a servant
Lk 22:27 ". . . I am among you as one who serves." *See also* **Mt** 20:28 pp **Mk** 10:45

Jesus Christ acts as a servant
By coming to dwell among humanity as a man
Php 2:6–7 [Christ Jesus] who, being in very nature God, did not consider equality with God something to be grasped, but made himself nothing, taking the very nature of a servant, being made in human likeness. *See also* **2Co** 8:9
By obeying God's will
Jn 4:34 "My food," said Jesus, "is to do the will of him who sent me and to finish his work." *See also* **Jn** 5:30; 6:38; 14:31; **Heb** 10:5–7; **Ps** 40:6–8
By ministering to his disciples Jn 13:1–17
By dying on the cross
Mt 20:28 "just as the Son of Man did not come to be served, but to serve, and to give his life as a ransom for many." pp **Mk** 10:45
See also **Mt** 26:39 pp **Mk** 14:36 pp **Lk** 22:42; **Php** 2:8

The exaltation of Jesus Christ the servant
He will complete his task Jn 17:4; 19:30
He will be exalted by God
Ac 3:13 ". . . the God of our fathers, has glorified his servant Jesus . . ." *See also* **Isa** 52:13; **Ac** 3:26; **Php** 2:9–11

Jesus Christ's obedience and servanthood an example to believers
Jn 13:14–15 ". . . I have set you an example that you should do as I have done for you." *See also* **Php** 2:5; **1Pe** 2:21 *See also* Jesus Christ, death of; Jesus Christ, example of; Jesus Christ, humility; Jesus Christ, love of; Jesus Christ, obedience; Jesus Christ, suffering.

Jesus Christ as shepherd
A title for Jesus Christ indicating believers' dependence on him as he protects, tends and guides those whom he knows intimately.

Prophecies about the shepherd Messiah
Eze 34:23 "I [the Sovereign LORD] will place over them one shepherd, my servant David, and he will tend them; he will tend them and be their shepherd." *See also* **Eze** 37:24; **Mic** 5:2; **Mt** 2:6; **Mic** 5:4; **Zec** 13:7; **Mt** 26:31 pp **Mk** 14:27

Jesus Christ's role as the good shepherd
He has compassion for the helpless
Mt 9:36 . . . he [Jesus] had compassion on them [the crowds], because they were harassed and helpless, like sheep without a shepherd. *See also* **Mk** 6:34; **Jn** 11:52
He seeks lost sheep
Mt 18:12–14 ". . . If a man owns a hundred sheep, and one of them wanders away, will he not leave the ninety-nine on the hills and go to look for the one that wandered off? And if he finds it, I tell you the truth, he is happier about that one sheep than about the ninety-nine that did not wander off. In the same way your Father in heaven is not willing that any of these little ones should be lost." pp **Lk** 15:3–7
See also **Mt** 10:6; 15:24; **Lk** 19:10; **Jn** 10:16

He knows his own sheep
Jn 10:14–15 ". . . I know my sheep and my sheep know me — just as the Father knows me and I know the Father . . ." *See also* **Mt** 25:32; **Jn** 10:27

His sheep know his voice
Jn 10:4 ". . . his sheep follow him because they know his voice." *See also* **Jn** 10:3,5,16,27

He provides for and protects his sheep
Jn 10:9 ". . . all who enter through me will be saved. They will come in and go out, and find pasture." *See also* **Jn** 10:28

He lays down his life for his sheep
Jn 10:11 "I am the good shepherd. The good shepherd lays down his life for the sheep." *See also* **Mt** 26:31 pp **Mk** 14:27; **Jn** 10:14–15, 17–18

He judges the sheep **Mt** 25:32–46

Jesus Christ shepherds his flock
Christians are Jesus Christ's flock
Lk 12:32 "Do not be afraid, little flock, for your Father has been pleased to give you the kingdom." *See also* **Mt** 10:16; **Jn** 10:16; **Ac** 20:29; **Ro** 8:36

Under-shepherds are appointed over Jesus Christ's flock
Jn 21:15–17 . . . Jesus said, "Feed my lambs." Again Jesus said, "Simon son of John, do you truly love me?" He answered, "Yes, Lord, you know that I love you." Jesus said, "Take care of my sheep." The third time he said to him, "Simon son of John, do you love me?" Peter was hurt because Jesus asked him the third time, "Do you love me?" He said, "Lord, you know all things; you know that I love you." Jesus said, "Feed my sheep." *See also* **Ac** 20:28; **1Pe** 5:2–4

Jesus Christ the risen Lord is Shepherd
Rev 7:17 "For the Lamb at the centre of the throne will be their shepherd; he will lead them to springs of living water . . ." *See also* **Heb** 13:20; **1Pe** 2:25; 5:4 *See also God as shepherd; God, titles and names of; Jesus Christ, compassion; Messiah, coming of.*

Jesus Christ, anger of
Jesus Christ's controlled emotion arising from his unswerving opposition to evil and his determination to eradicate it.

Causes of Jesus Christ's anger
Petty legalism in religious observance **Mt** 15:3; 23:1–4; **Mk** 3:4–5
Attempts to prevent access to him **Mk** 10:14
People leading others into sin **Mt** 18:6–7 pp **Mk** 9:42 pp **Lk** 17:1–2

Demonstrations of Jesus Christ's anger
Purging the temple **Mt** 21:12–13 pp **Mk** 11:15–17 pp **Lk** 19:45–46; **Jn** 2:14–16
Cursing the fig-tree **Mk** 11:14 pp **Mt** 21:19

Jesus Christ's words in anger
Against demons
Mt 17:18 Jesus rebuked the demon, and it came out of the boy . . . pp **Mk** 9:25 pp **Lk** 9:42 *See also* **Mk** 1:25–26 pp **Lk** 4:35

Against disciples
Lk 9:55–56 But Jesus turned and rebuked them [James and John] . . . *See also* **Mt** 16:23 pp **Mk** 8:33

Against Pharisees
Mt 23:13 "Woe to you, teachers of the law and Pharisees, you hypocrites! You shut the kingdom of heaven in people's faces. You yourselves do not enter, nor will you let those enter who are trying to." *See also* **Mt** 12:34; 15:7–9 pp **Mk** 7:6–8; **Mt** 23:15–16,23–33; **Lk** 11:42–44; 13:15; **Jn** 8:44

Against unbelief
Mt 17:17 "O unbelieving and perverse generation," Jesus replied, "how long shall I stay with you? How long shall I put up with you? . . ." pp **Mk** 9:19 pp **Lk** 9:41 *See also* **Mt** 12:39–45 pp **Lk** 11:29–32; **Mk** 8:38; **Lk** 11:50–51

Against false prophets
Mt 7:15 "Watch out for false prophets. They come to you in sheep's clothing, but inwardly they are ferocious wolves."

Against the rich
Lk 6:24–26 "But woe to you who are rich, for you have already received your comfort . . ."

Against unrepentant cities
Mt 11:20 Then Jesus began to denounce the cities in which most of his miracles had been performed, because they did not repent. *See also* **Mt** 11:21–24 pp Lk 10:13–15

Jesus Christ reflects the anger of God
Jn 3:36 ". . . those who reject the Son will not see life, for God's wrath remains on them." *See also* **Mt** 5:21–22,29; 22:7,13; 25:30,46; **Lk** 21:23

The anger of the glorified Christ
Against the unbelieving world
Rev 6:16 They [the kings and leaders of the earth] called to the mountains and the rocks, "Fall on us and hide us from the face of him who sits on the throne and from the wrath of the Lamb!"

Against the wayward church
Rev 2:16 Repent therefore! Otherwise, I will soon come to you and will fight against them with the sword of my mouth. *See also* **Rev** 2:5,22–23; 3:3,16 *See also God, anger of; Jesus Christ, justice of; Jesus Christ, righteousness.*

Jesus Christ, ascension
The return of Jesus Christ to his Father in order to establish his kingdom, having completed his work on earth.

Jesus Christ's ascension described
Ac 1:9–11 After he [Jesus] said this, he was taken up before their very eyes, and a cloud hid him from their sight . . . *See also* **Mk** 16:19; **Lk** 24:51; **Ac** 1:2; **Eph** 4:10; **1Ti** 3:16; **Heb** 9:24; **1Pe** 3:22; **Rev** 12:5

Predictions of Jesus Christ's ascension
In the OT
Eph 4:7–8 But to each one of us grace has been given as Christ apportioned it. This is why it says: "When he ascended on high, he led captives in his train and gave gifts to people." *See also* **Ps** 68:18

Jesus Christ looks forward to his ascension as his return to his Father
Jn 16:28 I came from the Father and entered the world; now I am leaving the world and going back to the Father." *See also* **Jn** 6:62; 7:33; 14:28; 16:10,5; 17:11,13; 20:17

Jesus Christ establishes his kingdom by his ascension
He ascended to send the Holy Spirit
Jn 16:7 ". . . Unless I [Jesus] go away, the Counsellor will not come to you; but if I go, I will send him to you." *See also* **Jn** 7:39; 14:16–19,25–26; 15:26–27; **Ac** 2:33

He ascended to prepare a place for his people
Jn 14:2–4 "In my Father's house are many rooms; if it were not so, I would have told you. I am going there to prepare a place for you . . ."
He ascended to exaltation and glory Lk 24:26; **Ac** 2:33; **Eph** 1:20–21; **1Pe** 3:22

He ascended to exercise his high priestly ministry
Heb 4:14 Therefore, since we have a great high priest who has gone through the heavens, Jesus the Son of God, let us hold firmly to the faith we profess. *See also* **Heb** 7:25; 9:24

He ascended so that believers may follow him
1Th 4:17 After that, we [believers] who are still alive and are left will be caught up together with them [the dead in Christ] in the clouds to meet the Lord in the air. And so we will be with the Lord for ever.

Jesus Christ's ascension indicates the manner of his return
Ac 1:11 "You Galileans," they [the two men dressed in white] said, "why do you stand here looking into the sky? This same Jesus, who has been taken from you into heaven, will come back in the same way you have seen him go into heaven." *See also* **Mt** 24:30 pp Mk 13:26 pp Lk 21:27; **Rev** 1:7 *See also Holy Spirit, promise of; Jesus Christ, exaltation; Jesus Christ, high priest; Jesus Christ, prophecies concerning; Jesus Christ, resurrection; Jesus Christ, second coming.*

Jesus Christ, attitude to Old Testament

Jesus Christ's teaching was based largely on the OT, which he treated as God's inspired and authoritative word, but which he had the authority to interpret.

Jesus Christ recognises the OT as Scripture

Jesus Christ calls the OT "Scripture"
Jn 10:35 ". . . the Scripture cannot be broken . . ." *See also* **Mk** 12:10,24 pp **Mt** 22:29; **Lk** 4:21; **Jn** 5:39; 7:38; 13:18

Jesus Christ underlines the authority of the OT
Jn 5:46–47 "If you believed Moses, you would believe me, for he wrote about me. But since you do not believe what he wrote, how are you going to believe what I say?"

The OT is authoritative over Jesus Christ's opponents
Mt 23:23 "Woe to you, teachers of the law and Pharisees, you hypocrites! You give a tenth of your spices—mint, dill and cummin. But you have neglected the more important matters of the law—justice, mercy and faithfulness. You should have practised the latter, without neglecting the former." *See also* **Mt** 5:19–20; 23:2–3; **Mk** 2:24–27 pp **Mt** 12:2–6 pp **Lk** 6:2–4

The OT is authoritative over Satan
Mt 4:4 Jesus answered, "It is written: 'People do not live on bread alone, but on every word that comes from the mouth of God.'" pp **Lk** 4:4 *See also* **Dt** 8:3; **Mt** 4:7 pp **Lk** 4:12; **Dt** 6:16; **Mt** 4:10 pp **Lk** 4:8; **Dt** 6:13

Jesus Christ regards the OT as being fulfilled in himself

Jesus Christ regards his ministry as fulfilling the OT
Mt 5:17–18 "Do not think that I [Jesus] have come to abolish the Law or the Prophets; I have not come to abolish them but to fulfil them . . ." *See also* **Mt** 11:4–6 pp **Lk** 7:22–23; **Mt** 26:56 pp **Mk** 14:49; **Lk** 4:17–21; **Isa** 61:1–2; **Jn** 15:25; **Ps** 35:19; 69:4

Jesus Christ regards his death as fulfilling OT prophecy
Lk 18:31–32 Jesus took the Twelve aside and told them, "We are going up to Jerusalem, and everything that is written by the prophets about the Son of Man will be fulfilled. He will be turned over to the Gentiles. They will mock him, insult him, spit on him, flog him and kill him." *See also* **Mt** 12:39–40; 26:28 pp **Lk** 22:20; **Mt** 26:31 pp **Mk** 14:27; **Zec** 13:7

Other aspects of the OT fulfilled or affirmed by Jesus Christ **Mt** 7:12; 11:10 pp **Lk** 7:27; **Mal** 3:1; **Mt** 13:14–15 pp **Mk** 4:12 pp **Lk** 8:10; **Isa** 6:9–10; **Mt** 17:11–12 pp **Mk** 9:12–13; **Mal** 4:5; **Mt** 24:15 pp **Mk** 13:14 pp **Lk** 21:20; **Da** 9:27; 11:31; 12:11

Jesus Christ confirms the OT teaching about judgment

Mt 12:41–42 "The people of Nineveh will stand up at the judgment with this generation and condemn it; for they repented at the preaching of Jonah, and now one greater than Jonah is here. The Queen of the South will rise at the judgment with this generation and condemn it; for she came from the ends of the earth to listen to Solomon's wisdom, and now one greater than Solomon is here." pp **Lk** 11:30–32 *See also* **Mt** 11:23 pp **Lk** 10:12–15

Jesus Christ interprets OT teaching

Jesus Christ interprets OT teaching about the Sabbath **Mk** 2:25–28 pp **Mt** 12:3–8 pp **Lk** 6:3–5
Jesus Christ interprets OT teaching about religious practices **Mt** 9:13; **Hos** 6:6; **Mt** 15:7–8 pp **Mk** 7:6–7; **Isa** 29:13
Jesus Christ interprets OT teaching about purity **Mk** 7:18–19 pp **Mt** 15:17
Jesus Christ interprets OT teaching about family life **Mt** 5:31–32; 15:4–6 pp **Mk** 7:10–13; **Ex** 20:12; **Dt** 5:16; **Ex** 21:17; **Lev** 20:9; **Mt** 19:1–9 pp **Mk** 10:2–9
Jesus Christ interprets OT teaching about retaliation **Mt** 5:38–42

Jesus Christ refers to the OT in his teaching

Mt 19:18 pp **Mk** 10:19 pp **Lk** 18:20; **Ex** 20:12–16;

Dt 5:16-20; **Mt** 22:31-32 pp Mk 12:26-27 pp Lk 20:37-38; **Ex** 3:6; **Mt** 24:37-39 pp Lk 17:26-27

Jesus Christ uses the language of the OT
Mt 27:46 pp Mk 15:34; **Ps** 22:1; **Mk** 4:29; **Joel** 3:13; **Mk** 8:18; **Isa** 6:10; **Mk** 9:48; **Isa** 66:24

Jesus Christ appeals to the OT in its entirety
Lk 11:50-51 ". . . from the blood of Abel to the blood of Zechariah . . ." *See also* **Lk** 24:27,44

Jesus Christ treats the OT as a true historical record
The patriarchs: **Mt** 8:11; **Jn** 8:56,58
Moses: **Mt** 8:4 pp Mk 1:44 pp Lk 5:14; **Mt** 19:8 pp Mk 10:5
Mt 6:29 pp Lk 12:27
The prophets: **Mt** 5:12 pp Lk 6:23; **Lk** 4:25-27; **Jn** 6:45 *See also Jesus Christ, death of; Jesus Christ, mission; Jesus Christ, preaching and teaching; Jesus Christ, prophecies concerning; Jesus Christ, temptation; Scripture, inspiration and authority.*

Jesus Christ, authority
The right of Jesus Christ to speak and act on his Father's behalf in forgiving sin, pronouncing judgment and promising eternal life to those who believe in him.

Jesus Christ's authority underlines his divine status
Jn 8:28 So Jesus said, "When you have lifted up the Son of Man, then you will know that I am the one I claim to be, and that I do nothing on my own but speak just what the Father has taught me. *See also* **Jn** 8:58; 14:6; **1Co** 1:24; **Col** 2:10

The origin of Jesus Christ's authority
It is given by God the Father
Jn 3:35 "The Father loves the Son and has placed everything in his hands." *See also* **Mt** 28:18; **Lk** 10:22; **Jn** 5:26-27; 7:16; 10:18; 12:49-50; 17:2

It is limited by the Father
Mk 10:40 ". . . to sit at my [Jesus'] right or left is not for me to grant. These places belong to those for whom they have been prepared."
See also **Mt** 24:36 pp Mk 13:32; **Php** 2:6-8

It is questioned by others
Mt 12:24-28 But when the Pharisees heard this, they said, "It is only by Beelzebub, the prince of demons, that this fellow drives out demons." . . . pp Mk 3:22-26 pp Lk 11:15-20
See also **Mt** 21:23-27 pp Mk 11:27-33 pp Lk 20:1-8; **Jn** 2:18

The authority of Jesus Christ is seen in his works
He has authority over nature **Mt** 8:23-27 pp Mk 4:36-41 pp Lk 8:22-25; **Mt** 14:22-33 pp Mk 6:45-51 pp Jn 6:15-21; **Mt** 21:18-22 pp Mk 11:12-14, 20-24
He has authority over sin **Mt** 9:1-8 pp Mk 2:3-12 pp Lk 5:18-26; **Lk** 7:37-38,44-50
He has authority over sickness **Mt** 8:14-15 pp Mk 1:30-31 pp Lk 4:38-39; **Mt** 20:29-34 pp Mk 10:46-52 pp Lk 18:35-43; **Ac** 3:16; 4:30
He has authority over evil **Mk** 1:23-27 pp Lk 4:33-36; **Lk** 10:17
He has authority over death **Mt** 9:18-25 pp Mk 5:22-42 pp Lk 8:40-55; **Mt** 28:1-7 pp Mk 16:1-6 pp Lk 24:1-8 pp Jn 20:1-17; **Lk** 7:11-16; **Jn** 11:38-44

The authority of Jesus Christ is seen in his teaching
Jesus Christ claims authority for his own words
Lk 4:18 "The Spirit of the Lord is on me, because he has anointed me to preach good news to the poor . . ." *See also* **Mt** 5:21-22, 27-28; 12:41-42; 17:5 pp Mk 9:7 pp Lk 9:35; **Mk** 2:5,10; 8:38; 10:15; 13:26, 31; **Jn** 4:24-26; 6:63; 7:15-18; 12:48-50; 13:13; 14:6; 15:3

His authority is recognised by others
Mt 7:28-29 When Jesus had finished saying these things, the crowds were amazed at his teaching, because he taught as one who had authority, and not as their teachers of the law.
See also **Mt** 22:33,46; **Mk** 1:22,27 pp Lk 4:32

His authority is questioned and opposed by others Mt 26:65–68; Lk 4:28–30

Jesus Christ delegates his authority to others
His followers preach in his name Mt 10:7; 28:18–20
His followers continue his works Mt 10:1 pp Mk 6:7 pp Lk 9:1–2; Mt 10:8; Mk 3:15; 6:13; 16:17–18; Lk 10:1–12; Jn 14:12; Ac 3:6,16
His followers pronounce his forgiveness and judgment Mt 18:18; Mk 6:11; Lk 22:28–30; Jn 20:22–23; 1Co 6:2–3

The results of Jesus Christ's authority
He receives honour and glory
Jn 5:22–23 "... the Father judges no-one, but has entrusted all judgment to the Son, that all may honour the Son just as they honour the Father ..." *See also* Jn 11:4; 17:5
He arouses amazement Mt 9:33; 12:23
He is opposed Mt 12:14 pp Mk 3:6 pp Lk 6:11
He is feared Lk 8:37 pp Mt 8:34
His disciples are opposed Ac 16:16–24

The authority of the exalted Christ
He is Lord Eph 1:20; Php 2:9–11; Col 3:1; 1Pe 3:22; Rev 3:21
He is Lord of creation Col 1:16–17
He is Lord of the church Eph 1:22; 5:23; Col 1:18
He is judge Ac 10:42; 17:31
He is Saviour Jn 3:15; 14:3; Col 1:19–20; Tit 2:13; Heb 7:24–25; 9:28
He is interceder Ro 8:34; Heb 7:25; 9:24; 1Jn 2:1   *See also* forgiveness; Jesus Christ's ministry; Jesus Christ as judge; Jesus Christ as king; Jesus Christ as Saviour; Jesus Christ, divinity; Jesus Christ, exaltation; Jesus Christ, head of the church; Jesus Christ, power of; Jesus Christ, responses to; Jesus Christ, the Lord.

Jesus Christ, baptism of
In obedience to God's will Jesus Christ was baptised in the River Jordan by John. The event was sealed by the descent of the Holy Spirit and the Father's voice of approval.

John tries to prevent Jesus Christ from being baptised
Mt 3:13–14 ... Jesus came from Galilee to the Jordan to be baptised by John. But John tried to deter him, saying, "I need to be baptised by you, and do you come to me?"

The necessity of Jesus Christ's baptism
Mt 3:15 Jesus replied, "Let it be so now; it is proper for us to do this to fulfil all righteousness." Then John consented.   *See also* Mk 10:38; Lk 12:50

The events surrounding Jesus Christ's baptism
The baptism itself
Mk 1:9 ... Jesus came from Nazareth in Galilee and was baptised by John in the Jordan. pp Mt 3:13 pp Lk 3:21
Jesus Christ prays while being baptised
Lk 3:21 ... Jesus was baptised too. And as he was praying, heaven was opened
The Holy Spirit descends on Jesus Christ
Mk 1:10 As Jesus was coming up out of the water, he saw heaven being torn open and the Spirit descending on him like a dove. pp Mt 3:16 pp Lk 3:22   *See also* Jn 1:32–34
The voice of the Father is heard
Mt 3:17 ... a voice from heaven said, "This is my Son, whom I love; with him I am well pleased." pp Mk 1:11 pp Lk 3:22   *See also* Mt 17:5 pp Mk 9:7 pp Lk 9:35   *See also* God, fatherhood; Holy Spirit in life of Jesus Christ; Jesus Christ, obedience; Jesus Christ, prayers of; Jesus Christ, sinlessness; Jesus Christ, sonship of; Jesus Christ, temptation; Trinity.

Jesus Christ, birth of
Jesus Christ was born to a poor unmarried Jewish couple in the village of Bethlehem. As Son of God, he was conceived by the Holy Spirit in the womb of his mother Mary.

Jesus Christ's birth is prophesied in the OT
The prophecy of a coming ruler
Isa 9:6–7 For to us a child is born, to us a

son is given, and the government will be on his shoulders. And he will be called Wonderful Counsellor, Mighty God, Everlasting Father, Prince of Peace. Of the increase of his government and peace there will be no end. He will reign on David's throne and over his kingdom, establishing and upholding it with justice and righteousness from that time on and for ever. The zeal of the LORD Almighty will accomplish this.

The prophecy of a virgin's son
Isa 7:14 "Therefore the Lord himself will give you a sign: The virgin will be with child and will give birth to a son, and will call him Immanuel."

The prophecy concerning his birthplace
Mic 5:2 "But you, Bethlehem Ephrathah, though you are small among the clans of Judah, out of you will come for me one who will be ruler over Israel, whose origins are from of old, from ancient times."

Jesus Christ was conceived by the Holy Spirit and born of a virgin

Mt 1:18 This is how the birth of Jesus Christ came about: His mother Mary was pledged to be married to Joseph, but before they came together, she was found to be with child through the Holy Spirit.
Mt 1:23 "The virgin will be with child and will give birth to a son, and they will call him Immanuel"—which means, "God with us."
See also **Mt** 1:20; **Lk** 1:34–35

Jesus Christ's incarnation
Jn 1:14 The Word became flesh and made his dwelling among us. We have seen his glory, the glory of the One and Only, who came from the Father, full of grace and truth.
Gal 4:4 But when the time had fully come, God sent his Son, born of a woman, born under law, *See also* **Ro** 8:3; **2Co** 8:9; **Php** 2:7–8; **1Ti** 3:16; **1Jn** 4:2

The circumstances of Jesus Christ's birth
An angel informs Mary that she is to be the mother of the Messiah
Lk 1:26–38 . . . But the angel said to her, "Do not be afraid, Mary, you have found favour with God. You will be with child and give birth to a son, and you are to give him the name Jesus . . ."
Mary responds in praise Lk 1:46–55
An angel explains to Joseph why Mary's baby is so special
Mt 1:18–25 . . . an angel of the Lord appeared to him in a dream and said, "Joseph son of David, do not be afraid to take Mary home as your wife, because what is conceived in her is from the Holy Spirit. She will give birth to a son, and you are to give him the name Jesus, because he will save his people from their sins." . . .
The birth of Jesus Christ takes place
Lk 2:1–7 . . . she [Mary] gave birth to her firstborn, a son. She wrapped him in cloths and placed him in a manger, because there was no room for them in the inn.
Angels announce Jesus Christ's birth to some shepherds Lk 2:8–20
The Magi search for Jesus Christ's birthplace and Herod tries to kill him Mt 2:1–18
See also incarnation; Jesus Christ as king; Jesus Christ, genealogy; Jesus Christ, humanity; Jesus Christ, humility; Jesus Christ, prophecies concerning; Jesus Christ, Son of David; Jesus Christ, Son of God; Messiah, coming of.

Jesus Christ, childhood
As an infant Jesus Christ was consecrated in the temple, accompanied by prophetic utterances regarding his future ministry. His childhood was characterised by a growth in wisdom and grace and, in particular, a strong desire to learn of God his Father and to understand the Scriptures.

Jesus Christ was consecrated as an infant
Lk 2:22 When the time of their purification according to the Law of Moses had been completed, Joseph and Mary took him to Jerusalem to present him to the Lord
See also **Lk** 2:23–24

Indications of Jesus Christ's future ministry were revealed
Through the words of Simeon
Lk 2:30–32 "For my eyes have seen your

salvation, which you have prepared in the sight of all people, a light for revelation to the Gentiles and for glory to your people Israel."
See also **Lk** 2:25–29,34–35

Through the words of Anna
Lk 2:38 Coming up to them [Mary, Joseph and Jesus] at that very moment, she gave thanks to God and spoke about the child to all who were looking forward to the redemption of Jerusalem.

The visit of the Magi
Mt 2:1–12

The escape to Egypt
Mt 2:13–15 . . . an angel of the Lord appeared to Joseph in a dream. "Get up," he said, "take the child and his mother and escape to Egypt. Stay there until I tell you, for Herod is going to search for the child to kill him." So he got up, took the child and his mother during the night and left for Egypt, where he stayed until the death of Herod . . .

The return from Egypt
Mt 2:19–20 After Herod died, an angel of the Lord appeared in a dream to Joseph in Egypt and said, "Get up, take the child and his mother and go to the land of Israel, for those who were trying to take the child's life are dead."
See also **Mt** 2:15; **Hos** 11:1; **Mt** 2:21

Jesus Christ lives in Nazareth
Mt 2:22–23 . . . he [Joseph] went and lived in a town called Nazareth. So was fulfilled what was said through the prophets: "He will be called a Nazarene."   See also **Lk** 2:39

Jesus Christ grows up
Lk 2:40 . . . the child [Jesus] grew and became strong; he was filled with wisdom, and the grace of God was upon him.   See also **Lk** 2:52

Jesus Christ visited the temple
He celebrates the Passover there **Lk** 2:41–42
He stays behind in the temple **Lk** 2:43–45, 48–50

He displays his understanding of the Scriptures there
Lk 2:46–47 . . . Everyone who heard him [Jesus] was amazed at his understanding and his answers.

The obedience of Jesus Christ
Lk 2:51 Then he [Jesus] went down to Nazareth with them [Mary and Joseph] and was obedient to them . . .

Mary and Joseph remember the sayings and events of Jesus Christ's childhood
Lk 2:19,33,51   See also **Jesus Christ, attitude to Old Testament; Jesus Christ, birth of; Jesus Christ, family of; Jesus Christ, humanity; Jesus Christ, obedience; Jesus Christ, prophecies concerning; Jesus Christ, Son of God; Jesus Christ, wisdom.**

Jesus Christ, compassion
Jesus Christ's pity and loving concern for the lowly and the needy. His words and deeds show God's merciful and gracious nature in action.

Jesus Christ shows the compassion of God
2Co 1:3 Praise be to the God and Father of our Lord Jesus Christ, the Father of compassion and the God of all comfort,   See also **2Ch** 36:15; **Ps** 86:15; **Hos** 11:4,8–9; **Lk** 1:72,78; 15:20

The compassion of Jesus Christ is the basis of Christian confidence
Heb 4:14–16 Therefore, since we have a great high priest who has gone through the heavens, Jesus the Son of God, let us hold firmly to the faith we profess. For we do not have a high priest who is unable to sympathise with our weaknesses, but we have one who has been tempted in every way, just as we are—yet was without sin. Let us then approach the throne of grace with confidence, so that we may receive mercy and find grace to help us in our time of need.

The demonstration of Jesus Christ's compassion
In supporting the weak
Mt 12:20 "A bruised reed he will not break,

and a smouldering wick he will not snuff out, till he leads justice to victory." See also **Isa** 42:3; **Mt** 19:14 pp Mk 10:14 pp Lk 18:16

In healing the sick
Mt 14:14 When Jesus landed and saw a large crowd, he had compassion on them and healed their sick. pp Lk 9:11 See also **Mt** 20:34 pp Mk 10:52 pp Lk 18:42–43; **Mk** 1:41 pp Mt 8:3 pp Lk 5:13; **Lk** 13:12

In comforting the bereaved
Lk 7:13 When the Lord saw her [the widow of Nain], his heart went out to her and he said, "Don't cry." See also **Lk** 8:50 pp Mk 5:36; Jn 11:33–35; 19:25–27; 20:14–16

In feeding the hungry
Mt 15:32 Jesus called his disciples to him and said, "I have compassion for these people; they have already been with me three days and have nothing to eat. I do not want to send them away hungry, or they may collapse on the way." pp Mk 8:2–3 See also **Mt** 14:16 pp Mk 6:37 pp Lk 9:13 pp Jn 6:5–6

In finding and forgiving lost sinners
Mt 9:36 When he [Jesus] saw the crowds, he had compassion on them, because they were harassed and helpless, like sheep without a shepherd. pp Mk 6:34 See also **Isa** 40:11; **Mt** 18:14; 23:37–38 pp Lk 13:34–35; **Lk** 7:47–48; Jn 8:10–11

In giving rest to those who are burdened or abandoned
Mt 11:28–29 "Come to me, all you who are weary and burdened, and I will give you rest. Take my yoke upon you and learn from me, for I am gentle and humble in heart, and you will find rest for your souls." See also **Mk** 1:40–41 pp Mt 8:1–3 pp Lk 5:12–13; **Lk** 11:46; 15:1–2; 17:12–14

Jesus Christ's compassion is a model for Christians to follow
Lk 10:36–37 "Which of these three do you think was a neighbour to the man who fell into the hands of robbers?" The expert in the law replied, "The one who had mercy on him." Jesus told him, "Go and do likewise." See also **Jn** 13:34; 17:18; **Php** 2:1 See also forgiveness; God, compassion; God, grace and mercy; Jesus Christ, grace and mercy; Jesus Christ, love of; Jesus Christ, miracles; Jesus Christ, power of.

Jesus Christ, cross of
The death of Jesus Christ is of central importance to the Christian faith. Through Christ's death, sinners are reconciled to God and to their fellow human beings. Paul summarises the gospel as "the message of the cross"

Jesus Christ foretold his death on the cross
Mt 20:18–19 "We are going up to Jerusalem, and the Son of Man will be betrayed to the chief priests and the teachers of the law. They will condemn him to death and will turn him over to the Gentiles to be mocked and flogged and crucified. On the third day he will be raised to life!" pp Mk 10:33–34 pp Lk 18:31–32 See also **Mt** 26:2; **Jn** 3:14–15; 8:28; 12:32–33; 18:32

The facts of Jesus Christ's death on the cross
Carrying Jesus Christ's cross
Jn 19:17 Carrying his own cross, he [Jesus] went out to the place of the Skull (which in Aramaic is called Golgotha). See also **Mt** 27:32 pp Mk 15:21 pp Lk 23:26

Jesus Christ refused the comfort of wine, which would have lessened the pains of his suffering **Mt** 27:34 pp Mk 15:23

Jesus Christ was nailed to the cross
Lk 23:33 When they came to the place called the Skull, there they crucified him, along with the criminals—one on his right, the other on his left. pp Mt 27:35 pp Mk 15:24–25 pp Jn 19:18

Jesus Christ's words from the cross **Lk** 23:34,43; Jn 19:26–27; **Mt** 27:46 pp Mk 15:34; **Ps** 22:1; **Lk** 23:46; Jn 19:28–30

Signs accompanying Jesus Christ's death on the cross
Darkness over the whole land for three hours: **Mt** 27:45; **Mk** 15:33 pp Lk 23:44–45

The temple curtain torn from top to bottom: **Mt** 27:51 pp Mk 15:38 pp Lk 23:45; **Mt** 27:52–53

Jesus Christ, death of

People at the scene of the cross
The Roman centurion and his men: **Mt** 27:35–36,54 pp **Mk** 15:39 pp **Lk** 23:47

The two criminals crucified with Jesus Christ: **Mt** 27:38 pp **Mk** 15:27 pp **Lk** 23:32–33 pp **Jn** 19:18; **Mt** 27:44; **Lk** 23:39–43

Mt 27:39–43 pp **Mk** 15:29–32 pp **Lk** 23:35–37
Jesus Christ's mother and other women: **Mt** 27:55–56 pp **Mk** 15:40–41 pp **Lk** 23:27–31 pp **Jn** 19:25; **Lk** 23:49 **Jn** 19:26–27

Responsibility for the cross
The cross as God's plan
Ac 2:23 "This man [Jesus of Nazareth] was handed over to you by God's set purpose and foreknowledge; and you, with the help of wicked people, put him to death by nailing him to the cross." *See also* **Isa** 53:10; **Mt** 26:39 pp **Mk** 14:36 pp **Lk** 22:42; **Mt** 26:42; **Jn** 14:30–31; **Ac** 4:25–28; **Ps** 2:1–2; **Rev** 13:8

The crowd's call for Jesus Christ's crucifixion
Mt 27:21–22 pp **Mk** 15:12–14 pp **Lk** 23:18–21 pp **Jn** 19:15; **Mt** 27:25; **Ac** 2:36; **1Th** 2:14–15

Jewish and Roman leaders' responsibility
Mt 27:1,20 pp **Mk** 15:11; **Mt** 27:26 pp **Mk** 15:15 pp **Jn** 19:16; **Lk** 23:24–25; **Jn** 19:6–7; **Ac** 4:10; **1Co** 2:8

The triumph of the cross
Col 2:15 And having disarmed the powers and authorities, he [God] made a public spectacle of them, triumphing over them by the cross.

The cross brings glory to Jesus Christ
Jn 17:1 After Jesus said this, he looked towards heaven and prayed: "Father, the time has come. Glorify your Son, that your Son may glorify you." *See also* **Jn** 12:28; 13:31–32; 17:5; **Php** 2:8–11; **Heb** 12:2; **Rev** 5:8–14

The cross brings reconciliation
Eph 2:13–17 . . . His [Jesus'] purpose was to create in himself one new humanity out of the two, thus making peace, and in this one body to reconcile both of them to God through the cross, by which he put to death their hostility . . . *See also* **Ro** 5:9–10; **2Co** 5:18–19; **Col** 1:20

Identification with the crucified Christ releases believers from their old way of life
Gal 2:20 I [Paul] have been crucified with Christ and I no longer live, but Christ lives in me. The life I live in the body, I live by faith in the Son of God, who loved me and gave himself for me. *See also* **Ro** 6:5–13; **Gal** 5:24–25; 6:14; **Col** 2:13–14

Jesus Christ's cross is central to the Christian message
1Co 2:2 For I [Paul] resolved to know nothing while I was with you except Jesus Christ and him crucified. *See also* **Ac** 2:23–24; 3:13; 5:30; 13:27–29; **Gal** 3:1

Jesus Christ's cross is the symbol of Christian discipleship
Mt 16:24 Then Jesus said to his disciples, "Those who would come after me must deny themselves and take up their cross and follow me." pp **Mk** 8:34 pp **Lk** 9:23 *See also* **Mt** 10:38; **Jn** 21:18–19 *See also* forgiveness; Jesus Christ, death of; Jesus Christ, glory of; Jesus Christ, obedience; Jesus Christ, prophecies concerning; Jesus Christ, suffering; Jesus Christ, victory.

Jesus Christ, death of
The death of Jesus Christ by crucifixion is of central importance to the NT. Through the faithful, obedient death of Christ, God grants sinners forgiveness and eternal life. The Christian sacraments of baptism and the Lord's Supper focus upon the death of Christ.

Jesus Christ's death was foretold
In time and in eternity
Rev 13:8 . . . the Lamb that was slain from the creation of the world. *See also* **Isa** 53:10–12; **Zec** 12:10; **Jn** 1:29,36

By Jesus Christ himself
Mt 16:21 From that time on Jesus began to explain to his disciples that he must go to Jerusalem and suffer many things at the hands of the elders, chief priests and teachers of the law, and that he must be killed and on the third day be raised to life. pp **Mk** 8:31 pp **Lk** 9:22 *See also* **Mt** 17:22–23; 26:12 pp **Jn** 12:7; **Jn** 16:16,28; 18:4

Jesus Christ willingly planned to give his life
Jn 10:11 "I [Jesus] am the good shepherd. The good shepherd lays down his life for the sheep." *See also* Jn 10:15,17–18; 13:1; 15:13; 1Jn 3:16

Plots to kill Jesus Christ
Mk 3:6 Then the Pharisees went out and began to plot with the Herodians how they might kill Jesus. pp Mt 12:14 *See also* Mt 26:4 pp Mk 14:1; Lk 13:31; 19:47; Jn 5:18; 7:25; 8:37,40

The manner of Jesus Christ's death
Jesus Christ died by crucifixion
Lk 23:33 When they came to the place called the Skull, there they crucified him, along with the criminals—one on his right, the other on his left. pp Mt 27:35 pp Mk 15:24–25
The moment of death
Mk 15:37 With a loud cry, Jesus breathed his last. pp Mt 27:50 pp Lk 23:46 pp Jn 19:30 *See also* Jn 19:33
Events accompanying Jesus Christ's death Mt 27:45, 51–53
Jesus Christ's burial
Mt 27:58–60 . . . Joseph took the body, wrapped it in a clean linen cloth, and placed it in his own new tomb that he had cut out of the rock . . . pp Mk 15:43–46 pp Lk 23:51–53 pp Jn 19:38–42

The unique character of Jesus Christ's death
Jesus Christ's body did not decay
Ac 2:31 "Seeing what was ahead, he [David] spoke of the resurrection of the Christ, that he was not abandoned to the grave, nor did his body see decay." *See also* Ps 16:10; Ac 2:27; 13:36–37
Jesus Christ descended to the dead
Ro 1:4 . . . who through the Spirit of holiness was declared with power to be the Son of God, by his resurrection from the dead: Jesus Christ our Lord. *See also* 1Pe 3:18–22
Jesus Christ was raised bodily from the dead
Lk 24:36–40 . . . Look at my hands and my feet. It is I myself! Touch me and see; a ghost does not have flesh and bones, as you see I have." . . . *See also* Jn 21:12–13; Ac 10:41; 25:19
Death had no power over Jesus Christ
Ac 2:24 But God raised him from the dead, freeing him from the agony of death, because it was impossible for death to keep its hold on him. *See also* Ro 6:9–10; Rev 1:18
Jesus Christ's death was a unique sacrifice
Heb 7:27 Unlike the other high priests, he [Jesus] does not need to offer sacrifices day after day, first for his own sins, and then for the sins of the people. He sacrificed for their sins once for all when he offered himself. *See also* 1Co 5:7; Eph 5:2; Heb 9:26,28; 10:10,12; 1Jn 2:2; 4:10

Achievements of Jesus Christ's death
Jesus Christ's death establishes the new covenant
Lk 22:20 In the same way, after the supper he [Jesus] took the cup, saying, "This cup is the new covenant in my blood, which is poured out for you." pp Mt 26:28 pp Mk 14:24 pp 1Co 11:25 *See also* Heb 9:15; 13:20
Jesus Christ's death is a victory
Col 2:14–15 . . . And having disarmed the powers and authorities, he [God] made a public spectacle of them, triumphing over them by the cross. *See also* Heb 2:9,14–15; Rev 12:11
Jesus Christ's death brings redemption
Rev 5:9 And they sang a new song: "You [the Lamb] are worthy to take the scroll and to open its seals, because you were slain, and with your blood you purchased for God members of every tribe and language and people and nation." *See also* Mk 10:45 pp Mt 20:28; Ac 20:28; Gal 3:13; Eph 1:7; Tit 2:14; 1Pe 1:18–19
Jesus Christ's death brings forgiveness and cleansing
1Jn 1:7 . . . the blood of Jesus, his Son, purifies us from all sin. *See also* Heb 9:14; Rev 1:5; 7:14
Jesus Christ's death brings sanctification
Heb 13:12 And so Jesus also suffered . . . to make the people holy through his own blood. *See also* Heb 10:14; 1Pe 1:2

Believers identify with Jesus Christ in his death
Ro 6:3–8 ... don't you know that all of us who were baptised into Christ Jesus were baptised into his death? ... *See also* **2Co** 5:14–15; **Gal** 2:20; **Col** 2:11; **2Ti** 2:11 *See also* forgiveness; Jesus Christ as Lamb; Jesus Christ as redeemer; Jesus Christ, resurrection; salvation; sin.

Jesus Christ, divinity

The equality and identity of Jesus Christ as God is clearly stated in the NT, and is also implied by the words and deeds of Jesus Christ. The OT prophecies also point to the divinity of the coming Messiah.

The NT writers affirm Jesus Christ's divinity
Heb 1:8 But about the Son he [God] says, "Your throne, O God, will last for ever and ever, and righteousness will be the sceptre of your kingdom." *See also* **Ps** 45:6; **Jn** 1:1–2,18; **Ro** 9:5; **Php** 2:6; **Tit** 2:13; **2Pe** 1:1

Statements which imply Jesus Christ's divinity
Mt 1:23 "The virgin will be with child and will give birth to a son, and they will call him Immanuel"—which means, "God with us." *See also* **Isa** 7:14; **Lk** 1:35; **Col** 1:15; 2:2,9; **1Ti** 1:17; **1Jn** 5:20

Jesus Christ's unity with the Father and the Holy Spirit in the Godhead
Mt 28:19 "Therefore go and make disciples of all nations, baptising them in the name of the Father and of the Son and of the Holy Spirit," *See also* **Jn** 14:16; **2Co** 13:14; **Eph** 1:13–14; 2:18,22; 3:14–17; 4:4–6

Jesus Christ's eternal nature indicates his divinity
Jesus Christ precedes creation
Col 1:17 He [Jesus] is before all things, and in him all things hold together. *See also* **Mic** 5:2; **Jn** 17:5,24; **2Ti** 1:9; **1Pe** 1:20; **1Jn** 1:1; 2:13

Jesus Christ is everlasting
Jn 8:58 "I tell you the truth," Jesus answered, "before Abraham was born, I am!" *See also* **Heb** 1:12; **Ps** 102:27; **Heb** 7:3,24; 13:8; **Rev** 1:8; 5:13; 22:13

Jesus Christ's pre-existence indicates his divinity
Jn 6:62 "What if you [the disciples] see the Son of Man ascend to where he was before!" *See also* **Jn** 3:13,31; 6:41–42; 13:3; 16:28

Jesus Christ's manifestation of God's glory indicates his divinity
Heb 1:3 The Son is the radiance of God's glory and the exact representation of his being ... *See also* **Mt** 17:2 pp **Mk** 9:2–3 pp **Lk** 9:29; **Jn** 1:14; **1Co** 2:8; **2Co** 4:4; **Jas** 2:1

Jesus Christ's divinity in the OT
The divinity of the coming Messiah Isa 9:6; 40:3; **Jer** 23:6; **Mal** 3:1
NT passages which apply OT passages about God to Jesus Christ
Ro 10:13 ... "Everyone who calls on the name of the Lord will be saved." *See also* **Joel** 2:32; **Jn** 12:40–41; **Isa** 6:10; **Ro** 9:33; **Isa** 8:14; **Eph** 4:8; **Ps** 68:18

Jesus Christ's claims to divinity
He claimed to be one with the Father
Jn 5:17–18 ... For this reason the Jews tried all the harder to kill him; not only was he breaking the Sabbath, but he was even calling God his own Father, making himself equal with God. *See also* **Jn** 10:30–33,36–38; 12:45; 14:7,9–11; 17:11,21
He demonstrated his authority to forgive sin
Lk 5:20–24 ... The Pharisees and the teachers of the law began thinking to themselves, "Who is this fellow who speaks blasphemy? Who can forgive sins but God alone?" ... pp **Mt** 9:2–6 pp **Mk** 2:5–10 *See also* **Lk** 7:47–48

Jesus Christ's actions imply his divinity
Mt 8:26–27 ... The disciples were amazed and asked, "What kind of man is this? Even the

winds and the waves obey him!" pp Mk 4:39–41 pp Lk 8:24–25   See also **Mt** 12:8 pp **Mk** 2:28 pp Lk 6:5; **Lk** 8:39 pp **Mk** 5:19–20

Jesus Christ's resurrection confirms his divinity
Ac 2:36 "Therefore let all Israel be assured of this: God has made this Jesus, whom you crucified, both Lord and Christ."   See also **Ro** 1:4; **Php** 2:9–11

Jesus Christ's names and titles point to his divinity
Jesus Christ as judge
Jn 5:27 "And he [the Father] has given him [the Son] authority to judge because he is the Son of Man."   See also **Mt** 25:31–33; **Mk** 8:38 pp Mt 16:27 pp Lk 9:26; **Ac** 17:31; **Ro** 2:16; **2Co** 5:10
Jesus Christ as "I am"
Jn 11:25 Jesus said to her [Martha], "I am the resurrection and the life. Those who believe in me will live, even though they die;"   See also Jn 6:35; 8:12; 10:7,11; 14:6; 15:1; 18:5–6
Jesus Christ as Saviour
Ac 5:31 "God exalted him [Jesus] to his own right hand as Prince and Saviour that he might give repentance and forgiveness of sins to Israel."   See also **Ac** 4:12; **Eph** 5:23; **Heb** 7:25
Jesus Christ as Lord
Ro 10:9 . . . if you confess with your mouth, "Jesus is Lord," and believe in your heart that God raised him from the dead, you will be saved.   See also **Lk** 1:43; 2:11; **Jn** 13:13; **1Co** 12:3; **2Co** 4:5; **Rev** 19:16
Jesus Christ as creator
Col 1:16 For by him [Jesus] all things were created: things in heaven and on earth, visible and invisible, whether thrones or powers or rulers or authorities; all things were created by him and for him.   See also **Jn** 1:3,10; **Ac** 3:15; **Ro** 11:36; **1Co** 8:6; **Heb** 1:2,10; **Ps** 102:25
Jesus Christ as shepherd
Heb 13:20 . . . our Lord Jesus, that great Shepherd of the sheep,   See also **Jn** 10:11–16; **1Pe** 2:25; 5:4

Those who recognised Jesus Christ's divinity
The disciples
Jn 20:28 Thomas said to him [Jesus], "My Lord and my God!"   See also **Mt** 16:16 pp Mk 8:29 pp Lk 9:20
The demons Mk 3:11; **Lk** 4:41 pp Mk 1:34

The consequences of recognising Jesus Christ's divinity
Jesus Christ is worshipped as God
Lk 24:52 Then they [the disciples] worshipped him [Jesus] and returned to Jerusalem with great joy.   See also **Mt** 2:11; 28:9,17; **Jn** 9:38; **2Ti** 4:18; **2Pe** 3:18; **Rev** 1:5–6; 5:12–13; 7:10
Prayer is addressed to Jesus Christ Ac 7:59–60; 9:13; **1Co** 16:22; **Rev** 22:20   See also forgiveness, Jesus Christ's ministry; Holy Spirit in life of Jesus Christ; Jesus Christ as judge; Jesus Christ as Saviour; Jesus Christ, glory of; Jesus Christ, humanity; Jesus Christ, resurrection; Jesus Christ, sonship of; Jesus Christ, the Lord; Jesus Christ, titles and names of; Jesus, the Christ.

Jesus Christ, exaltation
Having completed his work on earth, Jesus Christ is raised to God's right hand where he receives honour, power and glory.

Jesus Christ is exalted to God's right hand
1Pe 3:21–22 . . . Jesus Christ, who has gone into heaven and is at God's right hand—with angels, authorities and powers in submission to him.   See also **Mt** 26:64 pp Mk 14:62 pp Lk 22:69; **Ac** 2:33; 3:20–21; 7:55–56; **Heb** 1:3; 12:2

Jesus Christ is exalted because he first humbled himself
Lk 24:26 "Did not the Christ have to suffer these things and then enter his glory?"
See also **Php** 2:6–11; **1Ti** 3:16; **Rev** 5:6–14; 7:17; 22:3

Jesus Christ's exaltation follows his resurrection and ascension
1Pe 1:21 . . . God, who raised him [Christ]

from the dead and glorified him . . . *See also* **Mk** 16:19; **Ac** 13:37; **Eph** 1:20

Jesus Christ's exaltation is predicted in the OT
As God's servant
Isa 52:13 See, my [God's] servant will act wisely; he will be raised and lifted up and highly exalted.

Jesus Christ is exalted by God the Father
Php 2:9–11 Therefore God exalted him [Jesus] to the highest place and gave him the name that is above every name, that at the name of Jesus every knee should bow . . . *See also* **Ac** 2:36; 5:31

The work of the exalted Christ
As Saviour
Ac 5:31 "God exalted him [Jesus] to his own right hand as Prince and Saviour that he might give repentance and forgiveness of sins to Israel." *See also* **Heb** 7:25
As high priest and advocate
Ro 8:34 . . . Christ Jesus, who died—more than that, who was raised to life—is at the right hand of God and is also interceding for us. *See also* **Heb** 4:14; 7:24–26; 8:1–2; 9:24; **1Jn** 2:1
In giving the Holy Spirit and spiritual gifts to his people
Ac 2:33 "Exalted to the right hand of God, he [Jesus] has received from the Father the promised Holy Spirit and has poured out what you now see and hear." *See also* **Eph** 4:8–13
In making every authority subject to him
Eph 1:20–22 . . . he [God] raised him [Christ] from the dead and seated him at his right hand in the heavenly realms, far above all rule and authority, power and dominion, and every title that can be given, not only in the present age but also in the one to come. And God placed all things under his feet and appointed him to be head over everything . . . *See also* **1Co** 15:24–26; **Php** 2:9–11; **Heb** 2:7–9; 10:12–13; **1Pe** 3:22; **Rev** 17:14; 19:16

Believers should lead lives that are mindful of Jesus Christ's exaltation
Believers are exalted with Jesus Christ
Eph 2:6 . . . God raised us up with Christ and seated us with him in the heavenly realms in Christ Jesus, *See also* **Rev** 3:21
Believers should be concerned with heavenly values
Col 3:1–4 Since, then, you have been raised with Christ, set your hearts on things above, where Christ is seated at the right hand of God . . . *See also* **Php** 3:20; **Heb** 12:2–3
See also Jesus Christ as king; Jesus Christ as Saviour; Jesus Christ as servant; Jesus Christ, ascension; Jesus Christ, authority; Jesus Christ, glory of; Jesus Christ, head of the church; Jesus Christ, majesty of; Jesus Christ, resurrection; Jesus Christ, the Lord.

Jesus Christ, example of
Jesus Christ sets his disciples an example, especially in servanthood, self-denial and endurance of suffering, so that they may become like him.

Jesus Christ calls believers to follow his example
Jn 13:14–16 " . . . I have set you an example that you should do as I have done for you . . ." *See also* **Heb** 3:1; 12:2–3; **1Pe** 2:21; **1Jn** 2:6

The qualities of Jesus Christ which set an example for believers
Self-denial
Php 2:4–5 Each of you should look not only to your own interests, but also to the interests of others. Your attitude should be the same as that of Christ Jesus: *See also* **Mt** 10:38; 16:24 pp **Mk** 8:34 pp **Lk** 9:23; **Lk** 14:27; **Heb** 12:2
Endurance of suffering
1Pe 2:21–23 To this you were called, because Christ suffered for you, leaving you an example, that you should follow in his steps . . . *See also* **Mt** 10:24–25; **Jn** 15:20; **1Th** 2:14–15; **Heb** 12:3
Service Mt 20:25–28 pp **Mk** 10:42–45; **Jn** 13:13–17
Faithfulness Heb 3:1–2
Love Eph 5:1–2,25; **1Jn** 3:16

Patience 1Ti 1:16
Forgiveness of others Eph 4:32; Col 3:13
Gentleness and humility Mt 11:29
Purity 1Jn 3:3
Prayer Lk 11:1

God wants his people to follow Jesus Christ's example and be conformed to his image
Ro 8:29; 1Co 15:49

Those who followed Jesus Christ's example
1Co 11:1; 1Th 1:6; Ac 7:60   *See also Christlikeness; forgiveness; Jesus Christ as servant; Jesus Christ, holiness; Jesus Christ, humility; Jesus Christ, love of; Jesus Christ, suffering.*

Jesus Christ, faithfulness
The total reliability and constancy of Jesus Christ is shown in his personal character, and made known by his words and works.

Jesus Christ's faithfulness is seen in his character
He is faithful by nature
Rev 19:11 I [John] saw heaven standing open and there before me was a white horse, whose rider is called Faithful and True . . .
See also **Rev** 1:5; 3:14
The promised Messiah is faithful
Isa 11:5 Righteousness will be his belt and faithfulness the sash round his waist.
See also **Isa** 42:3
Jesus Christ is faithful because he never changes
Heb 13:8 Jesus Christ is the same yesterday and today and for ever.   *See also* **Heb** 1:11–12; **Ps** 102:26–27
Jesus Christ is faithful because he is the truth
Jn 1:14 . . . We have seen his glory, the glory of the One and Only, who came from the Father, full of grace and truth.   *See also* **Jn** 1:17; 14:6

Jesus Christ's faithfulness demonstrated in his obedience
He is faithful to his Father
Heb 3:6 But Christ is faithful as a son over God's house . . .   *See also* **Lk** 2:49; **Jn** 5:30; 6:38; 8:29; 14:31; **Heb** 3:2
He kept faithfully to his work
Lk 4:43 But he [Jesus] said, "I must preach the good news of the kingdom of God to the other towns also, because that is why I was sent." pp Mk 1:38   *See also* **Jn** 4:34; 9:4; 12:27; 17:4; 19:30; **Heb** 2:17–18

Jesus Christ's faithfulness is seen in his words
In his predictions about events
Mt 16:28 "I [Jesus] tell you the truth, some who are standing here will not taste death before they see the Son of Man coming in his kingdom." pp Mk 9:1 pp Lk 9:27
Mt 24:2 "Do you see all these things?" he [Jesus] asked. "I tell you the truth, not one stone here will be left on another; every one will be thrown down." pp Mk 13:2 pp Lk 21:6
See also **Mt** 21:2 pp Mk 11:2 pp Lk 19:30; **Mk** 26:21 pp Mk 14:18 pp Lk 22:21 pp Jn 13:21; **Mt** 26:34 pp Mk 14:30 pp Lk 22:34 pp Jn 13:38; **Jn** 16:20; 21:18–19
In his promises about eternal life
Jn 5:24 "I [Jesus] tell you the truth, those who hear my word and believe him who sent me have eternal life and will not be condemned; they have crossed over from death to life."   *See also* **Mt** 19:28–29 pp Mk 10:29–30 pp Lk 18:29–30; **Lk** 23:43; **Jn** 6:47,53–54; 8:51
In his promise of authority for believers
Mt 17:20 He [Jesus] replied, ". . . I tell you the truth, if you have faith as small as a mustard seed, you can say to this mountain, 'Move from here to there' and it will move. Nothing will be impossible for you."   *See also* **Mt** 16:19; 18:18; 21:21 pp Mk 11:23; **Mt** 28:18–19; **Lk** 10:19
In his promise about the Holy Spirit
Jn 14:26 "But the Counsellor, the Holy Spirit, whom the Father will send in my name, will teach you all things and will remind you of everything I have said to you."   *See also* **Lk** 24:49; **Jn** 14:16; 15:26; 16:7; **Ac** 1:4,8; 2:38–39; 10:44–46; **Ro** 5:5; **1Co** 12:7

Jesus Christ's promises about the future are faithful

Jn 14:2–3 "In my Father's house are many rooms; if it were not so, I would have told you. I am going there to prepare a place for you. And if I go and prepare a place for you, I will come back and take you to be with me that you also may be where I am." *See also* **Mt** 16:27; 26:64; **Jn** 14:28

Jesus Christ is faithful to believers in all circumstances

2Ti 2:13 . . . if we are faithless, he [Christ Jesus] will remain faithful, for he cannot disown himself. *See also* **Mt** 18:20; 28:20; **Jn** 17:9; **Ac** 18:9–10; **2Th** 3:3; **Heb** 10:23 *See also God, faithfulness; Holy Spirit, promise of; Jesus Christ, obedience; Jesus Christ, prophecies concerning; Jesus Christ, second coming.*

Jesus Christ, family of

Jesus Christ belonged to a human family and experienced family relationships during his earthly ministry. Such relationships underline the fact of Christ's humanity.

Jesus Christ was born into a family
He is placed in a family tree Mt 1:1–17; Lk 1:34–37; 3:23–38
His birth was a natural one
Lk 2:5–7 . . . she [Mary] gave birth to her firstborn, a son . . . *See also* Lk 2:21–22
He grew up within a family
Lk 2:48 When his [Jesus'] parents saw him, they were astonished. His mother said to him, "Son, why have you treated us like this? Your father and I have been anxiously searching for you." *See also* Lk 2:51–52

Jesus Christ's family is mentioned during his earthly ministry
Mt 13:55–56 "Isn't this the carpenter's son? Isn't his mother's name Mary, and aren't his brothers James, Joseph, Simon and Judas? Aren't all his sisters with us? Where then did this man get all these things?" pp Mk 6:3 *See also* **Mt** 12:46–47 pp Mk 3:31–32 pp Lk 8:19–20; Jn 2:1,12

Jesus Christ's natural brothers
James
Gal 1:19 I [Paul] saw none of the other apostles—only James, the Lord's brother. *See also* Mt 13:55 pp Mk 6:3
Jude
Jude 1 Jude, a servant of Jesus Christ and a brother of James . . . *See also* Mt 13:55 pp Mk 6:3

The nature of Jesus Christ's relationships with his family
He was obedient to and caring towards his parents
Lk 2:51 Then he [Jesus] went down to Nazareth with them [Mary and Joseph] and was obedient to them . . . *See also* Jn 19:26–27
The will of his heavenly Father took precedence over the wishes of his natural family
Jn 2:3–4 When the wine was gone, Jesus' mother said to him, "They have no more wine." "Dear woman, why do you involve me?" Jesus replied, "My time has not yet come."
See also Mt 12:48–50 pp Mk 3:33–35; Lk 2:48–49; Jn 7:6–8
His family did not fully understand his ministry
Jn 7:3–5 Jesus' brothers said to him, "You ought to leave here and go to Judea, so that your disciples may see the miracles you do. No-one who wants to become a public figure acts in secret. Since you are doing these things, show yourself to the world." For even his own brothers did not believe in him. *See also* Mk 3:21
Jesus Christ's natural family were among the first Christians
Ac 1:14 They all [the eleven apostles] joined together constantly in prayer, along with the women and Mary the mother of Jesus, and with his brothers. *See also* 1Co 9:5 *See also Jesus Christ, birth of; Jesus Christ, childhood; Jesus Christ, genealogy; Jesus Christ, humanity; Jesus Christ, obedience.*

Jesus Christ, genealogy

Jesus Christ's human ancestry is traced back in two separate lines to David and thence back to

Adam. Jesus' descent from David is of importance for his Messianic claims.

Jesus Christ is descended from Adam
Lk 3:23–38

Jesus Christ is descended from Abraham
Gal 3:16 The promises were spoken to Abraham and to his seed. The Scripture does not say "and to seeds", meaning many people, but "and to your seed", meaning one person, who is Christ. *See also* **Ac 3:25–26**

Jesus Christ is descended from Isaac
Ge 21:12; 26:2–4; Gal 3:16

Jesus Christ is descended from Jacob
Ge 28:13–14; Mt 1:2; Lk 3:34

Jesus Christ is descended from the tribe of Judah
Heb 7:14 For it is clear that our Lord descended from Judah . . . *See also* **Ru 4:18–22**

Jesus Christ is descended from Jesse
Isa 11:1 A shoot will come up from the stump of Jesse; from his roots a Branch will bear fruit.
Ro 15:12 . . . "The Root of Jesse will spring up, one who will arise to rule over the nations; the Gentiles will hope in him."

Jesus Christ is descended from David
Jesus Christ's human lineage
Mt 1:1–17 A record of the genealogy of Jesus Christ the son of David, the son of Abraham . . . Thus there were fourteen generations in all from Abraham to David, fourteen from David to the exile to Babylon, and fourteen from the exile to the Christ.
Lk 2:4 So Joseph also went up from the town of Nazareth in Galilee to Judea, to Bethlehem the town of David, because he belonged to the house and line of David. *See also* **1Ch 3:10–19; Lk 3:23–31**
Jesus Christ as the Son of David
Rev 22:16 "I, Jesus . . . am the Root and the Offspring of David, and the bright Morning Star." *See also* **Mt 1:20; 20:30–31 pp Mk 10:47–48 pp Lk 18:38–39; Mt 21:9,15; Lk 1:27,32; Jn 7:42**

Jesus Christ is greater than David
Mt 22:41–45 He [Jesus] said to them [the Pharisees], "How is it then that David, speaking by the Spirit, calls him 'Lord'? . . ." pp Mk 12:35–37 pp Lk 20:41–44 *See also* **Ps 110:1; Rev 5:5; 22:16**

Jesus Christ is greater than Solomon
Mt 12:42 . . . one greater than Solomon is here. pp Lk 11:31

Jesus Christ as the son of Joseph and Mary
Mt 13:55 "Isn't this the carpenter's son? Isn't his mother's name Mary, and aren't his brothers James, Joseph, Simon and Judas?" pp Mk 6:3
Jn 6:42 They [the Jews] said, "Is this not Jesus, the son of Joseph, whose father and mother we know? . . ." *See also* **Mt 1:16; Lk 4:22; Jn 1:45** *See also Jesus Christ as king; Jesus Christ, family of; Jesus Christ, humanity; Jesus Christ, Son of David; Jesus Christ, Son of God; Jesus Christ, sonship of; Messiah, coming of.*

Jesus Christ, glory of
Jesus Christ's radiance and splendour reflects the glory of the Father, and is both revealed to and reflected in the lives of believers.

Jesus Christ's glory existed before the incarnation
Jn 17:5 ". . . Father, glorify me [Jesus Christ] in your presence with the glory I had with you before the world began." *See also* **Jn 1:14; 17:24**

Jesus Christ's glory is God's glory
God's glory is reflected in Jesus Christ
Heb 1:3 The Son is the radiance of God's glory . . . *See also* **Jn 12:41; 13:32; 2Co 4:4, 6**
Jesus Christ brings glory to his Father
Jn 14:13 ". . . so that the Son may bring glory to the Father." *See also* **Jn 13:31; 17:1,4; Ro 16:27; Eph 1:12; Jude 25**

The Holy Spirit glorifies Jesus Christ
Jn 16:14 "He [the Spirit of truth] will bring glory to me [Jesus] by taking from what is mine and making it known to you."

Jesus Christ's glory is revealed on earth
Through his miracles
Jn 2:11 This, the first of his miraculous signs, Jesus performed at Cana in Galilee. He thus revealed his glory . . .   *See also* **Jn** 11:4,40
To his disciples
Lk 9:28–32 . . . As he [Jesus] was praying, the appearance of his face changed, and his clothes became as bright as a flash of lightning . . . Peter and his companions were very sleepy, but when they became fully awake, they saw his glory . . .   pp **Mt** 17:1–2 pp **Mk** 9:2–3   *See also* **Jn** 1:14; **Ac** 9:3; 22:6; 26:13; **2Pe** 1:17
In his death and resurrection
Jn 12:23 Jesus replied, "The hour has come for the Son of Man to be glorified."   *See also* **Jn** 7:39; 12:16; **Ac** 3:13–15; **1Pe** 1:21; **Heb** 2:9

The glory of the exalted Christ
His appearance
Rev 1:13–16 . . . among the lampstands was someone "like a son of man", dressed in a robe reaching down to his feet and with a golden sash round his chest. His head and hair were white like wool, as white as snow, and his eyes were like blazing fire. His feet were like bronze glowing in a furnace, and his voice was like the sound of rushing waters. In his right hand he held seven stars, and out of his mouth came a sharp double-edged sword. His face was like the sun shining in all its brilliance.   *See also* **Ac** 7:55–56; **Rev** 2:18; 19:11–16
He receives glory from all creation
Rev 5:13 Then I heard every creature in heaven and on earth and under the earth and on the sea, and all that is in them, singing: "To him who sits on the throne and to the Lamb be praise and honour and glory and power, for ever and ever!"   *See also* **Heb** 13:21; **2Pe** 3:18; **Rev** 1:6; 5:11–12; 7:9–12

Jesus Christ's glory will be revealed at the second coming
Mt 16:27 ". . . the Son of Man is going to come in his Father's glory with his angels . . ."   pp **Mk** 8:38 pp **Lk** 9:26   *See also* **Mt** 24:27,30 pp **Mk** 13:26 pp **Lk** 21:27; **Mt** 25:31; **2Th** 1:7; 2:8; **Tit** 2:13; **1Pe** 4:13

Jesus Christ's glory is shared by believers
As they become like him
2Co 3:18 . . . we, who with unveiled faces all reflect the Lord's glory, are being transformed into his likeness with ever-increasing glory, which comes from the Lord, who is the Spirit.   *See also* **Jn** 17:22; **Col** 1:27
At the end of time
1Co 15:49 . . . just as we have borne the likeness of the earthly, so shall we bear the likeness of the heavenly.   *See also* **Ro** 8:17–18; **Php** 3:21; **Col** 3:4   *See also* glory; God, glory of; Jesus Christ, death of; Jesus Christ, divinity; Jesus Christ, exaltation; Jesus Christ, majesty of; Jesus Christ, miracles; Jesus Christ, perfection; Jesus Christ, resurrection; Jesus Christ, second coming; Jesus Christ, transfiguration.

Jesus Christ, grace and mercy
The qualities of Jesus Christ by which he is compassionate, accepting and generous. In his ministry, Christ demonstrates these qualities towards those whom he encounters. Believers should model themselves upon Jesus Christ in this respect.

The grace and mercy of God made known in Jesus Christ
Jn 1:14 The Word became flesh and made his dwelling among us. We have seen his glory, the glory of the One and Only, who came from the Father, full of grace and truth.

Jn 1:16–17 From the fulness of his grace we have all received one blessing after another. For the law was given through Moses; grace and truth came through Jesus Christ.   *See also* **Lk** 2:40,52; **2Co** 8:9; **Tit** 2:11

Grace and mercy in the ministry of Jesus Christ
Jesus Christ responds to pleas for mercy
Mt 9:27–30 As Jesus went on from there, two blind men followed him, calling out, "Have mercy on us, Son of David!" ... he touched their eyes and said, "According to your faith will it be done to you"; and their sight was restored ... *See also* **Mt** 15:22; 20:29–34 pp **Mk** 10:46–52 pp **Lk** 18:35–42

His teaching reflects his grace and mercy
Lk 6:35–36 "But love your enemies, do good to them, and lend to them without expecting to get anything back. Then your reward will be great, and you will be sons of the Most High, because he is kind to the ungrateful and wicked. Be merciful, just as your Father is merciful."
See also **Hos** 6:6; **Mt** 6:12–15 pp **Lk** 11:4; **Mt** 9:10–13 pp **Mk** 2:15–17 pp **Lk** 5:29–32; **Mt** 18:21–35; **Lk** 10:30–37; **Eph** 4:32

Grace and mercy in relation to salvation
The grace of Jesus Christ
Ac 15:11 "... it is through the grace of our Lord Jesus that we are saved ..." *See also* **Ro** 3:24; 5:15; **Eph** 2:4–5,8; **2Ti** 1:9

The mercy of Jesus Christ
Lk 23:34 Jesus said, "Father, forgive them, for they do not know what they are doing." ... *See also* **Mt** 9:2 pp **Mk** 2:3–5 pp **Lk** 5:18–20; **Lk** 7:37–38,48; **Ro** 5:6,15; **1Ti** 1:13–14

Eternal life is a gift of grace and mercy
Ro 5:21 ... just as sin reigned in death, so also grace might reign through righteousness to bring eternal life through Jesus Christ our Lord. *See also* **Ro** 6:23; **Tit** 3:7

The grace and mercy of Jesus Christ and the Christian life
The need to rely upon the grace of Jesus Christ
2Co 12:9 But he said to me, "My grace is sufficient for you, for my power is made perfect in weakness." Therefore I will boast all the more gladly about my weaknesses, so that Christ's power may rest on me.

2Ti 2:1 ... be strong in the grace that is in Christ Jesus. *See also* **Eph** 4:7; **2Pe** 3:18; **Heb** 4:16

Prayers for the grace of Jesus Christ
Ro 1:7 ... Grace and peace to you from God our Father and from the Lord Jesus Christ.
See also **Ro** 16:20; **1Co** 16:23; **Gal** 1:3; 6:18; **Eph** 6:24; **Php** 4:23; **2Jn** 3; **Rev** 22:21 *See also forgiveness; God, grace and mercy; grace and Jesus Christ; Jesus Christ as Saviour; Jesus Christ, compassion; Jesus Christ, love of; Jesus Christ, miracles; salvation.*

Jesus Christ, head of the church

Jesus Christ rules and governs his people and directs them towards the fulfilment of God's purposes. All power and authority within the church derive from Jesus Christ as the head.

Jesus Christ rules the universe in the interest of the church
Eph 1:22–23 And God placed all things under his feet and appointed him to be head over everything for the church, which is his body ... *See also* **Eph** 1:10; **Col** 1:18

All power and authority within the church derive from Jesus Christ as the head
Jesus Christ is recognised as head of the church
Eph 4:15 ... we will in all things grow up into him who is the Head, that is, Christ.
See also **Eph** 5:23; **Col** 2:19

Within the church Jesus Christ alone rules with authority
Mt 23:8–10 "But you are not to be called 'Rabbi', for you have only one Master ... Nor are you to be called 'teacher', for you have one Teacher, the Christ. *See also* **Jn** 13:13; **2Co** 4:5

The church owes obedience to its head
Jn 14:15 "If you love me, you will obey what I command." *See also* **Jn** 14:21,23; **Eph** 5:24; **1Jn** 3:24

All human authority in the church derives from its head
Eph 4:11 It was he [Christ] who gave some to

be apostles, some to be prophets, some to be evangelists, and some to be pastors and teachers, *See also* **Gal** 1:1

Jesus Christ is the cornerstone and builder of the church
Eph 2:20–22 . . . In him [Christ Jesus] the whole building is joined together and rises to become a holy temple in the Lord. And in him you too are being built together . . . *See also* **Mt** 16:18; **Ac** 4:11; **Ps** 118:22; **1Pe** 2:4–6

Jesus Christ's role as head of the church
He loves the church
Eph 5:25 . . . Christ loved the church and gave himself up for her *See also* **Jn** 10:11; **Eph** 5:2,23; **1Jn** 3:16
He cares for the church
Rev 7:17 "For the Lamb at the centre of the throne will be their shepherd; he will lead them to springs of living water. And God will wipe away every tear from their eyes." *See also* **Jn** 10:14–15,27–28; 17:12; **Eph** 5:29–30
He provides for the growth of the church
Col 2:19 . . . the Head, from whom the whole body, supported and held together by its ligaments and sinews, grows as God causes it to grow. *See also* **Eph** 4:15–16
He prays for the church
Jn 17:20–26; **Ro** 8:34; **Heb** 7:25
He judges the church
Rev 2:23 ". . . all the churches will know that I [the Son of God] am he who searches hearts and minds, and I will repay each of you according to your deeds." *See also* **Ro** 14:10–12; **2Co** 5:10; **Eph** 6:8
He will present the church blameless before God
Eph 5:27 . . . to present her [the church] to himself as a radiant church, without stain or wrinkle or any other blemish, but holy and blameless. *See also* **2Co** 4:14; **Col** 1:22; **Jude** 24 *See also church; Jesus Christ as judge; Jesus Christ as shepherd; Jesus Christ, authority; Jesus Christ, love of; Jesus Christ, power of; Jesus Christ, pre-eminence; Jesus Christ, the Lord.*

Jesus Christ, high priest
Jesus Christ, being a truly human high priest, perfectly represents humanity before God. He made atonement for sins by his own sacrificial death. Being a truly divine high priest, this act of Christ's was perfect, once for all and of eternal value.

The ministry of Jesus Christ as high priest
He made atonement for sin
Heb 2:17 . . . he [Jesus] might make atonement for the sins of the people. *See also* **Heb** 8:3; 9:7,11–12; 13:11–13
He represents human beings before God
Heb 5:1 Every high priest is selected from among human beings and is appointed to represent them in matters related to God, to offer gifts and sacrifices for sins. *See also* **Ro** 8:34; **1Jn** 2:1–2
He entered the Most Holy Place
Heb 9:24 For Christ did not enter a sanctuary made with human hands that was only a copy of the true one; he entered heaven itself, now to appear for us in God's presence. *See also* **Heb** 4:14; 6:19–20; 9:7,12
He makes believers perfect
Heb 10:14 . . . by one sacrifice he [Jesus] has made perfect for ever those who are being made holy. *See also* **Heb** 10:10; 13:12
He brings believers close to God
Heb 10:19–22 . . . we [believers] have confidence to enter the Most Holy Place by the blood of Jesus . . .
He helps those being tempted
Heb 2:18 . . . he [Jesus] is able to help those who are being tempted. *See also* **Heb** 4:15; 5:2
He intercedes continually
Heb 7:24–25 . . . Jesus lives for ever, he has a permanent priesthood. Therefore he is able to save completely those who come to God through him, because he always lives to intercede for them. *See also* **Jn** 17:20; **Ro** 8:34

Jesus Christ, the human high priest
As a man he is able to represent human beings
Heb 2:17 . . . he [Jesus] had to be made like

his brothers and sisters in every way, in order that he might become a merciful and faithful high priest in service to God ... See also **Heb** 5:1
He is divinely appointed
Heb 5:5–6 ... Christ also did not take upon himself the glory of becoming a high priest. But God said to him, "You are my Son; today I have become your Father." ... See also **Heb** 3:1–2

Jesus Christ, the divine high priest
He is sinless
Heb 7:26–27 Such a high priest meets our need—one who is holy, blameless, pure, set apart from sinners, exalted above the heavens ...
He is eternal
Heb 6:20 ... He has become a high priest for ever ... See also **Heb** 5:6; 7:17,21,28
His atoning work was completed once for all
Heb 7:27 ... He [Jesus] sacrificed for their sins once for all when he offered himself. See also **Heb** 9:12,25–26,28; 10:10
He is exalted
Heb 8:1 ... We [believers] do have such a high priest, who sat down at the right hand of the throne of the Majesty in heaven, See also **Zec** 6:13; **Heb** 7:26

Jesus Christ's high priesthood was of the order of Melchizedek
Heb 6:20 ... He [Jesus] has become a high priest for ever, in the order of Melchizedek. See also **Ps** 110:4; **Heb** 5:6,10; 7:1–4,14–17

Responses to Jesus Christ's high priesthood
Heb 4:14–16; 10:19–22; 12:1–3, 28–29
See also access to God; Jesus Christ, sinlessness.

Jesus Christ, holiness
The holiness of Jesus Christ is seen in his divine nature and work, as he stands apart from and above the created world with divine power, authority and purity. Recognition of the holiness of Jesus Christ leads both to a realisation of sin and unworthiness and to worship and adoration.

The holy character of Jesus Christ
Its divine origin
Lk 1:35 ... "The Holy Spirit will come upon you [Mary], and the power of the Most High will overshadow you. So the holy one to be born will be called the Son of God." See also **Jn** 1:1–2; 3:31; 8:23; 13:3; 17:14,16
Its divine nature
Col 2:9 For in Christ all the fulness of the Deity lives in bodily form, See also **Jn** 1:14; 10:30,38; 14:10; **Php** 2:6; **Heb** 1:3
Its divine purity
Heb 7:26 Such a high priest meets our need—one who is holy, blameless, pure, set apart from sinners, exalted above the heavens. See also **2Co** 5:21; **Heb** 4:15; **1Pe** 1:19; 2:22; **1Jn** 3:3,5
Its divine power
Ac 4:30 "Stretch out your hand to heal and perform miraculous signs and wonders through the name of your holy servant Jesus." See also **Ac** 10:38

The holy work of Jesus Christ
He is set apart as God's servant
Ac 4:27 "... Herod and Pontius Pilate met together with the Gentiles and the people of Israel in this city [Jerusalem] to conspire against your holy servant Jesus, whom you [God] anointed." See also **Mk** 10:45 pp **Mt** 20:28; **Jn** 14:31; **Ac** 3:26; **Php** 2:7–8; **Heb** 10:7
His life is consecrated to the will and purpose of God
Mt 26:39 ... he [Jesus] fell with his face to the ground and prayed, "My Father, if it is possible, may this cup be taken from me. Yet not as I will, but as you will." pp **Mk** 14:35–36 pp **Lk** 22:42 See also **Mt** 26:42; **Jn** 12:49–50; 14:31
He is appointed as the judge of sinners Jn 5:22,26–27; **Ac** 17:31; **2Co** 5:10
He makes God's people holy
Heb 13:12 ... Jesus also suffered outside the city gate to make the people holy through his own blood. See also **Jn** 17:19; **Eph** 5:25–27; **Heb** 2:11; 10:10,14; **1Pe** 2:4–5,9–10

Declarations of the holiness of Jesus Christ
By David: **Ps** 16:10; **Ac** 2:27; 13:35
Mk 1:24 pp Lk 4:34; **Lk** 1:35
By Peter: **Jn** 6:69; **Ac** 3:14
Rev 3:7

Results of recognising the holiness of Jesus Christ
Awareness of sin and unworthiness
Lk 5:8 When Simon Peter saw this, he fell at Jesus' knees and said, "Go away from me, Lord; I am a sinful man!"   *See also* **Mt** 8:8 pp Lk 7:6–7
Fear Mt 8:28–34 pp Mk 5:9–17 pp Lk 8:26–37; **Rev** 1:17
Adoration and worship Rev 5:8–14   *See also access to God; God, holiness of; holiness; Jesus Christ as judge; Jesus Christ as servant; Jesus Christ, divinity; Jesus Christ, miracles; Jesus Christ, obedience; Jesus Christ, perfection; Jesus Christ, responses to; Jesus Christ, righteousness; Jesus Christ, sinlessness.*

Jesus Christ, humanity
Scripture stresses the total humanity of Jesus Christ. Although sinless, Christ shared in the general condition of humanity, including suffering and death.

Jesus Christ was a man
By his own claims
Jn 8:40 "... you [the Jews] are determined to kill me [Jesus], a man who has told you the truth that I heard from God..."   *See also* **Mt** 8:20 pp Lk 9:58
In statements made by others
Jn 19:5 When Jesus came out wearing the crown of thorns and the purple robe, Pilate said to them [the crowds], "Here is the man!"
See also **Mt** 8:27; **Mk** 15:39 pp Lk 23:47; **Lk** 15:2; 23:18; **Jn** 1:33; 4:42; 7:12; 15, 27; 9:33; 11:47; **Ac** 2:22–23

Jesus Christ shared in the general condition of humanity
He assumed human nature
Jn 1:14 The Word became flesh and made his dwelling among us...   *See also* **Php** 2:7–8; **Heb** 2:14; **1Jn** 4:2
He had a human descent
Ro 1:3 regarding his [God's] Son, who as to his human nature was a descendant of David,
See also **Mt** 1:1; 13:54–56 pp Mk 6:2–3; **Ro** 9:5
He had a normal body which could be handled and touched
1Jn 1:1 That which was from the beginning, which we have heard, which we have seen with our eyes, which we have looked at and our hands have touched—this we proclaim concerning the Word of life.   *See also* **Mt** 14:36 pp Mk 6:56; **Lk** 2:28; **1Ti** 3:16
He had a soul
Mt 26:38 Then he [Jesus] said to them, "My soul is overwhelmed with sorrow to the point of death. Stay here and keep watch with me." pp Mk 14:34   *See also* **Isa** 53:11

Jesus Christ partook of human experience
He was born
Gal 4:4 ... God sent his Son, born of a woman...   *See also* **Lk** 2:6–7
He grew and developed Lk 2:40,52
He was hungry
Mt 21:18 ... as he [Jesus] was on his way back to the city, he was hungry. pp Mk 11:12   *See also* **Mt** 4:2 pp Lk 4:2
He was thirsty
Jn 19:28 ... Jesus said, "I am thirsty."   *See also* **Jn** 4:7
He was tired
Jn 4:6 Jacob's well was there, and Jesus, tired as he was from the journey, sat down by the well...
He slept Mt 8:24 pp Mk 4:38 pp Lk 8:23
He was tempted
Heb 2:18 ... he [Jesus] himself suffered when he was tempted...   *See also* **Mt** 4:1 pp Mk 1:13 pp Lk 4:2; **Heb** 4:15
He suffered
1Pe 4:1 ... Christ suffered in his body...   *See also* **Col** 1:22; **Heb** 5:7–8; 10:10; **1Pe** 2:24
He died
Mt 27:50 And when Jesus had cried out again

in a loud voice, he gave up his spirit. pp Mk 15:37 pp Lk 23:46 pp Jn 19:30   *See also* **Heb 2:9,14**

The risen Christ has human characteristics
Lk 24:37–43 They [the disciples] were startled and frightened, thinking they saw a ghost. He [Jesus] said to them, "Why are you troubled, and why do doubts rise in your minds? Look at my hands and my feet. It is I myself! Touch me and see; a ghost does not have flesh and bones, as you see I have." . . .   *See also* **Jn 20:27**

The returning Christ retains his human identity
Ac 1:11 ". . . This same Jesus, who has been taken from you into heaven, will come back . . ."

Jesus Christ was a sinless human being
Heb 4:15 For we [believers] do not have a high priest who is unable to sympathise with our weaknesses, but we have one who has been tempted in every way, just as we are—yet was without sin.   *See also* **Lk 23:41,47; Heb 7:26**

The necessity of Jesus Christ's humanity
As a man Jesus Christ made atonement for sin
Ro 5:18–19 . . . For just as through the disobedience of the one man the many were made sinners, so also through the obedience of the one man the many will be made righteous.   *See also* **Ro 5:12–17; 1Ti 2:5; Heb 2:17**

As a man Jesus Christ gives the gift of resurrection
1Co 15:21 For since death came through a human being, the resurrection of the dead comes also through a human being.   *See also* **1Co 15:45; Php 3:20–21**

As a man Jesus Christ is able to help others in their need
Heb 2:18 Because he himself suffered when he was tempted, he is able to help those who are being tempted.   *See also* **Heb 4:15–5:2**

As a man Jesus Christ is the perfect example
Php 2:5–8   *See also* **Holy Spirit in life of Jesus Christ; incarnation; Jesus Christ, birth of; Jesus Christ, death of; Jesus Christ, genealogy; Jesus Christ, perfection; Jesus Christ, Son of Man; Jesus Christ, suffering; Jesus Christ, temptation.**

Jesus Christ, humility
The obedient submission of Jesus Christ to his Father, seen in his willingness to become a human being for humanity's sake, his freedom from self-interest and his willingness to serve others.

Jesus Christ's willingness to become a human being
Php 2:6–7 . . . [Jesus] Who, being in very nature God, did not consider equality with God something to be grasped, but made himself nothing, taking the very nature of a servant, being made in human likeness.   *See also* **Ro 8:3; 2Co 8:9**

Jesus Christ's humility predicted in the OT
Mt 12:19–20; Isa 42:2–3; 50:4–6
The suffering servant: **Mt 8:17; Ac 8:32–33; Isa 53:2–7; 1Pe 2:22; Isa 53:9; 1Pe 2:24**
The coming king: **Mt 21:5 pp Jn 12:15; Zec 9:9 Zec 12:10**
The shepherd struck: **Mt 26:31 pp Mk 14:27; Zec 13:7**

The poverty of Jesus Christ's birth and upbringing
Lk 2:7,12,16,22–24

Jesus Christ's obedience to his human parents
Lk 2:51 Then he [Jesus] went down to Nazareth with them and was obedient to them [Joseph and Mary] . . .

Jesus Christ's obedience to his heavenly Father
Jn 5:30 ". . . I [Jesus] seek not to please myself but him who sent me."   *See also* **Jn 8:29; 15:10; Ro 5:19; 15:3; Php 2:8; Heb 5:8**

Jesus Christ's dependence on his heavenly Father
Jn 5:19 ". . . the Son can do nothing by himself; he can do only what he sees his Father doing, because whatever the Father does the Son also does." *See also* **Jn** 5:30; 17:7

Jesus Christ's submission to baptism
Mt 3:13-15 Then Jesus came from Galilee to the Jordan to be baptised by John. But John tried to deter him, saying, "I need to be baptised by you, and do you come to me?" Jesus replied, "Let it be so now; it is proper for us to do this to fulfil all righteousness." Then John consented. pp Mk 1:9 pp Lk 3:21

Jesus Christ's humble acceptance of ill treatment
1Pe 2:23 When they hurled their insults at him [Jesus], he did not retaliate; when he suffered, he made no threats. Instead, he entrusted himself to him who judges justly. *See also* **Mt** 26:63 pp Mk 14:61; **Mt** 26:66-67 pp Mk 14:64-65; **Mt** 27:14 pp Mk 15:5; **Mt** 27:28-30 pp Mk 15:17-19 pp Jn 19:2

Jesus Christ's acceptance of the cross
Php 2:8 And being found in appearance as a human being, he [Jesus] humbled himself and became obedient to death—even death on a cross! *See also* **Mt** 26:39 pp Mk 14:36 pp Lk 22:42; **Mt** 26:53; **Lk** 23:34; **Heb** 5:7

Jesus Christ's humility with other people
Children: **Mt** 19:13-15 pp Mk 10:13-16 pp Lk 18:15-17
Beggars: **Mt** 20:29-34 pp Mk 10:46-52 pp Lk 18:35-43
Mk 1:40-42; **Jn** 4:5-9

Jesus Christ's servant attitude
Mk 10:45 "For even the Son of Man did not come to be served, but to serve, and to give his life as a ransom for many." . . . pp Mt 20:28
See also **Mt** 12:19-20; **Jn** 13:4-5,12; **2Co** 10:1

Jesus Christ's teaching about humility
Mk 9:33-37 . . . Jesus called the Twelve and said, "Anyone who wants to be first must be the very last, and the servant of all." pp Mt 18:1-5 pp Lk 9:46-48 *See also* **Mt** 23:8-12; **Mk** 10:42-45 pp Mt 20:26-28; **Lk** 14:7-11; 18:9-14

Jesus Christ's humility as a model for others
Jn 13:12-17 ". . . Now that I [Jesus], your Lord and Teacher, have washed your feet, you also should wash one another's feet. I have set you an example that you should do as I have done for you . . ." *See also* **Mt** 11:29-30; **Eph** 5:25; **Php** 2:5; **1Pe** 2:21 *See also* Jesus Christ as Lamb; Jesus Christ as servant; Jesus Christ, obedience; Jesus Christ, suffering.

Jesus Christ, joy of
Jesus Christ brings joy to his people, who are able to rejoice at the coming of their Saviour and Lord, and all the benefits which he brings to them.

Jesus Christ's joy originates in God
From his intimate relationship with his Father and the Spirit
Lk 10:21 At that time Jesus, full of joy through the Holy Spirit, said, "I praise you, Father, Lord of heaven and earth, because you have hidden these things from the wise and learned, and revealed them to little children. Yes, Father, for this was your good pleasure." pp Mt 11:25-26 *See also* **Isa** 11:2-3; **Mt** 3:16-17 pp Mk 1:10-11 pp Lk 3:22; **Mt** 12:18; **Isa** 42:1; **Ac** 2:28; **Ps** 16:11
From his awareness of God's purposes
Heb 12:2 . . . [Jesus] who for the joy set before him endured the cross, scorning its shame, and sat down at the right hand of the throne of God. *See also* Jn 8:29

Jesus Christ's coming brings great joy
His birth
Lk 2:10-11 ". . . I [the angel] bring you good news of great joy that will be for all the people. Today in the town of David a Saviour has been born to you; he is Christ the Lord."
See also **Mt** 2:10; **Lk** 1:44; 2:20,28-32

His resurrection and ascension
Jn 16:20-22 "... Now is your time of grief, but I [Jesus] will see you again and you will rejoice, and no-one will take away your joy." *See also* **Mt** 28:8-9; **Lk** 24:40-41,50-53; **Jn** 20:20

Jesus Christ gives joy to his people
He brings joy to his disciples
Jn 17:13 "... I [Jesus] say these things while I am still in the world, so that they [his disciples] may have the full measure of my joy within them." *See also* **Isa** 61:1-3; **Jn** 15:11; **Ro** 12:12; **Php** 1:26

Being in his presence is likened to the joy of a wedding
Mt 22:1-10 Jesus spoke to them [the chief priests and the Pharisees] again in parables, saying: "The kingdom of heaven is like a king who prepared a wedding banquet for his son..." *See also* **Mt** 9:14-15 pp **Mk** 2:18-19 pp **Lk** 5:33-34; **Mt** 25:1-10; **Jn** 3:29; **Rev** 19:7,9

To know Jesus Christ brings great joy to others
Lk 15:7 "I [Jesus] tell you [Pharisees and teachers of the law] that in the same way there will be more rejoicing in heaven over one sinner who repents than over ninety-nine righteous persons who do not need to repent."
See also **Mt** 8:11; **Lk** 15:10,22-24,31-32; **Jn** 8:56 *See also* God, joy of; God, purpose of; Holy Spirit, joy of; Jesus Christ, ascension; Jesus Christ, birth of; Jesus Christ, resurrection appearances.

Jesus Christ, justice of
The teaching and lifestyle of Jesus Christ show him to be just and impartial in his judgments and dealings with people. At the end of the age, God has appointed Jesus Christ to judge and rule with justice.

Justice was a quality displayed in Jesus Christ's life
Mt 12:18-21 "Here is my servant whom I have chosen, the one I love, in whom I delight; I will put my Spirit on him, and he will proclaim justice to the nations ... A bruised reed he will not break, and a smouldering wick he will not snuff out, till he leads justice to victory ..." *See also* **Isa** 42:1-4

Jesus Christ was just and impartial in his dealings with people
Mk 9:10-12 pp **Mk** 2:15-17 pp **Lk** 5:29-31; **Mt** 15:21-28 pp **Mk** 7:24-29; **Jn** 4:9, 27

Justice in the teaching of Jesus Christ
Mt 23:23 "Woe to you, teachers of the law and Pharisees, you hypocrites! You give a tenth of your spices—mint, dill and cummin. But you have neglected the more important matters of the law—justice, mercy and faithfulness. You should have practised the latter, without neglecting the former." pp **Lk** 11:42 *See also* **Mt** 5:17-48; 7:1-5 pp **Lk** 6:37-42; **Lk** 12:58-59; 14:13-14; **Jn** 7:24; 8:7

Parables which teach justice
Lk 18:1-8 ... And will not God bring about justice for his chosen ones, who cry out to him day and night? Will he keep putting them off? ... *See also* **Mt** 20:1-16; 25:14-30 pp **Lk** 19:12-27; **Lk** 16:19-31

Jesus Christ will judge the nations with justice
Ac 17:31 "For he [God] has set a day when he will judge the world with justice by the man he has appointed. He has given proof of this to everyone by raising him from the dead."
See also **Ps** 72:1-2; **Isa** 11:4; **Jn** 5:30; 8:15-16; **Rev** 19:11

Jesus Christ will rule the nations with justice
Isa 9:6-7 ... Of the increase of his government and peace there will be no end. He will reign on David's throne and over his kingdom, establishing and upholding it with justice and righteousness ... *See also* **Isa** 2:2-4; 32:1 "Branch" is a Messianic title: **Jer** 23:5-6; 33:15-16 **Mic** 4:1-3; **Rev** 19:11-16 *See also* God as judge; Jesus Christ as judge; Jesus Christ as king; Jesus Christ, grace and mercy; Jesus Christ, preaching and teaching; Jesus Christ, righteousness; Jesus Christ, victory.

Jesus Christ, kingdom of

The present and future realm in which Jesus Christ exercises full authority, and through which he triumphs over all opposition.

Jesus Christ's kingdom is a heavenly kingdom

It is not of this world
Jn 18:36 Jesus said, "My kingdom is not of this world . . . my kingdom is from another place." See also **Rev** 5:6; 7:10; 21:1,3

The kingdom was given to him by God
Da 7:14 "He [one like a son of man] was given authority, glory and sovereign power; all nations and people of every language worshipped him. His dominion is an everlasting dominion that will not pass away, and his kingdom is one that will never be destroyed." See also **Ps** 72:1; **Da** 2:44; **Mt** 28:18; **Jn** 16:15

The kingdom is his by right
Col 1:15-16 . . . For by him [Christ] all things were created: things in heaven and on earth, visible and invisible, whether thrones or powers or rulers or authorities; all things were created by him and for him. See also **Heb** 1:8; **Ps** 45:6; **Rev** 22:13

Jesus Christ inherits the kingdom promised to David
Lk 1:32 "He [Jesus] will be great and will be called the Son of the Most High. The Lord God will give him the throne of his father David, See also **Ro** 15:12; **Isa** 11:10; **Rev** 2:27; **Ps** 2:9

Jesus Christ reveals God's kingdom on earth

Jesus Christ brought in God's kingdom
Mt 4:17 From that time on Jesus began to preach, "Repent, for the kingdom of heaven is near." See also **Mt** 3:2; 10:7; 12:28 pp Lk 11:20; **Mk** 1:15; **Lk** 17:20-21

Miracles are a sign of the kingdom
Jn 6:14-15 After the people saw the miraculous sign that Jesus did, they began to say, "Surely this is the Prophet who is to come into the world." Jesus, knowing that they intended to come and make him king by force, withdrew again to a mountain by himself. See also **Mt** 8:26-27 pp Mk 4:39-41 pp Lk 8:24-25; **Mt** 11:2-5 pp Lk 7:19-22

Authority over life and death: **Lk** 7:11-15; **Rev** 1:17-18

Parables are a sign of the kingdom
Mt 13:1-52 . . . The disciples came to him [Jesus] and asked, "Why do you speak to the people in parables?" He replied, "The knowledge of the secrets of the kingdom of heaven has been given to you, but not to them . . ." See also **Mk** 4:1-34; **Lk** 8:4-15; 13:18-21

Jesus Christ exercises kingdom authority today

Believers enter Jesus Christ's kingdom immediately
Lk 23:42-43 . . . Jesus answered him [a criminal on the cross], "I tell you the truth, today you will be with me in paradise." See also **Mt** 5:3 pp Lk 6:20; **Mt** 11:11

Believers are redeemed from the kingdom of darkness
Col 1:12-13 . . . For he [the Father] has rescued us from the dominion of darkness and brought us into the kingdom of the Son he loves, See also **Eph** 5:5

Believers enjoy the blessings of Jesus Christ's kingdom now
Mt 16:19 "I [Jesus] will give you [Peter] the keys of the kingdom of heaven; whatever you bind on earth will be bound in heaven, and whatever you loose on earth will be loosed in heaven." See also **Da** 7:22,27; **Lk** 12:32; 22:29-30; **Jas** 2:5; **Rev** 1:5-6,9; 3:21

Jesus Christ rules over every authority now
1Pe 3:22 who [Jesus Christ] has gone into heaven and is at God's right hand—with angels, authorities and powers in submission to him. See also **Eph** 1:20-23; **Php** 2:9; **Col** 2:10; **Heb** 12:2; **Rev** 12:10; 19:16

Jesus Christ's kingdom will be fully established at his return

His kingdom will come with power at a specific moment
Mt 25:31 "When the Son of Man comes in his

glory, and all the angels with him, he will sit on his throne in heavenly glory." See also Zec 9:10; **Mt** 24:30-31 pp Mk 13:26-27 pp Lk 21:27; **2Ti** 4:1

His kingdom will replace all earthly authority
Rev 11:15 The seventh angel sounded his trumpet, and there were loud voices in heaven, which said: "The kingdom of the world has become the kingdom of our Lord and of his Christ, and he will reign for ever and ever." See also **1Co** 15:24-25,50-52; **Php** 3:20-21

All creation will acknowledge Jesus Christ's kingship
Php 2:10-11 ... at the name of Jesus every knee should bow, in heaven and on earth and under the earth, and every tongue confess that Jesus Christ is Lord, to the glory of God the Father. See also **Ps** 2:6-8; **Rev** 5:13

His kingdom lasts for ever
Lk 1:33 "... he [Jesus] will reign over the house of Jacob for ever; his kingdom will never end." See also **Isa** 9:7 See also Jesus Christ as king; Jesus Christ, majesty of; Jesus Christ, miracles; Jesus Christ, parables; Jesus Christ, pre-eminence; Jesus Christ, second coming; Jesus Christ, Son of David; kingdom of God; Son of Man.

Jesus Christ, knowledge of

Jesus Christ has perfect insight into God's purposes and into human nature by reason of his intimate relationship with the Father, but he has accepted limited knowledge as a consequence of his humanity.

Jesus Christ's knowledge of his Father
Mt 11:27 "All things have been committed to me by my Father. No-one knows the Son except the Father, and no-one knows the Father except the Son and those to whom the Son chooses to reveal him." pp Lk 10:22 See also **Jn** 7:29; 8:26,55; 10:15; 11:41-42; 15:15; 17:25

Jesus Christ's complete knowledge
Jn 16:30 "Now we [Jesus' disciples] can see that you know all things and that you do not even need to have anyone ask you questions. This makes us believe that you came from God." See also **Jn** 21:17

Jesus Christ's foreknowledge of events
Jesus Christ's knowledge of his mission
Jn 8:14 Jesus answered, "Even if I testify on my own behalf, my testimony is valid, for I know where I came from and where I am going ..." See also **Jn** 13:1,3; 16:28; 18:4; 19:28

Jesus Christ's knowledge of his death and resurrection
Mt 16:21 From that time on Jesus began to explain to his disciples that he must go to Jerusalem and suffer many things at the hands of the elders, chief priests and teachers of the law, and that he must be killed and on the third day be raised to life. pp Mk 8:31 pp Lk 9:22 See also **Mt** 20:18-19 pp Mk 10:33-34 pp Lk 18:31-33

Jesus Christ's knowledge of his betrayer
Jn 6:64 ... For Jesus had known from the beginning which of them did not believe and who would betray him. See also **Mt** 26:20-25 pp Mk 14:17-20; **Jn** 13:11,18,21-26

Jesus Christ's knowledge of the disciples' desertion and Peter's denial Mt 26:31-34 pp Mk 14:27-30 pp Lk 22:31-34

Jesus Christ's knowledge of human beings
Jesus Christ knows every human heart
Jn 2:24-25 But Jesus would not entrust himself to them, for he knew all people. He did not need human testimony about them, for he knew what was in people. See also **Ac** 1:24; **Rev** 2:23

Jesus Christ discerns evil thoughts and motives
Mt 22:18 But Jesus, knowing their [the Pharisees'] evil intent, said, "You hypocrites, why are you trying to trap me?" pp Mk 12:15 pp Lk 20:23 See also **Mt** 9:3-4 pp Mk 2:6-8 pp Lk 5:21-22; **Mt** 12:14-15,24-25 pp Lk 11:15-17; **Lk** 6:7-8; **Jn** 5:42; 6:15

Jesus Christ knows those whose faith is not genuine Mt 7:21-23

Jesus Christ knows people's situations and needs
Jn 1:47-49 ... "How do you know me?"

Nathanael asked. Jesus answered, "I saw you while you were still under the fig-tree before Philip called you." . . . *See also* **Mk** 6:34; **Lk** 19:5; **Jn** 4:16–19,28–29; 5:6

Jesus Christ's knowledge of believers
Jesus Christ knows those who are his
Jn 10:14 "I [Jesus] am the good shepherd; I know my sheep and my sheep know me—"
See also **Jn** 10:27; 20:15–16; **2Ti** 2:19
Jesus Christ knows those who call on him in faith
Mk 5:24–34 . . . At once Jesus realised that power had gone out from him. He turned around in the crowd and asked, "Who touched my clothes?" "You see the people crowding against you," his disciples answered, "and yet you can ask, 'Who touched me?'" But Jesus kept looking around to see who had done it . . . pp **Mt** 9:18–22 pp **Lk** 8:43–48 *See also* **Mt** 9:2 pp **Mk** 2:5 pp **Lk** 5:20
Jesus Christ knows believers' deeds
Rev 2:2 "I [Jesus] know your [the Ephesian Christians'] deeds, your hard work and your perseverance. I know that you cannot tolerate wicked people, that you have tested those who claim to be apostles but are not, and have found them false." *See also* **Mt** 10:42 pp **Mk** 9:41; **Mt** 16:27; 25:37–40; **Rev** 2:3,19,23
Jesus Christ knows believers' needs Mk 6:48; **Rev** 2:9–10,13; 3:8
Jesus Christ knows his disciples' misunderstandings and disputes Mt 16:5–8 pp **Mk** 8:14–17; **Mk** 9:33–35 pp **Lk** 9:46–48; **Jn** 6:60–61; 16:17–19
Jesus Christ knows those who are half-hearted Rev 2:2–5; 3:1–2,15–18

Jesus Christ's knowledge of the Scriptures
Lk 24:27 And beginning with Moses and all the Prophets, he [Jesus] explained to them what was said in all the Scriptures concerning himself.
See also **Mt** 4:4 pp **Lk** 4:4; **Mt** 5:21; 12:3–7; 22:29–32 pp **Mk** 12:24–27 pp **Lk** 20:34–38; **Mt** 24:37–39 pp **Lk** 17:26–29

Limitations of Jesus Christ's knowledge
Jesus Christ acquired knowledge by usual human means Mt 4:12; 14:13; **Mk** 6:38; 9:21; **Lk** 2:46,52; **Jn** 9:35
Things that Jesus Christ did not know on account of his humanity
Mt 24:36 "No-one knows about that day or hour, not even the angels in heaven, nor the Son, but only the Father." pp **Mk** 13:32 *See also* **Ac** 1:7 *See also* God, all-knowing; Holy Spirit, inspiration; Jesus Christ, divinity; Jesus Christ, humanity; Jesus Christ, mind of; Jesus Christ, prophecies concerning; Jesus Christ, wisdom; knowing God; Scripture, understanding.

Jesus Christ, love of
Jesus Christ's total giving of himself, shown supremely in his obedient suffering and death on the cross, reveals God's amazing love for sinners. It continues to motivate and inspire Christians today.

The supreme quality of Jesus Christ's love
Eph 3:17–19 . . . And I [Paul] pray that you [Ephesians], being rooted and established in love, may have power, together with all the saints, to grasp how wide and long and high and deep is the love of Christ, and to know this love that surpasses knowledge . . . *See also* **Ro** 8:35, 38–39
It caused him to leave his eternal glory
2Co 8:9 For you know the grace of our Lord Jesus Christ, that though he was rich, yet for your sakes he became poor, so that you through his poverty might become rich. *See also* **Php** 2:6–8
It moved him to give his life for others
1Jn 3:16 This is how we know what love is: Jesus Christ laid down his life for us . . .
See also **Jn** 10:11,14–15; 15:13; **Eph** 5:2; **Rev** 1:5
He loves sinners
Lk 23:34 Jesus said, "Father, forgive them, for they do not know what they are doing." . . .
See also **Lk** 13:34 pp **Mt** 23:37; **Lk** 23:43
He loves each believer
2Th 2:13 But we ought always to thank God for you, brothers and sisters loved by the Lord . . . *See also* **Jn** 10:3–5

Examples of Jesus Christ's love
His compassion for the needy Mt 9:36 pp Mk 6:34; **Mt** 14:14; 15:32 pp Mk 8:1–2; **Lk** 7:13
His love for children Mt 19:13–15 pp Mk 10:13–16 pp Lk 18:15–17
His love for his mother Jn 19:26–27
His love for his followers
Jn 13:1 . . . Having loved his own who were in the world, he [Jesus] now showed them the full extent of his love.
Lazarus: **Jn** 11:1–7,17–22,32–44
The "disciple whom Jesus loved" is widely thought to have been John, the author of the Gospel: **Jn** 13:23; 20:2; 21:7,20

Jesus Christ's love stems from the Father
He receives the Father's love
Jn 3:35 "The Father loves the Son and has placed everything in his hands." *See also* **Mt** 17:5 pp Mk 9:7 pp Lk 9:35; **Mk** 1:11 pp Mt 3:17 pp Lk 3:22; **Jn** 5:20; 14:31
His love reveals the Father's love
Ro 5:8 But God demonstrates his own love for us in this: While we were still sinners, Christ died for us. *See also* **Jn** 3:16; **Eph** 2:4–5; **1Jn** 4:9–10

Jesus Christ's love motivates the church
His love indwells believers
Jn 17:26 "I [Jesus] have made you [the Father] known to them [the disciples], and will continue to make you known in order that the love you have for me may be in them and that I myself may be in them." *See also* **Jn** 15:9–10; **Gal** 2:20; **1Ti** 1:14; **1Jn** 4:12
His love disciplines believers
Rev 3:19 "Those whom I [Jesus] love I rebuke and discipline. So be earnest, and repent."
See also **Heb** 12:5–6; **Pr** 3:11–12; **Rev** 3:9
His love inspires authentic Christian attitudes
Jn 13:34–35 "A new command I [Jesus] give you: Love one another. As I have loved you, so you must love one another. By this everyone will know that you are my disciples, if you love one another." *See also* **Lev** 19:18; **Dt** 6:5; **Mt** 5:43–44; 22:35–39 pp Mk 12:28–31 pp Lk 10:25–27; **Lk** 6:27; **Jn** 15:12; **1Jn** 3:10

His love inspires Christian marriage
Eph 5:25 Husbands, love your wives, just as Christ loved the church and gave himself up for her *See also* **Eph** 5:28–30
His love inspires a desire for spiritual gifts
1Co 14:1 Follow the way of love and eagerly desire spiritual gifts, especially the gift of prophecy.
His love motivates Christians to live for God
2Co 5:14–15 For Christ's love compels us, because we are convinced that one died for all, and therefore all died. And he died for all, that those who live should no longer live for themselves but for him who died for them and was raised again. *See also* **Ro** 8:37; **1Co** 16:14; **Col** 2:2; **1Th** 1:3; **Heb** 10:24 *See also church; God, love of; Holy Spirit and love; Jesus Christ, compassion; Jesus Christ, cross of; Jesus Christ, death of; Jesus Christ, grace and mercy.*

Jesus Christ, majesty of
The glorious splendour of Jesus Christ's royal authority belongs to him by right and is reaffirmed through his exaltation to the Father's right hand.

Jesus Christ shared in God's majesty before time began
Jn 17:5 "And now, Father, glorify me in your presence with the glory I had with you before the world began." *See also* **Jn** 17:24; **Col** 1:15; **Heb** 1:3; **Rev** 22:13

Jesus Christ renounced his majesty to become a human being
Php 2:6–8 Who [Christ Jesus], being in very nature God, did not consider equality with God something to be grasped, but made himself nothing, taking the very nature of a servant, being made in human likeness. And being found in appearance as a human being, he humbled himself and became obedient to death—even death on a cross! *See also* **Isa** 53:2–3; **Mt** 20:28 pp Mk 10:45; **Jn** 13:3–5; **2Co** 8:9

Jesus Christ's majesty seen in his earthly ministry
At the transfiguration
2Pe 1:16 We did not follow cleverly invented

stories when we told you about the power and coming of our Lord Jesus Christ, but we were eye-witnesses of his majesty. *See also* **Mt** 17:2 pp **Mk** 9:2–3 pp **Lk** 9:29

At the entry into Jerusalem
Mt 21:9–10 The crowds that went ahead of him and those that followed shouted, "Hosanna to the Son of David!" "Blessed is he who comes in the name of the Lord!" "Hosanna in the highest!" When Jesus entered Jerusalem, the whole city was stirred and asked, "Who is this?" pp **Mk** 11:9–10 pp **Lk** 19:37–38 pp **Jn** 12:13 *See also* **Mt** 21:5 pp **Jn** 12:15; **Zec** 9:9

Jesus Christ's majesty is reaffirmed through his exaltation

Jesus Christ is exalted to the throne of God's majesty
Heb 1:3 . . . After he [Jesus] had provided purification for sins, he sat down at the right hand of the Majesty in heaven. *See also* **Ac** 5:31; **Heb** 8:1; **1Pe** 3:22

A vision of the glorified Christ in his majesty
Rev 1:13–16 . . . among the lampstands was someone "like a son of man", dressed in a robe reaching down to his feet and with a golden sash round his chest. His head and hair were white like wool, as white as snow, and his eyes were like blazing fire. His feet were like bronze glowing in a furnace, and his voice was like the sound of rushing waters. In his right hand he held seven stars, and out of his mouth came a sharp double-edged sword. His face was like the sun shining in all its brilliance. *See also* **Rev** 5:6–8; 14:14

Jesus Christ is majestic in his absolute pre-eminence
Col 1:18 . . . so that in everything he [Jesus] might have the supremacy. *See also* **Da** 7:13–14; **Ac** 2:36; **1Co** 15:25; **Php** 2:10–11; **Rev** 19:16

Jesus Christ's majesty is shown by his authority as judge of all
Mt 25:31 "When the Son of Man comes in his glory, and all the angels with him, he will sit on his throne in heavenly glory." *See also* **Ac** 17:31; **2Ti** 4:1

All humanity will see Jesus Christ's majesty
Mt 26:64 "Yes, it is as you [Caiaphas] say," Jesus replied. "But I say to all of you: In the future you will see the Son of Man sitting at the right hand of the Mighty One and coming on the clouds of heaven." pp **Mk** 14:62 *See also* **Mt** 24:30 pp **Mk** 13:26 pp **Lk** 21:27; **2Th** 1:7–10; **Rev** 1:7; 5:13; 6:15–17; 7:9–10 *See also* God, majesty of; Jesus Christ as king; Jesus Christ, authority; Jesus Christ, divinity; Jesus Christ, exaltation; Jesus Christ, glory of; Jesus Christ, humanity; Jesus Christ, pre-eminence; Jesus Christ, second coming; Jesus Christ, the Lord; Jesus Christ, transfiguration; Jesus Christ, triumphal entry.

Jesus Christ, mind of
The centre of Jesus Christ's thought, understanding and motivation, characterised by a total dedication to God. Christians are called upon to have the same mind as Christ.

The intellectual capacity of Jesus Christ's mind

In childhood
Lk 2:47 Everyone who heard him [Jesus] was amazed at his understanding and his answers. *See also* **Lk** 2:40,52

In adulthood
Jn 7:15 The Jews were amazed and asked, "How did this man [Jesus] get such learning without having studied?" *See also* **Mt** 7:28; 13:54 pp **Mk** 6:2; **Mk** 1:22 pp **Lk** 4:32; **Mk** 11:18

Jesus Christ's mind was pure
Heb 7:26 Such a high priest meets our need—one who is holy, blameless, pure, set apart from sinners . . . *See also* **Lk** 1:35; **Jn** 10:30; **Heb** 4:15

Examples of Jesus Christ's use of his mind

In overcoming temptation Mt 4:4 pp **Lk** 4:4; **Dt** 8:3; **Mt** 27:42 pp **Mk** 15:32 pp **Lk** 23:37
Against opposition Mt 22:18–22 pp **Mk** 12:15–17 pp **Lk** 20:22–26

Jesus Christ's mind is more than intellect

His thinking is supported by prayer
Lk 6:12-13 One of those days Jesus went out to a mountainside to pray, and spent the night praying to God. When morning came, he called his disciples to him and chose twelve of them, whom he also designated apostles: *See also* **Lk 5:16; 22:41-43** pp **Mt 26:39** pp **Mk 14:35-36**

His thinking is tempered by understanding
Isa 11:2 The Spirit of the LORD will rest on him—the Spirit of wisdom and of understanding, the Spirit of counsel and of power, the Spirit of knowledge and of the fear of the LORD—
See also **Mt 9:35-36; Lk 4:22; Jn 2:24-25**

His mind experiences anguish
Jn 12:27 "Now my heart is troubled, and what shall I say? 'Father, save me from this hour'? No, it was for this very reason I came to this hour." *See also* **Mt 26:38** pp **Mk 14:34; Mt 27:46** pp **Mk 15:34; Ps 22:1; Lk 12:49-50; 22:44; Jn 13:21**

Jesus Christ's mind is extraordinary

He has unusual insight
Mk 2:8 Immediately Jesus knew in his spirit that this was what they were thinking in their hearts, and he said to them, "Why are you thinking these things?" pp **Mt 9:4** pp **Lk 5:22**
See also **Mt 12:25** pp **Lk 11:17; Lk 6:8; 9:47; Jn 1:47-48; 4:17-18; 11:4**

He understands the future
Mk 8:31 He [Jesus] then began to teach them that the Son of Man must suffer many things and be rejected by the elders, chief priests and teachers of the law, and that he must be killed and after three days rise again. pp **Mt 16:21** pp **Lk 9:22**
See also **Mt 26:21** pp **Mk 14:18; Lk 22:34,37; Isa 53:12; Jn 3:14; 4:49-50; 13:33; 18:4**

Jesus Christ's mind did not know all things
Mt 8:10 pp **Lk 7:9; Mk 9:21; 13:32**

Jesus Christ's strength of mind made him resolute
Lk 9:51 As the time approached for him to be taken up to heaven, Jesus resolutely set out for Jerusalem. *See also* **Mt 27:14** pp **Mk 15:5; Jn 6:6; 12:27**

Jesus Christ's mind was not always understood
Mk 9:32 . . . they [the disciples] did not understand what he meant and were afraid to ask him about it. pp **Lk 9:45** *See also* **Mk 3:21-22; Lk 2:50; 18:34; Jn 3:10; 8:27; 12:16**

Christians should have the same mind as Christ

In his attitude
1Pe 4:1 Therefore, since Christ suffered in his body, arm yourselves also with the same attitude, because all who have suffered in their bodies are done with sin. *See also* **1Co 2:16; Isa 40:13; Php 2:5; 3:8; Col 2:2-3**

In his knowledge of Scripture **Mt 7:28-29; 22:29; Lk 2:47; 24:27; Jn 5:39**

In his awareness of God **Jn 8:16,28,55; 14:10-11; 17:1,6**

In the love in which Jesus Christ's mind is exercised **Lk 11:42; Jn 14:23; 1Co 13:2**
See also Christlikeness; Jesus Christ, authority; Jesus Christ, knowledge of; Jesus Christ, love of; Jesus Christ, prophecies concerning; Jesus Christ, wisdom.

Jesus Christ, miracles
Supernatural acts of Jesus Christ, revealing and confirming his Messianic credentials, and the coming of God's kingdom. The miracles of Christ are to be seen as an integral part of his ministry.

Examples of the kind of miracles Jesus Christ performed

Authority over natural forces
Mt 8:27 The disciples were amazed and asked, "What kind of man is this? Even the winds and the waves obey him!" pp **Mk 4:41** pp **Lk 8:25**
See also **Mt 14:19-20** pp **Mk 6:41-43** pp **Lk 9:16-17** pp **Jn 6:11-13; Mt 14:25** pp **Mk 6:48** pp **Jn 6:19; Mt 17:27; Lk 5:4,6; Jn 2:9**

Healing the sick
Mt 4:24 News about him [Jesus] spread all over Syria, and people brought to him all who

were ill with various diseases, those suffering severe pain, the demon-possessed, those having seizures, and the paralysed, and he healed them. *See also* **Mt** 8:13 pp Lk 7:10; **Mt** 8:15 pp Mk 1:31 pp Lk 4:39; **Mt** 9:22 pp Mk 5:29 pp Lk 8:44; **Mt** 9:29–30; 12:13 pp Mk 3:5 pp Lk 6:10; **Mk** 7:35; **Lk** 17:14; **Jn** 4:52–53; 5:8–9; 9:6–7

Casting out demons
Mk 1:34 . . . He [Jesus] also drove out many demons, but he would not let the demons speak because they knew who he was. pp Mt 8:16 pp Lk 4:41 *See also* **Mt** 9:33; 12:22 pp Lk 11:14; **Mt** 17:18 pp Mk 9:25–26 pp Lk 9:42

Raising the dead
Lk 7:14–15 . . . The dead man sat up and began to talk, and Jesus gave him back to his mother. *See also* **Mt** 9:25 pp Mk 5:41–42 pp Lk 8:54–55; **Jn** 11:43–44

The purpose of Jesus Christ's miracles
To bring healing and wholeness
Lk 8:35 . . . When they [the people] came to Jesus, they found the man from whom the demons had gone out, sitting at Jesus' feet, dressed and in his right mind . . . *See also* **Mt** 15:28; **Lk** 17:14–15; **Jn** 9:38

To reveal God's kingdom
Mt 12:28 "But if I [Jesus] drive out demons by the Spirit of God, then the kingdom of God has come upon you." pp Lk 11:20 *See also* **Mt** 11:4–5 pp Lk 7:22

To fulfil God's word
Mt 8:16–17 When evening came, many who were demon-possessed were brought to him [Jesus], and he drove out the spirits with a word and healed all the sick. This was to fulfil what was spoken through the prophet Isaiah: "He took up our infirmities and carried our diseases." *See also* **Isa** 53:4; **Mt** 12:15–17; **Lk** 4:18–19; **Isa** 61:1–2; **Lk** 4:21

To bring glory to God
Jn 11:4 When he heard this, Jesus said, "This sickness will not end in death. No, it is for God's glory so that God's Son may be glorified through it." *See also* **Mt** 15:31; **Jn** 2:11

To show Jesus to be the Messiah
Ac 2:22 "People of Israel, listen to this: Jesus of Nazareth was a man accredited by God to you by miracles, wonders and signs, which God did among you through him, as you yourselves know." *See also* **Mt** 11:3–5 pp Lk 7:19–22; **Jn** 5:36; 10:25,37–38; 11:42

Varying responses to Jesus Christ's miracles
Terror and fear
Mk 4:41 They [the disciples] were terrified and asked each other, "Who is this? Even the wind and the waves obey him!" pp Lk 8:25 *See also* **Mt** 8:34; **Mk** 5:15 pp Lk 8:35

Wonder and amazement
Lk 4:36 All the people were amazed and said to each other, "What is this teaching? With authority and power he [Jesus] gives orders to evil spirits and they come out!" pp Mk 1:27 *See also* **Mt** 9:33; 12:23; **Lk** 9:43; 11:14

Faith and gratitude
Lk 19:37 When he [Jesus] came near the place where the road goes down the Mount of Olives, the whole crowd of disciples began joyfully to praise God in loud voices for all the miracles they had seen: *See also* **Mk** 5:18–20 pp Lk 8:38–39; **Lk** 17:15–16; **Jn** 9:38; 14:11; 20:30–31

Opposition and hatred
Jn 15:24 ". . . But now they have seen these miracles, and yet they have hated both me [Jesus] and my Father." *See also* **Mt** 11:20–21 pp Lk 10:13; **Mt** 12:24 pp Mk 3:22 pp Lk 11:15; **Jn** 12:10–11,37–38

Limitations on Jesus Christ's miracles
Jesus Christ restricted his miracles because of superficial faith
Jn 2:23–24 Now while he was in Jerusalem at the Passover Feast, many people saw the miraculous signs he was doing and believed in his name. But Jesus would not entrust himself to them, for he knew all people. *See also* **Mt** 12:38–39 pp Lk 11:29; **Mt** 16:1–4 pp Mk 8:11–12; **Jn** 2:18; 6:30

Miracles require faith
Mt 13:58 And he [Jesus] did not do many miracles there because of their lack of faith. pp Mk 6:5 *See also* **Mt** 14:28–31; 17:14–20

Jesus Christ's miracles performed through others
Through the disciples during Jesus Christ's lifetime Mt 10:1 pp Mk 3:14–15 pp Lk 9:1–2; Mk 9:38 pp Lk 9:49; Lk 10:17
Through the apostles after Jesus Christ's ascension Ac 3:6,16; 4:10; 5:12; 6:8; 8:6–7; 16:18; 19:11; 2Co 12:12
Through the church 1Co 12:10,28–29 *See also* faith; God, glory of; Jesus Christ, kingdom of; Jesus, the Christ; kingdom of God; miracles; signs.

Jesus Christ, mission
The work that Jesus Christ was sent to do, including both his healing and preaching ministry, but particularly his work of salvation. Jesus Christ sends Christians to continue his work by proclaiming his message of salvation.

Jesus Christ was called to his mission from the beginning of time
Isa 49:1 . . . Before I [the servant of the LORD] was born the LORD called me; from my birth he has made mention of my name.
See also Mic 5:2; 1Pe 1:20

Jesus' mission as Messiah was foretold
His mission to help and heal the poor
Isa 61:1–3 The Spirit of the Sovereign LORD is on me, because the LORD has anointed me to preach good news to the poor . . .
See also Isa 11:3–5; 32:3–4; 35:5–6; 42:3,7
His mission to rule and establish the kingdom of God
Isa 9:6–7 . . . a child is born, to us a son is given, and the government will be on his shoulders . . . He will reign on David's throne and over his kingdom, establishing and upholding it with justice and righteousness from that time on and for ever . . . *See also* Ge 49:10; Ps 132:11; Jer 23:5–6; Da 2:44
His mission to establish justice and peace
Isa 11:4–5 . . . with righteousness he will judge the needy, with justice he will give decisions for the poor of the earth . . . *See also* Isa 2:4; 9:4–7; 42:4

His mission to suffer and die
Isa 53:3–10 He [God's servant] was despised and rejected by others, a man of sorrows, and familiar with suffering . . . *See also* Isa 50:6; 52:14; Da 9:26; Mk 8:31; Lk 24:26–27; Ac 8:32–35
His mission was fulfilled in humility and poverty
Zec 9:9 . . . your king comes to you, righteous and having salvation, gentle and riding on a donkey, on a colt, the foal of a donkey.
See also Isa 42:2–3; 49:7
His mission was for all nations
Isa 49:6 . . . "It is too small a thing for you [the servant of the LORD] to be my [the LORD's] servant to restore the tribes of Jacob and bring back those of Israel I have kept. I will also make you a light for the Gentiles, that you may bring my salvation to the ends of the earth."
See also Isa 11:10; 42:1–6; 55:4–5

Aspects of Jesus Christ's mission
Preaching and teaching
Lk 4:43 . . . "I [Jesus] must preach the good news of the kingdom of God to the other towns also, because that is why I was sent." pp Mk 1:38
See also Mt 4:17; 5:2; Mk 1:21; Jn 8:2; 18:37
Sacrificial service
Mt 20:28 ". . . the Son of Man did not come to be served, but to serve, and to give his life as a ransom for many." pp Mk 10:45 *See also* Lk 22:27; Jn 13:13–16; Php 2:7
Healing
Mt 4:23 Jesus went throughout Galilee . . . healing every disease and sickness among the people. *See also* Mt 14:14; Mk 1:34; Lk 4:40; 5:15; Jn 9:4–7
Judgment
Jn 9:39 Jesus said, "For judgment I have come into this world, so that the blind will see and those who see will become blind." *See also* Lk 12:49; Jn 3:17–18; 5:22; 8:10–11,26; 12:47–48

Criteria for the direction of Jesus Christ's mission
Obedience to his Father's will
Jn 6:38 ". . . I [Jesus] have come down from

heaven not to do my will but to do the will of him who sent me." *See also* **Mt** 26:39 pp **Mk** 14:36 pp **Lk** 22:42; **Jn** 4:34; 14:31; 18:11

The fulfilment of the Law and the Prophets
Mt 5:17 "Do not think that I [Jesus] have come to abolish the Law or the Prophets; I have not come to abolish them but to fulfil them." *See also* **Mt** 13:35; 26:54; **Lk** 4:18–21; 18:31; **Ro** 3:21

Jesus Christ's saving death is the supreme aspect and focus of his mission

Jesus Christ came to save and to give life
Jn 10:10 ". . . I [Jesus] have come that they may have life, and have it to the full." *See also* **Mt** 1:21; **Lk** 19:10; **Jn** 3:17; **1Ti** 1:15; **2Ti** 1:10

Jesus Christ came to suffer and to die
Mt 16:21 . . . Jesus began to explain to his disciples that he must go to Jerusalem and suffer many things at the hands of the elders, chief priests and teachers of the law, and that he must be killed . . . pp **Mk** 8:31 pp **Lk** 9:22 *See also* **Mt** 20:28 pp **Mk** 10:45; **Jn** 12:27; **Ro** 3:24–25; **Col** 1:20; **1Jn** 4:10

Jesus Christ was aware of the personal cost of his mission
Lk 12:50 ". . . I [Jesus] have a baptism to undergo, and how distressed I am until it is completed!" *See also* **Mt** 26:38–39 pp **Mk** 14:34–36 pp **Lk** 22:42

The mission of Jesus Christ continues today

Jesus Christ's own work continues
Heb 7:24–25 . . . Jesus lives for ever, he has a permanent priesthood. Therefore he is able to save completely those who come to God through him, because he always lives to intercede for them. *See also* **Ro** 8:34; 15:18; **2Co** 4:10–11; **Heb** 6:20; 9:12,14; 13:21

Christians are called to share in Jesus Christ's mission
Jn 20:21 ". . . As the Father has sent me [Jesus], I am sending you [the disciples]." *See also* **Mt** 28:19–20; **Mk** 16:15; **Jn** 14:12

See also church, purpose; Holy Spirit and mission; Jesus Christ as Saviour; Jesus Christ as servant; Jesus Christ, cross of; Jesus Christ, miracles; Jesus Christ, suffering; Messiah, coming of; Trinity, mission of.

Jesus Christ, obedience

The selfless obedience of Jesus Christ to the will of God his Father, through which the redemption of humanity is accomplished. Christ also shows himself willing to submit to earthly authorities and sets an example which believers are called to imitate.

Jesus Christ was totally obedient to his Father's will

Obedience was central to Jesus Christ's life and thought
Jn 4:34 "My food," said Jesus, "is to do the will of him who sent me and to finish his work.
Heb 10:9 . . . he [Jesus] said, "Here I am, I have come to do your [God's] will." . . . *See also* **Mt** 3:15; 8:9–10 pp **Lk** 7:8–9; **Jn** 5:30; 6:38; 14:31; **Heb** 10:7; **Ps** 40:7–8

Jesus Christ's obedience meant ultimate personal cost
Mt 26:39 . . . he [Jesus] fell with his face to the ground and prayed, "My Father, if it is possible, may this cup be taken from me. Yet not as I will, but as you will." pp **Mk** 14:36 pp **Lk** 22:42
Php 2:8 . . . he [Jesus] humbled himself and became obedient to death—even death on a cross! *See also* **Isa** 50:5–6; 53:10–12; **Mt** 16:21 pp **Mk** 8:31 pp **Lk** 9:22; **Jn** 10:18; 13:1; **Heb** 5:8

Jesus Christ's obedience was necessary for God's salvation plan
Ro 5:18–19 . . . through the obedience of the one man the many will be made righteous. *See also* **Mt** 27:40–42 pp **Mk** 15:30–31 pp **Lk** 23:35–37; **Lk** 24:26; **Jn** 17:2–4,26; 19:30

Jesus Christ's obedience was shown in his human relationships

He was obedient to his parents
Lk 2:51 . . . he [Jesus] went down to Nazareth with them [Mary and Joseph] and was obedient to them . . .

He was obedient to secular authorities Mt 17:24–27; 22:17–21 pp Mk 12:15–17 pp Lk 20:22–25
He was obedient to the Jewish law Mt 5:17–18; 22:37–40 pp Mk 12:29–31 pp Lk 10:26–28; **Mk** 2:23–28; **Jn** 7:19; 10:37–38

Believers should follow Jesus Christ's example of obedience
Obedience to God's will is paramount
Mt 19:17 ". . . If you want to enter life, obey the commandments."   *See also* Mt 7:21; 12:50 pp Mk 3:35 pp Lk 8:21; Jn 15:10; **Eph** 6:6
Christlike obedience expresses love for God
2Jn 6 And this is love: that we walk in obedience to his [God's] commands. As you have heard from the beginning, his command is that you walk in love.   *See also* Jn 14:15,20–21; 15:12
Obedience should characterise believers' lives
Ro 1:5 . . . we [Paul and his fellow-workers] received grace and apostleship to call people from among all the Gentiles to the obedience that comes from faith.   *See also* Ac 5:29; **2Co** 2:9   *See also* God, will of; Jesus Christ as Saviour; Jesus Christ as servant; Jesus Christ, baptism of; Jesus Christ, cross of; Jesus Christ, example of; Jesus Christ, humility; Jesus Christ, Son of God; Jesus Christ, suffering; law, Jesus Christ's attitude.

Jesus Christ, opposition to
Jesus Christ encountered criticism, grumbling and plotting because he was seen as a threat to the religious and political hierarchy, and because he exposed sin.

Opposition by different groups
By family and friends
Lk 4:24–29 . . . All the people in the synagogue [at Nazareth] were furious when they heard this. They got up, drove him out of the town, and took him to the brow of the hill on which the town was built, in order to throw him down the cliff.   *See also* Mt 13:55–57 pp Mk 6:3–4; **Mk** 3:21; Jn 7:3–5

By religious leaders
Mt 12:14 But the Pharisees went out and plotted how they might kill Jesus. pp Mk 3:6 pp Lk 6:11   *See also* Jn 11:47–53
By political leaders Mt 2:13–14; Lk 13:31

Opposition through criticism and accusation
Criticism of Jesus Christ's choice of company
Mt 9:11 When the Pharisees saw this, they asked his disciples, "Why does your teacher eat with tax collectors and 'sinners'?" pp Mk 2:16 pp Lk 5:30   *See also* Lk 7:39; 19:7
Criticism for breaking with tradition Mt 15:1–2 pp Mk 7:5; **Lk** 10:16; 11:38
Accusations of Sabbath-breaking
Jn 5:16 . . . because Jesus was doing these things on the Sabbath, the Jews persecuted him.   *See also* Mt 12:2 pp Mk 2:24 pp Lk 6:2; Mt 12:10 pp Mk 3:2 pp Lk 6:7; **Lk** 13:14; 14:1
Accusations of blasphemy
Jn 10:33 "We are not stoning you for any of these," replied the Jews, "but for blasphemy, because you, a mere human being, claim to be God."   *See also* Mt 9:3 pp Mk 2:6–7 pp Lk 5:21; Mt 26:65 pp Mk 14:64; Jn 5:18; 10:36
Accusations of being demon-possessed
Jn 10:20 Many of them [the Jews] said, "He [Jesus] is demon-possessed and raving mad. Why listen to him?"   *See also* Mt 12:24 pp Mk 3:22 pp Lk 11:15; Jn 7:20; 8:48

Reasons for opposing Jesus Christ
Because of hatred
Jn 15:23–25 ". . . they [the world] have hated both me [Jesus] and my Father. But this is to fulfil what is written in their Law: 'They hated me without reason.'"   *See also* Jn 7:7; 8:40; 15:18
Because people's minds are closed
Jn 8:43–44 ". . . you [the Jews] are unable to hear what I [Jesus] say. You belong to your father, the devil, and you want to carry out your father's desire. He was a murderer from the beginning, not holding to the truth, for there is no truth in him. When he lies, he speaks his native language, for he is a liar and the father of lies."   *See also* Jn 8:37; **2Co** 4:4

Jesus Christ knew where opposition would lead
Mt 16:21 ... Jesus began to explain to his disciples that he must go to Jerusalem and suffer many things at the hands of the elders, chief priests and teachers of the law, and that he must be killed and on the third day be raised to life. pp Mk 8:31–32 pp Lk 9:22   *See also* **Mt 17:22–23** pp Mk 9:31; **Mt 20:17–19** pp Mk 10:32–34 pp Lk 18:31–32; **Lk** 9:44

Unsuccessful opposition before the crucifixion
Early attempts to arrest Jesus Christ
Jn 10:39 Again they [the Jews] tried to seize him, but he escaped their grasp.   *See also* **Jn** 7:30,32,44
Attempts on Jesus Christ's life
Jn 8:59 ... They [the Jews] picked up stones to stone him, but Jesus hid himself, slipping away from the temple grounds.   *See also* **Lk** 4:28–30; **Jn** 7:19; 10:31

Opposition that led to the crucifixion
Plots by the Jewish leaders
Mt 26:3–4 Then the chief priests and the elders of the people assembled in the palace of the high priest, whose name was Caiaphas, and they plotted to arrest Jesus in some sly way and kill him. pp Mk 14:1–2 pp Lk 22:2   *See also* **Mt** 21:46 pp Mk 12:12 pp Lk 20:19; **Jn** 11:57
The chief priests stirred up the crowd
Mt 27:20–23 ... the chief priests and the elders persuaded the crowd to ask for Barabbas and to have Jesus executed ... pp Mk 15:11–14 pp Lk 23:21   *See also* **Jn** 19:15
Rejection by political authorities
Mt 27:26 Then he [Pilate] released Barabbas to them. But he had Jesus flogged, and handed him over to be crucified. pp Mk 15:15 pp Lk 23:24–25   *See also* **Lk** 23:7–12; **Jn** 19:16; **Ac** 4:25–27; **Ps** 2:1–2
The mockery of the Roman soldiers **Mt** 27:27–31 pp Mk 15:16–20
The betrayal by Judas Iscariot **Mt** 26:14–16 pp Mk 14:10–11 pp Lk 22:3–6; **Mt** 26:47–50 pp Mk 14:43–45 pp Lk 22:47–48; **Jn** 18:2–5

Opposition at the crucifixion
Mt 27:39–44 pp Mk 15:29–32 pp Lk 23:35–39; **Jn** 19:21

Opposition to Jesus Christ in apostolic preaching
Ac 3:13–15 "... You [people of Israel] handed him [Jesus] over to be killed, and you disowned him before Pilate, though he had decided to let him go. You disowned the Holy and Righteous One and asked that a murderer be released to you. You killed the author of life ..."   *See also* **Ac** 2:23; 4:10; 5:30; 7:52–53; 10:39; 13:27–29

Saul of Tarsus opposes Jesus Christ
Ac 9:4–5 He fell to the ground and heard a voice say to him, "Saul, Saul, why do you persecute me?" "Who are you, Lord?" Saul asked. "I am Jesus, whom you are persecuting," he replied.   *See also* **Ac** 22:7–8; 26:14–15
See also gospel, responses; Jesus Christ, responses to; Jesus Christ, suffering; Jesus Christ, trial.

Jesus Christ, parables
A central feature of Jesus Christ's teaching was the use of extended similies and short stories about the kingdom of God, based on human experience. Christ used them frequently to call for a response to his message.

Parables are a central feature of Jesus Christ's teaching
Mt 13:34–35 Jesus spoke all these things to the crowd in parables; he did not say anything to them without using a parable ...   *See also* **Ps** 78:2; **Mk** 4:33–34

Different characteristics of Jesus Christ's parables
They vary in complexity and length Mt 7:6; 13:18–23 pp Mk 4:13–20 pp Lk 8:11–15; **Mt** 13:37–45,52
They vary in their use of metaphors, word pictures, objects and actions Mt 5:13–16; 13:44; 18:2–3; 21:18–22 pp Mk 11:12–14 pp Mk 11:20–24; **Lk** 15:8–10

They have different levels of meaning
Often the full impact of a parable may be lost if the Jewish context is not understood: Lk 10:30–37; 15:11–32

They draw on human experience Mt 13:33 pp Lk 13:20–21; Mt 18:12–14 pp Lk 15:4–7; Lk 7:41–43

The themes of Jesus Christ's parables
The kingdom of God
Mk 4:30 Again he [Jesus] said, "What shall we say the kingdom of God is like, or what parable shall we use to describe it?" pp Lk 13:18   See also Mt 13:31–32 pp Mk 4:31–32 pp Lk 13:19–21; Mt 13:44–45; Mk 4:26–29

Relationship with God
Lk 15:20 "So he [the lost son] got up and went to his father. But while he was still a long way off, his father saw him and was filled with compassion for him; he ran to his son, threw his arms around him and kissed him."   See also Mt 7:9–11 pp Lk 11:11–13; Mt 18:12–14 pp Lk 15:4–7; Lk 18:7–8

Right behaviour
Lk 10:37 . . . Jesus told him [the expert in the law], "Go and do likewise."   See also Mt 7:24–27 pp Lk 6:47–49; Lk 13:6–9; 15:27

The time of the end
Mt 25:34 "Then the King will say to those on his right, 'Come, you who are blessed by my Father; take your inheritance, the kingdom prepared for you since the creation of the world.'"   See also Mt 25:1,14–19 pp Lk 19:11–15; Mk 13:35; Lk 12:35–36,40 pp Mt 24:44; Lk 16:22–23

Jesus Christ speaks about himself
Mt 21:37 "Last of all, he [the landowner] sent his son to them. 'They will respect my son,' he said." pp Mk 12:6 pp Lk 20:13   See also Mt 22:2; 25:10

The "I am" sayings of Jesus Christ are brief picture parables: Jn 6:35; 8:12; 10:14; 15:1

Understanding Jesus Christ's parables
Further explanation is sometimes needed
Mt 13:36 Then he [Jesus] left the crowd and went into the house. His disciples came to him and said, "Explain to us the parable of the weeds in the field."   See also Mt 13:18 pp Mk 4:13 pp Lk 8:11; Mt 15:15 pp Mk 7:17

The meaning is sometimes hidden
Lk 8:9–10 . . . He [Jesus] said, "The knowledge of the secrets of the kingdom of God has been given to you, but to others I speak in parables, so that, 'though seeing, they may not see; though hearing, they may not understand.'" pp Mt 13:11–16 pp Mk 4:11–12   See also Isa 6:9–10

Responses to Jesus Christ's parables
The parables demand action
Mt 5:14–16 ". . . In the same way, let your light shine before others, that they may see your good deeds and praise your Father in heaven." See also Mt 4:24; 7:5–6; 13:43,45–46; 25:13,40,45; Lk 12:21,32–33

Positive responses
Mt 13:16 "But blessed are your eyes because they see, and your ears because they hear." See also Mt 7:28–29; 13:51

Rejection of Jesus Christ and his parables
Lk 20:19 The teachers of the law and the chief priests looked for a way to arrest him [Jesus] immediately, because they knew he had spoken this parable against them. But they were afraid of the people. pp Mt 21:45–46 pp Mk 12:12 See also Lk 16:14

Examples of Jesus Christ's parables
Mt 13:1–23 pp Mk 4:1–20 pp Lk 8:4–15; Mt 13:47–52; 18:12–14 pp Lk 15:4–7; Lk 10:25–37; 15:11–32; 18:9–14   See also heaven; Jesus Christ, preaching and teaching; Jesus Christ, second coming; kingdom of God; last things.

Jesus Christ, patience of
Jesus Christ supremely displays God's patient character in his work of salvation. The patience of Jesus Christ is seen in his relationships with people and in his perseverance through trial and suffering to death. Followers of Christ are called to demonstrate patience in all their relationships and circumstances.

The patience of Jesus Christ in his earthly ministry

His patience with people
Lk 22:32-34 "But I [Jesus] have prayed for you, Simon, that your faith may not fail. And when you have turned back, strengthen your brothers." . . . *See also* **Mt** 20:20-28 pp **Mk** 10:35-45; **Mt** 26:69-75 pp **Mk** 14:66-72 pp **Lk** 22:55-62 pp **Jn** 18:16-27; **Mk** 4:13-20; **Lk** 23:33-34; **Jn** 21:15-19

His patience with God's timing of events
Jn 12:27 "Now my [Jesus'] heart is troubled, and what shall I say? 'Father, save me from this hour'? No, it was for this very reason I came to this hour." *See also* **Mk** 1:34 pp **Lk** 4:41; **Mk** 7:36; 8:30; 9:9; **Jn** 2:4; 7:6,30; 12:23; 13:1; 16:32; 17:1

His patience in suffering
Mt 26:39-42 . . . He [Jesus] went away a second time and prayed, "My Father, if it is not possible for this cup to be taken away unless I drink it, may your will be done." pp **Mk** 14:35-36 pp **Lk** 22:42 *See also* **Mt** 26:59-68; 27:28-50; **2Th** 3:5; **Heb** 5:7-9; 12:2-3; **1Pe** 2:21-25

Jesus Christ reflects God's own patient character
Ex 34:6-7; **Nu** 14:18-20; **Mt** 18:26-27; **Ro** 10:21; **1Pe** 3:20; **2Pe** 3:8

Jesus Christ's patience brings about God's salvation
1Ti 1:16 . . . I [Paul] was shown mercy so that in me, the worst of sinners, Christ Jesus might display his unlimited patience as an example for those who would believe on him and receive eternal life. *See also* **Ro** 2:4; **2Pe** 3:15

Jesus Christ's patience must be appropriated by his followers

In relation to people
Eph 4:2 . . . be patient, bearing with one another in love. *See also* **Mt** 18:26-35; **1Co** 13:4; **Gal** 5:22; **Col** 1:11; 3:12; **1Th** 5:14; **2Ti** 4:2; **Jas** 5:7-8

In enduring life's circumstances and sufferings
1Pe 2:20-23 . . . if you suffer for doing good and you endure it, this is commendable before God. To this you were called, because Christ suffered for you, leaving you an example, that you should follow in his steps . . . *See also* **Lk** 8:15; 21:19; **Ro** 5:3-4; 8:25; 12:12; **Col** 1:11; **1Th** 1:3; **Tit** 2:2; **Heb** 12:1-3; **Jas** 1:2-4; 5:8; **1Pe** 5:8-10; **Rev** 1:9; 13:10; 14:12

In communicating the gospel
2Ti 4:2 Preach the Word; be prepared in season and out of season; correct, rebuke and encourage—with great patience and careful instruction. *See also* **Tit** 2:2

In living and waiting for the Lord's coming
Jas 5:7-8 . . . be patient and stand firm, because the Lord's coming is near. *See also* **Ro** 8:25; **1Th** 1:3

Examples of Jesus Christ's patience found in his followers
2Co 1:5-6; 6:4-6; **2Ti** 3:10-11; **Rev** 1:9; 3:10
See also forgiveness; God, patience of; Jesus Christ as Saviour; Jesus Christ, example of; Jesus Christ, obedience; Jesus Christ, second coming; Jesus Christ, suffering.

Jesus Christ, perfection
Jesus Christ perfectly radiates the glory of God, exactly representing his Father's likeness. Christ's work is complete and he is free from all impurity.

Jesus Christ represents perfection and absoluteness

His perfection was established through obedient suffering
Heb 5:8-9 . . . he [Jesus] learned obedience from what he suffered and, once made perfect, he became the source of eternal salvation for all who obey him *See also* **Heb** 2:10; 7:28

All things find fulfilment in Christ
Eph 1:22-23 And God placed all things under his feet and appointed him to be head over everything for the church, which is his body, the fulness of him who fills everything in every way. *See also* **Eph** 1:9-10; 4:13,15-16; **Col** 1:17-18

Jesus Christ radiates God's glory
Heb 1:3 The Son is the radiance of God's

glory . . .   *See also* **Mt** 17:2 pp **Mk** 9:3 pp **Lk** 9:29; **Jn** 1:14; **2Co** 4:4,6; **2Pe** 1:17; **Rev** 1:14–16

Jesus Christ exactly represents the Father's likeness
Heb 1:3 . . . the exact representation of his [God's] being . . .   *See also* **Jn** 1:18; 12:44–45; 14:7,9–10; **Php** 2:6; **Col** 1:15

The fulness of God dwells in Jesus Christ
Col 1:19 For God was pleased to have all his fulness dwell in him [Jesus],   *See also* **Col** 2:9

Jesus Christ's work is totally complete
Heb 12:2 . . . Jesus, the author and perfecter of our faith, who for the joy set before him endured the cross, scorning its shame, and sat down at the right hand of the throne of God. *See also* **Heb** 7:25

Christians will finally participate in Christ's perfection
2Co 3:18 And we, who with unveiled faces all reflect the Lord's glory, are being transformed into his likeness with ever-increasing glory, which comes from the Lord, who is the Spirit.   *See also* **1Co** 13:9–12

Jesus Christ is without impurity
1Jn 3:5 . . . in him [Jesus] is no sin. *See also* **Jn** 8:46; **2Co** 5:21; **Heb** 4:15; 7:26; **1Pe** 1:19; 2:22; **Isa** 53:9; **1Jn** 3:3,7   *See also God, perfection; Jesus Christ, divinity; Jesus Christ, glory of; Jesus Christ, high priest; Jesus Christ, holiness; Jesus Christ, majesty of; Jesus Christ, obedience; Jesus Christ, sinlessness; Jesus Christ, Son of God; Jesus Christ, suffering; Jesus Christ, transfiguration.*

Jesus Christ, power of
The historical and ongoing effective authority of Jesus Christ over natural elements, over human life and ultimately over sin, forces of evil, Satan and death.

Jesus Christ's power is from God
Ac 10:38 ". . . God anointed Jesus of Nazareth with the Holy Spirit and power . . . he went around doing good and healing all who were under the power of the devil, because God was with him."

God's creative power is exercised through Jesus Christ
Jn 1:3 Through him [Jesus] all things were made; without him nothing was made that has been made.   *See also* **1Co** 8:6; **Col** 1:16; **Heb** 1:2

God's infinite power is given to Jesus Christ
Mt 28:18 Then Jesus came to them [the disciples] and said, "All authority in heaven and on earth has been given to me."   *See also* **Mt** 9:6 pp **Mk** 2:10 pp **Lk** 5:24; **Mt** 19:26 pp **Lk** 1:37; **Lk** 1:35; **Jn** 3:34–35; 5:19–20; 13:3; **Php** 2:9

Jesus Christ's power is revealed on earth

Jesus Christ's power over nature
Mt 8:26–27 . . . Then he got up and rebuked the winds and the waves, and it was completely calm. The disciples were amazed and asked, "What kind of man is this? Even the winds and the waves obey him!" pp **Mk** 4:39–41 pp **Lk** 8:24–25   *See also* **Mt** 14:25 pp **Mk** 6:48 pp **Jn** 6:19; **Mt** 21:19 pp **Mk** 11:14; **Mk** 11:21

Jesus Christ's power over sickness
Mt 4:23 Jesus went throughout Galilee . . . healing every disease and sickness among the people.   *See also* **Mt** 8:2–3 pp **Mk** 1:40–42 pp **Lk** 5:12–13; **Mk** 5:27–30 pp **Mt** 9:21–22 pp **Lk** 8:44–46; **Lk** 5:17; **Ac** 10:38

Jesus Christ's power over human life
Mt 11:5 "The blind receive sight, the lame walk, those who have leprosy are cured, the deaf hear, the dead are raised, and the good news is preached to the poor." pp **Lk** 7:22   *See also* **Mt** 9:18–25 pp **Mk** 5:22–42 pp **Lk** 8:41–55; **Jn** 11:43–44

Jesus Christ's power over his own life
Jn 10:18 ". . . I [Jesus] have authority to lay it [my life] down and authority to take it up again. This command I received from my Father."   *See also* **Heb** 7:16

Jesus Christ's power over human behaviour
Mt 4:20 At once they [Simon Peter and Andrew] left their nets and followed him [Jesus]. pp **Lk** 5:11   *See also* **Mt** 9:9 pp **Mk** 2:14 pp **Lk** 5:27–28; **Mk** 15:5; **Jn** 11:29; 19:10–11

Jesus Christ's power over forces of evil
Mt 8:16 . . . many who were demon-possessed were brought to him [Jesus], and he drove out the spirits with a word and healed all the sick. pp Mk 1:32–34 pp Lk 4:40–41 *See also* Mt 4:10–11 pp Mk 1:13 pp Lk 4:12–13; Mt 9:32–33; 12:22; 17:18 pp Mk 9:25 pp Lk 9:42; Jn 14:30

Jesus Christ has power over sin and death
Jesus Christ's crucifixion defeats the power of sin
Ro 6:6 For we [believers] know that our old self was crucified with him [Jesus] so that the body of sin might be done away with, that we should no longer be slaves to sin— *See also* Isa 53:10–12; Mt 9:6; Jn 15:13; 1Co 15:3; Tit 2:14; Heb 9:28; 1Pe 2:24; Rev 5:9
Jesus Christ's resurrection defeats the power of death
Ro 6:9 For we [believers] know that since Christ was raised from the dead, he cannot die again; death no longer has mastery over him. *See also* Ps 16:10; Jn 2:19; 5:21; 17:2; Ac 2:24,32; Ro 1:4; Eph 1:19–20; Php 3:10
Jesus Christ's power over sin and death remains effective
Heb 7:25 . . . he [Jesus] is able to save completely those who come to God through him, because he always lives to intercede for them. *See also* Jn 6:40; Ro 8:2–3; 1Co 15:22; Heb 7:26–28; 1Pe 3:18

Jesus Christ's power remains available in human experience
Jesus Christ's forgiving power is effective today
Ac 13:38–39 ". . . through Jesus the forgiveness of sins is proclaimed to you. Through him everyone who believes is justified from everything you could not be justified from by the law of Moses." *See also* Jn 20:23; Ac 5:31; Eph 1:7
Jesus Christ's enabling power is effective today
Mt 28:18–20; Lk 9:1; 24:49; Jn 16:14; Ac 1:8; 1Co 12:4–6 *See also* forgiveness; God, power of; Holy Spirit in the world; Jesus Christ as creator; Jesus Christ, authority; Jesus Christ, death of; Jesus Christ, miracles; Jesus Christ, resurrection; sin.

Jesus Christ, prayers of
Prayer was the essence of Jesus Christ's relationship with the Father. He prayed for himself and his mission, and he continues to pray for all believers.

Jesus Christ's practice of prayer
He prayed regularly
Lk 5:16 But Jesus often withdrew to lonely places and prayed.
He often prayed alone
Mk 1:35 Very early in the morning, while it was still dark, Jesus got up, left the house and went off to a solitary place, where he prayed. *See also* Mt 14:23 pp Mk 6:46; Lk 6:12; 9:18

Prayer at specific times in Jesus Christ's life
Before his death: Mt 26:36–46 pp Mk 14:32–41 pp Lk 22:39–46; Jn 17:1–26
On the cross: Mt 27:46 pp Mk 15:34; Lk 23:34,46
Lk 3:21–22; 6:12–13; 9:28–29

Characteristics of Jesus Christ's prayers
Communion with his Father Mt 6:9 pp Lk 11:2; Mt 11:27 pp Lk 10:22
Submission to his Father
Heb 5:7 During the days of Jesus' life on earth, he offered up prayers and petitions with loud cries and tears to the one who could save him from death, and he was heard because of his reverent submission. *See also* Mt 6:10; 26:36 pp Mk 14:36 pp Lk 22:42
Giving praise and thanks to his Father
Mt 11:25–26 At that time Jesus said, "I praise you, Father, Lord of heaven and earth, because you have hidden these things from the wise and learned, and revealed them to little children. Yes, Father, for this was your good pleasure." pp Lk 10:21 *See also* Mt 14:19 pp Mk 6:41 pp Lk 9:16 pp Jn 6:11; Mt 15:36 pp Mk 8:6–7; Mt 26:26–27 pp Mk 14:22–23 pp Lk 22:17–19 pp 1Co 11:24; Lk 24:30; Jn 11:41–42

The scope of Jesus Christ's prayers
Mt 19:13–15 pp Mk 10:13–16 pp Lk 18:15–17
For his disciples: **Lk** 22:31–32; **Jn** 14:16; 17:6–19
Lk 23:34
For himself: **Jn** 12:27–28; 17:1–5
Jn 17:20–26

Jesus Christ's continuing ministry of prayer
Heb 7:25 . . . he [Jesus] is able to save completely those who come to God through him, because he always lives to intercede for them. *See also* **Ro** 8:34; **1Jn** 2:1

Jesus Christ's teaching about prayer
Mt 6:9–15 "This, then, is how you should pray . . ." pp Lk 11:2–4 *See also* **Mt** 5:44; 6:5–8; **Lk** 6:28; 18:1–8,9–14; 21:36 *See also Jesus Christ, cross of; Jesus Christ, death of; Jesus Christ, high priest; Jesus Christ, obedience; Jesus Christ, suffering; prayer.*

Jesus Christ, pre-eminence
Jesus Christ excels over all of creation and reigns supreme over everything in the created order.

The scope of Jesus Christ's pre-eminence
Over all people
Jn 17:2 "For you [God] granted him [Jesus] authority over all people . . ." *See also* **Mt** 25:31–32; **Ro** 10:12
Over his enemies
1Co 15:25–26 For he [Jesus] must reign until he has put all his enemies under his feet. The last enemy to be destroyed is death. *See also* **Ac** 2:32–35; **Ps** 110:1; **Eph** 4:8
Over every power and authority
Col 2:15 And having disarmed the powers and authorities, he [God] made a public spectacle of them, triumphing over them by the cross.
See also **Eph** 1:21
Over all traditions and institutions **Mt** 12:8 pp Mk 2:28 pp Lk 6:5
Over all things
1Co 15:28 . . . the Son himself will be made subject to him who put everything under him . . . *See also* **Mt** 11:27 pp Lk 10:22; **Mt** 28:18; **Jn** 3:35; 13:3; 16:33; **Ac** 10:36; **Php** 3:21; **Heb** 2:8

The pre-eminence of Jesus Christ in relation to others
To other prophets **Mt** 3:11; 12:41 pp Lk 11:32; **Jn** 1:26–27,30; 3:30; **Heb** 1:1–2
To the patriarchs **Jn** 1:17; 8:52–58; **Heb** 3:3–6
To Aaron and other high priests
Heb 8:1–6 . . . the ministry Jesus has received is as superior to theirs [the priests] as the covenant of which he is mediator is superior to the old one, and it is founded on better promises. *See also* **Heb** 4:14; 6:20; 7:23,26–28; 9:11–14,24–26
To angels
1Pe 3:22 [Jesus] who has gone into heaven and is at God's right hand—with angels, authorities and powers in submission to him.
See also **Heb** 1:4–14
To other lords and kings
Rev 17:14 . . . the Lamb will overcome them because he is Lord of lords and King of kings . . . *See also* **1Ti** 6:15; **Rev** 19:16

Descriptions of Jesus Christ's pre-eminence
He is the head
Col 2:10 . . . Christ, who is the Head over every power and authority. *See also* **Eph** 1:9–10,22; 4:15; 5:23–24; **Col** 1:18
He is the capstone
Mt 21:42 Jesus said to them, "Have you never read in the Scriptures: 'The stone the builders rejected has become the capstone; the Lord has done this, and it is marvellous in our eyes'?"
pp Mk 12:10–11 pp Lk 20:17 *See also* **Ps** 118:22; **Ac** 4:11; **Eph** 2:20; **1Pe** 2:7
He is the Chief Shepherd **Jn** 10:11; **Heb** 13:20; **1Pe** 5:4

The reasons for Jesus Christ's pre-eminence
His divine origin
Jn 3:31 ". . . The one who comes from heaven is above all." *See also* **Jn** 1:1–2; 17:24

His equality with the Father
Jn 10:30 "I [Jesus] and the Father are one." *See also* **Col** 1:19; 2:9
His authority derives from the Father **Jn 5:22–27**
He possesses the rights of the firstborn
Col 1:15–17 He is the image of the invisible God, the firstborn over all creation. For by him all things were created: things in heaven and on earth, visible and invisible, whether thrones or powers or rulers or authorities; all things were created by him and for him. He is before all things, and in him all things hold together. *See also* **Ro** 8:29; **Heb** 1:6
He has a superior name
Php 2:9 ... God exalted him [Jesus] to the highest place and gave him the name that is above every name, *See also* **Ac** 4:12; **Heb** 1:4
He is the First and the Last
Rev 1:17 "... I [Jesus] am the First and the Last." *See also* **Rev** 2:8; 22:13

Examples of events whereby Jesus Christ's pre-eminence is recognised
His entry into Jerusalem Mt 21:4–9 pp **Mk** 11:7–10 pp **Lk** 19:35–38 pp **Jn** 12:12–15; **Zec** 9:9
His resurrection Ro 1:4; **1Co** 15:21–23; **Rev** 1:5
His exaltation to the Father's right hand
Ac 5:31 "God exalted him to his own right hand as Prince and Saviour ..." *See also* **Ac** 2:33; 7:55; **Eph** 1:20–21; 4:8–10; **Php** 2:9–11; **Col** 3:1; **Heb** 8:1; 10:12; **1Pe** 3:22; **Rev** 3:21 *See also God, greatness of; Jesus Christ as king; Jesus Christ as prophet; Jesus Christ, authority; Jesus Christ, divinity; Jesus Christ, exaltation; Jesus Christ, head of the church; Jesus Christ, high priest; Jesus Christ, majesty of; Jesus Christ, Son of God; Jesus Christ, the Lord; Jesus Christ, victory.*

Jesus Christ, preaching and teaching

A vital feature of Jesus Christ's ministry, focusing on his authoritative proclamation of the kingdom of God.

Jesus Christ's mission as preaching and teaching
Lk 4:43 But he [Jesus] said, "I must preach the good news of the kingdom of God to the other towns also, because that is why I was sent." pp **Mk** 1:38 *See also* **Mt** 11:5 pp **Lk** 7:22; **Mk** 6:6; **Jn** 7:16; **Ac** 1:1

Jesus Christ was regarded as a teacher and prophet
Jn 1:38 Turning round, Jesus saw them [two disciples] following and asked, "What do you want?" They said, "Rabbi" (which means Teacher), "where are you staying?" *See also* **Mt** 16:14 pp **Mk** 8:28 pp **Lk** 9:19; **Mt** 23:10; 26:25; **Mk** 9:5; 10:51; **Jn** 13:13

The sources of Jesus Christ's preaching and teaching
Jesus Christ's words were grounded in Scripture
Lk 24:27 And beginning with Moses and all the Prophets, he [Jesus] explained to them [two of the disciples] what was said in all the Scriptures concerning himself. *See also* **Mt** 4:4 pp **Lk** 4:4; **Dt** 8:3; **Mt** 21:16; **Ps** 8:2; **Mt** 22:29–32 pp **Mk** 12:24–27 pp **Lk** 20:35–38
Jesus Christ's words came from God
Jn 7:16 Jesus answered, "My teaching is not my own. It comes from him who sent me." *See also* **Jn** 3:2; 8:28; 12:49–50
Jesus Christ spoke in the power of the Spirit
Ac 1:2 ... he [Jesus] was taken up to heaven, after giving instructions through the Holy Spirit to the apostles he had chosen. *See also* **Lk** 4:14–15; **Jn** 3:34; 6:63

The content of Jesus Christ's preaching and teaching
The kingdom of God
Lk 9:11 ... He welcomed them [the crowds] and spoke to them about the kingdom of God, and healed those who needed healing. *See also* **Mt** 4:17,23; 6:33; 13:24; **Mk** 1:15; **Jn** 3:3
God as Father
Jn 14:8–14 ... Jesus answered: "Don't you know me, Philip, even after I have been among you such a long time? Anyone who has seen me has seen the Father ..." *See also* **Mt** 6:31–32 pp **Lk** 12:30–31; **Mt** 10:32–33; 18:10;

Mk 11:25; Jn 5:17–23; 8:18–19

Jesus Christ's own identity
Jn 4:25–26 The [Samaritan] woman said, "I know that Messiah" (called Christ) "is coming. When he comes, he will explain everything to us." Then Jesus declared, "I who speak to you am he."   *See also* Mt 16:13–17 pp Mk 8:27–30 pp Lk 9:18–21; **Lk 4:20–21**; 24:44; Jn 10:11; 14:6–7

Jesus Christ's mission
Mk 9:31 because he [Jesus] was teaching his disciples. He said to them, "The Son of Man is going to be betrayed into human hands. People will kill him, and after three days he will rise." pp Mt 17:22–23 pp Lk 9:44   *See also* Mt 20:17–19 pp Mk 10:32–34 pp Lk 18:31–34; **Lk 19:9–10**; 24:46; Jn 6:51; 10:14–15

How people should live
Mt 5:48 "Be perfect, therefore, as your heavenly Father is perfect."   *See also* Mt 5:20–22,43–44; 7:12; 19:21–24 pp Mk 10:21–25 pp Lk 18:22–25; Mt 22:35–40 pp Mk 12:28–31; Lk 6:35; Jn 13:34–35; 15:12–13

The future
Mk 14:62 . . . "And you will see the Son of Man sitting at the right hand of the Mighty One and coming on the clouds of heaven." pp Lk 22:69   *See also* Mt 10:15 pp Lk 10:12; Mt 12:36–37; 24:1–2 pp Mk 13:1–2 pp Lk 21:5–6; Mt 24:36–44; 25:31–33; Lk 17:26–35

Jesus Christ criticised false teachings
Mt 15:6–9 ". . . Thus you [Pharisees and teachers of the law] nullify the word of God for the sake of your tradition . . ." pp Mk 7:6–7   *See also* Isa 29:13; Mt 7:15–16; 16:12; 23:2–4; Mk 12:38–39 pp Lk 20:45–46

The results of Jesus Christ's preaching and teaching
Jesus Christ invited a response
Mt 11:28–30 "Come to me, all you who are weary and burdened, and I will give you rest . . ."   *See also* Mt 13:23 pp Mk 4:20 pp Lk 8:15; Mt 22:8–10; Lk 14:21–24; Jn 5:24

Jesus Christ looked for an obedient response
Lk 11:28 He [Jesus] replied, "Blessed rather are those who hear the word of God and obey it."   *See also* Mt 7:24–27; 11:15; 13:23 pp Mk 4:20 pp Lk 8:15; Mt 28:20; Mk 4:9; Jn 14:23–24

People responded to Jesus Christ's preaching and teaching
Jn 12:42 Yet at the same time many even among the leaders believed in him . . .   *See also* Mt 8:19–22 pp Lk 9:57–60; Mt 13:10–15 pp Mk 4:10–12; Jn 4:39; 6:68–69

Characteristics of Jesus Christ's preaching and teaching
It had authority
Mt 7:28–29 When Jesus had finished saying these things, the crowds were amazed at his teaching, because he taught as one who had authority, and not as their teachers of the law.   *See also* Mt 21:23 pp Mk 11:28 pp Lk 20:2; Mt 22:22 pp Mk 12:17 pp Lk 20:26; Mk 1:22 pp Lk 4:32; Mk 1:27; Jn 7:15

Jesus Christ lived out what he preached and taught
Jn 10:38 ". . . even though you do not believe me, believe the miracles, that you may know and understand that the Father is in me, and I in the Father."   *See also* Mt 11:29; 16:24 pp Mk 8:34 pp Lk 9:23; Jn 13:15,34

Jesus Christ's preaching and teaching methods
His use of lessons drawn from people's experience
Mt 9:16–17 pp Mk 2:21–22 pp Lk 5:36–37; Mt 12:11–12; 18:12 pp Lk 15:4; **Lk 9:62**; 13:15–16

His use of parables
Mt 13:34 Jesus spoke all these things to the crowd in parables; he did not say anything to them without using a parable.   *See also* Mt 13:3 pp Mk 4:2 pp Lk 8:4

His use of everyday objects
Mt 6:26–29 pp Lk 12:23–27; Mt 22:19–21 pp Mk 12:15–17 pp Lk 20:24–25

His use of questions
Mt 6:25–28; 21:24–25 pp Mk 11:29 pp Lk 20:3–4; **Lk 10:36–37**   *See also* God, fatherhood; Holy Spirit in life of Jesus Christ; Jesus Christ as prophet; Jesus Christ, attitude to Old Testament; Jesus Christ, authority; Jesus Christ, parables; Jesus Christ, responses to; kingdom of God.

Jesus Christ, prophecies concerning

The OT points ahead to the person and ministry of Jesus Christ. Christ's fulfilment of OT prophecy is often noted by NT writers as a demonstration of God's faithfulness to his promises of salvation and as confirmation of the divine authority of Jesus Christ.

Jesus Christ fulfils OT prophecy
He fulfils the OT as a whole
Lk 24:27 . . . beginning with Moses and all the Prophets, he [Jesus] explained to them what was said in all the Scriptures concerning himself. *See also* **Mt** 5:17; **Lk** 24:44; **2Co** 1:20

He fulfils God's promises to Abraham
Gal 3:14 He [Christ] redeemed us in order that the blessing given to Abraham might come to the Gentiles through Christ Jesus . . . *See also* **Lk** 1:54–55,72–74; **Gal** 3:16

He fulfils God's promises through the prophets
Ac 10:43 "All the prophets testify about him [Jesus] . . ." *See also* **Mt** 26:56; **Ac** 3:18,24; 13:27; **Ro** 1:2; **1Pe** 1:10

Prophecies about Jesus Christ's birth
Mt 1:23 "The virgin will be with child and will give birth to a son, and they will call him Immanuel"—which means, "God with us." *See also* **Isa** 7:14; **Mt** 1:21; **Lk** 1:31–32; **Isa** 9:6; **Mt** 2:6–7; **Mic** 5:2; **Mt** 2:15; **Hos** 11:1

Prophecies about Jesus Christ's ministry
He brings good news
Lk 4:17–19 The scroll of the prophet Isaiah was handed to him [Jesus]. Unrolling it, he found the place where it is written: "The Spirit of the Lord is on me, because he has anointed me to preach good news to the poor . . ." *See also* **Isa** 61:1–2; **Mt** 4:13–16; **Isa** 9:1–2

He divides people and is rejected
Lk 2:34–35 Then Simeon blessed them and said to Mary, his mother: "This child is destined to cause the falling and rising of many in Israel . . ." *See also* **Mt** 3:11–12 pp **Mk** 1:7–8 pp **Lk** 3:16–17; **Mt** 21:42 pp **Mk** 12:10–11 pp **Lk** 20:17; **Ps** 118:22–23; **Jn** 13:18; **Ps** 41:9

He teaches in parables
Mt 13:35 So was fulfilled what was spoken through the prophet: "I will open my mouth in parables, I will utter things hidden since the creation of the world." *See also* **Ps** 78:2; **Mt** 13:13–15 pp **Mk** 4:11–12 pp **Lk** 8:10; **Isa** 6:9–10

Prophecies about Jesus Christ's death
The Lord's Supper
Mt 26:28 "This is my [Jesus'] blood of the covenant, which is poured out for many for the forgiveness of sins." pp **Mk** 14:24 pp **Lk** 22:20 *See also* **Isa** 53:12; **Jer** 31:34

The betrayal
Mt 27:9–10 Then what was spoken by Jeremiah the prophet was fulfilled: "They took the thirty silver coins . . ."
Matthew brings together two prophetic passages fulfilled by this incident: **Jer** 19:1–13; **Zec** 11:12–13
Jn 18:9; 6:39

The cross
Mt 27:46 About the ninth hour Jesus cried out in a loud voice, "*Eloi, Eloi, lama sabachthani?*"—which means, "My God, my God, why have you forsaken me?" pp **Mk** 15:34 *See also* **Ps** 22:1; **Mt** 27:35 fn; **Ps** 22:18; **Lk** 23:46; **Ps** 31:5

Prophecies about Jesus Christ's resurrection and ascension
Mt 12:39–40 He [Jesus] answered, "A wicked and adulterous generation asks for a miraculous sign! But none will be given it except the sign of the prophet Jonah. For as Jonah was three days and three nights in the belly of a huge fish, so the Son of Man will be three days and three nights in the heart of the earth." pp **Lk** 11:29–30 *See also* **Jnh** 1:17; **Ac** 2:25–28; **Ps** 16:8–11; **Ac** 2:31; 13:35; 2:34; **Ps** 110:1; **Eph** 4:8; **Ps** 68:18

Prophecies about Jesus Christ's titles
Jesus Christ as Son of God
Ac 13:32–33 ". . . What God promised our ancestors he has fulfilled for us, their children, by raising up Jesus. As it is written in the second

Psalm: 'You are my Son; today I have become your Father.'" *See also* **Ps** 2:7; **Heb** 1:5; 5:5; **Mt** 22:44 pp **Mk** 12:36 pp **Lk** 20:42; **Ps** 110:1; **Heb** 1:8–9; **Ps** 45:6–7

Jesus Christ as Son of Man
Mt 26:64 . . . "But I [Jesus] say to all of you: In the future you will see the Son of Man sitting at the right hand of the Mighty One and coming on the clouds of heaven." pp **Mk** 14:62 pp **Lk** 22:69 *See also* **Da** 7:13–14; **Mk** 8:31 pp **Lk** 9:22

Jesus Christ as Son of David
Rev 22:16 "I, Jesus, have sent my angel to give you this testimony for the churches. I am the Root and the Offspring of David, and the bright Morning Star." *See also* **2Sa** 7:12–16 pp **1Ch** 17:11–14; **Lk** 1:32–33; **Isa** 9:7; **Ac** 13:34; **Isa** 55:3; **Ro** 15:12; **Isa** 11:1

Jesus Christ as the coming Messianic king
Mt 26:31 pp **Mk** 14:27; **Zec** 13:7; **Mt** 21:4–5; **Zec** 9:9

Jesus Christ as the suffering servant
Ac 8:32–35 . . . Then Philip began with that very passage of Scripture and told him the good news about Jesus. *See also* **Isa** 53:7–8; **Mt** 12:17–21; **Isa** 42:1–4

Jesus Christ as the prophet who is to come
Ac 3:22 "For Moses said, 'The Lord your God will raise up for you a prophet like me from among your own people; you must listen to everything his prophet tells you.'" *See also* **Dt** 18:18; **Lk** 4:18–19; **Isa** 61:1–2; **Jn** 6:14

Jesus Christ as priest
Heb 7:21 . . . he [Jesus] became a priest with an oath when God said to him: "The Lord has sworn and will not change his mind: 'You are a priest for ever.'" *See also* **Ps** 110:4; **Heb** 5:5–6; 7:17 *See also Jesus Christ as prophet; Jesus Christ as servant; Jesus Christ, ascension; Jesus Christ, birth of; Jesus Christ, cross of; Jesus Christ, death of; Jesus Christ, parables; Jesus Christ, resurrection; Jesus Christ, Son of David; Jesus Christ, Son of God; Jesus Christ, Son of Man; Messiah, coming of.*

Jesus Christ, responses to
The NT records a number of responses to Jesus Christ on the part of those who encountered him, both positive and negative.

Negative responses to Jesus Christ
Rejection Mt 21:42; **Mk** 7:5–8; **Lk** 4:28–30; 10:16

Lack of faith
Mk 6:4–6 Jesus said to them, "Only in their home towns, among their relatives and in their own homes are prophets without honour." He could not do any miracles there, except lay his hands on a few sick people and heal them. And he was amazed at their lack of faith. Then Jesus went round teaching from village to village. pp **Mt** 13:57–58

Questioning his authority Mk 11:27–33 pp **Mt** 21:23–27 pp **Lk** 20:1–8

Hardening of hearts Mt 13:10–17; **Jn** 12:37–41

Attributing his power to satanic forces
Mt 9:33–34 And when the demon was driven out, the man who had been mute spoke. The crowd was amazed and said, "Nothing like this has ever been seen in Israel." But the Pharisees said, "It is by the prince of demons that he drives out demons."

Demanding his death Lk 23:20–24; **Jn** 10:22–40

Positive recognition of Jesus Christ's identity

As Messiah
Jn 1:41 The first thing Andrew did was to find his brother Simon and tell him, "We have found the Messiah" (that is, the Christ). *See also* **Lk** 2:11; 9:20; **Ac** 5:42

As King
Jn 1:49 Then Nathanael declared, "Rabbi, you are the Son of God; you are the King of Israel." *See also* **Mt** 2:1–2; 27:37

As Lord
Jn 6:68 Simon Peter answered him, "Lord, to whom shall we go? You have the words of eternal life." *See also* **Jn** 13:13

As Son of David
Mt 15:22 A Canaanite woman from that vicinity came to him, crying out, "Lord, Son of David, have mercy on me! My daughter is suffering terribly from demon-possession."

As Son of God
Ac 9:20 At once he [Paul] began to preach in the synagogues that Jesus is the Son of God.

As Teacher
Mt 19:16 Now someone came up to Jesus and asked, "Teacher, what good thing must I do to get eternal life?" pp Mk 10:17 pp Lk 18:18 *See also* **Mt** 23:10; **Jn** 11:28

Responses to Jesus Christ by those whom he healed
Faith
Mk 10:52 "Go," said Jesus, "your faith has healed you." Immediately he [Bartimaeus] received his sight and followed Jesus along the road. pp Lk 18:42 *See also* **Mt** 8:13; 9:27–31; **Jn** 4:43–54

Thankfulness Lk 17:11–19
Witnessing to others Lk 8:38–39; **Jn** 1:40–42,45–46; 5:10–15; 9:13–34

Responses to Jesus Christ by those whom he met and taught
Amazement
Mt 7:26–29 "But everyone who hears these words of mine and does not put them into practice is like a foolish man who built his house on sand. The rain came down, the streams rose, and the winds blew and beat against that house, and it fell with a great crash." When Jesus had finished saying these things, the crowds were amazed at his teaching, because he taught as one who had authority, and not as their teachers of the law. *See also* **Mk** 12:17

Delight Mk 12:37
Faith Mt 8:10; 9:2,22; 15:28; **Jn** 12:11,41–43
Repentance
Lk 19:8 But Zacchaeus stood up and said to the Lord, "Look, Lord! Here and now I give half of my possessions to the poor, and if I have cheated anybody out of anything, I will pay back four times the amount." *See also* **Mt** 11:20; **Mk** 6:12; **Lk** 13:2–5

Obedience Mt 28:20; **Jn** 15:20; 17:6
Worship Mt 2:2; 14:33
Worship is a response to Jesus Christ which is especially associated with the period after his resurrection: **Mt** 28:9; **Lk** 24:52

Responses to Jesus Christ by those whom he redeemed
Faith
Ac 16:31 They [Paul and Silas] replied, "Believe in the Lord Jesus, and you [the jailer] will be saved—you and your household." *See also* **Ro** 10:9–10; **1Jn** 3:23; 5:5

Obedience Ro 16:26; **Php** 2:12; **Heb** 5:8–9; **1Pe** 4:17
Calling on his name Ac 9:14,21; **Ro** 10:13; **1Co** 1:2
Giving thanks in his name Eph 5:20
Glorifying his name 2Th 1:12
Proclaiming him to the world
Ac 5:42 Day after day, in the temple courts and from house to house, they never stopped teaching and proclaiming the good news that Jesus is the Christ. *See also* **Ac** 8:5; 16:10; **Ro** 15:19; **Col** 1:28; **2Ti** 1:8 *See also* faith; Jesus Christ as redeemer; Jesus Christ, authority; Jesus Christ, opposition to; Jesus Christ, preaching and teaching; Jesus Christ, Son of God; Jesus Christ, Son of Man; worship.

Jesus Christ, resurrection
True Christian preaching is centred on the fact that God raised Jesus Christ from the dead so that believers may have victory over sin and death and receive the blessings of eternal life.

The resurrection of Jesus Christ is foretold
In Scripture
1Co 15:3–4 For what I [Paul] received I passed on to you as of first importance: that Christ died for our sins according to the Scriptures, that he was buried, that he was raised on the third day according to the Scriptures, *See also* **Ps** 16:10; 49:15; **Isa** 53:10–12; **Hos** 6:2; **Lk** 24:46; **Ac** 2:29–31; 26:22–23
By Jesus Christ
Mt 16:21 . . . Jesus began to explain to his disciples that he must go to Jerusalem and suffer many things at the hands of the elders, chief priests and teachers of the law, and that he must be killed and on the third day be raised to life. pp Mk 8:31 pp Lk 9:22 *See also* **Mt** 12:40; 17:9 pp Mk 9:9; **Mt** 17:22–23 pp Mk 9:31; **Mt** 20:18–19

pp Mk 10:33–34 pp Lk 18:31–33; **Mt** 26:32
pp Mk 14:28; **Jn** 2:19–22; 16:16

The resurrection is preached by the apostles
Ac 4:33 . . . the apostles continued to testify to the resurrection of the Lord Jesus . . . *See also* **Ac** 2:24–32; 10:40–41; 17:2–3,18,31

The certainty of the resurrection
Ac 1:3 . . . he [Jesus] showed himself to them and gave many convincing proofs that he was alive . . . *See also* **1Co** 15:3–8
These verses particularly stress the physical reality of the risen Christ: **Lk** 24:36–43; **Jn** 20:26–28

The necessity of the resurrection
1Co 15:17 And if Christ has not been raised, your faith is futile; you are still in your sins. *See also* **Jn** 20:9

The results of Jesus Christ's resurrection
God's power is demonstrated
Eph 1:19–20 . . . his [God's] incomparably great power for us who believe. That power is like the working of his mighty strength, which he exerted in Christ when he raised him from the dead and seated him at his right hand in the heavenly realms, *See also* **Ac** 2:24; **1Co** 6:14
The sonship of Jesus Christ is declared
Ro 1:4 . . . [Jesus] who through the Spirit of holiness was declared with power to be the Son of God, by his resurrection from the dead: Jesus Christ our Lord. *See also* **Ac** 13:33
The lordship of Jesus Christ is declared
Ro 14:9 . . . Christ died and returned to life so that he might be the Lord of both the dead and the living.
The lordship of Jesus Christ is seen in that he was raised to the right hand of God: **Ac** 5:30–31; **Eph** 1:20–22
2Co 5:15
The destruction of death's power is declared
Rev 1:18 "I am the Living One; I was dead, and behold I am alive for ever and ever! And I hold the keys of death and Hades." *See also* **Ac** 2:24; **Ro** 6:9

The benefits of Jesus Christ's resurrection for believers
It is the foundation of salvation
Ro 4:25 He was delivered over to death for our sins and was raised to life for our justification. *See also* **Jn** 11:25–26; **Ro** 10:9; **1Pe** 1:21; 3:21
It provides the power to live for God
Ro 6:4 . . . just as Christ was raised from the dead through the glory of the Father, we too may live a new life. *See also* **Ro** 7:4; 8:11; **Eph** 2:4–7; **Php** 3:8–11; **Col** 2:12; 3:1; **Heb** 13:20–21
The intercession of Jesus Christ depends upon it
Ro 8:34 . . . Christ Jesus, who died—more than that, who was raised to life—is at the right hand of God and is also interceding for us. *See also* **Heb** 7:25
It brings assurance of resurrection to eternal life
1Co 6:14 By his power God raised the Lord from the dead, and he will raise us also. *See also* **Ro** 6:5; **1Co** 15:20–22; **2Co** 4:14; **1Th** 4:14; **1Pe** 1:3–4 *See also Holy Spirit, indwelling; Jesus Christ as Saviour; Jesus Christ, ascension; Jesus Christ, death of; Jesus Christ, preaching and teaching; Jesus Christ, prophecies concerning; Jesus Christ, resurrection appearances; Jesus Christ, Son of God; Jesus Christ, the Lord; Jesus Christ, victory.*

Jesus Christ, resurrection appearances
Jesus Christ appeared to various groups and individuals on several occasions after his death, prior to his ascension into heaven.

The resurrection appearances of Jesus Christ on the third day
To Mary Magdalene
Jn 20:10–18 . . . Mary stood outside the tomb crying . . . she turned round and saw Jesus standing there, but she did not realise that it was Jesus . . . Mary Magdalene went to the disciples with the news: "I have seen the Lord!" And she told them that he had said these things to her. *See also* **Mk** 16:9–11
To the women at the tomb **Mt** 28:1–10 pp Mk 16:1–8 pp Lk 24:1–12

To Peter Lk 24:34; 1Co 15:5
To the two travellers to Emmaus Mk 16:12–13; Lk 24:13–16,30–32
To the disciples in the upper room
Mk 16:14 ... Jesus appeared to the Eleven as they were eating; he rebuked them for their lack of faith and their stubborn refusal to believe those who had seen him after he had risen. pp Lk 24:36 pp Jn 20:19

Further appearances of Jesus Christ
To the disciples in the upper room Jn 20:26; 1Co 15:5
Other appearances
Jn 21:1 Afterwards Jesus appeared again to his disciples, by the Sea of Tiberias ... *See also* Mt 28:16–17; 1Co 15:6–7
Jesus Christ appears at his ascension Mk 16:19; Lk 24:50–51; Ac 1:9

Jesus Christ's resurrection body
It was different from his pre-crucifixion body
Jn 20:26 ... Though the doors were locked, Jesus came and stood among them [the disciples] and said, "Peace be with you!" *See also* Mk 16:12; Jn 20:14, 19 pp Lk 24:36
It was a body of flesh and blood
Lk 24:39 "Look at my hands and my feet. It is I myself! Touch me and see; a ghost does not have flesh and bones, as you see I have." *See also* Lk 24:42–43; Jn 20:20

Jesus Christ foretold his resurrection appearances
Jn 16:16 "In a little while you will see me no more, and then after a little while you will see me."

Responses to Jesus Christ's resurrection appearances
Fear and alarm
Lk 24:37 They [the disciples] were startled and frightened, thinking they saw a ghost. *See also* Mt 28:10
Doubt and disbelief
Mk 16:11 When they heard that Jesus was alive and that she [Mary Magdalene] had seen him, they did not believe it. *See also* Mt 28:17; Mk 16:13–14; Lk 24:11–12; Jn 20:9, 13–14,25
Belief and joy
Mt 28:8 So the women hurried away from the tomb, afraid yet filled with joy, and ran to tell his [Jesus'] disciples. *See also* Lk 24:31–32,41; Jn 20:16,18,27–29
Understanding and worship
Mt 28:9 Suddenly Jesus met them [the women]. "Greetings," he said. They came to him, clasped his feet and worshipped him. *See also* Lk 24:8,45–47; Jn 2:22; Ac 2:31–33

The significance of Jesus Christ's resurrection appearances
They gave proof of Jesus Christ's deity
Jn 20:28–29 Thomas said to him [Jesus], "My Lord and my God!" ... *See also* Lk 24:31–34; Jn 20:8; Ac 10:41–42
Christian life and faith depend on the trustworthiness of the witnesses' testimony
1Co 15:17 ... if Christ has not been raised, your faith is futile; you are still in your sins. *See also* Jn 20:31; Ac 3:15; Ro 1:4; 1Co 15:1–58; 1Th 4:14; 1Pe 1:3 *See also Jesus Christ, ascension; Jesus Christ, resurrection.*

Jesus Christ, righteousness
Jesus Christ pleased his Father perfectly in his life on earth and in his death. He now gives believers a new status before God and a new power for living.

The promised Messiah will be righteous
Zec 9:9 Rejoice greatly, O Daughter of Zion! Shout, Daughter of Jerusalem! See, your king comes to you, righteous and having salvation, gentle and riding on a donkey, on a colt, the foal of a donkey. *See also* Ps 45:7; Isa 53:11; Jer 23:5–6; 33:15
The promised Messiah will establish righteousness Ps 72:1–4; Isa 9:7; 11:3–5

Jesus Christ's own righteousness
Righteousness is characteristic of Jesus Christ
Ac 22:14 "Then he [Ananias] said: 'The God of

our ancestors has chosen you [Paul] to know his will and to see the Righteous One and to hear words from his mouth.'" See also Ac 3:14; 7:52; 2Ti 4:8; Heb 1:8-9; 1Jn 2:1,29; 3:7

Jesus Christ's obedience shows his righteousness
Jn 8:28-29 ". . . I [Jesus] always do what pleases him [the Father]." See also Jn 4:34; 6:38; 12:49-50; 14:31; Php 2:8; Heb 5:8-9; 10:9

Jesus Christ judges righteously
Jn 5:30 ". . . my [Jesus'] judgment is just, for I seek not to please myself but him who sent me." See also Rev 19:11

Jesus Christ is declared not guilty
Lk 23:14-15 ". . . I [Pilate] have examined him [Jesus] in your presence and have found no basis for your charges against him. Neither has Herod, for he sent him back to us; as you can see, he has done nothing to deserve death." See also Lk 23:4; Jn 19:6; Ac 3:13

Jesus Christ's righteousness recognised by others
Lk 23:47 The centurion, seeing what had happened, praised God and said, "Surely this was a righteous man." See also Mk 10:17-18 pp Lk 18:18-19; Lk 23:41; Ac 10:38

Consequences of Jesus Christ's righteousness

God justifies believers on account of the righteousness of Jesus Christ
Ro 5:18-19 . . . just as the result of one trespass was condemnation for all people, so also the result of one act of righteousness was justification that brings life for all people . . . See also Ro 3:23-26; 1Pe 3:18; 2Pe 1:1

All who believe share in the righteousness of Jesus Christ
1Co 1:30 . . . Christ Jesus . . . that is, our righteousness . . . See also Ro 3:21-22; 4:6,24; 9:30; 10:3-4; 2Co 5:21

Believers live by and for Jesus Christ's righteousness
Php 1:11 filled with the fruit of righteousness that comes through Jesus Christ . . . See also Ro 6:18; 8:10; 1Pe 2:24 See also faith, origins of; God, righteousness; holiness; believers' growth in; Jesus Christ, holiness; Jesus Christ, obedience; Jesus Christ, sinlessness; Messiah, coming of.

Jesus Christ, second coming
Jesus Christ will return visibly and in glory at the end of history to raise the dead, judge the world, destroy all evil and opposition to God and consummate his kingdom. Believers are encouraged to be prepared for his return, waiting with eagerness and joy.

The second coming is foretold
In the OT
Da 7:13-14 "In my vision at night I looked, and there before me was one like a son of man, coming with the clouds of heaven. He approached the Ancient of Days and was led into his presence. He was given authority, glory and sovereign power; all nations and people of every language worshipped him. His dominion is an everlasting dominion that will not pass away, and his kingdom is one that will never be destroyed." See also Ps 72:2-4; Isa 2:2-4 pp Mic 4:1-3; Isa 11:4-9; 40:5

By Jesus Christ
Mt 24:30 "At that time the sign of the Son of Man will appear in the sky, and all the nations of the earth will mourn. They will see the Son of Man coming on the clouds of the sky, with power and great glory." pp Mk 13:26 pp Lk 21:27 See also Mt 16:27; 25:31; Mk 14:62; Lk 12:40; Jn 14:3,28

By the angels at Jesus Christ's ascension
Ac 1:11 ". . . Jesus, who has been taken from you into heaven, will come back in the same way you have seen him go into heaven."

By the apostles
Php 3:20 But our citizenship is in heaven. And we eagerly await a Saviour from there, the Lord Jesus Christ, See also Ac 3:20-21; 1Co 1:7; 11:26; 1Th 1:10; 3:13; 4:16; 2Th 1:7-10; Heb 9:28

NT terms for the second coming
"Parousia"
Meaning literally "presence" or "coming", the term was used in the NT world of a royal visit: Mt 24:3; Jas 5:7-8; 2Pe 3:4; 1Jn 2:28

Jesus Christ, second coming

"Apocalypsis"
Meaning literally "unveiling", "apocalypsis" suggests that the second coming will make visible that which is already true of Jesus Christ but presently hidden from human sight: Lk 17:30; 1Co 1:7; 2Th 1:7; 1Pe 1:7; 4:13

"Epiphaneia"
Meaning literally "appearing" or "manifestation", the term suggests coming out into view from a hidden background: 2Th 2:8; 1Ti 6:14; 2Ti 4:1; Tit 2:13

Events that will precede the second coming

The universal preaching of the gospel
Mt 24:14 "And this gospel of the kingdom will be preached in the whole world as a testimony to all nations, and then the end will come." pp Mk 13:10   See also Mt 28:19–20; Ac 1:7–8

The persecution of believers
Mt 24:9 "Then you will be handed over to be persecuted and put to death, and you will be hated by all nations because of me." pp Mk 13:9 pp Lk 21:12   See also Mt 24:21 pp Mk 13:19; Mt 24:22 pp Mk 13:20; Mk 13:12–13 pp Mt 24:12–13 pp Lk 21:16–17; 2Ti 3:1; Rev 7:14

Apostasy, nominal religion and godlessness
1Ti 4:1 The Spirit clearly says that in later times some will abandon the faith and follow deceiving spirits and things taught by demons.   See also Mt 24:10; 2Ti 3:1–5; 2Pe 3:3–4

The revelation of the antichrist
1Jn 2:18 . . . this is the last hour; and as you have heard that the antichrist is coming, even now many antichrists have come. This is how we know it is the last hour.   See also Da 7:20–22; 2Th 2:3–4; 1Jn 4:3; Rev 13:1–10

The appearance of false Christs and false prophets
Mt 24:24 "For false Christs and false prophets will appear . . ." pp Mk 13:22   See also Mt 7:15; 24:5 pp Mk 13:6 pp Lk 21:8; Mt 24:11; Lk 17:23; 2Jn 7

Wars and rumours of wars
Mt 24:6–7 "You will hear of wars and rumours of wars, but see to it that you are not alarmed. Such things must happen, but the end is still to come. Nation will rise against nation, and kingdom against kingdom . . ." pp Mk 13:7–8 pp Lk 21:9–10

Famines and earthquakes
Mt 24:7–8 ". . . There will be famines and earthquakes in various places. All these are the beginning of birth-pains." pp Mk 13:8 pp Lk 21:11

Cosmic changes
Mt 24:29 "Immediately after the distress of those days the sun will be darkened, and the moon will not give its light; the stars will fall from the sky, and the heavenly bodies will be shaken.'" pp Mk 13:24 pp Lk 21:25–26

The timing of the second coming

At God's appointed time
Ac 3:20–21 ". . . that he [God] may send the Christ, who has been appointed for you— even Jesus. He must remain in heaven until the time comes for God to restore everything, as he promised long ago through his holy prophets." See also Mt 24:36 pp Mk 13:32; Lk 17:20–30; Ac 1:7; 2Pe 3:9

Unexpectedly
1Th 5:1–2 . . . the day of the Lord will come like a thief in the night.   See also Mt 24:27 pp Lk 17:24; Mt 24:43–44 pp Lk 12:39–40; 2Pe 3:10; Rev 3:3; 16:15

After a delay
Mt 25:5 "The bridegroom was a long time in coming, and they all became drowsy and fell asleep."   See also Mt 25:19; 2Pe 3:3–9

Imminently
Mt 24:30–34 ". . . Even so, when you see all these things, you know that it is near, right at the door. I tell you the truth, this generation will certainly not pass away until all these things have happened." pp Mk 13:26–30 pp Lk 21:27–32 See also Jn 21:22; Ro 13:11–12; Jas 5:8–9; Rev 3:11; 22:7,20

The manner of the second coming

Jesus Christ's personal return
Ac 1:11 ". . . This same Jesus, who has been taken from you into heaven, will come back in the same way you have seen him go into heaven."   See also Ac 3:20; 1Th 4:16; Heb 9:28

A visible and glorious return
Rev 1:7 Look, he is coming with the clouds, and every eye will see him, even those who pierced him; and all the peoples of the earth will mourn because of him. So shall it be! Amen. *See also* **Mt** 24:30 pp **Mk** 13:26 pp **Lk** 21:27; **Mt** 26:64; **Ac** 1:9

With the sound of a trumpet Mt 24:31; **1Co** 15:52; **1Th** 4:16

With angels Mt 16:27; 24:31; **2Th** 1:7

The purpose of the second coming
To raise the dead
1Co 15:22–23 For as in Adam all die, so in Christ all will be made alive. But each in his own turn: Christ, the firstfruits; then, when he comes, those who belong to him. *See also* **Jn** 5:28–29; **1Co** 15:52; **1Th** 4:16

To judge all people
Ps 96:13 they [the trees of the forest] will sing before the LORD, for he comes, he comes to judge the earth. He will judge the world in righteousness and the peoples in his truth. *See also* **Ps** 98:9; **Mt** 16:27; 25:31–32; **2Ti** 4:1; **Rev** 20:11–15; 22:12

To judge the wicked
2Th 1:7–10 ... This will happen when the Lord Jesus is revealed from heaven in blazing fire with his powerful angels. He will punish those who do not know God and do not obey the gospel of our Lord Jesus. They will be punished with everlasting destruction and shut out from the presence of the Lord and from the majesty of his power on the day he comes to be glorified in his holy people and to be marvelled at among all those who have believed ... *See also* **Mt** 24:51; **Ro** 2:5; **2Pe** 3:7; **Jude** 15

To separate the wicked from the righteous
Mt 25:31–32 "When the Son of Man comes in his glory, and all the angels with him, he will sit on his throne in heavenly glory. All the nations will be gathered before him, and he will separate the people one from another as a shepherd separates the sheep from the goats." *See also* **Mt** 24:40–41 pp **Lk** 17:34–35

To destroy all evil and opposition to God's kingdom
2Th 2:8 And then the lawless one will be revealed, whom the Lord Jesus will overthrow with the breath of his mouth and destroy by the splendour of his coming. *See also* **1Co** 15:24–26; **Rev** 20:10,14

To reward believers Mt 24:46–47; **Lk** 12:37; **2Ti** 4:8; **1Pe** 5:4; **1Jn** 3:1

To gather the church together Jn 14:3; **1Th** 4:17; **2Th** 2:1

To bring final salvation Lk 21:28; **Heb** 9:28

To transform the saints into his likeness 1Co 15:51–52; **Php** 3:20–21; **Col** 3:4

To end the present age Mt 24:3; **1Co** 15:24; **2Pe** 3:10,12

To restore and renew all things Ac 3:21; **2Pe** 3:13; **Rev** 21:1–5

Reactions at Jesus Christ's second coming
Mt 24:30; **2Th** 1:10

Present implications of the second coming for believers
They must always be watchful and ready
Mt 24:42–44 "Therefore keep watch, because you do not know on what day your Lord will come ... be ready, because the Son of Man will come at an hour when you do not expect him." *See also* **Mt** 25:10; **Mk** 13:35; **Lk** 12:35–36

They must be faithful stewards Mt 25:14–30 pp **Lk** 19:12–27

They must eagerly expect his coming
1Co 1:7 Therefore you do not lack any spiritual gift as you eagerly wait for our Lord Jesus Christ to be revealed. *See also* **Lk** 21:28; **Php** 3:20; **Tit** 2:13

They must endure suffering with patient endurance Mt 24:13; **1Pe** 1:6–7

They must wait patiently 1Th 1:10; **Jas** 5:7–8

It is an incentive to holiness
1Jn 3:2–3 ... we know that when he appears, we shall be like him, for we shall see him as he is. All who have this hope in them purify themselves, just as he is pure. *See also*

Col 3:4–5; 1Ti 6:14; 2Pe 3:11; 1Jn 2:23,28
It is an incentive to mission
2Ti 4:1–2 . . . in view of his [Jesus'] appearing and his kingdom, I [Paul] give you this charge: Preach the Word; be prepared in season and out of season; correct, rebuke and encourage—with great patience and careful instruction.   *See also* **2Pe** 3:12   *See also last things.*

Jesus Christ, sinlessness

The complete absence of sin, only in Jesus Christ. Christ demonstrated complete obedience to God in spite of his human frailty, enabling him to be a perfect atoning sacrifice and to give his righteousness to sinners.

Jesus Christ fully experienced human weakness
Php 2:7; Heb 2:14,17

Jesus Christ was tempted to sin
Mt 4:2–3 pp Lk 4:2–3; Mk 1:12–13; 8:32 pp Mt 16:22; Mk 14:36 pp Mt 26:39 pp Lk 22:42; Mk 15:29–30 pp Mt 27:40; Lk 23:37

Jesus Christ resisted the temptation to sin
Heb 4:15 For we do not have a high priest who is unable to sympathise with our weaknesses, but we have one who has been tempted in every way, just as we are—yet was without sin.   *See also* Mt 4:4 pp Lk 4:4; Mt 16:23 pp Mk 8:33

Jesus Christ committed no sin
He only spoke the truth
1Pe 2:22 "He [Christ] committed no sin, and no deceit was found in his mouth."   *See also* Isa 53:9,7; Jn 8:46; Heb 7:26
He fulfilled the law
Mt 5:17 "Do not think that I [Jesus] have come to abolish the Law or the Prophets; I have not come to abolish them but to fulfil them."   *See also* Mt 3:15; Lk 24:27,44; Ro 10:4
He was fully obedient to his human parents
Lk 2:51; Jn 19:26

He was fully obedient to his heavenly Father
Jn 17:4 "I [Jesus] have brought you [the Father] glory on earth by completing the work you gave me to do."   *See also* Jn 5:19,36; 8:28,49; 12:49–50; 14:31; Heb 5:7–8
He was innocent according to Roman law
Lk 23:14–15 ". . . I [Pilate] have examined him in your presence and have found no basis for your charges against him. Neither has Herod, for he sent him back to us; as you can see, he has done nothing to deserve death."   *See also* Mt 22:21 pp Mk 12:17 pp Lk 20:25; Mt 27:19,24; Lk 23:4,22; Ac 13:28

Jesus Christ's sinlessness was recognised by others
Lk 23:47 The centurion, seeing what had happened, praised God and said, "Surely this was a righteous man."   *See also* Lk 23:41

Jesus Christ was perfect
Heb 7:28 . . . the Son, who has been made perfect for ever.   *See also* Jn 1:14; Col 1:19; 2:9; Heb 1:3; 2:10; 5:9

Jesus Christ's sinlessness qualified him to be the perfect sacrifice
2Co 5:21 God made him who had no sin to be sin for us . . .   *See also* Isa 53:10; Ro 8:3; 1Pe 1:19; 3:18; 1Jn 3:5

Jesus Christ's sinlessness is the grounds of believers' sanctification
Heb 10:14 . . . by one sacrifice he has made perfect for ever those who are being made holy.   *See also* Isa 53:11; Ro 5:19; 8:4; Heb 10:10   *See also Jesus Christ, holiness; Jesus Christ, humanity; Jesus Christ, obedience; Jesus Christ, perfection; Jesus Christ, righteousness; Jesus Christ, sonship of; Jesus Christ, temptation; law.*

Jesus Christ, Son of David

A Messianic title. Jesus Christ comes as a descendant of David to fulfil God's promises in the OT of a future king who would establish the kingdom of God on earth.

OT promises of a future king from David's line

2Sa 7:12–14 "'When your days are over and you rest with your ancestors, I will raise up your offspring to succeed you, who will come from your own body, and I will establish his kingdom. He is the one who will build a house for my Name, and I will establish the throne of his kingdom for ever. I will be his father, and he shall be my son...'" pp 1Ch 17:11–13

Isa 16:5 In love a throne will be established; in faithfulness a man will sit on it—one from the house of David—one who in judging seeks justice and speeds the cause of righteousness. *See also* Ps 132:11–12,17; Isa 9:7; 11:1; Jer 23:5; 33:15; Eze 34:23–24; 37:24–25; Jn 7:42

NT statements verifying that Jesus Christ is descended from David

Mt 1:1 A record of the genealogy of Jesus Christ the son of David, the son of Abraham: *See also* Lk 3:23,31; Ro 1:3; 2Ti 2:8; Rev 22:16

Jesus Christ inherits the throne of David

Lk 1:32–33 ... The Lord God will give him the throne of his father David, and he will reign over the house of Jacob for ever; his kingdom will never end." *See also* Lk 1:69; Jn 1:49; 18:37; Mt 27:37 pp Mk 15:26 pp Lk 23:38 pp Jn 19:19

Jesus Christ is called "Son of David"
By those seeking healing

Mt 20:30–31 Two blind men were sitting by the roadside, and when they heard that Jesus was going by, they shouted, "Lord, Son of David, have mercy on us!" ... pp Mk 10:47–48 pp Lk 18:38–39 *See also* Mt 9:27; 15:22

At his triumphal entry into Jerusalem

Mt 21:9 The crowds that went ahead of him and those that followed shouted, "Hosanna to the Son of David!" "Blessed is he who comes in the name of the Lord!" "Hosanna in the highest!" pp Mk 11:10 *See also* Mt 21:15

Grounds for identifying Jesus Christ as the Son of David
His human descent

Ro 1:3 regarding his [God's] Son, who as to his human nature was a descendant of David, *See also* Mt 1:1

His birth in Bethlehem Mic 5:2; Jn 7:42
His healing ministry

Mt 12:22–23 Then they brought him a demon-possessed man who was blind and mute, and Jesus healed him, so that he could both talk and see. All the people were astonished and said, "Could this be the Son of David?" *See also* Jn 7:31

His ultimate victory Rev 5:5

Jesus Christ is more than a merely human king descended from David

Mk 12:35–37 While Jesus was teaching in the temple courts, he asked, "How is it that the teachers of the law say that the Christ is the son of David? David himself, speaking by the Holy Spirit, declared: 'The Lord said to my Lord: "Sit at my right hand until I put your enemies under your feet."' David himself calls him 'Lord'. How then can he be his son?" The large crowd listened to him with delight. *See also* Ps 110:1; Jn 18:36 *See also* Jesus Christ as king; Jesus Christ, genealogy; Jesus Christ, kingdom of; Jesus Christ, miracles; Jesus Christ, the Lord; Jesus Christ, triumphal entry; Jesus Christ, victory; Messiah, coming of.

Jesus Christ, Son of God

A title emphasising Jesus Christ's deity, his office as Messiah and his pre-eminence as the object of the church's faith and worship and as the content of its gospel.

"Son of God" in the OT
Israel as God's son

Ex 4:22–23 "Then say to Pharaoh, 'This is what the LORD says: Israel is my firstborn son...'" *See also* Jer 31:9,20; Hos 11:1

The future Messiah/king as God's Son

Ps 2:7 I will proclaim the decree of the LORD: He said to me, "You are my Son; today I have become your Father." *See also* Ps 89:27; Ac 13:33; Heb 1:5; 5:5

Jesus Christ is the Son of God

Jesus Christ affirms he is God's Son
Jn 10:36 ". . . Why then do you [some Jews] accuse me of blasphemy because I said, 'I am God's Son'?" *See also* **Lk** 22:70 pp **Mt** 26:63–64 pp **Mk** 14:61–62; **Jn** 19:7; **Rev** 2:18

The Father affirms Jesus Christ is his Son
Mt 3:17 And a voice from heaven said, "This is my Son, whom I love; with him I am well pleased." pp **Mk** 1:11 pp **Lk** 3:22 *See also* **Mt** 17:5 pp **Mk** 9:7 pp **Lk** 9:35; **2Pe** 1:17

Others affirm Jesus Christ is God's Son
Mt 14:33 Then those who were in the boat worshipped him, saying, "Truly you are the Son of God." *See also* **Mk** 15:39 pp **Mt** 27:54; **Jn** 1:34; **Ro** 1:4; **Heb** 4:14; **2Jn** 3

Demons affirm Jesus Christ is God's Son
Mk 5:7 He [a man with an evil spirit] shouted at the top of his voice, "What do you want with me, Jesus, Son of the Most High God? Swear to God that you won't torture me!" pp **Mt** 8:29 pp **Lk** 8:28 *See also* **Mk** 3:11; **Lk** 4:41

"Son of God" as a taunt
By the devil in the wilderness: **Mt** 4:3 pp **Lk** 4:3; **Mt** 4:6 pp **Lk** 4:9
By the crowd at the cross: **Mt** 27:40,43

"Son of God" stresses Jesus Christ's deity

Jesus Christ is the Son of God the Father
Jn 3:35 "The Father loves the Son and has placed everything in his hands." *See also* **Mt** 11:27 pp **Lk** 10:22; **Mt** 24:36 pp **Mk** 13:32; **Jn** 5:20–22; **Heb** 1:1–2; **1Jn** 1:3; 2:22–23; **2Jn** 9

"Son of God" implies Jesus Christ's equality with God
Jn 5:18 For this reason the Jews tried all the harder to kill him; not only was he breaking the Sabbath, but he was even calling God his own Father, making himself equal with God. *See also* **Jn** 5:23; 10:30,33; 14:9–10

"Son of God" implies Jesus Christ's obedience to the Father
Jn 5:19 Jesus gave them [the Jews] this answer: "I tell you the truth, the Son can do nothing by himself; he can do only what he sees his Father doing, because whatever the Father does the Son also does." *See also* **Mt** 26:39 pp **Mk** 14:36 pp **Lk** 22:42; **Mt** 26:42; **Jn** 8:28; 12:49; 14:31; 15:10; **Ro** 5:19; **Heb** 5:8; 10:9

Jesus Christ as "Son of God" is the Messiah

"Son of God" as a Messianic title for Jesus Christ
Mt 26:63–64 . . . The high priest said to him, "I charge you under oath by the living God: Tell us if you are the Christ, the Son of God." "Yes, it is as you say," Jesus replied . . . pp **Mk** 14:61–62 pp **Lk** 22:70–23:2 *See also* **Mt** 16:16; **Mk** 1:1; **Lk** 1:32; 4:41; **Jn** 1:49; 11:27

"Son of God" as one sent by God
Gal 4:4 But when the time had fully come, God sent his Son . . . *See also* **Mt** 21:37 pp **Mk** 12:6 pp **Lk** 20:13; **Jn** 3:16–17; **Ro** 8:3,32; **1Jn** 4:9

Grounds for regarding Jesus Christ as the Son of God

The virgin birth
Lk 1:35 The angel answered, "The Holy Spirit will come upon you [Mary], and the power of the Most High will overshadow you. So the holy one to be born will be called the Son of God."

Jesus Christ's resurrection
Ro 1:3–4 . . . who through the Spirit of holiness was declared with power to be the Son of God, by his resurrection from the dead: Jesus Christ our Lord.

Jesus Christ's works
Jn 10:36–38 ". . . even though you do not believe me, believe the miracles, that you may know and understand that the Father is in me, and I in the Father." *See also* **Jn** 5:17,19,36; 14:11

Jesus Christ's oneness with the Father
Jn 10:30 "I [Jesus] and the Father are one." *See also* **Jn** 12:45; 14:10; 17:21

Jesus Christ as Son of God is the object of the church's faith
Jn 6:40 "For my Father's will is that everyone who looks to the Son and believes in him shall

have eternal life, and I will raise him up at the last day." *See also* **Jn** 3:36; 20:31; **Ac** 8:37 fn; **Gal** 2:20; **1Jn** 3:23; 4:15; 5:5,13

Jesus Christ as Son of God is the content of the church's gospel
Ro 1:9 God, whom I [Paul] serve with my whole heart in preaching the gospel of his Son . . . *See also* **Ac** 9:20; **2Co** 1:19; **1Jn** 5:9–12 *See also* faith; gospel; Jesus Christ, divinity; Jesus Christ, mission; Jesus Christ, obedience; Jesus Christ, sonship of; Jesus, the Christ; Messiah, coming of; Trinity.

Jesus Christ, Son of Man

Jesus Christ's preferred title for himself. The term points to the humanity and servanthood of Christ, but also reflects Daniel's vision of the son of man as a coming figure of judgment and authority.

Jesus Christ as the Son of Man in his human nature
OT use of "son of man" to mean "human being"
Nu 23:19 "God is not human, that he should lie, nor a human being, that he should change his mind" . . . *See also* **Job** 25:6; 35:8; **Ps** 8:4; 80:17; 144:3
Jesus Christ describes himself as Son of Man to stress his humanity
Mt 8:20 Jesus replied, "Foxes have holes and birds of the air have nests, but the Son of Man has nowhere to lay his head." pp Lk 9:58
See also **Mt** 11:19 pp Lk 7:34; **Mt** 16:13,15; **Lk** 6:22; **Jn** 9:35
Blasphemy against the Son of Man is forgivable
Mt 12:32 "Anyone who speaks a word against the Son of Man will be forgiven, but anyone who speaks against the Holy Spirit will not be forgiven, either in this age or in the age to come." *See also* **Lk** 12:10

Jesus Christ as the Son of Man in his prophetic ministry
The OT use of "son of man" as a title for Ezekiel Eze 2:1
Jesus Christ preaches God's word
Mt 13:37–43 He [Jesus] answered, "The one who sowed the good seed is the Son of Man . . ."
Jesus Christ offers the words of eternal life
Jn 6:27 "Do not work for food that spoils, but for food that endures to eternal life, which the Son of Man will give you . . ." *See also* **Jn** 6:53,63,68

Jesus Christ as the Son of Man in his suffering and death
Jesus Christ as a servant
Mt 20:28 "just as the Son of Man did not come to be served, but to serve, and to give his life as a ransom for many." pp Mk 10:45
Jesus Christ came to suffer, die and be raised
Lk 24:6–7 "He [Jesus] is not here; he has risen! Remember how he told you, while he was still with you in Galilee: 'The Son of Man must be delivered into the hands of sinful men, be crucified and on the third day be raised again.'" *See also* **Mt** 12:40 pp Lk 11:30; **Mt** 17:9 pp Mk 9:9
Predictions of Jesus Christ's death: **Mt** 17:22–23 pp Mk 9:31 pp Lk 9:44; **Mt** 20:18 pp Mk 10:33 pp Lk 18:31; **Mt** 26:24 pp Mk 14:21 pp Lk 22:22; **Mk** 8:31 pp Lk 9:22; **Jn** 3:14; 12:23; 13:31

Jesus Christ as the Son of Man in his authority and dominion
The vision of the son of man
Da 7:13–14 "In my [Daniel's] vision at night I looked, and there before me was one like a son of man, coming with the clouds of heaven. He approached the Ancient of Days and was led into his presence. He was given authority, glory and sovereign power; all nations and people of every language worshipped him. His dominion is an everlasting dominion that will not pass away, and his kingdom is one that will never be destroyed."
Son of man meaning "son of Adam"
Ge 1:26 Then God said, "Let us make human beings in our image, in our likeness, and let them rule over the fish of the sea and the birds of the air, over the livestock, over all the earth, and over all the creatures that move along the ground."
See also **Ro** 5:14; **1Co** 15:45; **Heb** 2:6–9; **Ps** 8:4–6

Jesus Christ had authority on earth
Mt 9:6 "But so that you may know that the Son of Man has authority on earth to forgive sins . . ." pp Mk 2:10 pp Lk 5:24 *See also* **Mt** 12:8 pp Mk 2:28 pp Lk 6:5

Jesus Christ is now ascended into glory
Ac 7:55–56 . . . "Look," he [Stephen] said, "I see heaven open and the Son of Man standing at the right hand of God." *See also* **Rev** 1:13; 14:14

Jesus Christ will come to judge and reign over all
Mt 16:27–28 "For the Son of Man is going to come in his Father's glory with his angels, and then he will reward everyone according to what they have done . . ." pp Mk 8:38 pp Lk 9:26
See also **Mt** 10:23; 24:30 pp Mk 13:26 pp Lk 21:27; **Mt** 24:44 pp Lk 12:40; **Mt** 26:64 pp Mk 14:62 pp Lk 22:69; **Lk** 18:8; 21:36; **Jn** 5:27 *See also* Jesus Christ as judge; Jesus Christ as king; Jesus Christ as prophet; Jesus Christ as servant; Jesus Christ, authority; Jesus Christ, death of; Jesus Christ, exaltation; Jesus Christ, humanity; Jesus Christ, suffering; Jesus, the Christ; Son of Man.

Jesus Christ, sonship of
Jesus Christ is described as Son of David, Son of Man and Son of God. His sonship speaks of his divinity and humanity and is closely associated with his role as promised Messiah, suffering Saviour, risen Lord and coming judge and king. It also speaks of his intimate, obedient and unique relationship with his Father and of his mission to enable people to become children of God through faith in him.

Jesus Christ as the Son of David
He is physically descended from David
Mt 1:1 A record of the genealogy of Jesus Christ the son of David, the son of Abraham:
See also **Mt** 1:2–20; **Lk** 1:27,32; 2:4,11; 3:23–38; **Ro** 1:3; **2Ti** 2:8; **Rev** 22:16

He is the promised royal Messiah of David's line
Isa 16:5 In love a throne will be established; in faithfulness a man will sit on it—one from the house of David—one who in judging seeks justice and speeds the cause of righteousness.

See also **2Sa** 7:12–16 pp 1Ch 17:11–14; **Ps** 89:1–4; 132:11,17; **Isa** 9:7; 11:1; **Jer** 23:5–6; 33:15–16; **Eze** 34:23–24; 37:24–25
Zec 3:8; 6:12

He is both the Son and Lord of David
Mt 22:41–45 While the Pharisees were gathered together, Jesus asked them, "What do you think about the Christ? Whose son is he?" "The son of David," they replied. He said to them, "How is it then that David, speaking by the Spirit, calls him 'Lord'? For he says, 'The Lord said to my Lord: "Sit at my right hand until I put your enemies under your feet."' If then David calls him 'Lord', how can he be his son?" pp Mk 12:35–37 pp Lk 20:41–44 *See also* **Ps** 110:1

Jesus Christ as the Son of Man
Mk 2:10 ". . . the Son of Man has authority on earth to forgive sins. . . ." pp Mt 9:6 pp Lk 5:24
Jn 3:13 No-one has ever gone into heaven except the one who came from heaven—the Son of Man. *See also* **Da** 7:13–14; **Mk** 2:28 pp Mt 12:8 pp Lk 6:5; **Jn** 1:51; 6:27; 8:28

Jesus Christ as the Son of God
His divine origin and divinity
Lk 1:32–35 . . . The angel answered, "The Holy Spirit will come upon you [Mary], and the power of the Most High will overshadow you. So the holy one to be born will be called the Son of God." *See also* **Jn** 1:13,18; 5:18; 17:5,24

His intimate relationship with the Father
Mk 14:36 *"Abba*, Father," he said, "everything is possible for you . . ." *See also* **Mt** 3:17 pp Mk 1:11 pp Lk 3:22; **Lk** 2:49; **Jn** 1:18,32–34; 3:35; 5:20; 8:38; 14:31; 17:23

His knowledge of the Father's will
Mt 11:25–27 . . . "All things have been committed to me by my Father. No-one knows the Son except the Father, and no-one knows the Father except the Son and those to whom the Son chooses to reveal him." pp Lk 10:21–22; **Mk** 4:1–11 pp Lk 4 :1–13; **Mt** 12:50; **Jn** 3:17; 8:55; 10:17, 36; 14:31; 17:8 *See also* **Jn** 6:45–46; 8:55; 14:13–16; 15:15

His obedience to the Father's mission
Mt 26:42 He [Jesus] went away a second time

and prayed, "My Father . . . may your will be done." pp Mk 14:36 pp Lk 22:42   See also **Mt 3:13–17** pp Mk 1:9–11 pp Lk 3:21–22; **Mt 4:1–11** pp Lk 4:1–13; **Mt 12:50**; **Jn 3:17**; 8:55; 10:17, 36; 14:31; 17:8

His sharing in the Father's work Jn 3:34; 4:34; 5:17,21–26; 6:40; 8:16; 9:4; 12:49–50; 14:11

His role as promised Messiah
Mt 16:16 . . . "You [Jesus] are the Christ, the Son of the living God." pp Lk 9:20   See also 2Sa 7:12–14 pp 1Ch 17:11–13; Ps 89:26–27; Isa 9:6–7; **Mt 1:23**; Isa 7:14; **Mt 2:15**; Hos 11:1; **Mt 26:63–64** pp Mk 14:61–62 pp Lk 22:70; **Lk 4:41**; 22:29–30; Jn 1:49; 11:27; 20:31; Ac 13:33; Heb 1:5; 5:5; Ps 2:7

His sharing the Father's character and being
Heb 1:3 The Son is the radiance of God's glory and the exact representation of his being . . . See also Jn 1:14; 5:26; 6:57; 10:30; 17:5

The uniqueness of his sonship
Jn 3:16 "For God so loved the world that he gave his one and only Son . . ."   See also Jn 1:18; 3:18; Heb 1:3

Jesus Christ's disciples become children of God through him
Gal 4:4–7 . . . God sent his Son, born of a woman, born under law, to redeem those under law, that we might receive adoption as God's children . . .   See also **Mt 12:50**; Jn 3:16–18; 5:23–24; 6:40; 11:26–27; 14:1–2; 20:31; **Ro 8:13–17**; **Eph 1:5–6**

Jesus Christ as the son of natural parents
Mt 1:16,25; 13:55 pp Mk 6:3; Lk 2:7,48; 3:23; 4:22; Jn 1:45; 6:42; Ac 1:14   See also Abba; Jesus Christ, authority; Jesus Christ, divinity; Jesus Christ, family of; Jesus Christ, genealogy; Jesus Christ, prophecies concerning; Jesus Christ, Son of David; Jesus Christ, Son of God; Jesus Christ, Son of Man; Messiah, coming of; Trinity.

Jesus Christ, suffering
Jesus Christ's life was characterised by suffering, though the worst experiences were reserved for his final days. His sufferings are both redemptive and an example to believers.

Jesus Christ's sufferings foretold
In the OT Ps 22:6–8,16–18; Isa 50:6; 52:13–53:12; Zec 9:9–10; 12:10; 13:7; **1Pe 1:11**

In Jesus Christ's predictions
Mt 16:21 From that time on Jesus began to explain to his disciples that he must go to Jerusalem and suffer many things at the hands of the elders, chief priests and teachers of the law, and that he must be killed and on the third day be raised to life. pp Mk 8:31 pp Lk 9:22
See also Mt 20:17–19 pp Mk 10:32–34 pp Lk 18:31–32; Jn 12:32–33

Jesus Christ's suffering during his lifetime
As a child Mt 2:13–15

Because of his family
Mk 3:20–21 . . . When his [Jesus'] family heard about this, they went to take charge of him, for they said, "He is out of his mind."
See also Jn 7:3–5

Because of the crowds' unbelief
Mk 9:19 "O unbelieving generation," Jesus replied, "how long shall I stay with you? How long shall I put up with you? . . . pp Mt 17:17 pp Lk 9:41
See also Mt 12:39 pp Lk 11:29; Mk 8:11–12

Because of the disciples' slowness
Mk 8:17–21 Aware of their discussion, Jesus asked them [his disciples]: "Why are you talking about having no bread? Do you still not see or understand? Are your hearts hardened? Do you have eyes but fail to see, and ears but fail to hear? And don't you remember? . . ." pp Mt 16:8–11

Because of the religious leaders
Mt 12:14 But the Pharisees went out and plotted how they might kill Jesus. pp Mk 3:6 pp Lk 6:11   See also Jn 5:18; 7:1; 8:48

Because of human suffering
Lk 19:41 As he [Jesus] approached Jerusalem and saw the city, he wept over it   See also Mk 7:34; Lk 7:13; Jn 11:33–35

Jesus Christ's suffering at the time of his death
He was inwardly troubled
Jn 12:27 "Now my [Jesus'] heart is troubled,

and what shall I say? 'Father, save me from this hour'? No, it was for this very reason I came to this hour." *See also* Mt 26:36–42 pp Mk 14:32–39 pp Lk 22:40–44; Jn 13:21

He was betrayed Mt 26:21–25 pp Mk 14:17–21 pp Lk 22:21–23; Mt 26:47–49 pp Mk 14:43–45 pp Lk 22:47–48 pp Jn 18:2–5; Jn 13:18–30

He was humiliated

Mt 27:27–30 . . . They [the governor's soldiers] stripped him [Jesus] and put a scarlet robe on him, and then twisted together a crown of thorns and set it on his head. They put a staff in his right hand and knelt in front of him and mocked him. "Hail, king of the Jews!" they said . . . pp Mk 15:16–19   *See also* Mt 26:67–68 pp Mk 14:65 pp Lk 22:63–65; Mt 27:26 pp Mk 15:15 pp Lk 23:22; Lk 23:11; Jn 18:22; 19:1

He was crucified

Lk 23:33 When they came to the place called the Skull, there they crucified him, along with the criminals—one on his right, the other on his left. pp Mt 27:35 pp Mk 15:25 pp Jn 19:18

He suffered separation from God

Mt 27:46 About the ninth hour Jesus cried out in a loud voice, *"Eloi, Eloi, lama sabachthani?"*—which means, "My God, my God, why have you forsaken me?" pp Mk 15:34 pp Lk 23:46   *See also* Ps 22:1

Jesus Christ's attitude to his suffering
He did not retaliate in his suffering

1Pe 2:23 When they hurled their insults at him [Christ], he did not retaliate; when he suffered, he made no threats. Instead, he entrusted himself to him who judges justly.   *See also* Mt 27:12–14 pp Mk 15:3–5; Lk 23:34

He grew through the experience of suffering

Heb 5:8 Although he [Jesus] was a son, he learned obedience from what he suffered
See also Heb 2:10

Jesus Christ's sufferings were necessary for salvation

Lk 24:26–27 "Did not the Christ have to suffer these things and then enter his glory? . . ."   *See also* Lk 24:46–47; Ac 3:18; 17:3; 26:23

Jesus Christ suffered as a unique sacrifice Heb 7:27; 9:25–26

The Christian experience of suffering
Believers share in Jesus Christ's sufferings

2Co 1:5 For just as the sufferings of Christ flow over into our lives, so also through Christ our comfort overflows.   *See also* Mt 25:34–40; Ac 9:4–5 pp Ac 22:7–8; 26:15; Ro 8:17; Php 3:10; 1Pe 4:13

Jesus Christ's sufferings are an example for believers

1Pe 2:21 To this you were called, because Christ suffered for you, leaving you an example, that you should follow in his steps.   *See also* Jn 16:18–20; Php 2:5–7   *See also* God, suffering of; Jesus Christ as servant; Jesus Christ, compassion; Jesus Christ, cross of; Jesus Christ, example of; Jesus Christ, humanity; Jesus Christ, opposition to.

Jesus Christ, temptation
Repeated yet unsuccessful efforts made by Satan and by human beings to deflect Jesus Christ from his Father's will.

The wilderness temptations

Mk 1:13 . . . he [Jesus] was in the desert for forty days, being tempted by Satan . . .

Tempted to turn stones into bread

Mt 4:2–3 . . . The tempter came to him and said, "If you are the Son of God, tell these stones to become bread." pp Lk 4:2–3

Tempted to abuse miraculous power

Mt 4:5–6 . . . "If you are the Son of God," he said, "throw yourself down. For it is written: 'He will command his angels concerning you, and they will lift you up in their hands, so that you will not strike your foot against a stone.'" pp Lk 4:9–11   *See also* Mt 12:38; 16:1 pp Mk 8:11; Lk 11:16; Jn 2:18

Tempted by the offer of an easy route to power

Mt 4:8–9 . . . the devil took him to a very high mountain and showed him [Jesus] all the kingdoms of the world and their splendour. "All this I will give you," he said, "if you will bow down and worship me." pp Lk 4:5–7

Tempted to doubt he was God's Son
Mt 4:3 The tempter came to him and said, "If you are the Son of God . . ." pp Lk 4:3
See also **Mt** 4:6 pp Lk 4:9; **Mt** 27:40

Temptation continued throughout Jesus Christ's life
Lk 22:28 "You [the disciples] are those who have stood by me [Jesus] in my trials."
Opponents tempted Jesus Christ with trick questions Mt 22:15 pp Mk 12:13 pp Lk 20:20
Jesus Christ tempted to sidestep the cross
Mt 16:21–23 From that time on Jesus began to explain to his disciples that he must go to Jerusalem and suffer many things at the hands of the elders, chief priests and teachers of the law, and that he must be killed and on the third day be raised to life. Peter took him aside and began to rebuke him. "Never, Lord!" he said. "This shall never happen to you!" Jesus turned and said to Peter, "Get behind me, Satan! You are a stumbling-block to me; you do not have in mind the concerns of God, but human concerns." pp Mk 8:32–33   *See also* **Mt** 26:39–44 pp Mk 14:35–41 pp Lk 22:41–44; **Mt** 27:40 pp Mk 15:30

Jesus Christ steadfastly resisted temptation
Jesus Christ resisted temptation by trusting God's word
Mt 4:4 Jesus answered, "It is written: 'People do not live on bread alone, but on every word that comes from the mouth of God.'" pp Lk 4:4   *See also* **Mt** 4:7 pp Lk 4:12; **Mt** 4:10 pp Lk 4:8
Jesus Christ resisted temptation by obeying his Father
Heb 5:7–8 During the days of Jesus' life on earth, he offered up prayers and petitions with loud cries and tears to the one who could save him from death, and he was heard because of his reverent submission. Although he was a son, he learned obedience from what he suffered
See also **Mt** 26:39 pp Mk 14:36 pp Lk 22:42; **Mt** 26:42

Results of Jesus Christ's temptations
Satan left Jesus Christ alone
Mt 4:11 Then the devil left him [Jesus], and angels came and attended him. pp Lk 4:13
Jesus Christ remained sinless
Heb 4:15 . . . we have one who has been tempted in every way, just as we are—yet was without sin.   *See also* **Jn** 8:46; **1Pe** 2:22
Jesus Christ helps those who are being tempted
Heb 2:18 Because he himself suffered when he was tempted, he is able to help those who are being tempted.   *See also* **Heb** 4:14–16   *See also Jesus Christ, sinlessness; Jesus Christ, victory; law, Jesus Christ's attitude.*

Jesus Christ, the Lord
A title that signifies Jesus Christ's absolute authority and the basis on which people may know him. It is especially associated with his resurrection and return.

Lord as a title of respect for the earthly Jesus Christ
Mt 8:25 The disciples went and woke him [Jesus], saying, "Lord, save us! We're going to drown!"   *See also* **Mt** 15:25,27 pp Mk 7:28; **Mt** 21:3 pp Mk 11:3 pp Lk 19:31

Lord as a mark of Jesus Christ's authority as a teacher
1Th 4:15 According to the Lord's own word, we tell you that we who are still alive, who are left till the coming of the Lord, will certainly not precede those who have fallen asleep.   *See also* **Ac** 11:16; 20:35; **1Co** 7:10

Lord as a sign of Jesus Christ's divinity
Jesus Christ's divinity
Jn 20:28 Thomas said to him [Jesus], "My Lord and my God!"   *See also* **1Co** 8:6; **2Co** 3:17–18; **Eph** 4:5; **2Th** 2:16; **2Pe** 1:2
The day of Christ Jesus
Php 1:6 . . . he who began a good work in you will carry it on to completion until the day of Christ Jesus.   *See also* **1Co** 1:8; **2Co** 1:14; **Php** 1:10; 2:16; **Rev** 1:10

Jesus Christ is ruler over all
Rev 17:14 They will make war against the Lamb, but the Lamb will overcome them because he is Lord of lords and King of kings . . . *See also* **Dt** 10:17; **Rev** 19:16

Jesus Christ is the Saviour
Ro 10:13 . . . "Everyone who calls on the name of the Lord will be saved." *See also* **Joel** 2:32; **Ac** 2:21

Jesus Christ is Lord of the Sabbath
Mt 12:8 "For the Son of Man is Lord of the Sabbath." pp Mk 2:28 pp Lk 6:5

Jesus the Messiah is Lord
Ac 2:36 "Therefore let all Israel be assured of this: God has made this Jesus, whom you crucified, both Lord and Christ." *See also* **2Co** 4:5; **Col** 3:24

"Jesus is Lord" is the basic Christian statement of faith
Ro 10:9 . . . if you confess with your mouth, "Jesus is Lord," and believe in your heart that God raised him from the dead, you will be saved. *See also* **Ac** 11:20; 16:31; 20:21; **1Co** 12:3; **2Co** 4:5; **Php** 2:10–11

Jesus is Lord because of the resurrection
Ro 1:4 . . . who through the Spirit of holiness was declared with power to be the Son of God, by his resurrection from the dead: Jesus Christ our Lord. *See also* **Ac** 4:33; **Ro** 4:24; 14:9; **Heb** 13:20

Lord is a natural title for the risen Christ
Lk 24:34 . . . "It is true! The Lord has risen and has appeared to Simon." *See also* **Lk** 22:61; **Ac** 1:21; 7:59; **1Co** 9:1,5; **1Th** 4:17

Jesus Christ's lordship is the basis for his relationship with Christians
It is a personal relationship
Php 3:8 . . . I consider everything a loss compared to the surpassing greatness of knowing Christ Jesus my Lord, for whose sake I have lost all things . . . *See also* **Ac** 16:15; **Ro** 5:11; 14:8; **1Co** 6:17; **2Pe** 2:20

"The name of the Lord" expresses this relationship
1Co 6:11 . . . But you were washed, you were sanctified, you were justified in the name of the Lord Jesus Christ . . . *See also* **Ac** 8:16; 15:26; 19:5; 21:13; **Eph** 5:20; **Col** 3:17

"Jesus our Lord" expresses this relationship
Eph 6:24 Grace to all who love our Lord Jesus Christ with an undying love. *See also* **1Co** 15:57; **2Co** 8:9; **Gal** 6:14; **Eph** 5:20; **1Th** 5:28; **2Ti** 1:8

"In the Lord" as an expression of this relationship
Phm 16 . . . He [Onesimus] is very dear to me [Paul] but even dearer to you [Philemon], both as a person and as a fellow believer in the Lord. *See also* **Ro** 16:12; **Eph** 6:10; **Php** 1:14; 2:29; 3:1; **Phm** 20

The "grace of the Lord" as God's provision for this relationship
1Ti 1:14 The grace of our Lord was poured out on me [Paul] abundantly, along with the faith and love that are in Christ Jesus. *See also* **2Co** 13:14; **2Th** 3:18; **Phm** 25; **2Pe** 3:18; **Jude** 21

Jesus Christ's lordship is the basis for Christian obedience
Col 2:6 So then, just as you received Christ Jesus as Lord, continue to live in him, *See also* **Ro** 12:11; **Col** 3:23; **2Th** 1:8; **2Ti** 2:19; **1Pe** 3:15

Jesus Christ's lordship will be fully revealed
1Th 4:16 For the Lord himself will come down from heaven, with a loud command, with the voice of the archangel and with the trumpet call of God . . . *See also* **1Co** 1:7; **Php** 3:20; **1Th** 5:23; **2Th** 1:7; **1Ti** 6:14

Jesus Christ's lordship signifies his absolute authority
Jesus Christ as judge of all
1Co 4:4 . . . It is the Lord who judges me. *See also* **1Co** 11:32; **2Co** 10:18; **1Th** 4:6; **2Th** 1:8–9

Jesus Christ as Lord of all
Ro 10:12 For there is no difference between Jew and Gentile—the same Lord is Lord of all and richly blesses all who call on him, *See also*

Ac 10:36; **1Co 8:6**; **Php 2:10–11**; **Col 1:16–17**
See also Jesus Christ, authority; Jesus Christ, divinity; Jesus Christ, exaltation; Jesus Christ, majesty of; Jesus Christ, pre-eminence; Jesus Christ, resurrection; Jesus Christ, second coming; Jesus, the Christ.

Jesus Christ, titles and names of

These, in their rich variety, throw light on either the person of Jesus Christ or on some aspect of his ministry.

Titles relating to Jesus Christ's identity
The exact image of God
Heb 1:3 The Son is the radiance of God's glory and the exact representation of his being . . .
See also **Jn 14:9**; **2Co 4:4**; **Col 1:15**
The first and last, the Alpha and Omega
Rev 22:13 "I [Jesus] am the Alpha and the Omega, the First and the Last, the Beginning and the End." *See also* **Rev 1:17**; **2:8**; **21:6**
The Word of God
Jn 1:1 In the beginning was the Word, and the Word was with God, and the Word was God.
See also **Mal 3:1**; **Jn 1:14**; **1Jn 1:1**; **Rev 19:13**
The last Adam
1Co 15:45 . . . "The first Adam became a living being"; the last Adam [Jesus], a life-giving spirit. *See also* **Ro 5:14**
The bright Morning Star
Rev 22:16 "I, Jesus, have sent my angel to give you this testimony for the churches. I am . . . the bright Morning Star." *See also* **2Pe 1:19**
The rising sun **Mal 4:2**; **Lk 1:78**
The Living One
Rev 1:18 "I [Jesus] am the Living One; I was dead, and behold I am alive for ever and ever! . . ." *See also* **Jn 5:26**; **11:25**
The Amen
Rev 3:14 ". . . These are the words of the Amen, the faithful and true witness, the ruler of God's creation." *See also* **2Co 1:20**
The true light
Jn 1:3–9 . . . The light shines in the darkness, but the darkness has not understood it . . . The true light [Jesus] that gives light to everyone was coming into the world. *See also* **Isa 9:2**; **Lk 2:32**; **Jn 3:19–21**; **8:12**; **12:46**
The Righteous One
Ac 3:14 "You [people of Israel] disowned the Holy and Righteous One [Jesus] . . ." *See also* **Jer 23:6**; **33:15–16**; **Ac 7:52**; **22:14**
The Lion of Judah **Rev 5:5**
The king of the Jews **Mt 2:1–2**; **27:37**

The "I am" sayings of John's Gospel
Jn 8:58 "I tell you the truth," Jesus answered, "before Abraham was born, I am!" *See also* **Jn 6:35**
The light of the world: **Jn 8:12**; **9:5**
Jn 10:7–10, 11–14; **11:25**; **14:6**; **15:1–5**

Titles relating to Jesus Christ's ministry
The seed of Abraham
Gal 3:16 The promises were spoken to Abraham and to his seed. The Scripture does not say "and to seeds", meaning many people, but "and to your seed", meaning one person, who is Christ. *See also* **Ge 12:7**; **13:15**; **24:7**
The Root and Offspring of David
Rev 22:16 "I, Jesus . . . am the Root and the Offspring of David . . ."
The faithful witness
Rev 1:5 . . . Jesus Christ, who is the faithful witness . . . *See also* **Isa 55:4**; **Jn 18:37**; **Rev 3:14**
Immanuel
Mt 1:23 "The virgin will be with child and will give birth to a son [Jesus], and they will call him Immanuel"—which means, "God with us."
See also **Isa 7:14**; **8:8**
The capstone
Mt 21:42 Jesus said to them, "Have you never read in the Scriptures: The stone the builders rejected has become the capstone; the Lord has done this, and it is marvellous in our eyes'?" pp **Mk 12:10** pp **Lk 20:17** *See also* **Ps 118:22**; **Ac 4:11**; **Eph 2:20–21**; **1Pe 2:6–7**
The rock
1Co 10:4 . . . they [God's people] drank from the spiritual rock that accompanied them, and that rock was Christ. *See also* **Isa 8:14**; **28:16**; **Ro 9:32–33**; **1Pe 2:8**

The bridegroom
Jn 3:29 ". . . The friend who attends the bridegroom waits and listens for him, and is full of joy when he hears the bridegroom's voice. That joy is mine, and it is now complete." *See also* **Mt 9:15** pp **Mk 2:19–20** pp **Lk 5:34–35; Mt 25:1–10; Rev 19:7; 21:2**

The firstborn among many brothers Ro 8:29
The firstfruits 1Co 15:23
The firstborn from the dead Rev 1:5
The heir of all things Heb 1:2

Titles relating to Jesus Christ's authority
Lord
Ac 2:25 "David said about him: I saw the Lord always before me. Because he is at my right hand, I will not be shaken.'" *See also* **Mt 7:21; Lk 6:46; Jn 6:68; Ro 10:13; 1Co 3:5; Col 3:23; 1Th 4:16–17; 2Pe 1:11**

The head of the church Eph 1:22–23; 4:15; 5:23; Col 2:19

The Chief Shepherd
1Pe 5:4 . . . when the Chief Shepherd appears, you will receive the crown of glory that will never fade away. *See also* **Mt 2:6; Mic 5:2; Jn 10:11; 1Pe 2:25; Heb 13:20**
Prince Ac 5:31
Rabbi Jn 1:38,49; 20:16

Titles emphasising Jesus Christ's saving work
Jesus: the LORD saves
Mt 1:21 "She [Mary] will give birth to a son, and you [Joseph] are to give him the name Jesus, because he will save his people from their sins."
Man of sorrows Isa 53:3
The Passover lamb
1Co 5:7 . . . Christ, our Passover lamb, has been sacrificed.
A horn of salvation Lk 1:69
The consolation of Israel Lk 1:68; 2:25,38
The deliverer and Redeemer Ro 11:26; Isa 59:20

The author and perfecter of salvation
Heb 2:10 In bringing many sons to glory, it was fitting that God, for whom and through whom everything exists, should make the author of their salvation perfect through suffering. *See also* **Heb 5:9; 12:2**

Titles stressing Jesus Christ's mediatory status
The Mediator 1Ti 2:5
The high priest
Heb 3:1 Therefore, holy brothers and sisters, who share in the heavenly calling, fix your thoughts on Jesus, the apostle and high priest whom we confess. *See also* **Heb 2:17; 6:20**
The Son of Man
Lk 19:10 "For the Son of Man came to seek and to save what was lost." *See also* **Mt 11:19; Lk 5:24; Jn 3:13; 6:53; Ac 7:56; Rev 1:13** *See also* Immanuel; Jesus Christ as Lamb; Jesus Christ as Saviour; Jesus Christ as shepherd; Jesus Christ, high priest; Jesus Christ, Son of David; Jesus Christ, Son of God; Jesus Christ, Son of Man; Jesus Christ, the Lord; Jesus, the Christ; Messiah, coming of.

Jesus Christ, transfiguration
The revelation of the glory of Jesus Christ, shortly before his death, at which his disciples caught sight of him in his full majesty. The transfiguration brought home to the disciples that Jesus Christ is the Son of God.

The glory of Jesus Christ is revealed at the transfiguration
Jesus Christ prepares for his glory to be revealed
Lk 9:28 . . . he [Jesus] took Peter, John and James with him and went up onto a mountain to pray. pp **Mt 17:1** pp **Mk 9:2**
Jesus Christ is visibly transfigured
Mt 17:2 There he was transfigured before them. His face shone like the sun, and his clothes became as white as the light. pp **Mk 9:2–3** pp **Lk 9:29**
The disciples are eye-witnesses of Jesus Christ's glory
Mt 17:6 When the disciples heard this, they fell face down to the ground, terrified. *See also* **Mk 9:9; Lk 9:32; Jn 1:14; 2Pe 1:16**

Moses and Elijah appear at the transfiguration

Lk 9:30–31 Two men, Moses and Elijah, appeared in glorious splendour, talking with Jesus. They spoke about his departure, which he was about to bring to fulfilment at Jerusalem. pp Mt 17:3 pp Mk 9:4

God's voice is heard at the transfiguration

Mt 17:5 . . . a voice from the cloud said, "This is my Son, whom I love; with him I am well pleased. Listen to him!" pp Mk 9:7 pp Lk 9:35   See also Mt 3:17 pp Mk 1:11 pp Lk 3:22; 2Pe 1:17–18

The disciples' response to the transfiguration

Peter's wish to build shelters Mt 17:4 pp Mk 9:5–6 pp Lk 9:33
Fear Mt 17:6–7; Mk 9:6; Lk 9:34
Questioning and confusion Mt 17:10 pp Mk 9:10–11
They keep to themselves what they have seen and heard
Lk 9:36 . . . The disciples kept this to themselves, and told no-one at that time what they had seen. pp Mt 17:9–10 pp Mk 9:9–10
See also God, fatherhood; God, revelation; Jesus Christ, baptism of; Jesus Christ, glory of; Jesus Christ, majesty of; Jesus Christ, perfection; Jesus Christ, Son of God; Jesus Christ, sonship of.

Jesus Christ, trial

Jesus Christ, falsely accused of blasphemy towards God and treason towards Rome, humbly endured his trial as a fulfilment of the purposes of God.

The preliminary hearing before Annas
Jn 18:12–14, 19–23

The trial before Caiaphas and the Sanhedrin

Jesus Christ is sent to the ruling high priest
Mt 26:57 pp Mk 14:53 pp Jn 18:24; Lk 22:54
False evidence is sought
Mt 26:59–60 The chief priests and the whole Sanhedrin were looking for false evidence against Jesus so that they could put him to death. But they did not find any, though many false witnesses came forward. Finally two came forward pp Mk 14:55–56
False accusations are made Mt 26:60–61 pp Mk 14:57–59

Jesus Christ's trial centres upon his Messianic claims

Jesus declares himself to be the Christ
Mt 26:63–64 . . . The high priest said to him [Jesus], "I charge you under oath by the living God: Tell us if you are the Christ, the Son of God." "Yes, it is as you say," Jesus replied. "But I say to all of you: In the future you will see the Son of Man sitting at the right hand of the Mighty One and coming on the clouds of heaven." pp Mk 14:61–62   See also Lk 22:66–70
Jesus Christ is charged with blasphemy Mt 26:65–66 pp Mk 14:63–64; Mt 27:1 pp Mk 15:1
Jesus is mocked as the Christ Mt 26:67–68 pp Mk 14:65 pp Lk 22:63–65

The trial before Pilate

The Sanhedrin hand Jesus Christ over to Pilate
Mt 27:2 pp Mk 15:1; Lk 23:1; Jn 18:28–32
Jesus Christ accepts the title of king
Jn 18:36–37 Jesus said, "My kingdom is not of this world . . . "You are a king, then!" said Pilate. Jesus answered, "You are right in saying I am a king. In fact, for this reason I was born, and for this I came into the world, to testify to the truth . . ."   See also Mt 27:11 pp Mk 15:2; Lk 23:2–3; Jn 19:9–12; 1Ti 6:13
Pilate decides Jesus Christ is innocent
Lk 23:4 . . . Pilate announced to the chief priests and the crowd, "I find no basis for a charge against this man."   See also Lk 23:14–15,22; Jn 18:38; 19:4–6; Ac 13:28
Pilate sends Jesus Christ to Herod Lk 23:5–10
Herod sends Jesus Christ back to Pilate Lk 23:11–12
Pilate seeks to release Jesus Christ
Jn 19:12 . . . Pilate tried to set Jesus free . . .
See also Mt 27:15–18 pp Mk 15:6–10; Mt 27:19; Lk 23:16, 20, 22; Jn 18:38–39; 19:6,15

Jesus Christ, triumphal entry

The crowd demand the release of Barabbas and the crucifixion of Jesus Christ
Mt 27:20 . . . the chief priests and the elders persuaded the crowd to ask for Barabbas and to have Jesus executed. pp Mk 15:11 *See also* **Mt** 27:21–23 pp Mk 15:12–14; **Lk** 23:18,21,23; **Jn** 18:40; 19:6–7,12,15

The crowd's demands prevail
Mk 15:15 Wanting to satisfy the crowd, Pilate released Barabbas to them. He had Jesus flogged, and handed him over to be crucified. pp Mt 27:26 *See also* **Mt** 27:24–25; **Lk** 23:23–25; **Jn** 19:16; **Ac** 3:13–14

Jesus Christ is mocked as king
Jn 19:2–3 The soldiers twisted together a crown of thorns and put it on his head. They clothed him in a purple robe and went up to him again and again, saying, "Hail, king of the Jews!" And they struck him in the face. *See also* **Mt** 27:27–31 pp Mk 15:16–20; **Jn** 19:15

Jesus Christ's response to his trial
Isa 53:7 He [the servant] was oppressed and afflicted, yet he did not open his mouth; he was led like a lamb to the slaughter, and as a sheep before her shearers is silent, so he did not open his mouth. *See also* **Mt** 26:62–63 pp Mk 14:60–61; **Mt** 27:12,14 pp Mk 15:5; **Lk** 23:9; **Jn** 19:9; **Ac** 8:32–35; **1Pe** 2:23

Jesus Christ's trial confirms he is God's servant
Ac 4:27–28 "Indeed Herod and Pontius Pilate met together with the Gentiles and the people of Israel in this city to conspire against your [God's] holy servant Jesus, whom you anointed. They did what your power and will had decided beforehand should happen." *See also* **Isa** 53:10; **Jn** 19:8–11; **Ac** 2:23 *See also* God, purpose of; Jesus Christ as king; Jesus Christ as Lamb; Jesus Christ as servant; Jesus Christ, cross of; Jesus Christ, death of; Jesus Christ, Son of God; Jesus Christ, suffering; Jesus, the Christ.

Jesus Christ, triumphal entry

Jesus Christ rode into Jerusalem on a colt, royally yet humbly, to the rejoicing of his followers, but provoking opposition from the Jewish religious leaders.

The colt used in Jesus Christ's entry into Jerusalem
Jesus Christ's instructions to his disciples
Lk 19:29–31 As he [Jesus] approached Bethphage and Bethany at the hill called the Mount of Olives, he sent two of his disciples, saying to them, "Go to the village ahead of you, and as you enter it, you will find a colt tied there, which no-one has ever ridden. Untie it and bring it here. If anyone asks you, 'Why are you untying it?' say, 'The Lord needs it.'" pp Mt 21:1–3 pp Mk 11:1–3
The obedience of the disciples Mt 21:6 pp Mk 11:4–6 pp Lk 19:32–34

Jesus Christ's entry into Jerusalem
Jn 12:14–15 Jesus found a young donkey and sat upon it, as it is written, "Do not be afraid, O Daughter of Zion; see, your king is coming, seated on a donkey's colt." pp Mt 21:4–5 *See also* **Isa** 62:11; **Zec** 9:9

The response of the crowd to Jesus Christ's entry into Jerusalem
Proclamation of Jesus Christ's kingship Mt 21:8 pp Mk 11:8 pp Lk 19:36; **2Ki** 9:13
Proclamation of Jesus' messiahship
Mt 21:9 The crowds that went ahead of him and those that followed shouted, "Hosanna to the Son of David!" . . . pp Mk 11:9–10 pp Lk 19:37–38 *See also* **Ps** 118:26
Proclamation of Jesus Christ's victory
Jn 12:13 They took palm branches and went out to meet him . . . *See also* **Lev** 23:40; **Ps** 118:27; **Rev** 7:9

The response of the Pharisees to Jesus Christ's entry into Jerusalem
Lk 19:39–40 *See also* Jesus Christ as king; Jesus Christ as Saviour; Jesus Christ, humility; Jesus Christ, kingdom of; Jesus Christ, majesty of; Jesus Christ, opposition to; Jesus Christ, Son of David; Jesus Christ, Son of Man; Jesus Christ, victory; Jesus, the Christ.

Jesus Christ, victory

Jesus Christ triumphs over and disarms all the powers of evil arrayed against him. Believers are able to share in this victory through faith in Jesus Christ.

The scope of Jesus Christ's victory
Over temptation
Heb 4:15 . . . we have one [a high priest] who has been tempted in every way, just as we are—yet was without sin. *See also* **Mt** 4:1–11 pp **Lk** 4:1–13

Over sin
Ro 5:20–21 . . . But where sin increased, grace increased all the more, so that, just as sin reigned in death, so also grace might reign through righteousness to bring eternal life through Jesus Christ our Lord. *See also* **1Jn** 3:5,8

Over Satan
Jn 12:31 ". . . now the prince of this world will be driven out." *See also* **Lk** 10:18–19; **Jn** 14:30; 16:11; **Heb** 2:14–15

Over evil spirits Mk 1:23–27 pp **Lk** 4:33–36

Over all powers
Col 2:15 And having disarmed the powers and authorities, he made a public spectacle of them, triumphing over them by the cross. *See also* **Ro** 8:38–39; **1Co** 15:24–25; **Eph** 1:21–22; 4:8; **Ps** 68:18

Over the world
Jn 16:33 ". . . I have overcome the world." *See also* **2Th** 2:8; **1Jn** 5:4–5; **Rev** 17:12–14; 19:11–21

Over death
Ro 6:9 For we know that since Christ was raised from the dead, he cannot die again; death no longer has mastery over him. *See also* **Ac** 2:24; **1Co** 15:26,54–57; **2Ti** 1:10; **Rev** 1:18

The manner of Jesus Christ's victory
By the written word of God Mt 4:4–10 pp **Lk** 4:4–12

By his death on the cross
Heb 2:14 . . . he [Jesus] too shared in their humanity so that by his death he might destroy him who holds the power of death—that is, the devil— *See also* **Col** 2:15; **Rev** 12:11

By God's authority
Lk 11:20 "But if I [Jesus] drive out demons by the finger of God, then the kingdom of God has come to you." pp **Mt** 12:28

By his spoken word
Mt 8:16 . . . he [Jesus] drove out the spirits with a word and healed all the sick. *See also* **Mt** 8:8 pp **Lk** 7:7; **Mt** 8:13

Consequences of Jesus Christ's victory
Assurance for believers Jn 16:33; **1Th** 4:13; **Rev** 5:5

Victory for believers
1Co 15:57 But thanks be to God! He gives us the victory through our Lord Jesus Christ. *See also* **Ro** 7:21–25; 8:37; 16:20 *See also Jesus Christ as king; Jesus Christ as redeemer; Jesus Christ as Saviour; Jesus Christ, authority; Jesus Christ, cross of; Jesus Christ, resurrection; Jesus Christ, temptation; Jesus Christ, the Lord.*

Jesus Christ, wisdom
Jesus Christ's deep understanding of God, people and situations derived from his relationship with God his Father and from knowledge of his word. Christ's wisdom is seen in his words, actions and dealings with people.

The wisdom of Messiah was foretold and recognised in Jesus Christ
Isa 11:2 The Spirit of the Lord will rest on him [the Messiah]—the Spirit of wisdom and of understanding, the Spirit of counsel and of power, the Spirit of knowledge and of the fear of the Lord— *See also* **Pr** 8:22–23; **Isa** 52:13; **Jn** 1:1; 4:29; **1Co** 1:24,30; **Col** 2:2–3

Wisdom was characteristic of Jesus Christ's childhood
Lk 2:40 And the child grew and became strong; he was filled with wisdom . . . *See also* **Lk** 2:46–47,52

Wisdom was characteristic of Jesus Christ's ministry
Jesus Christ's wisdom was exceptional
Mt 13:54 Coming to his home town, he [Jesus] began teaching the people in their synagogue, and they were amazed. "Where did this man get this wisdom and these miraculous

powers?" they asked. pp Mk 6:2   See also **Mt 12:42** pp Lk 11:31; **Mk** 11:18; **Jn** 7:15

Jesus Christ's wisdom in teaching
Mt 7:29 . . . he [Jesus] taught as one who had authority, and not as their teachers of the law.   See also **Mt** 11:4–5 pp Lk 7:22; **Mt** 13:34; 16:12; 17:13; **Mk** 1:22 pp Lk 4:32; **Lk** 24:8; **Jn** 2:17

Jesus Christ's wisdom in dealing with people
Jn 4:29 "Come, see a man who told me everything I ever did. Could this be the Christ?"   See also **Mt** 18:2–3 pp Mk 9:36–37 pp Lk 9:47–48; **Mt** 20:25–26 pp Mk 10:42–43; **Jn** 8:10–11

Jesus Christ's wisdom in dealing with opposition
Lk 14:5–6 Then he [Jesus] asked them [the Pharisees and experts in the law], "If one of you has a child or an ox that falls into a well on the Sabbath day, will you not immediately pull it out?" And they had nothing to say. pp Mt 12:11–12   See also **Mt** 22:18–22 pp Mk 12:15–17 pp Lk 20:23–26; **Mt** 27:14 pp Mk 15:5

Jesus Christ's wisdom arose from his relationship with God
It was based on prayer
Mt 26:36 Then Jesus went with his disciples to a place called Gethsemane, and he said to them, "Sit here while I go over there and pray." pp Mk 14:32 pp Lk 22:41

Lk 5:16 But Jesus often withdrew to lonely places and prayed.   See also **Mt** 14:23 pp Mk 6:46; **Mk** 1:35; **Lk** 6:12

It was based on Scripture
Mt 4:4 Jesus answered, "It is written: 'People do not live on bread alone, but on every word that comes from the mouth of God.'" pp Lk 4:4   See also **Dt** 8:3; **Mt** 5:17; 22:29; **Lk** 24:27

Jesus Christ's life embodies the wisdom of God's will and purposes
Jn 8:29 The one who sent me [Jesus] is with me; he [the Father] has not left me alone, for I always do what pleases him."   See also **Jn** 5:30; 8:16,28; 14:10   See also God, wisdom of; Jesus Christ, childhood; Jesus Christ, compassion; Jesus Christ, knowledge of; Jesus Christ, mind of; Jesus Christ, opposition to; Jesus Christ, prayers of; Jesus Christ, preaching and teaching; Jesus Christ, Son of God.

Jesus, the Christ

"Christ" means "Messiah" or "anointed one". As the Christ, Jesus is the one who fulfils all OT expectations. Paul's phrase "in Christ" indicates the intimate relationship between Jesus Christ and his people.

The Christ as the anointed one
The act of anointing in the OT
1Sa 16:13 So Samuel took the horn of oil and anointed him in the presence of his brothers, and from that day on the Spirit of the LORD came upon David in power . . .   See also **Ex** 40:15; **Lev** 8:12; **1Sa** 10:1; **1Ki** 1:39

Anointed OT leaders
Priests: **Ex** 29:7; **Lev** 4:3,5; 6:20; 16:32
Kings: **1Sa** 24:6,10; 26:9,11,16,23; **Ps** 18:50; 20:6; 132:10

The OT promise of a future anointed leader
Isa 11:1–2 A shoot will come up from the stump of Jesse; from his roots a Branch will bear fruit. The Spirit of the LORD will rest on him . . .   See also **Isa** 42:1; **Jer** 23:5–6

Jesus' own claims to be the Christ
Jn 4:25–26 The woman said, "I know that 'Messiah' (called Christ) 'is coming. When he comes, he will explain everything to us.'" Then Jesus declared, "I who speak to you am he." See also **Mt** 23:10; 26:63–64 pp Mk 14:61–62; **Jn** 10:24–25

Jesus recognised as the Christ
Mt 16:16 Simon Peter answered, "You [Jesus] are the Christ, the Son of the living God." pp Mk 8:29 pp Lk 9:20   See also **Lk** 2:26–32; 4:41; **Jn** 1:41–42; 11:27

Jesus' demand that his identity as the Christ should not be publicised
Mt 16:20 Then he [Jesus] warned his disciples not to tell anyone that he was the Christ. pp Mk 8:30 pp Lk 9:21   See also **Mt** 12:16; **Lk** 4:41

Grounds for affirming Jesus as the Christ

Jesus Christ's birth in Bethlehem
Mt 2:4–6 When he [King Herod] had called together all the people's chief priests and teachers of the law, he asked them where the Christ was to be born. "In Bethlehem in Judea," they replied . . . *See also* **Mic** 5:2; **Lk** 2:4–7

Jesus Christ's spiritual anointing from God
Ac 10:38 "how God anointed Jesus of Nazareth with the Holy Spirit and power, and how he went around doing good and healing all who were under the power of the devil, because God was with him." *See also* **Mt** 3:16 pp **Mk** 1:10 pp **Lk** 3:22; **Jn** 3:34; **Ac** 4:27

Jesus Christ's proclamation of Jubilee
Lk 4:17–21 . . . "The Spirit of the Lord is on me, because he has anointed me to preach good news to the poor. He has sent me to proclaim freedom for the prisoners and recovery of sight for the blind, to release the oppressed, to proclaim the year of the Lord's favour." . . . *See also* **Isa** 61:1–2

Jesus Christ's healing ministry
Mt 8:16–17 When evening came, many who were demon-possessed were brought to him, and he drove out the spirits with a word and healed all the sick. This was to fulfil what was spoken through the prophet Isaiah: "He took up our infirmities and carried our diseases." *See also* **Isa** 53:4; **Mt** 11:2–5 pp **Lk** 7:18–23; **Jn** 7:31

Jesus Christ's prophetic ministry
Jn 4:29 "Come, see a man who told me everything I ever did. Could this be the Christ?" *See also* **Mt** 21:45–46; 26:67–68; **Jn** 4:19; 7:26

Jesus Christ's suffering, death and resurrection
Lk 24:26 "Did not the Christ have to suffer these things and then enter his glory?" *See also* **Lk** 24:46; **Ac** 3:18; 17:3; 26:23; **1Pe** 1:11

Jesus Christ's fulfilment of prophecy
2Co 1:20 For no matter how many promises God has made, they are "Yes" in Christ . . . *See also* **Mt** 1:22–23; **Isa** 7:14; **Mt** 26:21–24 pp **Mk** 14:18–21; **Ps** 41:9; **Mt** 21:4–7 pp **Jn** 12:14–15; **Zec** 9:9; **Mt** 21:8–9 pp **Mk** 11:9–10 pp **Lk** 19:37–38 pp **Jn** 12:12–13; **Ps** 118:26; **Ac** 2:22–36

God's establishment of Jesus Christ as king
Lk 1:32–33 "He [Jesus] will be great and will be called the Son of the Most High. The Lord God will give him the throne of his father David, and he will reign over the house of Jacob for ever; his kingdom will never end." *See also* **Ps** 2:6–7; **Isa** 9:6; **Lk** 22:29

Messianic titles used of Jesus
Son of David **Mt** 1:1; 15:22; 21:9; 20:30–31 pp **Mk** 10:47–48 pp **Lk** 18:38–39; **2Ti** 2:8
Son of God **Mt** 14:33; 27:54 pp **Mk** 15:39; **Jn** 1:34
The Prophet **Mt** 21:11; **Jn** 6:14; 7:40
King of the Jews **Mt** 2:2; 27:37 pp **Mk** 15:26 pp **Lk** 23:38 pp **Jn** 19:19; **Mk** 15:32; **Jn** 12:13
High priest **Heb** 2:17; 4:14–15; 5:5; 6:20; 7:26; 8:1

Israel's rejection of Jesus as the Christ
Jesus' messiahship was largely rejected by the Jews
Mt 27:22 "What shall I do, then, with Jesus who is called Christ?" Pilate asked. They all answered, "Crucify him!" *See also* **Jn** 1:11; 8:13; 11:37; **Ac** 7:52–53; 17:3–5

Jesus was accused of blasphemy because of his claims to be the Christ
Mk 14:61–64 . . . Again the high priest asked him, "Are you the Christ, the Son of the Blessed One?" "I am," said Jesus . . . The high priest tore his clothes. "Why do we need any more witnesses?" he asked. "You have heard the blasphemy. What do you think?" They all condemned him as worthy of death. pp **Mt** 26:63–66

That Jesus is the Christ is a central Christian belief
Jn 20:31 But these [miraculous signs] are written that you may believe that Jesus is the Christ, the Son of God, and that by believing you may have life in his name. *See also* **Jn** 11:27; **1Jn** 5:1

The apostles' message was that Jesus is the Christ
Ac 5:42 Day after day, in the temple courts and

from house to house, they never stopped teaching and proclaiming the good news that Jesus is the Christ. *See also* **Ac** 2:36; 9:22; 10:38; 18:5,28

Jesus Christ is the representative head of the church
Baptism is into Christ
Gal 3:27 for all of you who were baptised into Christ have clothed yourselves with Christ.
See also **Ac** 2:38; 10:48; **Ro** 6:3
Jesus Christ lives within believers
Gal 2:20 "I [Paul] have been crucified with Christ and I no longer live, but Christ lives in me . . ." *See also* **Ro** 6:8; 8:1; 16:7; **1Co** 1:30; **Eph** 1:13; **Col** 3:1 *See also* abiding in Christ; Jesus Christ as king; Jesus Christ as prophet; Jesus Christ, head of the church; Jesus Christ, high priest; Jesus Christ, miracles; Jesus Christ, prophecies concerning; Jesus Christ, resurrection; Jesus Christ, Son of David; Jesus Christ, Son of God; Messiah, coming of.

---

justification, Jesus Christ's work

On account of the death and resurrection of Jesus Christ, the demands of the law of God are met, and believers are granted the status of being righteous in the sight of God.

Justification is grounded in the death of Jesus Christ
Jesus Christ's death shields believers from God's wrath
Ro 5:9 Since we have now been justified by his [Christ's] blood, how much more shall we be saved from God's wrath through him! *See also* **Ro** 3:24; 4:25; 5:18; **1Pe** 2:24
Jesus Christ's death fulfils the demands of the law of God
Ro 8:3–4 For what the law was powerless to do in that it was weakened by the sinful nature, God did by sending his own Son in the likeness of sinful humanity to be a sin offering. And so he condemned sin in our sinful nature, in order that the righteous requirements of the law might be fully met in us, who do not live according to the sinful nature but according to the Spirit. *See also* **Ro** 3:25–26; **Gal** 3:13; **1Jn** 2:2

Justification is grounded in the resurrection of Jesus Christ
Ro 4:25 He [Jesus the Lord] was delivered over to death for our sins and was raised to life for our justification.
Ro 10:9–10 That if you confess with your mouth, "Jesus is Lord," and believe in your heart that God raised him from the dead, you will be saved. For it is with your heart that you believe and are justified, and it is with your mouth that you confess and are saved. *See also* **Ac** 2:22–39; 4:10–12; 17:30–31; **1Pe** 3:18–21

Justification means believers are reckoned as righteous through the death of Jesus Christ
Ro 5:19 For just as through the disobedience of the one man [Adam] the many were made sinners, so also through the obedience of the one man [Jesus Christ] the many will be made righteous.
1Co 1:30 It is because of him that you are in Christ Jesus, who has become for us wisdom from God—that is, our righteousness, holiness and redemption.
2Co 5:21 God made him [Jesus Christ] who had no sin to be sin for us, so that in him we might become the righteousness of God.
See also **1Co** 6:9–11; **Php** 3:8–9

Justification is received by faith
Ro 1:17 For in the gospel a righteousness from God is revealed, a righteousness that is by faith from first to last, just as it is written: "The righteous will live by faith." pp **Gal** 3:11
See also **Hab** 2:4; **Ro** 5:1; **Eph** 2:8
The example of Abraham
Ge 15:6 Abram believed the LORD, and he [the LORD] credited it to him as righteousness.
See also **Ro** 4:1–5,9–22; **Gal** 3:6–9,16–18
The example of David Ro 4:6–8; **Ps** 32:1–2
Apostolic teaching on the need of faith for justification
Ac 13:39 "Through him [Jesus] everyone who believes is justified from everything you could not be justified from by the law of Moses."
See also **Ro** 3:22,25,27–30; 4:5; 5:1; 9:30–32; 10:10; **1Co** 6:11; **Gal** 2:16; 3:8,14; **Eph** 2:8

Justification is a gift of God's grace
Ro 3:24 [all who believe] . . . are justified freely by his [God's] grace through the redemption that came by Christ Jesus.   *See also* **Ro** 5:15–17; 8:33; **Tit** 3:7

Not by works or the law
Gal 3:11 Clearly no-one is justified before God by the law, because, "The righteous will live by faith."   *See also* **Ro** 3:20; 4:5; **Gal** 2:16,21; 3:2–5,24; 5:4–6; **Eph** 2:8–9   *See also faith; God, anger of; God, grace and mercy; Jesus Christ as Saviour.*

kingdom of God

Or, less frequently, "kingdom of heaven", the kingly rule of God in the lives of people and nations. It refers to the recognition of the authority of God, rather than a definite geographical area, and begins with the ministry of Jesus Christ.

kingdom of God, coming

The kingdom of God comes into being wherever the kingly authority of God is acknowledged. Although God is always sovereign, Scripture looks to a future "realm" or "reign" of salvation. This has come in Christ and yet will come in its fulness only when Jesus Christ returns.

God is sovereign over Israel and over the whole earth
Ps 47:7–8 For God is the King of all the earth . . . God reigns over the nations . . .
See also **Ex** 15:18; **1Sa** 12:12; **1Ch** 16:31; 28:5; 29:11–12; **Ps** 9:7–8; 45:6; 93:1–2; 103:19; 145:11–13; **Isa** 37:16; **Da** 4:34–35

The coming reign of God
Its expectation
Isa 51:4–5 "Listen to me, my people; hear me, my nation: The law will go out from me; my justice will become a light to the nations. My righteousness draws near speedily, my salvation is on the way, and my arm will bring justice to the nations . . ."
Mk 15:43 Joseph of Arimathea . . . who was himself waiting for the kingdom of God . . . pp Lk 23:51   *See also* **Isa** 2:2–4 pp Mic 4:1–3; **Isa** 32:1; **Jer** 3:17; **Da** 2:44; 7:18,21–22,27; **Zec** 8:22; 14:9; **Mk** 11:10

Its association with the coming of the Messiah
Isa 9:6–7 For to us a child is born, to us a son is given, and the government will be on his shoulders. And he will be called Wonderful Counsellor, Mighty God, Everlasting Father, Prince of Peace. Of the increase of his government and peace there will be no end. He will reign on David's throne and over his kingdom, establishing and upholding it with justice and righteousness from that time on and for ever . . .
Da 7:14 He [one like a son of man] was given authority, glory and sovereign power; all nations and people of every language worshipped him. His dominion is an everlasting dominion that will not pass away, and his kingdom is one that will never be destroyed.   *See also* **Isa** 11:1–9; **Jer** 23:5–6; **Mic** 5:2

The kingdom of God was central in the preaching of Jesus Christ and the apostles
Mt 24:14 "And this gospel of the kingdom will be preached in the whole world as a testimony to all nations, and then the end will come."
Lk 8:1 . . . Jesus travelled about from one town and village to another, proclaiming the good news of the kingdom of God . . .
Ac 28:31 Boldly and without hindrance he [Paul] preached the kingdom of God and taught about the Lord Jesus Christ.   *See also* **Mt** 4:17,23; 9:35; 10:7; **Mk** 1:13–14; **Lk** 4:43; 9:2, 11; 10:9; **Ac** 1:3, 6–8; 8:12; 19:8; 20:25; 28:23

The kingdom of God has come in Christ: it is present
Mt 11:12 From the days of John the Baptist until now, the kingdom of heaven has been forcefully advancing . . .   *See also* **Mt** 3:1–2; 4:17; 13:31–32 pp Mk 4:30–32 pp Lk 13:18–19; **Mt** 13:33 pp Lk 13:20–21; **Mt** 16:28 pp Mk 9:1 pp Lk 9:27; **Lk** 11:20; 16:16; 17:20–21

The kingdom of God will come in its fulness only when Jesus Christ returns: it is future

Lk 22:18 "For I [Jesus] tell you I will not drink again of the fruit of the vine until the kingdom of God comes." pp Mt 26:29 pp Mk 14:25   See also **Mt** 6:10 pp Lk 11:2; **Mt** 25:31,34; **Lk** 22:16; **1Co** 15:24; **2Ti** 4:18; **Rev** 11:15; 12:10   See also church; God, sovereignty; Jesus Christ as king; Jesus Christ, parables; Jesus Christ, second coming; last things; Messiah, coming of.

---

kingdom of God, entry into

Entering or inheriting the kingdom of God is the privilege of those who acknowledge and live by the rule of God and have become part of the new order of salvation and righteousness in Christ.

Entry into the kingdom of God is of vital importance
It is costly
Mt 13:44 "The kingdom of heaven is like treasure hidden in a field. When a man found it, he hid it again, and then in his joy went and sold all he had and bought that field."
Ac 14:22 . . . "We must go through many hardships to enter the kingdom of God," . . . See also **Mt** 8:19–20 pp Lk 9:57–58; **Mt** 13:45–46; **Lk** 18:29–30; **2Th** 1:5; **Rev** 1:9
It is a matter of urgency
Lk 9:59–62 . . . "Let the dead bury their own dead, but you go and proclaim the kingdom of God." Still another said, "I will follow you, Lord; but first let me go back and say good-bye to my family." Jesus replied, "No-one who takes hold of the plough and looks back is fit for service in the kingdom of God." pp Mt 8:21–22

Conditions of entry into the kingdom of God
Childlike trust
Mk 10:15 ". . . anyone who will not receive the kingdom of God like a little child will never enter it." pp Lk 18:17   See also **Mt** 18:3
To be born again of God's Spirit
Jn 3:3 . . . "I [Jesus] tell you [Nicodemus] the truth, no-one can see the kingdom of God without being born again."   See also **Jn** 3:5; **1Co** 15:50
Obedience to God's will
Mt 7:21 "Not everyone who says to me [Jesus], 'Lord, Lord,' will enter the kingdom of heaven, but only those who do the will of my Father who is in heaven."

Warnings about entry into the kingdom of God
The way is narrow
Lk 13:24–28 "Make every effort to enter through the narrow door . . ."   See also **Mt** 7:13–14; 23:13
The wicked will not inherit the kingdom
1Co 6:9–10 Do you not know that the wicked will not inherit the kingdom of God? Do not be deceived: Neither the sexually immoral nor idolaters nor adulterers nor male prostitutes nor homosexual offenders nor thieves nor the greedy nor drunkards nor slanderers nor swindlers will inherit the kingdom of God.   See also **Mt** 5:20; **Mk** 9:43–47; **Gal** 5:19–21; **Eph** 5:5
The need for readiness and watchfulness
Mt 24:42–44 "Therefore keep watch, because you do not know on what day your Lord will come . . . So you also must be ready, because the Son of Man will come at an hour when you do not expect him."   See also **Mt** 24:37–39 pp Lk 17:26–27; **Mt** 25:13; **Lk** 12:35–40
Entry is not based on outward appearances nor granted to all who claim to know the Lord
Mt 7:21–23 ". . . Many will say to me [Jesus] on that day, 'Lord, Lord, did we not prophesy in your name, and in your name drive out demons and perform many miracles?' Then I will tell them plainly, 'I never knew you. Away from me, you evildoers!'"   See also **Mt** 13:24–30,47–50; **Lk** 13:25–27

The kingdom of God is a kingdom of grace
It belongs to those qualified by God
Col 1:12–13 . . . who [the Father] has qualified you to share in the inheritance of the saints in the kingdom of light. For he has rescued us from the dominion of darkness and brought us into the kingdom of the Son he loves . . .

See also **Lk** 12:32; 22:29–30

It belongs to the poor and the poor in spirit
Lk 6:20 . . . "Blessed are you who are poor, for yours is the kingdom of God." pp Mt 5:3
See also **Mt** 11:5 pp **Lk** 7:22; **Mt** 19:23–24 pp **Mk** 10:23–25 pp **Lk** 18:24–25; **Jas** 2:5; 5:1

It belongs to the childlike
Mt 19:14 Jesus said, "Let the little children come to me, and do not hinder them, for the kingdom of heaven belongs to such as these." pp Mk 10:14 pp Lk 18:16

It belongs to sinners
Mk 2:17 . . . "It is not the healthy who need a doctor, but the sick. I have not come to call the righteous, but sinners." pp Mt 9:12–13 pp Lk 5:31–32 *See also* **Mt** 21:31

It belongs to those who are persecuted for Jesus Christ's sake
Mt 5:10 "Blessed are those who are persecuted because of righteousness, for theirs is the kingdom of heaven." pp Lk 6:22–23

It belongs to Gentiles as well as to Jews
Mt 8:11 "I say to you that many will come from the east and the west, and will take their places at the feast with Abraham, Isaac and Jacob in the kingdom of heaven." *See also* **Mt** 21:43; 22:8–10; **Lk** 14:21–24 *See also grace; Holy Spirit and regeneration; salvation.*

kingdom of God, qualities

Those who have entered the kingdom must live according to its values, anticipating the reign of peace which will come when Jesus Christ returns.

The kingdom of God does not conform to the standards of this world
Jn 18:36 Jesus said, "My kingdom is not of this world. If it were, my servants would fight to prevent my arrest by the Jews. But now my kingdom is from another place."
Ro 14:17 For the kingdom of God is not a matter of eating and drinking, but of righteousness, peace and joy in the Holy Spirit,

Those who inherit the kingdom of God are to bear its fruit
1Th 2:12 . . . urging you to live lives worthy of God, who calls you into his kingdom and glory. *See also* **Mt** 25:34–36; **2Pe** 1:10–11

The kingdom of God is and will be a kingdom of peace
Peace between people
Isa 2:2–4 . . . They [the nations] will beat their swords into ploughshares and their spears into pruning hooks. Nation will not take up sword against nation, nor will they train for war any more. pp Mic 4:1–4
Jas 3:18 Peacemakers who sow in peace raise a harvest of righteousness. *See also* **Isa** 9:5; 19:24–25; **Mic** 5:4–5; **Mt** 5:9

The peace and prosperity of all creation
Isa 11:6–9 The wolf will live with the lamb, the leopard will lie down with the goat, the calf and the lion and the yearling together; and a little child will lead them . . . *See also* **Isa** 35:1–2,9; 41:17–19; **Eze** 47:9,12; **Hos** 2:21–22

The kingdom of God is a kingdom of forgiveness
Mt 6:12 pp **Lk** 11:4; **Mt** 18:21–35; **Lk** 17:3–4

Status in the kingdom of God
Mt 18:1–5 ". . . those who humble themselves like this child are the greatest in the kingdom of heaven . . ." pp Mk 9:33–37 pp Lk 9:46–48
Mt 20:25–28 ". . .whoever wants to become great among you must be your servant . . ." pp Mk 10:42–45 pp Lk 22:25–27 *See also* **Mt** 5:19; 11:11 pp **Lk** 7:28; **Mt** 19:30 pp **Mk** 10:31 *See also Christlikeness; forgiveness; Holy Spirit, fruit of; Jesus Christ, kingdom of.*

knowing God

A faith-relationship and love-relationship with God involving mind, heart and will, and bringing experience of his presence and power. To know God is to worship him and be transformed by him. Human knowledge of God, which begins with knowledge about him, comes through God's self-revelation.

knowing God, effects

Knowing God has a transforming effect on a person spiritually and morally and makes that person bold in actions for God. Not knowing God in the present will result in dissatisfaction and degeneration into wickedness and in the future will bring eternal alienation from him.

The effects of knowing God
Spiritual transformation: from death to life
Col 1:9 For this reason, since the day we heard about you [Colossian believers], we [apostles] have not stopped praying for you and asking God to fill you with the knowledge of his will through all spiritual wisdom and understanding. *See also* **Jn** 17:3; **Gal** 4:8–9; **Eph** 1:17; 3:19; **Col** 2:2

Moral transformation: from evil to good
Pr 2:1–6 My son, if you accept my words and store up my commands within you . . . then you will understand the fear of the LORD and find the knowledge of God. For the LORD gives wisdom, and from his mouth come knowledge and understanding.

2Co 10:5 We [believers] demolish arguments and every pretension that sets itself up against the knowledge of God, and we take captive every thought to make it obedient to Christ.

1Th 4:3–5 It is God's will that you should be sanctified: that you should avoid sexual immorality; that each of you should learn to control your own body in a way that is holy and honourable, not in passionate lust like the heathen, who do not know God; *See also* **Ro** 16:26; **Eph** 4:17–24; **Php** 1:9–11; **Col** 1:10; **1Jn** 3:10; 4:8

Boldness of action for God
Jer 32:38–39 "They [the people of Israel] will be my people, and I will be their God. I will give them singleness of heart and action, so that they will always fear me for their own good and the good of their children after them."

Da 11:32 "With flattery he [the king of the North] will corrupt those who have violated the covenant, but the people who know their God will firmly resist him." *See also* **Ps** 138:3; **Pr** 28:1; **Ac** 6:8–10; **2Co** 3:12; **1Pe** 1:13

Biblical images of knowing God
Like parent and child
2Sa 7:14 "'I [the LORD] will be his [David's offspring's] father, and he shall be my son. When he does wrong, I will punish him with a rod wielded by human beings, with floggings inflicted by human hands.'" pp 1Ch 17:13

1Jn 3:1 How great is the love the Father has lavished on us [believers], that we should be called children of God! And that is what we are! The reason the world does not know us is that it did not know him.

God disciplines like a parent: **Heb** 12:6; **Pr** 3:12; **Dt** 8:5 **Ps** 2:7; 27:10; 68:5; 89:26; 103:13; **Isa** 49:15; 66:12–13; **Hos** 11:1; **Mt** 5:45,48; 6:6–9,18,32; **Lk** 15:11–32; **Jn** 14:21; **1Co** 1:3

Like husband and wife
Isa 62:5 As a young man marries a young woman, so will your [Israel's] people marry you; as a bridegroom rejoices over his bride, so will your God rejoice over you.

Jer 3:14 "Return, faithless people," declares the LORD, "for I am your husband . . ." *See also* **Isa** 54:5; **Jer** 2:2; 3:20; 31:32; **Hos** 2:16; **Eph** 5:25; **Rev** 19:7; 21:2

Like king and subject
Ps 97:1 The LORD reigns, let the earth be glad; let the distant shores rejoice. *See also* **1Sa** 8:7; **Ps** 5:2; 10:16; 29:10; 44:4; 84:3; 95:3; 99:1; 145:1; **Mt** 6:33 pp **Lk** 12:31; **1Ti** 1:17; 6:15

Like shepherd and sheep
Ge 48:15 Then he [Jacob] blessed Joseph and said, "May the God before whom my fathers Abraham and Isaac walked, the God who has been my shepherd all my life to this day,"

Ps 23:1–2 The LORD is my [David's] shepherd, I shall not be in want. He makes me lie down in green pastures, he leads me beside quiet waters,

Isa 40:11 He [the LORD] tends his flock like a shepherd: He gathers the lambs in his arms and carries them close to his heart; he gently leads those that have young. *See also* **Ps** 28:9; 80:1; **Eze** 34:16; **Mic** 7:14; **Jn** 10:11; **Rev** 7:17

The peril of not knowing God
Lack of satisfaction and degeneration in the present
Ro 1:21–32 . . . Furthermore, since they did

not think it worth while to retain the knowledge of God, he gave them over to a depraved mind, to do what ought not to be done . . .

Tit 1:15–16 To the pure, all things are pure, but to those who are corrupted and do not believe, nothing is pure. In fact, both their minds and consciences are corrupted. They claim to know God, but by their actions they deny him. They are detestable, disobedient and unfit for doing anything good. *See also* **Ex** 5:2; **Jer** 4:22; **Ro** 10:2–3; **1Th** 4:3–5

Eternal punishment in the future
Mt 7:22–23 "Many will say to me [Jesus] on that day, 'Lord, Lord, did we not prophesy in your name, and in your name drive out demons and perform many miracles?' Then I will tell them plainly, 'I never knew you. Away from me, you evildoers!'"

Ro 1:18–19 The wrath of God is being revealed from heaven against all the godlessness and wickedness of those who suppress the truth by their wickedness, since what may be known about God is plain to them, because God has made it plain to them. *See also* **Ro** 2:5; **2Th** 1:8 *See also God as shepherd; God, fatherhood; God, feminine descriptions of; God, human descriptions of; Jesus Christ as king; sin.*

knowing God, nature of

To know God is not merely to know things about him, such as his character, but also to experience his presence and power. To know God is to be transformed by him. Human knowledge of God is as a result of God's revelation of himself.

The origin of knowing God
Knowing God depends on revelation
Ro 11:33–36 Oh, the depth of the riches of the wisdom and knowledge of God! How unsearchable his judgments, and his paths beyond tracing out! "Who has known the mind of the Lord? Or who has been his counsellor?" "Who has ever given to God, that God should repay the gift?" For from him and through him and to him are all things. To him be the glory for ever! Amen. *See also* **Isa** 40:13; **Dt** 29:29; **Nu** 12:6; 23:3; **Job** 12:22; **Isa** 40:5; 65:1; **Eze** 20:5; **Da** 2:20–23, 28; **Am** 4:13; **Mt** 11:25–27 pp Lk 10:21–22; **Ro** 16:25–26; **Gal** 1:12; **Eph** 3:4–5

God gives knowledge of his reality through creation
Ro 1:20 For since the creation of the world God's invisible qualities—his eternal power and divine nature—have been clearly seen, being understood from what has been made, so that they are without excuse. *See also* **Ps** 8:1; 19:1–4; 97:6; **Ac** 14:17; 17:24–27

God gives knowledge of his mercy and his will through Scripture, both law and gospel
Ro 1:17 For in the gospel a righteousness from God is revealed, a righteousness that is by faith from first to last, just as it is written: "The righteous will live by faith." *See also* **Dt** 31:13; **Ac** 10:36; **1Co** 1:20–21; **Heb** 8:10–11; **Jer** 31:33–34

God gives knowledge of himself through Jesus Christ
Mt 11:27 "All things have been committed to me [Jesus] by my Father. No-one knows the Son except the Father, and no-one knows the Father except the Son and those to whom the Son chooses to reveal him." pp Lk 10:22 *See also* **Jn** 3:2; 8:19; 10:32; 14:7; 16:30; 17:3; **Col** 2:2; **2Ti** 1:9–10; **1Pe** 1:20–21

God gives knowledge of himself and his ways through the Spirit
Eph 1:17 I [Paul] keep asking that the God of our Lord Jesus Christ, the glorious Father, may give you the Spirit of wisdom and revelation, so that you may know him better. *See also* **Isa** 11:2; **Jn** 14:16–17,26; 15:26; 16:12–15; **Ac** 4:31; **1Co** 2:9–11; 12:8; **Eph** 3:16–19; **1Pe** 1:12

God gives knowledge of his greatness and grace through experience of him, submission to him and in answer to prayer
Ps 56:9–11 Then my [David's] enemies will turn back when I call for help. By this I will know that God is for me. In God, whose word I praise, in the LORD, whose word I praise—in God I trust; I will not be afraid. What can human beings do to me? *See also* **Ex** 9:29; **Ps** 17:6–7; 66:19–20; **Isa** 41:19–20; 45:3–6; 50:4; 60:16; **Jer** 22:16; 24:7; **Eze** 6:7

last things

The nature of knowing God
Knowing his character
Jnh 4:2 He [Jonah] prayed to the LORD, "O LORD, is this not what I said when I was still at home? That is why I was so quick to flee to Tarshish. I knew that you are a gracious and compassionate God, slow to anger and abounding in love, a God who relents from sending calamity."   *See also* **Dt** 7:9; **Ps** 9:10; 36:10; 135:5; **1Th** 4:3–5; **1Jn** 4:8,16

Knowing his words and works
Am 3:7 Surely the Sovereign LORD does nothing without revealing his plan to his servants the prophets.   *See also* **Ge** 41:25; **Ex** 6:6–7; 7:5, 17; 18:11; **Dt** 29:29

Samuel: **1Sa** 3:7,21

David: **1Sa** 17:46; **2Sa** 7:21 pp **1Ch** 17:19; **2Sa** 7:27 pp **1Ch** 17:25

2Ki 8:10; 19:19; **Ps** 147:19; **Eze** 20:9; **Lk** 2:26; **Jn** 17:8; **Ac** 2:22; 22:14

To know Jesus Christ is to know God
Jn 14:6 Jesus answered, "I am the way and the truth and the life. No-one comes to the Father except through me."

Col 1:15 He [Christ] is the image of the invisible God . . .   *See also* **Mt** 16:16–17; **Jn** 8:19; 15:15; 16:15; 17:26; **Col** 2:2–3; **1Jn** 5:20

To know God is to experience his salvation
Jn 17:3 "Now this is eternal life: that they may know you, the only true God, and Jesus Christ, whom you have sent."   *See also* **Ps** 17:6–7; **Isa** 25:9; 43:12; 52:10; 56:1; **1Jn** 5:13,20

See also God as Saviour; God, revelation; Holy Spirit; teacher; law; life, spiritual; revelation; Scripture.

---

last things
The doctrine of the last things ("eschatology") includes the subjects of death, the second coming of Jesus Christ, the resurrection of the dead, the last judgment, heaven and hell.

Death
Physical death is universal
Job 30:23 "I know you [God] will bring me down to death, to the place appointed for all the living."   *See also* **2Sa** 14:14; **Ro** 5:12

The timing of natural death is beyond human control
Ecc 8:8 No-one has power over the wind to contain it; so no-one has power over when death comes . . .   *See also* **Ps** 90:10; **Mt** 6:27; **Jas** 4:14

Death is not to be feared by the believer
Ps 23:4 Even though I walk through the valley of the shadow of death, I will fear no evil, for you are with me; your rod and your staff, they comfort me.   *See also* **Ps** 116:15; **Pr** 14:32; **Ro** 14:8; **Php** 1:21; **Rev** 14:13

For believers, death is likened to falling asleep
Jn 11:11–13 . . . "Our friend Lazarus has fallen asleep; but I am going there to wake him up." . . . Jesus had been speaking of his death, but his disciples thought he meant natural sleep.   *See also* **Mk** 5:39; **Ac** 13:36; **1Co** 15:6

At the second coming, believers still living on earth will not experience death
1Th 4:15–17 . . . we who are still alive, who are left till the coming of the Lord, will certainly not precede those who have fallen asleep . . . the dead in Christ will rise first. After that, we who are still alive and are left will be caught up together with them in the clouds to meet the Lord in the air. And so we will be with the Lord for ever.   *See also* **1Co** 15:51–52

Death is the penalty for unforgiven sin
Ro 6:23 . . . the wages of sin is death, but the gift of God is eternal life in Christ Jesus our Lord.   *See also* **1Ch** 10:13; **Pr** 11:19; **Ro** 5:12

The second coming of Jesus Christ
The second coming is foretold
Mt 26:64 ". . . In the future you will see the Son of Man sitting at the right hand of the Mighty One and coming on the clouds of heaven." pp **Mk** 14:62   *See also* **Lk** 21:27; **Ac** 1:11; **Heb** 9:28

The timing of the second coming is known only to God the Father
Mt 24:36 "No-one knows about that day or hour, not even the angels in heaven, nor the Son, but only the Father." pp **Mk** 13:32   *See also* **Mal** 3:1; **Mt** 24:44 pp **Lk** 12:40; **Rev** 16:15

last things

God's purpose at the second coming is to gather his people together, to reward the faithful and judge the wicked
Mt 16:27 "For the Son of Man is going to come in his Father's glory with his angels, and then he will reward everyone according to what they have done."   *See also* **Da** 7:13–14; **Mt** 25:31–32; **Jn** 14:3; **1Co** 4:5; **1Th** 4:16–17; **1Pe** 5:4; **1Jn** 3:2; **Jude** 14–15

The right attitude towards the second coming
1Jn 2:28 And now, dear children, continue in him, so that when he appears we may be confident and unashamed before him at his coming.   *See also* **Mk** 13:35; **Ac** 3:19–20; **1Ti** 6:13–14; **2Pe** 3:11

The resurrection of the dead
All will be raised
Jn 5:28–29 ". . . all who are in their graves will hear his voice and come out—those who have done good will rise to live, and those who have done evil will rise to be condemned."
See also **Da** 12:2; **Ac** 24:15

Believers in Jesus Christ will be raised to eternal life
Jn 6:40 "For my Father's will is that all those who look to the Son and believe in him shall have eternal life, and I will raise them up at the last day."   *See also* **Jn** 11:25; **2Co** 4:14; **1Th** 4:16

Unbelievers will be condemned
Jn 5:29 ". . . those who have done evil will rise to be condemned."   *See also* **Mt** 25:46

Believers will be given resurrection bodies
1Co 15:42–44 So will it be with the resurrection of the dead. The body that is sown is perishable, it is raised imperishable . . . it is sown a natural body, it is raised a spiritual body. If there is a natural body, there is also a spiritual body.   *See also* **1Co** 15:50–53

The last judgment
All face judgment after death
Heb 9:27 Just as people are destined to die once, and after that to face judgment,   *See also* **Ro** 14:12; **1Pe** 4:5; **Rev** 20:11–12

Judgment is entrusted to Jesus Christ
Jn 5:22 "Moreover, the Father judges no-one, but has entrusted all judgment to the Son,"
See also **Ac** 10:42; 17:31; **Rev** 1:18

Those who have not responded to Christ will be condemned
Jn 12:48 "There is a judge for those who reject me and do not accept my words; that very word which I spoke will condemn them at the last day."
See also **2Th** 1:7–8; **2Pe** 3:7; **Jude** 15; **Rev** 20:15

Believers will not be judged for sin
Jn 5:24 "I tell you the truth, those who hear my word and believe him who sent me have eternal life and will not be condemned; they have crossed over from death to life."   *See also* **Jn** 3:18; **Ro** 8:1–2,33–34

Believers will be judged on how they have lived their Christian lives
2Co 5:10 For we [Christians] must all appear before the judgment seat of Christ, that everyone may receive what is due to them for the things done while in the body, whether good or bad.
See also **1Co** 4:5; **Heb** 9:28; **1Jn** 4:17

Heaven
God's throne is in heaven where he is continuously worshipped
Rev 4:9–10 Whenever the living creatures give glory, honour and thanks to him who sits on the throne and who lives for ever and ever, the twenty-four elders fall down before him who sits on the throne, and worship him who lives for ever and ever . . .   *See also* **Isa** 6:1–3

God's will is perfectly served in heaven
Mt 6:10 "'your kingdom come, your will be done on earth as it is in heaven.'"   pp **Lk** 11:2
See also **1Ki** 22:19

At Jesus Christ's second coming, a new heaven and earth will replace the old
Rev 21:1 Then I saw a new heaven and a new earth, for the first heaven and the first earth had passed away . . .

The redeemed will enjoy life in the presence of God in the new heaven
1Th 4:17 . . . And so we will be with the Lord for ever.   *See also* **Mt** 5:8; **Php** 3:20; **Jude** 24; **Rev** 21:1–4

All life in heaven is sustained by God
Rev 22:1-2 Then the angel showed me the river of the water of life, as clear as crystal, flowing from the throne of God and of the Lamb down the middle of the great street of the city . . . *See also* **Jn** 6:58; **Rev** 2:7; 21:23

Hell
Hell is the destiny of human beings who reject God
Mt 25:41 "Then he [the King, Jesus] will say to those on his left, 'Depart from me, you who are cursed, into the eternal fire prepared for the devil and his angels.'" *See also* **Mt** 13:41-42; **Ro** 2:8; **Heb** 10:26-27; **Jude** 6; **Rev** 17:8
Those in hell are finally separated from God
2Th 1:9 They will be punished with everlasting destruction and shut out from the presence of the Lord . . . *See also* **Mt** 25:46
Hell is a place of fire, darkness and weeping
Rev 20:15 All whose names were not found written in the book of life were thrown into the lake of fire. *See also* **Mt** 8:12; **2Pe** 3:7; **Jude** 7
Jesus Christ himself frequently warned about the dangers of hell
Lk 12:5 "But I will show you whom you should fear: Fear him who, after the killing of the body, has power to throw you into hell . . ." *See also* **Mt** 5:29-30; 13:40 *See also* **God as judge; heaven; Jesus Christ, second coming.**

---

law
The God-given regulation of the life of the people of God in relationship with him. As the command of God, it enables and gives shape to the relationship between God and human beings on the one hand, and between fellow human beings on the other.

---

law and gospel
The law, which bears witness to the grace of God, points ahead to its fulfilment and climax in the gospel of Jesus Christ. The gospel does not abolish the law, but fulfils it, by allowing it to be seen in its proper light.

Human beings cannot fulfil the law by their own efforts
Ro 3:20 Therefore no-one will be declared righteous in his [God's] sight by observing the law . . .
Gal 2:15-16 "We who are Jews by birth and not 'Gentile sinners' know that a person is not justified by observing the law, but by faith in Jesus Christ. So we, too, have put our faith in Christ Jesus that we may be justified by faith in Christ and not by observing the law, because by observing the law no-one will be justified." *See also* **Ac** 13:39; **Ro** 4:13-15

The law brings knowledge of human sin and the need for redemption
Ro 3:20 . . . through the law we become conscious of sin.
Ro 5:20 The law was added so that the trespass might increase . . . *See also* **1Ti** 1:9-10; **1Jn** 3:4

The law points to the coming of Jesus Christ
Gal 3:24 So the law was put in charge to lead us to Christ that we might be justified by faith.

Believers are not justified by works of the law, but through faith in the blood of Jesus Christ
Ro 3:28 For we maintain that a person is justified by faith apart from observing the law.
Gal 3:11 Clearly no-one is justified before God by the law, because, "The righteous will live by faith." *See also* **Hab** 2:4; **Ro** 4:1-5; **Gal** 3:10-14; **Eph** 2:15

The relationship between believers and the law
Dying to the law through Jesus Christ
Gal 2:19 "For through the law I died to the law so that I might live for God."
The law remains valid for believers
Ro 7:11-12 For sin, seizing the opportunity afforded by the commandment, deceived me, and through the commandment put me to death. So then, the law is holy, and the commandment is

holy, righteous and good.
1Ti 1:8 We know that the law is good if one uses it properly.
1Pe 1:15–16 But just as he who called you is holy, so be holy in all you do; for it is written: "Be holy, because I am holy." *See also* **Lev** 11:44–45; 19:2; 20:7; **Ro** 7:7–11; 13:8–10; **Jas** 2:8–11

The Holy Spirit enables believers to fulfil the law through Jesus Christ
Ro 8:3–4 For what the law was powerless to do in that it was weakened by the sinful nature, God did by sending his own Son in the likeness of sinful humanity to be a sin offering. And so he condemned sin in our sinful nature, in order that the righteous requirements of the law might be fully met in us, who do not live according to the sinful nature but according to the Spirit. *See also* **Jer** 31:31–34; **Eze** 11:19–20; **Gal** 5:13–18
See also gospel; grace and salvation; Jesus Christ as Saviour; life, spiritual; sin.

---

law, Jesus Christ's attitude
Jesus Christ accepted the authority of the OT law and saw himself as coming to fulfil its purpose.

Jesus Christ's disputes with the Pharisees and teachers of the law
The Pharisees and teachers of the law accuse Jesus Christ's disciples of not following tradition
Mk 7:5 So the Pharisees and teachers of the law asked Jesus, "Why don't your disciples live according to the tradition of the elders instead of eating their food with 'unclean' hands?" pp **Mt** 15:2
Jesus Christ accuses the Pharisees and teachers of the law of hypocrisy
Mk 7:6–8 He [Jesus] replied, "Isaiah was right when he prophesied about you hypocrites; as it is written: These people honour me with their lips, but their hearts are far from me. They worship me in vain; their teachings are merely human rules.' You have let go of the commands of God and are holding on to human traditions." pp **Mt** 15:7–9 *See also* **Isa** 29:13

Jesus Christ gives examples where human tradition is observed rather than God's law
Mk 7:10–13 pp **Mt** 15:3–6; **Mt** 23:1–36 pp **Mk** 12:38–39 pp **Lk** 20:45–46
The Pharisees accuse Jesus Christ of breaking the Sabbath
Mk 2:23–24 One Sabbath Jesus was going through the cornfields, and as his disciples walked along, they began to pick some ears of corn. The Pharisees said to him, "Look, why are they doing what is unlawful on the Sabbath?" pp **Mt** 12:1–2 pp **Lk** 6:1–2
Jesus Christ demonstrates his authority over the Sabbath
Mk 2:27–3:4 Then he [Jesus] said to them, "The Sabbath was made for people, not people for the Sabbath. So the Son of Man is Lord even of the Sabbath." Another time he went into the synagogue, and a man with a shrivelled hand was there. Some of them were looking for a reason to accuse Jesus, so they watched him closely to see if he would heal him on the Sabbath. Jesus said to the man with the shrivelled hand, "Stand up in front of everyone." Then Jesus asked them, "Which is lawful on the Sabbath: to do good or to do evil, to save life or to kill?" But they remained silent. pp **Mt** 12:8–10 pp **Lk** 6:5–7
Jesus Christ challenges the religious leaders to think about principles not rules
Mk 3:4 Then Jesus asked them, "Which is lawful on the Sabbath: to do good or to do evil, to save life or to kill?" But they remained silent. pp **Lk** 6:9 pp **Mt** 12:11–12 *See also* **Lk** 13:10–17

Jesus Christ came to fulfil the law
Mt 5:17 [Jesus said] "Do not think that I have come to abolish the Law or the Prophets; I have not come to abolish them but to fulfil them."
Mt 5:21–22 "You have heard that it was said to the people long ago, 'Do not murder, and anyone who murders will be subject to judgment.' But I [Jesus] tell you that anyone who is angry with a brother or sister will be subject to judgment. Again, anyone who says to a brother or sister, 'Raca,' is answerable to the Sanhedrin. But anyone who says, 'You fool!' will be in danger of the fire of hell." *See also* **Ex** 20:13

Mt 5:27–28 "You have heard that it was said, 'Do not commit adultery.' But I [Jesus] tell you that anyone who looks at a woman lustfully has already committed adultery with her in his heart." *See also* **Ex 20:14**

Jesus Christ asserts the continuing validity of the law
Mt 5:18–19 "I [Jesus] tell you the truth, until heaven and earth disappear, not the smallest letter, not the least stroke of a pen, will by any means disappear from the Law until everything is accomplished. Anyone who breaks one of the least of these commandments and teaches others to do the same will be called least in the kingdom of heaven, but whoever practises and teaches these commands will be called great in the kingdom of heaven."

Lk 10:25–28 On one occasion an expert in the law stood up to test Jesus. "Teacher," he asked, "what must I do to inherit eternal life?" "What is written in the Law?" he replied. "How do you read it?" He answered: "'Love the Lord your God with all your heart and with all your soul and with all your strength and with all your mind'; and, 'Love your neighbour as yourself.'" "You have answered correctly," Jesus replied. "Do this and you will live." pp Mt 22:37–39 pp Mk 12:29–34 *See also* **Lk 10:29–37; 16:16**

Jesus Christ himself was obedient to the law and its commands
In honouring his parents Lk 2:41–51
In being baptised
Mt 3:13–15 Then Jesus came from Galilee to the Jordan to be baptised by John. But John tried to deter him, saying, "I need to be baptised by you, and do you come to me?" Jesus replied, "Let it be so now; it is proper for us to do this to fulfil all righteousness." Then John consented.
In resisting temptation Lk 4:1–13
In observing the Passover
Lk 22:7–8 Then came the day of Unleavened Bread on which the Passover lamb had to be sacrificed. Jesus sent Peter and John, saying, "Go and make preparations for us to eat the Passover."

In submitting to the will of God
Mt 26:39 Going a little farther, he fell with his face to the ground and prayed, "My Father, if it is possible, may this cup be taken from me. Yet not as I will, but as you will." pp Mk 14:35–36 pp Lk 22:41–42 *See also Jesus Christ, attitude to Old Testament; Jesus Christ, obedience; Jesus Christ, opposition to.*

law, letter and spirit
A rigid adherence to the letter of the law often masks hypocrisy and neglect of its spirit, namely having God at the centre of one's life and putting others before oneself, or recognising that the law points to Jesus Christ.

The letter of the law
Overemphasis on keeping some parts of the law
Mk 7:1–8 . . . The Pharisees and all the Jews do not eat unless they give their hands a ceremonial washing, holding to the tradition of the elders. When they come from the market-place they do not eat unless they wash. And they observe many other traditions, such as the washing of cups, pitchers, kettles . . . pp Mt 15:1–2 *See also* **Isa 29:13; Mt 9:10–13** pp Mk 2:15–17 pp Lk 5:29–32

Hypocrisy with regard to keeping the law
Mk 7:9–13 ". . . Moses said, 'Honour your father and your mother,' and, 'Anyone who curses father or mother must be put to death.' But you [Pharisees and teachers of the law] say that if anyone says to father or mother: 'Whatever help you might otherwise have received from me is Corban' (that is, a gift devoted to God), then you no longer let them do anything for their father or mother. Thus you nullify the word of God by your tradition that you have handed down. And you do many things like that." pp Mt 15:3–6 *See also* **Mt 23:1–33; Lk 11:37–52; 18:9–14; Jn 9:1–16; Ro 2:17–24; Isa 52:5**

The spirit of the law
Jesus Christ and the law
Mt 5:17–6:19 "Do not think that I [Jesus] have come to abolish the Law or the Prophets; I

have not come to abolish them but to fulfil them. I tell you the truth, until heaven and earth disappear, not the smallest letter, not the least stroke of a pen, will by any means disappear from the Law until everything is accomplished. Anyone who breaks one of the least of these commandments and teaches others to do the same will be called least in the kingdom of heaven, but whoever practises and teaches these commands will be called great in the kingdom of heaven . . ."   *See also* **Mt** 19:16–30 pp **Mk** 10:17–30 pp **Lk** 18:18–30

Jesus Christ's attitude to the Sabbath
Mk 2:23–3:6 . . . he [Jesus] said to them [the Pharisees], "The Sabbath was made for people, not people for the Sabbath . . ." pp **Mt** 12:1–14 pp **Lk** 6:1–11   *See also* **Mk** 1:21–28 pp **Lk** 4:31–37; **Lk** 13:10–17; 14:1–6; **Jn** 5:1–16; 7:21–24

Jesus Christ's treatment of the woman taken in adultery
Jn 8:2–11 . . . The teachers of the law and the Pharisees brought in a woman caught in adultery. They made her stand before the group and said to Jesus, "Teacher, this woman was caught in the act of adultery. In the Law Moses commanded us to stone such women. Now what do you say?" . . . When they kept on questioning him, he straightened up and said to them, "Let anyone of you who is without sin be the first to throw a stone at her." . . . Jesus straightened up and asked her, "Woman, where are they? Has no-one condemned you?" "No-one, sir," she said. "Then neither do I condemn you," Jesus declared. "Go now and leave your life of sin."

The greatest commandment
Mt 22:34–40 . . . an expert in the law, tested him [Jesus] with this question: "Teacher, which is the greatest commandment in the Law?" Jesus replied: " 'Love the Lord your God with all your heart and with all your soul and with all your mind.' This is the first and greatest commandment. And the second is like it: 'Love your neighbour as yourself.' All the Law and the Prophets hang on these two commandments." pp **Mk** 12:28–34   *See also* **Mt** 25:31–46

The importance of obedience and right attitudes outweighs that of outward actions
Ro 2:25–29 . . . A person is not a Jew who is only one outwardly, nor is circumcision merely outward and physical. No, a person is a Jew who is one inwardly; and circumcision is circumcision of the heart, by the Spirit, not by the written code. Such a person's praise is not from others, but from God.   *See also* **1Sa** 15:22–23; **Ps** 51:16–17; **Pr** 21:3; **Isa** 1:11–17; **Jer** 7:21–23; **Hos** 6:6; **Am** 5:21–24; **Mic** 6:6–8; **Gal** 3:1–5

The spirit of the law is embodied in the new covenant
2Co 3:3–6 . . . He [God] has made us [apostles] competent as ministers of a new covenant—not of the letter but of the Spirit; for the letter kills, but the Spirit gives life.   *See also* **Jn** 4:19–24; **Ro** 7:4–6; 8:1–11; **1Co** 15:45–46; **2Co** 3:13–18; **Gal** 5:18; **Heb** 7:18–22; 8:1–13; **Jer** 31:31–34   *See also Holy Spirit; teacher; Jesus Christ as Saviour; Jesus Christ, attitude to Old Testament; Sabbath; sin.*

---

law, Old Testament
OT laws and legal traditions govern every aspect of the life of the covenant people of God.

Kinds of OT law
Criminal law
Ex 21:12–14 "Anyone who strikes someone a fatal blow shall surely be put to death. However, if it is not done intentionally, but God lets it happen, that person is to flee to a place I will designate. But if anyone schemes and kills someone deliberately, that person shall be taken from my altar and put to death."

Civil law
Dt 16:18–20 Appoint judges and officials for each of your tribes in every town the LORD your God is giving you, and they shall judge the people fairly. Do not pervert justice or show partiality. Do not accept a bribe, for a bribe blinds the eyes of the wise and twists the words of the righteous. Follow justice and justice alone, so that you may live and possess the land the LORD your God is giving you.   *See also* **Dt** 15:12–18

Social law
Ex 22:21-22 "Do not ill-treat or oppress an alien, for you were aliens in Egypt. Do not take advantage of a widow or an orphan."
See also Dt 24:19-22

Cultic law
Cultic law deals explicitly with the ritual or religious life of the people of God. Leviticus chapters 1-7 are totally devoted to this kind of law: **Lev** 1:10-13; 4:13-21; 7:11-18

Examples of OT law
Conditions for freeing servants
Ex 21:2-6 "If you buy a Hebrew servant, he is to serve you for six years. But in the seventh year, he shall go free, without paying anything..." pp Dt 15:12-18 *See also* **Ex** 21:3-11; **Lev** 25:39-55

Dealing with injuries
Ex 21:23-25 "But if there is serious injury, you are to take life for life, eye for eye, tooth for tooth, hand for hand, foot for foot, burn for burn, wound for wound, bruise for bruise." *See also* **Mt** 5:38

Property is to be protected
Ex 22:1 "Whoever steals an ox or a sheep and slaughters it or sells it must pay back five head of cattle for the ox and four sheep for the sheep." *See also* **Lev** 6:1-7; **Lk** 19:8

The rights of aliens must be respected
Ex 22:21 "Do not ill-treat or oppress an alien, for you were aliens in Egypt." *See also* **Lev** 19:33; **Dt** 10:19

Justice must be universally respected
Ex 23:2-3 "... When you give testimony in a lawsuit, do not pervert justice by siding with the crowd, and do not show favouritism to the poor in a lawsuit." *See also* **Lev** 19:15

The Sabbath must be observed by all
Ex 23:12 "Six days do your work, but on the seventh day do not work, so that your ox and your donkey may rest and the slave born in your household, and the alien as well, may be refreshed." *See also* **Ex** 20:8-11

Three annual festivals are to be celebrated
Ex 23:15-16 "Celebrate the Feast of Unleavened Bread... Celebrate the Feast of Harvest with the firstfruits of the crops you sow in your field. Celebrate the Feast of Ingathering at the end of the year..." *See also* **Ex** 12:17; **Dt** 16:16

Worship must be in accordance with God's will and must be kept pure Dt 12:1-7; 13:6-8
Certain foods are declared to be unclean Lev 11:1-23 pp Dt 14:3-20

A tenth of all produce must be given to God
Dt 14:22 Be sure to set aside a tenth of all that your fields produce each year. *See also* **Lev** 27:30

Cultic laws are grounded in the holiness of God
Lev 11:44 "'I am the LORD your God; consecrate yourselves and be holy, because I am holy...'"
Lev 19:1-2 The LORD said to Moses, "Speak to the entire assembly of Israel and say to them: 'Be holy because I, the LORD your God, am holy.'" *See also* **1Pe** 1:16
Full details were given for each type of offering: burnt, grain, fellowship, sin and guilt offerings. Only perfect animals were to be offered: **Lev** 1:3; 2:1-2; 3:1-2; 4:27-28; 5:17-18

Rules governing infectious or contagious diseases
Lev 13:2 "When anyone has a swelling or a rash or a bright spot on the skin that may become an infectious skin disease, they must be brought to Aaron the priest or to one of his sons who is a priest."
Lev 15:13 "'When people are cleansed from their discharge, they are to count off seven days for their ceremonial cleansing; they must wash their clothes and bathe themselves with fresh water, and they will be clean.'"

There must not be unlawful sexual relations
Lev 18:6 "'No-one is to approach any close relative to have sexual relations. I am the LORD.'"

A Day of Atonement must be held Lev 23:26-32 pp Lev 16:2-34 pp Nu 29:7-11
See also worship.

---

law, purpose of
The law covers and regulates every area of life of the covenant people of God in accordance with

the commands of God. Although the laws may be divided into categories of civil, criminal, social and cultic (or ritual) law, these distinctions are not clear-cut, and occasionally overlap with one another.

The origins of the law
Law as God's command is found in the story of creation
Ge 2:16–17 And the LORD God commanded the man, "You are free to eat from any tree in the garden; but you must not eat from the tree of the knowledge of good and evil, for when you eat of it you will surely die."

The law expresses the covenant relation between God and his people
Dt 4:44–45 This is the law Moses set before the Israelites. These are the stipulations, decrees and laws Moses gave them when they came out of Egypt

Dt 5:1 Moses summoned all Israel and said: Hear, O Israel, the decrees and the laws I declare in your hearing today. Learn them and be sure to follow them. *See also* **Ex 20:1–17** pp **Dt 5:6–21**; **Dt 10:12–13**; **30:1–16**

The purpose of the law
The law shows the proper response to the holiness of God
Lev 19:2 "Speak to the entire assembly of Israel and say to them: 'Be holy because I, the LORD your God, am holy.'"

The law ensures that the people continue to receive the blessings of the covenant promises
Dt 6:24–25 'The LORD commanded us to obey all these decrees and to fear the LORD our God, so that we might always prosper and be kept alive, as is the case today. And if we are careful to obey all this law before the LORD our God, as he has commanded us, that will be our righteousness." *See also* **Ge 22:17–18**; **Ex 20:12**; **Dt 6:3–7**

Breaking the law leads to forfeiting the covenant blessings
Jer 11:9–11 Then the LORD said to me [Jeremiah], "There is a conspiracy among the people of Judah and those who live in Jerusalem. They have returned to the sins of their ancestors, who refused to listen to my words. They have followed other gods to serve them. Both the house of Israel and the house of Judah have broken the covenant I made with their ancestors. Therefore this is what the LORD says: 'I will bring on them a disaster they cannot escape. Although they cry out to me, I will not listen to them.'" *See also* **Ex 32:1–4**

The law deepens the believer's knowledge of God through meditation
Ps 1:1–2 Blessed are those who do not walk in the counsel of the wicked or stand in the way of sinners or sit in the seat of mockers. But their delight is in the law of the LORD, and on his law they meditate day and night. *See also* **Dt 6:2**; **Ps 19:7–14**; **119:25–32,105–120**

The law will finally be written on believers' hearts
Jer 31:33 . . . "I will put my law in their minds and write it on their hearts. I will be their God, and they will be my people." *See also* **Eze 11:19–20**

The general principles underlying the law
Justice
Dt 16:20 Follow justice and justice alone, so that you may live and possess the land the LORD your God is giving you.
Righteousness
Dt 16:18 Appoint judges and officials for each of your tribes in every town the LORD your God is giving you, and they shall judge the people fairly.
Holiness
Lev 19:2 . . . "'Be holy because I, the LORD your God, am holy.'"
Love
Lev 19:18–19 "'Do not seek revenge or bear a grudge against one of your people, but love your neighbour as yourself. I am the LORD. Keep my decrees. Do not mate different kinds of animals. Do not plant your field with two kinds of seed. Do not wear clothing woven of two kinds of material.'" *See also* God, justice of; God, righteousness; holiness.

law, Ten Commandments

The basic laws given to Israel through Moses following the exodus from Egypt (Ex 20:1–17; Dt 5:6–21). The first four commandments safeguard Israel's special relation to God; the remaining six protect individuals within the community and promote their well-being.

The Ten Commandments are to govern the life of Israel as the people of God

Israel should obey God alone

Ex 20:2–3 "I am the LORD your God, who brought you out of Egypt, out of the land of slavery. You shall have no other gods before me." pp Dt 5:6–7   See also **Dt** 6:13–15

Idolatry forbidden

Ex 20:4–6 "You shall not make for yourself an idol in the form of anything in heaven above or on the earth beneath or in the waters below. You shall not bow down to them or worship them . . ." pp Dt 5:8–10   See also **Ex** 32:1–8; **Lev** 19:4; **1Co** 10:7

God's name should not be misused

Ex 20:7 "You shall not misuse the name of the LORD your God, for the LORD will not hold anyone guiltless who misuses his name." pp Dt 5:11   See also **Mt** 7:21

A day of rest is commanded

Ex 20:8–11 "Remember the Sabbath day by keeping it holy. Six days you shall labour and do all your work, but the seventh day is a Sabbath to the LORD your God. On it you shall not do any work, neither you, nor your son or daughter, nor male or female servant, nor your animals, nor the alien within your gates. For in six days the LORD made the heavens and the earth, the sea, and all that is in them, but he rested on the seventh day. Therefore the LORD blessed the Sabbath day and made it holy." pp Dt 5:12–15   See also **Ex** 16:23; **Lev** 19:3; **Isa** 56:2; **Jer** 17:21–22

Parents are to be honoured

Ex 20:12 "Honour your father and your mother, so that you may live long in the land the LORD your God is giving you." pp Dt 5:16   See also **Mt** 15:4; **Eph** 6:1–3

Murder is forbidden

Ex 20:13 "You shall not murder." pp Dt 5:17   See also **Ge** 4:8–16; **Mt** 5:21

Adultery is forbidden

Ex 20:14 "You shall not commit adultery." pp Dt 5:18   See also **Lev** 18:20; **2Sa** 11:2–5; **Mt** 5:27; **Heb** 13:4

Stealing is forbidden

Ex 20:15 "You shall not steal." pp Dt 5:19   See also **Lev** 19:11,13

False witness is forbidden

Ex 20:16 "You shall not give false testimony against your neighbour." pp Dt 5:20   See also **Lev** 19:11

Coveting is forbidden

Ex 20:17 "You shall not covet your neighbour's house. You shall not covet your neighbour's wife, or his male or female servant, his ox or donkey, or anything that belongs to your neighbour." pp Dt 5:21   See also **Lev** 19:17–18; **Job** 31:9–12; **Ro** 7:7

The circumstances surrounding the giving of the Ten Commandments

The Ten Commandments written on stone tablets

Ex 24:12 The LORD said to Moses, "Come up to me on the mountain and stay here, and I will give you the tablets of stone, with the law and commands I have written for their instruction." See also **Dt** 4:13; 9:9–10

The stone tablets broken

Ex 32:19 When Moses approached the camp and saw the calf and the dancing, his anger burned and he threw the tablets out of his hands, breaking them to pieces at the foot of the mountain.   See also **Dt** 9:16–17

A second set of stone tablets made

Ex 34:1 The LORD said to Moses, "Chisel out two stone tablets like the first ones, and I will write on them the words that were on the first tablets, which you broke."

Ex 34:28 Moses was there with the LORD forty days and forty nights without eating bread or drinking water. And he wrote on the tablets the words of the covenant—the Ten Commandments.   See also **Dt** 10:1–2

The second set of stone tablets put in the ark of the covenant
Ex 40:20 He took the Testimony and placed it in the ark ...   *See also* **Dt 10:1–2**   *See also* **Sabbath**.

---

life of faith

The way by which believers journey through this world and into the life to come. Jesus Christ himself is the way to life.

Life seen as travelling with God
Walking with God
Ge 17:1 When Abram was ninety-nine years old, the LORD appeared to him and said, "I am God Almighty; walk before me and be blameless."   *See also* **Ge 5:22,24; 6:9; 48:15; Ps 56:13; 89:15; Mic 4:5; Zec 10:12**

Journeying from the old to the new
Isa 43:19 "See, I am doing a new thing! Now it springs up; do you not perceive it? I am making a way in the desert and streams in the wasteland."   *See also* **Ex 18:8; Isa 40:3–5; Mic 2:13**

God's guidance along the way
Ex 13:21 By day the LORD went ahead of them [the Israelites] in a pillar of cloud to guide them on their way and by night in a pillar of fire to give them light, so that they could travel by day or night.   *See also* **Ex 23:20; Dt 1:32–33; 8:2; Ne 9:12,19; Ps 25:9; Jer 2:17; Gal 5:25**

God's ways
Walking in God's way
Isa 35:8 And a highway will be there; it will be called the Way of Holiness. The unclean will not journey on it; it will be for those who walk in that Way; wicked fools will not go about on it.
1Jn 2:6 Whoever claims to live in him [Jesus] must walk as Jesus did.   *See also* **Ge 18:19; Ex 18:20; Dt 10:12–13; 13:5; 28:9; Jos 22:5; Job 23:10–12; Ps 1:1–2; 18:30; 2Ti 3:10**

God teaches believers his way
Isa 48:17 This is what the LORD says—your Redeemer, the Holy One of Israel: "I am the LORD your God, who teaches you what is best for you, who directs you in the way you should go."   *See also* **1Sa 12:23; 1Ki 8:35–36 pp 2Ch 6:26–27; Ps 25:8–9,12; 86:11; 119:30; Pr 6:23; Isa 2:3; 30:20–21**

Characteristics of the way of life include holiness, obedience, trust, humility, joy and peace: **Ps 16:11; 23:2; Pr 8:20; Jer 6:16; Mic 6:8; Gal 5:22–23**

Sinners refuse to follow God's way
Isa 53:6 We all, like sheep, have gone astray, each of us has turned to our own way ...   *See also* **Isa 56:11; Ac 14:16; 2Pe 2:15**

All other routes end in death
Pr 14:12 There is a way that seems right to a person, but in the end it leads to death.   *See also* **Dt 11:28; 31:29; Jdg 2:17; 2Ki 21:22; Ps 1:6; Pr 15:10; 16:25**

Those who travel God's way are blessed
Pr 4:18 The path of the righteous is like the first gleam of dawn, shining ever brighter till the full light of day.   *See also* **Dt 5:33; 1Ki 8:23; Pr 11:5; Isa 26:7–8; Mt 5:3–12**

Jesus Christ is the way to life
Jn 14:6 ... "I am the way and the truth and the life. No-one comes to the Father except through me."
Col 2:3 in whom [Christ] are hidden all the treasures of wisdom and knowledge.   *See also* **Jn 8:12; Heb 12:2**

"the Way" was an early designation of Christianity, suggestive of the content of the church's message that Jesus Christ is the way to life: **Ac 9:2; 19:9,23; 22:4; 24:14,22**

Entrance to the way to life
Entrance is restricted
Mt 7:13–14 "Enter through the narrow gate. For wide is the gate and broad is the road that leads to destruction, and many enter through it. But small is the gate and narrow the road that leads to life, and only a few find it."   *See also* **Jn 10:9; 14:6**

Entrance is by faith
Heb 11:8–10 By faith Abraham, when called to go to a place he would later receive as his inheritance, obeyed and went, even though he did not know where he was going ...   *See also*

life, spiritual

Jn 3:15–16; **2Co** 5:7; **Heb** 11:6,13–16   *See also faith; God as redeemer; God as shepherd; Holy Spirit, teacher; Jesus Christ as Saviour; Jesus Christ, example of; Jesus Christ, preaching and teaching.*

life, spiritual

Life embraces more than physical existence; it includes humanity's relationship with God. Human beings come to life spiritually only through faith in the redeeming work of God in Jesus Christ. This spiritual life is a foretaste of the life which believers will finally enjoy to the full in the new heaven and earth. Life in the Spirit means keeping in step with the promptings and guidance of the Holy Spirit, and always being open to his gifts and empowerment.

The nature of spiritual life
It is new life
Ac 5:20 "Go, stand in the temple courts," he said, "and tell the people the full message of this new life."   *See also* **Ac** 11:18; **2Pe** 1:3; **1Jn** 3:14
It is true life
1Ti 6:19 In this way they will lay up treasure for themselves as a firm foundation for the coming age, so that they may take hold of the life that is truly life.
It is eternal life
Ro 5:21 so that, just as sin reigned in death, so also grace might reign through righteousness to bring eternal life through Jesus Christ our Lord.   *See also* **Da** 12:2; **Mt** 19:29; **Jn** 6:27; **1Jn** 5:11,20
It is abundant life
Ps 16:11 You have made known to me the path of life; you will fill me with joy in your presence, with eternal pleasures at your right hand.
Jer 17:8 "They will be like a tree planted by the water that sends out its roots by the stream. It does not fear when heat comes; its leaves are always green. It has no worries in a year of drought and never fails to bear fruit."   *See also* **Ps** 1:3; **Jn** 10:10

The origins and nature of spiritual life
Spiritual life is the work of the Holy Spirit
Jn 3:6 "Flesh gives birth to flesh, but the Spirit gives birth to spirit."
Jn 3:8 "The wind blows wherever it pleases. You hear its sound, but you cannot tell where it comes from or where it is going. So it is with everyone born of the Spirit."   *See also* **Eze** 36:26; **Jn** 3:3,5–7; **Ro** 8:11; **Tit** 3:5–7
Spiritual life unites believers to Jesus Christ
Eph 2:4–5 . . . God, who is rich in mercy, made us alive with Christ . . .   *See also* **Ro** 6:3–5; 8:10; **1Co** 12:13; **Col** 2:13; **1Jn** 5:12
Spiritual life makes believers the children of God
Jn 1:12–13 Yet to all who received him, to those who believed in his name, he [the Word] gave the right to become children of God . . .   *See also* **Dt** 30:20; **Mt** 6:9; **Ro** 8:15; **Jas** 1:18; **1Jn** 4:7; 5:1
Spiritual life brings people to know God
Jn 17:3 "Now this is eternal life: that they may know you, the only true God, and Jesus Christ, whom you have sent."   *See also* **Mt** 11:27
Spiritual life brings about faith
Jn 3:15 ". . . everyone who believes in him may have eternal life."
Jn 20:31 But these are written that you may believe that Jesus is the Christ, the Son of God, and that by believing you may have life in his name.   *See also* **Jn** 3:16,36; 5:24; 6:40; 11:25

Keeping in step with the Spirit
A new way of life is made possible
Gal 5:25 Since we live by the Spirit, let us keep in step with the Spirit.   *See also* **Ro** 8:5–6,9–16; **Gal** 5:16–18,22–24
Bondage to the written law is ended
Ro 2:29 . . . circumcision is circumcision of the heart, by the Spirit, not by the written code . . .   *See also* **Ro** 7:6; 8:2; **2Co** 3:6; **Gal** 5:17–18
Obedience to God is made possible
Ro 8:4 in order that the righteous requirements of the law might be fully met in us, who do not live according to the sinful nature but according to the Spirit.   *See also* **Eze** 36:27; **Ro** 8:13; **Gal** 5:16; **1Th** 4:7–8
Deepening unity is encouraged
Eph 4:3 Make every effort to keep the unity of

the Spirit through the bond of peace. *See also* **Col** 2:13; **Php** 2:1–4
Strength and encouragement are received Ac 9:31

Gifts for those living in the Spirit
Gifts are given for building up the church
1Co 12:4–11 . . . Now to each one the manifestation of the Spirit is given for the common good . . . *See also* **Ro** 12:6–8; **1Co** 12:27–30
Visions are given Ac 2:17; **Joel** 2:28; **Rev** 1:10,12–13; 4:2; 17:3; 21:10
Miracles are worked
Mt 12:28 "But if I [Jesus] drive out demons by the Spirit of God, then the kingdom of God has come upon you." *See also* **Ac** 10:38; **Ro** 15:19; **Gal** 3:5
Ministry is enhanced
2Co 3:6 He has made us competent as ministers of a new covenant—not of the letter but of the Spirit; for the letter kills, but the Spirit gives life. *See also* **2Co** 3:7–9

Those living in the Spirit receive revelation and guidance
God is revealed as Father
Gal 4:6 Because you are his children, he sent the Spirit of his Son into our hearts, the Spirit who calls out, "Abba, Father." *See also* **Ro** 8:14–16
God's purposes are revealed
1Co 2:9–10 . . . "No eye has seen, no ear has heard, no mind has conceived what God has prepared for those who love him"—but God has revealed it to us by his Spirit . . . *See also* **Ro** 15:13; **2Co** 5:2–5; **Gal** 5:5; **Eph** 1:17–18
Guidance is given to believers
Ac 8:29 The Spirit told Philip, "Go to that chariot and stay near it." *See also* **Ac** 10:19; 11:12; 13:2; 16:6–7; 20:22–23
Help is given to pray Ro 8:26–27; **Eph** 6:18; **Jude** 20

The Holy Spirit sanctifies those in whom he lives
Through the Spirit, Jesus Christ lives in believers Eph 3:16–17

The Spirit transforms believers
2Co 3:18 And we, who with unveiled faces all reflect the Lord's glory, are being transformed into his likeness with ever-increasing glory, which comes from the Lord, who is the Spirit. *See also* **Ro** 15:16; **2Th** 2:13; **1Pe** 1:2
The fruit of the Spirit is seen in believers' lives Ac 13:52; **Ro** 5:5; 8:6; 14:17; 15:30; **Gal** 5:22–23; **Col** 1:8; **1Th** 1:6

Examples of life in the Holy Spirit
Jesus Christ Mt 4:1 pp **Mk** 1:12 pp **Lk** 4:1; **Mt** 12:18,28; **Lk** 4:14,18; 10:21; **Ac** 10:38
Simeon Lk 2:25–27
Peter Ac 4:8; 10:19,44
Stephen Ac 6:5,10; 7:55
The first Christians Ac 4:31; 6:3–5; 11:24,27–29; 13:1–3; 15:28 *See also Holy Spirit and regeneration; Holy Spirit and sanctification; Holy Spirit in life of Jesus Christ; Holy Spirit in the church; Holy Spirit, fruit of; Holy Spirit, guidance; Holy Spirit, indwelling; Holy Spirit, life-giver; Jesus Christ, mission; knowing God.*

Lord's Day
As well as keeping the Sabbath, the first Christians assembled together on the first day of the week to commemorate Jesus Christ's resurrection through the Lord's Supper. The Lord's Day quickly became the focal point of the Christian week, eventually assuming the characteristics of the Jewish Sabbath, namely worship and rest.

The disciples continued to observe the Sabbath
Lk 23:56 . . . they [the women who had come with Jesus from Galilee] rested on the Sabbath in obedience to the commandment. *See also* **Ac** 13:14,42; 16:13; 17:2; 18:4

The Lord's Day commemorated Jesus Christ's resurrection
The resurrection took place on the first day of the week
Mk 16:9 When Jesus rose early on the first day of the week, he appeared first to Mary Magdalene,

out of whom he had driven seven demons.
See also **Mt** 28:1–7 pp **Mk** 16:1–7 pp **Lk** 24:1–6 pp **Jn** 20:1

The disciples assembled together on the first day of the week
Ac 20:7 On the first day of the week we [the believers gathered at Troas] came together to break bread . . . *See also* **Jn** 20:19–20,24–26

The Lord's Day took over the role of the Sabbath
1Co 16:2 On the first day of every week, each one of you should set aside a sum of money in keeping with your income, saving it up, so that when I come no collections will have to be made. *See also* **Rev** 1:10 *See also Jesus Christ, resurrection; Sabbath.*

Messiah, coming of

The coming of a figure chosen and anointed by God to deliver and redeem his people. Anointing was seen as a sign of being chosen by God for a special task of leadership or responsibility. The OT looked ahead to the final coming of such a figure to usher in a new era in the history of the people of God; the NT sees this expectation fulfilled in the person and work of Jesus Christ.

Anointing as a sign of being chosen by God
Anointing with oil
Lev 8:12 He [Moses] poured some of the anointing oil on Aaron's head and anointed him to consecrate him. *See also* **1Sa** 16:12–13; **2Sa** 2:4; 5:3 pp **1Ch** 11:3; **1Ki** 1:39; **2Ki** 9:6; **Ps** 89:20

Anointing with the Holy Spirit
Isa 61:1 The Spirit of the Sovereign LORD is on me, because the LORD has anointed me to preach good news to the poor. He has sent me to bind up the broken-hearted, to proclaim freedom for the captives and release from darkness for the prisoners, *See also* **Lk** 4:18; **Jdg** 14:19; **1Sa** 11:6; 16:13; **Isa** 11:2; **Mt** 12:18; **Isa** 42:1

Anointing as a sign of national and spiritual leadership
Anointed to be king
1Ch 29:22 . . . Then they [the whole assembly] acknowledged Solomon son of David as king a second time, anointing him before the LORD to be ruler . . . *See also* **Jdg** 9:7–15; **1Sa** 9:16; 15:17; **2Sa** 19:10; **1Ki** 1:34; **2Ki** 9:3; 11:12 pp **2Ch** 23:11; **2Ch** 22:7

Anointed to be priest
Ex 40:13–15 ". . . Anoint them [Aaron's sons] just as you anointed their father, so that they may serve me as priests. Their anointing will be to a priesthood that will continue for all generations to come." *See also* **Ex** 28:41; 29:7; **Lev** 7:35–36; 16:32; **Nu** 3:3

Anointed to be judge
The coming of the Spirit on some of the judges is a spiritual anointing: **Jdg** 3:10; 6:34; 11:29; 15:14

Anointed to be prophet **1Ki** 19:16; **Isa** 48:16; **Eze** 11:5; 37:1; **Mic** 3:8

The expectation of a future Messiah
The future anointed king
Ge 49:10 "The sceptre will not depart from Judah, nor the ruler's staff from between his feet, until he comes to whom it belongs and the obedience of the nations is his."
Isa 16:5 In love a throne will be established; in faithfulness a man will sit on it—one from the house of David—one who in judging seeks justice and speeds the cause of righteousness.
See also **Nu** 24:17; **2Sa** 7:12–14 pp **1Ch** 17:11–13; **Ps** 2:7–9; 45:6–7; 110:1–2; 132:11–12; **Isa** 9:6–7; **Eze** 37:24; **Mic** 5:2; **Zec** 9:9

The future anointed priest
Ps 110:4 The LORD has sworn and will not change his mind: "You are a priest for ever, in the order of Melchizedek." *See also* **Zec** 6:13

The future anointed prophet
Isa 61:1–2 The Spirit of the Sovereign LORD is on me, because the LORD has anointed me to preach good news to the poor. He has sent me to bind up the broken-hearted, to proclaim freedom for the captives and release from darkness for the prisoners, to proclaim the year of the LORD's favour and the day of vengeance of

our God, to comfort all who mourn. See also Dt 18:18

The future anointed judge Isa 2:4; 11:3–4; Mic 4:3

The future anointed servant of God
Isa 42:1–4 "Here is my servant, whom I uphold, my chosen one in whom I delight; I will put my Spirit on him . . ." See also Isa 49:1–6; 50:4–9; 52:13–53:12 See also Jesus Christ as king; Jesus Christ as servant; Jesus Christ, high priest; Jesus Christ, prophecies concerning; Jesus, the Christ.

miracles

Events that are totally out of the ordinary and that cannot be adequately explained on the basis of natural occurrences, such as those associated with the ministry of Jesus Christ. They are seen as evidence of the presence and power of God in the world or as demonstrating authority on the part of one of his servants.

miracles, nature of

Miracles may be performed directly by God or through a human agent. Those recorded in Scripture include healing, raising the dead, miracles of nature and the casting out of demons.

Miracles demonstrate God's greatness and power
Ps 77:14 You are the God who performs miracles; you display your power among the peoples. See also Ex 14:30–31; 34:10; Dt 3:24; 1Ki 18:37–39; Job 5:9; Ps 78:4; Lk 9:42–43

Miracles bringing God's judgment
Lev 10:1–2 . . . So fire came out from the presence of the LORD and consumed them [Nadab and Abihu], and they died before the LORD. See also Ge 19:24–26; Nu 12:10; 16:31–35; 1Ki 13:4–5; 2Ki 1:9–12; 2Ch 26:19–20; Ac 5:5,10; 13:11

Miracles which meet human need
The provision of food and water
Ex 17:6 "I [the LORD] will stand there before you by the rock at Horeb. Strike the rock, and water will come out of it for the people to drink." So Moses did this in the sight of the elders of Israel. See also Ex 15:25; Nu 11:31–32; 20:10–11; Jdg 15:18–19; 1Ki 17:5–6,8–16; 2Ki 2:19–22; 4:42–44; Mt 14:15–21; Mk 8:1–10

Healing
Ac 5:16 Crowds gathered also from the towns around Jerusalem, bringing their sick and those tormented by evil spirits, and all of them were healed. See also Nu 21:6–9; 2Ki 5:1–14; Lk 9:6; Ac 3:1–10; 9:33–34; 28:7–9

Exorcism
Ac 16:18 She [a slave girl] kept this up for many days. Finally Paul became so troubled that he turned round and said to the spirit, "In the name of Jesus Christ I command you to come out of her!" At that moment the spirit left her. See also Mk 6:13; 9:38 pp Lk 9:49; Lk 10:17; Ac 8:7

The raising of the dead
Jn 11:38–44 . . . The dead man [Lazarus] came out, his hands and feet wrapped with strips of linen, and a cloth around his face. Jesus said to them, "Take off the grave clothes and let him go." See also 1Ki 17:17–24; 2Ki 4:32–37; 13:21; Ac 9:36–41; 20:9–12

Miraculous births
Ge 18:10–14 ". . . Is anything too hard for the LORD? I [the LORD] will return to you at the appointed time next year and Sarah will have a son." See also Jdg 13:2–3; 1Sa 1:20; 2Ki 4:14–17; Lk 1:34–37

Miracles involving military victory
2Ch 32:21 And the LORD sent an angel, who annihilated all the fighting men and the leaders and officers in the camp of the Assyrian king. So he withdrew to his own land in disgrace . . . pp 2Ki 19:35–36 pp Isa 37:36–37 See also Ex 12:29–36; 14:26–28; Jos 10:12–14; 1Sa 7:10–12; 2Ki 6:18–23; 2Ch 20:22–26

Miraculous help in trouble
Da 6:27 "He [the living God] rescues and he saves; he performs signs and wonders in the heavens and on the earth. He has rescued Daniel from the power of the lions." See also Ps

91:11–12; **Da** 3:19–27; 6:19–23; **Mt** 8:23–27 pp Mk 4:36–41 pp Lk 8:22–25; **Ac** 12:6–11; 16:25–26

Gifts of supernatural strength
Jdg 14:5–6 . . . The Spirit of the LORD came upon him [Samson] in power so that he tore the lion apart with his bare hands as he might have torn a young goat . . . *See also* **Jdg** 14:19; 15:14–16; 16:26–30; **1Ki** 18:46

Nature miracles
2Ki 2:7–8 . . . Elijah took his cloak, rolled it up and struck the water with it. The water divided to the right and to the left, and the two of them [Elijah and Elisha] crossed over on dry ground. *See also* **Ex** 10:13–23; 14:15–22; **Jos** 3:14–17; **2Ki** 2:13–14; **Mt** 21:18–22 pp Mk 11:12–14 pp Mk 11:20–24; **Jn** 2:1–11

Miracles are part of God's plan of redemption
2Sa 7:23 "And who is like your people Israel—the one nation on earth that God went out to redeem as a people for himself, and to make a name for himself, and to perform great and awesome wonders by driving out nations and their gods from before your people, whom you redeemed from Egypt?" pp 1Ch 17:21 *See also* **Mk** 16:17–18; **Ac** 2:22–24; 14:3; **Heb** 2:3–4

Miracles occur at times of special significance
At the time of the exodus Ex 3:2–3; 7:3–4; 16:11–15; 17:6–7; **Nu** 17:8; **Dt** 4:34
At times of national religious crisis 1Ki 18:30–39; **2Ki** 3:16–25; 4:3–7,40–41; 6:5–7
In the time of Jesus Christ Mt 14:15–21 pp Mk 6:35–44 pp Lk 9:12–17 pp Jn 6:5–13; **Mt** 20:29–34 pp Mk 10:46–52 pp Lk 18:35–43; **Jn** 11:38–44
In the time of the first Christians Lk 10:17; **Ac** 8:6,13; 14:8–10,19–20; 19:11–12

Miracles are God's gift
They authenticate the message of his servants
Jn 10:38 ". . . even though you do not believe me [Jesus], believe the miracles, that you may know and understand that the Father is in me, and I in the Father." *See also* **Ex** 4:30–31; **Mt** 11:2–5 pp Lk 7:20–22; **Mk** 9:39; 16:20; **Jn** 14:11; **2Co** 12:12

They are given by God's sovereign will
1Co 12:8–11 . . . All these are the work of one and the same Spirit, and he gives them to each one, just as he determines. *See also* **Mt** 10:1 pp Lk 9:1; **1Co** 12:28–30; **Gal** 3:5

Miracles are not in themselves proof of God's work
They are no guarantee of genuine faith
Mt 7:22–23 "Many will say to me on that day, 'Lord, Lord, did we not prophesy in your name, and in your name drive out demons and perform many miracles?' Then I will tell them plainly, 'I never knew you. Away from me, you evildoers!'" *See also* **Lk** 16:27–31; **Jn** 2:23–24; **1Co** 13:1–2

They can be counterfeited
Mt 24:24 "For false Christs and false prophets will appear and perform great signs and miracles to deceive even the elect—if that were possible." *See also* **Ex** 7:11–12,22; 8:7; **Ac** 8:9–11; **2Th** 2:9; **Rev** 13:13; 16:14; 19:20
See also God, greatness of; God, power of; Jesus Christ, miracles; providence; signs.

---

miracles, responses
Miracles often depend upon faith on the part of those who will benefit from them. Human responses to miracles take various forms. Some respond in faith and obedience, whilst others are confirmed in their unbelief and rebellion.

Faith and obedience required in the working of miracles
1Ki 17:13–15 . . . She went away and did as Elijah had told her. So there was food every day for Elijah and for the woman and her family. *See also* **Ex** 14:16,21; **Nu** 21:8–9; **Jos** 3:13–17; **1Ki** 17:5; **2Ki** 4:41; 5:10–14; **Mt** 9:6–7 pp Mk 2:10–12 pp Lk 5:24–25; **Mt** 9:22 pp Mk 5:34 pp Lk 8:48; **Lk** 1:38; **Heb** 11:29–30

Miracles limited by lack of faith
Mt 13:58 And he [Jesus] did not do many miracles there [in Nazareth] because of their lack

of faith. pp Mk 6:5–6   See also **2Ki** 4:3–6; **Mt** 14:28–31; 17:14–20

Positive responses to miracles
Faith
Ex 14:31 And when the Israelites saw the great power the LORD displayed against the Egyptians, the people feared the LORD and put their trust in him and in Moses his servant.   See also **Ex** 4:30–31; **Jn** 7:31; **Ac** 9:33–35,40–42; 13:12
Amazement
Mt 15:31 The people were amazed when they saw the mute speaking, the crippled made well, the lame walking and the blind seeing. And they praised the God of Israel. pp Mk 7:37   See also **Da** 3:24; **Ac** 3:10; 8:13; 12:16
Praise and worship
Ac 3:8 He [the man crippled from birth] jumped to his feet and began to walk. Then he went with them [Peter and John] into the temple courts, walking and jumping, and praising God. See also **Ex** 15:11,21; **Ps** 9:1; **Da** 3:28; 4:2–3; 6:26–27; **Mt** 15:31; **Lk** 19:37; **Ac** 4:21–22
A closer attention paid to the word of God
Ac 8:6 When the crowds heard Philip and saw the miraculous signs he did, they all paid close attention to what he said.   See also **1Ki** 17:24

Temporary faith as a response to miracles
Jn 2:23–24 Now while he was in Jerusalem at the Passover Feast, many people saw the miraculous signs he was doing and believed in his name. But Jesus would not entrust himself to them, for he knew all people.   See also **Ex** 15:20–24; 16:1–3; 17:3; **Nu** 20:3–5; **Lk** 17:17–18; **Jn** 6:49

Negative responses to miracles
Fear Mk 5:15–17 pp Lk 8:36–37; **Ac** 5:5,11; 19:17
Disbelief
Ac 12:14–15 . . . "You're out of your mind," they [the people who were praying] told her [Rhoda]. When she kept insisting that it was so, they said, "It must be his [Peter's] angel."
See also **Ge** 17:17–18; 18:12–13; **Lk** 1:18,20

Hardness of heart
Ex 8:19 The magicians said to Pharaoh, "This is the finger of God." But Pharaoh's heart was hard and he would not listen, just as the LORD had said.   See also **Ex** 7:3–4; 11:10; **Ps** 78:32; **Mt** 11:20–22 pp Lk 10:13–14; **Jn** 9:18,28–29; 10:25–26; 12:37; 15:24
Opposition Jn 11:47–48; **Ac** 6:8–9; 16:19–21
Disobedience
Ps 106:7 When our ancestors were in Egypt, they gave no thought to your miracles; they did not remember your many kindnesses, and they rebelled by the sea, the Red Sea.   See also **Nu** 14:11,22–23; **Ps** 78:11–22,42–43
Jealousy Ac 8:13,18–19   See also faith; Jesus Christ, responses to; worship.

---

prayer
Fellowship with God through Jesus Christ, expressed in adoration, thanksgiving and intercession, through which believers draw near to God and learn more of his will for their lives. Scripture stresses the vital role of the Holy Spirit in stimulating and guiding prayer.

prayer and faith
Effective prayer depends on faith, especially on a willingness to trust in God's faithfulness to his promises to his people.

Faith is necessary in order to approach God
Heb 11:6 And without faith it is impossible to please God, because anyone who comes to him must believe that he exists and that he rewards those who earnestly seek him.

Faith is necessary to receive benefits from God
Mk 6:5–6 He [Jesus] could not do any miracles there, except lay his hands on a few sick people and heal them. And he was amazed at their lack of faith. Then Jesus went round teaching from village to village.
Jas 5:16–18 . . . The prayer of a righteous person is powerful and effective. Elijah was human

just as we are. He prayed earnestly that it would not rain, and it did not rain on the land for three and a half years. Again he prayed, and the heavens gave rain, and the earth produced its crops.   See also **Eph** 3:12; **Heb** 10:22

Faith is necessary for effective prayer
Mt 21:21–22 Jesus replied, "I tell you the truth, if you have faith and do not doubt, not only can you do what was done to the fig-tree, but also you can say to this mountain, 'Go, throw yourself into the sea,' and it will be done. If you believe, you will receive whatever you ask for in prayer."   pp Mk 11:22–24
Jas 1:5–8 If any of you lacks wisdom, you should ask God, who gives generously to all without finding fault, and it will be given to you. But when you ask, you must believe and not doubt, because the one who doubts is like a wave of the sea, blown and tossed by the wind. Those who doubt should not think they will receive anything from the Lord; they are double-minded and unstable in all they do.   See also **Jas** 5:14–15

Jesus Christ responded to people's need on the basis of faith
Mt 9:27–30 As Jesus went on from there, two blind men followed him, calling out, "Have mercy on us, Son of David!" When he had gone indoors, the blind men came to him, and he asked them, "Do you believe that I am able to do this?" "Yes, Lord," they replied. Then he touched their eyes and said, "According to your faith will it be done to you"; and their sight was restored . . .   See also **Mt** 8:5–13 pp Lk 7:1–10; **Mt** 9:20–22 pp Mk 5:25–34 pp Lk 8:43–48; **Mt** 15:21–28 pp Mk 7:24–30

Examples of notable prayers of faith
1Ki 18:36–37; **Jas** 5:17–18; **1Ki** 17:19–22; **2Ki** 4:32–35   See also faith.

prayer and God's will
Prayer is concerned not only with the well-being of the one who prays. A vital aspect of its purpose is to allow the will of God to be done, and to bring glory and honour to his name.

True motives for prayer
The desire that God's name be honoured
Mt 6:9–13 "This, then, is how you should pray: 'Our Father in heaven, hallowed be your name . . .'"   pp Lk 11:2–4   See also **Nu** 14:13–16; **Jos** 7:7–9; **2Sa** 7:25–26; **1Ki** 18:36–37; **Ps** 115:1; **Jn** 17:1
The desire that God's will be fulfilled
Mt 6:9–13 "This, then, is how you should pray: ' . . . your kingdom come, your will be done on earth as it is in heaven . . .'"   pp Lk 11:2–4   See also **Mt** 26:39 pp Mk 14:36 pp Lk 22:42; **Mt** 26:42; **Heb** 10:7

God answers prayer that accords with his will
1Jn 5:14–15 This is the confidence we have in approaching God: that if we ask anything according to his will, he hears us. And if we know that he hears us—whatever we ask—we know that we have what we asked of him.
Petitioners may enquire of God to discover his will
Ps 143:10 Teach me to do your will, for you are my God . . .   See also **Ge** 25:22–23; **Jdg** 1:1–2; **2Sa** 2:1; **1Ch** 14:14–15
The Holy Spirit helps believers to pray in God's will
Ro 8:26–27 In the same way, the Spirit helps us in our weakness. We do not know what we ought to pray for, but the Spirit himself intercedes for us with groans that words cannot express. And he who searches our hearts knows the mind of the Spirit, because the Spirit intercedes for the saints in accordance with God's will.

God's response to prayers allows believers to discern his will
2Co 12:7–9 To keep me [Paul] from becoming conceited because of these surpassingly great revelations, there was given me a thorn in my flesh, a messenger of Satan, to torment me. Three times I pleaded with the Lord to take it away from me. But he said to me, "My grace is sufficient for you, for my power is made perfect in weakness." Therefore I will boast all the more gladly about my weaknesses, so that Christ's

power may rest on me.   *See also* **Ex** 33:18–20; **2Sa** 12:15–18; **Job** 19:7–8; **Ps** 35:13–14

God does not respond to the prayers of the wicked
Jn 9:31 "We know that God does not listen to sinners. He listens to the godly person who does his will."   *See also* **Ps** 66:18; **Pr** 15:8; **Isa** 1:15; 59:1–2; **La** 3:44; **1Pe** 3:12   *See also God, purpose of; God, will of.*

---

prayer and worship
Worship is turning to God in awe, praise and joy, as his people realise how wonderful he is. Prayer is a natural part of worship: to know God is to want to worship him and pray to him.

Worship is a fundamental requirement of life
All nations are exhorted to worship God
1Ch 16:28–29 Ascribe to the LORD, O families of nations, ascribe to the LORD glory and strength, ascribe to the LORD the glory due to his name. Bring an offering and come before him; worship the LORD in the splendour of his holiness.
See also **Ps** 29:1–2; 96:9
Israel is commanded to worship God
2Ki 17:36 "But the LORD, who brought you up out of Egypt with mighty power and outstretched arm, is the one you must worship. To him you shall bow down and to him offer sacrifices."
See also **Ps** 95:6–7; 99:4–5

Right attitudes in worship are imperative
Reverence and humility characterise acceptable worship
Heb 12:28–29 Therefore, since we are receiving a kingdom that cannot be shaken, let us be thankful, and so worship God acceptably with reverence and awe, for our "God is a consuming fire."   *See also* **Ps** 5:7; 95:6; 138:2; **Ecc** 5:1
Honesty, without hypocrisy, characterises acceptable worship
Am 5:21–24 "I hate, I despise your religious feasts; I cannot stand your assemblies. Even though you bring me burnt offerings and grain offerings, I will not accept them. Though you bring choice fellowship offerings, I will have no regard for them. Away with the noise of your songs! I will not listen to the music of your harps. But let justice roll on like a river, righteousness like a never-failing stream!"   *See also* **Mt** 15:7–9 pp **Mk** 7:6–7; **Isa** 29:13; **Lk** 18:9–14; **Jn** 4:24

Prayer can focus on different aspects of God's character
Prayer can focus on God's holiness
Ex 15:11 "Who among the gods is like you, O LORD? Who is like you—majestic in holiness, awesome in glory, working wonders?"   *See also* **Ps** 77:13; 96:9; 99:5
Prayer can focus on God's glory
Ps 19:1–6 The heavens declare the glory of God; the skies proclaim the work of his hands . . .   *See also* **Ps** 29:1–2; 138:5; **Ro** 16:27; **Php** 4:20; **Jude** 25
Prayer can focus on God's majesty
Ps 104:1–4 . . . O LORD my God, you are very great; you are clothed with splendour and majesty . . .   *See also* **Ps** 8:1; 76:4; 96:4–6
Prayer can focus on God's kingship
Ps 97:1 The LORD reigns, let the earth be glad; let the distant shores rejoice.   *See also* **Ps** 9:7; 22:3; 93:1; 95:3; 102:12
Prayer can focus on God's love and compassion
Ps 103:1–18 . . . The LORD is compassionate and gracious, slow to anger, abounding in love . . .   *See also* **Ps** 111:4; 118:1–4; 145:17–20
Prayer can focus on God's justice and righteousness
Ps 97:2 Clouds and thick darkness surround him [the LORD]; righteousness and justice are the foundation of his throne.   *See also* **Ps** 7:17; 9:8; 97:6; 111:3
Prayer can focus on God's creative activity
Ne 9:6 "You alone are the LORD. You made the heavens, even the highest heavens, and all their starry host, the earth and all that is on it, the seas and all that is in them. You give life to everything, and the multitudes of heaven worship you."   *See also* **Ps** 90:2; 95:3–7; 102:25–27;

prayer as praise and thanksgiving

104:5–9,24–26   *See also God, glory of; God, holiness of; God, justice of; God, love of; God, majesty of; God, the Creator; Holy Spirit and prayer; worship.*

prayer as praise and thanksgiving

Prayer embraces praising God for who he is, thanking him for what he has already done, and looking forward with joy to what he has promised to do in the future.

Scripture exhorts God's people to praise and thank him

Php 4:6 Do not be anxious about anything, but in everything, by prayer and petition, with thanksgiving, present your requests to God.   *See also* **Ps** 66:1; 68:4; 95:1–2; 105:1–3; **Eph** 5:19–20; **Col** 4:2; **1Th** 5:16–18; **Heb** 13:15

Praise and thanksgiving in prayer for God's goodness towards his people

Praise and thanksgiving for deliverance and salvation

Ps 65:1–5 Praise awaits you, O God, in Zion; to you our vows will be fulfilled. O you who hear prayer, to you all people will come. When we were overwhelmed by sins, you forgave our transgressions . . .   *See also* **Ps** 66:5–6; 81:1–7; 124:1–8; **Jnh** 2:1–9

Praise and thanksgiving for provision of material needs

Mk 8:6 . . . When he [Jesus] had taken the seven loaves and given thanks, he broke them and gave them to his disciples to set before the people . . . pp **Mt** 15:36   *See also* **Ps** 65:9–13; **Mt** 26:26–27 pp **Mk** 14:22–23 pp **Lk** 22:19–20

Praise and thanksgiving for help in time of trouble

Ps 34:1–4 I will extol the Lord at all times; his praise will always be on my lips. My soul will boast in the Lord; let the afflicted hear and rejoice. Glorify the Lord with me: let us exalt his name together. I sought the Lord, and he answered me; he delivered me from all my fears.   *See also* **Ps** 30:1–12; 40:1–5; 103:1–5; 116:1–19

Praise and thanksgiving for the encouragement of other believers

Php 1:3–6 I thank my God every time I remember you. In all my prayers for all of you, I always pray with joy because of your partnership in the gospel from the first day until now, being confident of this, that he who began a good work in you will carry it on to completion until the day of Christ Jesus.   *See also* **Ro** 1:8; **2Co** 8:1; **Eph** 1:16; **2Th** 1:3

Notable songs of praise and thanksgiving

Ex 15:1–18
David, on his deliverance from Saul: **2Sa** 22:2–51; **Ps** 18:1–50
1Ch 16:8–36; **Lk** 1:46–55

prayer in the church

The prayer life of the NT provides a pattern from which the modern church can learn, both in terms of the importance of prayer, and also matters for prayer.

Prayer was at the centre of the life of the early church

They prayed when they met together

Ac 1:14 They all joined together constantly in prayer, along with the women and Mary the mother of Jesus, and with his brothers.
See also **Ac** 2:42; 4:23–31; 12:12; 20:36; 21:5

They prayed about the selection and ordination of Christian leaders

Ac 13:2–3 While they [the leaders of the church at Antioch] were worshipping the Lord and fasting, the Holy Spirit said, "Set apart for me Barnabas and Saul for the work to which I have called them." So after they had fasted and prayed, they placed their hands on them and sent them off.   *See also* **Ac** 1:24–25; 6:6; 14:23

They prayed during persecution

Ac 12:5 So Peter was kept in prison, but the church was earnestly praying to God for him.
See also **Ac** 7:59–60; 12:12; 16:22–25

They prayed for healing

Ac 9:40 Peter sent them all out of the room; then he got down on his knees and prayed.

Turning towards the dead woman, he said, "Tabitha, get up." She opened her eyes, and seeing Peter she sat up.   See also **Ac** 28:7–8

The apostles' teaching on prayer in church life
The importance of prayer
Col 4:2 Devote yourselves to prayer, being watchful and thankful.   See also **Ro** 12:12; **Eph** 6:18; **1Th** 5:17; **1Ti** 2:1; **1Pe** 4:7
Prayer for the spread of the gospel
Col 4:3–4 And pray for us, too, that God may open a door for our message, so that we may proclaim the mystery of Christ, for which I am in chains. Pray that I may proclaim it clearly, as I should.   See also **Eph** 6:19–20; **2Th** 3:1
Prayer for the sick
Jas 5:14 Is any one of you sick? Call the elders of the church to pray over you and anoint you with oil in the name of the Lord.
Prayer for sinners
1Jn 5:16–17 If you see your brother or sister commit a sin that does not lead to death, you should pray and God will give them life. I refer to those whose sin does not lead to death. There is a sin that leads to death. I am not saying that you should pray about that. All wrongdoing is sin, and there is sin that does not lead to death.   See also **Jas** 5:16
Prayer for God's servants
Ro 15:30 I urge you, brothers and sisters, by our Lord Jesus Christ and by the love of the Spirit, to join me in my struggle by praying to God for me.   See also **2Co** 1:11
Orderly conduct of public prayer
1Co 11:4–5 Every man who prays or prophesies with his head covered dishonours his head. And every woman who prays or prophesies with her head uncovered dishonours her head—it is just as though her head were shaved.
See also **1Co** 11:13–15

The practice of the apostles
Prayer was central to their ministry
Ac 6:3–4 ". . . We [the apostles] will turn this responsibility over to them [deacons] and will give our attention to prayer and the ministry of the word."

They prayed for the church
Col 1:9–10 For this reason, since the day we [Paul and Timothy] heard about you, we have not stopped praying for you and asking God to fill you with the knowledge of his will through all spiritual wisdom and understanding. And we pray this in order that you may live a life worthy of the Lord and may please him in every way: bearing fruit in every good work, growing in the knowledge of God,   See also **Eph** 1:16–21; 3:16–19; **Php** 1:9–11; **Col** 1:3; **1Th** 1:2; **2Th** 1:11–12   See also church, life of.

prayer, answers
God has promised to answer prayer for personal or corporate needs and for the needs of others.

God answers the prayers of individuals
God answers the psalmists' prayers
Ps 145:18–19 The LORD is near to all who call on him, to all who call on him in truth. He fulfils the desires of those who fear him; he hears their cry and saves them.   See also **Ps** 3:4; 6:8–9; 30:2–3; 66:19–20; 116:1–2; 118:5; 138:3
God answers Moses' prayers **Ex** 15:23–25; 17:4–7; **Nu** 11:10–17
God answers Hannah's prayer for a son
1Sa 1:27 "I prayed for this child, and the LORD has granted me what I asked of him."
See also **1Sa** 1:10–20
God answers the prayers of the prophets
Ps 99:6 Moses and Aaron were among his priests, Samuel was among those who called on his name; they called on the LORD and he answered them.   See also **1Sa** 7:9; **La** 3:55–57; **Jnh** 2:1–2; **Jas** 5:17–18
God answers the prayers of the kings of Israel **1Ki** 9:3; **2Ch** 18:31

God answers corporate petition
Answered prayer for deliverance from hardship
Dt 26:7–8 "Then we cried out to the LORD, the God of our ancestors, and the LORD heard our voice and saw our misery, toil and oppression. So the LORD brought us out of Egypt with a mighty hand and an outstretched arm, with great terror

and with miraculous signs and wonders."
See also **Ex** 2:23–25; 3:7–9; **Nu** 20:16; **1Sa** 12:8; **Ps** 81:7

Answered prayer for deliverance from enemies
1Sa 12:10–11 "They cried out to the LORD and said, 'We have sinned; we have forsaken the LORD and served the Baals and the Ashtoreths. But now deliver us from the hands of our enemies, and we will serve you.' Then the LORD sent Jerub-Baal, Barak, Jephthah and Samuel, and he delivered you from the hands of your enemies on every side, so that you lived securely."
See also **Jdg** 3:9,15; **2Ki** 19:19–20; **1Ch** 5:20

God answers the prayer of the oppressed
Jas 5:4 Look! The wages you failed to pay the workers who mowed your fields are crying out against you. The cries of the harvesters have reached the ears of the Lord Almighty.
See also **Ex** 22:22–23; **Job** 34:28

God answers prayer for healing
Jas 5:14–16 Is any one of you sick? Call the elders of the church to pray over you and anoint you with oil in the name of the Lord. And the prayer offered in faith will make you well; the Lord will raise you up. If you have sinned, you will be forgiven. Therefore confess your sins to each other and pray for each other so that you may be healed. The prayer of a righteous person is powerful and effective.   *See also* **Nu** 12:10–15; **1Ki** 17:21–22; **2Ki** 4:32–35; 20:1–6 pp 2Ch 32:24 pp Isa 38:1–6; **Mt** 8:2–3 pp Mk 1:40–42 pp Lk 5:12–13; **Ac** 9:40

God answers prayer for others
Dt 9:18–19 Then once again I fell prostrate before the LORD for forty days and forty nights; I ate no bread and drank no water, because of all the sin you [Israel] had committed, doing what was evil in the LORD's sight and so provoking him to anger. I feared the anger and wrath of the LORD, for he was angry enough with you to destroy you. But again the LORD listened to me.   *See also* **1Sa** 7:8–9; **Ac** 12:5–8

prayer, asking God
God wants his people to turn to him in prayer, individually and corporately, in times of need or crisis, and to bring requests to him as a Father.

God's people are commanded to bring their requests to him
Php 4:6 Do not be anxious about anything, but in everything, by prayer and petition, with thanksgiving, present your requests to God.
See also **1Ch** 16:11; **Mt** 7:7 pp Lk 11:9; **Jn** 16:24; **Eph** 6:18–20; **1Th** 5:17; **Jas** 5:13

Prayer for deliverance from difficulty
Ps 4:1 Answer me when I call to you, O my righteous God. Give me relief from my distress; be merciful to me and hear my prayer.
Ps 107:6 Then they cried out to the LORD in their trouble, and he delivered them from their distress.   *See also* **Ps** 40:2–3; **Jnh** 2:1–3; **Ac** 12:5

Prayer for deliverance from enemies
Ps 17:8–9 Keep me as the apple of your eye; hide me in the shadow of your wings from the wicked who assail me, from my mortal enemies who surround me.
Ps 35:4 May those who seek my life be disgraced and put to shame; may those who plot my ruin be turned back in dismay.   *See also* **2Ki** 19:9–11; **2Ch** 14:11

Prayers of individuals in time of crisis
Jacob's prayer Ge 32:9–12
David's prayers
Ps 28:1–9 To you I call, O LORD my Rock; do not turn a deaf ear to me. For if you remain silent, I shall be like those who have gone down to the pit. Hear my cry for mercy as I call to you for help, as I lift up my hands towards your Most Holy Place . . .   *See also* **Ps** 4:1; 5:1–3; 30:8–10; 142:1–7
Elijah's prayer
1Ki 19:4 . . . He [Elijah] came to a broom tree, sat down under it and prayed that he might die. "I have had enough, LORD," he said. "Take

prayer, asking God

my life; I am no better than my ancestors."
Jeremiah's prayer Jer 15:15–18
Jesus Christ's prayers
Mt 26:39 Going a little farther, he [Jesus] fell with his face to the ground and prayed, "My Father, if it is possible, may this cup be taken from me. Yet not as I will, but as you will." pp Mk 14:35–36 pp Lk 22:42–44

Individual petition to God in prayer
Individual prayer for guidance
Ge 24:12–14 Then he [Abraham's servant] prayed, "O Lord, God of my master Abraham, give me success today, and show kindness to my master Abraham. See, I am standing beside this spring, and the daughters of the townspeople are coming out to draw water. May it be that when I say to a girl, 'Please let down your jar that I may have a drink,' and she says, 'Drink, and I'll water your camels too'—let her be the one you have chosen for your servant Isaac. By this I will know that you have shown kindness to my master." *See also* **Jdg** 1:1–2; 6:36–40; **1Sa** 14:41; **2Sa** 2:1; **1Ch** 14:14–15
Individual prayer for healing
2Ki 20:1–11 ... Hezekiah turned his face to the wall and prayed to the Lord, "Remember, O Lord, how I have walked before you faithfully and with wholehearted devotion and have done what is good in your eyes." And Hezekiah wept bitterly ... pp Isa 38:1–10
Individual prayer for the birth of a child
1Sa 1:10–11 In bitterness of soul Hannah wept much and prayed to the Lord. And she made a vow, saying, "O Lord Almighty, if you will only look upon your servant's misery and remember me, and not forget your servant but give her a son, then I will give him to the Lord for all the days of his life, and no razor will ever be used on his head." *See also* **Ge** 25:21; 30:17

Corporate petition to God
Corporate prayer for deliverance
Ex 2:23 ... The Israelites groaned in their slavery and cried out, and their cry for help because of their slavery went up to God.

See also **Nu** 20:15–16; **Dt** 26:6–8; **Jdg** 3:9; 4:3; 6:7–10; **1Sa** 12:8
Corporate prayer for restoration Ps 44:23–26; 79:8–9; 80:4–7; 85:4–7
Corporate prayer for protection, especially at times of crisis
Ezr 8:21–23 There, by the Ahava Canal, I [Ezra] proclaimed a fast, so that we might humble ourselves before our God and ask him for a safe journey for us and our children, with all our possessions ... So we fasted and petitioned our God about this, and he answered our prayer. *See also* **2Ch** 20:12–13; **Ezr** 10:1; **Est** 4:16; **Ps** 74:18–23; **Da** 2:17–18

The first Christians prayed together when they met
Ac 1:13–14 When they arrived, they went upstairs to the room where they were staying. Those present were Peter, John, James and Andrew; Philip and Thomas, Bartholomew and Matthew; James son of Alphaeus and Simon the Zealot, and Judas son of James. They all joined together constantly in prayer, along with the women and Mary the mother of Jesus, and with his brothers. *See also* **Ac** 2:42,46–47; 16:13,16; 20:36; 21:5

The first Christians prayed together at times of crisis or important decisions
When threatened with punishment
Ac 4:24–31 When they [the Jerusalem believers] heard this [what the chief priests and elders had said to Peter and John], they raised their voices together in prayer to God ... *See also* **Ac** 12:5,12
When Barnabas and Saul were sent off by the church at Antioch Ac 13:3
When Paul and Silas experienced persecution Ac 16:25

Prayers for mercy and grace
Ps 143:1 O Lord, hear my prayer, listen to my cry for mercy; in your faithfulness and righteousness come to my relief.
Heb 4:16 Let us then approach the throne of grace with confidence, so that we may receive

mercy and find grace to help us in our time of need. See also **2Ch** 6:18–19; **Ps** 130:1–2; **Mt** 20:30–31

prayer, God's promises
God promises to hear and respond to the prayers of his people, when they pray in the name of his Son and according to his will.

God expects his people to make requests of him in prayer
Mt 7:7–11 "Ask and it will be given to you; seek and you will find; knock and the door will be opened to you. For everyone who asks receives; everyone who seeks finds; and to everyone who knocks, the door will be opened. "Which of you, if your children ask for bread, will give them a stone? Or if they ask for a fish, will give them a snake? If you, then, though you are evil, know how to give good gifts to your children, how much more will your Father in heaven give good gifts to those who ask him!" pp Lk 11:9–13   See also **Mt** 21:22

God promises to answer prayer in the name of Jesus Christ
Jn 14:13–14 "And I will do whatever you ask in my name, so that the Son may bring glory to the Father. You may ask me for anything in my name, and I will do it."
Jn 15:7 "If you remain in me [Jesus] and my words remain in you, ask whatever you wish, and it will be given you."   See also **Jn** 15:16; 16:23–24

God promises to respond to the prayers of his people in times of need
Ps 91:14–16 "Because you [who makes the Most High his dwelling] love me," says the LORD, "I will rescue you; I will protect you, for you acknowledge my name. You will call upon me, and I will answer you; I will be with you in trouble, I will deliver you and honour you. With long life will I satisfy you and show you my salvation."   See also **Ps** 50:14–15

God promises to hear the prayers of the oppressed
Ps 10:17 You hear, O LORD, the desire of the afflicted; you encourage them, and you listen to their cry,   See also **Ex** 22:22–23,26–27; **Ps** 102:19–20; **Isa** 41:17

God promises to hear the prayers of the truly penitent
2Ch 7:14 if my people, who are called by my name, will humble themselves and pray and seek my face and turn from their wicked ways, then will I hear from heaven and will forgive their sin and will heal their land.   See also **Eze** 36:37; **Zec** 10:6; 13:8–9

God promises to hear the prayers of his obedient people
1Jn 3:22 and receive from him anything we ask, because we obey his commands and do what pleases him.

The need in prayer to have confidence in God's promises
Mk 11:24 "Therefore I tell you, whatever you ask for in prayer, believe that you have received it, and it will be yours."
1Jn 5:14 This is the confidence we have in approaching God: that if we ask anything according to his will, he hears us.   See also **Mt** 18:19   See also faith and blessings.

prayer, persistence
An answer to prayer may not come immediately. Petitioners are to continue praying earnestly. This requires patience, determination and, at times, a willingness to wrestle with God for the desired outcome.

The principle of persistence in prayer
Prayer should be made with patience and perseverance
Ps 40:1 I waited patiently for the LORD; he turned to me and heard my cry.
Ps 88:1 O LORD, the God who saves me, day and night I cry out before you.   See also **1Ch** 16:11; **Ps** 116:2

Jesus Christ taught his disciples to persist in prayer

Lk 18:1–8 Then Jesus told his disciples a parable to show them that they should always pray and not give up. He said: "In a certain town there was a judge who neither feared God nor cared about people. And there was a widow in that town who kept coming to him with the plea, 'Grant me justice against my adversary.' For some time he refused. But finally he said to himself, 'Even though I don't fear God or care about people, yet because this widow keeps bothering me, I will see that she gets justice, so that she won't eventually wear me out with her coming!'" And the Lord said, "Listen to what the unjust judge says..." *See also* **Lk 11:5–10**

Persistence in prayer was exemplified in the early church

Ac 1:14 They all joined together constantly in prayer, along with the women and Mary the mother of Jesus, and with his brothers.
See also **Ac 2:42**

Paul exhorted the churches to practise persistent prayer

Eph 6:18 And pray in the Spirit on all occasions with all kinds of prayers and requests. With this in mind, be alert and always keep on praying for all the saints. *See also* **Ro 12:12; 1Th 5:17**

Examples of persistence in prayer
Abraham pleads persistently for Sodom

Ge 18:23–33 Then Abraham approached him [the LORD] and said: "Will you sweep away the righteous with the wicked? What if there are fifty righteous people in the city? Will you really sweep it away and not spare the place for the sake of the fifty righteous people in it? Far be it from you to do such a thing—to kill the righteous with the wicked, treating the righteous and the wicked alike. Far be it from you! Will not the Judge of all the earth do right?" ...

Jacob persists in wrestling with God

Ge 32:24–32 ... Then the man said, "Let me go, for it is daybreak." But Jacob replied, "I will not let you go unless you bless me." ...

Moses persists in interceding for Israel

Dt 9:25–29 ... "O Sovereign LORD, do not destroy your people, your own inheritance that you redeemed by your great power and brought out of Egypt with a mighty hand. Remember your servants Abraham, Isaac and Jacob. Overlook the stubbornness of this people, their wickedness and their sin..." *See also* **Ex 32:31–32**

Hannah persistently asks for a son

1Sa 1:10–11 In bitterness of soul Hannah wept much and prayed to the LORD. And she made a vow, saying, "O LORD Almighty, if you will only look upon your servant's misery and remember me, and not forget your servant but give her a son, then I will give him to the LORD for all the days of his life, and no razor will ever be used on his head."

Elijah persists in prayer about the rain

Jas 5:17–18 Elijah was human just as we are. He prayed earnestly that it would not rain, and it did not rain on the land for three and a half years. Again he prayed, and the heavens gave rain, and the earth produced its crops. *See also* **1Ki 18:36–44**

The psalmists persist in calling out to God **Ps 88:1–18; 119:147–149; 130:1–6**

Jesus Christ persisted in pursuing the Father's will

Lk 22:42–44 "Father, if you are willing, take this cup from me; yet not my will, but yours be done." ... And being in anguish, he prayed more earnestly, and his sweat was like drops of blood falling to the ground. pp **Mt 26:36–43** pp **Mk 14:32–40**

Persistence in prayer is exemplified in waiting for God

Mic 7:7 But as for me, I watch in hope for the LORD, I wait for God my Saviour; my God will hear me. *See also* **Ps 27:14; 33:20; 37:7; 38:15; 40:1; Isa 26:8**

---

prayer, relationship with God

Prayer is based on God's love for believers. Through his grace, he gives them things which they do not deserve, while through his mercy he shields them from those things which they do deserve.

God's children can turn to their Father in prayer

Under the old covenant

Isa 64:8–9 Yet, O LORD, you are our Father. We are the clay, you are the potter; we are all the work of your hand. Do not be angry beyond measure, O LORD; do not remember our sins for ever. Oh, look upon us we pray, for we are all your people. *See also* **Ps** 103:13–14; **Isa** 63:16

Under the new covenant

Mt 6:9–13 "This, then, is how you should pray: 'Our Father in heaven, hallowed be your name . . .'" pp Lk 11:2–4 *See also* **Mt** 6:6; 7:7–11 pp Lk 11:9–13; **Ro** 8:15; **Gal** 4:6

Jesus Christ's prayer life with his Father

Mk 14:36 "*Abba*, Father," he said, "everything is possible for you. Take this cup from me. Yet not what I will, but what you will." pp Mt 26:39, 42 pp Lk 22:42 *See also* **Jn** 17:1–26

It is possible to approach God in prayer because of Jesus Christ's sacrifice

Heb 10:19–22 Therefore, brothers and sisters, since we have confidence to enter the Most Holy Place by the blood of Jesus, by a new and living way opened for us through the curtain, that is, his body, and since we have a great priest over the house of God, let us draw near to God with a sincere heart in full assurance of faith, having our hearts sprinkled to cleanse us from a guilty conscience and having our bodies washed with pure water. *See also* **Eph** 3:12; **Heb** 7:15–19

Prayer reflects a longing after God

Ps 42:1–2 As the deer pants for streams of water, so my soul pants for you, O God. My soul thirsts for God, for the living God. When can I go and meet with God?

Jer 29:12–13 "Then you will call upon me and come and pray to me, and I will listen to you. You will seek me and find me when you seek me with all your heart." *See also* **Ps** 130:5–6; 145:18–19; **Pr** 8:17; **Isa** 26:9; 33:2; **La** 3:25 *See also* Abba; access to God; God, fatherhood; knowing God, nature of.

prayer, response to God

Prayer offers believers a means of acknowledging the character and purposes of God and the opportunity to seek guidance concerning his will for them.

The direction of prayer is upwards towards God

Ps 123:1–2 I lift up my eyes to you [LORD], to you whose throne is in heaven. As the eyes of slaves look to the hand of their master, as the eyes of a female servant look to the hand of her mistress, so our eyes look to the LORD our God, till he shows us his mercy. *See also* **Ps** 25:1; 86:4; 121:1–2; 143:8–10; 145:15

Fellowship with God through prayer

Ps 73:23–26 . . . I am always with you [the LORD]; you hold me by my right hand. You guide me with your counsel, and afterwards you will take me into glory. Whom have I in heaven but you? And earth has nothing I desire besides you. My flesh and my heart may fail, but God is the strength of my heart and my portion for ever. *See also* **Ex** 33:11; **1Ki** 8:57–59; **Ps** 16:2; 145:17–20; **Mt** 18:20

The habit of prayer

Lk 5:16 . . . Jesus often withdrew to lonely places and prayed. *See also* **Ne** 2:4; **Da** 6:10–11, 13

Contemplative prayer as a response to God's presence

Ps 27:4 One thing I ask of the LORD, this is what I seek: that I may dwell in the house of the LORD all the days of my life, to gaze upon the beauty of the LORD and to seek him in his temple. *See also* **1Ch** 16:10–11 pp Ps 105:3–4; **Ps** 27:8; **Isa** 55:6; **Jer** 29:13; **Ac** 17:27–28; **Heb** 11:6

Prayer of acceptance in response to God's call

1Sa 3:10 The LORD came and stood there, calling as at the other times, "Samuel! Samuel!"

Then Samuel said, "Speak, for your servant is listening." *See also* **Isa** 6:8; **Rev** 3:20

Prayer of confession
In response to God's holiness
1Jn 1:5–9 . . . God is light; in him there is no darkness at all . . . If we confess our sins, he is faithful and just and will forgive us our sins and purify us from all unrighteousness. *See also* **Isa** 6:3–7; 55:7–9

In response to sin being exposed
Ps 51:1–2 Have mercy on me, O God, according to your unfailing love; according to your great compassion blot out my transgressions. Wash away all my iniquity and cleanse me from my sin. *See also* **Ps** 51:3–12

Prayer of co-operation in response to God's purposes
Jn 15:7–8 "If you [Jesus' disciples] remain in me [Jesus] and my words remain in you, ask whatever you wish, and it will be given you." *See also* **Ps** 119:105–106; **Lk** 1:38; **Jn** 15:16

Prayer of confidence in response to God's mercy and grace
Heb 4:16 Let us [believers] then approach the throne of grace with confidence, so that we may receive mercy and find grace to help us in our time of need. *See also* **Ne** 1:4–7; **Ps** 123:1–2; **Jas** 1:5–8 *See also God, grace and mercy; God, holiness of; repentance.*

---

providence
The continuing and often unseen activity of God in sustaining his universe, providing for the needs of every creature, and preparing for the completion of his eternal purposes.

God's general providence
God sustains the created order
Ge 8:22 "As long as the earth endures, seedtime and harvest, cold and heat, summer and winter, day and night will never cease." *See also* **Ne** 9:6; **Isa** 40:26; **Col** 1:17; **Heb** 1:3

All life is dependent on God
1Ti 6:13 In the sight of God, who gives life to everything . . . *See also* **1Sa** 1:27; **Job** 1:21; **Ps** 127:3; **Ecc** 3:2; 9:9; **Eze** 24:16; **Da** 5:26; **Mt** 4:4; 10:29

God controls the elements
Ps 147:8 He [the LORD] covers the sky with clouds; he supplies the earth with rain and makes grass grow on the hills. *See also* **Job** 37:1–13; **Ps** 29:3–9; 135:6–7; **Mt** 5:45; **Ac** 17:25–28

God provides for the created world
Ps 145:15–16 The eyes of all look to you, and you give them their food at the proper time . . . *See also* **Job** 38:39–41; **Ps** 104:27–28; 136:25; 147:9; **Lk** 12:6–7; **Ac** 14:17; **1Ti** 6:17

God's providence through miraculous means
Job 5:9–10 "He [God] performs wonders that cannot be fathomed, miracles that cannot be counted. He bestows rain on the earth; he sends water upon the countryside." *See also* **Ex** 16:11–14; **Nu** 16:28–35; **Jdg** 15:18–19; **1Ki** 17:5–6; **2Ki** 4:42–44

God's providence in human history
God's control of human intentions
Hab 1:12 O LORD, are you not from everlasting? My God, my Holy One, we will not die. O LORD, you have appointed them [the Babylonians] to execute judgment; O Rock, you have ordained them to punish. *See also* **1Ki** 22:19–20; **2Ki** 19:27–28 pp **Isa** 37:28–29; **Isa** 10:15; **Hab** 1:6

God's providential actions on behalf of individuals
Ro 8:28 And we know that in all things God works for the good of those who love him, who have been called according to his purpose. *See also* **Job** 1:12; 2:6; **Ps** 107:12–14,24–29,33–38; **Isa** 38:17

God's saving purposes fulfilled through providence
Ge 50:20 "You [Joseph's brothers] intended to harm me, but God intended it for good to accomplish what is now being done, the saving of

repentance

many lives." *See also* **Ge** 22:13; 45:5–8; **2Ch** 36:22–23 pp **Ezr** 1:1–3; **Ezr** 6:14; **Isa** 44:28–45:1; **Ac** 2:23; 4:27–28; **Gal** 4:4–5

God's providence prepares for the completion of his ultimate purpose

God is forming a people for himself

Rev 21:3 And I [John] heard a loud voice from the throne saying, "Now the dwelling of God is with human beings, and he will live with them. They will be his people, and God himself will be with them and be their God." *See also* **Ex** 6:7; **Jer** 31:33; **2Co** 6:16; **Eph** 2:14–16; **1Pe** 1:3–5; **Rev** 7:9

God will bring all things under Jesus Christ's authority

Eph 1:9–10 And he [God] made known to us the mystery of his will according to his good pleasure, which he purposed in Christ, to be put into effect when the times will have reached their fulfilment—to bring all things in heaven and on earth together under one head, even Christ. *See also* **Isa** 45:22–23; 66:23; **1Co** 15:24–26; **Php** 2:10–11; **Col** 1:20; **Rev** 11:15

God will complete his purpose for creation

Ro 8:20–21 . . . the creation itself will be liberated from its bondage to decay and brought into the glorious freedom of the children of God. *See also* **Isa** 65:17; 66:22; **2Pe** 3:13; **Rev** 21:1

God directs all things for his glory

Ro 11:36 For from him and through him and to him are all things. To him be the glory for ever! Amen. *See also* **Ps** 46:10; **Ro** 9:23; 11:36; **Eph** 1:4–6,11–12 *See also creation and God; God, sovereignty; God, the provider; miracles, nature of.*

---

repentance

A change of mind leading to a change of action. It involves a sincere turning from sin to serve God and includes sorrow for, and confession of, sin and where possible restitution. At points, Scripture refers to God changing his plans in response to events.

repentance, importance

Repentance is of central importance because sin brings God's judgment and fellowship with God is only possible through full and sincere repentance. God, through his servants, calls people to repent as the only way to escape judgment and receive the forgiveness and restoration which he offers.

The call to repentance

Lk 5:32 "I [Jesus] have not come to call the righteous, but sinners to repentance."

Jas 5:19–20 . . . remember this: Those who turn sinners from the error of their ways will save them from death and cover over a multitude of sins. *See also* **Jer** 25:4–6; **Eze** 33:7–9; **Mk** 1:4 pp **Lk** 3:3; **Lk** 24:47; **2Ti** 2:24–26

Repentance opens the way for blessing

It is the only way to escape God's judgment

Eze 18:30–32 ". . . Repent! Turn away from all your offences; then sin will not be your downfall. Rid yourselves of all the offences you have committed, and get a new heart and a new spirit. Why will you die, O house of Israel? For I take no pleasure in the death of anyone, declares the Sovereign LORD. Repent and live!" *See also* **Job** 36:12; **Jer** 18:7–8; 26:3; **Hos** 11:5; **Jnh** 3:10; **Lk** 3:8–9; **Rev** 2:5

It prepares the way for God's kingdom

Mt 4:17 From that time on Jesus began to preach, "Repent, for the kingdom of heaven is near." pp **Mk** 1:14–15 *See also* **Mt** 3:2

It brings forgiveness and restoration

2Ch 7:13–14 ". . . if my people, who are called by my name, will humble themselves and pray and seek my face and turn from their wicked ways, then will I [the LORD] hear from heaven and will forgive their sin and will heal their land.

Isa 55:7 Let the wicked forsake their ways and the unrighteous their thoughts. Let them turn to the LORD, and he will have mercy on them, and to our God, for he will freely pardon. *See also* **Dt** 30:1–10; **Ne** 1:8–9; **Job** 22:23–25; 36:10–11; **Isa** 44:22; **Ac** 2:38–39; 3:19; 5:31; 11:18

God desires that all people should repent

He wants everyone to be saved
Eze 18:23 "Do I take any pleasure in the death of the wicked? declares the Sovereign LORD. Rather, am I not pleased when they turn from their ways and live?"

His patience with the unrepentant
2Pe 3:9 The Lord is not slow in keeping his promise, as some understand slowness. He is patient with you, not wanting anyone to perish, but everyone to come to repentance. *See also* **Isa** 65:2; **Ro** 2:4; **Rev** 2:21

His discipline encourages repentance
Jer 31:18–20 "I [the LORD] have surely heard Ephraim's moaning: 'You disciplined me like an unruly calf, and I have been disciplined. Restore me, and I will return, because you are the LORD my God . . .'" *See also* **Isa** 10:20–21; 19:22; **Hos** 2:6–7; 6:1

Taking God's opportunity for repentance

Isa 55:6 Seek the LORD while he may be found; call on him while he is near.
Ac 17:30–31 "In the past God overlooked such ignorance, but now he commands all people everywhere to repent. For he has set a day when he will judge the world with justice by the man he has appointed . . ." *See also* **Heb** 3:13–15; 4:7; **Ps** 95:7–8

Refusing God's opportunity for repentance

Examples of those who refuse to repent
Jer 35:15 "'Again and again I [the LORD] sent all my servants the prophets to you. They said, "Each of you must turn from your wicked ways and reform your actions; do not follow other gods to serve them. Then you shall live in the land I have given to you and your ancestors." But you have not paid attention or listened to me.'"
See also **Jer** 5:3; **Mt** 11:20; 21:32; **Rev** 9:20–21; 16:9–11

God confirms those who refuse to repent in their hardness of heart **Mt** 13:14–15 pp **Mk** 4:11–12 pp **Lk** 8:9–10; **Ac** 28:25–27; **Isa** 6:10

Repentance may not remove the effects of human sin
Nu 14:39–45; **1Sa** 15:24–26; **2Sa** 12:13–14; **Heb** 12:16–17 *See also forgiveness; God, compassion; gospel, requirements; kingdom of God.*

---

repentance, nature of

Scripture stresses the necessity of repentance from sin if individuals and communities are to have full fellowship with God. It also uses the term to refer to God's relenting of sending judgment on his people, usually in response to human repentance.

Repentance is a requirement for fellowship with God

2Ki 17:13 The LORD warned Israel and Judah through all his prophets and seers: "Turn from your evil ways. Observe my commands and decrees, in accordance with the entire Law that I commanded your ancestors to obey and that I delivered to you through my servants the prophets."
1Th 1:9 . . . you turned to God from idols to serve the living and true God, *See also* **Ps** 34:14; **Isa** 55:7; **Ac** 14:15; **Jas** 4:7–10

Repentance involves turning from sin

Sorrow for sin
Ps 51:17 The sacrifices of God are a broken spirit; a broken and contrite heart, O God, you will not despise.
2Co 7:8–10 . . . your sorrow led you to repentance. For you became sorrowful as God intended . . . Godly sorrow brings repentance that leads to salvation and leaves no regret . . .
See also **Job** 42:6; **Ps** 34:18; **Isa** 57:15; 66:2; **Joel** 2:12–13; **Lk** 18:13

Confession of sin
Lk 15:17–19 "'. . . I [the prodigal son] will set out and go back to my father and say to him: Father, I have sinned against heaven and against you . . .'" *See also* **Lev** 5:5; **Ps** 51:1–3; **Pr** 28:13; **Hos** 14:1–2

Forsaking specific sins **Ezr** 10:10–11; **Eze** 14:6; **Ac** 15:19–20

Making appropriate restitution **Nu** 5:6–7; **Lk** 19:8

revelation

Repentance involves turning to God
Faith in God

Isa 30:15 This is what the Sovereign LORD, the Holy One of Israel, says: "In repentance and rest is your salvation, in quietness and trust is your strength, but you would have none of it." *See also* **Lk** 22:32; **Ac** 11:21; 20:21; 26:18

Obedience

Eze 18:21–23 "But if the wicked turn away from all the sins they have committed and keep all my [the LORD'S] decrees and do what is just and right, they will surely live; they will not die . . ." *See also* **Mal** 3:7–10

Repentance demonstrated by actions

Ac 26:20 ". . . I [Paul] preached that they should repent and turn to God and prove their repentance by their deeds." *See also* **Isa** 1:16–17; **Da** 4:27; **Mt** 3:8 pp Lk 3:8; **Lk** 3:10–14

Repentance must be sincere

Jer 3:10 ". . . Judah did not return to me with all her heart, but only in pretence," declares the LORD.

Jer 24:7 "'I will give them a heart to know me, that I am the LORD. They will be my people, and I will be their God, for they will return to me with all their heart.'" *See also* **1Ki** 8:46–50 pp 2Ch 6:36–39; **Ps** 78:34–37; **Hos** 6:1–4

The repentance of God

Jer 26:3 "Perhaps they [Judah] will listen and each will turn from their evil ways. Then I [the LORD] will relent and not bring on them the disaster I was planning because of the evil they have done." *See also* **Ex** 32:14; **Ps** 106:45; **Hos** 11:8; **Joel** 2:13; **Am** 7:1–6 *See also faith; God, anger of; God, joy of; God, repentance of; sin.*

revelation

The making known of God's person, nature and deeds, in Scripture, history and supremely the person of Jesus Christ. God is also made known, to a limited yet important extent, through his creation.

revelation, creation

The creation bears witness to the wisdom and power of its creator. This natural knowledge of God is limited in its extent, but is sufficient to convince human beings of the existence of God and the need to respond to him.

The creation bears witness to its creator

Ps 19:1–6 The heavens declare the glory of God; the skies proclaim the work of his hands. Day after day they pour forth speech; night after night they display knowledge. There is no speech or language where their voice is not heard. Their voice goes out into all the earth, their words to the ends of the world . . . *See also* **Job** 36:22–37:18; **Am** 4:13; **Ac** 14:15–17

All human beings have a natural awareness of God

Ro 2:14–15 . . . when Gentiles, who do not have the law, do by nature things required by the law, they are a law for themselves, even though they do not have the law, since they show that the requirements of the law are written on their hearts, their consciences also bearing witness, and their thoughts now accusing, now even defending them. *See also* **Ac** 17:22–31

The limitations of a natural knowledge of God

Ro 1:18–21 . . . For since the creation of the world God's invisible qualities—his eternal power and divine nature—have been clearly seen, being understood from what has been made, so that they are without excuse. For although they knew God, they neither glorified him as God nor gave thanks to him, but their thinking became futile and their foolish hearts were darkened. *See also* **Ro** 1:32; **1Co** 1:20–21 *See also God, glory of; God, revelation; God, the Creator; knowing God, nature of.*

revelation, necessity

Finiteness and sin make it impossible to gain adequate knowledge of God through human effort alone. God in mercy makes himself known through the incarnation of the Son and the illumination of human minds to understand him.

The impossibility of fully knowing God without revelation

God is beyond unaided human knowing

Jn 1:18 No-one has ever seen God, but God the One and Only, who is at the Father's side, has made him known. *See also* **Ex** 33:20; **Isa** 55:8–9; **Jn** 6:46; **1Jn** 4:12

The human mind is limited

Job 11:7 "Can you [Job] fathom the mysteries of God? Can you probe the limits of the Almighty?" *See also* **Job** 9:4,10; 23:3–9; 26:14; 36:26; 37:5,23; **Ps** 139:6; 145:3; **Ecc** 3:11; **Isa** 40:13–14,28; **Ro** 11:33

The human mind cannot discern God of its own accord

2Co 4:4 The god of this age has blinded the minds of unbelievers, so that they cannot see the light of the gospel of the glory of Christ, who is the image of God. *See also* **Jn** 1:5; **Ro** 1:18–32; **1Co** 1:21; 2:14; **2Co** 3:14; **Eph** 4:17–18

God is known fully only through Jesus Christ

Heb 1:1–2 In the past God spoke to our ancestors through the prophets at many times and in various ways, but in these last days he has spoken to us by his Son, whom he appointed heir of all things, and through whom he made the universe.

1Jn 5:20 We know also that the Son of God has come and has given us understanding, so that we may know him who is true. And we are in him who is true—even in his Son Jesus Christ. He is the true God and eternal life. *See also* **Jn** 1:14–18; 17:3; **Col** 1:15–20 *See also God, grace and mercy; God, truth of; God, will of; Holy Spirit in the world; Jesus Christ, Son of God.*

---

revelation, New Testament

The NT fulfils and completes the revelation of God which began in the OT. Jesus Christ is the central focus of this self-revelation of God.

The unity and progress of revelation

The unity of OT and NT

Mt 5:17–18 "Do not think that I [Jesus] have come to abolish the Law or the Prophets; I have not come to abolish them but to fulfil them. I tell you the truth, until heaven and earth disappear, not the smallest letter, not the least stroke of a pen, will by any means disappear from the Law until everything is accomplished." *See also* **Ro** 3:21–22; **2Ti** 3:14–15; **2Pe** 3:15–16; **Rev** 22:18–19

The progress of NT revelation

Heb 1:1–2 In the past God spoke to our ancestors through the prophets at many times and in various ways, but in these last days he has spoken to us by his Son, whom he appointed heir of all things, and through whom he made the universe. *See also* **Heb** 2:1–4; 12:22–27

The NT fulfils and completes God's revelation of himself

Jesus Christ is the supreme revelation of God

Col 1:25–27 I [Paul] have become its [the church's] servant by the commission God gave me to present to you the word of God in its fulness—the mystery that has been kept hidden for ages and generations, but is now disclosed to the saints. To them God has chosen to make known among the Gentiles the glorious riches of this mystery, which is Christ in you, the hope of glory. *See also* **Jn** 1:9–18; 14:6; **Ac** 4:12; **Gal** 4:4; **Php** 2:6–8; **Heb** 2:14

Jesus Christ is the image of God

2Co 4:4 The god of this age has blinded the minds of unbelievers, so that they cannot see the light of the gospel of the glory of Christ, who is the image of God.

Col 1:15 He is the image of the invisible God, the firstborn over all creation.

Jesus Christ has the nature of God

Php 2:6 [Christ Jesus] Who, being in very nature God, did not consider equality with God something to be grasped

Jesus Christ is the exact representation of God

Heb 1:3 The Son is the radiance of God's glory and the exact representation of his being,

revelation, Old Testament

sustaining all things by his powerful word. After he had provided purification for sins, he sat down at the right hand of the Majesty in heaven.
Jesus Christ is the incarnate Word of God
Jn 1:14 The Word became flesh and made his dwelling among us. We have seen his glory, the glory of the One and Only, who came from the Father, full of grace and truth.

The role of the Holy Spirit in revelation
He is the divine agent of revelation
Jn 16:12–15 ". . . But when he, the Spirit of truth, comes, he will guide you into all truth. He will not speak on his own; he will speak only what he hears, and he will tell you what is yet to come. He will bring glory to me by taking from what is mine and making it known to you. All that belongs to the Father is mine. That is why I said the Spirit will take from what is mine and make it known to you."   *See also* **Jn** 14:16–17; 15:26; **1Jn** 4:6; 5:6; **Rev** 2:7,11,17,29; 3:6,13,22
He is the source of revelatory manifestations
1Co 12:7–11 Now to each one the manifestation of the Spirit is given for the common good. To one there is given through the Spirit the message of wisdom, to another the message of knowledge by means of the same Spirit, to another faith by the same Spirit, to another gifts of healing by that one Spirit, to another miraculous powers, to another prophecy, to another distinguishing between spirits, to another speaking in different kinds of tongues, and to still another the interpretation of tongues. All these are the work of one and the same Spirit, and he gives them to each one, just as he determines.   *See also* **Ac** 2:1–12; **Ro** 12:6; **1Co** 12:28–30; 13:8–12; 14:1–33; **Eph** 4:11

God's purposes in revelation
To reveal himself in Jesus Christ
Col 1:15–20 . . . For God was pleased to have all his fulness dwell in him, and through him to reconcile to himself all things, whether things on earth or things in heaven, by making peace through his blood, shed on the cross.   *See also* **Jn** 1:14; 12:44–45; 14:9; **2Co** 4:4; **Heb** 1:3

To reveal his plan through Jesus Christ
Eph 1:9–10 And he [God] made known to us [believers] the mystery of his will according to his good pleasure, which he purposed in Christ, to be put into effect when the times will have reached their fulfilment—to bring all things in heaven and on earth together under one head, even Christ.   *See also* **Ro** 16:25–27; **1Co** 2:7–10; **Eph** 3:3–11; **Col** 1:19–20   *See also God as redeemer; Holy Spirit, inspiration; Holy Spirit, teacher; Jesus Christ as redeemer; Jesus Christ, attitude to Old Testament; Jesus Christ, Son of God; Jesus Christ, transfiguration; salvation.*

revelation, Old Testament
The OT bears witness to God's revelation in the history of Israel and in the inspired testimony of the prophets and other writers of the period. This knowledge of God prepares the way for the full disclosure of God in Jesus Christ in the NT.

Revelation in Eden and before the flood
Ge 1:3 And God said, "Let there be light," and there was light.
Ge 2:16–18 And the LORD God commanded the man, "You are free to eat from any tree in the garden; but you must not eat from the tree of the knowledge of good and evil, for when you eat of it you will surely die." The LORD God said, "It is not good for the man to be alone. I will make a helper suitable for him."   *See also* **Ge** 1:29–30; 3:9–19; 4:6–7,9–15; 6:13–22

The covenant framework of OT revelation after the flood
God's covenant with Noah
Ge 9:8–11 Then God said to Noah and to his sons with him: "I now establish my covenant with you and with your descendants after you . . ."   *See also* **Ge** 6:18; 9:12–17
God's covenant with Abraham
Ge 17:7 "I [the LORD] will establish my covenant as an everlasting covenant between me and you [Abraham] and your descendants after you for the generations to come, to be your God and the God of your descendants after you."
See also **Ge** 15:9–21; 17:2,4,10–14; 22:16–18; **Ex** 6:2–6; **1Ch** 16:14–18; **Ps** 105:8–9

God's covenant with Moses at Sinai
Ex 34:27 Then the LORD said to Moses, "Write down these words, for in accordance with these words I have made a covenant with you and with Israel." *See also* **Ex** 24:3–8; 34:10–14; **Dt** 5:2–4; **Jer** 11:2–5

God's covenant with David
Ps 89:3–4 You [the LORD] said, "I have made a covenant with my chosen one, I have sworn to David my servant, 'I will establish your line for ever and make your throne firm through all generations.'" *See also* **2Sa** 7:8–16; **Ps** 132:11–12

The promise of a new covenant
Jer 31:31–34 "The time is coming," declares the LORD, "when I will make a new covenant with the house of Israel and with the house of Judah . . ." *See also* **Isa** 42:6; **Mt** 26:27–28 pp **Mk** 14:24 pp **Lk** 22:20 pp **1Co** 11:25; **Heb** 8:8–12; 9:15; 10:15–18

The recipients of OT revelation
The people of Israel
Am 3:2 "You only have I chosen of all the families of the earth . . ." *See also* **Ex** 19:3–6; **Dt** 7:6; **Isa** 65:1; **Eze** 20:5

On occasions God spoke to people outside the covenant community
Da 2:27–28 Daniel replied, "No wise man, enchanter, magician or diviner can explain to the king the mystery he has asked about, but there is a God in heaven who reveals mysteries. He has shown King Nebuchadnezzar what will happen in days to come . . ." *See also* **Ge** 41:25,28–32; **Da** 4:1–37; 5:17–28

Methods of OT revelation
Direct communication
Dt 18:18 "I [the LORD] will raise up for them [Israel] a prophet like you from among their people and I will put my words in that prophet's mouth. My prophet will tell them everything I command." *See also* **Ex** 4:12; **Nu** 12:8; 23:5; **Isa** 50:4; 51:16; **Jer** 1:9

Visions and dreams
Nu 12:6 he [the LORD] said, "Listen to my words: When there are prophets of the LORD among you, I reveal myself to them in visions, I speak to them in dreams." *See also* **Ge** 15:1; 28:12; 37:5–7,9; 46:2; **Nu** 24:4; **Dt** 13:1; **Jdg** 7:13–14; **Job** 33:14–15; **Eze** 1:1,26–28

Visible manifestations (theophanies)
Ge 18:1 The LORD appeared to Abraham near the great trees of Mamre while he was sitting at the entrance to his tent in the heat of the day. *See also* **Ge** 32:24–30; **Ex** 3:1–6; 34:4–7; **Nu** 11:25; 12:5; 14:10–12; **Jos** 5:13–15

Scripture
Dt 31:9 So Moses wrote down this law and gave it to the priests, the sons of Levi, who carried the ark of the covenant of the LORD, and to all the elders of Israel. *See also* **Ex** 17:14; **Nu** 33:2; **Isa** 30:8; **Jer** 36:2; 51:60

The content of OT revelation
Revelation of God's will and purposes
Ge 17:1–2 When Abram was ninety-nine years old, the LORD appeared to him and said, "I am God Almighty; walk before me and be blameless. I will confirm my covenant between me and you and will greatly increase your numbers." *See also* **Ge** 12:1–3; 15:1–5; **Ex** 19:5–6; 20:1–17 pp **Dt** 5:6–21; **Ex** 22:31; **Lev** 11:44–45; 19:1–2; 20:7–8

Revelation of God's plan
Ge 3:15 ". . . I [God] will put enmity between you [the serpent] and the woman, and between your offspring and hers; he will crush your head, and you will strike his heel." *See also* **Isa** 9:6–7; 11:1–10; 42:1; **Mic** 5:1–5; **Zec** 9:9–13

Revelation of God's character and being
Ex 3:11–15 . . . God said to Moses, "I AM WHO I AM. This is what you are to say to the Israelites: 'I AM has sent me to you.'" God also said to Moses, "Say to the Israelites, 'The LORD, the God of your fathers—the God of Abraham, the God of Isaac and the God of Jacob—has sent me to you.' This is my name for ever, the name by which I am to be remembered from generation to generation."

God's glory: **Ex** 40:34; **1Ki** 8:11; **Eze** 1:28
God is just and merciful: **Nu** 14:17–19; **Ps** 143:1
God's love: **Dt** 7:7–8; **La** 3:22

revelation, responses

God is righteous: **Ps 72:2**; 103:6; **Isa** 59:17
God is the sovereign creator: **Ps** 115:3; 135:5–6

The incompleteness of OT revelation
Heb 11:39–40 These [Old Testament saints] were all commended for their faith, yet none of them received what had been promised. God had planned something better for us so that only together with us would they be made perfect. *See also* **Heb** 1:1–2; **1Pe** 1:10–12 *See also God, purpose of; God, titles and names of; Holy Spirit in Old Testament; Scripture, sufficiency; word of God.*

revelation, responses
God requires and imparts a frame of mind that receives and responds to what he has made known.

God commands that his word be heeded
Mk 4:3 "Listen! A farmer went out to sow his seed." *See also* **Isa** 1:10; **Mk** 4:9; **Rev** 2:7

People do not naturally understand what God has revealed
They fail to recognise God's revelation in Jesus Christ
Mt 11:25–27 At that time Jesus said, "I praise you, Father, Lord of heaven and earth, because you have hidden these things from the wise and learned, and revealed them to little children . . . No-one knows the Son except the Father, and no-one knows the Father except the Son and those to whom the Son chooses to reveal him." pp Lk 10:21–22 *See also* **Jn** 5:37–40; 6:44–45; 10:24–26; 12:37–41; 14:9; **Ro** 9:31–10:4; **1Co** 1:18–25; 2:8; **2Co** 4:4
They fail to understand God's revelation in general
1Co 2:14 The person without the Spirit does not accept the things that come from the Spirit of God but considers them foolishness, and cannot understand them, because they are spiritually discerned. *See also* **Mk** 4:11–12 pp Mt 13:13–15 pp Lk 8:10; **Isa** 6:9–10; **Jn** 8:43–47; **2Co** 3:14–16; **2Th** 2:11–13

God has given his Spirit to illuminate the human mind
He reveals and teaches truth
1Co 2:12–13 We [believers] have not received the spirit of the world but the Spirit who is from God, that we may understand what God has freely given us. This is what we speak, not in words taught us by human wisdom but in words taught by the Spirit, expressing spiritual truths in spiritual words. *See also* **Jer** 31:31–34; **Mt** 16:17; **Jn** 3:3–10; 14:16–17,25–26; 16:12–15; **Php** 3:15
He reveals through prayer for understanding
Ps 119:18 Open my eyes that I may see wonderful things in your [God's] law. *See also* **Ps** 119:12,27; **Eph** 1:17–18

Understanding God's revelation carries special responsibility
Lk 12:47–48 ". . . From everyone who has been given much, much will be demanded; and from the one who has been entrusted with much, much more will be asked. *See also* **Mt** 13:11–12; 25:14–30 pp Lk 19:12–27

God's revelation of himself will only be fully understood at the second coming of Jesus Christ
1Co 13:12 Now we [believers] see but a poor reflection as in a mirror; then we shall see face to face. Now I know in part; then I shall know fully, even as I am fully known. *See also* **1Pe** 1:13; **1Jn** 3:2

The consequences of responding to revelation
Repentance
Ac 2:38 Peter replied, "Repent and be baptised, every one of you, in the name of Jesus Christ for the forgiveness of your sins. And you will receive the gift of the Holy Spirit." *See also* **Mt** 4:17; **Ac** 3:19; 26:20; **2Co** 7:10
Faith
Ro 10:17 Consequently, faith comes from hearing the message, and the message is heard through the word of Christ. *See also* **Ro** 10:8–10,14–15; **1Co** 2:4–5

Obedience

Ro 1:5 Through him [Jesus Christ] and for his name's sake, we received grace and apostleship to call people from among all the Gentiles to the obedience that comes from faith. *See also* **Jdg** 2:17; **Phm** 21; **1Pe** 1:2 *See also faith, necessity; gospel, responses; Jesus Christ, second coming; life, spiritual; repentance.*

Sabbath

The day of rest laid down for the people of God. The OT treated the seventh day of the week (Saturday) as the Sabbath, a custom continued in modern Judaism. The Christian church, in recognition of the importance of the resurrection of Jesus Christ, observed a day of rest on the first day of the week (Sunday).

Sabbath, in New Testament

The NT develops the OT teaching on the Sabbath in three important directions. It declares that the Sabbath should not be observed in a legalistic manner; the Sabbath-rest is treated as an important symbol of the Christian doctrine of salvation; and finally, the NT itself indicates how Sunday, rather than Saturday, came to be seen as the Christian Sabbath.

Gospel incidents connected with the Sabbath

Exorcism Mk 1:21–25 pp **Lk** 4:31–35
Healing Mt 12:9–14 pp **Mk** 3:1–6 pp **Lk** 6:6–11; **Mk** 1:30–31 pp **Lk** 4:38–40; **Lk** 13:10–17; 14:1–6; **Jn** 5:5–18; 9:1–16
Teaching Mk 6:2 pp **Mt** 13:54; **Lk** 4:16
Other references Mt 28:1 pp **Mk** 16:1; **Lk** 23:55–56; **Jn** 12:2

Jesus Christ's teaching regarding the Sabbath

Jesus Christ observes the Sabbath regulation
Lk 4:16 He went to Nazareth, where he had been brought up, and on the Sabbath day he went into the synagogue, as was his custom . . . *See also* **Mt** 24:20; **Ac** 1:12

Human well-being is more important than rigid observance of the Law
Mk 2:27–28 Then he [Jesus] said to them [the Pharisees], "The Sabbath was made for people, not people for the Sabbath. So the Son of Man is Lord even of the Sabbath." *See also* **Mt** 12:3

Ceremonial observance must give way before any higher, or more spiritual, motive
Mt 12:5–6 "Or haven't you read in the Law that on the Sabbath the priests in the temple desecrate the day and yet are innocent? I tell you that one greater than the temple is here." *See also* **Lk** 6:5

Sabbath reading of Scripture provided an opportunity for reaching the Jews

Ac 17:2 As his custom was, Paul went into the synagogue, and on three Sabbath days he reasoned with them from the Scriptures, *See also* **Ac** 13:14,27,42,44; 15:21; 16:13; 18:4

Sabbath observance was optional for Gentile Christians

Col 2:16 Therefore do not let anyone judge you by what you eat or drink, or with regard to a religious festival, a New Moon celebration or a Sabbath day.

The Lord's Day

Rev 1:10 On the Lord's Day I was in the Spirit, and I heard behind me a loud voice like a trumpet, *See also* **Jn** 20:19,26; **Ac** 20:7; **1Co** 16:2

The Sabbath-rest is seen as a symbol of the salvation of the people of God

Heb 4:1 Therefore, since the promise of entering his rest still stands, let us be careful that none of you be found to have fallen short of it.
Heb 3:18–19 And to whom did God swear that they would never enter his rest if not to those who disobeyed? So we see that they were not able to enter, because of their unbelief.
Heb 4:9 There remains, then, a Sabbath-rest for the people of God; *See also Jesus Christ, attitude to Old Testament; Jesus Christ, opposition to; Lord's Day; Scripture.*

Sabbath, in Old Testament

The Sabbath of rest is grounded in God's work of creation. Observance of a Sabbath day is distinctive of the people of God.

The Sabbath grounded in creation itself

Ge 2:3 And God blessed the seventh day and made it holy, because on it he rested from all the work of creating that he had done. *See also* **Ps** 118:24

The purpose of the Sabbath
To remember God's work in creation

Ex 20:8-11 "Remember the Sabbath day by keeping it holy. Six days you shall labour and do all your work, but the seventh day is a Sabbath to the LORD your God. On it you shall not do any work, neither you, nor your son or daughter, nor your male or female servant, nor your animals, nor the alien within your gates. For in six days the LORD made the heavens and the earth, the sea, and all that is in them, but he rested on the seventh day. Therefore the LORD blessed the Sabbath day and made it holy." *See also* **Ge** 2:2; **Ex** 35:2

To remember the exodus

Dt 5:12-15 "Observe the Sabbath day by keeping it holy, as the LORD your God has commanded you. Six days you shall labour and do all your work, but the seventh day is a Sabbath to the LORD your God. On it you shall not do any work, neither you, nor your son or daughter, nor your male or female servant, nor your ox, your donkey or any of your animals, nor the alien within your gates, so that your male and female servants may rest, as you do. Remember that you were slaves in Egypt and that the LORD your God brought you out of there with a mighty hand and an outstretched arm. Therefore the LORD your God has commanded you to observe the Sabbath day." *See also* **Ge** 8:4; **2Sa** 7:1,11; **Ps** 95:10-11; **Heb** 4:9; **Rev** 14:13

To be a sign of the relationship between Israel and God and to give refreshment

Ex 31:17 "'It will be a sign between me and the Israelites for ever, for in six days the LORD made the heavens and the earth, and on the seventh day he abstained from work and rested.'" *See also* **Dt** 5:12-14

The Law required the Sabbath to be a holy day free from work

Lev 23:3 "'There are six days when you may work, but the seventh day is a Sabbath of rest, a day of sacred assembly. You are not to do any work; wherever you live, it is a Sabbath to the LORD.'" *See also* **Ex** 34:21; 35:3; **Lev** 23:38; **Isa** 56:2; 58:13

The Sabbath was linked with celebration of the New Moon

2Ki 4:23 "Why go to him [Elisha] today?" he asked. "It's not the New Moon or the Sabbath." *See also* **Isa** 1:13; **Eze** 46:3; **Hos** 2:11; **Am** 8:5

Abuses of the Sabbath

Ex 16:27-28; **Nu** 15:32; **Ne** 13:15-18
Engaging in commerce: **Ne** 10:31; **Am** 8:5 **Jer** 17:21

Punishments for infringing the Sabbath law

The death penalty Ex 31:14; **Nu** 15:35
Disaster for Jerusalem Jer 17:27; **Eze** 20:13; 22:8,15

Sacrifices to be offered on the Sabbath

Bread Lev 24:8; **1Ch** 9:32
Burnt offerings Nu 28:9-10; **1Ch** 23:31; **2Ch** 2:4
Other offerings Eze 46:4 *See also* law, Old Testament.

salvation

The transformation of a person's individual nature and relationship with God as a result of repentance and faith in the atoning death of Jesus Christ on the cross. All humanity stands in need of salvation, which is only possible through faith in Jesus Christ.

salvation, nature of

Salvation involves a change in the relationship between God and a person. Salvation includes God's adoption of believers into his family, his acceptance of them as righteous and his forgiveness of their sins. It also includes personal renewal and transformation through the work of the Holy Spirit.

Salvation as a change in status before God

Access to God
Ro 5:1–2 Therefore, since we have been justified through faith, we have peace with God through our Lord Jesus Christ, through whom we have gained access by faith into this grace in which we now stand. And we rejoice in the hope of the glory of God. *See also* **Eph** 2:13; **Heb** 4:16

Adoption into the family of God Jn 1:12; **Ro** 8:22–24; **Gal** 4:4–7

Forgiveness of sin
Ac 5:30–31 "The God of our ancestors raised Jesus from the dead—whom you had killed by hanging him on a tree. God exalted him to his own right hand as Prince and Saviour that he might give repentance and forgiveness of sins to Israel." *See also* **Ps** 32:1–2; **Mt** 26:28; **Ac** 10:43; 13:38; **Eph** 1:7; **Col** 2:13

Heavenly citizenship
Php 3:20–21 But our citizenship is in heaven. And we eagerly await a Saviour from there, the Lord Jesus Christ, who, by the power that enables him to bring everything under his control, will transform our lowly bodies so that they will be like his glorious body. *See also* **Eph** 2:19; **Col** 3:1–2; **Heb** 12:22–24

Inheritance from God
Ro 8:17 Now if we are children, then we are heirs—heirs of God and co-heirs with Christ, if indeed we share in his sufferings in order that we may also share in his glory. *See also* **Col** 1:12; **Rev** 21:7

Peace with God
Eph 2:13–17 But now in Christ Jesus you who once were far away have been brought near through the blood of Christ. For he himself is our peace, who has made the two one and has destroyed the barrier, the dividing wall of hostility, by abolishing in his flesh the law with its commandments and regulations. His purpose was to create in himself one new humanity out of the two, thus making peace, and in this one body to reconcile both of them to God through the cross, by which he put to death their hostility. He came and preached peace to you who were far away and peace to those who were near. *See also* **Isa** 53:5; **Jn** 16:33; **Ro** 5:1–2; **Col** 3:15

Righteousness in the sight of God
Ro 1:17 For in the gospel a righteousness from God is revealed, a righteousness that is by faith from first to last, just as it is written: "The righteous will live by faith." *See also* **Isa** 61:10; **Ro** 3:22; 4:3–13,25–5:1; **1Co** 1:30; **2Co** 5:21; **Php** 3:8–9; **2Ti** 4:8; **Heb** 11:7

Salvation as a change in a person's nature

Becoming a new creation
2Co 5:17 Therefore, if anyone is in Christ, there is a new creation: the old has gone, the new has come! *See also* **Ro** 6:4; **Gal** 6:14–15; **Eph** 2:15

Deliverance from God's righteous condemnation
Ro 8:1–2 Therefore, there is now no condemnation for those who are in Christ Jesus, because through Christ Jesus the law of the Spirit of life set me free from the law of sin and death. *See also* **Isa** 50:8; **Ro** 5:15–17; 8:33–39; **Col** 1:22

Deliverance from the power of sin and evil
Gal 1:3–4 Grace and peace to you [Galatian believers] from God our Father and the Lord Jesus Christ, who gave himself for our sins to rescue us from the present evil age, according to the will of our God and Father, *See also* **Ro** 6:14; 7:21–25; 8:2–4; **1Pe** 2:24; **Rev** 1:5

Inner personal renewal
1Jn 1:7 But if we walk in the light, as he is in the light, we have fellowship with one another, and the blood of Jesus, his Son, purifies us from all sin. *See also* **Ps** 51:1–2,7; **Heb** 1:3; 10:19–22

salvation, necessity of 240

New birth
Jn 3:3–7 . . . Jesus declared, "I tell you the truth, no-one can see the kingdom of God without being born again." "How can anyone be born in old age?" Nicodemus asked. "Surely they cannot enter a second time into their mother's womb to be born!" Jesus answered, "I tell you the truth, no-one can enter the kingdom of God without being born of water and the Spirit. Flesh gives birth to flesh, but the Spirit gives birth to spirit. You should not be surprised at my saying, 'You must be born again.'" *See also* **Jas** 1:18; **1Pe** 1:23; **1Jn** 3:9

The presence of the Holy Spirit
Ro 8:10–11 But if Christ is in you, your body is dead because of sin, yet your spirit is alive because of righteousness. And if the Spirit of him who raised Jesus from the dead is living in you, he who raised Christ from the dead will also give life to your mortal bodies through his Spirit, who lives in you. *See also* **Gal** 5:2–25 *See also access to God; forgiveness; grace and salvation; Holy Spirit and regeneration; Holy Spirit, indwelling.*

---

salvation, necessity of

Scripture stresses that fallen human beings are cut off from God on account of their sin. All need to be saved, if they are to enter into a new relationship with God as their Creator and Redeemer. Salvation is not the result of human achievement, privilege or wisdom, but depends totally upon the graciousness of a loving God, supremely expressed in the cross of Jesus Christ. People must respond in repentance and faith if they are to benefit from God's offer of salvation in Christ.

The necessity of salvation
The universal rule of sin in human nature Isa 64:6; **Ro** 3:19–23; 5:12–18; 7:24; **Eph** 2:3
Sin cuts humanity off from God
Isa 59:1–2 Surely the arm of the Lord is not too short to save, nor his ear too dull to hear. But your iniquities have separated you from your God; your sins have hidden his face from you, so that he will not hear. *See also* **Ge** 3:22–24; **Eph** 2:1–5; 4:18

Sin enslaves humanity to evil Jer 13:23; **Hos** 5:4; **Zec** 7:11–12; **Ro** 7:14–20; **2Pe** 2:13–19

Salvation is grounded in the love of God
Salvation is not based on human achievement
Ro 3:28 For we maintain that a person is justified by faith apart from observing the law.
Eph 2:8–9 For it is by grace you have been saved, through faith—and this not from yourselves, it is the gift of God—not by works, so that no-one can boast. *See also* **Ac** 15:7–11; **Ro** 4:1–3; 5:1–2; **Gal** 2:16,21; **2Ti** 1:9
Salvation is grounded in God's love for his people
Eph 2:4–5 But because of his great love for us, God, who is rich in mercy, made us alive with Christ even when we were dead in transgressions—it is by grace you have been saved. *See also* **Dt** 7:1–8; **Jn** 3:16–17; **Ro** 5:8; **2Th** 2:16; **1Jn** 4:9–19
Salvation is grounded in God's grace
Ro 3:22–24 This righteousness from God comes through faith in Jesus Christ to all who believe. There is no difference, for all have sinned and fall short of the glory of God, and are justified freely by his grace through the redemption that came by Christ Jesus. *See also* **Jn** 1:16; **Ac** 15:11; **Ro** 5:15–17; **2Co** 6:1–2; **Eph** 1:5–8; 2:4–10; **1Ti** 1:14–15; **Tit** 2:11; 3:4–7; **Heb** 2:9

Salvation and the work of Jesus Christ
Salvation is grounded in the work of Jesus Christ
Ac 5:30–31 The God of our ancestors raised Jesus from the dead—whom you had killed by hanging him on a tree. God exalted him to his own right hand as Prince and Saviour that he might give repentance and forgiveness of sins to Israel.

1Ti 1:15 Here is a trustworthy saying that deserves full acceptance: Christ Jesus came into the world to save sinners—of whom I [Paul] am the worst. *See also* **Jn** 4:42; **Ac** 4:10–12; **Ro** 5:9–10; **Php** 3:20–21; **2Ti** 1:9–10; **Tit** 3:5–7; **Heb** 7:24–25; **1Jn** 4:14

Jesus Christ's death was totally sufficient for salvation
1Pe 3:18 For Christ died for sins once for all, the righteous for the unrighteous, to bring you to God. He was put to death in the body but made alive by the Spirit, *See also* **Jn** 17:1–4; **Ac** 4:10–12; **Gal** 1:3–4; **Eph** 1:5–10; **1Ti** 2:5–6; **2Ti** 1:9–10; **Heb** 10:10; **1Jn** 4:9–10; **Rev** 7:9–10

Salvation demands a human decision
Jn 3:36 "Those who believe in the Son have eternal life, but those who reject the Son will not see life, for God's wrath remains on them."
Ac 3:19 "Repent, then, and turn to God, so that your sins may be wiped out, that times of refreshing may come from the Lord," *See also* **Mk** 1:15; **Lk** 8:50; **Jn** 3:17–18; **Ac** 2:37–39; **Heb** 12:25; **1Pe** 2:4–8; **1Jn** 5:10 *See also faith and salvation; God as Saviour; God, love of; gospel; human race and redemption; Jesus Christ as Saviour; Jesus Christ, responses to; repentance; sin, deliverance from.*

Scripture
The biblical writings, inspired by the Holy Spirit, have been entrusted to the church to remind it of the central teachings of the gospel, to guard it from error and to enable it to grow into holiness. The church is required to be obedient to Scripture and revere it as the Word of God.

Scripture, inspiration and authority
Those writings that are acknowledged to be the word of God to be revered as issuing from him and as having his authority.

Recognition of a body of sacred writings
In the OT
Ne 8:1 all the people assembled with one accord in the square before the Water Gate. They told Ezra the scribe to bring out the Book of the Law of Moses, which the LORD had commanded for Israel. *See also* **Ex** 24:7; **Jos** 8:34; **2Ki** 22:8 pp **2Ch** 34:14; **2Ki** 23:2 pp **2Ch** 34:30; **2Ch** 35:12; **Ezr** 6:18; **Ne** 8:8; 9:3; 13:1

By Jesus Christ
Mt 22:29 Jesus replied, "You [Sadducees] are in error because you do not know the Scriptures or the power of God." *See also* **Lk** 4:21; 24:27,45
Mt 21:13 "It is written," he [Jesus] said to them, ' "My house will be called a house of prayer,' but you are making it a 'den of robbers'." pp **Lk** 19:46 *See also* **Isa** 56:7; **Jer** 7:11; **Mt** 4:4 pp **Lk** 4:4; **Dt** 8:3; **Mt** 4:7 pp **Lk** 4:12; **Dt** 6:16; **Mt** 4:10 pp **Lk** 4:8; **Dt** 6:13; **Mt** 21:42 pp **Mk** 12:10; **Ps** 118:22–23; **Mt** 26:31 pp **Mk** 14:27; **Zec** 13:7; **Mk** 7:6–7; **Isa** 29:13; **Lk** 7:27; **Mal** 3:1; **Jn** 7:38

By the apostles
2Ti 3:14–15 But as for you [Timothy], continue in what you have learned and have become convinced of, because you know those from whom you learned it, and how from infancy you have known the holy Scriptures, which are able to make you wise for salvation through faith in Christ Jesus. *See also* **Ac** 1:15–17; **Ro** 1:1–2; 15:4; **1Co** 15:3–4; **2Ti** 3:16–17

By the early church **Ac** 17:11

The inspiration of Scripture
2Ti 3:16 All Scripture is God-breathed . . .
See also **2Ki** 17:13–14; **Ne** 9:30; **Mt** 22:43–44 pp **Mk** 12:36; **1Co** 2:13; **Heb** 1:1–2; **1Pe** 1:10–11; **2Pe** 1:20–21

The authority of Scripture recognised in the OT
Ps 119:89 Your word, O LORD, is eternal; it stands firm in the heavens.
Jos 23:6 "be careful to obey all that is written in the Book of the Law of Moses, without turning aside to the right or to the left." *See also* **Jos** 1:8; **2Ki** 22:11; **Ezr** 10:1–4,9–12; **Ne** 13:1–3; **Isa** 40:8

The authority of Scripture recognised in the NT
Jn 10:34–36 ". . . the Scripture cannot be broken . . ." *See also* **Mt** 5:17–19; **Lk** 21:21–23; 16:17; **1Th** 2:13

Jesus Christ claims scriptural authority for his own words
Mt 24:34–35 ". . . Heaven and earth will pass away, but my words will never pass away." pp Mk 13:30–31 *See also* **Jn** 12:47–50; 14:10,23–24 *See also* Holy Spirit and Scripture; Holy Spirit, inspiration; Jesus Christ, attitude to Old Testament; law, Jesus Christ's attitude; revelation; word of God.

Scripture, purpose
Scripture has been given by God to lead people to faith and salvation. Through Scripture believers are nurtured in faith and led to spiritual maturity.

Scripture is intended to lead people to salvation
2Ti 3:14–15 . . . the holy Scriptures . . . are able to make you wise for salvation through faith in Christ Jesus. *See also* **Ps 19:7–11**; **Jn** 20:30–31; **Ro** 10:8

Scripture is intended to lead believers to maturity in faith
By its teaching
2Ti 3:16 All Scripture is God-breathed and is useful for teaching . . . *See also* **Dt** 6:6–9; **Ps** 19:7–8; 119:9,130; **Col** 3:16
By its rebuke and correction
2Ti 3:16 All Scripture is God-breathed and is useful for . . . rebuking, correcting . . . *See also* **Ps** 19:11–13; **1Co** 10:11–12; **Heb** 4:12–13
By training in righteousness
2Ti 3:16 All Scripture is God-breathed and is useful for . . . training in righteousness . . . *See also* **Dt** 29:29
By its illumination
Ps 119:105 Your [the LORD's] word is a lamp to my feet and a light for my path.
Ps 119:130 The unfolding of your [the LORD's] words gives light; it gives understanding to the simple. *See also* **2Pe** 1:19; **1Jn** 2:8
By its encouragement and reassurance
Ro 15:4 For everything that was written in the past was written to teach us, so that through endurance and the encouragement of the Scriptures we might have hope.

1Jn 5:13 I write these things to you who believe in the name of the Son of God so that you may know that you have eternal life.
See also **Ps** 19:8–9; 119:50–51,76; **Heb** 12:5–6
By its record of God's promises
1Ki 8:56 ". . . Not one word has failed of all the good promises he [the LORD] gave through his servant Moses."
Ps 119:140 Your [the LORD's] promises have been thoroughly tested, and your servant loves them. *See also* **Eze** 12:25; **Lk** 24:44; **2Co** 1:19–22
By its trustworthiness
1Ki 17:24 Then the woman said to Elijah, "Now I know that you are a man of God and that the word of the LORD from your mouth is the truth."
Ps 19:7–11 The law of the LORD is perfect, reviving the soul. The statutes of the LORD are trustworthy, making wise the simple . . .
Ps 33:4 For the word of the LORD is right and true; he is faithful in all he does. *See also* **Ps** 119:151,160; **Jn** 21:24; **Rev** 21:5

Scripture is essential for spiritual growth and maturity
Ps 1:1–3 Blessed are those who do not walk in the counsel of the wicked or stand in the way of sinners or sit in the seat of mockers. But their delight is in the law of the LORD, and on his law they meditate day and night. The are like trees planted by streams of water, which yield their fruit in season and whose leaves do not wither. Whatever they do prospers. *See also* **Mt** 4:4; **Jn** 15:5–8; 17:17; **Eph** 6:10–17; **2Ti** 3:14–17
See also faith; God, will of; salvation.

Scripture, sufficiency
Scripture is presented as being of itself sufficient for faith and for life.

God's written revelation is sufficient
Dt 4:1–2 Hear now, O Israel, the decrees and laws I [Moses] am about to teach you. Follow them so that you may live and may go in and take possession of the land that the LORD, the God of your ancestors, is giving you. Do not add

to what I command you and do not subtract from it, but keep the commands of the LORD your God that I give you.   See also **Dt** 12:32; **Jos** 1:7–8; **Pr** 30:5–6; **Jer** 26:2

The NT records the completion and fulfilment of the OT
Heb 1:1–2 In the past God spoke to our ancestors through the prophets at many times and in various ways, but in these last days he has spoken to us by his Son, whom he appointed heir of all things, and through whom he made the universe.   See also **Jn** 12:47–50; **Eph** 2:20

Warnings against turning from, or adding to, the apostolic gospel, as set forth in Scripture
Rev 22:18–19 I [Jesus] warn everyone who hears the words of the prophecy of this book: If any one of you adds anything to them, God will add to you the plagues described in this book. And if any one of you takes words away from this book of prophecy, God will take away from you your share in the tree of life and in the holy city, which are described in this book.
See also **Gal** 1:6–9; **Col** 1:25–2:8,18,20–23; **2Th** 2:1–2

Descriptions of Scripture point to its sufficiency
Scripture is good
Ro 7:12 So then, the law is holy, and the commandment is holy, righteous and good.
See also **1Ti** 1:8
Scripture is perfect
Ps 19:7 The law of the LORD is perfect, reviving the soul . . .   See also **Ps** 119:142; **Jas** 1:25
Scripture is eternal
Ps 119:89 Your word, O LORD, is eternal; it stands firm in the heavens.   See also **Mt** 5:18; 24:35; **1Pe** 1:24–25; **Isa** 40:6–8   See also *gospel*.

Scripture, understanding
God intends his word to be understood and has provided the directions and means for understanding it.

Scripture is intended to be clearly understood
It is accessible to ordinary people
Ps 119:130 The unfolding of your [the LORD's] words gives light; it gives understanding to the simple.   See also **Ps** 19:7
Some sections are difficult to understand
2Pe 3:15–16 Bear in mind that our Lord's patience means salvation, just as our dear brother Paul also wrote to you with the wisdom that God gave him. He writes the same way in all his letters, speaking in them of these matters. His letters contain some things that are hard to understand, which ignorant and unstable people distort, as they do the other Scriptures, to their own destruction.   See also **Heb** 5:11

God has prescribed the way to understand Scripture
Through public reading
1Ti 4:13 Until I come, devote yourself to the public reading of Scripture, to preaching and to teaching.   See also **Ne** 8:2–8; 13:1–3
Through diligent study
2Ti 2:15 Do your best to present yourself to God as one approved, a worker who does not need to be ashamed and who correctly handles the word of truth.   See also **Dt** 17:18–20; **Ac** 17:11
Through thoughtful meditation
Ps 1:1–3 . . . their [the righteous] delight is in the law of the LORD, and on his law they meditate day and night . . .   See also **Jos** 1:8; **Job** 23:12; **Ps** 119:15,27,48,97,148

Assistance in understanding through the Holy Spirit
1Co 2:9–12 However, as it is written: "No eye has seen, no ear has heard, no mind has conceived what God has prepared for those who love him"—but God has revealed it to us [believers] by his Spirit . . .   See also **Isa** 64:4; **Lk** 24:45; **Jn** 14:26; 16:13; **1Jn** 2:27

Assistance in understanding through ministers of the word
Ne 8:2–8 . . . They [the Levites] read from the

Book of the Law of God, making it clear and giving the meaning so that the people could understand what was being read.   See also **Eph 4:11–14; 1Ti 4:11–16; 2Ti 4:1–5**   See also *Holy Spirit, teacher, prayer.*

signs
Miraculous or supernatural confirmations of the existence and power of God or the miraculous demonstration of spiritual authority on the part of an individual.

signs, kinds of
Signs are miraculous events, supernatural phenomena or everyday things that are given a special significance. The term is used in John's Gospel to describe the miracles of Jesus Christ.

Miraculous signs
2Co 12:12 The things that mark an apostle—signs, wonders and miracles—were done among you with great perseverance.   See also **Ex 10:1; Ps 78:43; 105:27; Mt 24:24 pp Mk 13:22; Mk 16:17; Ac 2:43; Ro 15:19**

The signs of Jesus Christ in John's Gospel
Jn 2:11 This, the first of his miraculous signs, Jesus performed at Cana in Galilee. He thus revealed his glory, and his disciples put their faith in him.   See also **Jn 6:26; 9:16; 11:47**

Jesus Christ refers to Jonah as a sign
Mt 12:39–41 pp Lk 11:29–32

Prophetic signs
Ex 3:12 And God said, "I will be with you. And this will be the sign to you that it is I who have sent you: When you have brought the people out of Egypt, you will worship God on this mountain."   See also **1Sa 10:7–9; 1Ki 13:1–5; 2Ki 19:29 pp Isa 37:30; Isa 7:14–17; 8:18; 19:19–20; Lk 2:12**

Signs of protection
Ex 12:13,23; Jos 2:12–13,17–21

Signs given to guarantee promises
The rainbow
Ge 9:12 And God said, "This is the sign of the covenant I am making between me and you and every living creature with you, a covenant for all generations to come."   See also **Ge 9:13–17**
Circumcision
Ge 17:10–11 ". . . You are to undergo circumcision, and it will be the sign of the covenant between me and you."   See also **Ge 17:12–14; Ro 4:11**

Signs serve as reminders of past blessings
Monuments Jos 4:4–7
Religious observances
Passover: **Ex 13:9,16**
Sabbath: **Ex 31:12–17; Eze 20:12,20**

Signs associated with the birth of Jesus Christ
The virgin birth
Isa 7:14 "Therefore the Lord himself will give you a sign: The virgin will be with child and will give birth to a son, and will call him Immanuel."   See also **Mt 1:22–23; Lk 1:34–36**
The birthplace
Lk 2:12 "This will be a sign to you: You will find a baby wrapped in cloths and lying in a manger."   See also **Lk 2:7,16**
The star
Mt 2:1–2 After Jesus was born in Bethlehem in Judea, during the time of King Herod, Magi from the east came to Jerusalem and asked, "Where is the one who has been born king of the Jews? We saw his star in the east and have come to worship him."   See also **Mt 2:9–10**

Signs associated with the death of Jesus Christ
Darkness at midday
Mt 27:45 From the sixth hour until the ninth hour darkness came over all the land. pp Mk 15:33 pp Lk 23:44–45   See also **Am 8:9**
The curtain of the temple torn in two
Mt 27:51 . . . the curtain of the temple was torn in two from top to bottom. The earth shook

and the rocks split. pp Mk 15:38 pp Lk 23:45
The dead came back to life
Mt 27:51-53 ... The tombs broke open and the bodies of many holy people who had died were raised to life. They came out of the tombs, and after Jesus' resurrection they went into the holy city and appeared to many people.

Signs associated with the coming of the Holy Spirit
The sound like a violent wind
Ac 2:2 Suddenly a sound like the blowing of a violent wind came from heaven and filled the whole house where they were sitting.
Tongues of fire
Ac 2:3 They saw what seemed to be tongues of fire that separated and came to rest on each of them.
Speaking in other languages
Ac 2:4 All of them were filled with the Holy Spirit and began to speak in other tongues as the Spirit enabled them. *See also* **Ac** 2:5-11

Signs associated with the second coming of Jesus Christ
General signs
Mt 24:3-8 "... All these are the beginning of birth-pains." pp Mk 13:4-8 pp Lk 21:7-11
Signs preceding the second coming Mt 24:9-24 pp Mk 13:9-22 pp Lk 21:12-24
Signs simultaneous with the second coming Mt 24:27-31 pp Mk 13:24-27 pp Lk 21:25-27; **Lk** 17:24; **Ac** 2:19-20; **Joel** 2:30-31; **2Pe** 3:12-13

False signs
Dt 13:1-3 If a prophet, or one who foretells by dreams, appears among you and announces to you a miraculous sign or wonder, and if the sign or wonder spoken of takes place, and the prophet says, "Let us follow other gods" (gods you have not known) "and let us worship them," you must not listen to the words of that prophet or dreamer ... *See also* **Isa** 44:25; **Mt** 24:24 pp Mk 13:22; **2Th** 2:9; **Rev** 13:11-14; 16:14; 19:20   *See also* Holy Spirit, gift of; Jesus Christ, birth of; Jesus Christ, death of; Jesus Christ, miracles; Jesus Christ, preaching and teaching; Jesus Christ, second coming; miracles, nature of.

signs, purposes
Signs are given to confirm God's word. They may warn the rebellious or encourage the faithful. People may seek signs as a result of a genuine desire to serve God.

Signs are given to demonstrate God's power
Dt 34:10-12 ... For no-one has ever shown the mighty power or performed the awesome deeds that Moses did in the sight of all Israel.
See also **Dt** 4:34; 6:21-22; 7:19; 26:8; **1Ch** 16:11-12 pp Ps 105:4-5; **Jer** 32:21

Signs demonstrate the authority of God's servants
Moses and Aaron
Ex 4:1-9 ... Then the LORD said, "If they do not believe you or pay attention to the first miraculous sign, they may believe the second. But if they do not believe these two signs or listen to you, take some water from the Nile and pour it on the dry ground. The water you take from the river will become blood on the ground."
See also **Ex** 4:30-31; 7:8-12; **Nu** 17:1-9; **Ac** 7:36
Elijah 1Ki 18:36-38
Elisha 2Ki 2:13-14
Jesus Christ
Ac 2:22 "People of Israel, listen to this: Jesus of Nazareth was a man accredited by God to you by miracles, wonders and signs, which God did among you through him, as you yourselves know." *See also* **Jn** 2:23; 3:2; 7:21; 20:30
The apostles
2Co 12:12 The things that mark an apostle— signs, wonders and miracles—were done among you ... *See also* **Ac** 2:43; 5:12; 15:12

Signs may accompany the preaching of the gospel
Heb 2:3-4 ... This salvation, which was first announced by the Lord, was confirmed to us by those who heard him. God also testified to it by signs, wonders and various miracles, and gifts of the Holy Spirit distributed according to his will.
See also **Mk** 16:20; **Ac** 8:6; 14:3

Signs may warn the ungodly of impending judgment
Ex 8:22–23 " 'But on that day I will deal differently with the land of Goshen, where my people live; no swarms of flies will be there, so that you will know that I, the LORD, am in this land. I will make a distinction between my people and your people. This miraculous sign will occur tomorrow.' "

The prophets often acted out their messages for greater effect: **Isa 20:**1–4; **Eze 4:**1–3; 12:3–6,11; 24:15–24
Jer 44:29–30; **Lk** 2:34; **Php** 1:28

Signs may warn God's people against rebellion
Nu 17:10 The LORD said to Moses, "Put back Aaron's staff in front of the Testimony, to be kept as a sign to the rebellious. This will put an end to their grumbling against me, so that they will not die." *See also* **Nu** 16:38; 26:10; **Dt** 28:45–46; **1Sa** 2:34; 12:16–18

Signs may encourage faith
By giving guidance
1Sa 14:8–10 Jonathan said, "Come, then; we will cross over towards them and let them see us. If they say to us, 'Wait there until we come to you,' we will stay where we are and not go up to them. But if they say, 'Come up to us,' we will climb up, because that will be our sign that the LORD has given them into our hands." *See also* **Ge** 24:10–14; **Ex** 13:21–22; **2Sa** 5:23–24 pp 1Ch 14:14–15; **Mt** 2:9–10

By giving assurance of God's presence
Jdg 6:17–22 Gideon replied, "If now I have found favour in your eyes, give me a sign that it is really you talking to me . . ." *See also* **Ge** 28:10–17; **Ex** 3:1–5

By encouraging the fearful and doubting
Isa 38:7–8 " 'This is the LORD's sign to you that the LORD will do what he has promised: I will make the shadow cast by the sun go back the ten steps it has gone down on the stairway of Ahaz.' " So the sunlight went back the ten steps it had gone down. pp 2Ki 20:8–11 pp 2Ch 32:24 *See also* **Dt** 7:17–19; **Jdg** 6:36–40; **2Ki** 6:15–17

Signs need hold no terror for the godly
Jer 10:2 This is what the LORD says: "Do not learn the ways of the nations or be terrified by signs in the sky, though the nations are terrified by them." *See also* **Mt** 24:6 pp Mk 13:7 pp Lk 21:9

Seeking signs
When seeking signs is acceptable to God
Isa 7:11 "Ask the LORD your God for a sign, whether in the deepest depths or in the highest heights." *See also* **Jdg** 6:17; **Isa** 38:22

When seeking signs is condemned by God
Mt 16:1–4 ". . . A wicked and adulterous generation looks for a miraculous sign, but none will be given it except the sign of Jonah." Jesus then left them and went away. pp Mk 8:11–12 *See also* **Mt** 12:38–39 pp Lk 11:29; **Lk** 11:16; 12:54–56; 23:8; **Jn** 2:18; 4:48; 6:30; **1Co** 1:22
See also God, power of; Jesus Christ, authority; miracles; word of God.

---

sin
Primarily a wrong relationship with God, which may express itself in wrong attitudes or actions towards God himself, other human beings, possessions or the environment. Scripture stresses that this condition is deeply rooted in human nature, and that only God is able to break its penalty, power and presence.

---

sin and God's character
In his righteousness and holiness, God detests sin and its effects upon humanity. In his mercy and grace, he makes available a means of atonement, by the death and resurrection of Jesus Christ.

God's character and sin
God himself is perfect
Hab 1:13 Your eyes are too pure to look on evil; you cannot tolerate wrong . . .
1Jn 1:5 . . . God is light; in him there is no darkness at all. *See also* **Dt** 32:4; **Jos** 24:19; **Ps** 97:2; **Isa** 6:3

Jesus Christ is sinless
1Pe 2:22 "He committed no sin, and no deceit

was found in his mouth." *See also* **Isa** 53:9; **2Co** 5:21; **Heb** 1:9; 7:26–27; **1Jn** 3:5

God's people are to be holy
1Pe 1:15–16 But just as he who called you is holy, so be holy in all you do; for it is written: "Be holy, because I am holy." *See also* **Lev** 11:44,45; 19:2; 20:7; **Mt** 5:48; **1Th** 4:7; **1Jn** 3:3

God's attitude to sin
God knows all sin
Jer 16:17 "My eyes are on all their ways; they are not hidden from me, nor is their sin concealed from my eyes." *See also* **Job** 10:14; **Ps** 139:1–4; **Jer** 2:22; **Hos** 7:2; **Am** 5:12; **Heb** 4:13

God grieves over sin
Ge 6:6 The LORD was grieved that he had made human beings on the earth, and his heart was filled with pain. *See also* **Isa** 63:10; **Eph** 4:30

God hates sin
Ps 11:5 The LORD examines the righteous, but the wicked and those who love violence his soul hates. *See also* **Dt** 25:16; **2Sa** 11:27; **Ps** 5:5; **Pr** 6:16–19; **Zec** 8:17; **Lk** 16:15

Sin provokes God's anger
Ro 1:18 The wrath of God is being revealed from heaven against all the godlessness and wickedness of those . . . *See also* **2Ch** 36:16; **Eze** 20:8; **Am** 1:3; **Jn** 3:36; **Eph** 5:5–6; **Col** 3:5–6

God is also merciful and gracious
Ex 34:6–7 . . . "The LORD, the LORD, the compassionate and gracious God, slow to anger, abounding in love and faithfulness, maintaining love to thousands, and forgiving wickedness, rebellion and sin . . ." *See also* **Ne** 9:17,31; **Ps** 78:38; 103:8–14; **La** 3:22–23; **Mic** 7:18–19; **Ro** 11:32

God's patience with sinners
2Pe 3:9 . . . He is patient with you, not wanting anyone to perish, but everyone to come to repentance. *See also* **Ro** 2:4; 9:22; **1Ti** 1:16

Jesus Christ is the supreme revelation of God's love for sinners
Jesus Christ's ministry of forgiveness
1Ti 1:15 . . . Christ Jesus came into the world to save sinners . . . *See also* **Mt** 9:2 pp **Mk** 2:5 pp **Lk** 5:20–21; **Lk** 7:36–50; 15:1–10; 19:5–10; **Jn** 8:1–11

God's love shown in Jesus Christ's death
Ro 5:8 But God demonstrates his own love for us in this: While we were still sinners, Christ died for us. *See also* **Jn** 3:16–17; **Eph** 2:4; **1Pe** 3:18; **1Jn** 4:9–10

The risen Christ gives grace to sinful people
1Jn 2:1 . . . But if anybody does sin, we have one who speaks to the Father in our defence—Jesus Christ, the Righteous One. *See also* **Ro** 8:34; **Heb** 2:17–18; 4:15–5:2 *See also* God, all-knowing; God, anger of; God, grace and mercy; God, holiness of; God, love of; God, righteousness; grace; Jesus Christ, compassion; Jesus Christ, perfection.

---

sin, avoidance
God calls his people to avoid sin, and through Jesus Christ gives them the inner power to be victorious over it.

God's people are to resist sin
1Pe 2:11 Dear friends, I urge you, as aliens and strangers in the world, to abstain from sinful desires, which war against your soul. *See also* **Ps** 97:10; **Pr** 4:23–27; **1Co** 15:34; **Eph** 4:25–5:20; **Jas** 1:21

The Christian life is a constant struggle against sin
Heb 3:13 . . . so that none of you may be hardened by sin's deceitfulness. *See also* **Ac** 20:28; **Ro** 7:14–25; **Eph** 6:10–18; **1Pe** 5:8–9

God helps his people to resist sin
Release from sin through Jesus Christ's death
1Pe 2:24 He himself bore our sins in his body on the tree, so that we might die to sins and live for righteousness; by his wounds you have been healed. *See also* **Ro** 6:1–7; **Gal** 2:20; 5:24; **Col** 2:11–12

The avoidance of sin through new life in Jesus Christ
1Jn 3:9 Those who are born of God will not continue to sin, because God's seed remains in them; they cannot go on sinning, because they have been born of God. *See also* **2Co** 5:17; **1Pe** 1:23; **1Jn** 3:6; 5:18

sin, avoidance

Believers co-operate with Jesus Christ to avoid sin
Php 2:12–13 . . . continue to work out your salvation with fear and trembling, for it is God who works in you to will and to act according to his good purpose.

Believers are to put to death what is sinful in them
Col 3:5 Put to death, therefore, whatever belongs to your earthly nature: sexual immorality, impurity, lust, evil desires and greed, which is idolatry. *See also* **Ro** 6:11–14; 8:13

Believers are to exchange sinful for righteous behaviour
Ro 13:12–14 The night is nearly over; the day is almost here. So let us put aside the deeds of darkness and put on the armour of light . . .
See also **Eph** 4:22–24; **Col** 3:7–10; **1Ti** 6:11; **2Ti** 2:22

Believers are to allow the Spirit to inform and direct their conduct
Ro 12:2 Do not conform any longer to the pattern of this world, but be transformed by the renewing of your mind. Then you will be able to test and approve what God's will is—his good, pleasing and perfect will. *See also* **Ro** 8:5–8; **Gal** 5:16–25

Practical steps for overcoming sin and temptation
Meditation on Scripture
Ps 119:11 I have hidden your word in my heart that I might not sin against you. *See also* **Ps** 18:22–23; **Mt** 4:1–11 pp **Lk** 4:1–13; **2Ti** 3:16–17

Prayerful dependence upon God
Mt 6:13 "'And lead us not into temptation, but deliver us from the evil one . . .'" pp **Lk** 11:4 *See also* **Ps** 19:13; **Mt** 26:41; **1Co** 10:13; **Heb** 4:15–16

Active seeking of the good
Ro 6:19 . . . Just as you used to offer the parts of your body in slavery to impurity and to ever-increasing wickedness, so now offer them in slavery to righteousness leading to holiness.
See also **Ps** 34:14; **Isa** 1:16–17; **Am** 5:14–15; **1Th** 5:22; **3Jn** 11

Incentives for avoiding sin
The fear of God
Pr 16:6 . . . through the fear of the LORD evil is avoided. *See also* **Ex** 20:20; **Pr** 3:7; 8:13

The holiness of God
1Pe 1:15–16 But just as he who called you is holy, so be holy in all you do; for it is written: "Be holy, because I am holy." *See also* **Lev** 11:44–45; 19:2; 20:7; **1Co** 6:18–20; **1Th** 4:7

The expectation of Jesus Christ's return
1Pe 4:7 The end of all things is near. Therefore be clear minded and self-controlled so that you can pray. *See also* **2Co** 5:9–10; **1Th** 5:4–6; **2Pe** 3:10–14

A consideration of the consequences of sin
Gal 6:7–8 Do not be deceived: God cannot be mocked. People reap what they sow. Those who sow to please their sinful nature, from that nature will reap destruction; those who sow to please the Spirit, from the Spirit will reap eternal life.
See also **Mk** 9:42–48; **Ro** 6:21–23; **Heb** 6:7–8; 10:26–31

The need to be a good witness to unbelievers
1Pe 2:15 For it is God's will that by doing good you should silence the ignorant talk of foolish people. *See also* **1Pe** 3:1–2,15–16

The role of others in avoiding sin
Bad company is to be avoided
1Co 15:33 Do not be misled: "Bad company corrupts good character." *See also* **Dt** 7:1–4; **Ps** 1:1; **Pr** 1:10; **1Co** 5:1–13

A good example is to be followed
1Co 11:1 Follow my [Paul's] example, as I follow the example of Christ. *See also* **Php** 3:17; 4:9; **Heb** 12:1–3; **1Pe** 4:1–3

Believers are to support one another
Jas 5:19–20 My brothers and sisters, if one of you should wander from the truth and someone should bring that person back, remember this: Those who turn sinners from the error of their ways will save them from death and cover over a multitude of sins. *See also* **Mt** 18:15–17; **Gal** 6:1–2; **1Ti** 5:20; **Heb** 3:12 *See also* holiness; Holy Spirit and sanctification; Jesus Christ, high priest; Jesus Christ, holiness.

sin, deliverance from

The gospel reveals the purpose and power of God to deal with sin and all of its effects. Scripture uses a range of images to express the comprehensiveness of salvation.

God's removal of sin

Atonement for sin
Isa 6:7 With it [a live coal] he touched my mouth and said, "See, this has touched your lips; your guilt is taken away and your sin atoned for." *See also* **Ex** 32:30; **Lev** 4:27–31; **Pr** 16:6; **Ro** 3:25; **Heb** 2:17

Forgiveness of sin
Mic 7:18 Who is a God like you, who pardons sin and forgives the transgression of the remnant of his inheritance? You do not stay angry for ever but delight to show mercy.

Ac 13:38 "Therefore, my brothers and sisters, I want you to know that through Jesus the forgiveness of sins is proclaimed to you."
See also **1Ki** 8:35–36; **2Ch** 30:18–20; **Ps** 103:2–3; **Isa** 33:24; 55:7; **Joel** 3:21; **Mt** 26:27–28; **Lk** 24:46–47; **Eph** 1:7; **1Jn** 1:9

Cancellation of a debt
Mt 6:12 "'Forgive us our debts, as we also have forgiven our debtors.'" *See also* **Mt** 18:21–35; **Lk** 7:41–50

A covering over of sin
1Pe 4:8 Above all, love each other deeply, because love covers over a multitude of sins.
See also **Ps** 32:1; 85:2; **Jas** 5:20

The taking away of sin
Ps 103:12 as far as the east is from the west, so far has he removed our transgressions from us. *See also* **2Sa** 12:13; **Isa** 6:6–7; **Zec** 3:4; **Jn** 1:29; **Heb** 9:28; **1Jn** 3:5

Remembering sin no more
Isa 43:25 "I [the LORD], even I, am he who blots out your transgressions, for my own sake, and remembers your sins no more." *See also* **Ps** 25:7; **Jer** 31:33–34; **2Co** 5:19

God's deliverance for the sinner

The salvation of the sinner
1Ti 1:15 Here is a trustworthy saying that deserves full acceptance: Christ Jesus came into the world to save sinners—of whom I am the worst. *See also* **Ps** 28:8–9; **Mt** 1:21; **Lk** 19:9–10; **Jn** 3:17; **Heb** 7:25

The image of healing
Lk 5:31–32 Jesus answered them [Pharisees and teachers of the law], "It is not the healthy who need a doctor, but the sick. I have not come to call the righteous, but sinners to repentance."
pp **Mt** 9:12 pp **Mk** 2:17 *See also* **2Ch** 7:14; **Isa** 53:5; 57:18–19; **Hos** 14:4; **1Pe** 2:24

The image of cleansing
Ps 51:2 Wash away all my iniquity and cleanse me from my sin. *See also* **Lev** 16:30; **Eze** 36:25; **Jn** 13:1–11; **Heb** 10:22; **Ac** 22:16; **1Jn** 1:9

Redemption by God
Ps 130:8 He himself will redeem Israel from all their sins. *See also* **Isa** 44:22; **Tit** 2:14; **1Pe** 1:18–19

Justification before God
Gal 2:16 "... a person is not justified by observing the law, but by faith in Jesus Christ. So we, too, have put our faith in Christ Jesus that we may be justified by faith in Christ and not by observing the law, because by observing the law no-one will be justified." *See also* **Isa** 53:11; **Ro** 3:24–26; 4:5,25; 5:16–19; 8:33

Freedom from condemnation
Ro 8:1 Therefore, there is now no condemnation for those who are in Christ Jesus ... *See also* **Jn** 3:18; 8:3–11; **Ro** 8:34

Peace with God
Ro 5:1 Therefore, since we have been justified through faith, we have peace with God through our Lord Jesus Christ. *See also* **Isa** 53:5; **Lk** 2:14; **Eph** 2:17

Reconciliation with God
2Co 5:18 All this is from God, who reconciled us to himself through Christ ... *See also* **Ro** 5:9–11; **Col** 1:19–20

Sanctification to God
Heb 10:10 And by that will, we have been made holy through the sacrifice of the body of Jesus Christ once for all. *See also* **1Co** 6:11; **Eph** 5:25–26; **Col** 1:22

Freedom from sin and the sinful nature
Ro 7:24 What a wretched man I am! Who will

rescue me from this body of death?
1Pe 2:24 He himself bore our sins in his body on the tree, so that we might die to sins and live for righteousness . . . *See also* **Ro** 6:1–18; 8:1–9; **Gal** 5:24

A transition from death to life
Col 2:13 When you were dead in your sins and in the uncircumcision of your sinful nature, God made you alive with Christ . . . *See also* **Lk** 15:22–24; **Eph** 2:4–5

Receiving eternal life
Ro 6:23 For the wages of sin is death, but the gift of God is eternal life in Christ Jesus our Lord. *See also* **Jn** 3:16,36 *See also God as redeemer; salvation.*

---

sin, forgiveness of
Sinners must respond to God's offer of forgiveness through faith in Jesus Christ.

The conviction of sin
La 1:20 "See, O LORD, how distressed I am! I am in torment within, and in my heart I am disturbed, for I have been most rebellious. Outside, the sword bereaves; inside, there is only death."
Jn 16:8–9 "When he [the Counsellor] comes, he will convict the world of guilt in regard to sin and righteousness and judgment: in regard to sin, because people do not believe in me [Jesus];" *See also* **1Ki** 8:38–40; **Isa** 6:5; **Eze** 33:10–11; **Ac** 16:29

The inward response of faith
Ac 16:31 . . . "Believe in the Lord Jesus, and you will be saved . . ." *See also* **Mk** 1:14–15; **Jn** 3:36; 5:24; **Ac** 13:38–39; 16:25–34; **Ro** 3:22–26; 10:8–10; **Eph** 2:8

The outward response of baptism
Ac 22:16 "'And now what are you waiting for? Get up, be baptised and wash your sins away, calling on his [Jesus'] name.'" *See also* **Mk** 1:4–5 pp **Mt** 3:1–6 pp **Lk** 3:2–6; **Ac** 2:38; 8:36; **Col** 2:11–12; **1Pe** 3:21

Confession of sin
Pr 28:13 Those who conceal their sins do not prosper, but those who confess and renounce them find mercy.
1Jn 1:9 If we confess our sins, he is faithful and just and will forgive us our sins and purify us from all unrighteousness. *See also* **Lev** 16:20–22; 26:40–42; **2Sa** 12:13; **Ps** 32:3–5; **La** 3:40; **Lk** 15:17–20; **Ac** 19:18

Repentance
Turning towards God
Ac 3:19 "Repent, then, and turn to God, so that your sins may be wiped out . . ." *See also* **2Ch** 6:36–39; **Isa** 55:7; **Eze** 18:21; **Mt** 3:1–2 pp **Mk** 1:4 pp **Lk** 3:2; **Ac** 17:30; **2Co** 7:10; **1Th** 1:9

Turning away from sin
Jn 8:11 . . . "Then neither do I condemn you [the woman caught in adultery]," Jesus declared. "Go now and leave your life of sin." *See also* **Jer** 4:3–4; **Lk** 19:1–10; **Jn** 5:14; **Ro** 6:11–14; **1Pe** 2:11

The making of restitution
Lk 19:8 But Zacchaeus stood up and said to the Lord, "Look, Lord! Here and now I give half of my possessions to the poor, and if I have cheated anybody out of anything, I will pay back four times the amount." *See also* **Lev** 6:1–7; **Nu** 5:6–8; **Pr** 6:30–31; **Eze** 33:12–16

The forgiveness of others
Lk 11:4 "'Forgive us our sins, for we also forgive everyone who sins against us . . .'" pp **Mt** 6:12 *See also* **Mt** 6:14–15; 18:21–35; **Mk** 11:25; **Eph** 4:32; **Col** 3:13 *See also faith; gospel; Holy Spirit, conviction; repentance.*

---

sin, remedy for
Under the old covenant, sin was forgiven through sacrifice, prefiguring the atoning death of Jesus Christ, which brings forgiveness of sins under the new covenant.

Atonement for sins in the OT was through the shedding of blood
Lev 17:11 "'For the life of a creature is in the blood, and I have given it to you to make atonement for yourselves on the altar; it is the

blood that makes atonement for one's life.'"

Kinds of sin offering in the OT
The sin offering was for unintentional sins
Lev 4:1–5:13 The LORD said to Moses, "Say to the Israelites: 'When anyone sins unintentionally and does what is forbidden in any of the LORD's commands . . .'" *See also* **Nu** 15:22–31
The guilt offering was for unintentional sins, where restitution was required
Lev 5:14–6:7 ". . . In this way the priest will make atonement for them before the LORD, and they will be forgiven for any of these things they did that made them guilty." *See also* **Nu** 5:5–10
The annual Day of Atonement cleansed the nation of sin
Lev 16:1–34 ". . . This is to be a lasting ordinance for you: Atonement is to be made once a year for all the sins of the Israelites." . . . *See also* **Ex** 30:11–16; **Lev** 23:26–32; **Heb** 9:7
The priests made atonement on occasions of deliberate national sin Nu 16:46–48; 25:13

Sacrifices of atonement needed to be accompanied by repentance and a willingness to obey
Worshippers recognised the need for repentance and obedience
Pr 21:3 To do what is right and just is more acceptable to the LORD than sacrifice. *See also* **Ps** 40:6–8; 51:16–17
The prophets declared the need for obedience
1Sa 15:22 . . . "Does the LORD delight in burnt offerings and sacrifices as much as in obeying the voice of the LORD? To obey is better than sacrifice, and to heed is better than the fat of rams." *See also* **Isa** 1:11–17; **Jer** 7:21–23; **Hos** 6:6; **Mic** 6:6–8
The prophets warned of judgment to bring people to repentance
2Ki 17:13 The LORD warned Israel and Judah through all his prophets and seers: "Turn from your evil ways. Observe my commands and decrees, in accordance with the entire Law that I commanded your ancestors to obey and that I delivered to you through my servants the prophets." *See also* **Isa** 31:6–7; **Jer** 4:1–4; 35:15; **Eze** 3:16–19; **Jnh** 3:4–10

The death of Jesus Christ brings forgiveness for sin
Jesus Christ died on behalf of sinful humanity
Ro 5:6 . . . when we were still powerless, Christ died for the ungodly. *See also* **Mt** 26:26–28; **Jn** 10:11; 15:13; **Gal** 2:20
The early church proclaimed that Christ died for the sins of others
1Co 15:3 . . . Christ died for our sins according to the Scriptures, *See also* **Ro** 4:25; **Gal** 1:4; **1Pe** 3:18
Jesus Christ bore sin on the cross
2Co 5:21 God made him who had no sin to be sin for us, so that in him we might become the righteousness of God. *See also* **Isa** 53:10–12; **Heb** 9:28; **1Pe** 2:24
Jesus Christ has redeemed people by taking their place
Mt 20:28 ". . . the Son of Man did not come to be served, but to serve, and to give his life as a ransom for many." pp Mk 10:45 *See also* **Gal** 3:13; **1Ti** 2:6; **Tit** 2:14
Jesus Christ's death is sacrificial
Ro 3:25 God presented him as a sacrifice of atonement, through faith in his blood . . . *See also* **Ro** 8:3; **1Co** 5:7; **Eph** 5:2; **Heb** 7:27; 10:5–13; **1Jn** 2:2; 4:10
The shedding of Jesus Christ's blood brings forgiveness
1Jn 1:7 . . . the blood of Jesus, his Son, purifies us from all sin. *See also* **Jn** 1:29; **Eph** 1:7; **Heb** 9:12–22; 13:12; **1Pe** 1:18–19; **Rev** 7:14 *See also* forgiveness; Jesus Christ as Lamb; Jesus Christ as redeemer; Jesus Christ as Saviour; Jesus Christ, cross of; Jesus Christ, resurrection.

Son of Man
A Hebrew and Aramaic term, often used to mean a human being in general. In the Gospels Jesus Christ uses it to refer to himself in his earthly ministry and his future death, exaltation and coming as judge and Saviour.

Sons of men as a term for humanity in general
Human beings are inferior to God
Ps 115:16 The highest heavens belong to the LORD, but the earth he has given to the human race.   *See also* **Ps** 11:4; 33:13–14; 45:2
Human beings are dependent on God's care
Ps 8:4 what are mere mortals that you are mindful of them, human beings that you care for them?   *See also* **Ps** 36:7; 80:17; 107:8,15,21,31
Human beings are mortal
Ecc 9:3 This is the evil in everything that happens under the sun: The same destiny overtakes all. The hearts of people, moreover, are full of evil and there is madness in their hearts while they live, and afterwards they join the dead.   *See also* **Ecc** 3:18–19; **Eze** 31:14
Human beings are sinful and untrustworthy
Ps 146:3 Do not put your trust in princes, in human beings, who cannot save.   *See also* **Ps** 14:2–3 pp **Ps** 53:2–3; **Mic** 5:7

Son of Man as a term for individual men
The sons of Adam Ge 4:1–2; 5:3–4
Ezekiel
Eze 2:1 He [God] said to me, "Son of man, stand up on your feet and I will speak to you."   *See also* **Eze** 2:3,6,8; 3:1
Other people Job 25:6; **Da** 8:17

A son of man as a ruler of God's future kingdom
Da 7:13 "In my [Daniel's] vision at night I looked, and there before me was one like a son of man, coming with the clouds of heaven . . ."
Da 7:13–14 ". . . He approached the Ancient of Days and was led into his presence. He was given authority, glory and sovereign power; all nations and peoples of every language worshipped him. His dominion is an everlasting dominion that will not pass away, and his kingdom is one that will never be destroyed."
Da 7:27 "Then the sovereignty, power and greatness of the kingdoms under the whole heaven will be handed over to the saints, the people of the Most High. His [the son of man's] kingdom will be an everlasting kingdom, and all rulers will worship and obey him.' "   *See also* **Da** 7:18

Son of Man as a title for Jesus Christ
Used by Jesus Christ to emphasise his humanity and authority
Mk 2:10–11 "But that you may know that the Son of Man has authority on earth to forgive sins . . ." He [Jesus] said to the paralytic, "I tell you, get up, take your mat and go home." pp **Mt** 9:6 pp **Lk** 5:24
Mk 8:31 He [Jesus] then began to teach them that the Son of Man must suffer many things and be rejected by the elders, chief priests and teachers of the law, and that he must be killed and after three days rise again. pp **Lk** 9:22
The Son of Man receives God's kingdom
Ac 7:56 "Look," he [Stephen] said, "I see heaven open and the Son of Man standing at the right hand of God."   *See also* **Da** 7:13; **Mk** 14:62 pp **Mt** 26:64 pp **Lk** 22:69; **Heb** 2:6–9; **Ps** 8:4–6   *See also* human race; Jesus Christ, authority; Jesus Christ, second coming; Jesus Christ, Son of Man; Jesus Christ, sonship of; kingdom of God.

Trinity
The characteristically Christian doctrine about God. It declares that there is only one true God; that this God is three persons, the Father, the Son and the Holy Spirit, each of whom is distinct from, yet interrelated with, the others; and that all three persons are fully, equally and eternally divine.

Trinity, equality of
The Son and the Holy Spirit are equal to God the Father in eternity, nature and status. Within the Trinity the Father is head, first among equals; the Son and the Holy Spirit do the Father's will, glorifying him and making him known; and the Holy Spirit glorifies and makes known the Son.

The Son is equal with the Father
Jn 5:18 . . . he [Jesus] was even calling God his own Father, making himself equal with God.
See also **Jn** 5:23; 8:16; 14:9; 17:10; **Php** 2:6; **Col** 2:9

Ro 1:7 . . . Grace and peace to you from God our Father and from the Lord Jesus Christ. *See also* **1Co** 1:3; **Gal** 1:3; **Eph** 1:2; **1Th** 1:1; **1Ti** 1:2; **Phm** 3; **2Pe** 1:2

Rev 5:13 . . . "To him who sits on the throne and to the Lamb be praise and honour and glory and power, for ever and ever!" *See also* **Ro** 9:5; **Heb** 13:21; **2Pe** 3:18; **Rev** 7:10

The Holy Spirit is equal with the Father and the Son
2Co 13:14 May the grace of the Lord Jesus Christ, and the love of God, and the fellowship of the Holy Spirit be with you all. *See also* **Mt** 28:19; **1Pe** 1:2; **Rev** 1:4–5

The obedience of the Son to the Father
The Son submits to the Father in his incarnation
Php 2:6–7 Who, being in very nature God, did not consider equality with God something to be grasped, but made himself nothing, taking the very nature of a servant, being made in human likeness. *See also* **Mt** 24:36; **Jn** 4:34; 6:38; 14:28,31; **Ro** 5:19; **Heb** 5:8; 10:5–7; **Ps** 40:6–8
The Father is Jesus Christ's "head"
1Co 11:3 . . . the head of Christ is God. *See also* **1Co** 3:23; 8:6; 15:27–28

Equality and mutuality as the three persons glorify one another
The Son glorifies the Father
Ro 16:27 to the only wise God be glory for ever through Jesus Christ! Amen. *See also* **Jn** 14:13; **Eph** 1:5–6; 3:21; **Php** 2:11; **Col** 3:17; **1Pe** 4:11; **Jude** 25
The Father and the Son glorify one another
Jn 17:1 . . . he [Jesus] looked towards heaven and prayed: "Father, the time has come. Glorify your Son, that your Son may glorify you." *See also* **Jn** 8:54; 13:31–32; 17:4–5,24; **Ac** 3:13
The Spirit glorifies the Father and the Son
Jn 16:13–15 ". . . He [the Spirit of truth] will bring glory to me [Jesus] by taking from what is mine and making it known to you . . ." *See also* **Jn** 14:26; 15:26; **Eph** 1:13–14 *See also* God, glory of; God, revelation; Holy Spirit, divinity; Holy Spirit, personality; Holy Spirit, witness of; Jesus Christ, divinity; Jesus Christ, glory of; Jesus Christ, obedience.

Trinity, mission of
All three persons of the Trinity co-operate in God's work of salvation. For this purpose, the Father sends the Son and the Holy Spirit to redeem his people on earth and to live in and among them.

The Son and the Holy Spirit do God's work on earth
In the OT, the LORD alone is Saviour
Isa 43:11 "I, even I, am the LORD, and apart from me there is no saviour." *See also* **Ps** 19:14; 78:35; **Isa** 43:3; 49:26; 60:16; **Jer** 14:8; **Hos** 13:4
In the NT, the Son is the Saviour
Mt 1:21 ". . . you [Joseph] are to give him the name Jesus, because he will save his people from their sins." *See also* **Lk** 2:11; **Jn** 4:42; **Gal** 3:13; 4:5; **Tit** 2:13; 3:6
In the OT, the LORD lives among his people
Ex 29:45 "Then I will dwell among the Israelites and be their God." *See also* **Ps** 135:21; **Isa** 57:15; **Eze** 43:7; **Joel** 3:17; **Zec** 2:10–11
In the NT, the Spirit lives in the church
1Co 3:16 "Don't you [Corinthians] know that you yourselves are God's temple and that God's Spirit lives in you?" *See also* **Jn** 14:17; **Ro** 8:9,11; **2Ti** 1:14

Father and Son in the mission of Jesus Christ
The Father sends the Son
Gal 4:4 But when the time had fully come, God sent his Son . . . *See also* **Mt** 10:40; **Mk** 12:6; **Jn** 3:16–17; 7:28; 8:42; **1Jn** 4:9
The Son reveals the Father
Jn 8:38 "I [Jesus] am telling you what I have seen in the Father's presence, and you do what you have heard from your father." *See also* **Jn** 1:18; 15:15; 17:6,26; **Col** 1:15; **Heb** 1:3
The Son does the Father's work
Jn 5:19 . . . "I [Jesus] tell you the truth, the Son can do nothing by himself; he can do only

what he sees his Father doing, because whatever the Father does the Son also does." *See also* **Jn 4:34; 5:17; 9:3–4; 10:37; 14:10**

The Son speaks the Father's words
Jn 12:49–50 "For I [Jesus] did not speak of my own accord, but the Father who sent me commanded me what to say and how to say it . . ." *See also* **Jn 3:34; 8:28; 14:24; 17:8**

The Father testifies to the Son
Jn 5:37 "And the Father who sent me [Jesus] has himself testified concerning me . . ." *See also* **Jn 5:32; 8:18; 1Jn 5:9**

The sending of the Holy Spirit
The Father gives the Spirit
Lk 11:13 "If you [disciples] then, though you are evil, know how to give good gifts to your children, how much more will your Father in heaven give the Holy Spirit to those who ask him!" *See also* **Ac 5:32; 2Co 5:5; Gal 3:5; Eph 1:17; 1Jn 4:13**

The Son gives the Spirit
Jn 16:7 ". . . Unless I [Jesus] go away, the Counsellor will not come to you; but if I go, I will send him to you." *See also* **Mt 3:11 pp Mk 1:8 pp Lk 3:16; Jn 1:33; 20:22**

The Father sends the Spirit through Jesus Christ
Jn 14:16–17 "And I [Jesus] will ask the Father, and he will give you another Counsellor to be with you for ever—the Spirit of truth . . ." *See also* **Jn 14:26; 15:26; Ac 2:33**

The three persons share the work of salvation
The incarnation
Lk 1:35 The angel answered, "The Holy Spirit will come upon you [Mary], and the power of the Most High will overshadow you. So the holy one to be born will be called the Son of God."

Jesus Christ's baptism
Mt 3:16–17 As soon as Jesus was baptised, he went up out of the water. At that moment heaven was opened, and he saw the Spirit of God descending like a dove and lighting on him. And a voice from heaven said, "This is my Son, whom I love; with him I am well pleased." pp **Mk 1:10–11 pp Lk 3:21–22**

Jesus Christ's ministry
Ac 10:38 "how God anointed Jesus of Nazareth with the Holy Spirit and power, and how he went around doing good and healing all who were under the power of the devil, because God was with him." *See also* **Lk 10:21; Jn 3:34**

The work of redemption
1Pe 1:2 . . . chosen according to the foreknowledge of God the Father, through the sanctifying work of the Spirit, for obedience to Jesus Christ and sprinkling by his blood . . . *See also* **2Co 1:21–22; Gal 4:4–6; Eph 1:3–14; 2:18; 2Th 2:13–14; Tit 3:4–6**

Commissioning the disciples
Jn 20:21–22 Again Jesus said, "Peace be with you! As the Father has sent me, I am sending you." And with that he breathed on them and said, "Receive the Holy Spirit." *See also* **Ac 1:7–8**

Jesus Christ's exaltation
Ac 7:55 But Stephen, full of the Holy Spirit, looked up to heaven and saw the glory of God, and Jesus standing at the right hand of God. *See also* **Ac 5:31–32**

Proclaiming the gospel
Ac 2:38–39 Peter replied, "Repent and be baptised, every one of you, in the name of Jesus Christ for the forgiveness of your sins. And you will receive the gift of the Holy Spirit. The promise is for you and your children and for all who are far off—for all whom the Lord our God will call."

Building the church
Eph 2:22 And in him [Jesus] you too are being built together to become a dwelling in which God lives by his Spirit. *See also* **1Co 12:4–6** *See also* Holy Spirit in the world; Holy Spirit, baptism with; Holy Spirit, Counsellor; Holy Spirit, gift of; Jesus Christ as prophet; Jesus Christ, miracles; Jesus Christ, mission; Jesus Christ, preaching and teaching; salvation.

Trinity, relationships in
The actual term "the Trinity" is not found in Scripture, but the truths implied in a trinitarian understanding of God are clearly set out. The OT hints at a plurality of persons in the Godhead. The NT affirms that the Son and the Holy Spirit are divine.

Trinity, relationships in

There is only one God
Dt 6:4 Hear, O Israel: The LORD our God, the LORD is one. *See also* **Isa** 43:10–11; 44:8; **1Ti** 1:17; 2:5; **Jas** 2:19

OT indications of plurality in the Godhead
God refers to himself in the plural
Ge 1:26 Then God said, "Let us make human beings in our image, in our likeness . . ." *See also* **Ge** 3:22; 11:7; **Isa** 6:8

The angel of the LORD
Ge 16:11–13 The angel of the LORD [one who is identified with, yet distinct from, God] also said to her [Hagar]: "You are now with child and you will have a son . . ." She gave this name to the LORD who spoke to her: "You are the God who sees me," for she said, "I have now seen the One who sees me." *See also* **Ge** 18:1–33; **Ex** 3:2–6; **Jdg** 13:3–22

The word of God
The "word of the LORD" or "wisdom of God" is personified and identified with, yet distinct from, God: **Ps** 33:4; **Pr** 8:22–31

The Spirit of God
The Spirit of God is God's personal agent: **Ge** 1:2; **Ne** 9:20; **Job** 33:4; **Isa** 40:13 fn

The Messiah
The Messiah's divine nature is emphasised: **Ps** 110:1; **Isa** 9:6; **Jer** 23:5–6

Interchangeable expressions
Word, Spirit (or breath) and LORD are used interchangeably for God: **Ps** 33:6; **Isa** 48:16; 61:1

NT trinitarian references
Mt 28:19 "Therefore go and make disciples of all nations, baptising them in the name of the Father and of the Son and of the Holy Spirit," *See also* **2Co** 13:14; **Eph** 4:4–6; **Rev** 1:4–5

The unity of the three persons
The Son is fully united with the Father
Jn 10:30 "I [Jesus] and the Father are one." *See also* **Mk** 9:37 pp **Lk** 9:48; **Lk** 10:16; **Jn** 10:38; 12:44–45; 13:20; 14:7,9–11; 15:23

The Spirit is identified with God
2Sa 23:2–3 "The Spirit of the LORD spoke through me . . . The God of Israel spoke, the Rock of Israel said to me . . ." *See also* **Ps** 51:11; **Mt** 28:19; **1Co** 3:16

The three persons are distinct from one another
Jesus Christ addresses the Father directly **Mt** 11:25–26 pp **Lk** 10:21; **Mt** 26:39 pp **Mk** 14:36 pp **Lk** 22:42; **Mt** 26:42; 27:46 pp **Mk** 15:34; **Lk** 23:46; **Jn** 11:41–42; 17:1

The Father speaks to the Son from heaven **Mt** 3:17 pp **Mk** 1:11 pp **Lk** 3:22; **Mt** 17:5 pp **Mk** 9:7 pp **Lk** 9:35; **Jn** 12:27–28

The Spirit speaks to the Father on behalf of believers **Ro** 8:26–27

Other examples of the difference between the persons **Mt** 12:32; 24:36; **Jn** 7:39; 16:7; **1Ti** 2:5; **1Jn** 2:1

The relationship between the Father and the Son
Jesus Christ is God's unique Son
Jn 1:14 The Word became flesh and made his dwelling among us. We have seen his glory, the glory of the One and Only, who came from the Father, full of grace and truth. *See also* **Jn** 1:18; 3:16,18; **Ac** 13:33; **Heb** 1:5; **Ps** 2:7; **1Jn** 4:9

The relationship of Father and Son is unique
Mt 11:27 "All things have been committed to me [Jesus] by my Father. No-one knows the Son except the Father, and no-one knows the Father except the Son and those to whom the Son chooses to reveal him." pp **Lk** 10:22 *See also* **Jn** 6:46; 7:28–29; 8:55; 10:15; 17:25

The Father loves the Son
Jn 3:35 "The Father loves the Son and has placed everything in his hands." *See also* **Jn** 5:20; 10:17; 15:9; 17:24

The Father shares his divine life with the Son
Col 2:9 For in Christ all the fulness of the Deity lives in bodily form *See also* **Jn** 5:26; 6:57; **Col** 1:19

The Father delegates his authority to the Son
Jn 5:27 "And he [the Father] has given him [the Son] authority to judge . . ." *See also* **Mt** 28:18; **Jn** 3:35; 5:21–22; 16:15; **Rev** 2:26–27

Father and Son indwell each other
Jn 14:10–11 ". . . Believe me [Jesus] when I say that I am in the Father and the Father is in me . . ." *See also* **Jn** 10:38; 14:20; 17:21–23

The relationship between the Holy Spirit and the other two persons
The Spirit is "the Spirit of God" and "the Spirit of Christ"
Ro 8:9 You, however, are controlled not by the sinful nature but by the Spirit, if the Spirit of God lives in you. And if anyone does not have the Spirit of Christ, that person does not belong to Christ.

"the Spirit of God": **Ps** 106:33; **1Co** 2:14; **Php** 3:3; **1Jn** 4:2
"the Spirit of Christ": **Ac** 16:7; **Gal** 4:6; **Php** 1:19; **1Pe** 1:11

The Spirit's unique relationship with God
Mt 10:20 ". . . the Spirit of your Father . . ." *See also* **1Co** 2:10–11

The Spirit's unique relationship with the Son
Jn 1:33 "I [John the Baptist] would not have known him, except that the one who sent me to baptise with water told me, 'The man on whom you see the Spirit come down and remain is the one who will baptise with the Holy Spirit.'"
See also **Isa** 61:1; **Jn** 14:16–17,26; **Ac** 10:38
See also God, unique; God, unity of; Holy Spirit; Holy Spirit in life of Jesus Christ; Holy Spirit in Old Testament; Jesus Christ; Jesus Christ, authority; Jesus Christ, Son of God; Jesus Christ, sonship of; word of God.

---

types
An OT institution, person, place or event regarded as anticipating the person of Jesus Christ or some aspect of the Christian faith or life.

OT foreshadowings of Jesus Christ
Lk 24:25–27 He [Jesus] said to them [the disciples], "How foolish you are, and how slow of heart to believe all that the prophets have spoken! Did not the Christ have to suffer these things and then enter his glory?" And beginning with Moses and all the Prophets, he explained to them what was said in all the Scriptures concerning himself. *See also* **Lk** 24:44; **1Pe** 1:10–12

OT institutions as types
The Sabbath: Jesus Christ's finished work
Heb 4:3–6 . . . his [God's] work has been finished since the creation of the world. For somewhere he has spoken about the seventh day in these words: "And on the seventh day God rested from all his work" . . . It still remains that some will enter that rest . . . *See also* **Ge** 2:2–3; **Heb** 4:9–10

Marriage: Jesus Christ's union with his people
Eph 5:30–32 . . . we are members of his body. "For this reason a man will leave his father and mother and be united to his wife, and the two will become one flesh." This is a profound mystery—but I [Paul] am talking about Christ and the church. *See also* **Ge** 2:22–24; **Ps** 45:10–11; **Mt** 9:15, 25:1; **Jn** 3:29; **Eph** 5:25–27; **Rev** 19:7; 21:2

Circumcision: believers' union with Christ
Col 2:11 In him [Christ] you were also circumcised, in the putting off of the sinful nature, not with a circumcision done by human hands but with the circumcision done by Christ, *See also* **Ge** 17:9–14; **Ro** 2:29; **Php** 3:3

The tabernacle: Jesus Christ's coming among his people
Jn 1:14 The Word became flesh and made his dwelling among us. We have seen his glory, the glory of the One and Only, who came from the Father, full of grace and truth. *See also* **Ex** 25:8; 40:34–35

The tabernacle: the way to God
Heb 9:11–12 When Christ came as high priest of the good things that are already here, he went through the greater and more perfect tabernacle that is not made with human hands, that is to say, not a part of this creation. He did not enter by means of the blood of goats and calves; but he entered the Most Holy Place once for all by his own blood, having obtained eternal redemption. *See also* **Ex** 25:22; 30:6,36; **Nu** 17:4; **Heb** 9:8; 10:19–22

The high priesthood: Jesus Christ as intercessor
Heb 7:23–28 Now there have been many of

those priests, since death prevented them from continuing in office; but because Jesus lives for ever, he has a permanent priesthood. Therefore he is able to save completely those who come to God through him, because he always lives to intercede for them. Such a high priest meets our need—one who is holy, blameless, pure, set apart from sinners, exalted above the heavens. Unlike the other high priests, he does not need to offer sacrifices day after day, first for his own sins, and then for the sins of the people. He sacrificed for their sins once for all when he offered himself. For the law appoints as high priests men who are weak; but the oath, which came after the law, appointed the Son, who has been made perfect for ever.   *See also* **Ex** 29:1–7; **Lev** 16:11–17; **Heb** 4:14–16; 5:1–5; 9:11–12; 10:11–12

The priesthood: Christian worship and service
Heb 13:15–16 Through Jesus, therefore, let us continually offer to God a sacrifice of praise—the fruit of lips that confess his name. And do not forget to do good and to share with others, for with such sacrifices God is pleased.   *See also* **Ex** 19:6; 29:8–9; **1Pe** 2:5; **Rev** 1:6

Sacrifices: Jesus Christ as substitute
Ro 3:25 God presented him as a sacrifice of atonement, through faith in his blood . . .
See also **Lev** 4:13–15,25–35; **Isa** 53:4–12; **Mk** 15:25–37; **2Co** 5:15; **Gal** 2:20; **1Pe** 3:18

Sacrifice: believers' consecration
Ro 12:1 . . . I urge you, brothers and sisters, in view of God's mercy, to offer your bodies as living sacrifices, holy and pleasing to God—this is your spiritual act of worship.   *See also* **Lev** 1:1–9; **Nu** 15:1–12; **Php** 2:17; **2Ti** 4:6

The day of atonement: Jesus Christ as sin-bearer
Heb 9:28 . . . Christ was sacrificed once to take away the sins of many people . . .
See also **Lev** 16:1–34; **Heb** 9:7

Passover: deliverance from judgment
1Co 5:7 . . . Christ, our Passover lamb, has been sacrificed.   *See also* **Ex** 12:1–16; **Mt** 26:17 pp **Mk** 14:12 pp **Lk** 22:7; **Mt** 26:26–29 pp **Mk** 14:22–25 pp **Lk** 22:14–20; **Jn** 1:29; **1Pe** 1:18–19

Redemption: release from sin
Mt 20:28 ". . . the Son of Man did not come to be served, but to serve, and to give his life as a ransom for many." pp **Mk** 10:45   *See also* **Ex** 13:11–13; 21:28–32; **Job** 19:25; **Ps** 78:35; **Isa** 41:14; **Ro** 3:24; **1Co** 6:20

Redemption from the "curse of the law": **Gal** 3:13; 4:5
Eph 1:7; 1Ti 2:6; Tit 2:14; Heb 9:15

The temple: the church
2Co 6:16 . . . we are the temple of the living God. As God has said: "I will live with them and walk among them, and I will be their God, and they will be my people."   *See also* **1Ki** 6:1; 8:10–13; **1Co** 3:16; **Eph** 2:21–22; **1Pe** 2:5

OT places as types
The promised land: rest in Christ
Heb 4:8–11 . . . if Joshua had given them rest, God would not have spoken later about another day. There remains, then, a Sabbath-rest for the people of God; for those who enter God's rest also rest from their own work, just as God did from his. Let us, therefore, make every effort to enter that rest . . .   *See also* **Jos** 1:13; 11:23; 14:15

Jerusalem: the glorified church
Rev 21:1–3 Then I [John] saw a new heaven and a new earth, for the first heaven and the first earth had passed away, and there was no longer any sea. I saw the Holy City, the new Jerusalem, coming down out of heaven from God, prepared as a bride beautifully dressed for her husband. And I heard a loud voice from the throne saying, "Now the dwelling of God is with human beings, and he will live with them. They will be his people, and God himself will be with them and be their God."   *See also* **2Sa** 5:4–5; **Ps** 122:1–9; **Isa** 62:6–7; **Zec** 2:3–5; **Heb** 12:22–23; **Rev** 3:12; 21:9–10

Babylon: enmity to Jesus Christ
Rev 17:5 This title was written on her forehead:
MYSTERY
BABYLON THE GREAT
THE MOTHER OF PROSTITUTES
AND OF THE ABOMINATIONS OF THE EARTH.
See also **Isa** 13:19–22; **Rev** 18:2–3

OT people as types
Israel: the church
1Pe 2:9 But you [believers] are a chosen people, a royal priesthood, a holy nation, a people belonging to God, that you may declare the praises of him who called you out of darkness into his wonderful light. *See also* **Ge** 12:1–3; **Ex** 19:6; **Ro** 9:6–8; **Gal** 6:16; **Eph** 2:19

Adam: Jesus Christ as the head of his people
1Co 15:21–22 For since death came through a human being, the resurrection of the dead comes also through a human being. For as in Adam all die, so in Christ all will be made alive. *See also* **Ge** 3:17–19; **Ro** 5:12–20

Abraham: justifying faith in Jesus Christ
Ro 4:18–25 Against all hope, Abraham in hope believed and so became the father of many nations, just as it had been said to him, "So shall your offspring be." . . . This is why "it was credited to him as righteousness." The words "it was credited to him" were written not for him alone, but also for us, to whom God will credit righteousness—for us who believe in him who raised Jesus our Lord from the dead. He was delivered over to death for our sins and was raised to life for our justification. *See also* **Ge** 15:6; **Gal** 3:6–9

Melchizedek: Jesus Christ as priest-king
Heb 7:1–3 This Melchizedek was king of Salem and priest of God Most High. He met Abraham returning from the defeat of the kings and blessed him, and Abraham gave him a tenth of everything. First, his name means "king of righteousness"; then also, "king of Salem" means "king of peace". Without father or mother, without genealogy, without beginning of days or end of life, like the Son of God he remains a priest for ever. *See also* **Ge** 14:17–20; **Ps** 110:4; **Heb** 7:11–17

Sarah and Hagar: grace and law
Gal 4:22–26 . . . Abraham had two sons, one by the slave woman and the other by the free woman. His son by the slave woman was born in the ordinary way; but his son by the free woman was born as the result of a promise. These things may be taken figuratively, for the women represent two covenants. One covenant is from Mount Sinai and bears children who are to be slaves: This is Hagar. Now Hagar stands for Mount Sinai in Arabia and corresponds to the present city of Jerusalem, because she is in slavery with her children. But the Jerusalem that is above is free, and she is our mother. *See also* **Ge** 16:1–6; 21:10; **Gal** 4:27–31

David: Jesus Christ as king, shepherd and sufferer
Lk 1:31–33 "You [Mary] will be with child and give birth to a son, and you are to give him the name Jesus. He will be great and will be called the Son of the Most High. The Lord God will give him the throne of his father David, and he will reign over the house of Jacob for ever; his kingdom will never end." *See also* **2Sa** 7:11–16; **Ps** 78:70–72; 89:19–37; **Jn** 13:18; **Ps** 41:9; **Rev** 22:16

Solomon: Jesus Christ as wise ruler
Mt 12:42 "The Queen of the South will rise at the judgment with this generation and condemn it; for she came from the ends of the earth to listen to Solomon's wisdom, and now one greater than Solomon is here." *See also* **1Ki** 3:5–12

OT events as types
Noah's ark: salvation
1Pe 3:20–21 . . . In it [the ark] only a few people, eight in all, were saved through water, and this water symbolises baptism that now saves you also—not the removal of dirt from the body but the pledge of a good conscience towards God . . . *See also* **Ge** 7:7

Abraham offering Isaac: God giving his Son
Ro 8:32 He who did not spare his own Son, but gave him up for us all—how will he not also, along with him, graciously give us all things? *See also* **Ge** 22:9–14

Crossing the Red Sea: Christian commitment
1Co 10:1–2 . . . our ancestors were all under the cloud and that they all passed through the sea. They were all baptised into Moses in the cloud and in the sea. *See also* **Ex** 14:15–22

Water from a rock: Jesus Christ's provision
1Co 10:4 . . . they [Israelites] drank from the spiritual rock that accompanied them, and that rock was Christ. *See also* **Ex** 17:5–6

The bronze snake: Jesus Christ, the object of faith
Jn 3:14–15 "Just as Moses lifted up the snake in the desert, so the Son of Man must be lifted up, that everyone who believes in him may have eternal life." *See also* **Nu** 21:4–9 *See also Jesus Christ as king; Jesus Christ as Lamb; Jesus Christ, high priest.*

---

word of God

The utterances of God, especially as revealed in Scripture. This may take the form of commands or promises. The term can also refer to Jesus Christ as the incarnate Word of God.

The word of God revealed as law
God has made his commands and requirements known
Ps 147:19 He [God] has revealed his word to Jacob, his laws and decrees to Israel. *See also* **Ex** 20:1–17; 24:3; 34:27–28; **Dt** 5:5; **Isa** 2:3 pp Mic 4:2; **Mt** 15:6 pp **Mk** 7:13
God's law is to be obeyed
Dt 30:14 . . . the word is very near you; it is in your mouth and in your heart so that you may obey it. *See also* **Jos** 23:6; **Ps** 119:4; **Lk** 8:21; 11:28; **Jas** 1:22–23
Examples of disobedience and its consequences
Nu 15:31; **1Sa** 15:23–26; **2Sa** 12:9; **1Ch** 10:13; **2Ch** 34:21; **Isa** 5:24; **Jer** 8:9

The word of God as prophecy
The prophets spoke the words of God
Jer 1:9 Then the LORD reached out his hand and touched my mouth and said to me [Jeremiah], "Now, I have put my words in your mouth."
1Sa 3:1 . . . In those days the word of the LORD was rare; there were not many visions.
Jer 25:3 For twenty-three years—from the thirteenth year of Josiah son of Amon king of Judah until this very day—the word of the LORD has come to me [Jeremiah] and I have spoken to you again and again, but you have not listened. *See also* **1Ki** 17:24; **2Ki** 24:2; **2Ch** 36:12,15; **Isa** 16:13; 24:3; **Jer** 7:1; 14:1; **Am** 8:11–12; **Mal** 1:1

Prophetic introductory formulae
"The word of the LORD came to . . .": **Ge** 15:1; **1Sa** 15:10; **2Sa** 24:11; **1Ki** 6:11; **2Ki** 20:4 pp Isa 38:4; **Jer** 16:1; **Eze** 6:1; **Jnh** 1:1; **Zec** 1:1
"Hear the word of the LORD": **1Ki** 22:19; **2Ki** 20:16 pp Isa 39:5; **Isa** 1:10; **Jer** 2:4; **Hos** 4:1
"This is what the LORD says": **2Sa** 7:5 pp 1Ch 17:4; **2Ki** 1:6; **Isa** 37:6; **Jer** 2:5; **Eze** 2:4; **Am** 1:3; **Hag** 2:11
Prophetic predictions fulfilled
1Ki 12:15 . . . this turn of events was from the LORD, to fulfil the word the LORD had spoken to Jeroboam son of Nebat . . . *See also* **1Ki** 15:29; 16:12,34; 22:38; **2Ki** 1:17; 9:36; 10:17; 14:25; 15:12; 23:16; **2Ch** 36:21–22
The word "against" a people, indicating judgment Isa 9:8; 37:22; Jer 25:30; Am 3:1; Zep 2:5; Zec 9:1
True prophecy is inspired by God
2Pe 1:20–21 Above all, you must understand that no prophecy of Scripture came about by the prophet's own interpretation. For prophecy never had its origin in the human will, but prophets, though human, spoke from God as they were carried along by the Holy Spirit. *See also* **Ne** 9:30; **Jer** 23:16,25–26,30; **Eze** 13:1–3; **Mic** 3:8
A true prophet hears from God 2Ki 3:12; Jer 5:13; 23:18; 27:18
The prophetic word is to be heeded Ex 9:20–21; Jer 6:10; 25:3; Zec 7:12

The word of God as Scripture
Scripture is the written word of God
Da 9:2 . . . I, Daniel, understood from the Scriptures, according to the word of the LORD given to Jeremiah the prophet, that the desolation of Jerusalem would last seventy years. *See also* **Ro** 3:2; 15:4
NT writings are classified as Scripture 1Ti 5:18; 2Pe 3:16
Scripture is inspired and true Jn 10:35; 2Ti 3:15
The foundational importance of Scripture
It must not be distorted or changed: Dt 4:2; 12:32; Pr 30:6; 2Co 2:17; 4:2; 2Ti 2:15; Rev 22:19
It is to be read publicly: Ne 8:1–8; 1Ti 4:13
It is to be meditated upon: Ps 1:2; 119:15,97

It is the test of orthodoxy: **Isa** 8:20; **Ac** 17:11
Mt 22:29 pp Mk 12:24
It is the basis for preaching: **Ac** 17:2; 18:28
1Co 4:6

Jesus Christ as the incarnate Word of God
Jesus Christ is God in the flesh
Jn 1:1 In the beginning was the Word, and the Word was with God, and the Word was God. *See also* **Jn** 1:14; 12:45; **Col** 1:15; **Heb** 1:2; **1Jn** 1:1; **Rev** 19:13
Jesus Christ speaks the Father's words
Jn 8:40 ". . . you [the Jews] are determined to kill me [Jesus], a man who has told you the truth that I heard from God. Abraham did not do such things." *See also* **Mt** 22:16 pp Mk 12:14 pp Lk 20:21; **Jn** 7:18
Jesus Christ's words have sovereign power
Mt 8:8 pp Lk 7:7; **Mt** 8:16; **Heb** 1:3

The gospel as the word of God
It was preached by Jesus Christ
Mk 2:2 . . . he [Jesus] preached the word to them. *See also* **Mt** 13:19–23 pp Mk 4:14–20 pp Lk 8:11–15; **Mk** 4:33; **Lk** 4:43 pp Mk 1:38; **Lk** 5:1
It was preached by the first Christians
1Th 2:13 . . . when you received the word of God, which you heard from us [the apostles], you accepted it not as a human word, but as it actually is, the word of God . . . *See also* **Mk** 16:20; **Ac** 6:2; 8:4; 11:1; 13:5; 15:35–36; 17:13; **1Co** 14:36; **2Co** 2:17; 4:2; **Php** 1:14; **Col** 1:25; **2Ti** 4:2
It leads to numerical and spiritual growth within the church **Ac** 6:7; 12:24; 13:49; 19:20; **Col** 1:5–6; **1Th** 2:13
It must be preached **Ro** 10:14; **2Ti** 4:2

Descriptions of God's word
It is true: **Ps** 33:4; **Jn** 17:17
It is flawless: **2Sa** 22:31 pp Ps 18:30; **Pr** 30:5
It is infallible: **1Ki** 8:56; **2Ki** 10:10
Ps 103:20
It is eternal: **Ps** 119:89,152; **Isa** 40:8; **1Pe** 1:25
Ps 119:103; 138:2; **Isa** 45:23; **Eph** 6:17; **2Ti** 2:9; **Heb** 4:12; **1Pe** 1:23

Comparisons of the word of God with everyday things
Food: **Dt** 8:3; **Job** 23:12; **Ps** 119:103; **Jer** 15:16; **Eze** 2:8; 3:1; **1Pe** 2:2
Ps 119:105
Fire: **Jer** 5:14; 20:9; 23:29
Jer 23:29; **Heb** 4:12

The word of God has power
It is active
Isa 55:11 ". . . It [God's word] will not return to me empty, but will accomplish what I desire and achieve the purpose for which I sent it."
It brings about creation
Ps 33:6 By the word of the LORD were the heavens made, their starry host by the breath of his mouth. *See also* **2Pe** 3:5
It governs and maintains the created order
Heb 1:3 The Son is the radiance of God's glory and the exact representation of his being, sustaining all things by his powerful word . . . *See also* **Ps** 147:18
It gives life
Dt 8:3 . . . human beings do not live on bread alone but on every word that comes from the mouth of the LORD. *See also* **Isa** 55:2–3; **Mt** 4:4 pp Lk 4:4
It consecrates secular things **1Ti** 4:5
It restrains from evil **Ps** 17:4; 119:11
It heals and rescues **Ps** 107:20
It has power to save
Jas 1:21 . . . humbly accept the word planted in you, which can save you. *See also* **2Ti** 3:15; **1Pe** 1:23
It brings about the growth of the kingdom of God **Mt** 13:23 pp Mk 4:20 pp Lk 8:15
It builds up the saints **Ac** 20:32 *See also God, revelation; gospel; Holy Spirit and preaching; Holy Spirit, inspiration; law; revelation; Scripture, inspiration and authority.*

---

worship
The praise, adoration and reverence of God, both in public and private. It is a celebration of the worthiness of God, by which honour is given to his name.

worship of God
God alone is worthy of worship; the worship of other gods is forbidden. In the NT worship is offered to the Son of God.

God alone is to be worshipped
He alone is worthy of worship
1Ch 16:25 For great is the LORD and most worthy of praise; he is to be feared above all gods.   *See also* **Ps** 48:1; 96:4–5; 145:3; **2Sa** 22:4

The worship of God the Father
Jn 4:23 "Yet a time is coming and has now come when the true worshippers will worship the Father in spirit and truth, for they are the kind of worshippers the Father seeks."   *See also* **Php** 2:11

The worship of God the Son
Mt 2:11 On coming to the house, they [the Magi] saw the child with his mother Mary, and they bowed down and worshipped him. Then they opened their treasures and presented him with gifts of gold and of incense and of myrrh.
Mt 14:33 Then those who were in the boat worshipped him [Jesus], saying, "Truly you are the Son of God."
Jn 20:28 Thomas said to him [Jesus], "My Lord and my God!"   *See also* **Mt** 28:16–17; **Jn** 9:35–38; **Php** 2:9–11; **Heb** 1:6; **Rev** 5:8–14

Angels worship God
Ps 103:20 Praise the LORD, you his angels, you mighty ones who do his bidding, who obey his word.
Ps 148:1–2 Praise the LORD. Praise the LORD from the heavens, praise him in the heights above. Praise him, all his angels, praise him, all his heavenly hosts.   *See also* **Ps** 29:1–2; **Isa** 6:1–4; **Eze** 10:1–18; **Rev** 4:8–9

The worship of other gods forbidden
Ex 20:3 "You shall have no other gods before me." pp Dt 5:7
2Ki 17:35–36 When the LORD made a covenant with the Israelites, he commanded them: "Do not worship any other gods or bow down to them, serve them or sacrifice to them. But the LORD, who brought you up out of Egypt with mighty power and outstretched arm, is the one you must worship. To him you shall bow down and to him offer sacrifices."   *See also* **Ex** 34:14; **Dt** 6:13–14; **Ne** 9:6; **Ps** 86:9–10; 97:7; **Ac** 10:25–26; 14:13–18

The worship of angels forbidden
Col 2:18 Do not let anyone who delights in false humility and the worship of angels disqualify you for the prize . . .   *See also* **Rev** 19:9–10; 22:8–9   *See also* God, living; God, truth of; Jesus Christ, exaltation; Jesus Christ, Son of God.

worship, acceptable attitudes
True worship is not the mechanical repetition of rituals, but should be wholehearted and reverent. It should be based upon trustful and obedient lives, in that obedience is itself to be seen as an act of worship.

Worship should be in accordance with God's commands
Ge 22:2 Then God said, "Take your son, your only son, Isaac, whom you love, and go to the region of Moriah. Sacrifice him there as a burnt offering on one of the mountains I will tell you about."   *See also* **Ge** 12:1,7–8; **Dt** 30:16–20; **1Sa** 15:22; **Ps** 40:6–8; **Jer** 7:2; **Da** 3:28; **Ac** 13:2; **Ro** 12:1

Worship should not be mechanical
Jn 4:23–24 "Yet a time is coming and has now come when the true worshippers will worship the Father in spirit and truth, for they are the kind of worshippers the Father seeks. God is spirit, and his worshippers must worship in spirit and in truth."   *See also* **Heb** 10:1

Worship should give God the honour due to him
1Ch 16:29 pp Ps 96:8–9

Worship of mere human devising is unacceptable
Isa 29:13 The Lord says: "These people come

near to me with their mouth and honour me with their lips, but their hearts are far from me. Their worship of me is based on merely human rules which they have been taught." See also **Lev** 10:1; **Mt** 15:7–9 pp Mk 7:6–7; **Php** 3:3; **Col** 2:23

Worship should be orderly and reverent
1Co 14:40 But everything should be done in a fitting and orderly way. See also **1Ch** 16:37–42; **1Ki** 18:30–39; **1Co** 14:26

Worship should be grounded in godly and obedient living
Mic 6:6–8 With what shall I come before the LORD and bow down before the exalted God? Shall I come before him with burnt offerings, with calves a year old? Will the LORD be pleased with thousands of rams, with ten thousand rivers of oil? Shall I offer my firstborn for my transgression, the fruit of my body for the sin of my soul? He has showed you, O people, what is good. And what does the LORD require of you? To act justly and to love mercy and to walk humbly with your God.
Ro 12:1 Therefore, I [Paul] urge you, brothers and sisters, in view of God's mercy, to offer your bodies as living sacrifices, holy and pleasing to God—this is your spiritual act of worship. See also **Ps** 15:1–5; 24:3–4; **1Ti** 2:10

The proper attitude of worshippers
Preparation for worship
1Co 11:28 We ought to examine ourselves before we eat of the bread and drink of the cup. See also **Lev** 16:3–4; **2Sa** 12:20; **2Ch** 7:1; **Mt** 2:11
Wholeheartedness
Dt 6:5 Love the LORD your God with all your heart and with all your soul and with all your strength. See also **Ex** 34:14; **Dt** 10:12; **Jos** 22:5; **1Sa** 12:24; **Ps** 27:4; **Mt** 22:37 pp Mk 12:30; **Lk** 10:27
Confidence in approaching God
Heb 10:22–23 let us draw near to God with a sincere heart in full assurance of faith, having our hearts sprinkled to cleanse us from a guilty conscience and having our bodies washed with pure water. Let us hold unswervingly to the hope we profess, for he who promised is faithful. See also **Ge** 4:4; **Jas** 4:8; **Heb** 7:19; 11:4 See also holiness.

worship, elements
Praise and thankfulness are important elements of worship, which also includes confession of sin, the reading of Scripture and music.

Worship with awe
Dt 10:12 And now, O Israel, what does the LORD your God ask of you but to fear the LORD your God, to walk in all his ways, to love him, to serve the LORD your God with all your heart and with all your soul, See also **Lev** 10:1–3; **2Ch** 7:3; **Ps** 2:11; 68:35; 96:9; **Ecc** 5:1

Worship includes trust
Ps 4:5 Offer right sacrifices and trust in the LORD. See also **Ps** 37:7; **Heb** 11:6

Worship includes praise
Ps 22:22 I will declare your name to my people; in the congregation I will praise you.
Ps 107:32 Let them exalt him in the assembly of the people and praise him in the council of the elders.
Heb 13:15 Through Jesus, therefore, let us continually offer to God a sacrifice of praise—the fruit of lips that confess his name. See also **2Ch** 31:2; **Ne** 9:5–6; **Ps** 150:1–6; **Heb** 2:12; **Rev** 7:11–12

Worship includes thanksgiving
Ps 100:4 Enter his gates with thanksgiving and his courts with praise; give thanks to him and praise his name.
Rev 11:16–17 And the twenty-four elders, who were seated on their thrones before God, fell on their faces and worshipped God, saying: "We give thanks to you, Lord God Almighty, the One who is and who was, because you have taken your great power and have begun to reign." See also **2Ch** 7:3; **Ps** 50:14,23; **Eph** 5:19–20; **Php** 4:6; **Rev** 7:11–12

Worship with joy
Ps 95:1 Come, let us sing for joy to the LORD . . . *See also* **Ps** 27:6; 43:4; 100:2; **Lk** 24:52–53; **Ac** 2:46–47

Worship includes the confession of Jesus Christ as Lord
Heb 13:15 Through Jesus, therefore, let us continually offer to God a sacrifice of praise—the fruit of lips that confess his name.

Worship includes confession of sin
Hos 14:2 Take words with you and return to the LORD. Say to him: "Forgive all our sins and receive us graciously, that we may offer the fruit of our lips." *See also* **Lev** 16:21; **Ne** 9:2; **Ps** 66:18

Worship includes the reading of God's word
Col 3:16 Let the word of Christ dwell in you richly as you teach and admonish one another with all wisdom, and as you sing psalms, hymns and spiritual songs with gratitude in your hearts to God.
1Ti 4:13 Until I come, devote yourself to the public reading of Scripture, to preaching and to teaching. *See also* **Ne** 8:5–6; 9:3

Worship includes music and song
Ps 95:2–3 Let us come before him [the LORD] with thanksgiving and extol him with music and song. For the LORD is the great God, the great King above all gods. *See also* **2Sa** 6:5; **Ps** 100:2; **Eph** 5:19–20

Worship includes dance
Ps 149:3 Let them praise his name with dancing and make music to him with tambourine and harp. *See also* **Ex** 15:20; **Ps** 30:11
See also faith; Holy Spirit and praise; Scripture.

worship, hindrances
True worship goes beyond mere form and can therefore be hindered by a wrong relationship to God or to others.

Worship that is merely formal is unacceptable
1Sa 15:22 But Samuel replied: "Does the LORD delight in burnt offerings and sacrifices as much as in obeying the voice of the LORD? To obey is better than sacrifice, and to heed is better than the fat of rams." *See also* **Isa** 1:13; **Eze** 33:31; **Hos** 6:6; **Mt** 6:5; **2Ti** 3:5

Worship is hindered by wrong relationships
To God
Ps 66:18 If I had cherished sin in my heart, the Lord would not have listened;
Mt 15:7–9 . . . "These people honour me with their lips, but their hearts are far from me. They worship me in vain; their teachings are merely human rules.'" pp **Mk** 7:6–7 *See also* **Isa** 29:13; **Ps** 32:5–6; **Isa** 59:2; 64:7; **Jas** 4:3
To others
Isa 1:11–17 "The multitude of your sacrifices—what are they to me?" says the LORD . . . "Seek justice, encourage the oppressed. Defend the cause of the fatherless, plead the case of the widow."
Mt 5:23–24 "Therefore, if you are offering your gift at the altar and there remember that your brother or sister has something against you, leave your gift there in front of the altar. First go and be reconciled to them; then come and offer your gift." *See also* **Am** 5:21–24

worship, places
Under the old covenant, there were rules governing the places where worship might be offered but under the new covenant the earthly location is of no importance.

Worship at places commemorating some act of God
Ge 12:7 The LORD appeared to Abram and said, "To your offspring I will give this land." So he built an altar there [Shechem] to the LORD, who had appeared to him. *See also* **Ge** 8:20; 26:23–25; 35:1

Worship at a place chosen by God
Dt 12:13–14 Be careful not to sacrifice your

worship, reasons

burnt offerings anywhere you please. Offer them only at the place the LORD will choose in one of your tribes, and there observe everything I command you.   See also **Ge** 22:2; **Dt** 14:23–25; **1Ch** 21:18–19; **2Ch** 7:15–16

Worship in certain sacred places
Dt 12:5 But you are to seek the place the LORD your God will choose from among all your tribes to put his Name there for his dwelling . . .
See also **Ex** 3:12; **Dt** 26:2; **1Sa** 1:3,28; **Isa** 27:13; **Jn** 4:20

Worship at the Tent of Meeting
Ex 25:8–9 "Then have them [the Israelites] make a sanctuary for me [the LORD], and I will dwell among them. Make this tabernacle and all its furnishings exactly like the pattern I will show you [Moses]."   See also **Ex** 29:42–43; 33:10; **Lev** 17:1–5

Worship at the temple in Jerusalem
1Ch 22:1 Then David said, "The house of the LORD God is to be here, and also the altar of burnt offering for Israel."   See also **2Ch** 7:15–16; 29:27–30; **Ne** 8:6; **Lk** 1:8–10; 2:37; **Ac** 8:27

Worship in a synagogue
Lk 4:16 He [Jesus] went to Nazareth, where he had been brought up, and on the Sabbath day he went into the synagogue, as was his custom. And he stood up to read.   See also **Ac** 13:15; 15:21; 17:2

Worship in the home
Da 6:10 Now when Daniel learned that the decree had been published, he went home to his upstairs room where the windows opened towards Jerusalem. Three times a day he got down on his knees and prayed, giving thanks to his God, just as he had done before.   See also **Mt** 6:6; **Ro** 16:5; **1Co** 16:19; **Col** 4:15; **Phm** 2

The earthly location for worship is unimportant
Jn 4:21–24 Jesus declared, "Believe me, woman, a time is coming when you will worship the Father neither on this mountain nor in Jerusalem . . . a time is coming and has now come when the true worshippers will worship the Father in spirit and truth, for they are the kind of worshippers the Father seeks. God is spirit, and his worshippers must worship in spirit and in truth."   See also **Ge** 24:26; 47:31; **Jdg** 7:15; **Job** 1:20

In heaven worship is perfect
Lk 2:13; **Heb** 12:22; **Rev** 4:9–11; 5:13–14; 7:9–12; 19:4–7   See also **heaven.**

worship, reasons
The supreme reason for human existence is to worship God for his love, greatness and saving deeds.

To worship is a divine command
Mt 4:10 Jesus said to him, "Away from me, Satan! For it is written: 'Worship the Lord your God, and serve him only.'"   pp **Lk** 4:8   See also **Dt** 6:13; **Ex** 23:25; **2Ki** 17:36; **1Ch** 16:29; **Ps** 22:23; 29:2; 68:26; 113:1; 117:1; 148:11–13; 150:6; **1Ti** 2:8; **Rev** 14:7

God's people are to be a worshipping people
1Pe 2:9 But you are a chosen people, a royal priesthood, a holy nation, a people belonging to God, that you may declare the praises of him who called you out of darkness into his wonderful light.   See also **Ex** 19:5–6; **Ps** 105:1–6; **Isa** 43:21; **Rev** 1:5–6

Worship is the response of God's people
To God's love
Ex 4:31 . . . And when they [the elders of the Israelites] heard that the LORD was concerned about them and had seen their misery, they bowed down and worshipped.   See also **Dt** 6:5; 12:7; 26:10–11; **2Ch** 7:3; **Ps** 95:6–7; 117:1–2; 138:2

To God's holy presence
1Ch 16:29 . . . Bring an offering and come before him; worship the LORD in the splendour of his

holiness. pp Ps 96:8–9   See also Ex 33:10; Lev 10:3; Jos 5:13–15; Ps 29:2; 99:5; Rev 4:8; 15:4

To God's greatness
Ps 95:1–3 Come, let us sing for joy to the LORD; let us shout aloud to the Rock of our salvation. Let us come before him with thanksgiving and extol him with music and song. For the LORD is the great God, the great King above all gods.   See also Ex 3:12; Ps 22:27–28; 66:1–4; 96:1–3; Rev 15:3–4

To the deeds of God
Ge 8:20 Then Noah built an altar to the LORD and, taking some of all the clean animals and clean birds, he sacrificed burnt offerings on it. See also Ge 12:7

The signs and wonders in Egypt and Sinai: Ex 4:29–31; 12:27; 15:1,20

Ezr 3:10–11; Isa 19:21; Da 3:28; Mt 9:7–8 pp Mk 2:12 pp Lk 5:25–26; Ac 3:8

To the fear of God
Ps 22:23 You who fear the LORD, praise him! All you descendants of Jacob, honour him! Revere him, all you descendants of Israel!

Heb 12:28 Therefore, since we are receiving a kingdom that cannot be shaken, let us be thankful, and so worship God acceptably with reverence and awe,   See also Ps 2:11; Ac 10:2   See also God, goodness of; God, greatness of; God, holiness of; God, love of; prayer and worship.

---

worship, results
Worship not only gives God what is due to him but also results in many benefits for his people.

True worship brings benefits for God's people
Blessing
Ex 23:25–26 "Worship the LORD your God, and his blessing will be on your food and water. I will take away sickness from among you, and none will miscarry or be barren in your land. I will give you a full life span."   See also Dt 11:13–15

Guidance
Ac 13:2–3 While they [prophets and teachers in the church at Antioch] were worshipping the Lord and fasting, the Holy Spirit said, "Set apart for me Barnabas and Saul for the work to which I have called them." So after they had fasted and prayed, they placed their hands on them and sent them off.   See also Isa 58:6–11; Nu 7:89

Deliverance
Ac 16:25–26 About midnight Paul and Silas were praying and singing hymns to God, and the other prisoners were listening to them. Suddenly there was such a violent earthquake that the foundations of the prison were shaken. At once all the prison doors flew open, and everybody's chains came loose.   See also Ps 50:14–15

Joy
1Ch 29:21–22 The next day they [the Israelites] made sacrifices to the LORD . . . They ate and drank with great joy in the presence of the LORD that day . . .   See also 2Ch 29:30; Ps 43:4; Isa 56:7; Lk 24:52

A sense of God's presence
2Ch 5:13–14 . . . and the priests could not perform their service because of the cloud, for the glory of the LORD filled the temple of God. pp 1Ki 8:10–11   See also Ex 40:35

A deeper sense of Jesus Christ's lordship
Php 2:9–11 Therefore God exalted him [Jesus] to the highest place and gave him the name that is above every name, that at the name of Jesus every knee should bow, in heaven and on earth and under the earth, and every tongue confess that Jesus Christ is Lord, to the glory of God the Father.   See also Rev 1:10–18

Boldness to witness
Ac 4:31 After they [the Jerusalem Christians] prayed, the place where they were meeting was shaken. And they were all filled with the Holy Spirit and spoke the word of God boldly.   See also Ps 57:9; Ac 18:9–10

True worship convicts sinners
1Co 14:24–25 But if an unbeliever or someone who does not understand comes in while everybody is prophesying, such people will be convinced by all that they are sinners and will be judged by all, and the secrets of their hearts will be laid bare. So they will fall down and worship God, exclaiming, "God is really among you!" See also church, life of; Holy Spirit, conviction; Holy Spirit, guidance.

worship, times

Scripture stresses the importance of regular worship, while at the same time recognising that believers may worship God spontaneously.

Examples of regular worship
On a daily basis
Ac 2:46–47 Every day they [all the believers] continued to meet together in the temple courts. They broke bread in their homes and ate together with glad and sincere hearts, praising God . . . *See also* **Ex** 29:38–43; **Ps** 141:2; **Eze** 46:13–15
Several times a day
Da 6:10 . . . Three times a day he [Daniel] got down on his knees and prayed, giving thanks to his God, just as he had done before. *See also* **1Ch** 16:37; **Ps** 119:164; **Ac** 3:1; **Heb** 10:25
On holy days
2Ch 8:12–13 On the altar of the LORD that he had built in front of the portico, Solomon sacrificed burnt offerings to the LORD, according to the daily requirement for offerings commanded by Moses for Sabbaths, New Moons and the three annual feasts . . . *See also* **Eze** 46:3
At the three annual pilgrim festivals
Dt 16:16 Three times a year all your men must appear before the LORD your God at the place he will choose: at the Feast of Unleavened Bread, the Feast of Weeks and the Feast of Tabernacles . . .

Passover (or the Feast of Unleavened Bread): **Ex** 12:1–20; **Lk** 2:41
Pentecost (or the Feast of Weeks): **Ex** 34:22; **Ac** 2:1
The Feast of Tabernacles (or Ingathering): **Ex** 23:16; **Lev** 23:33–36; **Nu** 29:12–39; **Dt** 16:13–15
On the Day of Atonement
Lev 16:34 "This is to be a lasting ordinance for you: Atonement is to be made once a year for all the sins of the Israelites." And it was done, as the LORD commanded Moses. *See also* **Ex** 30:10; **Lev** 16:3–33; 23:26–32
On Sabbath days
Lk 4:16 He [Jesus] went to Nazareth, where he had been brought up, and on the Sabbath day he went into the synagogue, as was his custom . . . *See also* **Lev** 24:5–8; **Nu** 28:9–10

Examples of spontaneous worship
In response to an awareness of the closeness of God **Ex** 34:8; **Jdg** 7:15
In response to the experience of God's mercy
Ex 4:29–31 Moses and Aaron brought together all the elders of the Israelites, and Aaron told them everything the LORD had said to Moses. He also performed the signs before the people, and they believed. And when they heard that the LORD was concerned about them and had seen their misery, they bowed down and worshipped. *See also* **1Sa** 1:19–28
In response to the presence and power of Jesus Christ
Mt 28:8–9 So the women hurried away from the tomb, afraid yet filled with joy, and ran to tell his disciples. Suddenly Jesus met them. "Greetings," he said. They came to him, clasped his feet and worshipped him. *See also* **Mt** 14:33; **Lk** 24:52

Worship should not be dependent on circumstances
Php 4:6 Do not be anxious about anything, but in everything, by prayer and petition, with thanksgiving, present your requests to God. *See also* **Job** 1:20–21; **Da** 6:10; **Ac** 16:25; **1Th** 5:16–18

The continuous worship of God in heaven
Rev 4:10–11; 5:14; 7:11; 11:1; 19:4
See also Jesus Christ, power of; Sabbath.

Index

A
Abba 3
abiding in Christ 3
access to God 4
activity of God *See* God, activity of 29
anger, of God *See* God, anger of 31
   of Jesus Christ *See* Jesus Christ, anger of 132
ascension of Jesus Christ *See* Jesus Christ, ascension 133
asking God in prayer *See* prayer, asking God 224
assurance and Holy Spirit *See* Holy Spirit and assurance 90
authority of Scripture *See* Scripture, inspiration and authority 241

B
baptism of Jesus Christ *See* Jesus Christ, baptism of 136
birth of Jesus Christ *See* Jesus Christ, birth of 136
blasphemy against Holy Spirit *See* Holy Spirit, blasphemy against 101
blessings and faith *See* faith and blessings 13

C
Christ *See* Jesus Christ 123
   Jesus the *See* Jesus, the Christ 196
Christian life, grace and *See* grace and Christian life 79
Christlikeness 5
church 7
   Holy Spirit in the *See* Holy Spirit in the church 99
   Jesus Christ head of the *See* Jesus Christ, head of the church 149
   life of 7
   nature of 8
   prayer in the *See* prayer in the church 222
   purpose 9
   unity 11
coming of Messiah *See* Messiah, coming of 216
Commandments, Ten *See* law, Ten Commandments 212
community of redeemed, heaven *See* heaven, community of redeemed 82
compassion, of Jesus Christ *See* Jesus Christ, compassion 138
   of God *See* God, compassion 33
creation and God 12

Creator, God as *See* God, the Creator 60
   Jesus Christ as *See* Jesus Christ as creator 124
cross of Jesus Christ *See* Jesus Christ, cross of 139

D
death of Jesus Christ *See* Jesus Christ, death of 140
divine glory *See* glory, divine and human 22
divinity of Jesus Christ *See* Jesus Christ, divinity 142

E
entry into kingdom of God *See* kingdom of God, entry into 200
equality of Trinity *See* Trinity, equality of 252
eternal, God the *See* God, the eternal 61
exaltation of Jesus Christ *See* Jesus Christ, exaltation 143
example of Jesus Christ *See* Jesus Christ, example of 144

F
faith 13
   and blessings 13
   and prayer *See* prayer and faith 219
   and salvation 14
   life of *See* life of faith 213
   nature of 15
   necessity 16
   origins of 17
faithfulness, of God *See* God, faithfulness 34
   of Jesus Christ *See* Jesus Christ, faithfulness 145
family of Jesus Christ *See* Jesus Christ, family of 146
fellowship with God 18
feminine descriptions of God *See* God, feminine descriptions of 36
forgiveness 19
   divine 19
   Jesus Christ's ministry 20
   of sin *See* sin, forgiveness of 250
freedom through Jesus Christ 20
fruit of Holy Spirit *See* Holy Spirit, fruit of 105

G
gift of Holy Spirit *See* Holy Spirit, gift of 106

Index

glory 21
  divine and human 22
  human *See* glory, divine and human 22
  of God *See* God, glory of 36
  of Jesus Christ *See* Jesus Christ, glory of 147
  revelation of 23
God 24
  activity of 29
  all-knowing 30
  and creation *See* creation and God 12
  and human race *See* human race and God 119
  anger of 31
  as judge 24
  as redeemer 25
  as Saviour 26
  as shepherd 27
  as Spirit 28
  character of and sin *See* sin and God's character 246
  compassion 33
  faithfulness 34
  fatherhood 35
  feminine descriptions of 36
  glory of 36
  goodness of 37
  grace and mercy 38
  greatness of 40
  holiness of 41
  human descriptions of 42
  joy of 43
  justice of 44
  kingdom of *See* kingdom of God 199
  living 46
  love of 47
  majesty of 48
  mercy *See* God, grace and mercy 38
  names of God *See* God, titles and names of 66
  patience of 49
  perfection 49
  power of 50
  present everywhere 52
  purpose of 53
  repentance of 55
  revelation 55
  righteousness 57
  sovereignty 58
  suffering of 59
  the Creator 60
  the eternal 61
  the Father *See* God 24
  the Holy Spirit *See* Holy Spirit 90
  the LORD 62
  the Lord 63
  the provider 64
  the Rock 65
  the Son *See* Jesus Christ 123
  titles and names of 66
  transcendent 68
  truth of 68
  truthfulness 69
  unchangeable 70
  unique 70
  unity of 71
  will of 72
  will of and prayer *See* prayer and God's will 220
  wisdom of 74
  word of *See* word of God 259
  worship of *See* worship of God 261
  zeal of 75
God of the fathers 28
God's will and prayer *See* prayer and God's will 220
goodness of God *See* God, goodness of 37
gospel 75
  and law *See* law and gospel 206
  basics of 75
  promises 76
  requirements 77
  responses 78
grace 79
  and Christian life 79
  and Holy Spirit 80
  and Jesus Christ 80
  and salvation 81
  of God, mercy *See* God, grace and mercy 38
  of Jesus Christ *See* Jesus Christ, grace and mercy 148
greatness of God *See* God, greatness of 40

H

head of the church, Jesus Christ *See* Jesus Christ, head of the church 149
heaven 82
  community of redeemed 82
  inheritance 83
  kingdom of *See* kingdom of God 199
  nature of 84
  worship and service 86
holiness 86
  believers' growth in 87
  in behaviour 86
  of God *See* God, holiness of 41
  of Jesus Christ *See* Jesus Christ, holiness 151
  purpose 89
Holy Spirit 90
  and assurance 90

and grace *See* grace and Holy Spirit 80
and love 91
and mission 91
and peace 92
and praise 93
and prayer 93
and preaching 94
and regeneration 94
and sanctification 95
and Scripture 96
anointing 100
baptism with 100
blasphemy against 101
conviction 102
Counsellor 102
descriptions 103
divinity 104
filling with 105
fruit of 105
gift of 106
guidance 107
in creation 96
in life of Jesus Christ 97
in Old Testament 98
in the church 99
in the world 99
indwelling 108
inspiration 108
joy of 109
life-giver 110
personality 110
power 111
presence of 112
promise of 113
resisting 114
sealing of 115
sovereignty 115
teacher 116
titles and names of 117
wisdom 118
witness of 118
human descriptions of God *See* God, human descriptions of 42
human glory *See* glory, divine and human 22
human race 119
and God 119
and redemption 120
and sin 121
destiny 122
humanity *See* human race 119
of Jesus Christ *See* Jesus Christ, humanity 152
humankind *See* human race 119

humility of Jesus Christ *See* Jesus Christ, humility 153

I
Immanuel 122
incarnation 123
inspiration of Scripture *See* Scripture, inspiration and authority 241

J
Jesus Christ 123
and grace *See* grace and Jesus Christ 80
anger of 132
as creator 124
as judge 124
as king 125
as Lamb 126
as prophet 127
as redeemer 128
as Saviour 129
as servant 131
as shepherd 131
as the truth *See* God, truth of 68
ascension 133
attitude to Old Testament 134
authority 135
baptism of 136
birth of 136
childhood 137
compassion 138
cross of 139
death of 140
divinity 142
exaltation 143
example of 144
faithfulness 145
family of 146
genealogy 146
glory of 147
grace and mercy 148
head of the church 149
high priest 150
holiness 151
Holy Spirit in life of *See* Holy Spirit in life of Jesus Christ 97
humanity 152
humility 153
joy of 154
justice of 155
kingdom of 156
knowledge of 157
love of 158
majesty of 159

mind of 160
miracles 161
mission 163
obedience 164
opposition to 165
parables 166
patience of 167
perfection 168
power of 169
prayers of 170
pre-eminence 171
pre-existence of See Jesus Christ, divinity 142
preaching and teaching 172
prophecies concerning 174
responses to 175
resurrection 176
resurrection appearances 177
righteousness 178
second coming 179
sinlessness 182
Son of David 182
Son of God 183
Son of Man 185
sonship of 186
suffering 187
temptation 188
the Lord 189
titles and names of 191
transfiguration 192
trial 193
triumphal entry 194
victory 194
wisdom 195
Jesus, the Christ 196
joy, of God See God, joy of 43
 of Holy Spirit See Holy Spirit, joy of 109
 of Jesus Christ See Jesus Christ, joy of 154
judge, God as See God as judge 24
 Jesus Christ as See Jesus Christ as judge 124
justice, of God See God, justice of 44
 of Jesus Christ See Jesus Christ, justice of 155
justification, Jesus Christ's work 198

K

king, Jesus Christ as See Jesus Christ as king 125
kingdom of God 199
 coming 199
 entry into 200
 qualities 201
kingdom of Jesus Christ See Jesus Christ, kingdom of 156
knowing God 201

 effects 202
 nature of 203
knowledge of Jesus Christ See Jesus Christ, knowledge of 157

L

Lamb, Jesus Christ as See Jesus Christ as Lamb 126
last things 204
law 206
 and gospel 206
 Jesus Christ's attitude 207
 letter and spirit 208
 Old Testament 209
 purpose of 210
 Ten Commandments 212
letter of the law See law, letter and spirit 208
life of faith 213
life, of church See church, life of 7
 spiritual 214
LORD, God the See God, the LORD 62
Lord, God the See God, the Lord 63
Lord, Jesus Christ See Jesus Christ, the Lord 189
Lord's Day 215
love, and Holy Spirit See Holy Spirit and love 91
 of God See God, love of 47
 of Jesus Christ See Jesus Christ, love of 158

M

majesty, of God See God, majesty of 48
 of Jesus Christ See Jesus Christ, majesty of 159
man See human race 119
mankind See human race 119
mercy, of God See God, grace and mercy 38
 of Jesus Christ See Jesus Christ, grace and mercy 148
Messiah, coming of 216
mind of Jesus Christ See Jesus Christ, mind of 160
miracles 217
 nature of 217
 of Jesus Christ See Jesus Christ, miracles 161
 responses 218
mission, and Holy Spirit See Holy Spirit and mission 91
 of Trinity See Trinity, mission of 253

N

names, of God See God, titles and names of 66
 of Holy Spirit See Holy Spirit, titles and names of 117
 of Jesus Christ See Jesus Christ, titles and names of 191
necessity of salvation See salvation, necessity of 240

O

origins of faith *See* faith, origins of 17

P

parables, of Jesus Christ *See* Jesus Christ, parables 166
patience, of God *See* God, patience of 49
   of Jesus Christ *See* Jesus Christ, patience of 167
peace, and Holy Spirit *See* Holy Spirit and peace 92
perfection, of Jesus Christ *See* Jesus Christ, perfection 168
power, of God *See* God, power of 50
   of Jesus Christ *See* Jesus Christ, power of 169
praise, and Holy Spirit *See* Holy Spirit and praise 93
   and thanksgiving, prayer as *See* prayer as praise and thanksgiving 222
prayer 219
   and faith 219
   and God's will 220
   and Holy Spirit *See* Holy Spirit and prayer 93
   and Jesus Christ *See* Jesus Christ, prayers of 170
   and worship 221
   answers 223
   as praise and thanksgiving 222
   asking God 224
   God's promises 226
   in the church 222
   persistence 226
   relationship with God 227
   response to God 228
preaching, and Holy Spirit *See* Holy Spirit and preaching 94
   of Jesus Christ *See* Jesus Christ, preaching and teaching 172
presence of Holy Spirit *See* Holy Spirit, presence of 112
promise of Holy Spirit *See* Holy Spirit, promise of 113
prophecies concerning Jesus Christ *See* Jesus Christ, prophecies concerning 174
prophet, Jesus Christ as *See* Jesus Christ as prophet 127
providence 229
provider, God the *See* God, the provider 64
purpose of God *See* God, purpose of 53

R

redeemer, God as *See* God as redeemer 25
   Jesus Christ as *See* Jesus Christ as redeemer 128
redemption, and human race *See* human race and redemption 120
regeneration and Holy Spirit *See* Holy Spirit and regeneration 94
repentance 230
   importance 230
   nature of 231
   of God *See* God, repentance of 55
resurrection, of Jesus Christ *See* Jesus Christ, resurrection 176
revelation 232
   creation 232
   necessity 232
   New Testament 233
   of glory *See* glory, revelation of 23
   of God *See* God, revelation 55
   Old Testament 234
   responses 236
Rock, God the *See* God, the Rock 65

S

Sabbath 237
   in New Testament 237
   in Old Testament 238
salvation 238
   and faith *See* faith and salvation 14
   and grace *See* grace and salvation 81
   nature of 239
   necessity of 240
sanctification and Holy Spirit *See* Holy Spirit and sanctification 95
Saviour, God as *See* God as Saviour 26
   Jesus Christ as *See* Jesus Christ as Saviour 129
Scripture 241
   and Holy Spirit *See* Holy Spirit and Scripture 96
   inspiration and authority 241
   purpose 242
   sufficiency 242
   understanding 243
sealing of Holy Spirit *See* Holy Spirit, sealing of 115
second coming, of Jesus Christ *See* Jesus Christ, second coming 179
servant, Jesus Christ as *See* Jesus Christ as servant 131
service, in heaven *See* heaven, worship and service 86
shepherd, God as *See* God as shepherd 27
   Jesus Christ as *See* Jesus Christ as shepherd 131
signs 244
   kinds of 244
   purposes 245
sin 246
   and God's character 246
   and human race *See* human race and sin 121
   avoidance 247
   deliverance from 249
   forgiveness of 250
   remedy for 250
Son of David, Jesus Christ *See* Jesus Christ, Son of David 182
Son of God, Jesus Christ *See* Jesus Christ, Son of God 183

Son of Man 251
   Jesus Christ *See* Jesus Christ, Son of Man 185
sonship of Jesus Christ *See* Jesus Christ, sonship of 186
Spirit *See* Holy Spirit 90
   God as *See* God as Spirit 28
spirit of the law *See* law, letter and spirit 208
suffering, of God *See* God, suffering of 59
   of Jesus Christ *See* Jesus Christ, suffering 187

T

teaching of Jesus Christ *See* Jesus Christ, preaching and teaching 172
Ten Commandments, law *See* law, Ten Commandments 212
thanksgiving, prayer as *See* prayer as praise and thanksgiving 222
titles and names, of God *See* God, titles and names of 66
   of Holy Spirit *See* Holy Spirit, titles and names of 117
   of Jesus Christ *See* Jesus Christ, titles and names of 191
transfiguration, of Jesus Christ *See* Jesus Christ, transfiguration 192
Trinity 252
   equality of 252
   mission of 253
   relationships in 254
truth, Jesus Christ as the *See* God, truth of 68
   of God *See* God, truth of 68

types 256

U

understanding Scripture *See* Scripture, understanding 243
unity of God *See* God, unity of 71

W

will of God *See* God, will of 72
   and prayer *See* prayer and God's will 220
wisdom, of God *See* God, wisdom of 74
   of Jesus Christ *See* Jesus Christ, wisdom 195
witness of Holy Spirit *See* Holy Spirit, witness of 118
word of God 259
world, Holy Spirit in the *See* Holy Spirit in the world 99
worship 260
   acceptable attitudes 261
   and prayer *See* prayer and worship 221
   elements 262
   hindrances 263
   in heaven *See* heaven, worship and service 86
   of God 261
   places 263
   reasons 264
   results 265
   times 266

Z

zeal of God *See* God, zeal of 75

The New International Version

First published in 1979, the NEW INTERNATIONAL VERSION has become the world's most popular modern English Bible translation.

More than 100 scholars from diverse denominational backgrounds worked for 15 years to complete this distinctive translation. Their principal concern was to be faithful to the original texts, and to reflect the literary and stylistic diversity within the Bible.

The result is a Bible eminently suitable both for private study and public reading.

All Popular editions feature:
* topical headings which enhance ease of reading and understanding
* poetic passages printed as poetry
* table of weights and measures
* explanations of original names, measures and phrases in the footnotes
* clear, readable print
* Bible Guide containing
  The Bible at a glance
  The land and people of the Bible
  Well-known events in the life of Jesus
  Plan of the Bible
  Key events in the Bible
  Bible maps

A large range of popular-sized Bibles are available in the NIV:
Red cased	ISBN 0 340 25382 7
Brown cased	ISBN 0 340 26969 3
Paperback	ISBN 0 340 27818 8
Children's, illustrated	ISBN 0 340 26970 7
With Introductory Helps	ISBN 0 340 34601 9

As well as a range of popular-sized **Inclusive Language editions:**
Ideal for Bible study and those interested in the dynamics of Bible translation. Suitable for church use particularly when reading aloud to a mixed congregation.

Blue cased	ISBN 0 340 59140 4
Illustrated cased, green	ISBN 0 340 67134 3
Women's cased, blue	ISBN 0 340 65179 2
Paperback	ISBN 0 340 67136 X

Cased inclusive language editions come with an attractive dust jacket featuring an impressionist painting, making these editions ideal for giving as gifts.

A number of leather editions are also available in both ranges, for more details contact your local bookshop or the publisher.

Original language study tools

Deepen your understanding of Scripture by studying the texts in their original language:

Hebrew-Greek Key Study Bible
Edited by Spiros Zodhiates Th.D   ISBN 0 340 69396 7 US text

Combines the essential study tools for Hebrew and Greek with the NIV translation. Contains a competely new numbering system and lexical aids explaining the meanings and usage of key words.

Interlinear NIV Parallel Old Testament
Edited by John R. Kohlenberger III   ISBN 0 340 42588 1 US text

The Hebrew Old Testament with interlinear translation alongside the NIV text.

Interlinear NRSV-NIV Parallel New Testament in Greek and English
Edited by Alfred Marshall   ISBN 0 340 64299 8 US text
A parallel Bible giving the NRSV and the NIV Bible texts, as well as an interlinear New Testament showing the 21st edition of Nestlé's *Novum Testamentum Graece* Greek and a word-for-word English translation.

A selection of Bible study software with original language tools is also available from Hodder & Stoughton, for more details contact your local bookshop or the publisher.